Family Secrets

Richard Fallis, *Series Editor*

William Butler Yeats, 1899. Pencil sketch by Josephine Webb.
Courtesy of Society of Friends, Dublin.

FAMILY
SECRETS
• • •
William Butler Yeats
and His Relatives

WILLIAM M. MURPHY

SYRACUSE UNIVERSITY PRESS

First Edition 1995
95 96 97 98 99 00   6 5 4 3 2 1

Published in the United States of America by
Syracuse University Press, Syracuse, New York 13244–5160
and by arrangement with Gill and Macmillan, Dublin, Ireland.

This book has been supported by a grant
from the National Endowment for the Humanities,
an independent federal agency.

The paper used in this publication meets the minimum requirements
of American National Standard for Information Sciences—
Permanence of Paper for Printed Library Materials, ANSI 239.48–1984. ∞™

Library of Congress Cataloging-in-Publication Data
Murphy, William Michael, 1916–
Family secrets : William Butler Yeats and his relatives / William
M. Murphy.
p.   cm.—(Irish studies)
Includes bibliographical references (p.   ) and index.
ISBN 0-8156-0301-0
1. Yeats, W. B. (William Butler), 1865–1939—Biography.   2. Yeats,
W. B. (William Butler), 1865–1939—Family.   3. Poets, Irish—20th
century—Biography.   4. Pollexfen family.   5. Yeats family.
6. Family—Ireland.   7. Ireland—Biography.   I. Title.   II. Series:
Irish studies (Syracuse, N.Y.)
PR5906.M87   1994
821'.8—dc20
[B]   94-19006

Manufactured in the United States of America

To
Harriet Doane Murphy

William M. Murphy is Thomas Lamont Research Professor of Ancient and Modern Literature at Union College. He is author of *Prodigal Father: The Life of John Butler Yeats (1839–1922)*, which was a finalist for the National Book Award in Biography in 1979, and *The Yeats Family and the Pollexfens of Sligo;* editor of *Letters from Bedford Park: A Selection from the Correspondence of John Butler Yeats;* and coeditor of *Letters to William Butler Yeats*. His numerous articles on Yeats and the Yeats family have appeared in scholarly publications throughout the academic world.

Contents

Illustrations

Preface

The vast body of scholarship dealing with William Butler Yeats has been confined mostly to his literature. The few publications combining biography with criticism—Joseph Hone's two biographies (1915 and 1942), Richard Ellmann's *Yeats: The Man and the Masks* (1948), and A. Norman Jeffares's two biographies (1949, 1989)—devoted themselves chiefly to a relationship between the life and the works. Valuable though their contributions are, they have of necessity neglected a range of Yeats's experiences involving his relationships with the other members of his family.

One of the reasons for the neglect has been the difficulty of access to materials that would allow such a study. With the death of Mrs. William Butler Yeats in 1968, a vast new body of letters, diaries, memoirs, and other papers was made available for the first time, through the generosity of the poet's children, Anne and Michael Yeats. Making use of it, I published in 1971 *The Yeats Family and the Pollexfens of Sligo* (Dublin: Dolmen), the first full account of the family of the poet's mother, and in 1978 *Prodigal Father: The Life of John Butler Yeats (1839–1922),* (Ithaca and London: Cornell University Press), a study of the life of the poet's father and of his relationships with his children.

Since that time two other large blocks of material dealing with the Yeats family have become available. One is the collection of letters from John Butler Yeats to Rosa Butt, which had been kept under lock and key in the Bodleian Library until 1979 by a restriction imposed by the donor. The second was the enormous bulk of letters from Lily Yeats to her cousin Ruth Pollexfen Lane-Poole, the originals of which were given to Michael Yeats by Mrs. Lane-Poole's daughter, Mrs. Charles Burston, in 1982. Through the kindness of the poet's children, I was given access to both sets of

xiii

letters, which I transcribed into readable typescript: three 250-page volumes of the Rosa Butt letters; seven, of selections only, from the Ruth Pollexfen letters. Recently, new material on the Dun Emer Industries became available to me through the kindness of Sheila Pim and the collateral descendants of Evelyn Gleeson and Augustine Henry. From these, and from material made available earlier, it became possible to create a family biography showing the intimate and continuing connections between different sets of family members. It is on these materials that the present book is based.

As with *Prodigal Father* I want to make clear that this work does not attempt, except incidentally, literary or artistic criticism. It is intended to be simple biography, the story of people's lives, in this case of the four children of John Butler Yeats in their relations with one another and with him, and, partly, of a hitherto unknown portion of his. If others can find food for critical or psychological feasts in it, they are welcome to the banquet. If William Butler Yeats's poetry and prose, or the paintings and writings of Jack Yeats, become more comprehensible because of this narrative, I am happy to leave it to others to draw the connections. My interest is in the personalities and characters of the people involved. I do not approach the subject from the point of view of a Freudian or a Jungian, of a Deconstructionist or a New Historicist, of a Marxist or a Benthamite. I do not try to force eagles into pigeonholes. No one can escape his own prejudices, and mine will be apparent. But, to the best of my abilities, I have tried to write as a simple humanist with a bent toward common sense and the open mind, a position I feel comfortable with. If there are philosophical fathers behind the outlook in this volume they are the three Thomases: Jefferson, Paine, and Doubting. I apologize to my readers in advance if any passage in the book should give comfort to the wardens of Political Correctness.

The sections (or chapters) of the book are not arranged chronologically except where convenience allows. The first three follow more or less in order, as do the fifth and sixth (which should be treated as a unit). Each is a separate essay that may be read independently, although a reading of any will enrich one's understanding of the others. Those with the stamina to go the whole road will therefore find, and I hope excuse, some necessary repetitions, which I have tried to keep to a minimum. The last essay, on John Butler Yeats and Rosa Butt, deals with a confined subject private to the two principals, yet it too enhances the meaning of the other sections.

I am under no illusion that the story of Lily and Lollie Yeats would be of interest to the world if they were not the sisters of a great poet. The lives they led have counterparts all over the world in obscure destinies that seldom find a voice except in fiction. Yet these two, with their talents and achievements, stand as striking representatives of their kind. To me their lives represent an unusual kind of triumph and are worth recording for their own sakes. Their brother Jack, whose life and art have been studied and recorded well (by, among others, Hilary Pyle, Terence De Vere White, Robin Skelton, Martha Caldwell, and Marilyn Gaddis Rose—and, more recently, by John W. Purser), appears in a new light when viewed as a member of the remarkable family of which he was the youngest. It is my hope that the book will possess an interest and fascination even for ordinary readers who have no particular interest in, or special knowledge of, William Butler Yeats. For them I have provided a brief prologue outlining some of the important events in his life.

•   •   •

Most of the matter in this book is new, based on material unavailable or unknown to me before 1978. But I have not hesitated to make use of material I have published elsewhere; some of the monographs were printed in limited editions and are hard to obtain, and some of the articles appear in scholarly journals read only by specialists. I have treated *Prodigal Father* as I would any other published book, quoting from it where appropriate.

•   •   •

As with my earlier publications on the Yeats family, I owe so much to so many people that it would take more paragraphs than I have at my disposal to thank them all in detail for their contributions. Three scholars who are themselves preparing definitive works on Yeats have generously shared their findings with me: Dr. John Kelly, of St. John's College, Oxford, who is editing the complete letters of William Butler Yeats; Dr. Ann Saddlemyer, Master of Massey College of the University of Toronto, who is writing a biography of George Yeats, wife of the poet; and Dr. Roy Foster, of Hertford College, Oxford, who is preparing a full-length biography of William Butler Yeats. To all three I owe a debt of thanks. Without their cooperation many a loose end would have remained untied. I must express my deep regret that Dr. F. S. L. Lyons, former Provost of Trinity College, Dublin, died at all too young an age in 1983 while he was engaged in writing the life of William Butler Yeats. He and I worked together on the letters of Lily Yeats to Ruth Pollexfen, and it was my hope that we would continue both our collaboration and our friendship for many years to come. The world is impoverished by his loss. He was one of the most brilliant and dedicated of scholars, and we are all indebted to him.

Other scholars, some in non-Yeatsian fields, have also been of great help to me. Avis Berman, biographer of Juliana Force, let me know, among other things, of an important set of letters in the library of the University of Glasgow. Elizabeth Bergmann Loizeaux called to my attention a valuable collection of letters at the University of Delaware, and she has been of great help in solving other problems in connection with publication. Michael Stanford has helped me with Yeats materials at the Stanford University Library. Harry Diakoff let me have copies of some very important letters, which I have put, I hope, to good use. I give particular thanks to Mrs. Charles Burston, daughter of Ruth Pollexfen Lane-Poole, for her generosity in sending the letters of Lily Yeats to her mother to Michael Yeats. George Mills Harper generously gave me free run of his extensive collection of Yeatsiana; his friendship and support over a quarter of a century have been of great value to me.

Many people who either knew the members of the Yeats family or possessed material about them have generously shared their treasures with me. Dr. Patrick H. Kelly, Dean of Trinity College, Dublin, gave me full access to the private papers of his great-aunt Evelyn Gleeson, and Sheila Pim of Dublin shared with me her findings on the history of the Dun Emer Industries. Mrs. Hannah Cadbury Taylor has given her memories of the Yeats sisters, provided illustrations, and been of inestimable help in other ways. Mrs. Elizabeth Curran Solterer, daughter of Constantine Curran, provided detailed information about life at Gurteen Dhas. Kathleen Franks and Noni Franks Townsend of Dublin shared their intimate knowledge of their neighbors Lily and Lollie Yeats. Rosemary Hemming of Birmingham was able to give me invaluable information about her great-aunt Anne Boston. The late Dorothy Healy of Portland, curator of the Maine Women Writers Collection, shared her knowledge of things Irish and provided invaluable documents; I am particularly unhappy that her death just before this book was completed has made it impossible for her to see it in its final version. Dr. Maureen Murphy, Dean of Hofstra College, provided information on Cuala. Hilary Pyle of Dublin, biographer of Jack Yeats and Susan Mitchell, has shared her knowledge with me. Thomas A. Conroy, great-nephew of John Quinn, and his father, the late Dr. Thomas F. Conroy, have been generous in allowing me the use of John Quinn's letters. Dr. Barbara Phillips of Bath, England, has kindly allowed me permission to quote from the letters of Dr. Augustine Henry, her great-uncle. Dr. Robert Montgomery of Ballycastle, Northern Ireland, sent me information about the Pollexfens that I would not otherwise have seen. Dr. Richard Londraville and Janis Londraville provided copies of important letters of Jeanne Robert Foster. Professor Phillip L. Marcus of Cornell University and Dr. John Kelly of Oxford used their good offices in my search for the letters of John Butler Yeats to Rosa Butt. Brian Cassidy of Bath, England, was of great assistance in tracking down the letters of Lily Yeats to Ruth Pollexfen Lane-Poole; I am grateful to him and his wife Margaret for their help and friendship.

Three of my colleagues at Union College have done me the kindness to read the manuscript from beginning to end. Professor Harry Marten continued a constructive critical role first begun with his reading of *Prodigal Father*. Professor Adrian Frazier not only offered valuable comments but also suggested the title the book now bears. Professor James McCord wielded his scalpel on the prose. To all I am deeply indebted. Thora Girke, Secretary of the English Department, has proved indispensable with her talents and intelligence and generous contributions of time; without her my labors would have been much more difficult. It seems insufficient to mention her name only briefly, as I do here. To other members of the department who have followed the course of my work with interest I am grateful for their encouragement and support. For help with the baffling arcana of computerdom, I owe thanks to the members of the Peschel Computer Center at Union College: David V. Cossey, Director, and Robert M. Babb, Susan Brienza, Walter Cook, Mary McKnight, and Felix Wu.

To many others I owe more generalized thanks for kindnesses and services of various sorts (I give their names in alphabetical order): the late Neal W. Allen, Jr., Paul Andrews, Douglas Archibald, Heather Doane Atkinson, Dr. Ruth Barton, Suzanne Benack, Eloise Bender, the late Harold E. Blodgett, Harold W. Blodgett, Nicola Gordon Bowe, Louise Bowen, the late Van Wyck Brooks, Edward Fawcett Brown, Caesar M. P. Bryan, Gerald Bryan, Donna Burton, Warner Cadbury, Mary Cahill, Martha Caldwell, Janet and Francis Carroll, John Chandler, Wayne K. Chapman, Hilda Clohesy, Fraser Cocks, Josephine Coffin, Norman Colbeck, the late Padraic Colum, Bruce Connolly, the late Constantine P. Curran, Ingrida Dambergs, Thomas D'Andrea, the late Joseph Doty, William Dumbleton, the late Oliver Edwards, Leonard Elton, Ruth Anne Evans, Richard J. Finneran, Mary Fitzgerald, Ellen Fladger, Kathleen Franks, Frances-Jane French, Dr. Miriam Friedenthal, Larry Friedman, Daphne Fullwood, Joan Gaines, David Gerhan, the late Beatrice Lady Glenavy, Warwick Gould, Patricia Hampl, Maurice Harmon, Bobby Harper, the late James A. Healy, Peter Heinegg, Patrick Henchy, the late Thomas Henn, Richard Hirsch, Michael Holroyd, R.W. Hunt, Ann Hyde, the late Ruth Jameson, Colton Johnson, L. Rebecca Johnson, E. J. Kahn, Jr., Vincent Kinane, the late Sheelah Kirby, Eleanor and Frederick Klemm, Maribeth Krupczak, Joan Todhunter Lambe, Jennifer Lyons, the late Séan MacBride, Andrew McGowan, the late Thomas MacGreevy, Norman Mackenzie, Mr. and Mrs. J. Robert Maguire, Elizabeth Mansfield, Peggy McMullen, Jeffery Meyers, the late Liam Miller, Eleanor Munro, Dr. James W. Nelson, the late Carl Niemeyer, the late Nora Niland, the late Nora Connolly O'Brien, William H. O'Donnell, Jean O'Hara, James Olney, the late Glenn O'Malley, Harold Orel, Mme. Aimé Perrimond, Percy and Emily Phelps, the late Ezra Pound, the late Olive Purser, the late Benjamin L. Reid, Ann Rittenberg, Daniel Robbins, Marilyn Gaddis Rose, Mrs. Hans Rosenhaupt, Ann Seemann, Lydia Shackleton, Robin Skelton, Helen Farr Sloan, Jordan Smith, Colin Smythe,

Cornelia Starks, Ruth Stevenson, the late Samuel S. Stratton, the late Lola Szladits, the late Edwin Tolan, Richard Thompson, Donald Torchiana, Van Vechten and Bettina Trumbull, James Underwood, Helen Vendler, Terry Weiner, the late Terence De Vere White, Anne Wickens, Ruth Widmann, and Brenda Wineapple. To the many whose names I have unintentionally overlooked I offer my apologies; my gratitude to them is no less than to those I have named.

I should long ago have acknowledged my debt to the teachers and guides of my salad days, most now departed, whose influence on me, direct and indirect, has been profound, and profoundly appreciated: James Gillies, James B. Munn, Hyder E. Rollins, Theodore Morrison, and Douglas Bush. I must express again my deep obligation to the late Mrs. Jeanne Robert Foster, friend of John Butler Yeats and John Quinn, who first aroused my interest in the Yeats family and gave me access to her own invaluable collection of material. To my early mentor, the late David Worcester, I owe more than to anyone else except my father.

Many institutions lent their support during the course of my research, and I give thanks to all: to the libraries of Union College; Trinity College, Dublin; and the University of Glasgow; the Bodleian Library, Oxford; the National Library of Ireland; Reading University; the libraries of Stanford University, the University of British Columbia, York University, the University of Toronto, the University of Kansas, Colby College, the State University of New York at Buffalo, the State University of New York at Stony Brook, Southern Illinois University, and the University of Texas; the University of Victoria; the University of Delaware; the New York State Library; the libraries of Harvard, Yale, Princeton, and Brown; and the New York Public Library, the Henry L. Huntington Library, and the Library of Congress. The library of the Society of Friends, Dublin, has generously allowed me the use of drawings in its possession.

Over the years grants and fellowships have enabled me to pursue my studies. Of these the American Philosophical Society was the first grantor at a time when help and confidence were most needed. The American Council of Learned Societies provided a grant, and the Henry L. Huntington Library a Visiting Fellowship. The Ford Foundation Fund at Union College and the Union College Faculty

Development Fund have given several grants over a period of many years. The Rockefeller Foundation provided a Residency at the Study and Conference Center in Bellagio, Italy, where I was given valuable freedom to complete the manuscript. To all these I give thanks.

Peter Klose, of Dutchess Community College in Poughkeepsie, New York, has prepared many of the illustrations for reproduction, and I owe him a debt for his care and skill in giving life to photographs that are often faded from age. Rex Roberts of Dublin also provided excellent copies of other illustrations.

To the members of my own family I owe thanks for support of various kinds. Doris Smith has helped preserve an atmosphere of calm and efficiency in the household and made my work much easier than it would otherwise have been; her presence over twenty-five years has been almost that of a family member, and a treasured one.

My gratitude for the greatest patience and forbearance is expressed in the dedication.

Finally, this book (and others that I have written) would not have been possible without the complete cooperation of the members of the Yeats family over a period of twenty-eight years. They have offered material, information, and the gift of friendship and hospitality, but have made no attempt to censor anything I have written, even declining to read texts before publication. Anne Yeats and Michael Yeats, the curators of the family papers, have generously permitted use of previously unpublished material. Gráinne (Mrs. Michael) Yeats has shared with me her memories of Lily and Lollie Yeats. The grandchildren of William Butler Yeats have been helpful in a variety of ways over a period of many years: Caitríona Yeats, Siobhan Yeats, Síle Yeats, and Padraig Yeats. I believe I express the opinion of all Yeats scholars in saying that without their selfless help the achievements in the field would be much poorer. To all of them I offer thanks and the hope that this account of their talented relatives will not be displeasing to them.

Though many have helped with contributions of material and helpful suggestions, all mistakes and errors of judgment are mine alone and in no way the responsibility of those who have so generously helped me.

Prologue

The name of William Butler Yeats is, among the literate, one of the best-known of modern times. Lovers of poetry quote and allude to his "Lake Isle of Innisfree" and "The Second Coming," found in almost every anthology of English literature. Lovers of the drama give thanks for his part in the establishing of Dublin's Abbey Theatre and for the plays he wrote for it. Students of the occult pore over his arcane experiments to establish a link between the mundane and the otherworldly. Those devoted to the heritage of ancient Ireland find rich resources in his stories of ancient Celtic heroes. Devotees of the arts and crafts value his contributions to the Dun Emer and Cuala Industries, which produced books and embroideries of high quality. Historians of modern Ireland give consideration to the effects of his political activity, and the inspiration of his nationalist poetry, on the founding of the nation. Few poets have led lives of such richness and diversity or exercised such an influence on contemporaries and those of later generations.

Almost from the day of Yeats's death in 1939, a process of canonization and, some would say, deification began. W. H. Auden, himself regarded as a major poet of a later generation, honored Yeats with an elegy that is quoted as often as Yeats's own poetry. T. S. Eliot wrote an essay of appreciation that, like its subject, has developed a life of its own. A flood of other tributes followed, and books and articles have appeared in abundance. It would be virtually impossible today for anyone to read all the writings about him. Two scholarly journals—one published in England, one in America—are devoted solely to Yeats. In Sligo, where Yeats spent much of his childhood, the Yeats International Summer School recently celebrated its thirtieth anniversary. The testimony to the durability of his reputation is impressive, and there is no sign of its slackening.

Even during the seventy-three years of his life (1865–1939), Yeats was the subject of extensive criticism and analysis. A standard bibliography gives a partial list of books written about Yeats during his lifetime that numbers twenty. Yet in all these, and in the posthumous mountains of publications, little is to be found about the people closest to him, those with whom he grew up and shared the pleasures and agonies of family life: his parents, his two sisters, and his brother. The chapters that follow attempt to remedy the deficiency. In them little will be found about Yeats's career as a poet or occultist or dramatist or theater manager, except where such are entwined with his relationships with the other members of his family. But since his own career is involved with theirs, a decent respect for what the general reader brings to a perusal of this book requires that a brief summary of the poet's life be offered.

Yeats was born to a Protestant, Anglo-Irish family on 13 June, 1865 in Sandymount, Ireland, a suburb of Dublin. His father, John Butler Yeats, was at the time a law student at the King's Inns in Dublin, and a half year later was admitted to the bar. JBY, as he was known, was an iconoclast of sorts, a skeptic, a student of Darwin and Huxley and Comte. Finding the profession of law a deception devoted to winning victory rather than seeking truth, he abandoned it in favor of a career in art. WBY's mother, Susan Pollexfen Yeats, disapproved of her husband's decision but lacked the resources to fight him. They went off to London, where JBY began a career marked by one spectacular failure after another. He studied constantly to improve his technique but lacked the confidence and the conscience to seek pay for the works he painted. His improvidence and fecklessness were to exert a profound influence on his children, who were deprived of the advantages normally accorded the children of the favored Anglo-Irish. None ever received a formal education or inherited a sum of capital that might have been of help in the society into which they were born.

What John Butler Yeats did possess, however, in addition to enormous talent as an artist, was boundless enthusiasm and intelligence. He developed a reputation as one of the best conversationalists of his era. He read widely, almost indiscriminately, not only to himself but to his children. He believed in the supremacy of art and hated the notion of "getting on," an ambition he saw and disapproved of in his wife's family, the Pollexfens of Sligo. He bequeathed to his children—not least to "Willie," the eldest child —the notion that success in the world derived from achievement in artistic creation, not from the accumulation of wealth. As he lived to the ripe age of eighty-two, his influence remained constant and steady even as his way of life brought uncertainty and trouble to those who had to care for him. Willie was the one who bore the brunt of his insistences and was the one for whose development he felt himself in great measure responsible. Of all the members of the family JBY was the dominant one; without him the Yeats family as we know it would not have existed.

The young William Butler Yeats spent his life moving from London to Sligo and back again. Not till he was in late adolescence did the family settle in Dublin, the city most closely associated with his name and fame. There, in his late teens, he began to write poetry and became interested in occult studies, a subject that was to engage him for the rest of his life, an interest second only to his poetry. Under the spell of his father's friends, he also became a dedicated Irish nationalist, one who believed that the people of Ireland should be allowed to work out their own destinies without interference from the English, who had dominated the country for seven hundred years. Before he reached manhood the ideas and interests that were to dominate his life had been fully developed.

It was on the family's return to London in the late 1880s that the most fateful event of his private life occurred. In late January 1889, a beautiful, stately young lady named Maud Gonne visited the Yeats home at Blenheim Road in Bedford Park, a suburb of London, and Yeats instantly fell in love with her. She did not reciprocate his feelings, and for the next thirty years he pursued her fruitlessly, writing poems to her and assisting her in her political plans, which were wildly, almost insanely, committed to violence. At the time she met him, she was having an illicit affair with a French journalist named Lucien Millevoye, by whom she had two children. The older, a son, died young. The second, Iseult Gonne, she brought up alone under the fiction, believed by nobody, that Iseult was her niece. In the early 1900s she married John MacBride, by whom she had a son Séan, later to hold high office in the United Nations. She never accepted Yeats's ardent suit; even after her husband was executed for his part in the Easter Rising of 1916, she refused to marry him.

Much of Yeats's early poetry was written with Maud in mind. Much also was written out of another of his consuming interests, the life of the ancient men and women of Irish heroic history, Cuchulain, Diarmuid and Grania, Oisin, Deirdre. His *The Celtic Twilight*(1893), a collection of poems and essays on ancient times, gave its name to the period and was one of the titles that helped to bring him fame. One of his early poems, "The Lake Isle of Innisfree," in which he spoke of his hatred of London and his longing to return to the beautiful Sligo of his boyhood, was so rich in imagery and so unusual in the magic of its music that it brought him a recognition that in a way established his reputation. Robert Louis Stevenson, writing from far-off Samoa, praised Yeats for the beauty of the simple three-stanza lyric. By his mid-twenties Yeats had become a poet of international reputation.

During those London years Yeats joined an occult society called the Order of the Golden Dawn. In the section to which he belonged, called the Isis-Urania Temple, he met an older, wealthy Englishwoman named Annie Horniman, who fell in love with him. She shared his interest in occult studies and in the drama and provided the financial help necessary for the staging of one of his early plays. She was a strait-laced, opinionated, righteous woman with a high opinion of her own talents that was shared by nobody who knew her. She possessed one deficiency in the pursuit of her dreams: she hated the Irish people, like many English middle-class possessors of inherited wealth believing herself inherently superior to the unwashed peasants who lived across the Irish Sea. She pursued Yeats as zealously as he pursued Maud Gonne, and with as much success. But because of her persistence she was to become one of the most influential participants in the formation of an Irish Theatre.

Yeats's interest in theater began in the early 1890s, coinciding with his pursuit of Irish legends and his studies in the occult. All three were to come together in his ambition to develop a drama that would be purely literary, one in which scene and action would mean little but poetry and expression almost everything. "Beautiful language beautifully spoken" was his ideal. When in the late 1890s he met Lady Augusta Gregory, he had found at last the kind of "powerful character" (his term for her) who could help bring about the realization of his dreams. She was about ten years older than Yeats, the widow of Sir William Gregory and the lifetime occupant of his estate at Coole Park in Ireland's County Galway. A woman of stern mien and impressive managerial talents, she took the young man under her wing and provided emotional support and encouragement for him for forty years. In Dublin they found a group of amateur actors under the direction of a pair of talented brothers, William and Frank Fay, and persuaded them to form with them an Irish Theatre devoted to the production of poetic plays on Irish themes. When financing was needed, Annie Horniman stepped forward with her riches and offered to support the project. Out of the strange and complicated partnership of so many diverse groups and people came the Irish National Theatre Society, known universally today as the Abbey Theatre, for the founding of which Yeats is generally given the credit, chiefly because he was the one who insisted on high standards and who had the energy and decisiveness to shunt aside those who were not contributing to the kind of theatre he wanted. The result was that he made enemies along the way, among them Annie Horniman, who, after having invested a good portion of her inheritance in the Abbey in hopeless pursuit of Yeats (who never gave her the slightest reason to believe he reciprocated her passion), found herself stranded outside the circle of power. Yeats had had the idea, Lady Gregory the determination and drive, the Fays the talent, Annie Horniman the money. Without any one of them, the Abbey would probably never have come into existence. Yet Yeats is the name chiefly associated with the founding and success of the Theatre.

His fame was so great by his mid-thirties that he was able to make a highly profitable lecture tour of the United States, guided by a curmudgeonly New York lawyer named John Quinn, whose close and not always willing association with the Yeats family would not end until shortly before his death in 1924. Returning to Dublin, Yeats found himself involved in a new venture entered into by his sisters Lily and Lollie, the Dun Emer Industries. Although the enterprise was supposed to provide them with a source of income, it proved instead to be an albatross about Yeats's neck, and it and its successor, the Cuala Industries, were to consume much of his time and energy till the day of his death.

His father proved another problem. In 1907 the sixty-eight-year-old artist traveled to New York to attend an exhibition of Irish goods with his daughter Lily. He never returned, remaining in New York till his death on 3 February 1922. During all these years he was a constant burden on John Quinn, who advanced sums of money for the old man's care, sums for which William Butler Yeats assumed the responsibility and ultimately repaid, often by selling Quinn manuscripts he would rather not have parted with.

As a poet Yeats developed from the Celtic romanticism of his early days. Critics find several distinct periods in the poetry of his later days, ranging from the symbolic to the realistic, from the impressionistic to the brutally direct. He revised constantly and published constantly. His drama, successful as poetry but seldom popular with paying audiences at the Abbey, moved through similar stages. Always Yeats was at the forefront of the literary world. When the Irish rose against their English occupiers in the Easter Insurrection of 1916, Yeats wrote a poem honoring the executed martyrs that became a kind of founding document of what would later be the Irish Republic. During the decade 1910–1920 he published the first volume of his autobiography and in 1917 married Bertha Georgie Hyde-Lees, an Englishwoman, after having been rejected for the last time by Maud Gonne and—in a perverse development—by her daughter Iseult too. He and Mrs. Yeats had two children, Anne Butler (born in 1919) and Michael Butler (born in 1921), both of whom survive.

When the Irish finally achieved the quasi-independence of a Free State in 1922, Yeats was named a senator of the new country, a position he held till 1928. In 1923 he was awarded the Nobel Prize for Literature. In 1926 he published *A Vision,* a peculiar work of occultism springing out of "automatic writing," a kind of communication with the other world carried out in his case by his wife's ability to write down answers given by a spirit to Yeats's questions. It augmented his fame in occult circles.

While on the Continent in 1927, Yeats fell ill with serious

congestion of the lungs. He was never totally well thereafter. In 1929 at Rapallo he was stricken with Malta fever. Although he continued writing plays, poems, and essays—and even undertook another lecture tour in America—his health gradually worsened. On 28 January 1939 he died in a hotel in southern France and was buried in the cemetery in Roquebrune. Because the Second World War broke out later that year, his remains stayed there until 1946, when they were disinterred, brought to Ireland, and reburied in the churchyard of St. Columba's Church in Drumcliff, County Sligo, where his great-grandfather had served as rector a hundred years earlier.

No simple account could do justice to the complicated career of one of the most energetic and multitalented geniuses of modern times. Each sentence of this brief summary could be expanded to a long paragraph or a short book. What it omits is discussion of Yeats's relationships with the other members of his family, particularly his two sisters and his brother. They are the principal subjects of the ensuing chapters.

Abbreviations

ABY	Anne Butler Yeats
AE	George Russell
AH	Augustine Henry
Cottie	Mrs. Jack Yeats
EG	Evelyn Gleeson
GHLY	Bertha Georgie Hyde-Lees (Mrs. William Butler) Yeats
George	Mrs. William Butler Yeats
Isaac	Isaac Butt Yeats
JBY	John Butler Yeats
Jack	Jack Yeats (John Butler Yeats, Jr.)
Jack Yeats	Jack Yeats
Jack B. Yeats	Jack Yeats
LAG	Lady Augusta Gregory
Lily	Susan Mary ("Lily") Yeats
Lollie	Elizabeth Corbet ("Lollie") Yeats
MBY	Michael Butler Yeats
Q	John Quinn
SPY	Susan Pollexfen (Mrs. John Butler) Yeats
TCD	Trinity College, Dublin
WBY	William Butler Yeats
Willie	William Butler Yeats
WMM	William M[ichael] Murphy

Family Secrets

1

The Yeatses, the Pollexfens, and Sligo

> The Pollexfens all disliked Willie. In their eyes he was not only abnormal, but he seemed to take after me. But however irritable ("the crossest people I ever met," my sister Ellen called them) they were slothful and so let him alone. And therefore in Willie's eyes they appear something grand like the figures at Stonehenge seen by moonlight.
> —John Butler Yeats to Lily Yeats,
> 1 February 1922

> The Pollexfens are as solid and powerful as the sea-cliffs, but hitherto they are altogether dumb. To give them a voice is like giving a voice to the sea-cliffs. By marriage to a Pollexfen I have given a tongue to the sea cliffs.
> —John Butler Yeats, "Memoirs"

> My grown-up uncles and aunts, my grandfather's many sons and daughters, came and went, and almost all they said or did has faded from my memory, except a few harsh words that convince me by a vividness out of proportion to their harshness that all were habitually kind and considerate. . . .
> I remember little of childhood but its pain.
> —William Butler Yeats,
> "Reveries Over Childhood and Youth"

The ordinary reader of literature, knowing the power of the name and the poetry of William Butler Yeats, might think of the Great Man as a lonely if commanding figure mounted on a distant throne, composing odes or creating theaters or summoning spirits from the vasty deep. G. K. Chesterton, a friend of the family, knew better. William Butler Yeats "might seem as solitary as an eagle," he wrote, "but he had a nest." Chesterton rolled the names off his pen, "Willie and Lily and Lollie and Jack," "names cast backwards and forwards in a unique sort of comedy of Irish wit, gossip, satire, family quarrels, and family pride."[1] It was a family of unusual cohesion, its members remaining in close communication with one another throughout their lives, each affecting the others in various ways. Chesterton neglected to provide the surnames of the families who provided their genetic material, especially the name of the family into which John Butler Yeats had married, that of the Pollexfens of Sligo, who were to have more of an influence on his children than the family of the name that they inherited.

When John Butler Yeats (called "JBY" or "old JBY" by his friends) was old and alone in New York City, his son the poet sent him an unexpected gift of cash. A surprised father wrote his daughter Lily, "It may be endlessly debated whether Willie is a Pollexfen or a Yeats. . . . It was like a Yeats to send this money and make no fuss about it. It was like a Pollexfen to have it to send."[2] Thus did the unsuccessful father note one of the differences between his own family and that of the poet's mother, Susan Pollexfen Yeats. It was one of many such distinctions he was to draw during his long life, distinctions so impressing his children that they drew them too. To them as to him, there were virtually only two families in their ancestry, Yeats and Pollexfen. Although it was a rich and goodly heritage that met in the Yeats children—a mixture of Anglo-Irish old and new, of Cornish and Devon gentry, of Huguenots, of smugglers, sea-captains, merchants, of officials in Dublin Castle, clergymen, soldiers—it was almost as if those bearing the names of Middleton, Corbet, Taylor, and Armstrong had never existed.[3] Simplistic though their conception may appear, it was one they clung to and found good reason for accepting. However inadequate it may appear to others as a way of explaining opposing or contradictory elements in their natures, to them it was unassailable. The simple division was one assumed by the Yeats family, not one imposed by its biographers.[4]

1. John Butler Yeats (1839–1922), 1863, before his marriage to Susan Pollexfen. *Courtesy of author.*

John Butler Yeats, proud of his own family, spoke and wrote to his children constantly about their Yeats ancestors, whom he described as "The Good People,"[5] warm, loving, unambitious. He wrote his daughter Lily: "You would be proud to have their blood. They were so clever and so innocent. I never knew and never will know any people so attractive."[6] The Pollexfens, on the other hand, were undemonstrative, often unkind to one another, selfish, and dour. They suffered from a solemnity, an inability to express their joy in life, that led at times to melancholia and emotional instability, failings not to be found in the ebullient Yeatses. In his children JBY saw both sets of genes. When he wrote to his brother Isaac about Lollie's emotional problems, he was drawn to his favorite comparison. "There are in her two races, the Yeats and the Pollexfen. Sometimes she is one and sometimes the other. When she is Yeats she is happy and making the best of things. When she is Pollexfen she makes the worst of things. . . . She has the Pollexfen tendency to be morbid and unhappy."[7]

John Butler Yeats had just taken his degree from Trinity College, Dublin, in 1862 when he traveled to Sligo to visit George Pollexfen, a schoolmate from his days at the Atholl Academy in the Isle of Man. He met George's sister Susan, proposed to her, and married her the following year, in September 1863, at St. John's Church, Sligo. Returning to Dublin, he studied law at the King's Inns, distinguished himself as the most prominent member of the class, then suddenly abandoned his career and moved to London to become an artist, horrifying his own family and incurring the displeasure of the commercial Pollexfens. Six children were born to Susan within ten years, four surviving: William Butler ("Willie") (1865–1939), Susan Mary ("Lily") (1866–1949), Elizabeth Corbet ("Lollie") (1868–1940), and John Butler, Jr. ("Jack") (1871–1957).[8] Their father, a brilliant and iconoclastic conversationalist, was the dominant parent—so powerful a personality that his weaker wife was reduced to the role of passive bystander. Yet, by the accidents of fate, it was her family rather than his that was to impress its peculiarities on their children.

They knew of their Yeats ancestry only through their father's stories and letters. In it were Armstrongs and Corbets associated with the glories of British imperialism—John Armstrong had been one of Marlborough's officers—and Taylors, powerful in Dublin Castle, where JBY's father, William Butler Yeats, was born. The earliest known Yeats in the family records was Jervis, listed in 1712 as a wholesale linen merchant in Dublin,[9] whose son and grandson, both named Benjamin, succeeded him in the business. The brightest star in the ancestral firmament was Mary Butler, believed by

2. Susan Mary Pollexfen (1841–1900) 1863, before her marriage to John Butler Yeats. *Courtesy of Michael B. Yeats.*

family legend to be descended from the powerful Butlers of Anglo-Norman times, the family of the Earls of Ormonde.[10] Through her the Yeatses came into possession of a property of 560 acres in County Kildare and a house in Dorset Street, Dublin. The income from it supported JBY's grandfather, Parson John Yeats, and his father, William Butler Yeats, for many years. Their heir, who might have used it to build a fortune, instead lost the property and its income before his eldest son, the poet, could come into control of it.[11]

The children of John Butler Yeats knew few of their father's relatives personally. His father had died three years before Willie was born, his mother while her grandchildren were still small. Lily's sole recollection of her grandmother, Jane Grace Corbet Yeats, confirms what her father said about the qualities of his family. She recalled staying with her once when ill at the age of six:

> I was never so happy before. She was demonstrative, called me pet names, caressed me. I followed her about. She gave me feathers to stuff a child's mattress, got them then and there from the cook who was plucking the chicken. I was put to bed by several Aunts. They ran about, laughed, and played. Grandmama Yeats had nicknames and pet names for things as well as grandchildren. Her scissors had a name. The house was full of old things, everything had a story.[12]

Because of their father's impulsive decision to try his hand at art in London, the children lived their earliest days among strangers. None remembered much of their first stay at Fitzroy Road.[13] The chief significant childhood experiences for the three oldest children began not in London or Dublin but in Sligo, where they lived for two and a half years—from July 1872, when Willie was just seven years old and Jack a baby of one, to November 1874. When it began, nobody in the family thought their stay would last beyond the summer months, because JBY, with optimistic hopes for a successful career as a portrait painter, had expected to return to London when the summer of 1872 came to an end. But he failed to make money in Ireland, the return was delayed, and by the time their stay ended, WBY was nine and a half years old. So the most impressionable years of the lives of the Yeats children were spent with the family of their mother, the Pollexfens, in the bustling port town of Sligo.

On all the children of the family that was the place that would exercise the most profound effect. "No one will ever see Sligo as we saw it," Willie told Lily in later years.[14] A beautiful town at the western edge of Ireland, it was bounded by green fields, mountains, and the sea. It had its own harbor for oceangoing ships, and nearby were lakes and cataracts, the massive stone outcropping of Ben Bulben, and the mound on Knocknarea thought to contain the remains of Queen Maeve. It was a neighborhood that proved ideal ground for the upbringing of impressionable children.

For the three older of the Yeats children it also provided virtually their only opportunity to become acquainted with members of their father's family. At nearby Drumcliff was St. Columba's Church, where the Reverend John Yeats, JBY's grandfather, had preached decades earlier as a clergyman of the Church of Ireland— the Irish Protestant equivalent of the Church of England. His daughter Mary Yeats (1821–1891), called "Mickey," still lived on the outskirts of Sligo, as did her brother Matthew, the land agent. (Their brother Thomas, considered by JBY to be the finest Yeats of all, had died in 1872 before the children could come to know him.) WBY mentions Mickey several times in his "Reveries" but does not record what Lily wrote, that everyone loved her. "I never felt lonely with her," she wrote in her scrapbook; "she was strict but always kind and had the same gay spirit Papa had." [15] Willie and the two sisters visited her during that first long stay, Lily recording in her scrapbook an occasion when some towheaded children named Wynne accompanied their aunt on a visit there. When the aunt went inside, the Yeats children and their cousins, children of Matthew's, savagely attacked the Wynne children and drove them into the house. Willie and Lollie climbed into a tree with some of their cousins and pelted the enemy from above; Lily remained on the ground, whirring a wet mop round them and flinging tufts of grass at them. [16] Otherwise the children saw little of their Yeats relatives, though in one way it was a deprivation JBY did not object to, for both Matt and Mickey "were one-book people, their book the Bible." He thought they would have been better off if they had chosen Shakespeare and Dickens. [17]

The rest of their Sligo experience was with their mother's relatives, the Pollexfens, surely one of the most fascinating families in literary history. John Butler Yeats might praise the members of his own family, but he saw that there were two streams feeding the river of his children's genius, and though he spoke to them of both, he scanted his own family in the process. When he wrote to Edward Dowden in response to Dowden's praise of WBY's early verses, he added: "It is curious that long ago I was struck by finding in his mother's people all the marks of imagination, the continual absorption in an idea—and that idea never one of the intellectual and reasoning faculty but of the affections and desires and the senses." They possessed what JBY called "magnetism," which he believed was transmitted to his children. It was the Pollexfens to whom he gave the credit for the artistic power and passion he saw in all his children.[18] But he saw other qualities too, some of which he did not wish to see transmitted to his children. Along with the suppressed poetry went a feeling for class distinctions, a love of money and consequent attachment to business, and, in some, emotional instability.

The Pollexfens were relative newcomers to Sligo. William Pollexfen had sailed into the town in the early 1830s to offer help to a bereaved cousin, Elizabeth Pollexfen Middleton, whose husband, William, had died of cholera. He ended up marrying her daughter, also called Elizabeth, and remained in Sligo for the rest of his life. There he joined his brother-in-law William Middleton in a grain supply company called "Middleton and Pollexfen," and with him also founded the Sligo Steam Navigation Company, which carried cargo chiefly between Sligo and Liverpool.

Even though the Middletons were the ones with roots in Sligo, it was William Pollexfen who impressed his own personality on his family and on the town he adopted. He had run away to sea at the age of twelve and developed into a tough and resourceful sailor, silent and courageous. He stood about five feet nine inches, broadly built but not stout, with a fresh complexion and blue eyes and, in his early days, dark hair and beard. He held himself upright and was clearly not a man to be pushed around. For a half-century he was to be one of the town's leading citizens. He and Elizabeth and their children lived in a big house at the edge of town called "Merville," a spacious mansion on sixty acres of land with a big yard and stables, and with a magnificent view of Ben Bulben.[19] By 1872 the family had been completed—six sons and five daughters —and it was among this crowd of young aunts and uncles, with a grandfather who attracted yet terrified them and a grandmother

3. William Pollexfen (1811–1892), about 1865. *Courtesy of Michael B. Yeats.*

whom they worshiped, that the Yeats children found an early taste of family life.[20]

When the Yeats children stayed in Sligo, they saw the Middletons only occasionally. Great-uncle William Middleton was a hearty, cheerful man, good at business; yet beside his brother-in-law he was a pale figure, coming and going "without notice," as his great-nephew saw it.[21] The Middletons "were liked," W. B. Yeats wrote, "but had not the pride and reserve, the sense of decorum and order, the instinctive playing before themselves, that belongs to those who strike the popular imagination."[22] When William Middleton died in 1882 the members of his family liquidated their holdings in the family business, which thereafter became the "W. & G. T. Pollexfen Company, Limited."

The Pollexfen aunts and uncles were all older than the Yeats children. Alice, the youngest, was eight years older than young Willie; Charles, the oldest, was a year older than Willie's father. Between them lay George (1839–1910), Susan (1841–1900), Elizabeth (1843–1933), John (1845–1900), William (1847–1913), Isabella (1849–1938), Fredrick (1852–1929), Alfred (1854–1916), and Agnes (1855–1926).

The family as a group was undemonstrative. The "capacity for affection" was there, JBY thought, but not "the actuality." "The whole family were brought up as if they did not belong to each other," he wrote.[23] He described his first visit to them, when they lived in a house in town: "The family gathered in force and sat together mostly in one room, and all disliking each other, at any rate alien mutually, in gloomy silence broken only by the sound of your grandmother turning over the leaf of a book, or by the creaking of some one's brace, or by a sigh from George Pollexfen."[24] Lily remarked on the contrast between the happy life at her Grandmother Yeats's home and what she saw at Merville: "There was no merry talk there. People walked soberly about. There were no pet names or caresses. Life was serious and silent, no merry talk at meals, no running to and fro."[25]

They were a strange people, almost instinctively unpleasant, "the crossest people I ever met," JBY's sister Ellen said of them.[26] The flame that burned within them failed to warm them. They were poets and mystics *ex nativitate* who rejected the natural impulses their God had given them. The Yeats family combination of which they formed a part was charged with lightning. JBY believed his children, if they had been Yeatses only, might have become something quite different, something blander; but with the Pollexfen admixture they were blessed with what their father later came to consider the perfect mixture of fuel and fire.[27]

It was Grandpapa Pollexfen, the "silent and fierce old man," who placed his stamp on those who inhabited Merville. Having run away to sea as a boy and fought his own way to a position of affluence and respectability, he saw the world as a battlefield in which one either conquered or was defeated. He would not ask his men on the Sligo steamers to do anything he would not do himself; once he dived beneath a ship in Sligo harbor to see what was wrong with the rudder when the men refused his command to go down. Having no education himself, he saw no need for it in others, and he bequeathed his views to his children. The Pollexfens, JBY declared, "regarded Intellect and Education with unconcealed contempt because to them it seemed to bring only poverty and failure."[28] William Pollexfen admired spirit and courage and resourcefulness and he despised people, including his own sons, who were deficient in them. Gruff and cross, he overawed his grandchildren by the power of his mere presence. When William Butler Yeats thought of him in later years, the figure of King Lear rose before him.[29] Lily found him terrifying: "Grandpapa Pollexfen we liked, admired, and avoided. . . . He never talked to anyone. . . . The past and the future had no interest for him at all. He was in such a state of irritation with the present moment that he could think of nothing else. He was quite unsuspicious so it was only what he saw that irritated, so there was everything to be said for 'keeping out of the master's way.' "[30] The only one of his descendants with whom he could get along was the young grandson Jack, whose own private and aloof nature he shared.[31]

He was impatient, a man of direct action. He was infuriated by the noise people made when tapping the top of a boiled egg. "His way," Lily wrote, "was to hold the egg firmly on its plate with his left hand, then with a sharp knife in his right hand to behead the egg with one blow. He didn't care where the rest of the egg went." When he uncorked a bottle of lemonade, he shook it violently, then removed the wire and cork, "and out blew the cork and most of the lemonade."[32]

Grandmama Pollexfen provided a moderating influence, but only in conduct and ceremony, not daring to question her husband's primacy in important matters. She was the only one who could manage the old man, calming his rages and caring for his simple

4. Elizabeth Middleton (Mrs. William) Pollexfen (1819–1892), about 1865. *Courtesy of Michael B. Yeats.*

needs. "She had a tranquillizing effect on all, but mostly on him," Lily wrote of her. "She smoothed all the wrinkles out of his life she could. . . . Sometimes when he was worse than usual she would look nervous and blink her eyes. He would look at her, give a short laugh, and be quiet."[33]

She was a calm and even-tempered woman who had been born

into a comfortable world and appreciated her good fortune. Her life was an easy one, and she grew apologetic when telling her granddaughter Lily Yeats about it. She was known and liked throughout the village for her kindness and good works, and the nuns at the convent where she had been a pupil remembered their old friendship, asking her from time to time for flowers and sub-scriptions.

When the Yeats children first came to Sligo, the Pollexfen family had already been living for several years at Merville, where Elizabeth Pollexfen presided with grace and dignity. Every day, clothed simply but correctly—"black silk dress, real lace cap, collar and cuffs, quilted black satin petticoat, thin cream-coloured stockings, and thin black shoes"—she drove about in the outside car or the phaeton and "looked about her all the time for people to whom she could give a gift."[34] She was the perfect lady: calm, ordered, generous, sensible.

Yet if she appealed to her grandchildren because of her kindness and gentleness, she had little influence on the upbringing of her sons, who, in the finest Victorian tradition, were the responsibility of their father. He let them know the kind of goal he wished them to aspire to and then left them to shift for themselves. It was he who inculcated in them those false values that his first son-in-law so vainly deplored. Among the Pollexfens there was "a very strong sense of property," JBY wrote WBY years later. "Their canons did not permit them to indulge in an affection for their children, so they clung the more to houses and lands."[35]

Something had warped their values, given them false gods to worship, and caused them, JBY thought, to suppress all that was finest and best in themselves. The icon of their kind was money, and the Pollexfens, said JBY, thought money "the finest and most serious thing in the world." Yet it did not penetrate their vitals. It merely "oppressed them, turning them away from their natural ways." They did not even know what to do with it.[36] Hence their uneasiness with John Butler Yeats, who gradually lost his inheritance and showed no capacity for regaining it, and so evoked their disapprobation, even scorn.

With their uncritical admiration for money went their feeling for class: one had to believe oneself better than others. It was a family blight in the Pollexfens that worried John Butler Yeats, as he was afraid it might infect his own children. "Class feeling destroys life," he once wrote Lily. "Because of it everyone . . . is ashamed to be their real selves, always pretending to like people and things they don't really like, and to dislike people and things they naturally would like." [37] He called it "a curse, a sort of imprisonment corrupting the people who benefit by it, and enraging and brutalizing the others." [38] He understood the source of the Pollexfen weakness, noting that class feeling is "of commercial origin but apes the ways of aristocracy." [39] Let a peasant procure more wealth than his neighbors and he wants to set himself up for a duke. True nobility, in JBY's view, was something quite different. The Pollexfens had mistaken one thing for another and in reaching for the symbol had lost the truth. He thought they were a nobility just as they were. They were aristocrats as they were poets. They should have left well enough alone.

Of the oldest Pollexfen child, Charles (1838–1923), the Yeats children fortunately saw little. One of the two brothers who were schoolmates of JBY's at the Atholl Academy in the Isle of Man, he was sour and unpleasant, with a cynicism that stood in contrast to JBY's idealism. The "haughtiest letter" JBY ever received was from Charles.[40] Yet even Charles had "magnetism," and JBY felt its force, just as he felt it in his brother George. Charles had fine qualities, but he drove people away, "as he was apt to be very insulting, and could endure nobody except abject slaves and flatterers." He never recovered from his sour Pollexfen upbringing and remained, in JBY's opinion, "a great fragment of human quartz." [41] By the time the Yeats children came to Sligo for their first long stay in 1872, he had departed for Liverpool to manage the Sligo Steam Navigation Company's office there.

Joining him there later was the youngest of the Pollexfen sons, Alfred Edward (1854–1916), the "stout and humorous" uncle[42] who to the Yeats children was the most engaging and likable of the lot. In a different family he might himself have become a man of letters. He had attended Foyle College in Derry for four years in his teens and returned to Sligo just in time to live side by side with his young nieces and nephews. At school he and a fellow student founded and edited the school magazine.[43] About the time the

5. The Pollexfen sons: *Top row:* Alfred (1854–1916); Fredrick (1852–1929); George (1839–1910). *Center:* Charles (1838–1923). *Right middle:* William Middleton (1847–1913). *Right lower:* John (1845–1900). *Courtesy of Michael B. Yeats.*

Yeatses returned to London after their first long sojourn, he left for Liverpool and stayed there for almost forty years. In Alfred JBY found a frustrated poet, a man of natural affection not quite submerged in the merchant with commercial values, for which Alfred

6. Charles Pollexfen and George Pollexfen, about 1871. *Courtesy of Michael B. Yeats.*

had no real respect. As a child he had cried when given a new hat and demanded the return of his old one, an act in which JBY saw "the stirring of affection."[44] He loved music. When a band came to Sligo, the young boy Alfred would follow it about and remain with it until someone came to bring him home. Yet when he learned a tune he instantly mimicked it as if to pretend it had no value. "He made derision of his own susceptibilities," charged JBY.

In the family was a talent for art and music, and JBY observed that all had "a wonderful facility in picking up and remembering anything in the papers written in rhyme," yet they "despised literature and poetry as being part of the idleness which they regarded as calamitous to morals."[45] Alfred played the concertina and might have become a good musician. He had no gift for business but did not know it, and the family refused to recognize it: "It was as if a Spartan suspected one of the family of being a coward."[46] His humor was his one gift, a rare one in the family.[47] He had "no intellect or not enough to speak about"[48] and was impervious to reason. He accepted everything as it came and remained cheerful and contented, a bachelor working as a quiet drudge in the office of his domineering older brother.[49]

His real nature revealed itself in his hobby. He loved Dickens and for many years held the post of secretary to the Dickens Society of Liverpool. "I am considered to be quite an authority, John," he told his brother-in-law.[50] Ironically, the man thus transfixed spent his days hunched over a desk as a minor clerk, like a character who had stepped out of one of his idol's novels. On the death of his brother George in 1910, he returned to Sligo to take his place in the family business, living alone in lodgings in town for the six years left him. He had simple tastes, almost no wants and, though liked by everyone, had few close friends. During his last days in a nursing home, he asked Lily to get him some postcards. She asked if she should buy a half-dozen. He said no: "he would not know what to do with more than three."[51]

When his brother John died of pneumonia in 1900, Alfred was surprised to find himself "sorry." The event was so unexpected that he had not had time to summon up the Pollexfen imperviousness and so was disturbed by his humane reaction. "It worried him. He spoke of it several times as a thing to be apologized for."[52] JBY saw a spirit trapped below the surface, imprisoned by his upbringing. He held Alfred in deep affection for his humor and kindliness and the depth of his nature; in a letter to his son the poet, JBY said of Alfred, after calling him "a mental simpleton": *"I feel that he has got something greater than either of us."*[53]

John Anthony Pollexfen (1845–1900), the brother whose death filled Alfred with such embarrassing sorrow, and who appears in William Butler Yeats's poetic tribute to Alfred as "the sailor John," shared the magnetism of his family. He was a sailor all his life. When he was a young boatswain, the captain of his ship fell mortally ill and in his extremity dismissed all the officers, all the stylish young men, "sons of rich Liverpool merchants," who were standing by, eager to pay attendance on him, and sent for John instead, who stayed with him till he died. John told JBY the story and expressed surprise, as the captain had paid no attention to him earlier and indeed had never spoken to him. "The primitive in the captain recognized it in John," wrote JBY.[54]

Alfred and John were not the only ones possessed of the poetic spirit. Two of the sisters displayed the rich inner qualities that JBY saw in his own children. Elizabeth (1843–1933) as a child was unable to learn the multiplication tables until a teacher was hired who set them to music, after which she learned them instantly.[55] JBY called her, in an approving sense, a "primitive." Another daughter, Isabella, was even more of one. Artistic, quiet, and pretty, she traveled to London during the seventies to stay with JBY and Susan and met her brother-in-law's friends. Among them was Oliver Madox Brown, the pre-Raphaelite painter who died young. He was attracted to Isabella and wanted to go to Sligo to meet her family. He was dissuaded by John Butler Yeats on the grounds, probably correct, that her family would not understand him or approve of him.[56] Later she married another artist, John Varley, a painter in a family of painters. Unlike some other members of the family, she had, JBY thought, intelligence. "She is somebody and you cannot easily set her aside." He believed she had a passion to rule but no opportunity to exercise it. Instead she filled up "the vacuum of her days by studying occult philosophy," in which her powerful imagination was a great help.[57] It was she who gave her nephew William Butler Yeats a copy of A. P Sinnett's *Esoteric Buddhism* and impelled him down the muddy road of "magic" studies where his emotions were to be mired for most of his life, and from which, paradoxically, was to come much of his finest poetry.

John Butler Yeats's later worries about his son's addiction to

7. William Middleton Pollexfen, about 1863. *Courtesy of Michael B. Yeats.*

occultism arose largely from his knowledge of the family's emotional problems.[58] The chief victim was William Middleton Pollexfen (1847–1913), the second of the name in his generation, the first having died at the age of two a year before the younger was born. Little is known of him except that he grew to adulthood, became an engineer, and, according to his nephew William Butler

Yeats, "designed the quays at Sligo and produced a pamphlet explaining his unsinkable wooden ship."[59] Then he went mad, had to be put away "when quite young,"[60] and lingered in a mental institution in Northampton, England, until his death at sixty-six in 1913.[61] His father left £2,500 for his care.[62] His mother told Lily it was her "one great sorrow." She "never forgot him for an hour even," wrote Lily. "Reports came regularly to Grandpapa from the doctors. He never opened the letter but passed it to Grandmama, who went away to read it alone."[63] Poor William, Lily wrote to her father, led the life "of a caged and wingless bird," and she dreamed of a white sea bird when he died.[64]

It was a touchy subject among the Pollexfens. William's affliction and incarceration were kept quiet, and Lily seems to be one of the few of her generation who knew the details. Two others besides William reached a condition that required special care. Elizabeth Orr became morbidly depressed after the deaths of William and Elizabeth Pollexfen, who died within six weeks of each other in the autumn of 1892, and quietly but insistently discussed their deaths with anyone who came into the kitchen, even the delivery boy. A term in an institution was found necessary before recovery could be effected. Her condition was only temporary. Her sister Agnes (1855–1926) suffered from a series of severe emotional breakdowns through a long life and spent time in an asylum; and one of William and Elizabeth's grandchildren suffered from a severe disorder resulting in multiple personality.[65]

Still, of the daughters in the family JBY thought Agnes the "most gifted and generous," one who "really had a big brain."[66] She was the opposite of his wife, Susan, with "a faculty for fluent action and thought. . . . I think she had a deeper insight in matters of feeling than any of the others but would seldom let you see what she thought." Of her, he wrote, "She had the nervous and cerebral energy the others lack, and she also had that mysterious energy which I cannot describe, but which is the pulse of universal life."[67] It was this "mysterious energy," this "pulse of universal life," that John Butler Yeats found in the Pollexfens generally and believed was transmitted to his children.

Elizabeth became entangled in her family's passion for proper marriages. When she was betrothed, JBY was amused to observe

8. Arthur Jackson (1853–1938). *Courtesy of Gerald Bryan.*

that the family of her husband, the Reverend Barrington Orr, "frankly stated that more money should be given because Elizabeth belonged to a family who were not gentlefolk." His own family, having made a fortune manufacturing soda water, believed itself perched on the summit of gentility. JBY recounted to Lily how surprised Barrington was to discover later that his wife was "always quite admirable among ladies."[68]

9. Alice Pollexfen Jackson (1857–1928). *Courtesy of Gerald Bryan.*

But it was the youngest of the daughters who was most affected by the commercial spirit. When the Yeatses began their two-year stay in Sligo, Alice (1857–1928) was a young girl attractive to Arthur Jackson, an ambitious and immensely able youth from Belfast who had joined the Pollexfen firm as a young man. In a classic move, he married the boss's daughter and, after his father-in-law's death in 1892, took control of the business and greatly increased its it profitability. His values, honest and respectable, were quite different from those of the Yeatses, who could never understand or sympathize with them. The Yeats children agreed with their father that Alice and Arthur were too concerned with money to be of any usefulness in the world. Though there were "rudiments of better things there," Lily was disappointed in Alice. "She had no brains and treated life altogether too much as a business to be run like a little shop, give nothing and get all you can. Her life was too easy." Arthur, who ended up the richest of the group, had "a generous manner," according to Lily, "but it was only manner." He could have helped out the Yeatses with timely infusions of cash but never did so. He thought himself a greater man than his wife's nephew the poet, regarding WBY's fame as a failure of the world's judgment.[69] He would have been astounded to learn that if Arthur Jackson's name is remembered today it is only because of his association with the poet he scorned. Lily thought the Jacksons might have been better had they been educated, but Arthur felt as his father-in-law did about the worth of anything not connected with business. Alice attended the Alexandra secondary school in Dublin but left it in her late teens, having absorbed all the polish her father felt necessary. Because she had easy access to money all her life, she could never understand why other people might not. Lily summed up Alice's social philosophy in a sentence: "If anyone was hard up, well, it was their own fault." With all their advantages, the Jacksons lived what the Yeatses thought shallow lives. "I don't think they could even read anything so difficult as *David Copperfield,*" Lily wrote, "or that they have even tried."[70]

The two sons in the family with whom the Yeats children were most involved were George and Fred. Fredrick (1852–1929) was his father's favorite (although his father did little but spoil him instead of instructing and disciplining him) and, according to John Butler Yeats, was a victim of the "evil brother Charles," who had taught him bad ways.[71] Fred attended Foyle College with his younger brother Alfred but stayed only a year.[72] He was perhaps not suited for formal schooling, being excitable and talkative. The other members of the family, even the mild and inoffensive Alfred, disliked him. "He was tiresome and aggravating," a niece of his recalls, "and was really the only one in the family who annoyed people."[73] He ran through money on yachts and horses and other pleasures and on gambling. In 1882, Fred married a young lady

10. Fredrick and Alfred Pollexfen, about 1870. *Courtesy of Michael B. Yeats.*

from County Cavan who bore him nine children. When they later divorced, it was Lily Yeats who became a kind of foster mother to two of his daughters, so Fred's adventures affected the Yeatses in a direct way. Because Fred had spent money so recklessly, his father cut him and his children out of his will. At the reorganization of the firm in 1892 Fred was excluded from participation. He and a friend were started up as coal merchants in Limerick, but the enterprise failed.[74] Fred was much in evidence in Sligo during the stay there of the Yeats children, and his very existence would vex them for years to come.

Of all the Pollexfens, George ("Uncle George") was the one who would most affect the Yeats children, as he had affected their father years earlier. Both George and Charles had been unpopular at the Atholl Academy. Having come to the school "badly educated" (as JBY put it), they always stood at the foot of the class. They were personally disagreeable, refusing to take part in sports or games. George could be surly, and Charles, when the fit was on him, "would allow no one to approach who were not his inferiors and flatterers." In their solid and brooding presence there was something forbidding. Even "the master let them alone. They were not the sort to be interfered with."[75]

Nevertheless, George Pollexfen fascinated John Butler Yeats, a one-sided affection in JBY's view. "I don't think George took any interest in me then or at any time," he wrote sixty years later in his memoirs, "but from the first I was greatly interested in him and never lost my interest."[76] JBY thought it was George's melancholy that first attracted him; he was "slow and tedious in all his movements,"[77] and, among people he did not know well or felt uncomfortable with, he was not merely unresponsive but chilly. "Socially," his schoolmate wrote of him, "he was worse than a bore, he was an iceberg. In his presence talk grew languid and then stopped." Yet "in the intimacy of personal conversation he was irresistible, also as a monologist, . . . a poet who in Wordsworth's phrase had not 'the sweet accomplishment of verse.' "[78] In the large dormitory at the school, where he slept with nine or ten other boys, he wore a face the headmaster never saw:

> Night after night he would keep these boys wide awake and perfectly still while he told them stories, made impromptu as he went along. . . . He was as rich in natural fertility as a virgin forest. . . . What he knew he presented without philosophy, without theories, without ideas, in a language that recalled the vision of the early poets. . . . He talked poetry though he did not know it.[79]

In him JBY recognized that Pollexfen quality which he called "magnetism," and which he was to call also "sincerity" or "intensity" or "primitivism," by which he meant a closeness to nature, an almost animal connection with earth, air, and water, the stuff of which poets and poetry are made. "Had George taken to writing he would have made a very remarkable and peculiar success," he told his brother Isaac, and his son the poet agreed with him.[80] Yet, except for George, the Pollexfens were inarticulate, "like the sea-cliffs," JBY said of them, powerful but dumb. It was a force that needed the catalyst of the Yeats ebullience to give it expression. "If the sea-cliffs could speak what a wild babbling there would be," he was to write in a famous phrase. "By marriage to a Pollexfen," he boasted, "I have given a tongue to the sea-cliffs."[81]

George thus became a solid rock to the Yeats family, often more literally than metaphorically. Despite his prominent position in the family business—the "G. T." of W. & G. T. Pollexfen Company, Limited, stood for George Thomas—he had no special capacity for making money. When Arthur Jackson came into the firm, he found that George had lost nearly £40,000.[82] George agreed to let Arthur run the company, put his own affairs into the hands of a worker named Doyle whom he had saved from drink, and limited himself to acting as a kind of foreman.[83] He was proud of his skill in casting horoscopes. Given the birthday of York Powell, the Regius Professor of History at Oxford, but with no further identification, he correctly forecast Powell's death the following year, though Powell was in his early fifties and in perfect health when the prediction was made.[84] He was equally accurate with a newborn child.[85] A third spectacular success, a precise analysis of the actress Mary Walker (Maire nic Shiubhlaigh), was somewhat clouded by her later admission that she had given him the wrong date of her birth.[86]

It was during one of his nephew Willie's visits in the early 1890s that the poet and the mystic developed the strong friendship that lasted till George's death. During one stay, when Uncle George was ill of an infection caused by vaccination, his nephew cast images for him and he recovered overnight.[87] He was convinced that Willie's mystical symbols had brought the cure, and thereafter their friendship was sealed. Yet he remained the difficult egoist

11. George Pollexfen, about 1906. *Courtesy of Michael B. Yeats.*

that Willie's father had known in the Isle of Man forty years earlier. "He never treated me quite as a grown man," WBY complained, "and had the selfishness of an old bachelor.—I remember still with a little resentment that if there was but one kidney with the bacon at breakfast he always took it without apology."[88]

After George's cure they spent long periods together, discussing horses and occultism and staring into a crystal ball. Occasionally

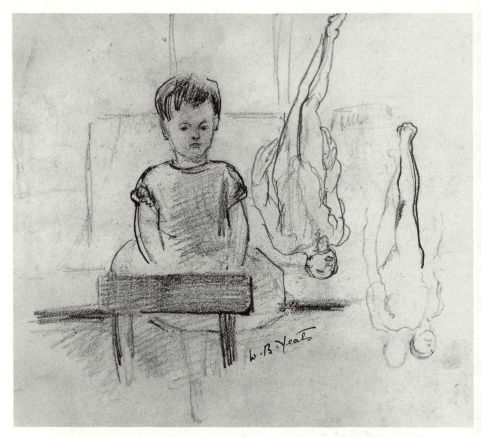

12. William Butler Yeats (1865–1939), about 1868. Unfinished
pencil sketch by JBY; identification in the hand of Lily Yeats.
Courtesy of Michael B. Yeats.

George served as first audience for his nephew's poetry,[89] and for
many years, according to a Sligo relative, he gave Willie an allowance of a pound a week. But when a mock funeral of the British
Empire staged by Irish Nationalists went unprotested by WBY,
George, a strong Unionist, stopped the allowance.[90]

The same lack of social grace that had scarred his image with
the masters at Atholl Academy continued until his death, but he
was loved by those who sought him out. York Powell found him

13. William Butler Yeats, about 1874. Pencil sketch by JBY; identification in hand of Lily Yeats. *Courtesy of Michael B. Yeats.*

unbelievably fascinating.[91] Never expecting anything of anyone, George was never disappointed. He neither liked nor disliked but took the world as it came. He was the classic egoist, utterly concerned with himself and not caring how he might appear to others. "If with George Pollexfen you always played safe," JBY wrote of him. "He never wanted to be agreeable or disagreeable. He was just himself, and since he was constantly dissatisfied with everything it was mostly a disagreeable self. He did not make a success at a small party, where he would sit on the edge of a chair like a thundercloud, or rather like an iceberg, freezing everybody, yet you soon knew him through and through, and his simplicity and lack of disguise became a real attraction in a world where everyone is frightened of everyone."[92] His actions were based on principle, so it was always easy for him to make a decision. "George would give you everything down to his last farthing *from principle,* but *not a farthing from good feeling,*" JBY told Lily.[93] Yet he agreed to help Lily with the education of Fredrick's children, not because he thought it morally correct, but because he liked Lily's company. People whom he did not care for, or who bothered him, or expected from him what he did not care to give, he disregarded. People who were financially irresponsible, like his old schoolmate and brother-in-law John Butler Yeats, he found repugnant. His last will and testament was based almost entirely on principle; he divided his estate equally among his brothers and sisters and their descendants with only minor modifications and exceptions.[94] To the one most in need of funds, John Butler Yeats, almost penniless in New York, he left nothing.[95]

•   •   •

As the Yeats children spent so much of their childhood in Sligo among their mother's family and so little among the Yeatses, it is not surprising that, except for the overwhelming personality of John Butler Yeats, the influence of the Pollexfens and the town they lived in was to leave the most lasting mark on them. For Willie it was not a blessing. The Pollexfens found him awkward and withdrawn and believed he shared too many of his father's qualities. "He was just like his feckless father, unsuccessful and therefore wicked," Papa told Lily in later years.[96] The Pollexfens were afraid their eldest grandson would grow up to be like his father; the father was afraid he would grow up to be like them.

Yet the passage of years eroded the bad memories and left mostly the residue of the good: those of the lovely town and the surrounding countryside, of the Irish servants and their charming superstitions, their belief in fairies and fairy raths, in a world that held mystery and meaning for its inhabitants. At Merville, Lily wrote, "The servants played a big part in our lives. They were so friendly and wise and knew so intimately angels, saints, banshees, and fairies."[97] When Lollie read a book of Irish folk tales in later

14. Lily Yeats (1866–1949), about 1875. Pencil sketch by JBY. *Courtesy of Michael B. Yeats.*

life, she was reminded of her childhood in Sligo. "To read them will bring all that good time back again. . . . All the talk among the servants was of the fairies."[98] Even in their old age the memory was still strong. "I get a longing often to see the waves roll in at the Rosses Point," Lily wrote her cousin Ruth in 1926, "to walk there on the Greenlands with the carpet of tiny flowers, wild thyme, lucky Larry, pansies, white clover—do you remember?— like jewels. To see Ben Bulben so majestic."[99]

"Sligo was our Paradise," Lily wrote in her old age.[100] William Butler Yeats tells us that when in later years he looked at his brother Jack's painting, *Memory Harbour,* a foreshortened impressionistic view of the main road at Rosses Point, with Sligo harbour off to the left, the Metal Man buoy in the channel, and the summer home of George Pollexfen at the top of the road just before it curves to the right, it filled him with "disquiet and excitement."[101] Lily

15. Lollie Yeats (1868–1940), 3 June 1877. Pencil sketch by JBY. *Courtesy of Michael B. Yeats.*

felt the same way about the Metal Man: "He is a figure of romance to all children—generations of those who like us had the good fortune to know Sligo in childhood." [102] The Sligo of their child-hood became to William Butler Yeats an ideal land, a dream world to which, though once an inhabitant, he could never return, a Paradise not to be regained.

16. Jack Yeats (1871–1957), 1874. Pencil sketch by JBY. *Courtesy of Michael B. Yeats.*

The children loved Sligo as they hated London, where there were no relatives of any kind, and outside were only the roadway and the pavements gray. At Sligo there were ships loading and unloading, the sight of Ben Bulben and Knocknarea, the stoning of raisins for the Christmas pudding, the Hazelwood Racecourse with "the crowds, the smell of bruised grass, the thud of the horses over the jumps."[103] Altogether, when the children thought of their childhood, the home that meant most to them, the place they most regarded as home, was Sligo, and, in Sligo, Merville. The homes in London and Dublin they regarded almost as temporary way stations, stopovers on the way to a return to Sligo. Jack spent most of his childhood in Sligo and lived there in memory for the rest of his life. In old age he wrote of it: "There is a rope of Sligo elemental air and the strands of it are so light that they can never be broken by the human will." [104] Willie, who wrote of his doings with his Pollexfen aunts and uncles that he could remember little of his childhood but its pain, also possessed another memory, of Sligo itself, of the harbor and river, of Innisfree and its imagined magic. That memory came in time to overpower the other. When he wrote nostalgically in later life, "I have walked on Sindbad's yellow shore and never shall another's hit my fancy," he could have been acting as spokesman for his whole family. [105]

2

Home Life among the Yeatses

"What a loss the Irish bar had when I turned artist. Still, had I remained a barrister and become a judge, there would have been no famous poet and Jack would not have been so distinguished, content only to be the sons of the Four Courts. . . . However, we are in God's hands, and I think we are a lucky family. My four sons and daughters have *realized* themselves."
—John Butler Yeats to Isaac Butt Yeats,
15 July 1919

"John Butler Yeats was the greatest literary father in history."
—Glenway Wescott (as reported by
Padraic Colum to William M. Murphy)

"Before John Butler Yeats the family was nothing. After him it could never be nothing again."
—Gráinne Yeats

In the Yeats household were two parents as opposite to each another as one could imagine. John Butler Yeats, the loquacious, intense artist and philosopher, was interested in little but ideas and their expression, which he pursued relentlessly and optimistically. "The great characteristic of his was his hopefulness," Lily wrote. "It was unquenchable. He lived on it. We all lived on it." [1] Money, worldly fame, success as ordinarily defined meant nothing to him. His wife, Susan Pollexfen, wanted only to be a conventional homebody, like her mother, with a prosperous house either in Dublin or London, or even Sligo, over which she could preside in comfort.

37

Her husband thought his inheritance of lands in Thomastown would provide the financial underpinning he required for the kind of life he wanted to live, but he had a poor head for money and gradually ran through everything he owned, finally selling off, at the age of sixty-eight, the estate that should have gone to his eldest son. The chief casualty of his fecklessness was his wife's happiness; its beneficiaries were, in many but not all ways, his children.

He had met Susan Pollexfen in Sligo when he was visiting her brother George in 1862, having just recovered from a rejection by another young lady whose identity is unknown. Years later he confessed to Rosa Butt that he was never really in love with Susan but had been caught on the rebound, yet he undeniably found her attractive. She was quiet and pretty, although with one blue eye and one brown eye, each of unambiguous color.[2] The land was Ireland and the season spring; under the spell of beautiful Sligo, John and Susan found themselves drifting together. Within a few days they were engaged. Two months later his father, the Reverend William Butler Yeats, died suddenly, the family properties passing to his eldest son. JBY spent most of that year studying law at the King's Inns in Dublin and saw little of his fiancée until he returned to Sligo the following summer. There, at St. John's Church, on 10 September 1863, the Pollexfens watched with pride and satisfaction as their daughter was married to an authentic Irish landlord, a descendant of the Butlers and of respectable clergymen and Castle officials, and a bright young star in the world of law. Susan and they could confidently look forward to his career as a successful barrister in Dublin or, if the Fates were gracious, London.

It was not long before the barrister and landlord disappointed his in-laws. After returning to Dublin and finishing his studies in law with distinction, he made an impulsive decision to abandon the law for life as an artist. In college he had been deeply influenced by the philosophical probings of his friends Edward and John Dowden and John Todhunter, who, like him, lived the life of the mind and were interested in first principles. He had rejected Christianity and become converted to Darwinism, choosing logic, fact, and reason over revelation and speculation. As the law came to look duller and less satisfying, he found himself increasingly more curious about art and its place in the universe of values. He had an

17. Susan Pollexfen Yeats (1841–1900), 1867. Pen sketch by JBY. *Courtesy of Michael B. Yeats.*

inborn talent for drawing, a skill that had made him popular among the students and teachers at Atholl Academy, where he had been a schoolboy from 1851 to 1857. In early 1867, in the face of the open hostility of his wife's family and the horrified apprehension of his own, he abandoned Dublin and the law and settled in London to begin, at the age of twenty-eight, the long and arduous training of the artist. The results for his economic well-being were disastrous. JBY proved a perfectionist who could not finish a picture ("You had to look for the crucial moment and snatch it from the easel when you thought it was right," Constantine Curran said).[3] He was never able to make a living from his art.

When he made the move to London, taking a house in Fitzroy Road, his older son Willie was only two years old, Lily just one; Lollie and Jack were still to come. So all their lives the children knew of their father as an unsuccessful painter, not as a prosperous breadwinner. To his impracticality as an artist he added an incapacity for business and finance. The family properties brought in about five hundred pounds a year, but much of the income was used to pay interest on mortgages with which the estate had been encumbered before he inherited it; and he periodically borrowed further against the properties as his need required. Susan Yeats's father was often called upon for infusions of cash to help tide things over.

The effect on Susan Yeats is not surprising. She did not possess the strong, decisive personality to enable her to stand up to so formidable an adversary as her husband,[4] who betrayed her family's expectations and her own as well. Even though it must be said in JBY's defense that he had not planned either his rebellion or his insolvency, both took place, and the combination crushed the weak Susan. She hated her life in London and made no attempt to disguise her feelings. She disliked the arty types who floated in and out of the Fitzroy Road house. Edwin Ellis was particularly annoying. "I don't wonder at all at poor little Mrs. Yeats's hatred of him," Todhunter wrote Edward Dowden. "He has not only estranged her husband from her, but he quietly ignores her existence."[5] The tensions were so great, the differences so irreconcilable that the young father, a stout believer in monogamy, drifted into an affair, which he later regretted, with a woman whose identity he would not reveal—his one straying from the marital range, if his word on the matter is to be accepted.[6] Their disenchantment with each other was so great that when Todhunter told JBY he was contemplating marriage, his friend warned him that it would be "a fatal mistake" and he would "repent it hereafter in sackcloth and ashes."[7]

For a while the marriage was in danger. Susan returned to her

18. Edwin Ellis (1848–1916), about 1868. *Courtesy of Michael B. Yeats.*

parents with the children whenever she could, and she complained constantly about her husband's fecklessness in abandoning the security of the bar for the uncertainties of the canvas. She even refused to recognize his choice. When she registered Lollie's birth in April 1868, she listed the father's profession as "Barrister." Two years later, resigning herself to the facts, she described him as "Artist" in registering Bobbie's birth, but her family was more stubborn. In 1873, Bobbie died suddenly of croup in Sligo while his father was away. William Middleton Pollexfen, not yet mad, was given the job of registering the death and described the child's father as "Barrister." There is no question where the Pollexfen preference lay.[8]

Because of the distribution of ages, Willie and Lily fell together as companions. Lily, born after only seven months of her mother's pregnancy, was afflicted with an errant thyroid gland, of unusual size and shape and with a tendency to wander about in her innards. It caused her constant distress, chiefly fatigue and difficulty in breathing. Undiagnosed till she was in her sixties, her illness was generally believed to be asthma. She and her more energetic older brother hit it off at once. Only fourteen months apart in age, they grew up almost as perfect contemporaries and continued a close relationship all their lives. Lily recalled her companionship at the time of their brother Robert's death in 1873: "Willy and I stayed together all those days and wandered about. I don't think we cried, we felt awed and excited, and drew rows and rows of ships with the flags half mast high. Someone told us the ships along the quays had put their flags at half mast and that excited us."[9] Lollie is not mentioned, nor is Jack, who, the youngest, was six years behind his older brother, almost a full generation in a child's perception of time. When Willie was ten, Jack was only four; when he was eighteen, Jack was twelve. There is no evidence to suggest that Willie ever took a serious fraternal interest in the kid brother and much to suggest that he did not.

Lollie fell between the oldest and youngest in a way that left her as a member of no group. Three years younger than Willie, from her earliest years she exhibited mannerisms that irritated him and others. While she and Lily, as the only two girls in the family, shared many experiences together, they were never as close as Lily and Willie. Lollie from the beginning felt isolated. Lily had another advantage: she was easygoing and likable, the one in the family who never annoyed anybody. Lollie annoyed everybody. WBY would probably have preferred Lily's company to Lollie's even if the ages of the sisters had been reversed.

The visits to Sligo, both during summers and at the Christmas

19. William Butler Yeats, about 1875. Three pencil sketches by JBY. *Courtesy of Michael B. Yeats.*

season, were the happiest for all the children. There they felt a sense of importance denied them in London. In Sligo they were part of an important family, even if a commercial rather than aristocratic one.[10] Lily has recorded many details of their days there.[11] One event, the wedding in August 1873 of Elizabeth Pollexfen to the Reverend Barrington Orr and her part in it, suggests the flavor of life there: the breakfast in the nursery, with special waiters brought in from Dublin to look after the wedding breakfast, Lily and Lollie in white muslin with blue sashes, Jack in a white dress and red sash, Willie in a blue knickerbocker sailor suit. She describes her grandfather's irritation at the beggars who hung about after the wedding party had left the church.

The carriage drove off but the beggars stayed. He took a carriage whip and drove them all before him out of the place. I remember one woman beginning, "My husband is a daycent man." Grandpapa gave his whip a crack and she scurried off. [12]

She recalled also the long sea voyage from Liverpool to Sligo on steamers of the family-owned Sligo Steam Navigation Company, and she wrote of one occasion when she asked Willie what had become of caterpillars he had collected, and he had answered, "Defunct." "I was impressed," wrote Lily, "quite a new word to me, spoken I am sure by Willy for the first time." [13] She remembered the "The Great Frost" on Lough Gill in the winter of 1881 or 1882. All seven miles of its water were frozen, and the Yeats children took advantage by learning how to skate. "For the first few days we four just stayed on the river near the shore and floundered about and fell. Every now and then someone with a kind heart and strong arm would help us for a while and then vanish. I remember Willy's long legs whirling in the air and seeing that he wore red socks. But in a few days we could all skate and away we went, up the river, through the narrows, and out into the lovely lake with its wooded islands." They skated all day for many days, and each day they went to look at a wild duck "frozen deep down in the ice with its pathetic yellow feet turned up." She couldn't be sure how long the frost lasted, but in her memory it seemed to remain "for months." [14]

When their father was in Sligo, they took long walks with him, and he would read to them—works like *The Merchant of Venice* and *Peau de Chagrin*. He made up stories for them. "Once when we were making little paper boats and sending them floating off on the river by the lake, he told us the history of one of these little boats, how it floated down the clear brown river through the town over the weir past the Rosses Point into the Atlantic, being spotted by the steamer from Liverpool, and finally came ashore at New York." [15]

If Sligo was their "Paradise," London was more like Purgatory. When the family returned there in November, 1874, the surroundings depressed the children. Their home at Edith Villas was small and uncomfortable. Yet it had its compensations, [16] for Willie and

Lily were now brought closer together, no outside companions being available. JBY encouraged them to explore the big city. With the excuse that one or both of them looked pale, he would say, "You want more oxygen. You better go for a long walk"; and he would give them a penny each. Lily describes one such day when they walked to the National Gallery and back. In the Gallery "Willie went straight to Frith's 'Derby Day,' and I went to a picture of King Charles signing some charter or other and looked at a baby that was low down in one corner of the picture, surrounded by ladies in waiting, one holding up a King Charles spaniel." They drank from all the fountains on the way and looked in the window of a confectioner's shop at a yacht "in full sail all made of sugar." [17] On another occasion she accompanied Willie to Kensington Park, where he sailed a small model boat made by one of the sea captains of the Sligo Steam Navigation Company. [18]

After the summer of 1876 in Sligo, John Butler Yeats hired a governess, Martha Jowitt, for the three younger children; she stayed three years. She was twenty-two when she came; Lily, who was ten, thought she was "quite elderly." "She taught us to read and write and to be tidy," said Lily; "she was a terror for neatness, often got us up out of bed to put our room tidy." [19]

In the meantime Papa took lodgings at Farnham Common near Slough to practice landscape painting and brought his eldest son Willie with him to begin his education. [20] When they returned to Edith Villas in 1877, Willie betook himself to the Godolphin School. Lily felt that the special relationship she had had with Willie had reached a turning point, for now he made friends with the boys at school and saw less of her. [21]

Susan played a lesser role in their lives than their dominant father. "Mama was very silent and very undemonstrative," Lily wrote of her. When the children were young, she had a few stories they liked to hear, like the one about the "wry mouth family," described by Lily as "a family with mouths all awry in different ways." The children acted out the roles with a candle on a chair. "We knelt round it and with twisted mouths blew in turns only getting the candle out when we all blew together, which was what the famous family had done." Susan Yeats let the children know they were poor, hinting that the cause was not their father's improvidence but the failure of the tenants in Kildare to pay their rent. One delinquent was Mrs. Flanagan. "When we wanted something badly," Lily wrote, "we were told we could not have it till Mrs. Flanagan paid her rent. We had a rag doll dressed in red knitted clothes. We called her 'Mrs. Flanagan,' and when the rent did not come we ill treated our Mrs. Flanagan, flung her downstairs. Being of rags she stood up to any bad treatment and was as tough as Mrs. Flanagan of Co. Kildare." [22] But such anecdotes are rare. In the children's recollections their mother seems a pale figure next to her husband.

Lily described her mother as "delicate," then modified the adjective: "No, 'delicate' is not the word. She was very strong in constitution, but her nervous system was easily upset, and her life was full of anxiety over money affairs and the care of children, and worry she could not stand." [23] She suffered the natural perils of all pre—twentieth century women, a series of unwanted pregnancies. "She had six children in ten years," Lily noted, "and was quite unable for the care and anxiety of life in London on an uncertain income." Her upbringing had not helped her. "As a girl in Sligo her life had been very easy, enough money, no cares." As a result, "she was not at all good at housekeeping, or childminding." She showed little sympathy for her offspring in their troubles. "When we were children and were ill she always said, 'Grin and bear it,' " and Lily felt that was exactly how her mother responded to her own life. [24] Mama was particularly annoyed by Willie, who always seemed to be doing the wrong thing, and, when JBY was away from home, he hated to open his wife's letters, knowing they would contain unflattering remarks about their eldest son. When Papa returned home on weekends he was no sooner in the house than he had to listen to "dreadful complaints of everybody and everything," but especially of Willie: "It was always Willie. Sometimes I would beg her to wait till after supper." He wrote one sorrowful sentence that perhaps tells us all we need to know about their relationship: "I always hoped she was not as unhappy as she seemed." [25]

In the spring of 1879, the Yeatses moved from Edith Villas (a house too small, with unhappy memories of Baby Jane Grace, who died there in 1876 before her first birthday) [26] to a brick house on Woodstock Road in newly developed Bedford Park in the western suburbs of London. It was the biggest and most elegant house the Yeatses ever lived in alone as a family. Miss Jowitt remained with the three younger children, teaching and disciplining them while Willie attended the Godolphin School. One room was reserved for classes. Lily's description of a day there is one of the earliest accounts of Lollie's unhappiness: "As we sat round the table in the schoolroom at our lessons with Miss Jowitt, if Lolly got into trouble over hers, she would start what we others called her 'whilaboloughing.' Tears of great size fell. There seemed to be no end of the supply. As they fell on the table she drew with her fingers pictures, using the tears as her medium, howling all the time." [27]

Lily loved the schoolroom, the only room in the house she remembered. When Willie wasn't away at school he joined the others. "It was our kingdom. We played while Miss Jowitt sat by the fire and read 'The Family Herald.' We were always making things, cardboard houses, painting and drawing. We had a magazine, 'The Cloud.' We acted. We loved dressing up and had a sheet we hung across the room and did shadow plays. Willy was serious about it. We others just romped about. None of us were any good except Jack, who was a good mimic and made us laugh. He always wanted a part in which he could wear Mama's wedding boots. They were white satin with elastic sides. He did like prancing about in them." [28]

She also enjoyed the garden, each child having a separate section. "Willy had dreams and plans, a forest of sunflowers with an undergrowth of love-lies-bleeding. A few sunflowers did come up. I don't think any of the undergrowth did." Jack's comic spirit went into his garden. "He mixed all his seeds together on a saucer before he sowed them, radish, mustard and cress, nasturtium, mignon-ette,—and up they all came in rich confusion." [29]

During the one summer vacation they spent outside Sligo, in 1879, all the children were together at Branscombe in Devon. [30] Papa, who remained in London during the weekdays, ordered the children not to go in the water, "adding that Mama was so reckless" they would all be drowned. [31] At the time Willie was fourteen and Jack eight, with the sisters between them at thirteen and eleven, and their stay together was one of family solidarity and happiness. They lived in an old farmhouse away from the village and near the sea. An orchard lay behind the house, in which were a dairy and stone kitchen. Lily remembers bathing in shallow pools, but only when Papa was present. They stayed inland and played in the fields and streams. Once Willie went off with local boys "looking for smugglers' caves." One day one of the boys said to him, "I saw thee and the little maids and little brother in church yesterday." Willie went about for days murmuring the sentence over and over to himself.[32]

It was Lily's record of their vacation that provides the first evidence of Jack's natural talent as an artist. "Every Saturday the daughter of the farm washed out the stone kitchen and with white chalk drew a sort of lace design on the floor close to the walls. We were fascinated." Jack was allowed to draw his own patterns for the floor; he also painted horses and huntsmen on a big flat stone used to keep the dairy door open.[33] Lily and Lollie pretended that big stones they had picked up and carried about were dolls. Jack promptly painted faces on them. When they bathed the dolls in a pool the faces came off, and Jack "put them on again."[34] His fascination with horses, one of the most common features of his later drawings and paintings, was evident even in the boy of eight.

All the children drew; six drawings survive of those done at Branscombe. Willie, Lollie, and Jack all drew the tree that stood behind the house they stayed in. Willie and Lily drew the local church, he showing the north wall, she the south. Jack drew a sketch of three men in sailor suits in a rowboat, a fourth standing on shore as they embarked.[35]

During the evenings Papa read *David Copperfield, Old Mortality,* and *The Antiquary* aloud to the children,[36] just as he had read to them in Sligo. In later years Lily claimed that though she lacked a formal education, she had learned as much as the schooled by simply being in the company of her father and hearing him talk and discuss the books he read to them.

At Branscombe William Butler Yeats was witness to a catch of fish that may have provided him with a famous line of poetry years later. A cobbler set up his work bench near the shore and watched for the ripples on the water that revealed the presence of mackerel. When he saw one he would run into the village with the news. "Men appeared from all directions," Lily wrote, "the boat was run

20. Drawings by Yeats children at Branscombe, Devon, 1879.
Courtesy of Michael B. Yeats.

out and the net cast about the shoal. We hurried to the shore and
saw the beautiful blue and silver fish leaping and tossing as the net
was brought in."[37] The "mackerel-crowded seas" Willie saw at
Devon were transmuted years later in a eulogy to Byzantium.

That was the last time all four children lived together until
eight years later. After the stay in Devon and a visit to Sligo, Jack
remained behind with his grandparents while the rest of the family
returned to London. For the next eight years, from his eighth to
his sixteenth year, Jack stayed with the Pollexfens, sporadically
attending school but chiefly soaking up the sights and sounds of
the place that was to provide him with most of the subject matter
of his art for the rest of his life. Lollie joined him there for a time,
while Lily, back in London with Willie and her parents, attended
the Notting Hill High School for a couple of terms. Because of her
poor health, Lily had to be removed from the school and sent to

Sligo, where she spent "a whole winter" with her grandparents and Jack in Merville, which they had to themselves, all the Pollexfen children having married or left. For Lily it was a bonus to her childhood years. "I rode every day on the red pony, with the coachman coming behind me on a big horse. Lovely warm days I remember in the soft air riding around Knocknarea through Hazelwood, or to Ballysodare." [38]

Despite JBY's efforts at improving his skill by studying landscape at Burnham Beeches, he still could not make a living in London. Toward the end of 1881, tempted by rumors of big money in Dublin, he moved the family to Howth, just north of Dublin across the bay. He rented a studio at York Street in the city, and Willie went in with him by train every day to attend the Erasmus Smith High School, a short distance away on Harcourt Street. Lily and Lollie occasionally visited their father at his studio, and one day John Doran, the bailiff at the Yeats estate in Thomastown, came on business and chatted with the two girls, then became formal and proper when Willie, the heir to the property, came in from school. [39]

The children liked Howth. It reminded Lollie of "the great difference of Dublin climate to this horrid climate [of London], so cold, foggy and dismal," enough "to give one the melancholies." She recalled "the glimpse of Howth Castle and the fine view of the harbour beneath, with the smoke of the village rising from the hollow and the pine woods beyond." [40] A couple of years later, the family moved again, this time to Terenure in Dublin. [41]

By then the inadequacies of John Butler Yeats as a breadwinner had reduced the family to a parsimonious existence. Every night all sat around a single lamp, "for the sake of a necessary thrift," as JBY put it. Willie, working quietly over his lessons, would begin composing verses, murmuring to himself, his voice growing louder and louder. "Then his sisters would call out to him, 'Now, Willie, stop composing.' And he would meekly lower his voice." The process would be repeated, the girls would again object, and finally Willie would be compelled to light another lamp and retire to the kitchen, "where he would murmur verses in any voice he liked to his heart's content." [42]

Through all the moves, through all the changes in her children's lives, Susan Pollexfen Yeats suffered and endured. There is no doubt that she was unhappy and that she had sufficient reason to be so. She underwent the embarrassment of constant indebtedness to butcher and baker. She longed for a home among people she felt comfortable with. The happiest years of her married life were probably those spent at the edge of the Irish Sea in Howth. Her husband, writing of that time, described her as sharing with Lily and Jack the "facility for understanding and being interested in poor people, and this not out of benevolence, but a sheer liking." Roseanna (Rose) Hodgins, the Yeats servant, herself from Howth, declared that her "mistress knew far more about the people at Howth than she herself did."[43] Among the surviving evidence there is no other testimony to her enjoyment of life. What she got from it was so far removed from her reasonable expectations that one can hardly accuse her of ingratitude. She entered upon a game with one set of rules only to find them changed almost as soon as the game began. From her point of view life was cruel and unfair, and John Butler Yeats was responsible.[44]

Yet the children saw things differently. William Butler Yeats is guarded in his comments about his mother. We learn of her love of telling stories to her children when the family was living in Howth, and of her sense of humor, briefly and cryptically mentioned. We learn that she was "unreasonable and habitual as the seasons."[45] Like her husband and her daughter Lily, WBY speaks also of her worry about money, the chief obvious source of her unhappiness. But he says nothing to indicate any deeper feelings about her, certainly nothing to imply affection. Lily's recollections, though more detailed, show the same reticence. Only a few of Susan's letters survive, written to Matthew Yeats, her husband's uncle and agent for his estate. In one of them she writes: "I know that you are doing all you can for us and I know we are very troublesome to you, but it can't be helped. I wish it could. We are in this unsettled state." She told Matt that JBY felt that his only course was "to paint pictures and pay models, and that comes to a lot of money."[46]

Lily, the family historian and archivist, who has most to say about the other members of the family, shows little sympathy for her mother's plight, suggesting that perhaps the children felt,

21. Susan Pollexfen Yeats, about 1881. Pencil sketch by JBY. *Courtesy of Michael B. Yeats.*

whatever their father's shortcomings, that Susan should have made an attempt to adjust to them. As a young housewife in London, even while ample funds were flowing in from the Thomastown rents, she was unapt at the simplest jobs. "Susan could not have boiled an egg," JBY told his brother Isaac sixteen years after his wife's death, and he hesitated to leave her at home with the children.[47] Willie noted that she took no interest in her husband's work as an artist[48] and made no attempt to familiarize herself with the subject matter of her husband's conversations with his friends—Dowden, Todhunter, and Edwin Ellis in the early London years; York Powell, John O'Leary, and others in the Dublin and later London years.[49] Even the kindly and generous Todhunter darkly alluded to her as having a "Philistine mind."[50] Significantly, in the correspondence of those outside the Yeats family, Susan Yeats is seldom mentioned except as a mere presence, "a silent flitting figure," as one acquaintance said of her;[51] it is almost as if she were not regarded as a member in good standing. "She was there as always," JBY wrote to Willie in later years, "disliking everybody and everything, yet accepting everybody and everything. She liked green countries and sky and the sea. I never knew how or why she liked them."[52] Yet during her lifetime he said nothing against her. "My father was always praising her to my sisters and me," William Butler Yeats wrote, "because she pretended to nothing she did not feel."[53]

If the Dublin years of the eighties were good for William Butler Yeats with his discovery of poetry, for the sisters the time was less fruitful. Papa insisted that they attend the Metropolitan Art School in Kildare Street,[54] and he planned to send them on to the Alexandra College. But at the last moment a bill requiring immediate payment had to be paid out of the Alexandra tuition money,[55] and the plan was scrapped.

It was during the seven-year stay in Dublin that Willie became interested in the occult, developed friendships with Charles Johnston and George Russell, and began writing poetry. Willie's discovery of what he called "Magic" and others call occultism came about when he read a copy of A. P. Sinnett's *Esoteric Buddhism,* provided for him by his aunt Isabella Pollexfen Varley. He took to its message at once.[56] His uncle George Pollexfen looked into crystal balls and waved magic wands about, and his sister Lily received remarkably predictive "visions," so his mind was well prepared to accept the existence of a spirit world as real, if less visible, than the tawdry one in which he had to spend his fleshly days.[57] From the beginning of his association with the spirit universe dates also the beginning of his disenchantment with his father, and of his

22. Lily and Lollie Yeats, about 1885. *Courtesy of National Library of Ireland.*

rebellion against him, while it also sealed further the bond between himself and Lily.

With no funds to pay for his education, William Butler Yeats, whose family tradition called on him to enter Trinity College, instead joined his sisters at the Metropolitan School of Art, studying there from May 1884 until April 1886.[58] He also became infatuated around this time with a young lady, Laura Armstrong, slightly older than himself and already engaged to be married to someone else. She inspired one of his early poems.[59] Little would be known of her if it were not for his short novel, *John Sherman*, written a few years later, in which she, "a most fascinating little vixen," provided the model for "the wicked heroine."[60] During the same period he also struck up a friendship with Katharine Tynan, a budding poet herself and one who recognized his qualities: "a white blackbird, a genius among the commonplace," she called him,[61] and she gave him encouragement at a time when he needed it.

At the Contemporary Club in Dublin, of which John Butler Yeats was a member, Willie met many of the intellectual luminaries of his time, like John O'Leary, Douglas Hyde, Michael Davitt, and, of the English visitors, William Morris. Thus began his association with the outside world of action and ideas; his dealings with his sisters and parents were now limited almost entirely to the dinner table in Terenure.

Except for Jack's long stay in Sligo with his grandparents, the Yeats family had remained together, with the occasional absences by JBY to execute sporadic portrait commissions or to improve his skill as a painter. Then, in 1887, JBY decided once again that he would never find his fortune in Dublin and abandoned his efforts to become "court painter" there. He moved again to London, where journey work might be available. Jack returned from Sligo to rejoin the family, and from then until 1894, when Jack married, the family lived together as a unit without interruption. But now the sons and daughters were no longer children. When that long and fruitful period began, Willie was twenty-two, Lily twenty-one, Lollie nineteen, Jack sixteen. They were to remain together till Jack was twenty-three; the seven years were to prove decisive in the development of each.

JBY returned to London dispirited, no longer planning to make a fortune by painting portraits. The family's low fortunes had hit bottom. The estate at Thomastown, heavily mortgaged, was sold to its tenants by John Butler Yeats under the terms of the Ashbourne Act; when the final payment of the purchase price came in 1907, most of the sum had been swallowed up by further debts and legal expenses. As there would be little income from that source after 1887, Papa tried sketching for commercial books and magazines.[62] He never succeeded. His elder son's comment in the fall of 1888 that his father, having finished a commission for *Atalanta,* was "once more dependent on stray drawings,"[63] serves as an epigraph of his work in the next decade. He simply did not know how to deal with the real world. Years later, after JBY was struck by a wagon in New York, John Quinn described the event to Lily: "Your father was as usual strolling through the traffic of New York like an Emperor in his garden," and Lily responded: "He went through life in much the same way."[64] Nevertheless, his depression during the Bedford Park years shows that he paid a price for his conduct and knew he was paying it.

When the family moved to London, William Butler Yeats was already, at twenty-two, a young man of both performance and promise, the author of a volume of published poetry praised by Edward Dowden and Katharine Tynan. The venerable and revered John O'Leary was one of his strongest supporters, supplying him with names of Londoners he should meet. Perhaps, if WBY had had his way, he would have moved into quarters of his own at once and attempted to establish himself as an independent spirit. Yet there is no suggestion in his letters that he considered abandoning his family or found its other members more than mildly annoying. He faithfully remained with them, even when he thought they stood in the way of his establishing his own identity. The sums he made by his writing and speaking went directly into the house coffers, "the swalley-hole," as the family called it.[65] Then, as in later life, he was generous with both money and moral support.[66]

The first of the residences after their return to London was a shabby place on Eardley Crescent, "old and dirty, dark and noisy," as JBY described it.[67] Lily called it "a horrible house," the garden only "a bit of cat-haunted sooty gravel." Behind the house was the newly built Earl's Court. When the Yeatses moved in, Buffalo Bill and his American Indians were performing there. To minimize complaints of noise from the nearby residents, the management gave every family in the neighborhood a season pass. The teenaged Jack, fresh from his years in Sligo, took full advantage of what was for him a gift from the gods: proud horses performing, Indians whooping and dancing, Buffalo Bill and his contingent firing guns with skill and accuracy. Even when Jack was at home he could tell by the sound from the auditorium "just what was happening at any moment of the day." [68]

Almost at once Willie moved into the center of Irish, artistic, nationalist, and occult circles in London. On 6 May 1887, he sat in the gallery at the House of Commons and heard T. M. Healy make "a rugged, passionate speech." [69] He met and was impressed by Ernest Rhys. [70] He talked regularly with his father's old friend John Todhunter. [71] He attended a meeting of "a woman's political association" (probably the Pioneers Club, one of whose members was Evelyn Gleeson, later a force in the history of the Yeats family as the founder of the Dun Emer Industries) [72] and was a guest at a meeting of the Home Rule Association Party where Mrs. William E. Gladstone spoke. [73] He was also invited to lecture on Irish folklore at the Southwark Literary Club, where Todhunter took the chair and Oscar Wilde's mother sent a representative. [74] Willie and Lily went to tea several times at Lady Wilde's, Oscar taking Lily aside and saying "flattering, pleasant things about Willy." [75] Fame had come early to a young man still unsure of his own identity.

Willie and his father both thought he should find work that would bring in money, but Willie was the more eager. Papa looked upon ordinary work—the nine-to-five job—as "evil" and hoped something would come along to make it "unnecessary." One indication of the family impracticality was that, as Willie told Katharine Tynan, in the matter of finding a job, "Neither Papa nor I know well how to set about it." [76] When he rejected an offer to write for the *Manchester Guardian* his father was relieved, saying, "You have taken a great weight off my mind." [77] WBY's income came from articles for American newspapers and plays for an artistic theater, and pieces on folklore that were later gathered together under the title *The Celtic Twilight,* which gave its name to a literary period.

The stay at Eardley Crescent was brief. Susan Pollexfen, trapped in the shabby surroundings, suffered a stroke. She was sent to her sister Isabella's home in Denby with the perennially ill Lily, and there in late 1887 she suffered another. JBY found a more pleasant and commodious house at 3 Blenheim Road in Bedford Park, near

23. William Butler Yeats, about 1885. *Courtesy of Michael B. Yeats.*

the Woodstock Road house where they had stayed in the early 1880s. Papa, Willie, Lollie, and Jack moved there in March 1888 and organized the household, and the following month Lily and the helpless Susan returned from Denby. For Susan Pollexfen Yeats it was to be the last move, as she remained in and about the Blenheim Road house, seldom stirring from it, until her death twelve years later at the age of fifty-nine.[78] She could do almost nothing to help herself or her family for the last years of her life.

The long residence in Blenheim Road marked a maturing of his children's talents that had been nurtured from their childhood by their restless father. He wrote of the Bedford Park years that they were "artistic and with complete freedom of thought. You went to church or not as you liked, and we talked about everything and avoided having fixed opinions. No one stayed in my house that did not benefit." Susan Mitchell, who became a paying guest in the late nineties and later went on to fame in Dublin as friend of George Russell and scourge of George Moore, gave credit to her stay among the Yeatses for her own education and broad point of view.[79]

JBY suggested to his eldest son that he write a novel, "partly of London, partly of Sligo." The dutiful son complied with an extravagant tale of ancient pre-Pyramidal peoples, the hero "a man of giant stature and of giant strength named Dhoya."[80] His father, disappointed, told Willie he wanted a story "about real people." The result was *John Sherman,* a novel published in 1891 and re-printed twice, in 1891 and 1892. Despite these indications of its appeal, Yeats refused to allow it to be reprinted among his works later, saying of it that it was "Written when I was very young and knew no better."[81] It had its genesis in both a nostalgia for Sligo and a dislike of London. "I feel like Robinson Crusoe in this dread-ful London," he told Katharine Tynan shortly after his arrival there.[82] He uttered similar sentiments continually: "this horrid London";[83] "What a horrid place this London is!";[84] "I sometimes imagine that the souls of the lost are compelled to walk through its streets perpetually. One feels them passing like a whiff of air."[85]

John Sherman is a revealing work, unlike anything else Yeats wrote in both tone and substance. Those who knew Willie inti-mately spoke of his humor, yet a reading of his works, in verse or prose, suggests chiefly an earnest, serious poet or pamphleteer. In *John Sherman,* however, the omniscient narrator maintains ironic, even mischievous, control, as he relates the adventures of the hero and his loved one, Margaret Leland.[86] The story is too complex to be summarized here in detail, but its broad outline is easy to sketch. John Sherman, an Irish country boy from Ballah (Yeats's fictional name for Sligo), moves to London to take a job, leaving behind a sweetheart, Mary Carton. Meeting Margaret Leland in the big city, he is tempted to forget his allegiance to Ballah and Mary

and to join the crowd of swells who have the connections that lead
to money and power. After some intricacies of plot, Sherman for-
sakes Margaret, returns to Ballah, marries Mary Carton, and lives
happily ever after.

John Sherman is far more valuable as a source of Willie's feelings
about life in the late 1880s than his autobiography, which is
marked by the indirection and vagueness characteristic of much of
his prose. Equally important as evidence of his father's influence is
the narrative technique of the book. John Sherman, although
clearly and principally William Butler Yeats, plays the roles at
times of Henry Middleton and Jack Yeats. The character William
Howard is at different times John Dowden, Edward Dowden,
Charles Johnston, and John Butler Yeats.[87] The structure and treatment match almost exactly those John Butler Yeats had made use
of in a series of stories, mostly unfinished, that he wrote in the early
1870s. The method is of course not original; the *roman à clef* is of
ancient lineage. Yet the devices in Willie's novel so closely resem-
ble his father's that it is not hard to see where they came from. In
later years Willie used the same technique in *The Speckled Bird,*
the unpublished autobiographical novel about his experiences with
Maud Gonne and his associates in the Order of the Golden Dawn.[88]

The composition of the early work that brought WBY lasting
fame, "The Lake Isle of Innisfree," was attended with a mundane
disappointment he doesn't mention in his autobiographical or fictional accounts.[89] Lily and Lollie were sitting in the living room
with a friend named Helen Acostos, all knitting or sewing in proper
Victorian fashion. Suddenly Willie burst in from the adjoining
room with the announcement that he had just completed a poem
and wanted them to listen while he recited it. It was "Innisfree."
When he finished, face flushed with enthusiasm, he waited for a
response. Miss Acostos turned to Lollie and said, "May I have a
paint brush?" Lily, always close to her brother, wondered how
anyone could have been so insensitive. Miss Acostos had not even
pretended to listen.[90] But, of course, at Blenheim Road WBY was
a prophet in his own country. Unlike many fortunate poets before
him who had cleared themselves of parental entanglements before
manhood, William Butler Yeats was to be closely involved with his
family until he was thirty years old. He might spend as much time

as he could with fellow poets in London, or with occultists in the Order of the Golden Dawn, or with John O'Leary or George Pollexfen in Ireland—or with Maud Gonne anywhere—but ordinarily he dined every night at home, in the presence of the two sisters and younger brother, with the dominant father at the head of the table holding forth like the Ancient Mariner, and Willie could not choose but hear. Mama dined alone upstairs. In such circumstances it was not easy for Willie to develop a sense of self-importance or independence.

The life at Blenheim Road is described with a vivid immediacy in two diaries, one kept by Lollie from 6 September 1888 to 24 May 1889,[91] the other by Lily from August 1895 to December 1896. The very first entry in Lollie's mentions Willie twice, once as reading aloud "all the evening to Papa," and as earning £5 for copying manuscripts (6 September 1888). A few days later (9 September) she records a striking scene:

> I am writing this in the kitchen and Miss J[owitt] is opposite to me writing about some new pupils and we can hear a murmur of talk from the dining-room where Papa and Willie are arguing something or other. Sometimes they raise their voices so that a stranger might fancy they were both in a rage. Not at all. It is only their way of arguing. I suppose it is because they are natives of the Emerald Isle.

A week and a half later she wrote a similar entry: "Papa and Willie had a hot argument on Metaphysics" (18 September).

Lollie's accounts are direct and simple, and often stark when she comments on the constant shortage of funds. On 20 September (while Jack was away on vacation in Sligo) she wrote of the happy part of their lives: "Papa has gone to dine at Dr. Hayes'. I don't like an evening he dines out at all. Lillie is writing to Jack, Mama is reading the story in the 'Pall Mall.' " Then follows the bad news: "I hope our affairs will improve as we have no butter, scarcely any sugar, and in fact want nearly everything. Late to bed." She records attending, with Lily, French classes at Kelmscott House on the Mall in Hammersmith, the home of William Morris. They had to walk both ways, there being no money in the house to pay for trams. On the twenty-second Dr. Todhunter came to Blenheim Road to help Willie read proofs, and later Willie went to visit William Ernest Henley.

The diary is full of such references, both to the activities of the family and to the perennial shortage of funds, but full too of the kind of commentary that indicates the Yeats feeling toward money. "The only penny in the house went on the *Pall Mall*," Lollie wrote on 25 September, "but I think it was worth it." Food had to be got "on tick," two words that appear often in the diary. "No money, *not a fraction* in the house, and no butter or marmalade or sugar or tea," she noted on the twenty-seventh. "What is to become of us I don't know as we owe something at all the shops." She felt embarrassed when the Gambles, neighbors in Bedford Park, gave her and Lily clothing the Gambles no longer needed, "a fawn-colored jacket, some dress stuff and old white satin evening dress all nice." Lollie wished people wouldn't give them things. "Makes you feel queer. One certainly has to pocket one's pride. All the same don't know what we should do without such gifts" (16 October).

Jack's name appears frequently in the diary, both as an attractive, likable teen-ager and as a talented cartoonist and businessman.[92] He studied briefly at an art school in Kensington but learned little there, being the kind of artist whose natural talent was such that schools could teach him nothing.[93] Before he had been in London long, he was selling sketches to magazines and drawing menu and race cards—forms on which restaurants and race tracks could print their offerings.[94] He also painted a design, described by Katharine Tynan as "a map of Sligo," on the ceiling of his older brother's study.[95] His interest in the arts extended even to the mechanical details: Lollie records a visit she and Jack paid to Emery Walker (almost a decade and a half before Evelyn Gleeson invited Lollie to join her in the business of Dun Emer) when the two men "talked a lot about etching, the process, etc." (2 December).

During the period the same themes emerge: of a family of artists working individually and of business people working in partnership, trying to bring in money to a family badly in need of it. Mama, though still able to read and to complain, flits through the pages of the diary as a shadowy figure, dependent and uncooperative—"feeble and unable to go out of doors or move about much,"

24. William Morris (1834–1896), 1880. Photograph by Abel
Lewis; engraved by Emery Walker. *Courtesy of Michael B. Yeats.*

Willie told Katharine Tynan in late January 1889—[96] while Papa,
the titular head of the family, works away fruitlessly, watching his
children outdo him.

Of all the associations described in the diary, none was more
important or more peculiar than that with the family of William
Morris, the cranky, inventive genius who combined talents for

literature and craftsmanship as few others have done. He was a
socialist of the theoretical sort, a dreamer of higher and better
societies, and a practical handyman whose ideas in interior decoration—particularly in hangings, wallpaper and furniture—were to
influence taste permanently. He had had a successful career as an
architect and had turned his hand to printing, his crowning
achievement being the Kelmscott Press edition of *The Canterbury
Tales,* on which he was working when the Yeatses knew him. WBY
had already met Morris at the Contemporary Club in Dublin and
had read his poems and liked them despite his father's objections to
them. Morris's successor as editor of the socialist periodical *Commonweal,* a young man named Herbert Halliday Sparling, was preparing an anthology of poetry to be called *Irish Minstrelsy* and sought
WBY's advice for improvement ("I fear it wants so much that it is
not improvable," WBY told John O'Leary). From the spring of
1887 onward,[97] Willie was a regular guest or visitor at Morris's
home. "It was now Morris himself that stirred my interest," WBY
wrote in his *Autobiographies,* "and I took to him first because of
some little tricks of speech and body that reminded me of my old
grandfather in Sligo." He conferred on Morris an unusual compliment: "If some angel offered me the choice, I would choose to live
his life, poetry and all, rather than my own or any other man's."[98]
There was another reason too for his choosing Morris, one that he
did not express openly until many years later. His father's intelligence and wit and devotion to a life of art were praiseworthy and
had helped shape, perhaps decisively, the mind and soul of William
Butler Yeats. But the other side of the paternal coin was the one
that most often turned up, that of the unsuccessful dreamer and
drifter. Personal success might be unimportant in an ideal world,
but in the real world it was the currency by which many measured
the wealth of a man's character, and by such standards John Butler
Yeats was deemed a failure. His son saw the failure not as the result
of lack of talent or defect of brain or education but of "sheer infirmity of will." Writing toward the end of his father's life to John
Quinn, Willie poured out feelings he had long suppressed:

> It is this infirmity of will which has prevented him from finishing
> his pictures and ruined his career. He even hates the sign of will

in others. It used to cause quarrels between me and him, for the qualities which I thought necessary to success in art or in life seemed to him "egotism" or "selfishness" or "brutality." I had to escape this family drifting, innocent and helpless, and the need for that drew me to dominating men like Henley and Morris.[99]

Morris allowed Kelmscott House to be used for meetings of socialist societies, for language classes, and for other cultural purposes. It lay within walking distance of Bedford Park, and soon WBY was attending regularly and taking part in the discussions of the intellectual and artistic who gathered there. It was there that WBY first made the acquaintance of George Bernard Shaw;[100] Walter Crane, Emery Walker, R. B. Cunninghame Graham, Henry Hyndman, and Prince Peter Kropotkin were others. Morris was sufficiently impressed by the young man that he asked him to contribute an article on Ireland to *Commonweal.*[101]

If Kelmscott House provided a good public forum for Morris's friends, it made a poor home for his family. Morris had married Jane Burden, one of the models he had employed during his early days as a painter, while he was still in his early twenties. Their daughter May was born within a year, and another daughter, Jenny, an epileptic, followed. Mrs. Morris, a beauty, was restless and dissatisfied, and her qualities were passed on to her elder daughter. The presence of Jenny put a stain on Jane Morris's image of what an elegant family should be, but Morris himself loved the handicapped daughter, the only one in the family for whom he showed affection.[102] "I never saw much sympathy between the members of the Morris household," wrote Lily. "There was always the barrier of uncontrolled bad temper between them."[103] (Mrs. Morris had already had an affair with Wilfred Scawen Blunt, the poet who later succeeded in bringing Lady Gregory under his blanket as well, so more than bad temper may have been involved). May, in her late twenties when the Yeatses met her, had developed a resentment against her parents and, partly because they disliked Sparling, she decided to marry him. Lily described Sparling as "a freak to look at, very tall, no chin, and very large spectacles," whose appearance contrasted with Morris's "fine head and shoulders," which, unhappily, were set on a body that was "much too short."[104] Willie

25. William Butler Yeats, 1889, before November. Pencil
sketch by Josephine Webb. *Courtesy of Society of Friends, Dublin.*

hadn't liked Sparling when he first met him, later thought him
acceptable, then reverted to his first opinion, being made "melancholy or irritable" by his "atheisms and negations." [105]

For a while it looked as though May and her lover would
become part of the Yeats family circle. Lily and Lollie, at their
father's insistence, had begun attending the French classes at Kelms-

cott, much to Willie's annoyance, as he felt their presence damaged his own image. Morris appeared at the classes from time to time. Once, after insisting that everyone speak French only, he himself "began the most comic mixture of French and English." [106] Lollie's account of how Willie appeared to others is well known:

> Willie's dramatic intense way of saying his French with his voice raised to telling distinctness and every pronunciation wrong as usual, seemed to amuse Mr. Sparling more than ever. He simply doubled up when Willie commenced. Willie of course divided it up into any amount of full stops where there weren't any, so Madame said, "Mr. Yaytes, you don't read poetry like that, do you?" "Yes, yes," he does, volunteered Mr. Sparling, and in truth [it] was rather like his natural way of reading. (18 January)

May and Sparling enjoyed the company of Lily and of Jack, whom they met at Blenheim Road, and accepted an invitation to attend a dance given by the Bedford Park Badminton Club if promised that the two would attend (8 December). Two days after the dance May sent Lily flowers, and not long afterward Lily and Lollie attended a party at the Morrises', where they helped grind the coffee and cut the cake and performed other little services for the occasion. May sang, accompanying herself on a guitar with colored ribbons "streaming out of it." Morris read from *Huckleberry Finn*. Lollie had Morris for a partner in a dance called the "Sir Roger" and because of Morris's quickness the two "*always* came out *ahead*" (29 December).

With her father's encouragement May had become expert in embroidery and had developed a clientele of wealthy women who ordered patterns she had partly worked, planning to finish them themselves. At the height of the friendliness between May and Sparling and the Yeatses, May asked Lily one day at French class whether she would like to help her with the embroidery. Lily was to go every day "from ten till dinner-time" until "she learned it thoroughly." "I think it is with the idea of making some money by it," wrote Lollie. "I hope it may succeed. At any rate it is very kind of Miss Morris" (23 November).

For a while the Yeatses seemed uncertain about May's purpose, but within two weeks it became clear. "This is a red letter day," Lollie wrote in large bold letters in her diary on Saturday, 8 December, "for today *Lilly* earned her first money. Miss Morris paid her *ten shillings* for her week's embroidery. We all tell her we mean now in the future to be very civil to her, as Miss Morris says she can earn ten shillings and may earn more every week. Jack at once remarked, 'I allus was a friend of your'n, warn't I?' in his best costermonger style" (8 December).[107] Three weeks later the news was even better. "Lilly is getting on famously at Miss Morris. She made 10/- first week and 11/3 last" (20 December). By early January her weekly take had risen to 17 shillings (9 January 1889).

May's apparent generosity was not as altruistic as it seemed, for she had more commissions for embroidery than she could handle. Lily became one of the first of many assistants, who performed the tedious work of filling up the spaces after May had worked the main design.[108] Lily's work with her would last for six years, and when it ended she was an accomplished embroiderer with a skill matched by few in the world of arts and crafts. When Evelyn Gleeson sought a partner for her venture in the Dun Emer enterprise some years later, Lily was an obvious candidate.

May tried to interest Lollie in embroidering too, but the experiment didn't last long. Lollie had to work at home to be with her invalid mother and was too excitable and adventurous for work that demanded patience and an even temper, qualities Lily possessed in abundance. Lollie described in her diary the kind of work that Lily did every day: "Began some background embroidery for Miss Morris on Wednesday. It is an immense screen. When it will be finished I can't tell, terribly monotonous work, the one stitch and colour all the time" (2 March 1889). William Morris himself shared her feelings, finding the difficulty of threading the needles so time-consuming and boring that he gave up the work after a short trial.[109]

Lily worked from ten in the morning to six at night. For the first six months, from September 1888 till March 1889, the embroidering was done in the dining room at Kelmscott House, "a beautiful room with three large portraits of Mrs. Morris by Rossetti and a drawing called 'Pomona.' " Lily enjoyed the work, and, as

26. May Morris (1862–1938), about 1890. *Courtesy of William Morris Gallery.*

she was present at lunch every day, she met the fascinating people who were guests there.[110]

Yet it was only the income that made working under May Morris bearable. May's early camaraderie soon faded. "May very seldom did any work," Lily wrote, "just used to look at mine." The atmosphere in Kelmscott House was oppressive, what with

Jenny's presence and the parents' disapproval of May's attachment
to Sparling. Mrs. Morris was constitutionally dissatisfied anyhow.
"She never spoke and always seemed unhappy," Lily said of her.
"She liked to be surrounded by people easy to talk to and flattering
and admiring, and instead she was surrounded by cranks and freaks
and bad tempers, people who never looked at her." Morris himself
got along with few except those outside the family who were sympathetic to his ideas. Kelmscott "was not at all a happy house,"
said Lily, "fear of Morris's violent temper and May's bad one being
felt all through the house."[111]

May was hardly a model employer. If Lily took a day off for
illness she was unpaid. If any of the workers were even five minutes
late in the morning, the time was subtracted from their lunch
hour.[112] Each worker was allowed two weeks of holiday a year. Lily
always took an extra week at her own expense. She left Euston
Station by the night mail after working at May's all day, returning
by the night train and reporting for work in the morning, all to
lengthen her stay in Sligo.[113] "It was Paradise to get away from
London and the workroom and May Morris's temper, even for only
a fortnight, to the green peace."[114]

May's "great ladies" were looking for work to fill up idle time,
but Lily suspected that they never finished the designs.[115] The
workers were kept busy. "They make cushion covers and mantel-
piece covers without end," Willie told Katharine Tynan.[116] Over
the years the other girls came and went, most staying only a short
time because of May's bad temper and meanness, leaving Lily alone
at last with two schoolgirls.[117]

Despite his otherwise advanced ideas, Morris "had respect for
the conventions" and on one occasion used Lily as cat's-paw in a
scheme to rescue May from the fires of impropriety. Mrs. Morris
was away and Morris was planning to leave town when May announced that she would invite Sparling (then still only her fiancé)
to stay at Kelmscott with her while her parents were absent. Morris
thereupon asked Lily to live in the house for a week as an unofficial
chaperone. When she agreed, "he went away laughing, saying,
'What a joke if May does not want you.' " So Lily slept for a week
in the house of the would-be sinners.[118]

Later May tried to thwart her parents by moving out of Kelmscott to a place at 8 Hammersmith Terrace. Lily described the new quarters as "three rooms over a vegetable shop in a slummy street." Morris came one day and cried out, "It is a hole. My, it is a hole." Later, after May and Sparling married, they took a house in Hammersmith, "a nice old house, very inconvenient."[119] After May's marriage Lily would often be asked by Morris, against her desire, to join the Sparlings when they were invited to dinner at Kelmscott. By having Lily present, Morris hoped "to ward off a family row." Despite Lily's acceptance by Morris as a social equal May continued to treat her as a mere worker, little more than a serf.

May was equally unpopular with other people. Lily recounts an occasion when a number of Morris's friends gathered in May's garden to watch the Oxford-Cambridge boat race. All left immediately afterward, telling May they had trains to catch, then went straight to Emery Walker's house a short distance away, where they enjoyed the rest of the afternoon without her.[120]

Lily's earnings were important to the household. Of the seventeen shillings she made during the week ending 2 January, more than five went for a carpet for Willie's study, a "great improvement," thought Lollie (9 January 1889). From ten shillings a week her earnings rose to thirty by the time she left six years later,[121] and it all went into the common pot.

Her father felt sufficiently guilty about the magnitude of her contribution that he told Willie he hoped she would be able to "bank her money, or most of it," rather than pour it all into the "swalley-hole," but as she had already been working for three years when Papa made his hopeful remark, it seems unlikely that the situation ever changed. "She is the only one in the house," he told his son, "whose work is quite without intellectual interest, sewing away amid such depressing associations and in near neighbourhood to the bitter and half-crazed Mrs. Sparling."[122]

While Lily worked, Lollie remained at home, taking care of Mama and writing stories for submission to a magazine called *The Vegetarian*. With other girls in what they called a "mutual improvement society" she helped produce a magazine called *The Pléiades*.[123] She wanted to become a good writer. Always she kept busy, with the talkativeness and intensity that got on other people's nerves.

She enjoyed listening to the conversation of her father and his friends, describing one evening in her diary: "Papa, Willie, and they [the male guests] had great talk and argument, politics, art, etc. L[ily] and I felt dreadfully out of it. I wonder do all girls feel that way, as if the conversation when men talk was altogether beyond them, or is it because we are uneducated and know so little of all these things? But all the same I enjoyed hearing the talk" (19 November).

On 26 November she learned that Jack had received 15 shillings for a sketch for the *Vegetarian,* while she still had heard nothing about her own story. That day her father, concerned for the welfare of his family, borrowed six eggs from a neighbor and made each of his children eat one. "I am sure it is a year since I ate one before," Lollie wrote, "but in spite of a hayey flavor I liked it" (26 November).

William Butler Yeats appears only rarely in Lollie's notices. At the age of twenty-three he was trying to establish himself as a serious writer and thinker, and he had little time for attending dances at the Bedford Park Club or playing badminton with his sisters. Once he and Jack attended a performance of *The Yeomen of the Guard,* probably on free tickets (2 January 1889). When Lollie records the dining of the family at a neighbor's, she notes that "Willie talked theosophy" (26 December), hardly a subject for dinner table conversation in most places.

Lollie recorded that on Sunday, 13 January, Willie was "off to Madame Blavatsky's," while Papa read to the family "scraps out of 'Madame de Stael's Life' " before taking off for the Calumet conversation club (13 January 1889). A few nights later "we had coffee and they talked politics, and debated as to whether there is any afterworld, and whether we have a previous existence" (17 January). It was the kind of gathering Lily had in mind years later when she said that her education came from listening to her father and his friends.

Their association with the prosperous belied the Yeatses' chronic insolvency. "Times very bad," wrote Lollie on 24 January. "Bills on all sides wanting paying. Butcher spoke today, and £7 taxes. Dismal lookout." Nothing in the diary, however, gave any hint of the most momentous event that would occur in the life of

William Butler Yeats only a few days later, on Wednesday, 30 January 1889, the day "the troubling" in his life began. Lollie combined her entries for the four days from the twenty-seventh through the thirtieth. More than half the entry concerns the death and burial of Dan O'Connell, the family cat, and a full paragraph is devoted to Lollie's working on Lily's dress. Then comes the fateful entry:

> Miss Gonne the Dublin beauty (who is marching on to glory over the hearts of the Dublin youths) called today, on Willie of course, but apparently on Papa. She is an immense height and very stylish and well dressed in a careless way. She came in a hansom all the way from Belgravia and kept the hansom waiting while she was here. Lilly noticed that she was in her slippers. She has a rich complexion, hazel eyes I think and is decidedly handsome. I could not see her well as her face was turned from me. [124]

Next evening Willie dined at Miss Gonne's (31 January). From the time of their first meeting, he became entangled in a dense emotional underbrush in which he never found a clearing and from which he could find no escape, for his passion for her was not returned. His infatuation with Miss Gonne was one-sided in more ways than one, for everyone else in his family came to dislike her intensely. [125]

With her brothers and sister working to bring in money, Lollie could not stay at home for long and decided to continue her education and combine it with teaching brushwork painting. One of the results was the collapse of her diary. After she began her schooling in May 1889, entries in the diary dwindle and finally become single sentences. From the twenty-first to the twenty-fourth, she writes only one or two lines per day; the next entry is dated almost two years later, 20 January 1891.

Lollie's education included attendance at the Froebel School as a "student teacher." [126] She began teaching at the Kindergarten School in March 1889 but received no pay for a whole year. [127] She ultimately earned both Elementary and Higher certificates. She studied history and grammar and also "drawing birds" (21, 22, 23 May 1889). What is clear is that by the time she had finished,

27. Maud Gonne (1866–1953), about 1889. Pencil sketch by
Josephine Webb. *Courtesy of Society of Friends, Dublin.*

Lollie was a thoroughly trained and skillful teacher of art. During
the next decade she taught at the Froebel Society, the Chiswick
High School, the Central Foundation Schools in London (where she
taught art to the teachers) and a number of other public schools,
and at several private schools, and taught privately the children of
wealthy parents in the London area.[128] She had a compulsion to

work. "I never wanted to stop," she wrote years later. She described a typical day: "At school at a quarter to nine when I was teaching at the Kindergarten, home at 2 for dinner, and after that off to Notting Hill (from Chiswick) to lectures (except when I had afternoon school) and worked all evening in preparation for exams, etc." [129] Eventually the strain of "combined housekeeping and kindergarten anxieties" were, according to Willie, "too much for her," and she had to flee to Dublin for rest. [130]

While becoming the chief breadwinner for the family, Lollie perfected a technique for doing brushwork painting, eventually publishing three books on the subject and earning a good income from the teaching of it. [131] She became increasingly prosperous, and for many years the money she made constituted the bulk of the family income. [132] Her father wrote years later that in one year she had made £300; [133] and even if the passage of time inflated his estimate of the figure, his recollection suggests something of the importance of her contribution. Lollie sporadically listed Willie's and Jack's incomes too: the last entries of her diary show for WBY a total of £28.16.2 for the period between December 1889 and November 1890, and of £27 between 25 February and 19 May of 1891; for Jack £27.13.4 between December 1890 and May 1891.

So the family remained together in Bedford Park for a period of about six years, close-knit and loyal. Differences among its members were reduced by the fact that the children spent so little time together at home, Lily away all day, Jack sketching and visiting, Lollie teaching part of the day and tending Mama for the rest, Willie away not only during the days but the evenings too, as his activities with Irish cultural and nationalist matters and with occult studies increased.

Like Willie, Jack found Lily the member of the family he most enjoyed talking to. Their father has given an account of their closeness:

All my family are strangely different from each other, but Jack and Lily are closest to each other. That's why they have always been such good friends. In London when Jack arrived late at night, in his polite way he would stop a while with me and talk and then ask if I thought Lily was awake. And long after when I climbed up to bed, as I passed her room I could hear laughter and talking. It was Jack and Lily.[134]

Finally, after seven years of unbroken family solidarity, four events changed the Yeats pattern substantially. On 24 August 1894, Jack married Mary Cottenham ("Cottie") White, a woman he had pursued for a couple of years. Jack had met her in 1892 while they were in art school together, resolved to make enough money to be worthy of her, and so took a job for two years with a newspaper in Manchester—a period he was to call "the least satisfactory working days" of his life.[135] He stayed there all week, returning to Bedford Park on weekends when the opportunity arose. Cottie had money of her own as life beneficiary of a trust that brought in an income ample enough to support the two of them through lean days. Knowing of JBY's reputation with money, Cottie had her lawyer draw up papers to ensure that the allowance she made to her mother was removed from her control.[136] After the marriage Jack remained in close touch with his family, but as he and Cottie set up their own home, first in Surrey and later in Devon, he became necessarily a remote member of it. Cottie was never close to the others; they all professed to admire her and never said anything openly critical of her, but there was always an uneasiness in their dealings with her.[137]

Then in April 1894, Lily's long association with May Morris came to an end. The relationship between them had grown progressively worse, and Lily had hung on bravely only because the family needed her salary. May needed Lily too, for she proved a superb embroiderer. Lily and a colleague, Ellen Wright, did the bedspread and hangings for Morris's bed in Kelmscott Manor, a work designed by May for the 1893 Exhibition.[138] In 1896 the *Irish Times* gave a notice of her embroidery in the Arts and Crafts Exhibition in Dublin; "quite proud to see my name in the paper," she wrote in her diary.[139] But the tensions eventually became unbearable, and, when at length Lily felt her health not good enough for continued work, she announced she would have to leave after May's return from vacation. May wrote what JBY called "a malicious and impudent letter," Lily wrote in reply an indignant letter of resignation (or rather JBY composed it and Lily signed it), and that ended the association forever. Lily never saw May again.[140] Morris, with whom Willie remained on friendly terms, died two years later just as his Kelmscott Chaucer was appearing.

The break of course meant the end of Lily's contribution to the family coffers. She began a diary of her own sixteen months later, which lasted from 1 August 1895 to 26 June 1897, with long gaps.[141] In it the family appears as it did in Lollie's diary six years earlier: close-knit, busy, active with neighbors and visitors, engaged in literature, art, and Irish nationalism. Many of her anecdotes show Lily's continued closeness to Willie and her support of his difficult career, at the same time exhibiting an observant eye for the ridiculous and amusing.

The Poet has not a halfpenny, so he has been hard at work all day at a story so as to make enough to pay his railway fares (2 August 1895).

Willie reduced to borrowing 2^d pence from me (5 August).

Willy gone to Mr. Henley's in all the glory of a new coat, black, a joy and at the same time a disappointment. Don't know what he expected. He hopes in the future to be a symphony in grey, has got as far as the gloves, and they are already buttonless (10 August).

In afternoon Nora Hopper called, looking so stolid, sensible, and nice in spite of the hundred and one chains, brooches, and bows she was hung over with. Willy read her his story, "Costello[e] the Proud," which he has just finished. Dora Isbister called but was thrown into such a state of alarm by Willy, who gave her one of his grandest bows under the impression that she was someone he has or thinks he has an aversion to. Can't discover who he thought she was, doesn't know himself, I expect (11 August).

W. B. is reading an article which he has written on Standish O'Grady in the "Bookman" to Mr. O'Leary, who says it is no more like him than the man in the moon. Then the whole lot of them begin talking together. I don't know who is doing the listening (11 August).

Willy has gone to see if Miss Allport is at home so as to have his story typewritten. The whole family of Allport have to be at home, I believe, to do a story of W. B.'s, what with writing and unknown Irish names (13 August).

W. B. writing a poem the last couple of days. To judge by the groaning coming from his room, must be a painful performance (15 August).

Willy in next door [at Elkin Mathews's house], yesterday he got an advance copy of his Poems. He can't part from it but sits not reading it but looking at the outside and turning it over and over (21 August).

Willy next door to meet George Moore's brother. Rose out, so have the place to myself. Willy still wrestling with poems, they seem to have a time of it together. He went out of the hall door groaning (22 August).

On way back [from visit] met Willy, who was in the agony of another lyric. He walked along with me, muttering and groaning. The passers by looked at me with sympathetic eyes. "Such a nice girl, out with that poor mentally afflicted gentleman" (1 September).

W. B. stuck himself in his best coat onto a sticky flypaper (1 September, third entry).

Willy is having his portrait painted by Mr. Foulkes, an occult rose in one corner. Papa says he can't paint a bit. W. B. won't mind as long as it is full of symbols and is hollow cheeked (4 September).

It is clear from the entries that the old association of brother and sister was as strong as ever.

Lily made no attempt to find another paying job, instead working about the Blenheim Road home and visiting Sligo. Her father was working on the illustrations for the Dent edition of the works of Daniel Defoe, and she served as model for all the characters except Crusoe and the man Friday.[142] It was not the kind of art he had hoped to base his reputation on. In his fifties he had to face the fact of his failure both as artist and as breadwinner and to witness the silent contempt, as he saw it, of his two sons. Finally, in the mid-nineties, after years of fruitless optimism, he gave way to the demons within and suffered a severe collapse.

JBY's visible symptoms were physical, chiefly indigestion, but it is not hard to conclude that they were psychosomatic in origin. His old friends and schoolmates were published poets and critics, distinguished ecclesiastics, prosperous barristers or judges or professors. He alone had never been able to make a go of it with his talents. Titular head of his own family, he saw a wife whose unhappiness caused her to escape at last into a world of fantasy and four children whose own labors had to support the household for which he felt himself morally responsible.[143] A revealing letter from T. W. Rolleston to Elkin Mathews in 1894 refers to John Butler Yeats as "a comparatively unknown man," and identifies him as "the father of W. B. Yeats."[144] It was in the same year that Robert Louis Stevenson wrote his famous letter from Samoa to WBY praising him for his "Lake Isle of Innisfree."[145] Nobody wrote to the father about the greatness of his portraits. Jack, always ready in times of need, carried his father off to a physician. The physical symptoms slowly disappeared, and the emotional sources again became slowly buried under the restorative layers of JBY's irrepressible optimism. Not until his complete separation from the family in 1907 and his assuming a new life, and almost a new identity, in New York were the demons buried deep, almost if not quite beyond retrieval.[146]

In 1895 came the other two changes in the family unity. Willie's letters to Katharine Tynan and others spoke less and less of what was going on at Blenheim Road as outside interests claimed more of his attention, though he kept living there. Then, shortly before his thirtieth birthday, he decided to take rooms in the Temple. His move meant that he would take his guaranteed monthly rent with him. ("I always contribute here of course," he had assured John O'Leary).[147] Lollie was left as virtually the sole support of the family, although Willie and Jack made gifts from time to time. Yet the chemistry had changed, and Lollie, the one member of the family least able to stand the strain and worry, had to bear the heaviest burden.

Lily was angry when, on vacation in Sligo, she heard the news.

Willie told Lollie he thought he could live on ten shillings a week. "Let him try," wrote Lily in her diary (4 October 1895). Her reaction to his move aroused in her one of the few bitter passages about her favorite brother. She wrote, then tried unsuccessfully to delete, an entry in her diary charging that if he could afford ten shillings at the Temple he could surely afford to pay the same sum at home (4 October),[148] where the money was needed. Lily had no way of knowing that Willie was about to enter on a discreet affair with Mrs. Olivia Shakespear, which required privacy.

Then came the other major change. While in Sligo, Lily was offered a nonpaying job as governess to the children of an English family in Hyères in southern France. Urged by all in the family to accept, she returned briefly to Bedford Park, where Willie prepared an astrological forecast for her—"devil a word of truth in it," she said of it when time had put it to the test—and showed her a new poem he had written.[149] Less than a week later she arrived in Hyères to begin her work. Within three months she fell ill with typhoid fever. Because of her congenital weakness, still undiagnosed, the effect on her system was devastating. Fortunately, her employers were compassionate, taking care of her completely, sending her at one time to Italy for recuperation, which was to seem endless. She did not return to Blenheim Road till December 1896 and for several years afterward was so weak could do nothing requiring exertion.[150] Lollie was forced to continue the duties of houseminding along with her regular work.

During the evenings Lollie visited with friends and on holidays took off for Sligo or other places. Lily declared some years later that she saw so little of Lollie during those years that she did not know how unattractive a companion she could be; that discovery was to be saved for the years in Dublin. Willie had described to his new friend Lady Augusta Gregory in a single word how he felt about Lollie; she was "dangerous." When Lady Gregory first met the sisters she noted that Lily was "pretty and soft and delicate"; "the other, 'the dangerous one,' " was, she suspected, the one who "keeps the house going."[151]

Lily had already noticed Lollie's need of a "philosophy." The nervous excitement and talkativeness that were to cause her so much trouble later were already in evidence. When Jack heard that Lollie had bought a bicycle, he confided to Lily: "The bicycle would do Lolly good, particularly—but only whisper this to the bicycle, *not* to Lolly—it is *difficult to talk on a bicycle.*"[152] Yet her teaching was highly regarded by those familiar with it. Her pupils won "high awards" at the annual exhibition of the Royal Drawing Society of Great Britain and Ireland, and Her Royal Highness Princess Louise "specially commended" her work.[153] Her three books on drawing: *Brushwork* (1896), *Brushwork Studies of Flowers, Fruit, and Animals* (1898), and *Elementary Brushwork Studies* (1899, though not officially published till 1900)[154] are evidence of her enthusiasm and industriousness. Yet her talents as teacher and artist, which gave her some standing and should have increased her self-confidence and serenity, were still not matched by her social graces. Papa hinted at her position in the scheme of things in a letter to Lady Gregory. Susan Mitchell (at Blenheim Road as a paying guest from 1897 to late 1899), had just taken off on a vacation with Lily, whom she chose as a companion to the exclusion of Lollie. The house, JBY said, was now a "desert." "Lollie's work lies outside and very enchanting she often finds it. In this house just now there is no unoccupied person into whose sympathetic ear one may drop a confidential remark."[155] Clearly Lollie's ear was not sympathetic. Despite her vacations in Dublin and Sligo,[156] nothing gave her the serenity she needed.

Life at Blenheim Road continued in the old pattern. A second tier of friends had replaced or augmented the early one. Frederick York Powell, the Regius Professor of History at Oxford, spent his weekends in Bedford Park and became one of the family's most faithful friends—"sympathetic unique York Powell," Willie called him.[157] Oliver Elton, the literary historian, and his young wife came to live in Bedford Park and began a lifelong association with the family; it was Elton who observed of JBY with admiration that he was "quite fantastically not on the make."[158] An insecure, shambling young man named Gilbert Keith Chesterton came to Bedford Park to court one of its residents, Frances Blogg, whom he later married at a wedding attended by JBY and the two daughters. The Chestertons remained close friends of the Yeatses, especially of Lily and Lollie, all their lives. Susan Mitchell wrote of the fascinations of life among the Yeatses, "a society where ideas were valued above all other possessions and where normal conversation ran on subjects, some of which I had indeed thought of, but which thinking I regretted in myself." The master hand behind her education was John Butler Yeats, as expansive of ideas and advice as he was short of money. Miss Mitchell describes his manner: "Mr. Yeats, that brave head thrown back, his eyes smiling, said things that seemed to me daring, witty, full of old wisdom and young folly, but said them always with a distinction and grace that made the mere saying significant." [159] Chesterton, one of the world's great conversationalists, thought JBY the best talker he ever met, with WBY taking second place behind him.

> He had that very rare but very real thing, entirely spontaneous style. . . . A long and elaborately balanced sentence, with dependent clauses alternative or antithetical, would flow out of such talkers with every word falling into its place. . . . That style, or swift construction of a complicated sentence, was the sign of a lucidity now largely lost. [160]

Finally, on 3 January 1900, after years of declining health, Susan Pollexfen Yeats died, suddenly and unexpectedly. She was buried three days later in the nearby Acton Rural Cemetery, little notice of her life or death appearing in the local newspapers. She was indeed almost a nonperson for the last fifteen years of her life. During them, after the strokes, she drifted slowly into a state of isolation while retaining many of her faculties. Lily described her as a "semi-invalid" who stayed in her room during her last years, "memory vague, not unhappy. She read the papers, looked out of the window with interest." [161] John Butler Yeats later wrote to his son Willie: "I often said of your mother that her affection was a matter that one *inferred*. No one ever saw it or heard it speak." [162] William Butler Yeats was cautious in his remarks about her in his published works. "I can see now that she had great depth of feeling, that she was her father's daughter. My memory of what she was like in those days has grown very dim, but I think her sense of personality, her desire of any life of her own, had disappeared in her care for us and in much anxiety about money." [163] Writing a private letter eight years after his mother's death, he made perhaps the most depressing yet accurate analysis of her place in the family:

"My mother was so long ill, so long fading out of life, that the last fading out of all made no noticeable change in our lives." [164]

The chief result of her death was quite simply the liberation of the family. For years JBY had wanted to move to another place in London, though he had never fixed on a precise location. Now, with characteristic indecision, he visited Paris for two weeks to see the paintings there, then took a vacation with Jack and Cottie in Devon. He wrote a young artist friend that he would like to come to Dublin if he could. [165] George Russell and Lady Gregory tried to whip up enthusiasm in Dublin to have JBY return as teacher and a kind of court painter, but gave up in frustration when the other artists complained that there were already too many painters in the city. As always, JBY could not make decisions that affected his own welfare.

He could and did make one that affected another's. Fredrick Pollexfen, the annoying brother of Susan and George, had been divorced from the wife who had borne him nine children, and a dispute arose over their care. Funds were in short supply, and the judge was not willing to grant custody to either parent. The children were made wards of the court. When JBY heard that the eldest child, Ruth, then in her middle teens, might not be properly cared for, he sent for her at once, and Ruth became a member of the household, and virtually a member of the family, until her marriage more than a decade later. Immediately JBY took her under his wing, educating her in the things he thought important. He found her "extremely ingenious and artistic, with an eye in her head." [166] More ominous for the future happiness of the household was that Ruth took to Lily instantly, and the two became like mother and daughter. [167] Like virtually everyone else, Ruth did not take to Lollie at all, and Lollie responded with a virulent jealousy, blaming her for having separated her sister from her. In retrospect, it is clear that Lollie would have been unhappy and jealous and frustrated if Ruth had never existed, but Ruth was a convenient target and remained so until Lollie's death forty years later. [168]

All the members of the family visited Jack in Devon. At one time JBY, Lily, and Ruth went as a group: [169] at another, Willie was in residence "working at a novel," probably *The Speckled Bird*. When they were not present, Jack wrote letters to the others regularly, letters in which he displayed the elfin wit and grotesque

28. Lollie Yeats (1868–1940), 1898. Pencil sketch by JBY.
Courtesy of Michael B. Yeats.

imagination that made him such a delightful companion. In one of
those letters, written to Lily on 10 May 1902, he asks in an offhand
sentence that constitutes the last paragraph: "Any fresh develop-
ments over the Gleeson business?" The "Gleeson business"
was to become very much the Yeats business. It was to change the
direction of Lily's and Lollie's lives and, in ways that might not

29. William Butler Yeats, 28 January 1899. Pencil sketch by JBY. *Courtesy of Michael B. Yeats.*

have happened if the "Gleeson business" had never arisen, the lives of Willie and Jack as well.

The Gleeson business was of course the Dun Emer Industries. Its establishment by Evelyn Gleeson, with the Yeats sisters as associates, began a new chapter in the life of the Yeats family.

3

Dun Emer, 1902–1908

> All the things made at Dun Emer are beautiful in
> the sense that they are instinct with individual feeling
> and have cost thought and care.
> —Dun Emer Industries Prospectus,
> Winter 1903

> The whole Dun Emer venture should have been
> thought out carefully at the start.
> —William Butler Yeats to Lady Gregory,
> 8 February 1904

The Dun Emer Industries was established in Dublin in 1902 to provide work for Irish girls while they learned the crafts of weaving, embroidery, printing, and other such skills. In 1908 one branch of it split off from the other and formed the Cuala Industries. Both were still operating forty years later. Both names have become part of the lore of Yeatsiana, for Lily and Lollie Yeats were involved in both.[1]

The commonly accepted history of the enterprises is that Lily and Lollie combined forces with Evelyn Gleeson to found Dun Emer, but later parted company with her because of her "difficult" personality and formed the Cuala Industries on their own. Lollie's letters, filed in their hundreds in university libraries around the world, provide the details on which the common assumptions are based.

Those privy to the secrets of Lollie's personality will not be surprised to learn that the real story is not quite the same as the accepted one. The Yeats sisters were not founders of Dun Emer except in the most tangential way, and the split between them and

86

Miss Gleeson was hardly the result of her faults of personality. Indeed, it is not unfair to say that Miss Gleeson, although not easy to get along with, might have succeeded with someone other than Lollie as a partner but that Lollie would not have succeeded with anyone.

Dun Emer came about from a fortuitous meeting of people and ideas, but the people were not the Yeatses and the ideas were not theirs but someone else's. The sole founding spirits of what became Dun Emer were two unlikely Irish friends: a botanist whose fame in China and England is greater than in Ireland and an English-born daughter of a wealthy Irish physician. He was Augustine Henry (1857–1930), she Evelyn Gleeson (1855–1944).[2] He had met Evelyn's brother Jim at college in Galway and came to know the rest of the family through him. Henry, whose first wife had died in 1894, became a kind of brother or Dutch cousin to Evelyn; his letters to her, preserved in the National Library of Ireland, provide a virtually complete history of their relationship.[3] A medical doctor, he had left Ireland in 1881 to join the Imperial Maritime Customs Service in China. To keep himself sane in the emptiness of the Far East, he took up botany as a hobby, collecting plants wherever he could and sending samples back to England for identification. Altogether he spent seventeen years in Asia, and by the time he returned to the British Isles he was one of the foremost botanists in the world; many species of plants, shrubs, and flowers bear his name. Ultimately he became associated with the gardens at Kew, served with H. J. Elwes as coauthor (and principal scholar) of one of the seminal works of botany, *The Trees of Great Britain and Ireland,* won many honors, and was appointed to a readership at Cambridge.

During all these years he corresponded faithfully with Evelyn Gleeson, whose father, Edward Moloney Gleeson, had retired from medical practice in England in 1859 and returned to Ireland in 1863 to found the Athlone Woollen Mills. Evelyn, aged eight, accompanied her father, later returned to England, and spent most of her young adult life in London, where Henry visited her frequently. Evelyn became the beneficiary of a trust fund, which provided her with an income that, though small, was large enough to allow her to live independently. In the early 1880s she studied

30. Augustine Henry (1857–1930), about 1890. *Courtesy of Dr. Barbara Phillips.*

painting at the *Atelier Ludovici* in London and developed an interest in tapestry and weaving. As early as 1883 Alexander Millar, a craftsman of carpets, complimented her on a "rug sketch" she had sent to him for criticism. In the early 1890s Miss Gleeson, active both in Celtic matters and in the renaissance of the manual arts inspired by the work of William Morris, was appointed secretary of the Irish Literary Society in London, one of the founders of which was William Butler Yeats. At its meetings she met Yeats and his sisters. She and Dr. Henry had often talked about doing something for Ireland but all during the nineties had not been able to develop a practical scheme that would provide an outlet for her interest in arts and crafts.

Then, at the turn of the century, Evelyn Gleeson was faced with an unusual responsibility. The husband of her sister, Constance MacCormack, was killed in a fall from a horse, and Constance and her two small daughters moved in with her. Something was needed to keep all hands occupied. Henry renewed talk of a scheme he referred to as "The Settlement." Its precise nature was vague. He wanted Evelyn, whose health had been poor, to get out of London and live in Dublin, where the air was purer.[4] They determined that with Henry's financial help Miss Gleeson would return to Dublin and establish some kind of studio or manufactory where Irish things might be crafted by young Irish girls.[5] "The intention," as Sheila Pim puts it, "was that the craft centre would train workers and create jobs, as well as raising standards."[6] The two old friends set about to put flesh on the bones of their dream.

Surprisingly, they had no thought at the outset of engaging in either printing or carpet weaving. They sought out friends in London to find people "fit for settlement," as Henry phrased it, but some of the people he interviewed didn't understand what he was trying to do, and others annoyed him. After rejecting some candidates, Henry wrote to the Yeats sisters on 18 January 1902 and raised the question of whether they might be interested in joining the enterprise.[7] They said they were, and Dun Emer was born.

To understand the course of subsequent events one must know something of the four principal people involved, for one of the rocks on which their association foundered was a clash of personalities. Of the four Lily, still weak from her bout with typhoid, was the least involved in the unpleasantness of the subsequent disagreements. Henry, like Lily, was quiet, mild-mannered, and self-effacing. From the evidence he appears to have been interested in Miss Gleeson's welfare in a wholly charitable and selfless way. Slow to anger, optimistic, he suffered from a naïveté in expecting grandiose results from mundane efforts, being totally innocent of experience in busi-

31. Evelyn Gleeson (1855–1944), in the 1880s. *Courtesy of Dr. Patrick H. Kelly.*

ness. As the payer of the piper, he was the one who ultimately had to call the tune, but he did so reluctantly.

Lollie was nervous, excitable, and energetic. Of the two sisters she was the one who conducted most of the negotiations with Henry and Miss Gleeson; in the voluminous surviving body of correspondence and other documentation, Lily appears rarely, content to leave matters to her sister. Her decision may have been unfortunate, for Lollie had the unpleasing quality—not noticed by herself—of rubbing other people the wrong way. She assumed the correctness of her position in all matters and showed remarkable energy in asserting what she regarded as her rights.

Evelyn Gleeson was equally annoying in her own way. Like so many of the ladies of her time who enjoyed the benefit of an unearned income—Annie Horniman, financier of the Abbey Theatre, comes to mind—she had developed a feeling of superiority and righteousness, and with younger people or those she thought dependent on her she could be condescending and patronizing, something of the *grande dame.* Although herself generous and thoughtful and, like Dr. Henry, genuinely interested in the philanthropic benefits that would flow from the scheme they planned together, she often impressed outsiders as arrogant and overbearing.

When Henry approached the Yeats sisters, he providentially struck unusually vulnerable prospects. Since the death of their mother Lily and Lollie had nervously considered the future. Their father wanted to move from the Blenheim Road house that held so many memories of trying times but was temperamentally unable to make a decision. In the fall of 1901 he had traveled to Dublin for an exhibition of his and Nathaniel Hone's paintings and remained there only because he could not afford the return fare to Bedford Park.[8] He had no thought of taking his daughters away from London, where he believed they would find success. When Lollie asked him in early 1902 what he would think of their all living in Dublin, he replied emphatically, "What would become of you and your work and your *life work generally,* which seems to lie in London?"[9] Lily then hinted to him that she and Lollie would reveal "some plan" to him shortly,[10] and soon the machinery that was to become Dun Emer was set in motion. Within a few weeks the future of the father and his daughters was determined, as it so often had been before, by the actions of others. Miss Gleeson discussed her plans with Barry O'Brien, president of the Irish Literary Society, with her cousin T. P. Gill, secretary of the Department of Agriculture and Technical Instruction for Ireland, and with Willie and Jack Yeats.[11] To what extent the brothers gave their approval to the nebulous project is unclear; apparently neither paid much

32. Evelyn Gleeson, about 1900. *Courtesy of Dr. Patrick H. Kelly.*

attention to it when it was unfolding. WBY was to say a couple of years later that "the whole Dun Emer venture should have been thought out carefully at the start," [12] but at the time he raised no objection to it and seems to have welcomed the experiment as a device for giving work to his sisters.

When Henry approached Lily and Lollie he raised two questions: whether they would like to join Miss Gleeson in "The Settlement" and whether they would help raise capital for the new company. The sisters heard and absorbed the first question but not the second. Henry knew they had no funds of their own but expected that they would direct some of their energies—and what he may have thought of as their influence—towards finding investors. Perhaps he thought William Butler Yeats might be able to raise money because of his connections. He knew that John Butler Yeats would not; like everyone else in Ireland, he was aware of the old man's habits. ("You must not lend him any money," he warned Miss Gleeson.)[13] But the sisters gave no thought to investment; they could see only the prospect of work and income. Henry saw things in one way, they in another, and so an early link in the chain of misunderstanding was forged.

The fact that Henry rather than Miss Gleeson was the one who approached the sisters was another accident that helped define the nature of the relationship among the partners. It is clear that from the beginning the Yeatses regarded him as the master hand, the sole founder, of the organization of which they would become a part, and Evelyn Gleeson as merely another subordinate like themselves rather than, as Henry regarded her, the chief executive officer of a company he and she jointly founded for her benefit. Lines of authority that should have been sharply drawn at the outset were blurred. Evelyn Gleeson herself was partly responsible for the image of herself as seen by the sisters, for she insisted from the beginning that the enterprise be a cooperative one and that in matters of policy the sisters have equal power with herself. Instead of flatly asserting her primacy when the relationship began, she created in the sisters a false sense of equality that the realities could not sustain.

Lollie, who was earning a good income from her teaching, could not afford to enter into a new scheme without some guarantee of financial security, and Lily would also have to be provided for. In his innocent way Henry solved the problem by announcing that he would contribute five hundred pounds to cover the salaries of the sisters for the first two years, the amount to be treated as a loan to be repaid out of profits. His purpose was to see the project succeed, not to make a free gift to the sisters. His interest was in Miss Gleeson, not in them. They were excellent candidates for the scheme he had in mind, Lollie with her painting talents and her energy, Lily with her acknowledged skill at embroidery, so to him the investment seemed a reasonable one, and he confidently believed he would be repaid as sales brought in floods of cash.

Contributing to the misunderstandings that were to arise was the fact that Henry was himself almost permanently away from the scene of action, either at his work in Kew or in Nancy, France, where he studied forestry. Not being able to discuss problems with him in face-to-face talks, both Miss Gleeson and the Yeats sisters were forced to write to him instead. He was a third party hundreds of miles away consulted by two antagonistic forces who worked within a few yards of each other.

Although Henry and Miss Gleeson approached the Yeats sisters because of their skills and their connection with Irish cultural interests, they had no specific plans for exploiting their talents. Lollie might be a good teacher of painting, but that was not enough for the kind of work they had in mind. Miss Gleeson was even unclear about what her own role would be. In March 1902, Henry urged her "to take up the learning of the carpet business *at once."* Except for the designs done for Alexander Millar years before, she had no knowledge of the subject; the future head of the carpet branch of Dun Emer did not begin to learn her trade till after she had founded a company to exploit it. Henry advised her to get in touch with Millar at once.[14] Nor did Lollie Yeats know anything about printing; when the question was raised of her running a printing press, she resisted, saying "she disliked machinery" and "was afraid of even a sewing machine."[15] Of those who began the venture, only Lily Yeats knew her craft. She had not lost the skill, learned in the six hard years with May Morris, of working embroidery.

Henry was confident he could find willing investors to join him. He had agreed to finance Miss Gleeson through the difficult early days until money would begin to flow in from the sales of goods, but he knew that further capital would be needed. The five-hundred-pound loan to Lily and Lollie, a staggeringly large one for the times, may have given the sisters a false notion of what they were getting into and raised hopes that could never be fulfilled, but it may also have been what decided them to join forces with Miss Gleeson. Constance MacCormack, the widowed sister, was to be regarded as a partner, but her role was to be limited to managing the domestic chores that would become an inevitable part of the business. She was to play virtually no part in the ensuing disagreements.

Contributing to some of the early difficulties was Henry's fascination with Lollie. He dealt chiefly with her and not with Lily, [16] and she in turn was the one who answered his letters and dealt with Miss Gleeson. She was the dynamo, and her energy and drive impressed Henry, who found her attractive and engaging, as did all who knew her only from a distance. "Miss Lolly Yeats was looking last night extremely charming," he wrote Evelyn Gleeson in April 1902; "she has a strange delicate beauty, and fine clothes always make her a Watteau picture." Six months later he confessed, "I like her very much"; he thought she reminded him somewhat of his late wife Caroline. [17] Miss Gleeson did not find it easy to deal with Lollie when the chief banker of the project was in her antagonist's corner.

In their enthusiasm the new partners moved fast. In late March 1902, even while a preliminary set of articles of association was being drafted, Miss Gleeson sent five pounds to Lily for materials for embroidery; Lily had already joined with Pamela Colman ("Pixie") Smith to start work on a curtain. [18] Shortly afterward Lollie agreed to study the craft of printing with a view to establishing a press. For a time Miss Gleeson thought the new enterprise might make furniture, but the idea was soon discarded. [19] Then, in mid-April, Evelyn Gleeson, with Mrs. MacCormack and Lollie, met to consider a document she had drawn up, entitled "Articles of the Society," containing twenty sections defining the purposes of the Society and the manner in which they would be realized. Its terms were partly responsible for the problems that arose later. They provided for the formation of a Society, not yet named, "equivalent to a partnership," for the purpose of "carrying on industries in one of the suburbs of Dublin, at a location to be determined by Evelyn Gleeson." She was to take a large house somewhere in the suburbs to serve both as residence for herself, Constance MacCormack and Constance's children, and as headquarters and workshop of the Society. She undertook to pay the rent out of her own means for the first two years. All profits from the sale of articles "made by its members or their employees" and of "vegetables, fruits or flowers from its gardens," and all profits from "lectures, lessons, publications or writings concerning the Society" were to go into the general fund[20] and "distributed to each of the members." Section 7, the provision for the benefit of Lily and Lollie, was to prove a principal cause of the later split: "in case the profits of the Society do not exceed £125 annually for each member, that £250 each year be made up to the two Miss Yeats, the sum required being taken out of the capital; and such sum be reckoned a loan to the Miss Yeats' until such time as the Society gives profits large enough to enable them to give the loan back." The document did not specify that the £500 so earmarked, though funneled through Evelyn Gleeson, came from Dr. Henry, even though Lily and Lollie knew he was the source of the funding.

The Articles further provided that "the Society will raise capital not exceeding £1000 at first," with no security promised except the signature of the members, that all matters would be decided at regular meetings of the partners, and that in case of a tie vote decision would be made by lot. Each member of the Society would be "independent in her own department, as regards cost and purchasing of materials, employment of lecturers, hours of work for herself and her employees." No requirements were imposed on hours worked or funds spent. Employees would be paid wages for at least two years until such time as there were profits to distribute.

Lily, who had been unable to attend the meeting because of illness, was pleased with the document but wondered whether Miss Gleeson might not "have rather too much to be responsible for"; she thought the offer of two years' free rent generous. Yet neither of the sisters offered to share the rent and had no other practical suggestions for changing the arrangements.[21]

Henry was so interested in helping Miss Gleeson that he took a rosy view of prospects. In addition to the loan to the Yeatses, he agreed to give Miss Gleeson whatever further funds she needed, all to "be repaid at any time before the day of Judgment." "I can afford all this quite easily," he assured her. "It is a loan for an interesting scheme and experiment."[22]

Alexander Millar gave a different analysis of the document. A hardheaded businessman, he assumed the worst. In a long, detailed letter to Evelyn Gleeson he dissected the articles point by point and concluded that the proposed enterprise was "midsummer madness, an absolutely crazy scheme." He informed her that a partnership made each partner "jointly and severally responsible" for all debts; Miss Gleeson might find all her assets, including her future income, wiped out. The fanciful notion that the Yeatses would be able to repay their £500 within two years was "extremely improbable." "You are all amateurs, and will be sure to waste a lot of money in experiments and mistakes." If there were no profits and a partner retired, there was no provision for the repayment of the partner's share of liabilities. Furthermore, he told her, no sane man would invest in it. "Let me strongly urge you not to put any money into the concern except what you can spare out of your income. You will infallibly lose it."

The arrangement was "very one-sided and unfair to you," he told her. "You are putting something into the concern and taking nothing out until a profit is made, while others are to take out substantial salaries, profit or no profit, though they are putting nothing in." Someone would be left holding the bag, and that someone would be Miss Gleeson.

From his careful reading of the document Millar was led to the suspicion that some crafty second party (clearly the Yeatses) had drawn it up and fobbed it off on Miss Gleeson. The clause dealing with the independence of each section, with no control of working hours, caught his eye at once. "The idea that anyone receiving a fixed salary should not be bound to do a certain definite amount of work for it is quite Gilbertian." He felt that particular proviso had not been drafted by her. "If it has been suggested by anyone who is to receive a salary it is a piece of colossal impudence." There was only one possible source to which he could have been referring.

He tried to interpret Miss Gleeson's dream in the light of the cold realities of day. She thought that customers would make a beaten path to the door of an arts and crafts shop on the outskirts of Dublin. Not so, Millar warned. "Do you expect intending buyers to come out to your suburban house? I fear that on this point you have not clearly thought the matter out." Millar had no financial interest in the enterprise and was motivated only by feelings of friendship for Miss Gleeson. "I can only say that any business firm starting on the lines you propose would not last 12 months even if all its members had a regular business training. So I have no hope of anything but disastrous failure in which you personally will have to bear all the loss." He was sorry to throw cold water on the project, "but even now I feel that I have not sufficiently expressed my sense of its utter hopelessness from a business point of view." The clause on working hours, he repeated, "has the mark of the artistic temperament all over it, but it won't work." [23]

Millar's penetrating dissection, largely justified by subsequent events, would have been enough to discourage any but the most idealistic. But despite Millar's dark suspicions, the Yeats sisters had had nothing to do with the Articles, the work of Miss Gleeson alone. She genuinely desired a partnership. She did not want the sisters to regard themselves as inferior members. She envisioned an association of dedicated artists working serenely together. Money was to be a disregarded annoyance. All would be sweetness and light. Like a compulsive gambler, believing in the teeth of the statistics that her horse must win, Miss Gleeson plunged ahead.

Nothing was said in the plans about printing as such, for Lollie did not decide what her role would be until just after the Articles were discussed. Once she decided to become a printer, Henry thought she should consult Millar and visit his shop to "see the printing being *done.*" [24] It was a fateful decision and one that may have kept the partnership alive longer than other circumstances might have allowed. For Lollie was able to make an arrangement with her brothers by which they became actively involved in the work of the Press. Jack's role was minor: he would help with designs for bookplates and colophons and other art work. Willie's was more important: he would act as editorial advisor of the Press, choosing titles, providing works of his own, and soliciting manuscripts from others. His participation in Dun Emer would bring prestige and good advertisement that might otherwise be lacking. [25]

Despite Miss Gleeson's evident generosity, almost at once cracks developed on the surface of the partnership. The sisters asked Barry O'Brien to approach Dr. Henry and propose that his £500 advance be settled on them directly rather than funneled through Miss Gleeson. An understandably angry and insulted Miss Gleeson almost ended the relationship at once, and would have if it had not been for Henry's support of the sisters. "I was very silly to have consented to go on with them," she wrote Henry a year later. "I look back and wonder that I allowed you to persuade me."[26] A serpent had appeared in the artsy-craftsy Eden before the first apple was ripe.

One of the facts of the relationship was that Evelyn Gleeson was more than a decade older than Lily and Lollie. They always addressed her as "Miss Gleeson," never as "Evelyn."[27] And, whether fairly or not, the sisters saw Miss Gleeson as arrogant and abrasive and as afflicted with delusions of class—"the dragged up Peasant," as JBY described her—one who liked to exercise a kind of noblesse oblige over those who worked with her. John Butler Yeats did not find this side of her attractive. "Miss Gleeson . . . owes many of her most charming qualities to her assumption of class," he wrote Lily years later. "If she had not that class notion she would be quite different with her work girls."[28]

Miss Gleeson pushed forward confidently, leasing a house called Runnymede in Dundrum, a suburb of Dublin.[29] In early August 1902, Lollie visited Dublin to look for housing, and on the twenty-second Henry sent £100 as the first installment of "the Settlement money."[30]

Inevitably, problems arose almost at once because of the lack of sufficient capital. Miss Gleeson had persisted in believing that the Yeatses could come up with money, and Henry insisted in June that they should ("This sounds wicked and mean, but it is Miss Yeats turn to seek a little capital"). By late July, Evelyn was writing to Henry about unspecified "disagreeable events," which he tried to convert into spurs to encourage her.[31] But of course the Yeatses had no money to contribute and were as financially impractical as ever. Far from having surplus funds at his disposal, John Butler Yeats wrote Willie that he did not know how he would raise the £48 necessary for the move to Dublin.[32] So the sisters tried to include that sum as an expense against the business, a maneuver that did not sit well with Henry. He thought the sisters misunderstood Miss Gleeson's situation, believing her a bottomless pit of pounds and shillings, and he suggested she be frank with them about the actual state of her affairs.[33]

The behavior of Lily and Lollie toward Henry's £500 and the £48 moving expenses reflects their feeling about the nature of the

33. Dun Emer Industries, 1903. *Front center, in black:* Evelyn Gleeson; *front:* Lollie with elbow on Lily's knee. *Courtesy of Michael B. Yeats.*

enterprise. They knew Henry was providing most of the money, which they welcomed, and therefore tried to deal with him whenever they could. Miss Gleeson was merely an annoyance, a partner they would have preferred not to have. They seemed never to realize that without Miss Gleeson there would have been no "Settlement." Miss Gleeson, however, had taken on more than she could bear. The capital investment she had hoped for never materialized, and unanticipated expenses—Runnymede proved costly to repair— soaked up the small surplus from her income. She should perhaps have waited longer to begin putting the industry into the business of production. Nevertheless, she had the house decorated and furnished,[34] and by early fall the business was off and running, complete with a gaggle of young Irish girls whose education in arts and crafts would provide them with both culture and funds.[35] Miss Gleeson changed the name of the house to Dun Emer, after the wife of the ancient Irish hero Cuchulain, renowned for her skill in needlework and weaving. (She had suggested to Alexander Millar that the name of the Society might be "Dark Rose," but he thought it a bad name that might be confused with "Dark Horse").

One reason advanced by the Yeatses for their difficulties with Miss Gleeson and her sister was that the two drank. The Yeatses had faults, but drinking was not among them, and Lily in particular loathed those who overimbibed. The references to drinking in the letters of Lily and JBY make clear that they regarded Miss Gleeson's input as excessive. Miss Gleeson, in her mid-forties and suffering from assorted physical ailments, and her sister, freshly widowed, surely had some excuse for seeking the palliative of Jameson's, but the Yeats sisters were unsympathetic to excuses and saw only the effects on the victims: argumentativeness, belligerence, and incoherence. JBY wrote to Willie of Miss Gleeson's "explosions of violent temper,"[36] and Lily told her cousin Ruth years later that if she and Lollie had been aware of Mrs. MacCormack's drinking they would never have joined the partnership.[37]

Nevertheless, it is still clear that even if there had been no clashes of temperament the arrangement could not have survived for long; in business the lack of money is the root of all evil. Lollie's idiosyncrasies clashing with those of Evelyn Gleeson and her sister merely assisted the inevitable. The Yeats sisters never understood their place in the institutional hierarchy and failed to behave with becoming restraint. Miss Gleeson had offered them partnership and cooperation; they assumed superiority and independence. Despite their position as partners in the formal sense, they were in fact completely beholden to Miss Gleeson for their livelihood. She was providing the money (even if some of it came from Dr. Henry), she owned Dun Emer, she was the legitimate founder. To her a certain deference was owed, but from the sisters she did not get it.

Events moved swiftly for the Yeatses. JBY and Lollie found a little house a mile and a half by road from Dun Emer, in Churchtown, near Dundrum, which they christened Gurteen Dhas, Irish for "pretty little field." By 1 October 1902 the furniture had been removed from Blenheim Road, and the family (JBY, Lily, Lollie, cousin Ruth Pollexfen) and the two servants (Rose and Maria) moved in before the end of the month.[38] Lollie was soon hard at work, as assertive as ever, reminding Henry again of his

34. The Dun Emer House, 1903. *Left to right:* Constance Mac-Cormack, her two children, Evelyn Gleeson. *Courtesy of Dr. Patrick H. Kelly.*

wife, or of "one-half" of her,[39] for the wife, though firm and decisive as Lollie, had also been reasonable.

Lollie had sought the advice of William Morris's friend Emery Walker and at his suggestion studied printing for a month at the Women's Printing Society in London. He had recommended that her press choose 14-point Caslon Old Style as its type, and Lollie had ordered a font even before she had printing machinery. That, an Albion Hand Press, was purchased from an Irish provincial printing house. Its cost, with accessories, was £25.3.2, all paid out of the general funds of the Society. Before long, further supplies of the lowercase letters *g* and *w* had to be acquired, adding to the

expense. Lollie set to work at once, and by early December had
some pages of William Butler Yeats's *In the Seven Woods* ready for
his inspection; George Russell's *Nuts of Knowledge* was scheduled to
follow. Willie told Lady Gregory that he had spoken to Bernard
Shaw about procuring "a very witty and unknown story" of his for
his sister's press, and that Shaw promised to proofread it "entirely
for the purpose of making the print look nice," as William Morris
had always done.[40] Yet Willie's attitude toward the Press was cava-
lierly possessive. From the beginning the sisters found him domineering. When he saw the preliminary proofs for *Seven Woods* he
was delighted and wrote enthusiastically to Lady Gregory about his
intention to give more material for Lollie to add to it. He and the
Dame of Coole then engaged in a protracted discussion about the
additions he proposed. She objected to some of his ideas,[41] and
while they debated between themselves, Lollie and the girls at the
Press cooled their heels. So began, again from the very beginning,
the second of the lasting antagonisms in Dun Emer, a long-running
bitterness between Willie and Lollie, the two members of the family who couldn't get along with each other. From the first, he
treated her as almost a simple laborer hired to do mean work for
the lofty artist; she regarded herself as an artist in her own right
and resented his assumptions of superiority. He also interfered in
what the sisters regarded as their own responsibilities. Lily wrote a
sharp letter to her father, complaining about WBY and voicing her
suspicion that he was being influenced by Lady Gregory. "From
their pedestal [they] direct and order others a great deal too much."
After *In the Seven Woods* appeared, "Willy was full of 'Do this, you
must do that,' etc., 'a press man is absolutely necessary,' and so
on." She told her father that Willie even "threatened us and bullied
generally." In those trying times she forged an unlikely bond with
her sister. "Lolly and I are hardened and know him and stood our
ground." It annoyed Lily that her older brother should regard himself as an authority in matters about which he knew little. She
wanted to get designs for her needlework from Jack, but Willy had
"pets" of his own to whom he wanted the work steered. The first of
these offered what Lily called "a ridiculous design," the second
promised a piece that never arrived, and the third sent one that was
not only "quite commonplace" but also of the wrong size.[42]

35. Dun Emer Printing Room, 1903. *In background:* George Russell (AE) (1867–1935); *in foreground:* Beatrice Cassidy, Esther Ryan. *Courtesy of Dr. Patrick H. Kelly.*

Still, as 1902 ended all looked promising, at least to those on the outside. The departments of Dun Emer devoted to embroidery, weaving, and tapestry were established in a large room on the first floor. The Press was in a separate room on the same floor, on its wall a large pastel mural by AE (George Russell).[43] Fortunately, the opening of Dun Emer coincided with the completion of Loughrea Cathedral, and the embroidery section was commissioned to make ten banners for it at four guineas each.[44] The design, by Jack, included the figure of St. Patrick as a boy. Since the priest in charge had never seen a representation of Ireland's patron saint as a boy, he wanted the figure changed to that of a woman. Lily refused, so the priest approached Miss Gleeson and had her overrule Lily, who thought Miss Gleeson should not have interfered.[45] But she did interfere and she got her way, another portent of coming troubles.[46]

36. Dun Emer Weaving Room, about 1903–1904. Lollie Yeats at extreme left; Jack Yeats's *A Broad Sheet* on wall of door. *Courtesy of Dr. Patrick H. Kelly.*

The Society had been in operation less than three months when Lollie began complaining about the difficulties of printing, and Miss Gleeson let Henry know. "My Gracious!" he replied; "does she expect to become a printer all at once? She is desperately clever: but still everything wants time to learn." Miss Gleeson approached the subject of her problems with Lollie warily, knowing of Henry's feelings about her and of his optimism about the success of the project, but she felt compelled to let him know that when Lollie received fees for drawing lessons she wanted to pocket the money herself, in direct violation of the clause in the Articles that called for a pooling of all earned fees. Henry's reply, though firm, was worded mildly: "If Lolly Yeats gives drawing lessons I am afraid the money for them must justly be paid into the Settlement, as that was the idea, wasn't it?"[47]

The dispute over Lollie's painting lessons revealed again the

37. Dun Emer Weaving Room, about 1904. *Courtesy of Dr. Patrick H. Kelly.*

lack of thought that had gone into the original agreement. Lollie had taken private students for years before Dun Emer was founded. Now she was expected to turn over the profits from her extra work to the Society. Such treatment would not encourage her to seek students or to teach them well. A cloud of Marxian unreality lay over the treatment of her private work, as it did over all the idealistic assumptions in the Articles.

The lack of practicality shown by both Henry and Miss Gleeson soon had its effect. The expenditure for launching the business had come to £194 by the end of the year. No money flowed in from investors, and sales were weak. By late December Henry was suggesting to Miss Gleeson that she seek help from her cousin Tom Gill, in charge of dispensing grants through the Department of Agriculture and Technical Instruction. "Tell him you have trained teachers and want pupils, that you haven't much capital, that else

38. Dun Emer Printing Room, about 1903. Lollie at table writing; Beatrice Cassidy at work table; Esther Ryan at type cases. *Courtesy of Library of Trinity College, Dublin.*

where they are giving grants to teach people." He pointed out that Dun Emer would meet the qualifications for an educational grant: "You have practically what amounts to a Technical School." He thought Lolly ought to give lessons in design as well as painting, the fees of course to revert to Dun Emer.[48]

More to the point was Henry's remark, in the same letter in

which the start-up costs were mentioned, about the reticence he had shown up to then in responding to Evelyn Gleeson's annoyance with the sisters. "I will be frank! There are certain things I never speak much about. When people are annoying, write to me absurdly, do mean things, and so on, I bury always these things. Yet they happen and make me very unhappy often."[49] The allusion was clear. The month was December 1902; Dun Emer had been in operation only three months.

Only a month later he asked her point-blank if she was having "any friction" with the Yeatses. If she was, he insisted, it was because of their "not clearly understanding the position." She ought to tell them frankly what her financial situation was so that they would not expect impossibilities of her. "They are partners in a way in your enterprise," and, he added, "they would be discreet if warned not to speak of your affairs."[50]

Asked thus specifically, Miss Gleeson responded directly. The Yeats sisters disliked her, she told him. He expressed amazement. If they did, he replied, "it displays a great amount of stupidity and want of sense." He wondered whether she couldn't "win them round." For one thing, the society was functioning with a full crew, and it would be disastrous if it were to break up. "You must consider that they are *indispensable implements* now: and you must try and see what is the origin of their curious behavior." She had dropped a phrase in her letter about whether he continued "to believe" in her, and he emphatically responded that he would no more fail to believe in her than he would "suddenly go strange in the mind."[51] Augustine Henry was not only her benefactor but a friend of thirty years. He had known the Yeatses for only a year. She should not question where his sympathies and loyalties lay.

Despite Miss Gleeson's fear that her enterprise might become a mere technical school, she took Henry's suggestion and, in the spring of 1903, filled out a questionnaire for an application for a grant from T. P. Gill's department. It listed five names as heads of departments: Evelyn Gleeson for Tufted Carpet-making, Lily Yeats for Embroidery, Elizabeth Yeats for Printing, May Kerley for Tapestry-weaving, and Norah Fitzpatrick for Bookbinding. Of these Lily and Lollie were listed as receiving salaries of £125 a year each, and May Kerley (a niece of Henry's) £50. Norah Fitzpatrick was

39. Dun Emer Printing Room, 1903. *Left to right:* Essie Ryan, Beatrice Cassidy, Lollie Yeats. *Courtesy of Michael B. Yeats.*

listed as a prospective member to begin work in May, with no salary listed. In answer to a question involving the source of funding, Miss Gleeson wrote, in words that could not have escaped the attention of the Yeats sisters: "The expenses are all met by Evelyn Gleeson from private sources." No mention was made of Augustine Henry.[52]

For a brief time that spring, the level of antagonism was lowered; Miss Gleeson told Henry that the sisters were becoming "more reasonable."[53] JBY was optimistic. "My daughters are very busy and content," he wrote Lady Gregory as 1903 began, "Lollie increasingly absorbed in her printing of Willie's book, Lily enjoying herself very much. I do not feel the slightest doubt but that in time everything will succeed. They take to the work as a duck takes to water."[54] Lollie took pleasure in noting that Frank Fay,

40. Lady Augusta Gregory (1855–1932). Pencil sketch by JBY.
Courtesy of J. Robert Maguire.

the actor, came to Dun Emer several times and read to the girls, making the time go "on flying wheels."[55] But the truce was not to last. There were too many tensions, too many people rubbing one another the wrong way.

William Butler Yeats continued to monitor the development of *In the Seven Woods*. He saw his sisters briefly in Dublin in March

41. Dun Emer Printing Room, 1903. Lollie at press. *Courtesy of Library of Trinity College, Dublin.*

1903, but only "amid a whirl of people." He wrote Sydney Cocker- ell about a colophon for the Press designed by Emery Walker, but showed by a remark in the letter ("I don't know to what extent my sisters are in a hurry")[56] that he wasn't fully aware of the pressures they labored under. The colophon itself was the cause of another dispute, rivaling the one over Lollie's painting fees. Lollie showed

Miss Gleeson the sketch for the pressmark. Miss Gleeson called it "pretty" but thought it somewhat "feeble." Without further consultation Lollie had it engraved, and Miss Gleeson learned of the action only after Lollie had shown it to the work-girls first. She then asked Lollie for a copy, but Lollie "got angry" and refused, saying she had none. "It does not really matter," Miss Gleeson noted sensibly to Henry, "only that is the way things are done."[57]

Henry urged Lollie to send him all the prospectuses so that he could drum up business and asked that his own name be put down as a regular subscriber.[58] In the summer of 1903 appeared the first prospectus, listing the proposed titles after the publication of *In the Seven Woods* and AE's *Nuts of Knowledge.* These included a prose story by Shaw (later abandoned); Douglas Hyde's translations of *The Love Songs of Connacht;* translations by Lady Gregory of historic and medieval Irish poems (not to appear for some years); and a book on speaking to the psaltery (published later but not by Dun Emer). "Other books will be announced shortly." The list of authors and titles, and the identification of William Butler Yeats as editor, gave the Press an advantage in publicity over the other operations of the Industries.

By mid-August, Henry had received his copy of *In the Seven Woods* and sent Lollie a letter of congratulations on it.[59] William Butler Yeats told John Quinn it was the first book of his that was "a pleasure to look at—a pleasure whether open or shut."[60] The format of the book was the one Dun Emer adhered to and Cuala later followed till it went out of business. The cover was of a kind of blue paper, with half-cover and spine of cloth, its outer measurement $8^3/8$ by $5^7/8$ inches. The pages measured $8^1/4$ by $5^3/4$ inches, the print area $5^3/8$ by $3^5/8$ inches. The title was printed on a strip of paper and pasted on the spine.[61] A London bookseller told a subscriber to the series that he was "lucky" to get a copy of the slim volume. It cost 10/6, and only 325 copies were printed. "Prices would run up to £2 a copy soon," he predicted.[62]

After publication of *In the Seven Woods,* Lollie made an accounting of expenses and receipts of the Printing Department. Under expenses she listed "printing Press paper Etc" as £53, "binding" as £8.2, "postage" as £4.1.3 and £2.0.6, "Girls pay" as £4.2. There were other small, miscellaneous expenses, but the two biggest

42. Dun Emer Industries, 1903. Lollie, Lily at left; Evelyn Gleeson, back row, second from right. *Courtesy of Library of Trinity College, Dublin.*

items not directly connected with the physical reproduction of the book were the author's royalty, £31.10, and Lollie's pay, £114.8. William Butler Yeats provided his services as editorial advisor free of charge, but he made no gift of his literary property.[63] Indeed, he wanted all contributors to be paid, as otherwise only "amateurish" work would be produced. "We pay for everything that my sisters print," he told Stephen Gwynn.[64] Under "Money Received" Lollie also listed her income from her painting classes, so clearly Miss Gleeson had won the dispute over assignment of that money. The summary showed receipts from printing as £163.8.5 and from painting as £20.12.0, a total of £184.00.05. Expenses came to £217.3.9, for a loss of £33.03.00.[65]

The expense of the Albion hand press itself could be amortized

43. Dun Emer Embroidery room, 1903. Lily in center; Loughrea
Cathedral banners in background. *Courtesy of Dr. Patrick H.
Kelly.*

over a period of years, so the deficit was not so great as to cause
alarm on its account, but the salary to Lollie was the Press's highest
single cost, and its income was not enough to support it. Lily
received the same amount for her work at embroidery, and it too
was not returning enough in profits to provide it. Pessimistic rum-
bles began to emanate from Dublin, where everybody knew everybody else's business. "All your friends are rather hopeless of Dun
Emer," Henry wrote to Miss Gleeson, but he considered that "a
good sign," for "nothing ever succeeded in Ireland by well-wishing,
as every one sees so many difficulties, is so critical, so despairing."
He recommended that she "fight on" and be "cheerful and defi-
ant." [66]

The successful launching of WBY's book of poems did not
lessen the friction between the partners. Lollie irritated Miss Glee-

son by speaking of the Press boastingly, and her refusal to let Miss Gleeson see the pressmark still rankled. Henry tried to calm the waters. "I don't see any wrong in Lolly Yeats speaking of her Press. It is after all *hers,* just as the weaving is yours and the embroidery is Lily Yeats. Of course it is not very courteous of her to keep her little press mark a secret from you. However you are all sensitive creatures: and don't get over trifles as easily as men do, who laugh at little things, after smarting over them for a *moment.*"[67] But again Henry was speaking from outside the country, this time from Kew, where he was working on *The Trees of Great Britain and Ireland.* He was not present to feel directly the acidic resentments that were corroding the partnership.

Evelyn Gleeson had been forced to ask the trustee of her funds to advance her £100 out of her next half-year's entitlement and had already spent it all. She asked Henry in November 1903 if he could lend her £100 to be paid at once, another £100 on the following 15 March, and £50 on 1 July. She would not accept the money as a gift. Standing on her honor, she flatly refused to let Henry be "the loser." "I hold myself responsible for the capital you have advanced, and whenever there is any profit you shall be the first to get your just return," she wrote him. She found it "very difficult to meet all the demands for ready money, which are considerable." If the grant from the Technical Board came through she might be able to buy the Dun Emer house, which she held on a lease, and perhaps "make the business pay." But she could not get cooperation from the Yeatses. Instead of coming to her with questions about Dun Emer they still wrote to him.[68] "I daresay Lolly Yeats writes me to use my *influence,*" Henry wrote her. "So don't be annoyed with her for that: it is natural enough." But that is precisely what annoyed Evelyn Gleeson. "The last thing I want to do is to *interfere* in any way," he insisted. He seemed not to realize that by accepting Lollie's letters and responding to them he was interfering.

His own computations showed a loss for the combined Industries, from the beginning to 9 November 1903, of £198.14.4. He thought a better method of accounting should be tried. Each division should stand on its own feet, he suggested, and each should be audited separately, by someone utterly reliable, like George Russell.[69] He urged Miss Gleeson to warn the Yeats sisters of their

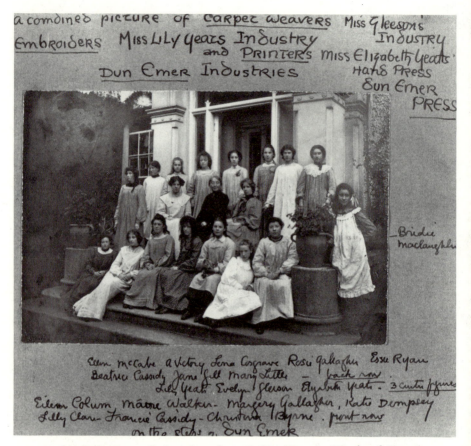

44. Dun Emer Industries, from Lollie Yeats's "Book of Dun Emer," 1903. *Courtesy of Library of Trinity College, Dublin.*

position: "You know I promised to advance £500: and that I am going to do: but after that of course I shall do no more: as you know of course: but perhaps the Yeats's don't know. So of course it is a little serious for them after end of the 2-years guaranteed period."[70]

Lollie's troubles widened. She and her brother the poet had always kept a respectful distance until Dun Emer forced them together. Lollie had accepted her brother's role as editorial adviser of the Press but regarded herself as the ultimate authority on its productions. He took the view that he was the boss, and he displayed as an editor the same kind of arrogance and righteousness that he had shown in some of his other roles. When Russell submitted the lyrics that were to be published as *The Nuts of Knowledge,* WBY found fault with them, pronouncing judgment on each and declaring which ones approached his own high standards and which did not. He would not allow Dun Emer to print those that did not meet with his approval. Both men were "stiff-necked," and finally Russell agreed to make a selection from all his verse rather than insisting that his original choices be published. In an amusing letter to John Quinn describing the controversy, Russell commented drily on Yeats's role as literary adviser: "If he will not let them print anything which is not on the level of a sacred book the output will be small." The event was another foretaste of the future at Dun Emer.[71]

Early in 1904 Miss Gleeson's application for help from the Technical Department was honored with a grant of £200 "in consideration of Dun Emer's educational work.[72] Instead of diminishing the conflict between Miss Gleeson and the sisters, the grant increased it, for Lollie apparently regarded it as a blow to her independence. Words were spoken. Lollie even got into a quarrel by letter with Lady Gregory over an unknown matter, perhaps something to do with the Russell book.[73] It is hard to know why Lollie should have objected to Miss Gleeson's grant, but apparently T. P. Gill, the dispenser of the funds, either assigned it to Miss Gleeson's part of the work only or imposed conditions on all the branches of the company that the sisters found irksome. As Gill was Miss Gleeson's cousin, suspicions naturally flowed through the Yeatsian veins. (John Butler Yeats wrote John Quinn that Miss Gleeson was a part of the Department's "fraudulent machinery.")[74] Miss Gleeson was so cowed by Lollie's fury that she thought of declining the grant, and only Henry's insistence that she take it changed her mind. In any event, he insisted, "it is not a question for flaring up about at all."[75]

But there was plenty of "flaring up" on both sides. It was clear that in the presence of such animosities no new plan would fully resolve the difficulties. Just as Miss Gleeson had applied for funds from T. E. Gill, now the sisters applied for a financial subsidy from

45. Dun Emer Embroidery Room, 1903. Lily Yeats at right foreground. *Courtesy of Library of Trinity College, Dublin.*

a private fund administered by the Arts and Crafts Society. In early March a grant for £100 came through,[76] and it was Miss Gleeson's turn to object. The grant was imposed on the condition that there be "careful auditing of the whole enterprise," a demand that offended both Miss Gleeson, who thought the Yeats sisters had insisted on inserting it as a criticism of her methods,[77] and the sisters, who didn't like the condition any more than she did. Neither side could accept with grace a grant won by the other, even if for the benefit of all. "If the Yeats were friends," Henry pointed out to Miss Gleeson, "their obtaining £100 would be a great pleasure to you. As you don't like them it is very annoying." If she refused to accept the grant in the name of Dun Emer, it would be "equivalent to treating the Yeats as mere employees, and soon getting rid of them."[78] The real difficulty, Henry noted, was "the impossibility of carrying on a partnership if the partners regard each other with dislike and suspicion, well or ill-founded." Yet he still wanted Miss Gleeson to treat the sisters as equal partners, though, as he acknowledged, "they had no money in: were paid salaries: and couldn't say anything with any footing regarding accounts, etc." She could assert her absolute authority over them if she wished, but then the partnership wouldn't work. From Miss Gleeson's point of view the arrangement wasn't working anyhow; she had put in a good portion of her own means, was taking all the risks, and was in debt to Henry. The Yeats sisters had put in nothing, were in debt to her but not in a position to repay, and were uncooperative and mean companions.[79] At one point, when Miss Gleeson announced the grant from Gill's department, Lollie's behavior was so bad that she felt it necessary to send a letter of apology. "I am very sorry that I was so excessively cross and rude this morning. I was out of temper with 'The Department' who understand Industries but not Art, and I stupidly vented my annoyance against them on you."[80]

Miss Gleeson again pressed the sisters for a capital contribution. To them she appeared in a "panic." As was to happen so often in family crises, the sisters turned to their elder brother, then prospering from his first money-making lecture tour of the United States. In view of the relationships, Lily was chosen to write the begging letter, which caught up with Willie in Chicago. He replied that he would have to wait till he returned to Ireland but wasn't sure he could do anything anyhow. He vented his frustration in a letter to Lady Gregory:

> I have said that the printing looks like a good investment, but that if I were a rich man I would require the opinion of some authority like Ricketts or Image or Whall as to the quality of the embroidery design. I hope my letter was not too cold, but I have written it again and again. . . . I have foreseen this moment all the while but it is annoying. If I give much it will go without effect (for it will not be enough) and if I give little I shall be blamed always. . . . I can think of nothing but going to George Pollexfen and having everything looked into, in a spirit of sound business, if he will consent to invest. I could then give whatever you thought right.

Of course, the crisis could blow over, he told her. Miss Gleeson's "panic" might pass and Lily's letter mean only "the depression of the moment."[81] But the whole business was annoying to him. From his point of view, the sisters should be managing their own affairs and not turning to him for rescue. He was contributing his services as "literary adviser,"[82] and that was enough. In another part of his letter to Lady Gregory he gave his frank opinion of their attempts to involve him: "family duties—just perhaps because they are rather thrust upon one—leave me colder than they should."[83] Those duties would plague him for the rest of his life, though no matter how unpleasant they were or how much he resented them, he ultimately always fulfilled them.

WBY returned from his American tour with a profit of £646, and it was natural that his family should stake a claim to it. JBY asked for a "loan" of £20, and the sisters thought some of the funds might help loosen Miss Gleeson's grip on them. Willie remained angrily aloof. George Pollexfen declined to spend money on anything that did not increase his own comfort, and he would not invest in any project that did not guarantee certain profit. Willie and Lollie grew unpleasant with each other, and Father had to admonish his son: "I daresay there have been mistakes made. Only don't let irritation or unreasonableness of any kind bear sway. To make Dun Emer a pecuniary success is a matter of life and death to Lily and Lollie. . . . Dun Emer is, as it appears to them, their one chance of ever having any sort of support in life. That is why they are so keen about things." He urged him to be *"gentle"* with Lollie, for if things "went wrong" with her and she grew exasperated, "she gets quite ill."[84]

Miss Gleeson's panic did not pass, and Henry finally admitted openly what he had wanted to deny, that Miss Gleeson and the Yeats sisters did not like each other. "I see great difficulties in managing with people whom you don't like, who are tactless," he told her. "I regret involving you in such a mess." The question was: "Have you the strength to carry on with people whom you *detest?* There is no use mincing matters: you dislike the Yeats *exceedingly* and your position is very difficult." Henry had by now lost all sympathy with the sisters, among other reasons because they had begun complaining about the commotion in Dun Emer, where

Mrs. MacCormack lived with her children and where, naturally, they scurried about and made noise. The sisters found even the din made by the workers unbearable. "It was impossible to take our lunch at Dun Emer," Lily wrote years later. "We had no private rooms, and the uproar made by the twenty girls at lunch hour was terrific."[85] Lollie behaved as if the house belonged to her rather than to Miss Gleeson. A reorganization would have to deal with that and other problems. Henry himself, almost casually, came up with what proved to be the structure of a new arrangement, though George Russell was the one who worked out the details. "One way would be for each industry to [be] absolutely independent, i.e., *for each person to make her things, pay her girls, and do her own correspondence. Then the association would be simply one of 3 artists, working in the same studio.*" Nobody would interfere with anybody else under his scheme, and everyone would "shut up talk and criticism." The ultimate effect would be that "three artists would have simply one address: no other connection."[86]

But under any reorganization, he insisted that the rights of Miss Gleeson and her sister to the ownership and use of the Dun Emer residence be made clear. By allowing it to be a workshop she was surrendering her *"privacy."* "People who come to work forget that the *house* or its affairs or inhabitants is absolutely *no* concern of others." All using the house must "pledge themselves" to consider it and its inhabitants as "non-existent."[87] He followed up with a letter to Lollie, who continued her complaints to him, and used "very direct but extremely polite language." He told her "that the Industries being in a private house had drawbacks, and that the difficulty lay in the fact that the doings of the inmates were not, as they ought to be, considered sacred by people who merely went to work there." He had let George Russell know what he thought and asked him to work out a new arrangement that would overcome Miss Gleeson's objections and yet be satisfactory to all involved. Henry then told Lollie that she must deal directly with Miss Gleeson. "I retire now from post of adviser *save to you*," he wrote Miss Gleeson; "I shall decline to say a word to anyone else."[88]

When Miss Gleeson remonstrated that she had never in so many words said she disliked the Yeatses, he replied, "When I said you detested the Yeats, I said only what I thought of them myself: as I dislike intensely what they have done and perhaps I dislike too much." He acknowledged "their good qualities"—without specifying them—"but they want *bossing* and *intimidating:* and if they were men they would hear from me."[89] Men were not sensitive in the same way women were, he told her; they were only sensitive to things like "meanness, lying, etc." In remarkably strong language he wrote, "The people with you ought to try to please you and not act like pigs."[90]

In August 1904, while Russell was working on a new agreement, the Press announced that of its first three publications, only the most recent, issued a month before, was still in print.[91] What it did not say was that another book, W. B. Yeats's *Stories of Red Hanrahan,* was already set in type and ready to go by the middle of the month but that the sisters were waiting for the reorganization. Russell's proposal proved only a slight improvement on the old, as the same people were involved, and the difficulties had always been personal, not organizational. Beginning 1 September 1904, Dun Emer became two separate enterprises, the Dun Emer Guild, Ltd., run by Evelyn Gleeson, and the Dun Emer Industries, Ltd., run by the Yeats sisters. Russell arranged to have both names officially registered, one in Miss Gleeson's name, the other in the names of Lily and Lollie. They constituted "two cooperative societies," though established technically as stock corporations.

The financial arrangements for the new Industries should have flashed a message to the sisters. Miss Gleeson and Mrs. MacCormack were each assigned 75 fully paid-up shares at a par value of £1 per share. Lily and Lollie and the seven girls working under them were given one share each. The disparity between their portion and that of the major owners and the equality of their portion with that of their supposed subordinates, showed clearly who was in power. In the division of stock the Yeatses were given £473.9.1½ worth of materials, furniture, and accounts due. With salaries of £526.8.0 advanced to the sisters during the period and with the cost of training workers and of goodwill thrown in, the transfer of funds to them came to £1,078.5.7½.[92] Henry thought the concessions made by Miss Gleeson quite generous. "Don't give the Yeats any more money," he counseled after hearing the details of the agreement.[93]

An account was made up, showing expenses from the beginning (late August 1902) to the end of the original Dun Emer (as of 17 September 1904.) It showed that purchases of £1,004.14.11 had been made for all branches, of which £445.3 went for the printing department, £349.9.10 for embroidery, and only £202.10 for weaving. The rest was for "general expenses." Income was £337.14 for printing, £273 for embroidery, and £164.6.10 for weaving, £22.11 for painting. Net loss for the sisters' two main enterprises came to £182.18.10, for Miss Gleeson's £37.15.0.[94]

Henry was hopeful. "If the Yeats would only be content with their little kingdom and eschewed an aggressive military policy, all would be well," he told Miss Gleeson just before the arrangements were concluded, and a few days later, "It is difficult to hope for: but I do hope that the Yeats will attain sense and on the new arrangement pull together decently. It is their correct course: and you, I know, will be olive-branch to repentants."[95]

In the new agreement the £500 advanced by Dr. Henry was not mentioned. In fact, no portion of it was ever repaid. As the debt was supposed to be reduced from profits, and as there were no profits, technically Lily and Lollie were guilty of no default. Henry, despite his earlier admonition, even urged Miss Gleeson to lend the sisters an additional £120 and give them £80 as a gift, for without a subvention their branches would fail.[96] She agreed but was prudent, treating the entire £200 as a loan. It was to be repaid at the rate of £15 yearly, an obligation the sisters agreed to. In accepting the small annual payments for the retirement of the loan principal, Miss Gleeson added a rider that was to prove crucial four years later. If any installment was in arrears by twenty-one days or more, Miss Gleeson was "forthwith to be entitled to take such steps as she may be advised to recover the balance then due." The Yeatses also would pay rent of £20 a year for the use of the Dun Emer building and were liable for their portion of expenses for tea and services.[97]

The negotiations had caused Miss Gleeson anguish, clearly revealed in her correspondence with Henry, but not visible to the sisters, who believed she was a mere dilettante, a rich amateur on an ego trip, an accusation for which she provided evidence against herself. "Her industry is just a toy she amuses herself with," Lollie wrote to John Quinn in 1906, "not a real business concern, but run I imagine by the Department. She goes away and neglects it for weeks, then comes back and is full of zeal for a few days, overpays some girls and pays others hardly anything, gives odd holidays and deducts the girls' pay for the day. They growl and grumble but are too afraid of her to speak out, and we have no grant but have to run the whole thing out of the sales, paying her rent &c, and it is hard work."[98]

For a while, according to Liam Miller, tensions decreased,[99] and when Miss Gleeson submitted another grant application it named all the departments as recipients. She even included a glowing testimonial to Lollie's talents as a teacher of drawing: she "pursues a system devised by herself," "perfected during many years that she has taught in London." "The result of her teaching has been most satisfactory as regards the workers here who came to her absolutely ignorant of the meaning of line and color. In my opinion no better system for developing original talent could possibly be found. It is an admirable method of teaching children to see for themselves and to render what they see."[100]

In her application Miss Gleeson names four girls as in the weaving branch, five in embroidery, and two in printing.[101] By December 1904, Henry was congratulating her on "getting so many orders," and suggested she think of "giving looms to people to work in their own homes."[102] Sheila Pim has pointed out that during the next few years all branches of Dun Emer were kept busy, including two new ones, bookbinding under Norah Fitzpatrick and enameling under Emily MacCarthy. Classes were established at Killarney and Glenbeigh to teach not only handicrafts but the Irish language as well. An agency for rugs was established with a company in Belfast. All branches were represented at exhibitions at the Royal Society in Dublin and at the Society for Artists at Work in London.[103] By the end of 1905 some thirty girls were employed, and the operation had become much more than the simple partnership of 1902. There was shifting around of the workers; Eileen Colum, for instance, transferred to the Press in early 1906 and stayed with it for the rest of her life.

As all still worked together in the same house, the same clashes of personality were inevitable, and, only six months into the new arrangement, Henry decided that the sisters must go,[104] even suggesting that Miss Gleeson might have to "ship" them "off the premises" by the following August.[105] He was glad she had been able to enlist Norah Fitzpatrick for bookbinding, but another girl they had been trying to sign as a worker wouldn't join because of the Yeats sisters.[106]

Just as WBY had annoyed Lollie by his delays with copy for *In the Seven Woods* and George Russell by denying him the right to choose his own poems for *Nuts of Knowledge,* so now he annoyed William Kirkpatrick Magee (who used the pen name John Eglinton) by insisting on the superiority of his own judgment to that of the author. Magee had to content himself with a note on a preliminary sheet of *Some Essays and Passages* (finished on 16 April 1905, published 25 August) that he "had no hand in the selection, which Mr. Yeats has done him the honour to make for the Dun Emer Press series," and he wanted the world to know that "if consulted he would hardly have approved of the inclusion of the last essay, written over twelve years ago, in which a metaphor is pressed to the point of being recommended as a gospel."[107]

The outside world knew little of the internal squabbles. A long piece in the *Irish Independent* of March 1905 gave a favorable account of Dun Emer, with black-and-white sketches of the press, of Lily, of Evelyn Gleeson, and of Jack's bookplate for John Quinn.[108] When Yeats's *Stories of Red Hanrahan* was published, G. K. Chesterton gave it a favorable review.[109] In 1906 one of Miss Gleeson's rugs won a silver medal at an international exhibition in Milan.[110] It is clear that, despite its personal and financial problems, Dun Emer was, artistically, a highly successful project. It did what Evelyn Gleeson and Augustine Henry had wanted it to do, taught young Irish girls how to make things with their hands and make money by so doing.

Lily wrote John Quinn of her satisfaction at being clear of Miss Gleeson. Yet, wondering how goods would be sold under the new arrangement, she asked if he knew of an importer in New York who would handle their products. "As Lolly and I have to make a living it is very important that we should get a market for ourselves." When the Industries sent goods to New York in early 1906 for a sale at Madison Square Garden, she told Quinn she hoped they would sell, "as we have had to overdraw at the bank a little." Lollie even discussed with A. H. Bullen some scheme of his for cooperating with the Press, but nothing came of it.[111]

The sisters found that running an independent business was not as easy as being in a partnership. They were assigned to a back room in Dun Emer and had to display their products there. Lily described to Quinn a frequent experience: "We are tormented by flocks of people, mostly old ladies. They finger all the work, ask numerous questions, and then go, some even with tears of emotion in their eyes at the thought of our noble work in such ideal surroundings, but they don't buy."[112]

The sisters discovered too that former partners could quickly become rivals. When a couple of John Quinn's American friends came to visit Lily and Lollie at the Industries, Miss Gleeson nailed them in her sales room, which they had to pass through to reach the sisters', and sold them a six-guinea rug before informing Lily and Lollie that the visitors were there. They bought only £5 worth from the sisters. Lollie's description of the scene is vivid: "Miss Gleeson was more than ever like the Mother Abbess yesterday. She stood smiling at my elbow all the time they were in the room, with her sister, a cousin, and some relatives grouped around like attendant nuns, so that no one could stir for the crowd packed into this little room, and she smiled and beamed and talked platitudes." The incident was typical. "You will think it horrid of us to mind Miss Gleeson taking possession of people who come to see us," she told Quinn, "but it so often happens now, and then they buy her things, which doesn't benefit our Industry at all."[113] Another of her nicknames for Miss Gleeson was "The Spider," for her way of trapping customers in her web.

In early 1906, Henry suggested to Miss Gleeson that she purchase the Dun Emer house, held on a lease, as that would enable her to borrow money against it. Her own small but steady income would enable her in time to pay off all her debts. What she needed to do, he urged, was to introduce "a few economies generally." One expense was having the Yeatses present, for though they paid rent "they cost something." His earlier suggestion that they leave in August 1905 had gone nowhere. Now he thought they should leave the premises when the next business year ended in August 1906.[114] By this time he was totally disenchanted with the sisters. When Lollie visited London for an exhibition and asked twice to see him, he told her he had no time.[115]

The differences were obviously irreconcilable. Henry might believe the sisters demanding and uncooperative, but they saw things otherwise. JBY told Willie that "their work at Dun Emer is terribly anxious." He threw in some hints. "It requires huge exertions to keep it going, yet if they had a little capital I believe they would work out something good. Their devotion is extraordinary." [116] To Miss Gleeson the sisters may have appeared derelict in not repaying their debts. To them the debts were terrifyingly omnipresent and unrepayable. They could make enough money to get along barely; they could not make enough to pay off what they owed. The petty maneuvering for customers became standard, and the sisters worked under perpetual tension. JBY wrote his friend Oliver Elton that Dun Emer was "a terrible strain on them, a sort of ever eating acid." [117]

The struggle between Lollie and her poet brother for control of the Press continued unabated. Without consulting him, Lollie had asked George Russell to make another selection of poems for the Press. The material—published later as *By Still Waters*—was the first over the selection of which the sparring siblings fought. Lollie announced that she had a fair copy of Russell's poems in hand and was ready to proceed. Her brother's approval would be merely a matter of form, she thought, since she was convinced she had the talent to make choices, and in this case Russell was the author and everyone knew he was a good poet. Willie viewed things differently. He promptly vetoed the selection, again declaring the poems not up to his own high standards. Lollie stood her ground and announced she would print them anyway. He wrote harsh and demanding letters, claiming his reputation would be damaged if they were allowed to appear. The pacific JBY tried to arbitrate. He told Willie that he agreed with his estimate of Russell's poems but that he ought to try to approach his sister differently. Perhaps his son should confine himself "to the mere giving of advice." There were other matters to be considered, he pointed out, than the family quarrel between brother and sister. Russell was involved too. "In amicable contests you and Russell should agree about a selection," he wrote; then he deftly inserted a needle in his son's arrogance. "A poet's selection from his own poetry ought to carry with it a certain authority. I suppose it was your own case." [118] Willie, of course, allowed no one to censor his own poems. But before WBY had received his father's letter of advice he had fired off another incendiary one to Lollie, and JBY exploded in exasperation:

> *Why do you write such offensive letters?* . . . You treat Lollie as if she was dirt. She is as clever a woman as you are, and in some respects much cleverer. She very naturally stands high in her own esteem as well as in that of other people, and she is entitled to be treated as a personage in her way.
>
> When you advise about choice of books for the Press, it should be advice and not haughty dictation backed up by menaces. After all *the press is Lollie's business* and it means our means of living. And she has often other things to consider besides the literary excellence of a particular book. There are questions of convenience and commercial expedience and policy, matters for tactful consideration not to be decided offhand by a literary expert.
>
> I think you ought to write a frank apology. If you want to withdraw from the business of advising it is easy to do in a temperate and kindly letter. This letter if not recalled *leaves a cleavage between you and Jack and Lily and Lollie.* I appeal from Philip drunk to Philip sober.

He added a note: "My own impression is that it would be best for all parties if you withdrew altogether from the position of literary adviser." If his son's letter was "unrecalled," it would mean "a bitter quarrel." [119]

Willie preferred the role of Philip drunk. Giving in to Lollie was not in his nature. His father expostulated with him again, urging that his relationship with Lollie "be put on some *workable* basis," but he got nowhere. [120] About the middle of August 1906, Willie resigned as adviser to the Press. Russell's text lay in type ready for printing, scheduled for publication in December.

The resignation was only a ruse, for Willie had no intention of giving up his power over such a valuable source of publicity and royalties. While the dispute was boiling, Lollie traveled to New York to sell Dun Emer goods at an Irish exhibition there, but not before she had asked Katharine Tynan for a volume of poems. Willie immediately wrote to Miss Tynan, one of his oldest friends, mentioning the "difference of opinion" between himself and his sister. He hinted that Lollie might yet be induced to come around to his way of thinking. But, he cautioned, "she will certainly not do so if she thinks she can have me on her own terms." He asked if Miss Tynan would deliver an ultimatum to Lollie: that she would not allow her book to be published unless Willie were to be the editor of it. "I have taken a great deal of trouble up to this and made things easier for her, and she won't know till she gets to the work, or tries to get another unpaid editor to do it, what a job it is." [121] Miss Tynan knew him so well, he added, that she must know he was not doing anything "capricious or ill-tempered." He was not dealing with logic, he said, "but with three very emotional people, my sisters and my father." [122]

The sisters took a different view; Lollie complained to her father that she and Lily had to work "very hard at a dull and slavish kind of work" for which they got "little reward," while WBY lived "very pleasantly," doing work he liked, "getting plenty of public and private consideration, everyone anxious to help and make smooth" his path. [123] His role as adviser was a peculiar one. He chose works of his own or of his friends, or insisted on his approval of works Lollie chose, yet he had no formal connection with the Industries at all. He earned royalties for his own works, and from the record these appear to be higher for him than for others, [124] but otherwise was not paid.

While Lollie was still in New York Willie made a proposal to her for a new arrangement. The details are not known, but, from Lollie's remarks in a letter to John Quinn, it appears that WBY wanted to make formal and binding his control over the publications of the Press. She appealed to Quinn for advice. "Can you make any suggestions on my side?" she asked. "I mean I want to keep some control in my own Press." She wanted Willie to have copy ready to meet deadlines—something he had not heretofore done—and she wanted to approve his choices just as he approved hers. "Perhaps you can think of some way of introducing these points into this wonderful legal document." Lily urged her to stand fast against their brother. "Don't have W. B. on top whatever you do," she warned. [125] WBY's position had been expressed in his letter to Katharine Tynan: "She [Lollie] would like me to go on editing various books, she on her part to put in others when the fancy pleased her, and this I won't have, as it means I know the gradual lowering of the standard of quality until it is like that of most Dublin publications." [126] AE and Quinn offered to mediate, and by mid-November a new arrangement had been entered into. Its details aren't known, but WBY apparently had to back down and acknowledge to some extent his sister's rights in her own business. WBY had written a long letter setting forth his position, but AE, with advice from Quinn, composed "a little agreement on a half sheet of paper with about a tenth of the words in Willie's letter," as Lollie put it. Willie "signed it like a lamb." Lollie, back in Dublin, felt triumphant. "I saw Willie at the play last night and he was quite amiable," she told Quinn. [127] Yet his editorial high-handedness was still in evidence. In one of Miss Tynan's poems he chose the first and last stanzas only, eliminating everything between. "How she will like it remains to be seen," said Lily. [128]

Lollie was unable to enjoy her stay in New York. It had been arranged by John Quinn, the New York lawyer who since his visit to Dublin in 1902 had become a staunch supporter of the entire Yeats family. It was he who had organized Willie's speaking tour in 1903–1904. [129] Lollie, staying with Mrs. Simeon Ford in Rye, wrote endless streams of letters to her family in Dublin, then shut them off abruptly and decided to return home, though her hostess urged her to stay. Years later she revealed the principal cause, a curious interpretation of people and events that can perhaps be understood only by those familiar with the Lollie Yeats seen by her sister and older brother. In New York she saw much of Quinn, a bachelor who was something of a lady's man, though he tried to limit himself to one woman at a time. He had just switched mistresses, discarding Miss Ada Smith for Mrs. Dorothy Coates, who played the part for another fifteen years. When Mrs. Coates saw Lollie and Quinn together, according to Lollie, she didn't like what she saw. "I thought her a horrid woman," Lollie told her father years later, "mean and vindictive, and she hated me on sight." Then came her remarkable, wholly imaginative, interpretation. "She of course feared J. Q. might get *interested in me*—and at that time—*(this is private of course)* I thought he was greatly interested in Lily, and so I was most anxious *not to annex him,* and couldn't get home to Ireland soon enough." [130]

This was not the kind of woman Miss Gleeson could deal with rationally. Miss Gleeson in turn, with her worries over money and health, and with her behavior as "Spider" and "Mother Abbess," was no more easy to handle. Exacerbating her fears and bad temper was a dispute over her brother's will. He had provided the trust of £6,958 from which she received her income, then in his will had established another trust for her of £6,500. The executor gratuitously asked the court to determine whether he had meant her to have both sums or whether the two were meant to be one and the same. It took years before the matter was settled—in her favor—but Miss Gleeson had to endure agonies of delay and worry as the case wound its tortuous way through the courts.[131] She had counted on an extra £180 a year from that source; when she heard of the executor's action, she felt she might have to shut Dun Emer down, or perhaps turn it into a cottage industry, with women working at home and with no central workplace. Henry counselled against such a move and urged instead that she try to sell the business to someone who could provide the management while she rented out the building.[132] To add to the assault on her nerves, at the very time she had to face Lollie's return from New York in 1906, her seventeen-year-old nephew died suddenly at Dun Emer of an undiagnosed brain tumor after having caused months of anxiety to his family because of his strange behavior.[133] Henry urged her to take a vacation in Florence at his expense, but she declined.

Relationships between the rival groups failed to improve. To Rosa Butt, John Butler Yeats referred to the founder of Dun Emer as "the always detested Miss Gleeson."[134] There was little attempt at cooperation. When Miss Gleeson's girls were invited to show their weaving at an exhibition in Clare Street, their advertisement made no mention of books or embroidery.[135] In a long article in the *British Warehouseman* on the Dun Emer Guild, no mention was made of the Yeats sisters at all; it was completely about Miss Gleeson and carpets and mats.[136]

The sisters had not been able to make more than one payment on their £200 loan, and Henry kept urging Miss Gleeson to get rid of them. All through 1907 the tensions grew, temporarily ameliorated by the prospect of an exhibition in New York of Irish goods. The circumstances of the invitation to it gave pleasure to

DUN EMER GUILD, LTD.,
DUNDRUM, Co. DUBLIN.
SECRETARY, EVELYN GLEESON.

WEAVING—Evelyn Gleeson.

BOOK-BINDING—Norah Fitzpatrick.

ENAMELLING—Emily MacCarthy.

46. Dun Emer Guild invoice, 1907. *Courtesy of Dr. Patrick H. Kelly.*

the sisters. P. T. Power, who had handled the exhibition that Lollie had attended in 1906, asked Lily for Irish products to sell in America and invited her to come to New York to manage a stall. He would pay travel and living expenses and try to encourage sales of her work. Lily thought he had made the same offer to Miss Gleeson.[137] Quinn had told Power about Dun Emer but mentioned only the sisters in connection with it; Power knew nothing of the separation of the branches. When he came to Ireland and sought Dun Emer, he naturally was met at the door by Miss Gleeson. She, thinking he had come to see her, and knowing he had already written Lily, asked the sisters to meet with her and Power at Dun Emer and give their advice in his interview with her. "Of course they went," JBY wrote Miss Butt, "rather pleased with themselves and their readiness to help a fellow worker not always very friendly to them." To Miss Gleeson's discomfiture, "Power commenced by saying that he wanted one Miss Yeats and two attendants to go at his expense to New York." After making sure Quinn approved, Lily agreed to go.[138]

To extricate himself from the misunderstanding, Power agreed to invite Miss Gleeson and pay for her travel, the two attendants to be transferred to her, but she would have to take a stall at her own expense. In early December, John Butler Yeats made a sudden decision to join Lily and insisted he would stay for a period of six weeks only. Lily had wanted him to be with her, as "Miss Gleeson will boss her less successfully if I am there."[139] Miss Gleeson, worried over the possible loss of her brother's legacy, had difficulty raising money for her own expenses in New York. In her desperation "she talked confidentially with Lilly," a rare occurrence. JBY wrote Rosa Butt: "Miss Gleeson humbled and frightened and crushed is a well-behaved woman, but how long will it last? They have had much experience with these moods of hers."[140] Lily thought Miss Gleeson might abandon her plans for the New York exhibition altogether and began to feel sorry for her, an unusual emotion in the relationship. Lily had had a dream some months earlier in which "she saw Dun Emer . . . all despoiled and vacant of its tenants, and looking desolate."[141]

In the end, both groups went, Lily with JBY, Miss Gleeson with "two girls and a Priest cousin and a nun." At first the *Lusitania* was selected for the voyage, with all parties traveling together, and it was at that point that Lily begged her father to join her. Then Power wrote to Miss Gleeson that he wanted all to go by the *Lucania* on 28 December. She gave the news "in her grandest manner," scoring a point over the Yeatses. Lily immediately cabled Power that she wished to go by the *Campania* on the twenty-first, and he agreed. This gave Lily an extra week in New York, and,

47. Evelyn Gleeson, about 1908. *Courtesy of Dr. Patrick H. Kelly.*

according to Papa, enabled her to "escape being patronized and *'exploited'* by Miss Gleeson." [142]

Anecdotes relating to the daily irritations at Dun Emer are rare, so JBY's account of an event connected with the departure is informative. One of the clever and silent girls who accompanied Miss Gleeson was liked by her fellow workers at Dun Emer. They contributed seventeen shillings to buy her a boa and muff as an embarkation gift. When Miss Gleeson heard of it she thought at once that Lily and Lollie had put the girls up to it. She "flew into a frightful rage and fell upon Lollie," then "called up the girls and frightened" them "into saying that they were forced into it." She forbade the presentation, then gave the girl an outfit that included a boa and a muff, presumably scoring another point. Petty maneuvering of this kind went on apparently all the time in what JBY called the "internecine war" at Dun Emer.[143]

The *Lucania* was a faster ship than the *Campania,* but JBY was happy not to be on it, for "it shakes you the whole way, night and day, such a tremendous throbbing and pulsating, shattering mind and body." His vision of Miss Gleeson's party on board is again suggestive of the view the Yeatses held of her. "Miss Gleeson will need her usual quantities of soothing liquor, and the others will take to their prayers."[144]

In New York, "in the biggest hall in Maddison gardens" (as JBY described it), Lily and Miss Gleeson kept separate stalls at opposite sides of the hall, Miss Gleeson and her two girls with looms, Lily with only her embroidery and books. They apparently avoided each other completely. A man sent by Power to interview Lily told her Miss Gleeson "was a bit worked up," but Lily didn't know quite what he meant by the remark.[145] Lily sold enough to send money back to Dublin, but she had to work all day, till eleven o'clock at night, and most of the profits came from sales to John Quinn's friends, whom he bullied into buying from her. Power himself was forced to spend £12 for a piece of embroidery. The first day Lily made £12, the second £6. A "pompous" millionaire came in one day and, after spending much time looking at her selections, spent only two shillings. Father watched Lily unobserved one day. "It was amusing to see the way she flew about, talking to all the possible customers, as I could guess rage in her heart because they would not buy." But there were compensations. Mark Twain came in one day and had a long chat with Lily and bought two books. He told her he had come "specially to see her," and asked about Willie and Jack. He also invited her to a "musical riot" at his home, an affair put on by his daughter, but Lily declined.[146] JBY thought she had too much of the Pollexfen in her "to quite admit such a frivolous thing as enjoyment," even though "she was always

48. Lily Yeats and John Butler Yeats on their arrival in New York, 29 December 1907. Photograph by Alice Boughton. *Courtesy of Rosemary Hemming.*

the best and gayest of company."[147] Quinn continued bullying his friends, and by late January Lily reported she had sold £140 worth of goods. She sent Lollie £80, held on to £20, and was owed the rest by Power and others. People told Lily how much they admired designs by Jack's wife, Cottie, and many asked for Jack. The Yeats name was magic in New York and undoubtedly helped spur sales. It was a magic Miss Gleeson lacked. When Miss Gleeson traveled away from New York, she asked whether Lily would sell goods for her on commission, but Lily declined, finding "a good excuse" for doing so.[148]

Augustine Henry had arranged talks for Miss Gleeson through friends he had made in America. After the exhibition closed she spoke in Boston before the Society of Arts and Crafts, and a reporter from the *Boston Herald* interviewed her. The result provides another amusing footnote to what was to become a standard tactic in the long-running war between Miss Gleeson and the Yeats sisters, a battle that raged even after the deaths of all three. Miss Gleeson gave the reporter a brief history of her own craft and explained the current workings of the organization: "I have established two cooperative societies, the Dun Emer Guild, and the Dun Emer Industries, to one or the other of which every pupil belongs. At the end of the year, after expenses are paid, each girl is given a share in the profits." Lily and Lollie were not mentioned at all. From a reading of the piece one would judge that Miss Gleeson was the sole driving force in Dun Emer. Whether she believed that—as she had some right to do—or was merely giving the back of her hand to the Yeatses is not easy to determine.[149] A similar piece in the *Pilot,* a Catholic newspaper, gave an account of the Dun Emer Guild and of Miss Gleeson (mentioning that she was related to both "the late beloved Mgr. Gleeson, Vicar General of the Diocese of Buffalo, New York" and "The late Archbishop Walsh of Toronto"), but again neither of the Yeats sisters was named.[150]

Lily's visit was a success financially. She sent home enough money to make everything "satisfactory at the Bank."[151] Father and daughter were supposed to leave no later than the middle of February, when JBY had an appointment in his studio in Dublin. But he temporized, saying he had good chances for commissions for portraits and would be a fool to go home while there was money to be made. Unspoken was his apprehension at returning to Gurteen Dhas and life with Lollie. Lily waited with him, hoping he would decide to accompany her, but she worried about being away from Dublin. "I can't draw any money from that miserable industry while I am away, and the money is wanted at home."[152] At last she returned in June, without him. He never returned at all, remaining in New York until his death in 1922, watched over by a harassed John Quinn. Thereafter he took part in the events at Dun Emer only through correspondence.[153]

Their decision to remain in New York beyond January was fateful, for after Miss Gleeson's return to Dublin (she sailed from New York on 15 February 1908), Lollie was left alone at Dun Emer to cope with her. JBY and Lily discussed the possibilities, and their predictions were correct in almost every detail. "Lolly alone with Miss Gleeson (Lilly not there to keep the peace), and with the account at the bank all right, Lilly thinks a row may spring up between her and Miss Gleeson," JBY wrote Miss Butt. "Lilly has done well in America, but it is doubtful whether Miss Gleeson has done so. Miss Gleeson therefore may be full of quarrel on her side. Lilly half expects to find Lollie and her girls in another house in Dundrum, and Lilly is in such good spirits that I don't think she much minds. At any rate she would not be there, and Lollie would enjoy the fight, with no one to interfere, a fair field and no quarter asked or given."[154]

That Miss Gleeson was not doing well is revealed in an account sheet showing receipts and expenditures from 1903 to 30 June 1908. Total expenses for the whole period (wages, materials, etc.) were £1,726.16.7½ and receipts £1,228.10.3, almost a £500 differential. It showed stock (presumably on hand) of £1,504.5.10½. The total profit from an auditor's point of view might appear to be about £1,000, but as that was represented solely by material goods in stock and not by money in the bank, Miss Gleeson was for practical purposes in the red.[155]

The war of publicity heated up. Miss Gleeson had spoken to an "American correspondent" who had written a piece on Dun Emer for Dublin's *Freeman's Journal* after her return. Like the *Herald* and *Pilot* articles, it made no mention of the Yeatses. Lollie was quick to respond to the errant journalist. Her letter was correct and sober, as were all printed pieces in the dispute: the formality and absence of rancor in the published letters by both sides stand in contrast to the things that were written in private. "There are two distinct societies at Dun Emer," Lollie wrote in her chiding response, "which are separately managed, financed, and altogether independent of each other." She described the different branches precisely.

49. Augustine Henry, about 1910. *Courtesy of Dr. Barbara Phillips.*

"Your correspondent writes as if these two were one Society, and the error, if uncorrected, might lead to confusion with our correspondents in matters of business. Both industries were represented at the Irish Industrial Exhibition in New York, but as distinct societies, and the arrangements by which Miss Gleeson's industry and our own were on exhibition were undertaken as independent enterprises by each Society." [156]

The inevitable break came about in late spring, while Lily was still in New York. Sheila Pim suspects that what touched it off was the arrival on the scene of friends of Dr. Henry's, who he hoped could be induced to put capital into Miss Gleeson's part of the business.[157] Whatever the immediate cause, the friction between Lollie and Evelyn Gleeson was the underlying and sufficient one. In May 1908 Lollie suddenly pulled up stakes, moving the Industries office out of Dun Emer and into another house, Lackeen Cottage at Churchtown, which overlooked the Milltown Golf Course and was nearer Gurteen Dhas.[158]

There she intended carrying on her business under the Dun Emer name, and so a final conflict erupted. Miss Gleeson felt the name belonged to her—a position hard to disagree with—but because the separation negotiated by George Russell had legally established "Dun Emer Industries" as a business name, Lily and Lollie could claim the right to it. Both Miss Gleeson and Dr. Henry became agitated at the future possibilities for confusion. Lawyers were consulted, threats made. But ultimately there could be but one conclusion, for Miss Gleeson held all the trump cards.[159]

Lollie had been unable to move the Albion Hand Press out of Dun Emer, and Miss Gleeson held it hostage. The sisters had repaid only £15 of the £200 loan Miss Gleeson had made to them in 1904. Now she was able to exercise the clause in the earlier agreement allowing her to "take such action as she may be advised to recover the balance then due."[160] Lollie tried appealing to Dr. Henry, on the ground that the £200 loan—like the earlier £500—had come from him and not Miss Gleeson, but he brushed her off sharply and took Miss Gleeson's side.[161] Under the circumstances Lollie could not win. Miss Gleeson, agitated by the dispute, agreed to refuse to press whatever legal claims she might have to the money if she could merely retain exclusive use of the Dun Emer name. In an agreement dated 6 July 1908, the sisters undertook to abandon the name "Dun Emer" and to refrain from producing the kinds of goods or enterprises—carpets, tapestries, and rugs, artistic bookbinding, and artistic enameling—that had been the province of Miss Gleeson's branch. In return, Miss Gleeson turned over the Albion Hand Press to Lollie and forgave the £185 debt. Again nothing was said about the original £500 contribution from Dr. Henry. The sisters promptly changed the name of their new cottage to "Cuala" (after the ancient barony of that name in which the building lay) and resumed business as "The Cuala Industries."

When the agreement was notarized on 6 July, Evelyn Gleeson and Constance MacCormack signed one copy that was sent to the Yeatses, the sisters signed another that was sent to Miss Gleeson. Apparently the principals did not wish to meet for the ceremony.[162]

Miss Gleeson vented her anger in a summary, written on a sheet of scrap paper, of the net gain to the sisters. At the bottom of a column of figures she wrote in large, bold lettering "SO ALTO-GETHER THEY GOT £821.7.0½."[163]

The sisters had decided to institute a new monthly publication to be called *Broadsides,* a large, four-page flier with a poem and an illustration to it by Jack Yeats, hand-colored by the girls. Jack put the whole publication together and did all the drawings for it.[164] The first issue, dated June 1908, bore the Dun Emer imprint and was ready to appear when Lollie moved out of Miss Gleeson's house. *Poetry and Ireland,* by W. B. Yeats and Lionel Johnson, had also been completely set in type, except for the colophon, with Dun Emer's name on the title page. The agreement provided that both could be published as they were, but Miss Gleeson refused to allow the Dun Emer name to be added to the colophon of the book. Both works therefore represent an interesting transition from one company to another: each was published by Cuala but bore Dun Emer's name.

So the long and unhappy association came to an end. When the split was made final, Miss Gleeson bitterly calculated the costs. She had invested and lost a goodly portion of her own money, though she resolved to continue with Dun Emer despite the difficulties, and the business was still going at the time of her death on 20 February 1944. The Yeatses, having given nothing but their time, talent, and sanity, had walked off with a flourishing business, a good printing press, and trained girls. Their newly occupied Cuala was also an improvement on Dun Emer, "delightful," Lily called it: "four rooms all freshly done up, a garden and a small orchard, and only a few minutes from our own house, so no more five mile tramps in all weather." They also thought Miss Gleeson was "perfectly mad" at their moving out, and that gave them pleasure.

50. Evelyn Gleeson, in her later years. *Courtesy of Dr. Patrick H. Kelly.*

They were at last "free of Dun Emer and the Mother Abbess." "She liked to have us there and to lead people to suppose we were in her employ and working under her." [165]

There is no indication that the Yeats sisters ever believed they had been handsomely treated. They had had to endure a woman they found crusty, excitable, and haughty, and in their later letters

AUGUSTIN HENRY.
1929

51. Augustine Henry, 1929. Portrait by Celia Harrison; kindness of Sheila Pim; permission of Dr. Barbara Phillips. *Courtesy of the National Botanic Gardens, Glasnevin.*

on the founding of Cuala (innumerable letters, most of them by Lollie), they do not mention the details of the distribution of the financial resources at the time of the split, the matter of most concern to Miss Gleeson. Lollie's account to James A. Healy written thirty years later is revealing. "We started in her house in Dundrum first in 1902. We all came over from London together and in two years I ran our Depts quite separately to her and in 1908 definitely broke all connection with Miss Gleeson. She kept the name Dun Emer for her carpets, and we moved our work, Printing and Embroidery, to a 4-room cottage near our own house. . . . We gave her the name of Dun Emer in exchange for some shares she had in our Industry, which was then cooperative." [166] Lollie thus told a story correct in every detail yet not entirely truthful. [167] The sisters even put their own twist on the financial problems. "The debt in the Society was all contracted before we got the management," Lily told Quinn. "The first two years Miss Gleeson did all the business part, and it was all mixed up with her weaving." [168] Her rancor toward Evelyn Gleeson prevented even the usually fair-minded Lily from acknowledging some indisputable facts.

Nor do the sisters explain fully why the original Dun Emer had twice to be split into two parts. Newspaper and magazine articles on the enterprises depend for their accuracy on whether Miss Gleeson or one of the Yeats sisters is the source, and neither side was willing to give much credit to its opponent. Libel laws kept each from speaking ill of the other, but no law required either to speak well. The fault lines in the foundation of the industries were apparent from the beginning, as Alexander Millar had correctly foreseen. They were probably enough in themselves to cause all the problems the women experienced. Yet, with all the money in the world, any business might have broken apart under the weight of the mutual animosities that revealed themselves so early in the partnership. To what extent Miss Gleeson is to be blamed is a judgment that the historian must leave to the impartial reader. Lollie's responsibility may be easier to assess, for her long subsequent partnership with her sister was no more successful than the one with Miss Gleeson.

In any event, after July 1908 Lily and Lollie were free of outside interference. From that time on, their only adversaries would be each other and their brother Willie. Cuala's history would be as troubled as that of Dun Emer, but it too, like Dun Emer, was somehow able to survive until the deaths of the sisters, and to outlast them.

4

William Butler Yeats
and "The Weird Sisters"

There is something of a fairy tale about their story
—both sisters given good gifts when they were born,
and neither able to use them to the full, Lily with her ill
health and Lollie with her fatal temperament. They both
had to work so hard to make a place for themselves at a
time when there was less sympathy for women's struggles. I wonder what they would have done today. It just
doesn't work out to the happy ending of a true fairy
story.

> —Hannah Cadbury Taylor
> to William M. Murphy, 1990

[Lily] is very valuable in my house. She keeps us all
together and is a sort of constant go-between among us
all. . . . She never misunderstands or gets cross or spiteful or depressed.

> —John Butler Yeats
> to Isaac Yeats, 29 December 1915

Lily has a bright and happy spirit and always looks
on the shiny side of things. Lollie looks on the worst
side of things, which is good for business but bad for
happiness and "sweet companionship."

> —John Butler Yeats
> to Rosa Butt, 15 December 1907

You were right about Lolly. She had very good
brains and many talents but frittered them all away for
want of balance. For the last twenty years I lived in dread
of her losing her balance altogether. They were twenty
years of Purgatory to me. It was curious that people
writing after her death said how distinguished she

145

looked and how much they admired her, but no one said
they loved her.

—Lily Yeats
to Ruth Pollexfen Lane-Poole, 23 November 1946

I desire the love of very few people, my equals or my
superiors. The love of the rest would be a bond or an
intrusion.

—William Butler Yeats
to George Russell, [8 January 1906]

Willie has a doctrinaire kind of mind. This is one of
his difficulties, and makes a difficulty with his friends.

—John Butler Yeats
to Lady Gregory, 1906

G.K. Chesterton's roll call of the names of the Yeats children
—"Willie and Lily and Lollie and Jack"—[1] has caused some
readers to think of the two sisters as merely different versions of
the same person. The sons of JBY have had their worshipers and
biographers, but the world knows little of the daughters, Susan
Mary, the elder, always known as "Lily," and Elizabeth Corbet,
two years younger, known as "Lollie."[2] There are two well-known
allusions to them in James Joyce's *Ulysses*. Enough in themselves to
guarantee them the immortality of a learned footnote, they are
less than flattering. Buck Mulligan, in Stephen Dedalus's tower,
parodies the wording of the colophon of the first book the sisters
produced for the Dun Emer Press: "Five lines of text and ten pages
of notes about the folk and fishgods of Dundrum. Printed by the
weird sisters in the year of the big wind." Later he calls them, in a
double entendre, "two designing females."[3] Joyce, who knew the
sisters, perhaps expressed in his wicked phrases the common Dublin
view of them. The off-rhyme euphony of their names has caused
them to be regarded as female counterparts of Tweedledum and
Tweedledee. Two sisters with sound-alike names and look-alike
handwritings, spinster ladies living together, working together in
an artsy-craftsy industry, both very much at the periphery of the
public vision: why shouldn't they be regarded almost as identical
twins, interchangeable at will?

52. Gilbert Keith Chesterton (1874–1936), about 1915. *Courtesy of Library of Congress.*

No assumption could be more wide of the mark. Lily's and Lollie's personalities differed from each other in almost every way. One was affable, pleasant, companionable; the other troubled, quarrelsome, unpleasant, jealous, talkative, paranoid. It was the tragedy of each that she had to live with the other, though in the Ireland of their time no other arrangement was realistically possible. Able and talented, but unmarried and with little money, the

way they took was the only one open to them. That they survived
at all under the circumstances and that they achieved what they
did is a tribute to the strength that came from their remarkable
heritage.

Lily, the elder of the two, was universally liked. Even as a child
her special qualities were evident. When JBY suggested to his wife,
then in Sligo, that she meet him with one of their young children,
he wrote: "Lilly would be the best. She is the best behaved and
would be the favorite with people."[4] She served as the moderate
center of the family, the one to whom all turned for emotional
support. She was one of the few people in the world, and the only
one in the family, close to her brother the poet. Her sister Lollie,
on the other hand, annoyed everyone close to her. William Butler
Yeats complained that he and she had fallen out "from the cradle."[5]
He told Lily: "She is a tragedy, really never happy, always doing
the wrong thing, restless, irritable, unloveable, unbalanced." The
last of these words, according to Lily, who knew her best, "sums
her up."[6] She had another quality whose ancestry was hard to
identify. "Where does her silliness come from?" William Butler
Yeats wanted to know.[7] One of their young cousins, who spent two
years with the sisters in the 1930s, said of her, "Sometimes you
would think Lollipop [her nickname for her] had no brains at all."[8]
Lollie was utterly unaware of the effect she had on others, once
telling Lily that "the mistake of her life" had been "that she always
considered other people instead of herself," and when she made
this remarkable assessment, Lily said, "she was not trying to be
funny."[9]

Lily Yeats was possessed of fundamental good nature, the source
of her strength and sanity. She shared with her father and brother
Jack "an extraordinary gift for making herself popular."[10] When
she stayed with her father in New York he noted that everybody in
the hotel, even the chambermaids and bellboys and the old ladies
in the lobby, took to her.[11] As a young woman she had a couple of
suitors, one of them the brother of the woman who became John
Masefield's wife,[12] but a person who had lived with a father and
brothers like hers could hardly have been satisfied with an ordinary
man. Lollie noticed that when John Quinn visited the Yeatses in
Dublin he and Lily found each other fascinating companions, and

she later asserted that he and John Millington Synge were the only ones Lily "took *that sort* of interest in."[13] Lily was an attractive younger woman, as her father's many portraits and sketches of her show. In her old age, a Dublin art teacher told her how lovely she had been as a girl, her "colouring like wild roses, so delicate." She had a grace of presence too. When Frank Fay instructed the actresses at the Abbey, he told them he wanted them to walk across the stage the way Lily Yeats walked across a room.[14]

Like all in the family, she had a talent for painting. In Hyères she did a flower picture, of yellow chrysanthemums in a brass bowl, which her employer hung along with landscapes by Edward Dowden's brother-in-law, Mr. West. One day a French painter of some standing came to the house, looked at the walls, tapped Lily's picture and said, "That is the work of an artist." "These," he said, pointing to West's, "are done by an amateur."[15] Her artistic talents found expression in her designs for Dun Emer and Cuala embroideries but were otherwise stifled by her health. Her principal contributions to the world, in addition to what resulted from the friendship with her brother Willie, were her wit and her very presence.

The New York judge Martin Keogh referred to her constantly as "the most amusing girl."[16] Letitia Overend, a friend, complimented her on being "interested in everything."[17] Oliver Elton told his son Leonard that Lily was "a special case," that nobody would meet a person like her "twice in one world."[18] The nurse who cared for her in her last days called her "the most wonderful and good and considerate patient I have ever had."[19] Papa depended so much on her good temper that he told her she was not allowed to get depressed. "I rely on you to keep cheerful," he told her,[20] and she seldom disappointed him. "My father and I were very great friends," she told a friend, "so that was good to begin with."[21] She was also the family "magpie," as JBY called her. She collected and saved every scrap of information about the Yeats family. "I treated her as my book of reference," said Jack.[22]

So it is not surprising that within her own family Lily was the one to whom everyone turned, even Lollie. "Lollie would go mad," JBY told Rosa Butt, "if it was not for Lily, who is a haven of refuge and a harbour of peace, with whom she may weep her sad bosom empty. Lily is a patient listener, a born listener. She controls by listening."[23] He wrote, "(between ourselves) I would not have Lollie in her place *for worlds.*"[24] To his brother Isaac he described Lily's importance: "She is very valuable in my house. She keeps us all together and is a sort of constant go-between among us all. George Pollexfen always consulted her about the family—*always.* He used to say, 'She has a head,' and then he would shake his own. The fact is she is constantly thinking about us all, and never forgets anything. She has a wonderful memory. She writes to me two or three times a week and is my constant comfort. I can talk to her about anything. She never misunderstands or gets cross or spiteful or depressed." He thought her single state was unfortunate. "I would have liked to see Lily married. She was intended for a domestic life with husband and children."[25]

Willie and she had a unique relationship. They shared special dreams about their childhood in the west of Ireland. "No one will ever see Sligo as we saw it," he told her.[26] When they were children in London they went on long walks together, and in later years he saw her whenever possible, seeking out her company as much as he avoided Lollie's. When he began his association with Madame Helena Blavatsky, he took Lily with him to her house, an event noted in her diary by Lollie, who was not invited.[27] When he wrote his "Reveries Over Childhood and Youth," Lily supplied him with the details of their Sligo days, most of which he had remembered only vaguely in a blur of warm feelings.[28] When he finished the draft, he asked Lily if she would listen to him as he read it, and he specifically excluded Lollie as a reader.[29] His ode "In Memory of Alfred Pollexfen" is but a rewording of one of Lily's letters to him.[30]

When Ruth Pollexfen joined the Yeats household in Bedford Park in 1899, she could have treated Lily and Lollie as equal older cousins. Instead, she chose Lily as her special protector and came to regard her as a mother. She and Lollie did not hit it off at all. Even those outside the family, paying guests like Susan Mitchell and Anne Boston, chose Lily's friendship and rejected Lollie's. When Miss Boston visited Dublin, she and Lily met secretly to escape Lollie's jealousy. When Ruth's daughter Charles visited Gurteen Dhas in 1936, it was to Lily she gravitated, and when her younger sister Mary followed her, the pattern was repeated. When the scholar Una Ellis-Fermor visited in 1938, Lollie grew angry because she chose to be "friendly" with Lily.[31] When John Quinn needed to write to Dublin about the problems he was having with John Butler Yeats, it was to Lily he wrote. The universal acceptance and admiration of her are indisputable. Those who knew her only in her declining years, when she was disabled by illness, do not find it easy to think of her as a vibrant, witty, thoroughly enjoyable companion, but so she was.

As a letter writer Lily had no equal in the family. Those familiar with her correspondence will understand the source of her charm. JBY confided to Isaac that he thought Lily's letters "as such" were "superior to Willie's," and added later, "I could make money out of those she sends to me. They are all good literature and at the same time always letters, dashed off in a moment."[32] Her writing is conclusive and epigrammatic, sparing of detail, marked by an astute selection of example and economical phrasing—direct, unpretentious, almost monosyllabic, often witty, and, when the occasion required, mordant and acid. Her poet brother's letters are naturally of more interest and more significance to the world of art and criticism, and they are still being probed by those in the scholarly world interested in what has become known, in an overused term, as the "creative process." Lily was not a philosopher or a critic but simply a person who saw the world about her and recorded what she saw with "humour and observation" (her brother's words).[33] "She can be very interesting about nothing at all," her father declared.[34] Her letters from Hyères he read faithfully to the Bedford Park neighbors. In New York, John Quinn asked JBY to save her letters for him to read. Her spelling was better than her brother's, her punctuation as undisciplined and free-spirited as his. Like his own writings, hers were meant to be read aloud; the sound of her voice is distinctive, always engaging and persuasive. In recounting the death of Lord Iveagh, she noted that his famous Guinness ancestor had been a servant in a great man's house at the time he developed his formula for stout. Now the descendants of his employer lived in genteel poverty in London, while the Guinnesses were the richest people in Ireland. Reflecting on the whims of fate, Lily ended her story simply: "I wish we were beer and not art." Of the illness of her physician's wife she wrote: "If she lives I suppose it will be Christian Science, if she dies the doctors."[35] At

53. Lily Yeats, New York, May 1908. From reproduction of pencil sketch by JBY. *Courtesy of Michael B. Yeats.* Provenance of original unknown.

the Grand Union Hotel in New York, she and her father occupied a suite on the same floor as Admiral Peary the year before the explorer made his assault on the Arctic.

I remember Peary at the hotel. I will never forget his voice. I heard it every morning ringing down the passage, "The papers and my mail." Then the door slammed. I used to think then that his wife might be the nearest thing to the North Pole he could ever get. You remember her, tall and cold and grim and handsome.[36]

She remembered a bibulous evening at Quinn's when Townsend Walsh overindulged: "Yes, I remember Mr. Walsh. He was writing his book on Boucicault between drinks. . . . He was trying to light his cigar, never getting his match within a foot of it."[37] Of two of her father's friends in New York she wrote: "Gregg has something to say but does not always say it. . . . Charlie [Johnston] has very little to say but says it at great length."[38]

It was passages such as these that caused her father to write to his brother Isaac: "Her letters are my solace and comfort. No one ever wrote better. They have all the graces of fine literary style and yet remain just letters. It is only a nice woman who can do that sort of miracle."[39] Once Lily asked a clergyman at St. George's if she could borrow for an arts and crafts exhibition an embroidered flag made by her and the girls at Cuala. He declined, arguing that "the flag had been consecrated and hung in the church and so could not be lent for exhibiting." Lily replied, "I see your point, but the rector and curate are also consecrated and they go out to tea." The next day he sent the flag, "saying my letter had made them change their point of view and made them laugh."[40] Tom Lyster, an Irish friend, told her she had a way of hitting the nail on the head without hurting her own fingers, and JBY agreed with him. She did it "so genially," he told her, "that I fancy the nail itself sometimes smiles."[41] Fred King, a friend of JBY's in New York, thought her letters worthy of publication.[42] JBY, alluding to Balzac's remark that he learned to write by writing to clever women, said: "I think Lily got her education *out of writing letters.*"[43] She could be mordant or merely observant, but always pointed, as the following sampling shows:

> *On the behavior of the wealthy during the First World War:* The rich are giving up sugar in their tea and subscribing to funds for the relief of the unemployed and at the same time dismissing their servants.[44]

On Ruth's seeking a good school for her daughter Charles: Don't try any freak school. They would be all right if the children at them were normal but they are all freaks also.[45]

On Charles's education: Don't let her run away with any false notions about the artistic temperament. . . . So many use "art" as a cloak for idleness and racketiness.[46]

On men: Jonas, who sweeps the roads as you will remember, looked at a passing short-skirted slim girl and remarked, "A man nowadays knows what he is getting. Long ago he didn't even know if she was straight or crooked." Old scamp, but he had an eye for a girl.[47]

On English attitudes toward the Irish: The English have a cool greed and annex our famous men. The Brontës Irish side is quite forgotten, except when they remember Branwell the brother. He used to be all Irish, but since someone started the story that he and not Emily had written *Wuthering Heights* he has ceased to be Irish.[48]

On the future Edward VIII: Did you see the Prince of Wales, seeing off Bernardo orphans being shipped to Australia and Canada, asked them to promise him to write regularly to their parents? Now, was he being funny or was it after lunch?[49]

On a gathering at Trinity College, Dublin: The Provost was very friendly and pleasant. After we and the general public had seated ourselves in the hall of the College, a voice said, "Ladies and gentlemen, the Provost." Up we stood, and the little man appeared to us again as if quite new.[50]

On a prosperous Dublin family: The men for generations have successfully done nothing but *have* married money, and that takes some doing.[51]

On an acquaintance who had been abandoned by her husband: Mrs. B——is an unhappy strung-up woman, deserted by the faithless B——. She looked miserable and angry and excited, and also looked as if she had made herself up a week before and then just allowed wind and weather to play havoc with her appearance.
I felt there might also have been Mr. B——'s story.[52]

> *On the pre-nuptial maneuvering of a young relative:* She will
> marry, don't worry. She means to. If she loses interest in the
> matter I won't. She has had one chance already but refused. I am
> glad she did. He was not the man nor she in love. She felt a little
> sentimental, that was all, and was funnily indignant when I
> described her feelings to her. She thought them very serious
> and deep. As she had two broken engagements already I didn't
> feel anxious about him, recovery likely to be rapid and com-
> plete.[53]

No general philosophy is to be found in the letters. Lily had no
agenda for political or artistic reform, no profound insights into the
fundamental mysteries of the universe; her views may be described
as a mile wide and an inch deep. One of the sources, perhaps the
principal source, of her optimism and placidity in the face of her
uncomfortable and confining life was her religious faith. Like her
sister and most of the Anglo-Irish of her time, she was a Protestant
belonging to the Church of Ireland, though it is not surprising
that she and Lollie attended services in different parishes.[54] Their
grandfather and greatgrandfather had been clergymen, but John
Butler Yeats had studied Bishop Joseph Butler's *Analogy of Religion*
and concluded that the Christian religion was "myth and fable,"
though he was by no means an "atheist" as the word is commonly
understood. He tried to bring up his children to be rationalists,
but he had a sneaking suspicion there might be a life after this
one, if not the one envisioned in conventional Christian theology.
Officially he worshiped fact and reason, neither of which he found
in the church of his forebears.

It was JBY's powerful character and intellect that undermined
any chance his children might have had for an easy, unthinking
acceptance of the orthodox. He made his views clear many times.
In a letter to his brother Isaac in 1916, he spoke of his Uncle Matt
Yeats, who had died decades earlier: "You know how I have always
hated what people call religion. Uncle Matt would have lived another ten years or so had it not been for religion. His religion was
a religion of fear, and so he was constantly praying, and *there is
nothing so fatiguing and so exhausting as praying.*"[55] His own uncertain
view was expressed in a letter to Lady Gregory: "I have never
believed in any religion, except the one doctrine of Predestination.
We are here for some use. Some *are in the reserve.* They are parents

or grandparents, ancestors from whom may come a remote descendant that will enter the fighting line and do a man's part."[56] Despite his misuse of the term "Predestination," his position is clear enough.

Lily worshiped her father, but in matters of religion she kept her views at a respectful distance from his.[57] She had visions (not dreams, but images that came to her in flashes when awake or more softly when she was in a state of semi-sleep) of discomforting accuracy that made it impossible for her to accept a purely mechanistic interpretation of the universe.[58] Of one belief particularly she was certain, with no suggestion of doubt whatever. She was convinced of immortality, of a personal afterlife of almost mundane proportions. "One could not go on if good-byes were forever," she wrote.[59] She even believed that she had lived before. "I think like you that life goes on," she told her father. "I am sure I have lived many times, and will live many times more, and I am sure I have been the mother of a great many children."[60] She knew she would meet John Butler Yeats again after death, was absolutely convinced of it, and she showed no apparent grief at the deaths of friends and acquaintances, certain they would be reunited with those they loved. When her father died, she wrote Willie: "I feel he has found his two children that died so long ago and is delighting in the likenesses he finds in them to his children here on this earth."[61] In writing of friends who had just died, Lily almost invariably spoke of their being reunited with a loved one. When a friend's mother died Lily wrote Ruth, "If what we hope is true, she was no longer weary but well and free from all suffering and anxiety and the weight of years, and met by her husband and others she had loved." And when a friend lay dying, she commented to Ruth: "I hope her illness will not be a long one. A quick goodbye and then the new life, which I am perfectly sure is a good life for her, and a brave going on for her sister."[62] After Willie died, she wrote Joseph Hone: "My affection for Willy is very deep and strong and has always been so. I miss him more every day, but never feel he is dead. He was so vital and vivid. I feel he is still vivid and vital, but just not where we are."[63]

When she advised Ruth on the upbringing of her three daughters, she insisted that they be taught "spiritual values" and urged to attend church faithfully.[64] A typical passage is the following, from a letter dealing with Ruth's daughter Charles:

> To go back to the need for a spiritual life. I think young people should be taught to realize that we have two lives, a physical and a spiritual, and that the last is most important. Charles has had a very happy life. No sorrow has come her way. She has felt no need for spiritual help and comfort, and is rather inclined to think it is not there. But now lately I have noticed that she is seeing and thinking and feeling that such a life is necessary and exists. She has read a good deal and heard Willy and others talk of it. He in a speech some time ago said, "The man who believes in nothing has made the world a poisonous place to live in."[65]

And a year later:

> We have rather fun with Charles accusing her of being entirely materialistic. She thinks when I say there is another side to life that I mean ghosts and nothing else. She ought to know and believe that "man does not live by bread alone."[66]

After Willy's death she wrote to Ruth:

> Remember this is only a very small part of our life. We are eternal. Be brave and patient. The next step will be a step up.[67]

What is surprising, then, is to discover that nowhere in the many passages in her letters and other writings that deal with religion does she say a word about "God" or "Jesus Christ," about "redemption" or "salvation," about "Hell" or "the Devil." She shows no interest in theological niceties and no awareness that they exist. All she knows is that everything will come right in the end. Moral as opposed to theological philosophy is her concern, and the strongest words she utters on the subject are more Hindu than Christian:

> I believe in another life, believe it without a shadow of a doubt, and believe that the way we take this life, the good we

do, the courage we show in trouble, and, most important, what we do for others, all means a higher state in the next life.[68]

Our obligation was to "fight manfully until the end," the only reason we were put on earth.[69]

Like many Protestants, Lily had reservations about the Catholic Church, not because of its theology or even its morals, but because of its refusal to let people think for themselves. An eleven-year-old Roman Catholic niece of one of her helpers visited Gurteen Dhas in 1942 and had to make up the religious training she would have got had she been at school.

> I am teaching her her catechism. She doesn't understand a word of it, but that does not seem to be wished. A lesson on the nature of God made me stop several times to look again and make sure I was not teaching her a speech by Hitler telling the world what he thinks he is.[70]

She observed once how Maria, the maid, left the house late one morning to go to Sunday Mass: "R.C.'s think they are in good time if they get in any time before the Gospel. So much for compulsory religion."[71] And whenever the subject of educating a young Church of Ireland child in Ireland is raised, Lily, like any proper Anglo-Irishwoman, expresses a fear that a mixed marriage might result.[72] The Yeatses, like other Anglo-Irish families, lived in complete harmony with their Catholic countrymen, whom they loved and admired, but they remained baffled by their religious practices.

Lily also had strong notions about what she called the "gentry" and was proud that the Yeats family could include itself in the group. Her father, who hated class distinctions of all kinds, what he called "class feeling,"[73] sometimes felt that his daughters might be afflicted with it. But it is clear from Lily's writings that her pride of family and her choice of friends rested on what she perceived as achievement and attitude. Her father had noted that "the aristocracy knows nothing of class," that it is only "the bourgeois" who loves class; what the aristocrat seeks is "cousinhood."[74] "Gentry" to her meant civilization and achievement, not the snobbery that

arises from mediocrity attached to money or station. She was tren-
chant in her comments on "half-sirs," people of no particular distinction who give themselves airs because they have accumulated
money and are ascending the social ladder. "The opinions of your
equals and superiors is valuable as well as pleasant," she wrote
Ruth. "By inferiors and superiors I don't mean class. Some imbecile
HRH might admire you very much and be at the same time your
inferior."[75] Her attitude was not snobbery as the term is commonly
understood but a preference for one set of standards over another,
for a cousinhood: for the more tolerant views of the Church of
Ireland as contrasted with those of the Church of Rome, for the
graciousness and good manners that flowed from those properly
brought up, for the beauty of "the rich man's flowering lawns"
rather than the ugliness of the "mean roof trees." Lily admired
people like John Quinn, in spite of their modest origins, and did
not care for those like Annie Horniman, in spite of their pretensions. She disliked many of the Anglo-Irish for the narrowness of
their minds and views, especially the West Britons with their knee-
jerk contempt for the Catholic Irish, and she admired the Catholics
who had escaped from the confinement of their upbringing, even if
a long rope might still keep them tethered there.

And no matter what other people might have thought about
the Jews during the dreadful thirties, Lily was their staunch supporter. She was horrified by Hitler's treatment of them. Many had
been forced to flee Germany (not realizing at the time how lucky
they were). "Where are they to go?" Lily asked Ruth. "They are a
great race, and have brains and many talents, and an astonishing
power of endurance."[76] She and Lollie and Ruth had met and become friends with a Jewish family in Frankfurt during one of their
visits to Germany during the first decade of the century. (She
learned in 1942 that one of them had been forced to flee the country
because of his race.) "This Jew baiting is horrible and will be much
regretted, I feel sure, by future generations. The Jews have brains
and are very valuable, with their music and many talents, excluding
that for finance, which is not only money-making. It is said that
all fine actors have either Irish or Jewish blood in them."[77]

• • •

Yet if others might see Lily as the mediator, the wit, the family anchor, she was forced to live with another part of her being, her congenitally poor health. For the last twenty-five years of her life, she was increasingly confined indoors, and for the last ten was hardly able to walk about; for the last five she was completely bedridden. Not the least of her sufferings was the fact that the source of her condition was not uncovered until she was in her early sixties, and by then it was too late for medical skills to be of any help. She had been born prematurely, with an abnormal thyroid gland that became enlarged and branched out into her chest, causing difficulty in her breathing and constant fatigue. As her uncle George had always been sluggish, stolid, and slow, it did not occur to her that her fatigue might be attributable to any other cause than her Pollexfen ancestry. Had she shared the good health of her sister Lollie, there is no telling how different her career might have been. As it was, she achieved far more than could reasonably have been expected of her.

•   •   •

William Butler Yeats called Lollie "my excitable sister Elizabeth" and described Lily as "a much more satisfactory person."[78] The characterizations were, coming from him, unusually mild. Lollie, always in good health, was nevertheless excitable, flighty, annoying, like a fly buzzing about one's head. "I am impatient by temperament," she admitted.[79] Yeats scholars know her through her letters, scattered in their hundreds in libraries throughout the United States and Canada—long, gossipy, heavy with exclamation points and underlined words and phrases. Like Lily's, her letters are fascinating, ("with the Pollexfen blood and tradition it could not be otherwise," JBY explained to Lady Gregory)[80] but with a difference—crammed with details, full accounts of daily activity, revelations of private thoughts and opinions, nothing omitted. Not many know the troubled person who wrote the letters. A handsome woman to whom men were attracted, always well-dressed and properly groomed,[81] her personality and mannerisms canceled out her physical charms; she remained isolated and lonely all her life, even when among other people.

The testimony to Lollie's effect on others comes from many

sources, from her father,[82] her brothers, her sister Lily, who knew her best, and her neighbors. Lollie did not hide her psychosis behind a placid demeanor. If she was troubled, she wanted everyone around her to be troubled too—no masks for her. Willie and Jack became victims of her wayward temperament, but the principal victim was the one with whom she lived and worked, her sister Lily.

If Lollie couldn't see herself as others saw her, it was not for lack of direct, sometimes brutal testimony. In the same book in which Chesterton lists the names of the Yeats children, he describes the formation in the 1890s of a social club in Bedford Park, where his future wife Frances Blogg resided, known as the "I.D.K." Chesterton, a kindly man, refrains from mentioning what was known informally as "Rule No. 1" of the club: "Lolly Yeats must never be allowed in as a member."[83] If Lollie was unaware of the hostility of the members of that club—and it is hard to see how she could have been—she could hardly have been oblivious to the feelings of her classmates at the Froebel School. It was the custom at the school's annual dance for the members to be introduced separately by one of their fellow students as they entered the ball-room from a side door. The names were called out in alphabetical order. Lollie, as a Yeats, was last in line. After the announcer introduced the next-to-last girl, she "looked straight at Lollie and shut the door in her face, saying, 'That is all now, Madame.' " Lollie had to open the door and enter on her own, joining a group of unappreciative companions.[84] Lollie herself told Lily the story, apparently not aware that she had been insulted.

Even then, in vigorous youth, Lollie repelled people. One of the reasons was her intense egoism, of which she seems to have been unaware—an exclusive focus on herself and her desires, a blindness to the concerns of others. She longed for command and public recognition. Her father told Rosa Butt that Lollie could not "live without movement and excitement and *visible success.*"[85] When she failed to achieve them, she took her frustrations out on those around her.

Lollie lived in a world of illusion, of a Cinderella romanticism, as Lily called it.[86] She thought of herself as a desirable beauty waiting to be rescued from scrubbing brush and broom by a dashing

54. Louis Claude Purser in the 1890s. Pencil sketch by Josephine Webb. *Courtesy of Society of Friends, Dublin.*

prince. The first of her suitors was Louis Purser, later a distinguished classical scholar at Trinity College, Dublin. During the Bedford Park days he had journeyed from Dublin to London regularly to see her. Yet just about the time the sisters were moving from London to Dublin, Louis cooled off. There was never an open break, no obvious breach of promise. Precisely what happened between them we can only conjecture. Lollie "gave her love" to Louis "in a real and serious sense" (the words are Lily's, whatever they mean) some time in 1902 or 1903, but after that he grew distant. In 1910, Lily felt compelled to write him, after he had asked her by letter to send his "love" to Lollie. "The barrier that has arisen neither *she* nor I understand. It is yours, not hers. If it is removable remove it, if not leave things as they are. . . . If you can make her even a little happy, do so. I write only from my affection for her and my knowledge of her misery. I use the word 'misery' as it is the only word that describes her state." [87] Louis's fires failed to reignite, and when Lollie suffered a nervous breakdown later in the year Lily thought that the affair—or non-affair—was largely to blame. John Butler Yeats, writing to Willie, told him that, remembering their mother, he feared for Lollie's condition. "I have often had my own dread that Lollie may lose her wits. The Pollexfen blood can't stand worry. At any rate Lollie can't. At times she becomes terribly depressed." [88]

Susan Mitchell once wrote to John Butler Yeats of Lollie's "repellent ways" but acknowledged at the same time that "she had never met anyone who had such a longing for affection and regard," perceptively recognizing the two elements in Lollie's personality. [89] The "repellent" part, unfortunately, was what people saw. The "longing for affection and regard" was concealed beneath the outward unpleasantness and, unhappily for her, few people responded to it.

Lollie was enterprising and daring, as her father recognized. "Of *all* my family Lollie is the most distinguished," he wrote his brother Isaac. "She has courage, ardour, and uprightness." She was "splendid in any emergency," he said, "as she is very courageous (although so nervous). She has both physical and moral courage. In the presence of any sort of danger she at once becomes cheerful and happy." But, he also noted, "She is so active and ambitious that she cannot bear to lead a humdrum existence." [90] To Rosa Butt he wrote, "A quiet life drives her into melancholia, and when she is unhappy she wants to share it with everybody else." [91]

To her energy and resourcefulness she added physical attractiveness, inevitably drawing the attention of eligible bachelors, Louis Purser being only the first. Dr. Augustine Henry makes clear

55. Susan Mitchell, about 1900. *Courtesy of Michael B. Yeats.*

in his early Dun Emer letters to Evelyn Gleeson that he found Lollie a radiant and charming being; his fascination with her helped spin the web at Dun Emer in which they all became entangled. Another suitor would come later, and the conclusion would be even more disastrous.

The only stage available to her where she could bask in the applause of the audience was the classroom, and there she was at her happiest and best. Everyone who studied drawing and painting under her spoke highly of her talents. She was inspiring, a thoroughly good teacher able to communicate her message with astonishing success. "She was a wonderful teacher," her sister wrote of her, "got results and exhilarated her pupils."[92] When she visited briefly at homes where children were present, she enthralled them with sketches and anecdotes.[93] The vigor of her personality and the dominance of her presence were undeniable; she was, her sister said, "a curious and remarkable character" who "fascinated and excited" people "by her vivid personality."[94] Even those who ultimately found her intolerable felt a secret sympathy for her, realizing her unhappiness and her inability to behave in a way that would remove it.[95]

Unlike Lily, who accepted what life brought and had the sense not to complain about what couldn't be changed, Lollie strove constantly and swept those around her into the vortex of her insecurities. She might make an instant favorable impression on her students yet showed no interest in following through. She "could not carry them on," wrote Lily, "just as she was a success with people right off, went no further."[96] When the applause faded Lollie faded too. To her sister she had "the most unhappy nature."[97] To her sister-in-law Mrs. William Butler Yeats she was like a character in a one-act play who wanted life to consist of a series of neatly resolved dramatic incidents.[98] She was constitutionally unable to be happy, and in her John Butler Yeats saw the same frightening symptoms he had observed in the Pollexfens. His letters to Isaac, the one close family member in whom he confided freely, are peppered with his concerns about her:

She is constantly anticipating something dreadful, so her letters are sometimes rather disquieting.[99]

Lollie is an abiding anxiety. Long ago I several times was most anxious about her—she is so constantly unhappy, too like "Grandpapa."[100]

> She has a terribly self-tormenting mind. She very easily gets unhappy. . . . I sometimes think the life she leads is far too quiet for her. She likes movement and success.[101]

> When Lollie is away she always writes as if she was on a pilgrimage of pain and sorrow, a long letter filled with complaints and groaning.[102]

Both Lily and Willie thought Lollie got her bad temper from William Pollexfen, who, however, had the fear of God to hold him in check, a restraint not available to Lollie.[103] Another Pollexfen trait Lollie displayed in abundance troubled Papa much more. He had to caution his brother Isaac not to share his letters with anyone else: "All I wrote to you yesterday about Lollie is quite confidential. Lily never speaks of it to anyone, and to me always speaks of it as nerves, as I to her—but it is depressive mania, and it affected more or less most of the Pollexfens. Three of them were in asylums."[104] The next day he repeated his fear. "She has the Pollexfen traits, a distinct tendency to what the doctors call depressive mania."[105]

To those who knew her only as an occasional houseguest or as a teacher, Lollie might be interesting, even fascinating. To those who had to live with her, she was a constant trial. The chief memory of her by those who knew her well is of her talkativeness: "a non-stop talker," Tom MacGreevy called her.[106] Her constant chatter was a way of keeping attention focused on herself, and it went on endlessly. Her speech was decisive and emphatic. She spoke as she wrote, in italics. She never realized how much she annoyed those who had to listen to her. When she wrote letters in the parlor at Gurteen Dhas, she bothered the others in the room by asking how certain words were spelled, what was so and so's address, how much postage was needed, when was the mail collected. If Lily was trying to read, Lollie would break in with gossip and babble about unimportant matters.[107] When annoyed, Lollie would purse her mouth till it was "the size of her eye," an expression used repeatedly by Lily.[108] And she was easily aroused. Once, when she visited her physician, Dr. Frank Purser, his first words to her were: "Well, who has been annoying you?"[109]

To her talkativeness she added fidgetiness, twitching restlessly like a Mexican jumping bean. She had a habit of jerking her left shoulder up that so annoyed her sister-in-law George Yeats, wife of WBY, that when her daughter Anne once made an involuntary motion of her shoulder, her mother chided her at once. "Stop that twitching. You'll get to be like Aunt Lollie." [110] When Lollie left the house for business or holidays the remaining inhabitants found the peace and silence overwhelming.

People with irritable natures look for a target at which to aim their arrows of annoyance. Lily, the older sister with whom Lollie lived cheek-by-jowl in Gurteen Dhas for forty years, was naturally the most obvious of targets, and it was she who took the arrows. Surprisingly, the two sisters had had little opportunity to rub against each other at Blenheim Road. "In the London days we saw very little of her," Lily wrote. "She was away all day, had her own friends and went away every holiday." [111] Not until the move to Dublin in 1902 were the two thrown together.

Although Lollie seldom tried to be companionable with her sister, she resented Ruth Pollexfen's attachment to Lily, and her jealousy became almost maniacal. Lily learned early to take precautions about Ruth's weekly letters from Australia after her marriage, instructing the servant Maria to put them in her room so that Lollie could not see that they had arrived. "A letter from you turns her black at once," Lily told Ruth. [112] Lollie believed her sister and Ruth were engaged in a whispering conspiracy against her and, when Ruth returned to Dublin with her first baby, did all she could to keep the two from seeing each other and forced them to meet in secret. When Hilda Pollexfen, Ruth's younger sister, came for a brief stay in 1904, [113] the same difficulty arose. In later years a young lady named Anne Boston came to live at Gurteen Dhas as a paying guest but had to leave because of Lollie's jealousy. [114] The break with Evelyn Gleeson at Dun Emer and the subsequent events at Cuala are made more understandable by a recognition of Lollie's problems.

One peculiarity of Lollie's, which Lily called a "warp," was unusual in the extreme. She refused to believe that other people could be ill, even those on the point of death. When Annie McElheron, one of the young Cuala workers, was taken to the hospital, Lollie insisted there was nothing wrong with her, even though the doctors found she needed surgery. Lollie refused to acknowledge

56. Anne Boston ("Phillida"). *Courtesy of Rosemary Hemming.*

the operation, insisting "there was nothing to fuss about," that Annie was "perfectly well."[115] When her nephew Michael Yeats had a "very delicate" operation, Lollie belittled the problem by insisting nothing was really the matter, even though the expensive surgery required four physicians.[116] When George wrote Lollie about Willie's being ill in Rapallo, Lollie insisted to Lily that it could not be true, that Willie "had little the matter" with him. Lily believed Lollie's problem was worth looking into. "Her warp is extraordinary and interesting seen as a case."[117] Yet Lollie may have come by it genetically and so perhaps not have been responsible for it. Susan Pollexfen Yeats had been much the same, Lily told Ruth, "a little like Lolly on other people's illnesses," her sole prescription for her sick children to "grin and bear it."

It was Lily's fatigue that most drew Lollie's ire. Her sister's affliction had always been thought to be a mild form of asthma, nothing more, and Lollie was sure, or pretended to be sure, that Lily was behaving as far more ill than she really was. It may indeed have been Lily's perpetual weakness, intensified by her bout with typhoid and the long recuperation, that caused Lollie's obsession about other people's illnesses. It certainly accounted for her otherwise inexcusable behavior at the time of Lily's collapse in 1923, when Lollie's malicious intervention misled the physician into a faulty diagnosis of her sister's condition.[118] For five years Lily, debilitated by her errant thyroid, had to live under the gaze of those who thought her a malingerer.

Even after she learned the truth about Lily's condition, Lollie continued to believe her sister wasn't as ill as she pretended to be and tried to poison other people's minds against her. One of her devices was to take people aside and ask them to tell Lily they thought she was looking well. When Oliver Edwards visited Gurteen Dhas to talk to Lily about the Yeats family tree, he said to her at intervals, "You are looking well."[119] An American visitor to Cuala, who had never seen Lily before, said even before shaking hands with her, "You are looking well."[120] When members of the Art Workers Guild came to Gurteen Dhas, their first words to Lily were, "You do look well." Lily was driven to exasperated frustration. "I am as helpless as if I was gagged and bound in chains," she told Ruth. "I can't shout, 'Stop, my sister is a neurotic and a liar.' They would then be perfectly sure of the truth of Lolly's fable."[121]

When James A. Healy, the New York stockbroker, developed an interest in the Cuala Press and the Yeats family in general in the late 1930s, the two sisters and Jack began an extended correspondence with him. Lily had long since been forced to give up her work at Cuala and live in enforced invalidism at home. When Healy wrote favorably of Lily, Lollie replied in a mean-spirited letter:

> She has no shares in Cuala and does not I think care what becomes of it! She never did. She really never liked running her Embroidery Department. She *likes* the kind of life she is living now. So it has been I and WBY who have had all along to try to keep Cuala on its feet. She was glad of the excuse of health to retire—and WB paid up her losses—and did not really mind

about the working stopping—not a bit. She has never liked any kind of active work. *She is built that way.*[122]

When Fred King, a friend of JBY's in New York, suggested to Lollie that Lily's letters should be published—but made no corresponding suggestion about Lollie's—she dismissed the idea lightly: "She *does* write good letters, but they are very personal, too personal to publish." She promised to tell Lily of his suggestion, but there is no evidence that she did.[123]

Her meanness and mendacity were at times damaging. When Lily made an amusing remark privately to Lollie about a friend of theirs who was about to marry and move to Africa, Lollie repeated it to the prospective bride in such a way as to make it appear offensive. The bride was naturally hurt by what she regarded as Lily's callousness.[124]

Lollie could also be mendacious for no apparent reason. When one of the Cuala girls was operated on for hammertoe, the physician, Sir Lambert Ormesby, arranged to have her admitted into a nursing home for recuperation. The girl had never had a free day in her life and was looking forward to a welcome rest. Lollie told the doctor and the authorities in the nursing home that Lily demanded the girl return to work at Cuala and that the girl had complained of being kept in bed against her will. An infuriated Sir Lambert ordered the girl to leave. The girl's mother appealed, trying "to explain Miss Lolly," whose ways were known to the Cuala girls, but Sir Lambert would have none of it. The girl was discharged, though she could hardly walk. Lily could do nothing because she didn't learn what had happened until after the event.[125] Neither of Lollie's charges had been true.

Indeed one of the principal daily worries in Lily's life was that she never knew what Lollie might be doing or saying away from Gurteen Dhas. Lollie told Willie and George that the girls at Cuala had complained about the embroidery department when they had not. She also spoke untruths indirectly, making "lying statements sound true by putting them into the mouths of others." She told Lily that Willie had informed her that Lily had tried to end her life by taking an overdose of drugs "in hopes of ending" her troubles, though Willie had said nothing of the kind.[126]

Lollie could cause trouble even in the most trivial matters by a skillful twisting of the truth. When Lily was almost totally confined to the fireside by her difficulty in breathing, she found it virtually impossible to leave the house. Her neighbor, Mrs. Franks, who lived a short way down the road, fell ill and wanted to receive visitors, but Lily found the walk too difficult. At the same time a Mrs. Eaton, who lived a little farther off, also fell ill. The Frankses and the Eatons didn't get along. One day a friend offered to drive Lily to visit Mrs. Eaton, and Lily accepted. Lollie promptly told the Frankses that although Lily wouldn't visit Mrs. Franks she had visited Mrs. Eaton, but she neglected to mention the ride and allowed them to believe that Lily had walked. The Frankses, offended, were cold to Lily for a long period afterward. "Isn't she a demon?" Lily wrote in exasperation to Ruth. "She has now turned everyone except my intimate friends against me." [127]

Maria O'Brien, the younger of the two Yeats servants, reported to Lily an exchange she heard in 1937 between Lollie and a visitor to Gurteen Dhas, Mrs. Crichton. The two went upstairs, out of earshot of Lily, and Mrs. Crichton asked, "Does your sister go into society?" (Lily had by then been long confined to home). "No," replied Lollie, "she is not at all as popular as I am. She never moves out of the house." When they came to Lily's room, Lollie said, "This is her room. It is North. I begged her to have my room, which is South, but nothing would induce her to." Lily wrote in resignation to Ruth, "It has the ring of truth about it." [128]

Mrs. Emmeline Cadbury, of the chocolate family, had long patronized Cuala and made generous annual gifts to both sisters, including £200 to Lollie to help her clear her debts. [129] Yet Lollie, who accepted the gifts without compunction, constantly complained of being bored when visiting the Cadburys. [130] But Lollie was bored with everything that didn't include herself as the center of attention. She reminds one of what Alice Longworth said of her father, Theodore Roosevelt: "He wants to be the bride at every wedding and the corpse at every funeral."

Lollie spent only as much time at Gurteen Dhas as she had to, preferring to find friends outside her home whom she could impress with her qualities and connections. Yet even there she could not be free of her demons. She joined the Royal Dublin Society, chiefly to make use of its library, but annoyed everyone there by demanding special treatment, "plunging about, shouting, trying to get through locked doors, breaking all the rules, then silencing all complaints with her name." [131]

To her mendacity Lollie added the "silliness" that so annoyed her elder brother and sister. An amateur psychologist visiting at Gurteen Dhas told Lily that the trouble with Lollie "is that mostly she is only seven years old." [132] Her unseemly brawls with the hired help, her fussing before Abbey nights, her foolish editorial decisions at the Dun Emer and Cuala Presses, were a trial to those about her. WBY and his wife, George, enjoyed Lily's visits to their home, but not Lollie's, and so they arranged to invite them separately. Lollie complained that they asked her to visit only "as a distasteful duty," [133] and in this belief she was absolutely correct. Willie couldn't stand her visits "unless in full health." [134] One night when he was at the Abbey Theatre and saw Lollie at a distance moving in his direction he shut himself in behind a door and let her walk by. [135]

When her Cinderella romanticism combined with her silliness, the result could prove devastating for her. Louis Purser was not the only forty-year-old to fix his attentions on Lollie. Another came along (his name is withheld, to protect the guilty), wined her and dined her, took her to the theatre, showered attentions on her. Lollie was in ecstasy. She was in love, she told Lily, and the man was in love with her. Lily wasn't the only one she told. She told friends, strangers on the street, people on trains and railway stations. Knowing her beloved had tea almost every afternoon at a shop in Grafton Street, she dressed in her finest finery and went there hoping to see him. She was "crazy about him," one of the witnesses to the affair said. Then one night he stole a kiss; perhaps there had been much holding of hands before the daring assault. Lollie was sure a proposal of marriage would follow.

The only discordant note in what is otherwise a familiar tune of the middle-aged Irishman seeking a bride is that when the affair took place Lollie was sixty years old. What her Lothario's intentions were are somewhat unclear, but among them marriage was not included. As soon as he learned of Lollie's wagging tongue he cut her off abruptly. One night, while Lollie thought the affair still flourished, she asked neighbors if they would invite the gentleman to their house so that she could entertain him properly. Lily's presence at Gurteen Dhas made having him there impossible, she said. They agreed and sent him an invitation. Lollie, in her best clothes, arrived early in anticipation of an exciting evening. An hour passed, then another. By ten o'clock it became clear that the suitor wasn't coming. Lollie, crestfallen, returned home, thoroughly "humiliated." The lover sent a letter to the hostess next day apologizing for not having appeared and adding, "You will understand." He then wrote a cruel letter to Lollie announcing that his interest was at an end. Not long afterward he married a young girl from Cork, and Lollie was left standing alone in the full view of those to whom she had boasted of her conquest.

"She made a fool of herself," said one who witnessed the events.[136] Lily was almost as embarrassed as her sister, having had to listen to the details of the affair while it was going on and to the excuses invented after it ended. She was "a bore," Lily said, "first for over 20 years about LCP [Louis Purser], and now a bore and an idiot for four [years] over this last madness."[137] She told Ruth that Lollie "never saw herself or events as they were." She thought the suitor, though attracted to Lollie, had been merely polite and friendly but had "lost his head for one evening" and then "got out of the difficulty in the very worst way possible."[138] Lily couldn't understand Lollie's blindness to the realities. "Surely she must know her age and what she looks like to others who are younger. And men are without pity towards the older woman."[139] Lollie never learned the lesson. She continued "simmering and floating in dreams" long after the business had ended, "self-indulgence and general silliness," Lily called it.[140]

It is no wonder that Lollie and her older brother did not hit it off. One of her problems with him sprang from her stout refusal to accept the notion that her brother was her superior in any way. "She thinks she is all Yeats and also just Willy in woman's form," Lily told Ruth.[141] She was angry that her talents were not recognized as the equal of his, and JBY once had to write Willie to urge his son to be more considerate of Lollie's ego.[142]

Naturally Willie would not accept Lollie's self-serving evaluation, especially from one he regarded as irrational and "silly." He could be difficult enough with people himself. L. A. G. Strong has written about his haughty manner: "He could magisterially resent a liberty, and the uninvited stranger was soon shown the door. He had no time for bores, or the self-satisfied and empty. He required of a man that he should have something to say, or else keep his mouth shut."[143] To have one who didn't meet his standards exist in the person of his own sister, for whose welfare he felt himself partly, if unwillingly, responsible, was maddening to him. Her unbusinesslike practices infuriated him, such as her decision to allow Cuala to publish commercially a book of poems by an author who could not pay, thus placing an additional financial burden on her brother.[144]

Some people bitten by a bee develop not an immunity to the venom but an increased sensitivity. Later bites cause more violent reactions than earlier ones. Willie seems to have reacted in such a way to Lollie's stings. His sensitivity to her "silliness" may also have been transferred to others and caused his impatience with and arrogance toward those whose idiosyncrasies, reminding him of Lollie, might not otherwise have bothered him. The two had fallen out "from the cradle," and matters had gone from bad to worse. Yet perhaps one source of the difficulties between them lay in the fact that they were much alike. One recalls W. H. Auden's words in his elegy on Yeats: "You were silly, like the rest of us." He and his sister shared the power to annoy others.[145] Her victims may have been less well known; he succeeded in his time in antagonizing people as talented and diverse as George Russell (AE), Annie Horniman, J. M. Synge, John Quinn, Joseph Holloway, Sean O'Casey, Duncan MacColl,[146] and Nora Connolly (daughter of the martyred James)[147] as well as, at different times and in different degrees, the members of his own family. JBY, liked by everyone, was disturbed by his son's penchant for antagonizing people. He wrote to Lily in 1908: "I wonder does he know how many enemies he makes. . . . Probably he will be very proud of making these enemies, but it is not through any good or estimable qualities that he makes these enemies, but the contrary."[148]

WBY might dismiss the unwanted guest, as Strong said, but some people could not be dismissed and had to be dealt with. Joseph Holloway describes WBY giving orders to the actors of the

Abbey company: ". . . a more irritating play producer never directed a rehearsal. He's ever flitting about and interrupting the players in the middle of their speeches, showing them by illustration how he wishes it done, droningly reading this passage and that in monotonous preachy sing-song, or climbing up the ladder on the stage and pacing the boards as he would have the players do. Ever and always he was on the fidgets, and made each and all of the players inwardly pray backwards. Frank Fay, I thought, would explode with suppressed rage at his frequent interruptions during the final speeches he had to utter." [149]

To have Willie and Lollie together made for an explosive combination. Once, when Willie knew he would have to discuss unpleasant Cuala business with Lollie, he invited her to dine with him at the Shelbourne Hotel, "saying that it was a good idea because there he could not shout at her." [150] He told Lily that he hated "these rows" with Lollie. "They almost make him ill," Lily told Ruth. Lily took advantage of his complaint to press her own case. "I said that I had her always and knew what it was like. In some ways it was worse for me, because I am ill and have no authority over her." [151] Lily told Ruth in 1929 that Lollie "keeps life from being soft, like fleas on dogs," [152] and she spoke as one who suffered most from the itches. In his constant quarrels with her over business at the Dun Emer and Cuala Presses, WBY found her arrogant in her attempts to usurp his place as editor, and books by George Russell, Katharine Tynan, Edward Dowden, and Ezra Pound appeared only after vitriolic disagreements between them. Yet to Lollie—and to many others—he seemed the arrogant one.

Their father saw the similarities clearly. "Like Lollie," he wrote to his brother Isaac about Willie, "he is not always easy to live with, having her tendency to melancholy, and like her when the fit is on him he does not in the least mind how he wounds your feelings. In this way they are both like their poor mother." [153] He wrote Lily in 1896 of a visit his son paid him in Bedford Park: "He has the greatest wish to be friendly and peaceable, but he can't manage it, and tho' I was sorry to see him go, for he is in good humour, both most attractive and affectionate, still wherever he is there is a constant strain and uneasiness." [154] He also noted another peculiarity of his son's behavior. "Willie thinks well of his fellow creatures except when he is fighting them," he told Rosa Butt.[155] Lily thought Lollie had no real friends, even when she wasn't fighting them, and commented on the absence of affection for her in the letters of condolence she received after Lollie's death.

Some part of Lollie's unending fury at her predicament might have come from Lily's passive resistance to her. Her "placidity and silence," George told her, were "just as maddening to Lollie" as Lollie's behavior was to her.[156] Lily learned early that the simplest word might lead to an argument. She never discussed her health with Lollie, leaving it to her physician to inform her. Her silences drove Lollie to further anger, yet Lily knew there was no hope of rational discussion. She had made up her mind when young that she would not allow herself to be done in by the Fates, yet she had two understandable wishes. "I would gladly take my life over again," she wrote Ruth, "if I could leave out Lolly and my unique gland."[157] For the first of these wishes she had the support of all Dublin. One of the witticisms that had wide circulation dealt with the home life of the Yeats sisters, of whom the neighbors said, though not in their presence, "They should have been divorced long ago."[158]

• • •

Lollie never crossed the border of sanity into schizophrenia and may be charitably said to have suffered no more than a severe personality disorder, an extreme neurosis. Whether William Butler Yeats resembled Lollie in any significant way may be a matter for dispute. But he confessed to experiences that suggest a similar cast of emotional disequilibrium. He admitted in a letter to John H. Pollock in 1935 that two years earlier he had "some sort of nervous breakdown."[159] He describes in his *Memoirs* some of the emotions he felt on an earlier occasion: "The feeling is always the same: a consciousness of energy, of certainty, and of transforming power stopped by a wall, by something one must either submit to or rage against helplessly."[160] Lily often claimed that Lollie was "just like her mother," and John Butler Yeats made the same observation.[161] Their comments make a passage in WBY's *Memoirs* tantalizing. "I begin to wonder whether I have and always have had some nervous weakness inherited from my mother. (I have noticed my own form of excitability in my sister Lolly, exaggerated in her by fits of prolonged gloom). It often alarms me; is it the root of madness?"[162] He spoke of being brought "almost to nervous breakdown" by "more than two hours of original composition."[163] In a provocative passage in a letter to Rosa Butt, John Butler Yeats had written: "A Pollexfen in a rage is like a dog gone mad. Everything is blotted out in a general blackness."[164]

Was WBY justified in his worry? We often look to the written lives of great men to learn why they behaved as they did, but rather than rely on the *DNB,* should we perhaps consult the DNA? Can the disturbance of mind that took such a toll on Susan Pollexfen Yeats and Lollie be reflected in what William Butler Yeats called his "nervous weakness," labeled distinctly by him "madness"? There was not only his mother but his uncle William Middleton Pollexfen, who was confined to a madhouse for forty years; his aunt Agnes Pollexfen Gorman, who served a term in an asylum; and a Pollexfen cousin of his own generation who also exhibited unambiguous signs of mental disorientation.[165] Certainly his fears seem overblown to his admirers, but whatever their foundation, there is no doubt that he surmounted them, as Lollie did not. If he was correct in his suspicion, perhaps whatever errant gene had made the Pollexfens so interesting was itself the source of his own poetic imagination. If to lack it meant he would be "normal," who would choose, for him, normality?

William Butler Yeats differed from his sister in one notable respect. He worked hard at what he did and went from strength to strength. She did not. He put his genius to work; she let hers sleep. Her painting never improved, nor did her work at the Press. She pottered about, utterly concerned with her person rather than her art, in striking contrast to her brother. There is a difference between wishing for greatness and working to achieve it.

It is clear that Joyce's clever phrases were wrong by half. As a novelist he was free to make whatever use he wished of his materials. The biographer, grappled to his evidence by hoops of steel, enjoys no such license and must conclude that there was only one designing woman, not two, not two weird sisters, but one.

Lily was charitable in her memories of Lollie, despite "her temper and jealousy," and was glad she had not openly quarreled with her, though "life with her was bondage." "I still feel affection for her," she told Ruth after Lollie's death, "and no bitterness," for Lily believed there were uncontrollable forces within her sister that explained and excused everything. "I just think she had a kink," she concluded, "and could not help it." [166]

5

Cuala
The Partnership, 1908–1923

Cuala, the wretched Industry, which eats up all one's mind, energy, and time, and comes to so little in the end.
> —Lily Yeats to John Quinn,
> November 1911

We toil all day and all the year round and only get in at the Industry something over £800 a year—to pay ourselves what no man over 25 would do clerk work for.
> —Lily Yeats to John Quinn,
> January 1913

Now, if my editorship is to continue there is something of more importance still. Lolly and you must both recognize that I am a man of letters and that as a matter of conscience I will not pass bad work on any financial plea. This is not a quixotic idea of mine, but a prejudice I share with many other men of letters.
> —William Butler Yeats to Lily Yeats,
> January 1912

L ily returned to Dublin in mid-1908 to a Cuala Industries fully furnished with the equipment and the people to carry out its objectives.[1] The new cottage was within easy walking distance of Gurteen Dhas,[2] and visible from it lay the pleasing greenery of the Milltown Golf Course. The printing press had come as a virtual gift from Dun Emer, and Beatrice Cassidy, Molly Gill, and Esther Ryan were already trained to work it. Eileen Colum, Padraic's sister, worked at coloring hand prints and assisting in administration, and experienced girls worked with Lily in the embroidery department. If a benefactor had given the sisters out of the blue a completely functioning business, they could not have done better.[3]

After the split, Cuala and Dun Emer existed side by side and continued to do so for many decades.[4] Dun Emer's supporters, many of them members of the original group that had formed the Abbey Theatre, were mostly political nationalists (rather than purely cultural nationalists, as Yeats professed to be), more interested in practical politics than in philosophy, as the Yeatses would discover at the Easter season in 1916.[5] Despite their support, Miss Gleeson found the going rough at Dun Emer. Lily heard that in late 1909 Miss Gleeson had threatened to close and had cut her girls' wages. "Anyway," Lily concluded (in a spirited display of the quality that made her, as her father claimed, "a good hater"), "She is an old beast and will be found out some day."[6]

Neither enterprise was a success financially, both sailing close to the wind, slowly accumulating deficits and relying on outside assistance to survive. Each was to learn that the business of arts and crafts is precarious enough on its own without needing the assistance of nettlesome personalities. There was no reconciliation: in the Yeats family correspondence Miss Gleeson continued to be called "the Demon" or the "Mother Abbess" or "The Spider."[7] When Roger Casement told John Butler Yeats that he liked Miss Gleeson, the old man retorted that she was "an unreliable Humbug."[8]

Today, when the names of Dun Emer and Cuala are invoked, it is of the Yeats sisters that people think. The reasons, having little to do with merit, are not hard to find. Most arts and crafts shops produce objects like carpets or tapestries (as Miss Gleeson's did), or pottery or sculpture or amateur art, and all these suffer from a common insufficiency: there is no law requiring that a record of their production be kept or their makers identified.[9] The hand of mortality lies heavy on such enterprises, and the names of most sink without a trace.

Cuala, with its printing press, was luckier. Books need to be copyrighted and registered with the names of their authors and publishers, and titles appear by the thousands in catalogues of

57. Cuala workers before Cuala building, 1908. *Courtesy of Michael B. Yeats.*

secondhand books. The Cuala Press thus had an advantage over Dun Emer that Miss Gleeson was denied. Her work, like Lily's, became dispersed throughout Ireland and England and, again like Lily's, is hard to find and identify today. If Cuala had consisted only of Lily's embroidery department, it too would probably be remembered—or forgotten—only to the extent that Dun Emer has been.

And Cuala had the Yeats name going for it. At the founding of Dun Emer in 1902, William Butler Yeats was already famous in the English-speaking world. During the years of Cuala his fame grew. Not only was he the editor of the Press, but many of the works it produced were his own. Lily was quick to recognize the built-in advantage. Surrendering the name of Dun Emer to Miss Gleeson was nothing. "Our own name is the really important thing," she wrote John Quinn, "and that she can't have."[10] What Miss Gleeson did enjoy in later years as a counterbalance to the Yeats name was the financial support of the Irish government,[11] but not even that could outweigh Cuala's advantages. Wealthy Americans in Ireland sought out Cuala because of the magnet of the Yeats name, and there was no "Spider" lurking in the web of the doorway to pounce on the unwary visitor.

When Lily returned from New York, it was also to a new household arrangement. Gurteen Dhas now held, in addition to the two servants, Roseanna Hodgins and Maria O'Brien, only the two sisters and their twenty-three-year-old cousin Ruth Pollexfen. Ruth's sister Hilda, also in Lily's care, was generally away at school; Lily in any event found it impossible to include her as a full-time member of the household, and her residencies at Gurteen Dhas were sporadic. John Butler Yeats's room, kept ready for his return, was in time taken over for other purposes. As the Cuala cottage was so close, Gurteen Dhas became almost an appendage to it. The sisters and JBY had held gatherings there regularly since 1902 with many artistic and literary people in attendance. These continued regularly for the next three decades, and the occasional presence at them of people like W. B. Yeats and Lady Gregory and Jack attracted other lions of Dublin society. The sisters also developed a schedule of At Homes; on Mondays one sister would stay home to receive visitors while the other managed Cuala alone.[12]

The sisters visited the Abbey regularly; as relatives of the founder, they were given free tickets to performances. Often Lily and Ruth attended plays together, walking the four miles there and back again.[13] Until her marriage Ruth worked at Cuala as she had at Dun Emer, choosing Lily's embroidery department rather than Lollie's printing, and she and Lily walked regularly together to Cuala in the mornings. Lollie naturally felt she was the odd person out.

Contributing to Lollie's unhappiness at the time was her realization that Louis Purser's long courtship of her was at an end. He had pursued her diligently for more than a decade, regularly making the sea voyage from Dublin to London to visit her during the 1890s. A conservative, self-effacing classics scholar at Trinity College, Louis was cautious in his approach to Lollie, and his expected proposal of marriage never came. About 1905, Lollie began to realize that his ardor had cooled noticeably, although he assumed the role of proofreader for the Dun Emer and Cuala books and continued in it until the mid-twenties. Instead of making a clean break with Lollie, he had simply ceased to be attentive, and Lollie, who had waited patiently for the chance to live comfortably as the wife of a college professor, found herself instead at the age of forty with no prospects. The emotional turmoil aggravated her normal peculiarities of personality, and Lily and Ruth became her victims.

The split with Dun Emer brought an unusual benefit to the sisters. John Quinn, whose life was to become so intertwined with that of the Yeatses, took their side against Miss Gleeson and became one of the major purchasers of Lollie's publications and Lily's embroideries. Quinn subscribed for the whole set of the new broadsides, and other Americans joined him; he and they continued to buy Cuala books during the following decade. When a new issue appeared, Quinn arranged for notices to appear in New York newspapers.[14] He ordered embroideries from Lily, even though he had no known interest in such objects, and in one case went so far as to order and pay for a second fire screen when the first was lost at sea uninsured.[15] He placed a standing order for three copies of each broadside and six of each book, and until his death in 1924 remained the sisters' most dependable customer.[16] Without the kind of support he offered, Cuala might well have foundered.

The prestige of the Press rested on its series of books, but Lollie devised other uses for the equipment to stimulate sales. As early as March 1909, Lily told Quinn of a new venture, copies of WBY's poems "written out with decorative initial letters," colored by hand and "framed in passe-partout,"[17] and in time the Press developed a business in Christmas cards and general greeting cards and published many books privately in the standard Cuala format. The cards and the prints of Jack's black-and-white drawings, colored by the girls, were "for many years among the most popular productions of the Press." Copies were run off as needed, and proceeds from their sale provided the bread and butter of the Press business.[18] Bookplates were offered at £3.10 per 500,[19] and in time the list of products was expanded to include "painted wooden things—bowls, boxes, frames of mirrors, backs of brushes, etc." Invitations to exhibitions and other events were also printed on special order.[20] The books, however, were expected to provide most of the profit.

Lily was similarly imaginative with her embroideries. Toward the end of 1917 a catalogue listed the offerings of her department: in colored linen there were table centers (from £1.5.0 to £3.3.0), sofa backs (£3.3.0) cushions (30/s), blotters (10/6), and handkerchief cases (from 4/s); in white linen were table centers (from 10/6) and tea cloths at £1.0.0. Evening and day dresses were embroidered to order from 10/6; blouses from 32/s, opera cloaks (£3.3.0) ("always in stock"), scarves, handbags, small boys' tunic suits, baby bonnets, matinee coats, cot and cradle covers, children's coats, bridge purses, card cases, handkerchief cases, pincushions, lavender bags. The landscape embroideries entitled "The Meadow" and "The Wood" were available at £8.8.0; for an embroidery mounted as a fire screen, the price rose to £10.10.0. Also available were portieres, flags, banners, and embroideries "for church purposes," "illuminated addresses" on vellum or parchment; and painted fans on silk, ivory, or mother-of-pearl sticks. Over the years thousands of items were produced and sold. The girls were kept busy continuously and paid regularly. Turnover in goods was high. Yet the bottom line in most years was written in red ink, the sisters never cracking the code of proper pricing.

One standard device for improving sales was never employed by the sisters: paid advertising. They issued brochures, listing what was available and what was to come, but these were mailed to old customers or placed on tables at exhibitions and sales.[21] Goods were sold at list price only, except to retail dealers who bought in bulk at a 33⅓ percent discount on cards, 20 percent on books and broadsides.[22] The sisters never gave free samples. Since all work was done by hand, large orders brought the same price per unit as small.[23] Reviews helped: Lollie told a friend they were "our only way of making it known to the world that Cuala has brought out a new book, and once there is a new review orders come in. And this way too we get *new* customers who if they buy the new book *get then all our lists* and often buy other things from Cuala also—and the circle widens."[24] Lollie had specific notions of the kind of customer she wanted: "people who *really want something* rather exclusive and are *ready to pay for it."* She named a couple who deliberately sought Cuala cards for Christmas, because "they *wanted something* every Tom, Dick, and Harry could not have." She was proud of Cuala's quality. "Our things can *never compete* with cheap manufactured things. They sell as *exclusive* and expressive things."[25]

One of the devices for increasing income was the holding of public sales both in Dublin and elsewhere, the 1908 sale in New York being merely a bigger and more well-publicized one than most. Over the years the sisters arranged sales in Belfast, Birmingham, London, and wherever else they could find customers.[26] Friends like the G. K. Chestertons and William and Emmeline Cadbury of Birmingham lent their names and sometimes their homes for the sales and persuaded wealthy friends to visit and buy. Yet the business still lost money, a total, including the last two Dun Emer years, of just under £500 from 1906 through 1910.

• • •

Once free of Miss Gleeson, Lollie was roused to a laudable pitch of creativity. She immediately planned two books of John Millington Synge's, his play, *Deirdre,* to be published first, then a selection from his poems; but Synge, mortally ill, had trouble finishing the play, and so the poems appeared first.[27]

With the poems Lollie again showed the kind of editorial temerity that had annoyed her brother earlier, asking Synge whether he thought it appropriate "from a business point of view" to include two that were strongly worded, "The Curse" and "Danny." How Willie and Synge responded to her intervention is not known, but both poems appeared in the finished edition. It was clear that Lollie did not intend to remain silent on editorial matters,[28] and equally clear that her word would not be heeded. She might regard herself as a literary critic; Synge and WBY looked upon her as a publisher whose job it was to print and sell what they gave her.

While the *Poems* were in press, Synge died. Lollie took *Deirdre,* which had been worked over by WBY, and published it as *Deirdre of the Sorrows* (a title Lollie claimed she herself chose).[29] It was done with greater care and elaboration than most books received, "ambitiously printed throughout in black and red, the scene descriptions and characters' names appearing in red throughout the text of the play." A photogravure print of a portrait of Synge by John Butler Yeats accompanied it.[30]

Despite the independence and freedom of the new arrangement,

58. John Millington Synge (1871–1909). Lithograph by Emery
Walker from pencil sketch by JBY. *Courtesy of author.*

as early as May 1909, Lily informed Quinn that Cuala was "over-
drawn at the bank" and had to print the Synge book quickly to
bring in money, and a year later she spoke of Cuala's "miserable
balance sheet."[31] To her father she gave figures: by the end of 1909,
despite "a good year," the overdraft at the bank was more than
£100.[32]

Life at Cuala was totally female. Usually both sisters (addressed by the girls as "Miss Lily" and "Miss Lolly") were present, each in her own section. The energetic Lollie handled the correspondence, answering letters and sending out bills. In early 1910 the sisters bought a second press and hired an extra girl for embroidery and for the coloring of Easter cards.[33] The young Cuala girls, utterly inexperienced in both trade and discipline, needed constant watching. One of them remembered years later how, when Lily arrived in the morning, she would say, "Pick up that thimble from the floor, whoever it belongs to." They were ready to exclaim, "It is not my thimble," but Lily "spiked that." One cold day she found several of them with their feet on the fender and sent them back to their work places. "There, an angel could not do good work with his feet on the fender." You needed "eyes on sticks when dealing with young ones," Lily remarked.[34] Yet the girls didn't mind the discipline, and the record shows that few left once hired. The sisters also encouraged their education and taste. They read good novels aloud to the girls whenever the opportunity arose. Behind Cuala they planted what had once been an orchard as a vegetable and herb garden. At one time they were producing potatoes, onions, lettuce, Brussels sprouts, cabbage, celery, marrow, broad beans, and scarlet runners, and mint, parsley, and thyme.[35]

The Cuala books were praised for their beauty, and at the Dublin Horse Show in August 1909 Lily won three prizes for her embroidery.[36] Yet all was not well, despite the public acclaim. During the six years with Miss Gleeson the sisters had, as it were, a common enemy, and the emotional solidarity brought on by their alliance may have helped to preserve some stability in their relationship. Once free of her, they had more time to develop their own tensions. Lily had never expected much of life, and her chronic illness had given her a fortitude, an acceptance of life's realities, that kept her sane. Lollie expected more of life than it had to give, and her unhappiness over Louis Purser's chilled attentions finally came to a head. In March 1910, Lily wrote her astonishing and revealing letter to Louis, demanding to know his intentions toward her sister and informing him of Lollie's "misery" at the cooling of his interest,[37] an appeal to which Louis did not respond. Adding to Lollie's misery was her jealousy of Ruth, who she thought was stealing her sister away from her. A partial solution to that problem seemed to appear when Ruth in early 1910 announced her engagement to be married to Charles Lane-Poole, a forester with the English service.[38] Lollie's problems had other roots, however, and Ruth's eventual move away from Gurteen Dhas solved nothing.[39] The epiphany Lollie hoped for—the romantic affair, the happy marriage, the public recognition—was always expected but never arrived, and she was unable to come to terms with the inevitable disappointment.

In September 1910, Uncle George Pollexfen died in Sligo,[40] and the sisters' share of his estate helped ease some of the financial tension at Cuala. Lily and Lollie were awarded two-thirds of the portion George left to their mother's descendants, Willie and Jack the other third.[41] Willie thought the sisters should net about £80 a year out of their share.[42] Lily was grateful for whatever it might be. "Even 6d a year certain will take some of the terrors out of the future for Lollie and me."[43] Much of their portion consisted of shares in the W. & G. T. Pollexfen Company and the Sligo Steam Navigation Company, both of which over the years not only provided income but served as security for loans.

When Lollie's condition grew worse, Lily laid plans to get her away for a long vacation.[44] Her father wrote Lollie casually, as if throwing off a few random thoughts in a general way. "I do think that you ought to seek change and rest and stay away as long as you can, . . . somewhere—*anywhere*—where you can stretch yourself at ease and talk out your thoughts. . . . You are never sufficiently careful of yourself. You don't often *enough take time to consider with yourself.*" Then he got to the heart of the matter. "When out of sorts you think it is somebody else's fault, anybody's. Most probably you blame the person that happens at the moment to be sitting nearest you, and then you *surprise* and offend them, instead of which you should stop and ask yourself whether *you yourself are not the wicked cause* of it all, by not taking things more quietly or giving yourself some needed change."[45] But the restless Lollie could not be advised.

Papa also wrote a strongly worded letter to Willie, marked *"Private."* "From various indications that have reached me and from what Lilly tells me, I am convinced Lollie is in some danger of some kind of mental disturbance." He wondered whether Willie might be able to raise money quickly on the security of the expected legacies. "Lollie is very like her grandfather. From him she gets her gloom and her ferocious irascibility. But she is also a Yeats, and the Yeats is wiry and recuperative."[46] He fired off another letter the next day: "I do not mean to suggest that she is in the least *out of her mind*," although that was exactly what he seemed to be suggesting. With Mrs. Julia Ford, Lollie's hostess in New York in 1906, he pulled no punches. Lollie, he told her, "is threatened with a serious breakdown." "She was depressed and unhappy, and an instant and prolonged change was necessary."[47] Yet Lily told her father of a fortnight she had spent in Germany with Lollie years earlier: "She was miserable, did not like the food, Paul Arndt irritated her, the sun burnt her nose." Later Lollie told Lily she had enjoyed the visit to Germany more than the one to New York. Lily was cool in her assessment, and unsparing. "She has no philosophy. She wants some sort of inner life—religious—something, even some fad, postage stamps, anything. She does not read except the easiest novels. She lets outside things possess her, the stones on the path, always either too hot or too cold, people irritate her, she flies at them, and then feels so much better, but they don't."[48] Yet this was the publisher of the Cuala Press, the coworker with whom Lily had to deal in the daily operations of the Industry. Minor but telltale glitches in her business procedures had already appeared. Quinn complained repeatedly about getting incorrect bills or receipts, and what happened to him was symptomatic of what happened to other customers too. The mistakes continued until Lollie's death.[49]

So Lollie was sent away. After a time in England, she went on to Italy and Switzerland, moving about discontentedly. She wrote letters "full of bitter delusions about everybody."[50] Lily hoped her absence would be prolonged,[51] but by April 1911 she was back at Gurteen Dhas just before Ruth Pollexfen's marriage to Charles Lane-Poole, excitable as ever. "Ruth's wedding excitement will keep Lolly in good humour for a while," Lily wrote her father, "but when Ruth has gone and we are left shuffling along together things will be pretty black." She blamed Lollie's "egotism and temper." "She often complains of her lack of friends, but it is her own fault. She is so irritable and will not let people be themselves." Everybody

59. Ruth Lane-Poole (née Pollexfen) (1885–1974) shortly after her marriage to Charles Lane-Poole. *Courtesy of Mrs. Charles Burston.*

bored her. "What she likes," said Lily, "is a series of new friends."[52] JBY told his brother Isaac that her trip "had not done her good but on the contrary made her worse," and he later wrote bluntly: "she's by no means sane."[53]

After the wedding Ruth left Gurteen Dhas, not to return except for two brief visits. Lily felt the loss keenly. "I feel wretched without my child," she told her father. "I have had her eleven years. We have been so closely united all the time and this last four years together all day at the Industry."[54] Yet all the while business had to go on, and sometimes the complexities were too great for the sisters to handle. When an offer came to Lollie in late 1911 from Mitchell Kennerley, the New York book dealer, she realized she knew too little about its implications and sought Quinn's advice. Kennerley wanted to become sole distributor for Cuala books in the United States, buying at a steep discount. The deal would have guaranteed Lollie a steady buyer, and Kennerley's offer was a flattering acknowledgment that her products were in demand. But she was reluctant to give up the American buyers she knew, who always paid full price.[55] Quinn pursued her query with his customary diligence, writing to Kennerley to get the full details of his offer, then advised Lollie to make sure her interests were covered, particularly her right to keep her regular American customers.[56] The deal eventually fell through,[57] its advantages all Kennerley's. Lollie had been in no condition to handle the matter anyhow, and soon she had to go away to Italy again for an even longer stay.[58]

So through most of the period from 1910 through 1912, Lily had to run both departments herself, despite her chronic fatigue. She called Cuala "the wretched Industry, which eats up all one's mind, energy, and time, and comes to so little in the end."[59] As 1913 began, her pessimism was at its peak. "We toil all day and all the year round and only get in at the Industry something over £800 a year—to pay ourselves what no man over 25 would do clerk work for." Her work was "made up of little things and little worries and little results and very little pay."[60]

Lollie and Willie continued the hostile professional relationship begun with the dispute over Katharine Tynan's poems. Now she thought she found an opportunity to have her own way and still satisfy the trying demands of her elder brother. Edward Dowden, one of JBY's oldest friends and one of WBY's earliest supporters, had died on 3 April 1913, after almost fifty years of service as professor at Trinity College, Dublin. As a younger man he had written poetry that had never received critical acclaim. Both JBY and his elder son thought he lacked courage: he refused to recognize Irish aspirations and sought instead acceptance by the English literary establishment, which paid little attention to him.[61] WBY regarded him as hypocritical—polite in personal conversation but hostile in print. The elder Yeats shrewdly noted that he was regarded in Ireland as English, in England as Irish. Now his widow, Dowden's second wife, came forward with a curious manuscript called *A Woman's Reliquary,* a collection of love poems to her whose authorship Dowden tried to conceal by asserting that he was merely editing poems given him by the niece of an anonymous writer. Lollie guessed at once who the author was and persuaded Mrs. Dowden "to write a note for the book which does allow readers to guess correctly." The concealment was another example of Dowden's timidity—his "false position"—and, in this case, one that he was wise to adopt. The poems in the collection are bad by almost any standard. But because Dowden had a reputation as a poet and was a distinguished literary critic and was, above all, a good friend of her father's, Lollie accepted the manuscript and agreed to publish it.

She made no attempt to consult WBY, who heard only indistinct rumors about her plan, and on 17 November 1913 three hundred copies of the book were printed and bound in standard Cuala form and published as part of the Cuala series. Willie was furious. After reading the poems in print, he wrote sourly to Lollie that they were even "worse" than he "feared" they would be. It was too late to stop publication, but he insisted that Lollie publish a circular in which it was made plain that WBY was not "responsible for the selection of this book."[62] It remains the one title in the series so described, but, as Willie well knew, denials seldom catch up with accusations, and some buyers were not aware that they were purchasing an unauthorized edition.[63] Lollie had insisted that she was only indulging "a quiet literary taste." Later in the year Willie told Lily that he hoped Lollie would be kept from "cherishing" such tastes "in the future."[64]

Later in the year Lollie published WBY's *Poems Written in Discouragement* as a private job order for him only. Although bearing Cuala's name as publisher, the eight-page pamphlet was issued in fifty copies only.[65] In January 1914, Cuala printed WBY's *The Hour-Glass* in an edition limited to fifty copies only, again meant only for WBY's friends. Willie paid for both titles; no copies were

60. Edward Dowden, about 1904. From *Letters of Edward Dowden and His Correspondents* (London: Dent, 1904).

sold. He was thus able to obtain needed gift copies of his work and help Cuala's cash flow at the same time.[66] Over the years the Press would profit from the job-printing of several dozen such privately financed books in the Cuala format.[67]

The war between brother and sister continued with only an occasional cease-fire. When *Responsibilities* appeared in early 1914,

Willie complained that Lollie was guilty of not catching several misprints and insisted that she add an errata sheet. She did so but provided only a few, and these in her own handwriting. To at least one she added the words: "These are alterations my brother made after the book was printed, so are not our misprints."[68] Yet she did not dare disregard his request. She tried to enlist her father's support in the contest, but he sided with Willie. "After all he is Editor, and were he not Editor your press would fail. . . . And as Editor his authority ought to be respected."[69]

By the spring of 1914, most of the Press's early titles had been sold out. Altogether, Lily was able to boast, "The Industry is thriving better, more money coming in, and the girls becoming more responsible." Yet they had the "bad old times" to pay for,[70] and the dream of a tidal flow of cash remained unrealized. Still, by the spring of 1914 Lily thought a corner had been turned. Lollie was back at work, not fully recovered—as she would never be— but at least able to carry on her part of the business, and Lily was relatively free of the physical incapacities to which her enlarged thyroid made her prone.

• • •

Then came the outbreak of war in early August, and whatever hopes the sisters may have had for a gradually increasing success for Cuala were dashed, if not quite shattered. Lily wrote despairingly to Quinn: "We are very hard hit by this terrible war. All the sales we were engaged for are abandoned, and we have twelve girls depending on us. Nothing is selling and all money going to war and relief funds."[71] Lollie asked her American customers to settle their balances, and most did so at once.[72] Both sisters had to show their spirit by volunteering for civic work, Lollie as a member of the Library Committee in Dundrum, Lily of the Women's Health Committee, reducing their time at Cuala.[73] Fortunately, Jack helped with expenses by contributing a pound a month to the household.[74] For the remaining years of the war, Cuala had to operate with reduced sales and profits, and every year the overdraft at the bank grew.

To add to the dislocations of the war, in the fall of 1914 Lily fell ill with "a kind of blood poisoning," thought to be the effect of faulty drains at Gurteen Dhas,[75] and now it was Lollie's turn to 'be in charge. She was eager to do so, welcoming the chance to exercise control over the entire business. "Cuala has had more orders than I expected, a good many orders to embroider dresses. I like looking after this, as I think I understand something about clothes, and these always pay well, and I like designing them."[76] Hitherto Lily had designed all the embroidery herself or adapted designs of others, but Lollie wanted Quinn to know of her own talents in Lily's line of work.

Lily's recuperation took longer than anyone had thought, and soon afterward she developed an abscess, accompanied by high fever, and the doctors diagnosed anthrax,[77] a rare but serious illness. When she finally returned to work in January 1915, she was able to go to Cuala only every other day.[78]

• • •

Luckily, Willie was still available to produce books for the Press, and these sold whether the world was at peace or war. One work he was eager to publish was his defense against what he regarded as an insulting account of him by George Moore.[79] Instead of responding directly, Yeats decided to write an account of his own life in his mid-twenties,[80] and the Cuala volume was the result. Willie could remember only the impressions of his boyhood in Sligo, not the details, so he called on Lily to provide him with the facts.[81] He planned using the title of a painting of Rosses Point by Jack called "Memory Harbour" ("everything happening and everything visible at once," Lily described it, "and everything at its best")[82] but finally settled for *Reveries Over Childhood and Youth* when he discovered the other title had been used for a book by another writer.[83]

Willie still smarted from Lollie's effrontery in publishing Dowden's book without his permission, yet one minor exchange between them reveals an amusing example of their similarities of behavior. He had written to ask her to send him twenty copies of *The Hour-Glass;* when she confirmed the request, she named a hundred copies. He replied: "It is not 100 copies that I want of *The Hour-Glass.* I said 20, but you better let me have 50."[84] It was a characteristic display all round: he gave her one figure, which she changed; he corrected her, then changed the number himself.

He determined to bypass her as much as possible in preparing

Reveries. When he had finished the manuscript, he wanted to make sure the facts were correct and so sought someone in the family to check it for accuracy. Lily was his first choice, Jack his second.[85] He did not involve Lollie at all. He hoped to keep her hands off what he wrote by not letting her see the manuscript before the final typed copy was sent to the printer. "I don't want to *invite* her criticism," he explained to Lily.[86] He told his father he had let Lily read the manuscript, "but Lollie is not to know this, as it would make her jealous."[87] He asked Lily technical questions about the book that should properly have been addressed to Lollie. "On general principles I prefer to write to you," he told her.[88]

But it was Lily who meddled with the text. Willie had written of a still living member of the Pollexfen family—not the mad William, still in a Northampton hospital—as emotionally disturbed, and Lily was afraid the family would be upset, even though the identity had been disguised. He tried to keep the reference in. "It could be a Yeats," he explained to Lily. She objected, triumphantly arguing that "they know the Yeats to be all sane." Willie removed the offending passage.[89]

When Lollie inevitably got the manuscript for typesetting, she and Willie entered into another of their disputes. Lollie gave her side of the story to Quinn: "We have a time of it putting in punctuation for W. B. He has a lordly way of disregarding it altogether, so we put it in as we go along and then let him have it in proof. His proof always delays us a good deal as he re-writes whole passages in proof, but with this book he hasn't rewritten so much. He has had bits of the MS back and made alterations for *it,* but he gets a good many revises and that delays us sometimes."[90] No matter how trivial the matter, Lollie and Willie could find cause for battle in it, and the occupant of the high ground was not always easy to identify.

Other crafts industries in Ireland had collapsed, and Lollie described in some detail to Quinn a scheme she had to spare Cuala a similar fate. She noted that even "The Royal Irish School of Embroidery," an old enterprise that had several prominent people —like Lady Mayo and Lady Fingal—as its supporters, and the "Royal Irish Industries," a shop in fashionable Grafton Street, had been forced to close.[91] Lollie thought Cuala could be saved by becoming a "Private Limited Company" rather than continuing as the "cooperative society" arranged by George Russell in the Dun Emer days. If confident investors could provide sufficient funds to pay off Cuala's debt (which Lollie told Quinn had risen to £665 by August 1915), the sisters could save the expense of about £40 a year in interest to the bank. They would also no longer have to fill out endless forms to the Irish agency that oversaw cooperative societies. Once free of debt and bureaucracy, they could make a profit and eventually pay a dividend to the investors. She had a promise from a friend, she told him, to buy fifty one-pound shares.[92] Quinn rose to the bait with a draft for £25, but the scheme went nowhere, though Lollie kept pursuing it till the day she died.

In their desperation the sisters sometimes resorted to high-pressure tactics, compelling unwilling friends to buy. Beatrice Lady Glenavy tells of being pestered by Lily to buy a set of Broadsides and of declining on the grounds that she did not like loose sheets. Lily thereupon had them bound and offered them triumphantly to her, and she felt she had to buy them, even though the binding had reduced their value.[93] Oliver Elton admitted that many people bought Cuala products at exhibitions as an indirect way of contributing to the Yeats sisters.[94]

Willie thought he had found a means for Lily to increase her income. He asked Sturge Moore to make a design for a table center he wanted Lily to embroider, and he hoped to find other designers too. She would do the work, and he would undertake to sell the goods. "I want you to do the best work possible, and I think of big prices. If there is a loss it will be mine."[95] He asked Lily for new designs of her own, which she would then produce in many copies, of tablecloths, napkins, and other small items, and he would then show them to "rich women." He would show one complicated design, featuring "sirens, unicorns, tigers, monkeys, and so on," to Olivia Shakespear, who would then praise it to her rich friends and perhaps persuade them to buy. "I think you would be well started," he told her. "I don't see why you shouldn't make a very good income."[96]

Lollie added to her own responsibilities and income by agreeing to conduct a class in drawing at St. Columba's School, and JBY noted the "good spirits" in her letters. "She is a case of the sword wearing out the scabbard," he wrote his brother Isaac. "If that sword is not kept busy and stays too long in the scabbard, the scabbard wears away, which means that to be happy Lollie must have constant and ever-renewed demands made on her *energy*—which is the sword. She ought to have been a man. The monotonous life woman is condemned to live is her hell."[97]

Lollie celebrated her agreement with St. Columba's by taking a vacation in Scotland and so missed the historic event that was about to unfold before the astonished eyes of all the Yeatses—the Dublin Easter Rising. In their correspondence during all the years stretching back to their arrival in Dublin in 1902, there is hardly a word about day-to-day political activity, merely an occasional mordant remark about the English. The Yeatses seemed unaware of the activities of the nationalists who had once been associated with them in the Irish Theatre. Indeed, there was a gulf that yawned between the so-called Anglo-Irish—broadly, the non-Catholic Irish, of English origins, the group to which the Yeatses belonged—and the Gaelic, Roman Catholic majority. The bridge connecting them across the gulf was shaky, supported chiefly by mutual politeness and forbearance. The historian Roy Foster has described the English colonial presence in Ireland as one "superimposed upon an ancient identity, alien and bizarre."[98] The Irish economic and social systems the English found there in the eleventh century were unconventional by "proper"—i.e., English—standards, and the religious even stranger. Long before the Reformation the Catholic Church in Ireland engaged in what the English thought queer practices, incomprehensible to them. Once when William Butler Yeats was staying at Edward Martyn's house, he annoyed Martyn by practicing occult rites in the room above the chapel where Martyn was praying. An irritated Martyn complained that his prayers could not reach the otherworldly saints he was addressing because Yeats's non-Catholic ritual blocked their passage. Although an outside observer might not see much difference in the nature of the two men's practices, Yeats's was not at all typical of the Anglo-Irishman, Martyn's all too typical of the Irish Catholic. Although Foster's remark was made about conditions in 1600, three hundred years of history had not eroded the fundamental differences between the two cultures. George Russell (AE), one of the most loved and respected of non-Catholic Irish, once suggested that Irishmen of all religions put aside their differences and come together in what later times would call "ecumenism." The response must have shocked Russell, and should have educated him. Thomas Bodkin, speaking for his coreligionists, declared that Russell's idea was unthinkable, that in proposing it he was offending the deepest sensibilities of his Catholic countrymen.[99] The girls at Cuala were not allowed to attend Ruth Pollexfen's wedding in a non-Catholic church and years later were denied the opportunity to attend memorial services for William Butler Yeats at St. Patrick's. It was not likely that their teachers would accept more latitude in other matters that, arising from religion, cut into all segments of Irish culture. In a parallel experience James Joyce describes the remoteness Stephen Dedalus felt when he heard his teacher, an Englishman converted to Catholicism, use the English "funnel" instead of the Irish (Gaelic) word "tundish." Stephen felt the enormous gap separating his view of the world from that of one bathed in a different linguistic sea.[100]

Lily Yeats, who regarded herself as Irish, had once contemplated the possibility of marriage with a Compleat Englishman and come to the conclusion that it would not have worked, that he would never have understood her position any more than she could have understood his.[101] She was Irish, he was English, and the two ran on different tracks, parallel tracks that could never meet. Lily could understand such a difference. What she may not have understood, for neither her letters nor those of the others in her family show such understanding, was that the Catholic Irish were even more remote, their ways not the ways of the non-Gaelic Irish whom they still regarded, if most of the time without open hostility, as descendants and representatives of unwanted intruders. Without realizing she was speaking of the very people who provided her working girls at Cuala, Lily had written John Quinn about her reaction to Joyce's *Dubliners:* it was, she said, "a never-to-be-forgotten book, a haunting book. At first I thought, how grey, how sordid; can such lives be lived even in the grey old houses about the north side of Dublin, built long ago for people who had leisure and money and talk, and now lived in by drab people. I saw the elderly women coming out and slipping into the city chapels for mouthfuls of prayer, seedy men coming out and slipping into greasy public houses for mouthfuls of porter. But of their lives I knew nothing, what went on behind the dirty windows, windows like those behind which James Stephens's charwomen lived, which were so dirty anyone wishing to look out had to open them. Since I read *Dubliners* I feel I know something of their lives." [102] Her father made the same admission to Lady Gregory about his family's ignorance of the vast underclass of Dublin. "In old days I knew there were such people, but never met them and never thought about them, and it was so with us all. We ignored these creatures. Now Joyce has dragged them into the light." [103] "These creatures," of course, constituted the vast majority of Dublin residents.

Yet Lily could understand little of their aspirations, which were quite different from hers; and her brother the poet, for all his assumption of the mantle of Irish cultural nationalism, with his worship of ancient Celtic warriors and their women ("broken-kneed heroes and barging heroines," Susan Mitchell called them), [104] was to his activist Catholic compatriots no less irrelevant, no less "alien and bizarre." Not many Irish recognized Yeats's map of their land. As Denis Donoghue perceptively noted, "Yeats invented a country and called it 'Ireland.' "

So it should have come as no surprise to the Yeatses that while they were worrying themselves over the solvency of Cuala, other Irishmen were plotting the overthrow of their colonial masters. The Sinn Fein (We Ourselves) movement for Irish independence had been gathering strength for years. Now, on Easter Monday 1916, a band of Irish patriots led by Padraic Pearse stormed the post office and several other key locations in Dublin and proclaimed the existence of an Irish Republic. The Rising did not last long; eventually it was put down and the leaders captured and most of them shot. Their deaths gave the Irish a pantheon of martyrs that sustained their cause in the coming decades and is still a powerful symbol in modern Ireland; it is no mistake to say that from an emotional point of view the origin of contemporary Republican Ireland dates from the Rising and not from later treaties with the English.

But the Rising did come as a surprise to the Yeatses. None of them knew anything about it until it happened, even though their employees did. Lily opened Cuala the next day only to find there were "no post, no papers, no trains." Lily was careful not to discuss anything with the girls. "Eileen Colum has a silly elated look," she told her father. "Two of the girls were gone yesterday when I went back after lunch," she wrote. "They both have Sinn Fein brothers. They both appeared again this morning looking haggard. I asked no questions." [105]

Both brothers were safe, but the authorities kept one as a prisoner for weeks without letting his family know, and his "distracted people," as Lily called them, "searched hospitals and morgues, running after rumours." Soldiers flooded in from England, martial law was imposed, transportation ceased except under tight regulation, villages formed committees to distribute food. By Saturday, Lily found she had only twenty-four shillings on hand, which she divided among the Cuala girls. The experience was unnerving: on the Monday evening of the Rising, Maria O'Brien, the Gurteen Dhas maid, saw a lorry pass by, and on it, "piled up and only partly covered were the unidentified dead" being carried to burial. "Dead men were on the roofs of houses, hung from telegraph lines, lay in the streets." Looting was inevitable, and Lily noted dryly that for months afterwards even her own friends "elaborately explained new boots." Two weeks later Lily managed to get into the city, and gave a moving description of what she saw: "Sackville Street was like a great plain covered with low heaps of smoking ruins. Smoke was also rising from the Liffey. It was impossible to tell where streets had been, where particular shops or hotels had been. It was an extraordinary sight. Trinity was full of soldiers. They looked very unwashed and slovenly, but some had washed their shirts and hung them out of the windows to dry." [106]

The Yeatses as a family deplored the Rising, regarding its leaders as "fools." "Did you ever hear or know of such a piece of childish madness, clever children?" Lily asked Quinn. "There is not one person in the whole of Ireland that is not the worse for this last fortnight's work." [107] Irish Nationalists all, the Yeatses had a vision of a better Ireland that did not include bloodshed and—except for Jack—did not require separation from England. [108] The motives of the leaders were indeed to them "alien and bizarre," and on the Rising itself the Yeatses' views were shared by many of even Gaelic Catholic Dubliners, who regarded the whole business as disruptive and foolhardy. Yet the English, who in almost a thousand years of enforced regimentation of unwilling people had learned nothing, thought they had solved the problem by swiftly executing the leaders. Instead, they brought sympathy to the "rebels" (so called, although, as one Irish patriot said, "You cannot 'rebel' against your own country"). "Till the first executions the feeling was against Sinn Fein," Lily noted, "but at the first execution feeling went round with a rush. The strongest Unionists shivered. A great mistake had been made." [109] "It was the greatest bit of mad folly," Lily wrote to Oliver Elton, "and now the shooting of *surrendered* men makes martyrs and heroes of them, and is for England a fatal blunder and mistake—a stupid blunder." [110] Lollie gave the common, and probably correct, view of the executions of Padraic Pearse and Thomas MacDonagh. "The whole thing is simply horrible," she told her father. "These men were high-minded, and fine men, led away by ideals of freedom for Ireland. They were in no sense violent men, gentle and scholarly." [111] English stupidity had transfigured "fools" into martyrs and given an impetus to Irish separatism that was to bear fruit not long afterward. [112] William Butler Yeats, kept out of the inner councils of the leaders, placed himself on high ground by writing "Easter 1916." [113] It was a poem that kept his memory green long after most of the men who died for Ireland had been forgotten, an impressive example of the superiority of language to ammunition. [114]

The effects of the Rising were naturally felt by Cuala. The sisters were stunned by the immediate rise in prices of essential materials. [115] New regulations for shipping goods to America added to the burden of labor and costs. [116] Luckily for the sisters, Uncle Alfred Pollexfen, who died four months after the Rising, left each of them some money, [117] and the portion of the old Pollexfen legacy put in trust for the mad son William was distributed in early 1917, each of the Yeats children getting £32. [118] These injections of cash, along with what remained of George's legacy, enabled them to hang on. But the half-yearly audit after the Rising showed they had fared poorly. When the cost of afternoon tea at Cuala rose to ten shillings a week, an expense borne by the sisters, they reluctantly abandoned it, the girls henceforth having to make tea at their own expense. To spur sales, Lily asked Ruth to act as her agent in Australia, [119] where Charles Lane-Poole had been assigned as a forestry official. Ruth thereafter served as a tireless promoter of Cuala products, particularly embroideries.[120]

Fortunately, the local patrons still supported Cuala. Even though there had been no public exhibitions away from Ireland since the war began, the 1917 Christmas Exhibition and Sale in Dublin proved successful. Lollie described it to an American friend:

> I was so afraid people would not be in the mood to spend perhaps that I sent out more invitations than I usually do and so we had a great crowd—at least about 150 people, and we had a splendid show of work *because* there have been less sales elsewhere to take it off. At a sale like that we only take in one or two books—it is all the hand-coloured prints (framed passe-partout) and the Embroideries. The girls all come in and do the selling. We take the things in early in the Dundrum taxi . . . and have some girls to help, and arrange the rooms before lunch. The visitors come in the afternoon. And we always have tea, and it is quite pleasant, quite a social gathering, not like a *Bazaar*. No one is asked to buy. . . . AE came, James Stephens, Susan Mitchell etc etc as well as Lady Ardilaun and others who have money and taste.[121]

They sought income in other ways. Gurteen Dhas had been renovated, and a spare bedroom was available upstairs,[122] so the sisters rented it out. By early 1917, Anne Boston (called "Phillida" by Lily), an English girl studying at Trinity for Honours in French and Literature, took the room and stayed for two months.[123] She would return many times over the years, well into the twenties, and provided needed extra funds. But, as with Susan Mitchell and Ruth Pollexfen and others, her friendship with Lily caused Lollie's jealousy to become so intense and unpleasant that eventually Miss Boston left permanently, taking her rental payments with her.

If Lollie believed her brother was difficult to work with, she found a new nemesis in Ezra Pound, who was involved in the next two Cuala publications, *Certain Noble Plays of Japan* (1916) and *Passages from the Letters of John Butler Yeats* (1917). For the first, Lollie had ordered a limited supply of paper to accommodate Pound's selections, which she thought would be of a certain length. Pound added an extra play, presenting Lollie with a dilemma. She had agreed to royalties on 400 copies but now found she could print only 350. From her point of view, she had behaved with business-like efficiency. Willie saw things differently:

> If your point is that Ezra sending you an extra play caused your supply of paper to run short I think you should have warned him of this and let him choose between a larger book with a smaller number of copies and the 400 copies of the original book. . . . I am anxious to guard you against anything of the nature of breach of contract. It would injure you to get the reputation of being unbusinesslike. I suggest your offering to Ezra an increase of percentage to make up for the reduction in the number of copies. Offer him say 14 percent instead of twelve. He agreed on certain terms and has kept his part of the bargain I think. I hate to have so often to write the man's point of view but I do it because I believe its acceptance a condition of success.[124]

Noticeably absent was any consideration by Willie of Lollie's posi-tion. She should have had an adequate supply of paper no matter what; Pound's addition to the text was irrelevant.

Ezra Pound specialized in stirring up trouble, so relations be-tween Willie and Lollie were not promising when Pound was cho-sen by Willie to edit their father's letters for a flat fee of £5.[125] Pound selected snippets of a few lines or a paragraph, deciding against complete letters or long passages. At first Lollie told JBY it was "one of the best books we have done." "It has been a lucky book all through—no hitches in the printing, it went on swim-mingly from beginning to end."[126] Not until later did Lollie, un-able to hide her resentment, tell Papa of her troubles with Pound in the process of editing.

Lily had given the first hint of the sisters' opinion of Pound in a letter to Quinn in the spring of 1917, after the book had come out. "What do you think of Ezra Pound's way of snipping it up into short barks?" she asked him. "Is he any good at all? He seems to me quite absurd. W. B. thinks he is a very big swan."[127] Pound and Willie conspired to treat the sisters as if they had no rights at all in a publication involving the Yeats family. In the letters Pound edited, JBY had made remarks about some people whose identity he would have preferred not to reveal. Willie and Pound wanted to give everyone's name in full, no matter who might be hurt. The sisters had to fight to convert the names to disguising capital letters.[128] Pound misprinted one word[129] and allowed a passage from Virgil to be misquoted, even though Louis Purser, still serving as copy editor, had called the errors to his attention. Lollie wrote indignantly to her father: "Mr. Pound is the worst proof-reader I ever met, and the book would have been full of mistakes if we had not been careful, and also got Louis to do it. He had a maddening way of putting back mistakes that we had carefully corrected. He has a kind of impudent cocksureness. Indeed I rather objected to this manner of his, hence the more modest tone of the preface."[130] Pound had responded to her complaints airily: "With the exception of your august brother I am about the worst corrector of proofs known to man."[131] Later in the year she wrote Pound another censorious letter with bad news about the return of unsold copies of his *Noble Plays* from booksellers. He responded in kind. When Lily complained to WBY, he defended Pound. "Ezra's letter is characteristic. He is violent by conviction; but Lolly also seems to have been characteristic. Why choose the moment when she wanted to get something out of him to tell him that four copies of his book had been returned? I wonder if she also told him that his book was not selling well?! That also would be just like her."[132] When Quinn replied to Lily that he thought highly of Pound, Lily retorted that he was "the only one I ever heard to think so." "Willy," she told him, "seems to regard him much as the cock does the rising sun; but all critics attack him, as we know, having published two books put together by him. After the Kaiser he seems quite the most hated man. As a proof-reader he is terrible, doesn't care, won't answer, won't return proofs."[133]

A short time later Pound wrote an "amicable" letter to Lily, after he had received thanks from JBY himself, who thought Pound had been "wonderfully sympathetic and clever."[134] "So all he wants, like many a man," said Lily, "is a little praise. And all the time what annoys people with him is this enormous conceit with himself. After all it may not be conceit but timidity."[135]

In 1917, after three years of war, the vise had tightened on all businesses. Lily described the straitened circumstances of life at

61. Ezra Pound, 1916. *Courtesy of Humanities Research Center, University of Texas.*

Gurteen Dhas and Cuala: food at double the prewar price, higher salaries for the girls to meet their costs, a decline in sales.[136] She was forced to ask Quinn whether he would pay for a pencil portrait of WBY done by JBY, even though she could not deliver it to him until after the war. He responded with a draft for £30.[137]

If the Dublin Rising had come as a surprise to the Yeatses,

62. George (Mrs. William Butler) Yeats (1892–1968), February 1920. Pencil sketch by JBY. *Courtesy of Michael B. Yeats.*

William Butler Yeats's marriage on 20 October 1917 was even more of a surprise to every member of the family except himself. He had bought an ancient castle at Ballylee, near Lady Gregory's estate at Coole, and now had a bride to take there, though they decided to live in Oxford till the castle was renovated. She, twenty-seven years his junior, was Bertha Georgie Hyde-Lees, henceforth called "George" by him and others. None of the family met her till months after the wedding. WBY sent a note to his father informing him of the marriage,[138] and an even later one to Quinn, who learned the news first from Lily and JBY.[139] The young wife could not have realized what she was getting into, for in marrying a poet she had married his family as well. Before many years had passed, she had become an active working associate at Cuala, eventually its sole operator, custodian of Lily in her last days, and, finally, curator of the family records and reputation.

At Gurteen Dhas the social life, good for Cuala, was as active as ever. In the early fall of 1918, Lily and Lollie entertained thirty-four people to meet G. K. Chesterton and his wife. Of those invited only two failed to come, Standish O'Grady, because he was at sea, and Mrs. J. R. Green, whose invitation was misaddressed. Susan Mitchell, always a catalyst at parties, was "one of the successes of the evening," Lily told her father. The high point was "a debate between Gilbert and AE, the rest of the company forming a ring four deep round them, Mr. Boyd on the outskirts throwing a well-aimed stone into the centre every now and then. The subject was, as you will guess right first time, the eternal subject of Ireland's future and present state."[140]

In the elections of late 1918, the Sinn Fein candidates won. *"It has swept the whole country,"* Lollie told her father. "I wonder what *they will do with this great success."* The Cuala girls were overjoyed. Lollie noted some of the paradoxes. "Most of the people elected are in prison. Such a taste for martyrdom have we here to be in prison now makes a man *sure* of election at the polls. It is a queer mixup." In a district that was heavily Unionist, Lollie voted for the Nationalist candidate.[141]

• • •

The war had lasted so long that when it finally ended, the girls found it hard to believe. For the Yeats family in general, but for Lily in particular, it brought only temporary joy, for two days before Armistice Day, John Butler Yeats came down with influenza, one of the victims of the epidemic that swept America. Fortunately, he survived, but the illness and recuperation lasted long, and Lily was at her wit's end coping with Quinn's almost daily cablegrams and wondering whether she should go to America and bring her father home. In the end, although she procured a passport, she did not go, realizing she could do nothing for her father that Quinn was not already doing. He did not come home, then or ever, living on for another four years in constantly declining health but full of enthusiasm to the end, and as ready to write long letters as he had ever been.[142] Then, as all his life, he was unable to make decisions, and so he followed the easiest course and remained where he was. He took no part in the sisters' plans for the publication of another selection of his letters, though he agreed passively to let the volume be done. Edited by Lennox Robinson, it was published in January 1920;[143] Lily thought Robinson, who chose longer passages than Pound's snippets, "much better" as an editor. Pound's methods, she told Quinn, "did not suit Papa's work."[144]

The newly elected Sinn Feiners, instead of going to Westminster as members of the British Parliament, chose to assert sovereignty over Irish affairs at home. In a daring act of defiance against their imperial oppressors, they organized a *de facto* government of their own, imposing unexpected demands on Ireland's inhabitants. Their methods were hardly kind and gentle. Lily called them "a set of irresponsible fanatics."[145] The Irish might be at last governing themselves, but not in a way or by a course of development that the Yeatses would have chosen. Lily's good friend—indeed, her best friend—Susan Mitchell was sympathetic to the Sinn Feiners and even declared herself to be completely Sinn Fein. "She and I always quarrel over it," Lily told Papa, "so we don't talk politics."[146]

But politics could not be avoided. On the night of 8 April 1919, Gurteen Dhas was the scene of an immense party for fifty people, given by the sisters in honor of the birth of Willie's and George's first child, their daughter Anne Butler, born on 24 February. Everyone of importance in their Dublin world—though not necessarily Evelyn Gleeson's Dublin world—was there. Lollie gave John Quinn a full account. "AE, James Stephens, Susan Mitchell, Ernest Boyd, Keating the artist and so on [were present]. The 50 people represented the most diverse political opinions, from extreme Protestant Unionist to Sinn Fein, and everyone who was at it seemed to enjoy themselves immensely. So it shows we are perhaps here in Ireland drawing together more and throwing down the doors of our watertight compartments. At any rate our Gurteen Dhas party will show those who were there that the doors *can* be thrown down without any very serious disaster." [147] The social and political importance of the Yeats sisters was measured by more than the balance sheet at Cuala Industries.

Lollie's description of the evening to her father provides amusing testimony to Lily's later weary charges that Lollie meddled with people and tried to improve them, stirring up waters that preferred to be placid. "Everyone, I think, enjoyed the party," Lollie wrote. "I had no talk myself, so busy making things go, introducing people and preventing the men getting into knots together and talking politics. . . . We had some guests of the extreme die-hard Unionist type, and also a good many Sinn Feiners. . . . I introduced them all together, and it did them all good. I wish I had a house of my own and money and could do this often. People don't mix together half enough. Of course one has to do the mixing with some skill. It is not *every* Sinn Feiner one could introduce to the old fashioned Unionist with happy results." [148] Lily remembered a remark by Aunt Isabella Varley: "The weather is very good if Lollie would only leave it alone." [149]

Sinn Fein's *de facto* government was not received with equanimity by the British, still twenty-five years away from learning how to disengage from empire. The Royal Irish Constabulary, defenders of the imperial faith, had been the object of guerrilla warfare by Irish Republicans, and the English soon sent in a ragtag bunch of military forces, known by their uniforms as the Black and Tans (later supplemented by the "Auxiliaries," clones of the Black and Tans but in different uniforms). These and the Sinn Feiners began shooting indiscriminately at each other, to the terror of the Irish citizens, whose leaders responded with their own brand of political effectiveness by ordering masses to be said all through the country every Saturday, "praying for the quick departure of our *protectors* and *guardians,* the military." Lily, never sympathetic to the Irish Church, hoped in this instance that the prayers "be heard as soon as spoken." [150] Lollie gave a report to Papa of the military trials that had supplanted civil ones in Dublin, of the murder of Canon Finlay, an eighty-year-old retired clergyman from Cavan, and the burning of his house, and of the killing of a girl student at Trinity College, probably by a "Sinn Fein shot meant for a soldier."[151]

Cuala was particularly affected by events. The Lord Mayor of Cork, Terence MacSwiney, had gone on a hunger strike in prison in protest against English methods in Ireland and in October had died. Cuala was under contract with Mrs. MacSwiney to embroider a Gaelic national dress for her, and the fabric had just arrived when the news of his death came.[152] By the middle of November 1920, Ireland had become almost anarchic. "Things have now got to such a state of barbarism that it is just reprisals on each side," wrote Lily to her father, "the Military with their machinery and regiments being able to kill and destroy the most, on Sinn Fein's side it is all an insult to the memory of men like MacSwiney. I don't think he would ever have approved the shooting of men in their beds."[153] The Dublin authorities had to impose a curfew. Willie was spared taking a position in the conflict by having his tonsils removed by Oliver St. John Gogarty and recuperating in England.[154] His Abbey Theatre suffered badly, like all businesses in Ireland, and ordinary men and women found it impossible to follow their normal routines. The sisters thought it prudent to have parties in the afternoon from four to six rather than in the evenings. In early 1921 they had twenty-two people as guests at one gathering, thirty at another, all leaving at once "in a flock" before dark so they would not be shot at.[155]

•   •   •

During all the years since John Butler Yeats had abandoned Gurteen Dhas, Lily's life with her sister had grown increasingly worse. The younger sister's irritating behavior was never-ending, affecting every breakfast and dinner, every business day at Cuala, every evening at home. Her jealousy over Lily's friends, her frustrations at her brother's treating her as a subordinate, her fussiness and talkativeness, her accusations of conspiracies had intensified, and no relief was in sight. Lily seldom revealed much to her father about the tensions at Cuala and Gurteen Dhas, for she knew he was old and ill, and her letters were meant to pacify, not upset. Yet she occasionally had to remind him that Lollie's "neurasthenia" was incurable, that any respite from her paranoid behavior was temporary. There were only occasional periods of quiescence. Miss Boston returned to Gurteen Dhas as a paying guest in the fall of 1920 to continue her studies at Trinity, and she and Lily resumed their friendship.[156] Lollie, annoyed by their closeness, had to content herself with a ten-day visit to the Cadburys' in Birmingham.[157] Lily thought the sojourn had done her good, she told her father. Lollie was "a reformed and changed woman." The Cadburys had all been knitting clothes for Austrian children, and Lollie had been converted. Some people were reformed "by 'getting religion' or taking the pledge, but Lolly has done it by taking to knitting. Instead of being on the rampage every evening from 7 to 11 she sits and knits and counts and peace reigns."[158] But that harmony, as always, was too good to last, and before long Lollie had returned to abnormal.

• • •

Despite the obvious political dangers, the sisters held their regular December sale of Cuala goods in Dublin in 1920 and, to their surprise, found it a success. "We expected nothing and got a good deal," Lily told JBY, "so we came home very cheerful in a taxi with the cashbox, but without our work as we feared to bring it back in the dark. In this sad country one is liable to be held up at any moment and searched by Military or Black and Tans, drunk and sober. You may also be fired at."[159] The widowed Mrs. Terence MacSwiney came in March to pay for the dress she had ordered before her husband's death.[160]

Willie and George, having tried living in Oxford, found it not as good as they hoped, the people proving "too dull." After the birth of their son Michael in the nearby town of Thame on 22 August 1921, they decided to move to Ireland, so they were henceforth to be on hand when crises developed in the sisters' affairs.[161] At Cuala the two irreconcilable antagonists again came to verbal blows. Lollie had told Willie she wanted more freedom to choose books for publication, a reminder to him of the Dowden fiasco. She wrote him with some heat that she knew she could make money if she had "a free hand," for she had "courage and enterprise." Willie took the letter as an ultimatum demanding his resignation and promptly agreed to it if he were not allowed the final word as editor. Lily responded with the words "We accept," which Willie took to mean his resignation was in force. What Lily had meant was that they accepted his terms, for the Cuala Press could not survive without him as editor, and they knew it. When Willie realized the meaning of Lily's words and saw that their revolt had failed, he expressed his position forcefully—in a letter to Lily, not Lollie, knowing its contents would be communicated:

> Now there are one or two things I must make plain. I cannot promise two books a year or books of any particular length. It grows more difficult, as time passes, to get books at all, and I could not get these if I did not write a great deal for the press myself. I resent, for instance, Lolly's perpetual complaints of the slow sale of "Noble Plays of Japan" because she must know that, on finding that I could get nothing but Ezra's book, I gave up weeks of my time to writing a long introduction in order to make the book sufficiently Irish to suit your press. But for Lolly's need I never would have written that essay. Then again, when Lady Gregory compiled her anthology of poetry from the Irish, she did so as a favour to me. I did not think the book would sell quickly and I told Lolly so, but I was glad to get it. The alternative was no book that year.
>
> Now if my editorship is to continue there is something of more importance still. Lolly and you must both recognize that I am a man of letters and that as a matter of conscience I will not pass bad work on any financial plea. This is not a quixotic idea of mine, but a prejudice I share with many other men of letters. I will get you the most profitable good work I can and will undertake this for two years more. At the end of two years we will consider the situation anew.[162]

When the typescript of his autobiographical monograph, *Four Years,* was sent to the Press, with all Willie's revisions and corrections duly noted, Lollie on her own put some passages within inverted commas (quotation marks, to use the American term) and, instead of the single inverted commas Willie preferred, chose the double. He wrote her acidly. If she insisted on having a girl at the press do the proofreading, he said, she should be made to undergo instruction and take a test to prove she knew what she was doing. Inverted commas were a typographical device with a specific, precise function. "Your girls seem to consider them as ornaments put in according to taste alone, double when they want a richer effect." [163]

Willie also put a stop to another of Lollie's devices to increase sales. She had regularly sent him Cuala books to autograph, a practice he resented. With *Four Years* he finally rebelled. "I hate signing books except for personal friends. I constantly find these books offered for sale at an increased price because signed." He suggested a new approach. "You announce 20 signed copies at enhanced prices (extra money to go to your girls' Xmas presents or some such thing). I would then get all my signing over at once." [164]

Another indication of his annoyance at what he saw as Lollie's lack of professionalism—of a knowledge of her own specialty after almost two decades on the job—is revealed in a second letter involving *Four Years:*

> You have not returned the first proofs with my corrections. This would have saved me trouble and have been safer. It is usual, and it is also worth noting, that proofs are property, and that I can sell them to collectors. George looks after such things so better return them even now. Always send back the corrected first proofs to an author as a guaranty that you have made his corrections. [165]

Then came an unexpected shock. The landlord of Cuala announced that he wanted the building for his son's use. The sisters protested, but a local board decided in favor of the landlord. [166] The lease expired in May 1922 (though the landlord allowed them to stay till the summer of 1923). "It is a blow," Lily wrote Papa, "no house anywhere to let. . . . We all like Cuala so much and it suited us so well in every way. The girls are very sad over it." [167] In the midst of their anxieties, Lily developed shingles, and Lollie had to assume her sister's work as well as her own. She "is being very good over the extra work," Lily told Papa, "irascible at times but on the whole calm." [168] Dr. Goff, the family physician, told Lily she needed to go away, but her response and the reason for it reflect the realities at Cuala. She agreed to go for a week to Ballinteer, only half an hour away. "That will do. I don't feel like going any further

off—no money, and I am shabby and disinclined to go further."
When she wrote these words, Lollie had also been at home with a
cold for three days.[169] Lily's illnesses became more frequent. Dr.
Goff, noticing her exhaustion as early as 1921, had suggested she
slow down, though not forbidding her her customary "hard work
and ordinary life."[170] When she returned to Cuala in mid-January
1922, it was for the mornings only.[171] To her worries she had to
add the usual fear that Lollie was giving a false account of her
condition to her father. "I had neuritis rather badly in my arm,"
she wrote him in October 1921, "but Dr. Goff is treating me and
I am very much better. I hope Lollie has not been drawing a fancy
portrait of me suffering from nerves. She accidentally read out part
of one of your letters, which made me think she had. If she has,
forget it. There is no truth in the story." He would see that for
himself when he returned to Dublin, as everyone thought he would,
in a month's time.[172]

But John Butler Yeats did not return to Dublin. He kept
delaying his departure from New York by a series of excuses, then
flatly announced to John Quinn that he simply would not leave.
While the family debated what further pressures might be brought
to bear on him, he died on 3 February 1922. For years Lily had
been writing soothing, humorous letters to him, trying always to
soften the blows about Lollie's illness by making things out to be
better than they were. Her father had been her best friend, she his,
and she readily admitted to Quinn that of all JBY's children she
had been "the favorite." "We were in perfect accord and never
irritated each other, which doesn't mean we did not see each other's
flaws. We saw them, but they just happened not to irritate. We
could talk together for hours and be silent together for hours."[173]
When the news of his death reached her in the midst of her own
illness,[174] the shock of it "of course was not good for her," as Lollie
put it to Quinn. Altogether she was in bed for six weeks and
"crawling about" for another six. Lollie was left to manage all the
affairs at Cuala.[175]

As if the personal problems in the Yeats family were not enough
to make the conduct of business difficult, a new round of violence
began in Ireland, this time featuring not the English against the
Irish but one set of Irishmen against another. The English had

finally agreed to allow the three southern provinces of Ireland to govern themselves as a separate country, and a division arose among the Irish about whether complete independence should be sought or some kind of loose association. Eamon De Valera and his Republicans wanted Ireland to be completely separated from England and particularly wished to see the odious Oath of Allegiance to the Crown abolished, an oath used all too often by England to punish Irishmen for fancied disloyalty to the king—as had been the case with the hapless Roger Casement, executed by the English for trying to stir up the Irish against the English. But De Valera's own emissaries to Westminster had broken their promise to him by signing a treaty establishing Ireland as a Free State with ties to the English crown and with the Oath of Allegiance intact. De Valera felt compelled to repudiate his colleagues and mounted a civil war against the Free State government. The "Troubles" that followed scarred the geography and the psyche of Ireland. In their folly the dissident forces set fire to the Four Courts, and valuable records accumulated over centuries were lost. The consequences that flowed from the civil war were to determine the divisions in Irish politics for decades to come, and to separate even members of the same family. The position of the Yeats sisters, and of most of those in Dundrum, was strongly in favor of the treaty. Lily called it "good news," and the telephone operator in Dundrum called out to whoever would listen, "Praise be to God Almighty—De Valera down and out." [176] Lollie spoke of "fine young people led into such madness by De Valera and other inflated fools," and when Michael Collins was assassinated, she wrote angrily of "the wretched *arid* person De Valera who has brought all this about!" (Even after De Valera's political rehabilitation a decade later, the Yeats view of him had not changed; Lollie called him "either a guileless child or a very astute man.") [177] Only Jack was in sympathy with the Republican cause.

The Cuala edition of JBY's memoirs, written with difficulty by the reluctant author over many years, was on the fall list, and almost all copies had been subscribed for, but after only forty pages had been put in type and eight printed, work had to be stopped because the mails were not functioning, a result of the "Troubles." [178] So JBY's partial autobiography (or memoir) did not appear until mid-September 1923. Condensed by Willie[179] and published under the title *Early Memories,* it provides an instructive example of the kind of carelessness that would have annoyed William Butler Yeats in Lollie but that he brushed away as trivial when indulged in by himself. In the preface Willie had shown his customary insouciance toward facts. John Quinn picked up his mistakes quickly and displayed irritation at their presence. "First, your father died the morning of February 3d and not on February 2nd, as stated by you. The second mistake is worse and consists in your statement that your father was *'taken ill in the night* and woke up and found his friends Mrs. Foster and John Quinn sitting at his bedside.'* That implies that Mrs. Foster and I were at your father's house in the middle of the night." In fact, both Quinn and Mrs. Jeanne Robert Foster had left early in the evening, and Quinn did not like to see in print anything suggesting that he was alone with a woman in the middle of the night, for such a report might be damaging if true; and by this time Mrs. Foster had long since displaced Dorothy Coates, Quinn's earlier mistress, so that Willie's casual mistake happened to correspond to the general, if not the specific, truth. This time the faults in the Cuala book could not be laid at Lollie's door.[180]

When Lily was at last able to write Quinn again after a lapse of six months, she reflected on the decisions she had made since 1908. Sometimes, she told him, she thought she should have stayed in New York with her father and looked for work. "But I was anxious about Ruth and her sister, who were in my care then, and anxious about the Industry, then starting with its new name and new place, and thought I was necessary to the girls and the Industry, which may be true and may not. All three might have done as well or better without me." Whatever the reasons, things had turned out well on all fronts.[181] All things considered—the poor capital underpinning of Cuala, Lollie's emotional problems, Lily's many illnesses, the war, the Black and Tans, the Troubles—Cuala's survival through the first fourteen years was remarkable.

A saving grace for Lily was the return of Ruth Pollexfen Lane-Poole from Australia in 1922 for a year's stay in Ireland and England. Her husband had been sent off to Papua to study forestry, and Ruth, about to have a third child, preferred the care of a specialist in Great Britain, her second birth having been a difficult one.[182] During her visit her sister Hilda was married to a Church of England clergyman, a Trinity College man, named Charles Graham[183] so Lily was able to take satisfaction in the second of her achievements as guardian, though Hilda had been to Lily more like a niece or distant relative than like a daughter, as Ruth had been. Lily's good fortune was of course Lollie's torment, for the sleeping jealousy awoke, and Lily and Ruth had to resort to the old practice of meeting secretly without letting Lollie know. The tensions arising from that combined with others to bring Lily closer and closer to the edge. At Gurteen Dhas, Maria O'Brien, the younger of the two maids, was drinking on the sly and failing to do her share of the work, putting the burden on the older Rose Hodgins, who was almost totally deaf and growing feebler every year.

Then, in May 1923, Cuala again became involved in Irish history. Lily had gone in early as usual, Lollie still nursing her emotions by having breakfast in bed. Lily described what happened: "I was in the usual place facing the window with my girls about me, when looking out the window I saw a young man with a bit of hawthorn in his buttonhole jump the wall. I just thought that he had come after sheep who had strayed off the golf links into the orchard. Then I saw a second man jump the wall. One of the girls stood up and looked out of the window and said, 'Raided.' So I got up and went into the middle room where the press was. The room seemed full of men. One was trying to read the type on the press, another the MS. I said, 'Who is in charge of this?' A man took his hat off and came towards me, saying, 'A raid by military orders. Can I speak to you alone?' So I opened the door of one sitting room and saw a man with a revolver at each of the two windows. The man in charge then asked me for two of my girls, giving their names, so I took them up to the kitchen where they were, and in a few minutes he took them away in a lorry. They had the whole house surrounded." Those taken away were the same two whose brothers had been imprisoned after the Rising. They returned after about six weeks, Lily saying they "seemed to have a very good time in prison."[184]

The other girls never moved while the arrests were being made but simply "went on with whatever they were doing as if nothing

were happening." After the soldiers had left, Sara Hyland leaned
back in her chair with a sigh of relief and said, "Thank God Miss
Lolly was not here." A few minutes later Lollie arrived and echoed
her remark: "Thank Goodness I wasn't here. I would have bitten
somebody." [185]

When the arrested girls returned to Cuala, neither Lily nor
Lollie asked them a word about what happened.[186] A chasm still
yawned between the two cultures. At Cuala the representatives of
each could live in symbiotic amity, but neither wished to know, or
could understand, the underlying assumptions of the other. The
two girls had been held on suspicion of supporting the IRA—they
were "two silly girls," said Lollie, "members of the Cuman-
na-Gael," and she thought them "very active in the Republican
cause." She had tried to talk them out of their politicking. "I
warned them they would be arrested, all no use." One of the girls,
Esther (Essie) Ryan, had been with the Press almost since the
beginning, and Lollie missed her services. She had to make do with
Eileen Colum, never reliable, and a new untrained girl, to manage
the presswork for JBY's *Early Memories*. "They were sure they could
never do it," said Lollie, "but I convinced them they could. It was
the only thing to do, as we could not get a man printer because of
the Trades Union," which would not allow an aged retired printer
to do the work, even for a nonprofit industry.[187] Arts and crafts
societies might be allowed to exist, but they must provide their
own labor and not upset the Irish market.

6

Cuala
The Separation, 1924–1940

We are not a normal family.
  —W. B. Yeats to Dr. Robert Simpson,
      3 April 1924

Cuala was looked upon as something of an incubus. One's attitude toward it was ambivalent. On the one hand its very existence presented a constant threat of some financial disaster, on the other hand it was an enterprise of such literary and artistic importance that everyone was willing to endure a good deal of family tension and inconvenience in order to preserve it.
  —Michael B. Yeats, in Liam Miller,
      The Dun Emer Press, Later the Cuala Press
      (Dublin: Dolmen, 1973), preface, 7–8

Cuala is the one outpost of chaos left in my life.
  —W. B. Yeats to Dorothy Wellesley,
      21 December 1937

As 1923 began, business looked promising. Papa's memoirs, ready to be published, had to be shunted aside so that two private books bringing in ready cash could be printed.[1] The problem of the relocation of the Cuala headquarters was on the verge of being solved: Willie and George would purchase "a large old Dublin house" and the sisters would rent it from them.

Then the blow fell, and Cuala entered a new phase of its life no one could have anticipated. Lily, who had never fully recovered from the illnesses of the year before, now suffered a complete col-

220

63. Lily Yeats at Gurteen Dhas, about 1922. *Courtesy of Anne B. Yeats.*

lapse. On a visit to England in mid-June 1923, she became so ill that she had to be taken to the Roseneath Nursing Home in London. Ruth Pollexfen Lane-Poole, still in England with her infant baby, rushed to her side and sent alarming reports to Willie, who wrote Lady Gregory that his sister might have "consumption of a very deadly kind" that could result in death "in a very short time."[2]

The diagnosis was soon changed, "tuberculosis" rapidly disappearing from the charts. At first Willie thought Lily's stay at Roseneath would be brief but soon learned she would need to be confined for months and that he and George would have to spend £400 a year thereafter for her care.[3] The chief cause of her troubles was of course the misplaced thyroid, but the symptoms were hard to analyze, and the anatomical villain was not identified till six years later. All that was certain was that Lily had suffered a massive physical breakdown and required medical care.

Just when money was most needed, William Butler Yeats was awarded the Nobel Prize in Literature. He told Edmund Gosse that he was grateful not only for the honor but "for the money."[4] In 1910 he had been granted a pension from the British government (on Gosse's recommendation) of £150 a year. Even with his other earnings from royalties and lectures, his income was not ample enough to enable him to support his sisters directly, especially since at the same time he was quietly paying the bills for his father's expenses in New York. At Cuala the overdraft at the bank rose every year, and in the spring of 1923 the financial wagon was rolling relentlessly toward the cliff. Lily's absence would weaken the embroidery branch, and the necessity of funding a new home for Cuala meant an additional expense. The medical bills would be piled on top of the rest, and there was no one to pay them except William Butler Yeats. The situation was so serious that Willie wrote Lady Gregory, "I imagine that whatever happens George and I will now become responsible for Cuala."[5]

So it was hardly surprising that when a journalist informed WBY of the award of the Nobel Prize, his first words were, "How much, Smyllie? How much is it?"[6] The remark may have been indiscreet, but it reflects Yeats's honest worry over his growing expenses.[7] John Quinn had been writing dyspeptically to WBY about the poet's finances and, after the announcement of the award, urged him strongly not to squander any of the $40,000 on frivolous expenses (like furnishing the castle at Ballylee), but to invest it carefully. Yet he agreed that some of it might properly be spent on Lily's health.[8]

William Butler Yeats has been so widely castigated by his detractors for his prickliness and for what some saw as his arrogance that one feature of his behavior has been overlooked—his silent generosity to the members of his family. He was under no legal obligation to support his father—whose fecklessness had lost a family estate that would have descended to his eldest son. Yet the son sent sums to him regularly and sold manuscripts to John Quinn to raise funds to defray his expenses. He watched over the affairs of his sisters when he could have looked the other way. With the Nobel Prize money in hand, he embarked on the most massive of his philanthropies. From then until his death sixteen years later, he provided his sisters with office space, made them repeated loans, and paid Lily's medical expenses. The real test of his generosity was that he never made it public; most of his friends and, later, students of his life seem unaware of its extent and duration.[9]

Now that Lily was seriously ill in a way that could not be denied, she seized the chance to say what she had been wanting to say for years. She wrote a revealing little document called first "My Will," and then, when she realized she had little to bequeath, "My wishes." Addressed to Willie and George, it lays bare the realities of daily life at both Cuala and Gurteen Dhas. She told of Maria O'Brien's constant pilfering and drinking, made easy by a household devoid of discipline because of Lollie's behavior.[10] Lily had endured agonies since the founding of Dun Emer, she told them, and especially in the decade and a half since Louis Purser's defection set her sister emotionally adrift. She told them what they must already have suspected. "I feel this is a break which had to come and I feel I ought to take advantage of it and make a complete separation from Lolly, for life with her for the past twenty years has been torture." She declared that it was "impossible ever to think of living with her again." Whatever happened, she was grateful to Willie and George "for this ease of body and mind they have given me." She was sure they would respond to her cry of desperation. "Whether I recover or not, while lying in bed I will get great happiness out of thinking that there can be a life for me of the freedom that I have all my life longed for."[11]

On learning of Lily's feelings, Willie and George were careful to keep Lollie away from her. Lollie hadn't been able to learn precisely what her sister's symptoms were and blamed Ruth Pollexfen Lane-Poole, whom she called a "maddening young woman," for keeping her in the dark. She was convinced there was nothing physically wrong with Lily, telling John Quinn her sister's illness could not be tuberculosis but merely *"neurasthenia."* Lollie, who was unable to recognize the symptoms in herself, could find them in others where they didn't exist.[12] Unfortunately for Lily, the doctors were unable to find the wandering thyroid, and their failure provided Lollie the opportunity she needed to press her own opinions on them. Sir Humphrey D. Rolleston had been placed in general supervision of Lily's case, with Dr. Robert Simpson, a specialist in lungs, in direct charge. Dr. Simpson's first report to WBY was pessimistic. He found a numbing of the nerves that control the breathing and thought the resulting exhaustion could "only end in heart failure."[13]

As Dr. Simpson could find no apparent cause for the troubles, he brought in as a consultant one E. D. Waggett, a specialist in diseases of the throat, who gave Lily a thorough examination and reported his findings to Dr. Simpson and Sir Humphrey. The patient, he concluded, suffered from "an expiratory asymmetry of her vocal cords," a condition Waggett attributed to "an ill-timed activity of the cortical centres." All she needed was training to restore the symmetry (what today is called "biofeedback"). With that, and with the taking of a cough syrup, her troubles should end. He told Lily, in Dr. Simpson's presence, that if she followed his advice she "would be cured in ten days." To show that he had been diligent in seeking all possible causes, he also told Dr. Simpson and Ruth Lane-Poole that "there was nothing of the nature of hysteria associated with her condition."[14]

Then Lollie roared into London, demanding to see Waggett. She was quick to express her opinion to him, and although there is no record of precisely what she said, it is not hard to draw conclusions, for after Waggett examined Lily a second time, on 12th March his diagnosis changed markedly. Dr. Simpson reported to WBY about Waggett's second talk with him. Waggett, he said, now insisted that Lily's problem was simply a "neurosis," and added that sooner or later the word "neurasthenic" would have to be used. (In the 1920s "neurasthenia" was the term loosely used for what in later years would be called "psychosis"; it was a polite way of suggesting that the patient was emotionally disturbed). Waggett

64. John Quinn, about 1920. *Courtesy of author.*

now refused to believe that Lily suffered from anything more than a delusion and told Dr. Simpson he had suggested she get out of bed and go back to work, and that she adopt a baby to give her something to do.

An angry Dr. Simpson made clear to WBY that he regarded Waggett's opinion as wholly unsupportable and that it had come entirely from Lollie's malicious intervention. He expressed his feelings strongly: if Lollie attempted to come to London again and stir up more trouble while Lily was still under his care, he would order the nurse not to allow her to come near Lily. He left no doubt that he thought Waggett had been taken in.[15]

Waggett's report to Willie was sent a week later. Willie should have been fully prepared for it by Simpson's letter. Lily, Waggett's report said, suffered no constitutional infirmity of any kind. Her problems were chiefly psychological, her "disorder" "purely functional." The "higher regions of the brain" were involved and needed *"something better to do."* He made derisive comments about her physical appearance and habits. "The patient has become extremely, genuinely feeble, and unduly fat, through her prolonged idleness, coupled with a large appetite and good food of which she absorbs a very large quantity." The problem was further complicated "by the fact that the patient has no desire to undertake any duties and is more than content to continue her present resting life." Then he tipped his hand on Lollie's interference:

> There is a very distinct difficulty, known to me at second hand only, arising out of a complicated conflict of family interest and family influences, into the details of which it would be quite improper for me to enter:—they come within the sphere of the family physician and the neurologist, who will be competing with the variations of those influences during the period of their treatment of the case:—nor would it be proper and advisable for me to suggest to you (on my second hand information) a course of action which might substitute a family quarrel for an illness which the patient appears to me to be thoroughly enjoying.[16]

His recommendation was "to get the patient back to normal life." His own "important contribution" was to discover that there was "no organic disease of the throat and no paralytic or spastic affection of the throat muscles indicative of organic disease in any part." He repeated to Willie what Simpson had already reported, that he thought Lily ought to adopt a baby "as a cure for having nothing" to keep her mind off her troubles.[17]

With the two letters before him, WBY's decision should have been simple. Incredibly, he accepted Waggett's opinion and rejected Simpson's. Just as Lollie had taken in Waggett, now Waggett took in WBY. "I have very little doubt that you have found the true solution,"[18] he told Waggett. He explained his position to Dr. Simpson:

> From my general knowledge of my sisters' temperaments I do not think his diagnosis improbable considered as a diagnosis of present conditions. The whole family are exceedingly nervous and suggestible. I remember once being crippled with rheumatism and my instant cure by an unexpected half hour's animated conversation. We are not a normal family.

He acknowledged that his sister Lollie was the one who possessed the family temperament "to excess."[19] He made no such charge against Lily, the most sensible of them all, yet by his decision placed upon her the burden of the Pollexfen legacy. Lollie, the paranoid, emerged as the pillar of sanity, Lily as the neurotic, and the turning of the tables had been accepted by one who should have known better.[20] So the "life of freedom" that Lily "all her life longed for" was not to be, then or ever. Willie had written to his wife, "She will never go back to Lolly,"[21] but back she went.

The problem of Cuala now commanded Willie's attention. It was a three-headed problem: a new workplace had to be found, the embroidery department had to be reorganized with someone other than Lily at its head, and something had to be done about the overdraft at the bank, which was approaching the staggering figure of £2,000. A second problem, this one with only two heads, was one Willie preferred not to deal with: how to arrange for the new lives of the sisters in the light of Lily's "wishes."

Lollie had long wanted to live near the center of Dublin, within easy walking distance of Trinity College and the Abbey Theatre and Stephens Green, in a home to which guests could come conveniently, a place where she could feel herself a part of the soul of Dublin. With Lily conveniently away, she found a house in Ranelagh that met her requirements. Lily told Lollie she approved of the house but neglected to add that she didn't wish to share it.[22] Yet she could not afford a place of her own, and even their combined incomes could not sustain the house in Ranelagh. The upshot was that both returned to Gurteen Dhas, and the life Lily said she could never return to was the one to which she returned, and she was to live it until her sister's death in 1940. With her brother's willingness to accept Waggett's incorrect diagnosis, there was really no other practical solution to her problems.

Willie and George, who had moved from Oxford to Dublin shortly after the birth of their son Michael Butler in August 1921, took a house at 82 Merrion Square, which became their principal residence for the next six years. While awaiting the resolution of Lily's illness, George and Willie settled the question of a new office for Cuala by allowing their own living quarters to be used. For the next year and a half, Cuala's letterhead bore the Merrion Square address. George, with Willie's encouragement, assumed management of the embroidery department. He looked on the crisis as an adventure and a challenge. He thought George would "improve" the embroidery business because "she knows what people wear and has seen modern art." His private feelings about Lily's embroidery, seldom expressed to outsiders, are made clear in remarks to Sturge Moore. "My sister's work had become too sere, a ghost of long past colours and forms." He was eager to be part of Cuala, looking forward to "living in a house where there is so much going on."[23]

Willie's support was encouraging but did not cure Lily's weakness, which ran a long course. Recuperation was slow. Almost a year after the onset of her illness, Lily wrote a letter to Quinn (her first letter to him in almost a year), from Calvados in France, where she was recuperating: "My difficult and noisy breathing is no better. It is caused they say by a very unusual condition of my vocal cords, which open when they ought to close and close when they ought to open, and also by a thickening I have of my bronchial tube."[24] Lollie saw things differently, boasting to Quinn in March 1924 as "good news" that as a result of her intervention, Lily "is now *out every day* and is to be out of *doors this week twice a day*."[25] Lily's voyage to this state of limited mobility had consumed almost a year, and in the early spring of 1925 she was still staying with friends in England, not yet strong enough to return to Dublin.

Lily's letter to Quinn marked another crucial juncture in her life. Only a few weeks after receiving it he died, at the age of fifty-four, having suffered from abdominal cancer for several years. Until her father's death Lily had written regularly to Quinn since her return from New York and had been able to confide in him as in no one else about matters affecting the family. He had watched over her aged father during his long fourteen-year "visit" to New York, had become a collector of William Butler Yeats's books and manuscripts, had been an early and faithful supporter of Dun Emer and Cuala. His death came as a surprise to the Yeatses. His letters had dropped in frequency, but the sisters "just thought he was disgruntled over things" in Ireland, then regretted they "had not at least written constantly, as we used to do." [26] Except for her father and older brother, he was the only male Lily could regard as a close and disinterested friend and advisor, and just at the time she was most in need of his advice and support fate deprived her of him.

When Lily returned to Gurteen Dhas in mid-1925, she found that Lollie's attitude had not changed, despite the trauma of her illness. She had written George in August 1924: "Lolly I find just the same, cross and full of venom. I have not yet found any topic we can talk on." [27] Lollie now handled the Press exclusively, George the embroidery; the two parts of the business could have functioned in different offices altogether. When, in March 1925, Lily began going in to Cuala in the Merrion Square house, she found she could only manage three days a week. [28] She and Willie talked privately about what to do. He said he would like to visit her at Gurteen Dhas provided Lollie would not be present, [29] and between them new plans would be devised.

The first was to end the long "temporary" stay in the home of Willie and George. A new office was rented on the second floor of a red-brick eighteenth-century house at 133 Lower Baggot Street, the embroidery rooms looking out over the street and so "rather noisy." Lily never got accustomed to the noise, longing always "for the quiet fields round the old Cuala." [30] The move was made by others, and Lily did not pay her first visit to the new offices until 2 April 1925. When Willie came for "a good talk," she learned that Lollie's only comment to George on leaving the Merrion Square quarters she had occupied for no payment was that "she was so glad to be at last in a place of her own." Lily's remark was spiked with the verbal acid of which she had a plentiful supply when talking of

Lollie: "Tactful! to the woman who had put us up rent free for a year and a half."[31]

From the very beginning of her return to work, Lily realized she would hardly be able to endure a full schedule. She "went in," as she put it, for a few hours a week only, and May Courtney, her most reliable girl, came out to Gurteen Dhas on other days and consulted with her. Neither branch of the Industries brought in a profit, partly because new taxes and restrictions by both the English and Free State governments curbed business,[32] and Lily told Ruth that she was forced to work merely to keep the household going.[33] At home Lollie was no less troublesome than before, refusing to believe there was anything wrong with her sister and slyly hinting to others that Lily was soldiering on the job. "She has the activity of a mosquito in spreading these lies and nearly everyone believes her," complained Lily.[34] George Yeats, now freed of full responsibility for the embroidery, had agreed to help out in emergencies but was "only half warm" over the idea, having "so much to do and so many interesting activities." All Lily could do was accept her lot and wait and hope.[35] George had wanted "to fling up Cuala and get back to her own life,"[36] but, trapped in the Yeatsian web, she would in fact be connected with Cuala continuously until her death in 1968.

Lily wrote Ruth about one transaction that typified their problems. One of her special orders, a rest gown for an Oxford lady, contained silk. A newly imposed English silk tax required Lily to specify the value of the silk in the gown, and this she gave as £1.6. The Oxford lady saw the amount on the packing slip and sent Lily a cheque for £1.6 along with a note saying the gown was "very nice." "I don't think even Woolworth could make one for £1.6," Lily told Ruth. "I feel quite mad over it, I was so disappointed."[37] Lily felt too embarrassed to send a bill for the correct amount. She conceived stratagems to circumvent the tariff. Once, when George Yeats was traveling to England, she took with her as personal clothing a silk shawl, a cloak, and a rest gown, then gave them to Hilda Pollexfen Graham in London, who in turn mailed them to Belfast for a Cuala sale. Since the second transfer was within the United Kingdom, there was no tax.[38]

Legally Cuala had been a cooperative society, with the two

65. Cuala Press Room, about 1925. *Courtesy of author.*

sisters functioning as partners, each able to substitute for the other. Managing the financial restructuring of Cuala was inconvenient, but Willie now achieved the change decisively. With his Nobel Prize money, he paid off the overdraft, then changed the society from a cooperative one to an independent one, each section being given a separate bank account.[39] So in 1925 the two branches underwent a further kind of separation, akin to the one that divided Dun Emer in 1904, with Willie assuming responsibility for their debt but also taking some Pollexfen and Steamer shares from the sisters as security.[40] The new arrangement was to prove a poison pill for Lollie. She was free of the enormous debt that had been as persistent and annoying as a nail in the shoe. But a nail appeared in the other shoe; the brother with whom she did not get along was now not merely an unofficial unpaid advisor of the Press but also a principal fiduciary with authority to look over her shoulder.

As in the days before the war, there were sales in Belfast and London, and, in Dublin, George Yeats opened up her home in Merrion Square annually for a Cuala sale. Holding the event at the

66. George (Mrs. William Butler) Yeats, about 1924. *Courtesy of Rosemary Hemming.*

Yeatses' home rather than at Cuala increased sales, as many came thinking they might run into the Great Man, who occasionally put in an appearance. George provided tea and hired two extra women to help out in addition to her permanent staff of three servants (not counting the nurse for Anne and Michael).[41] Lily and her girls worked away at a variety of small gifts, woollen purse bags, shawls, needle weaving sets, dinner sets of napkins and tablecloths—anything that would sell—[42] and the quality was high. The sales at Merrion Square were another indirect way in which Willie and George were able to help Cuala without laying out cold cash. "They certainly are good to let us upset the house, and fill it with a tramping crowd," said Lily. The Cuala girls did most of the necessary work. Lily was simply present and was "fairly dead" at the end of the day.[43] The annual sales there continued until late 1930, when Willie and George moved from Merrion Square to 42 Fitzwilliam Square. Christmas sales were thereafter conducted in the Cuala rooms, a less desirable arrangement for the sisters.

It was George rather than Willie who masterminded the sales at Merrion Square. Michael Yeats, their son, has written that it is "hard to exaggerate the importance of my mother's part in the affairs of Cuala." Her participation at the time of Lily's illness began a forty-five-year association with a business she did not seek, and she fought valiantly to discharge an obligation incurred by others. "During the twenties and thirties," her son has written, "her role was that of intermediary and general peacemaker between my father and his sisters."[44]

Old friends also continued to help by placing special orders.[45] When G. K. Chesterton and his wife came through Dublin in the spring of 1928, Frances Chesterton bought for £4.10 a heavy coat that Lily had just fashioned "out of a Donegal rug, fringe and all." Lily put embroidery on the "scarf ends" and declared it would make a good motor-coat. Frances said she wanted to use it for their trip to Rome the following month,[46] though whether she really needed it is not known.

Lily's long years of careful training of her helpers had paid off. "Cuala runs pretty well on the days I am not there," she told Ruth. "The girls are now grown women and know the money side as well as I do and are more thrifty and careful than I am."[47] The greatest benefit of the new arrangement was the independence of her business from Lollie's. "George did me a great service when she separated the embroidery quite from the Press. Lolly now can never say she has to do my work." She got some welcome support of her feelings about her sister. "Phillida and George say that the thing the matter with Lolly is that she hates any work and does extremely little, and they are right. I had not thought of it. She makes the noise and others do the work."[48] The embroidery branch was "always getting knockdown blows," Lily complained. "Duty, taxes all fall on it." Meanwhile "the printing goes free," and, since it was partly done by machine, could be produced cheaply.[49] The embroidery was hand-worked all the way, and the cost was high.

Willie's agreement with the sisters had been merely to give them a fresh start in a lumbering wagon, not a free ride in a spanking coach and four. By late 1925 he had cleared them of all debts, including Lily's medical and hospitalization charges of £245. With those and the guaranteed Cuala overdrafts, he had laid out a total of £2,010.11.1. He calculated the annual deficit over a twenty-year period, considering his own subsidies and those of the Cadburys and Anne Boston, as £135. "This seems roughly therefore the amount you have to make up annually by economies or increased sales."[50] With a large portion of their Pollexfen and Steamer shares at risk, he hoped to convert their potential liability into a spur to fiscal discipline. Willie had bought the shares back from the bank, guaranteeing the sisters the income from them,[51] the shares to be used as security against future debts and hence available to them in the form of overdrafts at the bank.

Relations at the Press never improved. Brother and sister disagreed; glitches recurred. Oliver St. John Gogarty's *An Offering of Swans* was published by Cuala in late 1923 after much delay, the Press having run out of paper for the binding and having to wait till Christmas week for more.[52] The miscalculation proved costly to the Yeatses. The edition was limited to only 300 copies (WBY's next book, scheduled for June, ran to five hundred), all of which sold at once. "We could easily have sold 100 more," Lollie told Van Wyck Brooks. The books instantly became collectors' items. Booksellers who could lay their hands on copies were selling them for a guinea each.[53] Money that could have flowed into the Cuala coffers went elsewhere.

In another attempt to indulge her "quiet literary taste," Lollie proposed publishing a book of Monk Gibbon's poems, Gibbon having made the suggestion to her. Willie refused, as he had refused an earlier request, made through her, by Padraic Colum. Whether his objection was based on a judgment of poetic merit or on a determination to discourage Lollie from acting as literary critic is not known, but his action may have soured his reputation with Gibbon.[54]

When Willie prepared an essay on Ezra Pound to be published by Cuala as part of *A Packet for Ezra Pound* (in fact, the essay was never published, though the *Packet* was), George Yeats wrote Pound that it would be her "unpleasant duty to get the sister to print same." She asked Pound to answer certain questions for her by mail so she could avoid having to deal with Lollie. "If you could reply on these points 'twill save me having her trotting round to 42 [Fitzwilliam Square] thrice daily for the sake of asking questions and having a little chat as well!"[55]

WBY's irritation with Lollie was not lessened when he learned of another of her willful rebellions. She had taught drawing to her niece Anne, who displayed remarkable talent, and showed one of her pictures in an Exhibition. But Lollie had assisted Anne, touching up the drawings to "improve" the final product. WBY put his foot down and ordered Lollie not to show any work of Anne's that was not completely her own. Lollie, who enjoyed the flattery that came to her when one of her students won an award—particularly the daughter of her distinguished relative—disregarded his order and showed another "improved" drawing, which took a prize. WBY made his daughter return it. Lollie flew into a rage at what she thought her brother's insensitive behavior, but his fury was greater than hers.[56]

Lily's financial position was considerably improved when, in 1925, Ruth and Charles Lane-Poole offered her a "tip" or gift[57] of £3 a month, which Lily cheerfully accepted. Her letters to Ruth from late 1925 until the end of her life give continual thanks for the contribution, without which she might have been denied some of the simple necessities. In explaining her acceptance of the "tip," Lily added: "I have only the 10/- a week I keep out of Cuala. Out of this I pay my train fares, postage, church, and all the odds and ends that come up every week." Meanwhile Lollie made £80 a year from her painting lessons, which she reserved for her own use. Lily kept the Lane-Poole gift a secret from Lollie, afraid she would try to invade it. When a division of expenses had to be made for fuel, taxes, and other household costs, Lollie always claimed she was paying more than her share.[58] Each sister kept her own books, and their affluence or lack of it was something they might complain about to each other, but neither discussed the details of her own fortunes.[59] At Cuala the cycle was consistent—good months followed by poor ones, all adding up to one mediocre year after another. The end of the rainbow was always several horizons away and never moved closer.

The sales of "small things" brought in so much money that Lily tried to devise additional embroideries that might increase the variety. She even paid to have her chief girl, Sara Hyland, take lessons in frame work "so that we can try Badge working for schools and colleges." "I don't think it is well paid," she told Ruth, "about £1 a day, but if it made anything it would help."[60]

She also pursued the big orders. Ruth was successfully drumming up business in Australia, having close connections through her husband to the seats of power, so there were injections of cash from that source also.[61] Cuala had already done screens for the Governor-General's House,[62] and now Ruth announced the biggest coup of all. The Duke and Duchess of York (later King George VI and Queen Elizabeth, parents of Elizabeth II) were to pay a visit to Canberra in 1927 and to stay at Government House. Lily was given the commission to design and embroider two bedspreads for the royal couple, a rare honor since Cuala was now part of the Free State, only tangentially associated with the United Kingdom.[63] It was a commission never again equalled by Cuala. Freke, the Dublin department store, displayed the Duke's bedspread in its window for five days, "just it, nothing else, and it made quite a stir." The *Manchester Guardian* gave a whole column to the bedspreads, along with a portrait of Cottie, who designed them.[64] The publicity was of enormous value to Lily, who had the satisfaction of knowing that the Governor-General had paid for it. On at least one occasion, the display merely aroused hopes that couldn't be fulfilled. A woman came into Cuala and asked for two bedspreads "the same as the Duke and Duchess's." When she heard the price, she lowered her expectations, asked what a single-bed size would cost, then murmured something about doing the work herself and slipped away.[65]

The fact that Ruth was placed in charge of the decoration and furnishing of the house and chose Cuala's embroidery without an open competition did not dampen Lily's enthusiasm at the assignment.[66]

Always holding Cuala back was the lack of sufficient money with which to expand and economize. Willie urged his sisters to collect their bills and try to turn a profit, "as he could not help again."[67] Although he probably had every intention of keeping to his stern threat, it proved an idle one. His interventions were to be, as always, frequent and reliable. Michael Yeats remembers even as a small boy "the constant atmosphere of tension that surrounded everything with Cuala and its affairs."[68] One of the reasons was the continued inability of the sisters to manage their books properly. In 1925 the outside auditors commented: "It may come as a surprise to the partners to learn that their goods are being sold at less than cost." They found that assets were £1,200 and liabilities £2,183. The overdraft that year was £1,976. WBY had to settle matters at the bank.[69]

Lollie particularly was so wound up in her own concerns that she paid little attention to the business end of the enterprise, and so the Press "never became a profitable industry." The earlier experiences with John Quinn were repeated with others. When people paid their bills, she sometimes threw away the records before checking their accuracy.[70] On one occasion she neglected to mail a book to a paid-up subscriber, sending two copies to another subscriber instead.[71] Michael Yeats, speaking particularly of the Press, has written, "My father was constantly expected to come to the rescue when financial difficulties arose, as when, for example, one of his own books was sold out in advance of publication but, as a result of some miscalculation, the firm lost £60 as a result." Lollie was unable to estimate figures properly, her "costings" being "eccentric." One of the account books showed "that a book sold retail at 9/6 actually cost 8/9 to produce. Allowing for booksellers' discounts, this did not leave much scope for profit."[72]

• • •

And always Lily had to live with the unpredictable Lollie. When her doctor ordered Lollie to walk every day to Cuala, a

67. Gurteen Dhas. Lollie in window; Maria O'Brien in doorway.
Courtesy of author.

danger arose. She would meet the postman on his morning rounds before he reached Gurteen Dhas, and Lily was afraid she would find and read Ruth's letters. She suggested that Ruth address them to Cuala instead, where May Courtney sorted through the mail first and could see that Lily got her letters without Lollie's knowing.[73]

Lollie didn't confine her troublesomeness to Gurteen Dhas, sometimes making unseemly displays before the employees at Baggot Street. One day she "had a nerve storm" over "the cleaning of the Cuala kitchen" and "said things that she could not possibly have known she was saying." Lily suspected that the Cuala girls "must believe her amazing fables," especially those about Lily's supposed hypochondria and malingering.[74] Ruth offered a way out by inviting Lily to come to Australia for a long visit, perhaps a permanent one. Lily would have liked to go, but the puritan side of her predominated. "We can just barely live by being together. And then Cuala—it would mean breaking up this house and Cuala or getting someone to board here and someone to take up my side

68. Gurteen Dhas living room, about 1925. *Courtesy of author.*

of Cuala, and then there would be my journey and clothes, and I might get ill on your hands, and I *certainly* would get old on your hands." So hopes of escape to the distant south were abandoned.[75]

The three and a half years from June 1925 to December 1928 had been trying ones for both sisters, the work in both branches of the Industries increasing in volume and intensity while profits were still elusive. Now, in the midst of their harried life, came another disturbance in the person of the forty-year-old gentleman from Cork who began paying attention to Lollie, who had reached her sixtieth birthday in 1928. Instead of her usual complaints, Lollie now filled the air at Gurteen Dhas with rhapsodic accounts of her new suitor, who she was sure was about to propose marriage to her. She boasted, publicly and indiscreetly, about her new alliance all over Dublin, and, when the courtship proved a mirage, the effect on Lollie's taut nerves was predictable: another emotional breakdown, almost as severe as the one brought on by the fading of Louis Purser's devotion twenty years earlier,[76] and the first attack of the angina pectoris that would lead to her death a decade later.

Lily had tried diligently to keep to the stern schedule expected

69. Cuala Embroidery Room, about 1925. *Courtesy of author.*

of her since her return to Cuala in 1925, but her breathing grew worse, and her fatigue at the end of the day was so great that she found movement of any kind difficult. Even if her symptoms had been psychosomatic, they still needed looking after, so her visits to the Dublin doctors were frequent. At length, one of them, noting the deterioration in her condition, decided that another X-ray was in order, and so in early 1929 the truth about her lifelong ailment was finally revealed:[77] an abnormally large and irregularly shaped thyroid gland pressed down on an assortment of nerves, muscles, and ligaments in her chest and throat. Depending on its position, she suffered from difficult breathing, chest pains, tingling of the fingers, flushing of the skin, chills, and a variety of other disabilities, and, always, from fatigue, which left her unable to work for more than short periods without coming close to exhaustion. "I am really extremely glad to know at last what is wrong and why I breathe as I do and why I have never felt very well," she wrote Ruth, then added what had perhaps always troubled her most: "I used to think myself sometimes that perhaps it was nothing, *'nerves,'* and then I felt mad with myself."[78] She hinted at the view she thought Willie, George, and others took of her since her stay at

Roseneath: "I know lots of people thought at the back of their mind that it was nerves."[79]

A chastened William Butler Yeats realized at last that he had been taken in by Waggett's incompetence and Lollie's manic interference. Although Lily's weakness was the result not of an "illness" but of a "condition" that was not fatal, it was clear that she could no longer carry on as a fully active member of Cuala. After she had gradually worked herself back to a full week at Baggot Street, it was now agreed that she should spend one full business day a week at home.[80]

Lily enjoyed embroidering. To her it was not merely a way to make money but a means of relaxation, and she welcomed the chance to work at it alone. "It is soothing," she told Ruth, "and gives you time to rest and think." To while away her free hours, she embroidered a book jacket for the copy of William Morris's Kelmscott edition of Chaucer that friends had presented Willie on his fortieth birthday in 1905, "olive and rose" in "pale gold and pinks and greens."[81] She was proud of her work, knew it was good, and never apologized for it.[82]

Lily tried to avoid unusually difficult commissions because of her low energy. She had sworn never to make another of her large embroideries, "The Garden," but when an order for one came through, she felt she had to take it, though, "the amount of work alarms me." She set a price of twelve guineas for it, unmounted.[83] Some people were willing to pay such sums for authentic handmade goods, but Lily complained to Ruth that the competition, which was once but a wisp of cloud, was now filling the sky. "There are so many d—— amateurs holding sales and selling cheap, bad work but cheap, and professional embroidery is now machine and cheap also."[84]

Life at Gurteen Dhas was further complicated by the death on 15 March 1930 of Roseanna Hodgins, the older of the two servants, who had been with the Yeatses for forty-five years. She had always provided a solid underpinning for the domestic life in the household. Maria O'Brien, who remained, still drank on the sly and was unreliable.

Perhaps Rose's death contributed to Lily's second great collapse. She had hardly begun work on the "Garden" project when, on Holy

70. Louis Purser, 1926. *Courtesy National Library of Ireland.*

Thursday, 2 April 1931, she felt "way down," and next day had a high temperature and "staggering palpitations" and couldn't sleep. For five days she remained in poor condition, and even in her recuperation was so weak she could hardly stand. "I go down like a stone and cannot get up again," she told Ruth.[85] For almost a month she was unable to write her weekly letter to Ruth, and for a couple of weeks she had to stay with George and Willie to rest up.[86] She never recovered even the little strength she had retained after the breakdown in London in 1923, and it was clear that she would no longer be able to participate actively in Cuala at all.

• • •

So another round of changes had to be made at the Industries. For a while Lily tried going in to Baggot Street three days a week but found she lacked the strength to do so.[87] Dr. Goff told her she would not get better and that nothing could be done for her.[88] By September 1931 she was staying permanently at home, managing her three remaining workers from a distance and doing odd jobs as they came along.[89]

Lily and Willie and George had a long discussion, and it was agreed that the embroidery branch would have to be closed. A sudden end would not be possible, for people might think both branches of Cuala were shutting down, so it was agreed that Lily would simply "fade out slowly," and Christmas 1931, three months ahead, was set as the tentative date. One of her girls left to get married, and in the meantime the other two could be kept busy with "little orders" until they found work elsewhere.[90] Lily hoped that old customers in England would pick up her remaining stock at bargain prices.[91] Through the difficult period George was a tower of strength, "good and generous," Lily told Ruth. "She is helping to wind me up at Cuala and does it so graciously, no fastening of a hook in your jaw over it."[92] On 3 December 1931, Cuala held its last sale of embroidery under Lily's direction, and she knew she would feel better when the anxiety had abated.[93]

But at the last minute the embroidery branch was saved, or at least partly so. Sara Hyland and May Courtney could not find work, despite their training, so they offered to continue the embroidering on their own, renting the room in Baggot Street from Lollie. George took care of the details of closing out Lily's part in the business. She wrote Willie on 4 January 1932: "Cuala is wound up —the Embroidery I mean. I have paid all the bills except the overdraft at the Bank. . . . Sara Hyland and May Courtney have decided to try and carry on as a 'Mendery and Dressmaking Establishment.' They pay their rent to Lolly and bear their proportion of telephone." Since each had part-time jobs outside, they would work

71. William and Emmeline Cadbury, *Courtesy of Hannah Cadbury Taylor.*

for lower rates than Cuala had paid. "They will act as agents for Lily's embroidery pictures, banners, Stations of the Cross, etc."[94] WBY paid off the overdraft at the bank, which had risen to £1,800, £1,000 in the embroidery account, £800 in the Printing. He took £1,000 out of his Nobel Prize money and gave another £200 in cash to enable Cuala to meet daily expenses. In return he awarded himself a thousand preference shares, which were worth no more than Cuala's future profitability.[95] Mrs. Cadbury also contributed £100, which was put into the Press account and for which she was given one hundred shares.[96] Lily was compelled to sell her remaining holdings in the Sligo Steam Navigation Company to Uncle Arthur Jackson who, ever the shrewd businessman, bought them at par, even though they paid 8 percent a year. From the sale Lily netted over £400. She was afraid she might have to sell her remaining Pollexfen shares too, leaving her with no capital at all to leave to Ruth's eldest daughter, as she had hoped to do. As a partial compensation, Willie and George agreed to make her a weekly contribution,[97] which, with the Lane-Pooles' £3 a month, would help her meet expenses. At Gurteen Dhas, Lily would conduct a small cottage industry, embroidering "little needle pictures," which Lollie's Cuala would sell for her on commission.[98]

Lollie took the news of the new arrangement "with temper" and was "as unpleasant" as she could be. She still refused to accept that anything was wrong with Lily, her "warp" blinding her vision, even though Willie insisted that in any public announcements the closing of the embroidery branch must be "put down entirely" to Lily's health.[99]

Under the new arrangement George and Willie would give Lily £7 a month if she would try to make another £7 from work she would produce at her leisure. Willie suggested she do "little pictures of famous houses," like that of Swift's lady friend Vanessa at Celbridge and of Lady Gregory's Coole; she had already done a picture of the Customs House and planned to do one of the Abbey Theatre.[100] Cousin Ida Varley Dewar-Durie sold "a very ancient garden screen," the first Lily ever worked, for £8 and sent her the proceeds.[101] George Russell drew one of his characteristic pictures of a "fairy among ferns and leaves" for her to work, and she hoped a rich American might buy it.[102] Except for the rich Americans, Lily felt the United States was "closed" to her because of its new high protective tariff.[103] Willie thought embroideries on AE's designs would be bought up by Americans "in quantities" and urged Lily to visit AE to see if he had drawings or paintings "that could be adapted."[104]

The break with Baggot Street was a substitute for the complete separation from Lollie that Lily had wished for years earlier, and it was one that in her view should have come sooner. "I never should have taken up the work after my illness," she told Ruth.[105] Now she would not be required to draw upon her limited physical energy. Before she could embroider, her materials needed to be stretched and marked, but Lily was unable to stoop, a necessary movement, so Sara Hyland agreed to do all the stretching and marking, Lily then sitting quietly at the frame in Gurteen Dhas and producing the finished work.[106] Since there was no pressure to do so, she went into Cuala once a week at her leisure and talked with her girls, who sought work on their own behalf and were paid a third of the price of whatever work of Lily's they could sell. To help them get started, the ever generous Emmeline Cadbury made them a gift of the first three months' rent owed to Lollie.[107] "I think now going into town will regain the old feeling of adventure and holiday it had in the old days when Cuala was at the cottage," Lily wrote to Ruth.[108]

Business was bad everywhere, as the worldwide depression was making its mark, and Cuala was not exempt from its effects. Lily was partly saved by her reputation. At the Arts and Crafts Exhibition in June 1932, her three Stations of the Cross, the ones done on speculation for Willie, were bought by "a rich American,"[109] who ordered eleven more to make up the full set.[110]

The rich American lady had bought herself a bargain, for the three Stations at the exhibition took first prize in the embroidery section; the judge, an expert from England, declared Lily's work "to be of exceptional high standard and beauty."[111] Lollie's nose was out of joint when she learned of the award. She was informed at Cuala early in the day but didn't tell her sister about it when she went home that night, leaving Lily to get the news from the secretary of the exhibition. "Jealousy is a disease," Lily wrote to Ruth for the hundredth time, though she knew making the remark would not cure Lollie. Lily received the news with satisfaction. "I rather expected to get the award as my work is easily the best there." Later Lollie learned she herself had won a medal for hand-printed books, so her envy subsided somewhat. Jack Yeats won two prizes at the same exhibition, one for a landscape, the second for a figure,[112] so the Yeats reputation continued undiminished.

If Lily's troubles with the Cuala girls in the embroidery department stemmed from her compassion for their possible loss of employment, Lollie's were of a different kind. She had to endure her
brother's selection of Mario Rossi's *Pilgrimage to the West,* in which
the author described Willie "as a big blue-eyed blond," being
obviously "not an observer but a gatherer of impressions," as Lily
put it. Willie refused to have the mistake corrected, since a poet
and philosopher had made it.[113] Lollie continued to run up an
overdraft every year.[114] WBY was exasperated by her failure to make
a go of what he thought should have been a profitable enterprise.
"The Press is going through a bad time," Lily told Ruth, "and all
she says is that she doesn't care. Willy said to me once that Lolly
never grows." She repeated her old charge: "The last Cuala book is
no better than the first." Lily diplomatically decided not to tell
Willie of her sister's habits at Cuala: "she never puts her teeth into
the work, barely reads the proofs, fiddles and fritters away her
day."[115] WBY tried discussing the Press with Lollie by telephone
but got into an argument with her instead.[116]

The issue involved on that occasion was basically Lollie's neglect
of the Press. The "lunacy" over her supposed sweetheart and her
"general childishness," as Lily called it, had meant she had not
given her mind to her work "for some years." WBY had ideas, one
of them a suggestion for a new set of broadsides, with a poem by
him and illustrations. Lollie rejected it, then changed her tune and
said she had been in favor of it all along. "Did you ever hear such
nonsense?" Lily asked Ruth.[117] The *Broadsides* finally appeared from
1935 to 1937.[118]

There was difficulty about proofreading also. In the old days
Louis Purser had done it as a favor, but after the new swain displaced him in Lollie's affections, he was no longer called on. Lollie
would do the proofs and bring them to Willie, and there would
inevitably be a row. Lily suggested that in the future WBY have
one of the Press girls come out with the proofs.[119]

Sometime in 1933, May Courtney had to leave Cuala because
of her mother's illness, and for almost a year Sara Hyland was the
sole representative of the embroidery division at the Baggot Street
rooms. The time was a difficult one for her. She owed a great deal
to Cuala, she had told Lily, but since Lily had left "things were

very different, and she could never get on with Miss Lolly." Lily hoped May would return soon, and after May's mother died on Good Friday in 1934, Lily was optimistic. But May announced she would not return, so Lily found a partner for Sara in Maureen Franks, the eighteen-year-old daughter of their Dundrum neigh-bor. They were to continue the old arrangement, the two girls paying rent to Lollie for the use of their space but otherwise conducting their own business and acting as agents for Lily.[120]

Yet Lollie insisted on acting as the commander-in-chief, ordering the girls around and interfering with their work. She imposed petty restrictions on them, like refusing to let them use the telephone. When Lily and Sara wanted to discuss things on the telephone, they waited until the afternoon when Lollie was away giving painting lessons. When customers for embroidery came, Lollie would enter and "give her opinion" about the goods. "People don't like it," Lily told Ruth.[121] And Lollie annoyed her older brother in the usual way by accepting for private publication a book of poems by a young poet, J. Lyle Donaghy, who was unable to pay for the work and therefore caused Cuala a further loss.[122]

Maureen Franks proved less forbearing than May. On one occasion Maureen's mother brought the Lord Mayor of Dublin into Cuala late in the day after Lollie had left. He looked at the Press and inspected the embroidery. Later he sent a messenger to buy Lily's embroidered picture, "The Abbey Theatre," but bought no books. Lollie was furious because she hadn't been consulted in the matter. She "refuses to see that the Franks can ask who they like into their workroom," Lily told Ruth, "and that it is no business of hers. She thinks she must be told of every move."[123]

Sara Hyland finally told Lily that she had had enough: "the strain of Lolly was more than she could stand any longer." She announced that as of 1 January 1935, she was leaving, but at the same time she agreed to do embroidery for Lily on commission.[124] Maureen Franks carried on alone, then quit after less than a year on the job. Lollie "got a shock," not realizing she herself was the reason for Maureen's leaving Cuala.[125] Adding to poor Lollie's excitability and unhappiness was that at precisely the time her ascendancy at Cuala was being assaulted, the aging Don Juan who had jilted her was in London marrying a young lady in her twenties.[126]

So from late 1934 on, the Cuala rooms were cleared of everyone but Lollie and her own staff. She became "less irritable," though she continued to show the same insensitivity as ever to those around her. If it was raining when she left Gurteen Dhas for Cuala, she did not hesitate to call Mr. Franks and ask for a ride into town in his car, despite her behavior toward the Frankses in the matter of the Lord Mayor and of Maureen.[127] Lily's embroideries were still available there, but after the departure of Maureen and Sara, almost no embroidery was sold at the Baggot Street building;[128] by the first week in May after Maureen left, only one picture had been disposed of.[129]

Willie encouraged Lily to keep producing her embroidered pictures, and she agreed: "I feel better with a needle in my hand."[130] When a small order to mend some old regimental flags came, Sara returned to Cuala to do the work, renting the old room temporarily.[131] But when a big order came from the Irish Free State, for three military flags, Sara didn't know whether she wanted to do the work or not because of Lollie's presence. "Sara works in a corner of my old room, the printers spread out over the rest. They don't make things easier for her, and Lollie wants a big percentage of the work." Lily decided not to advise Sara but to stay silent and let her make up her own mind.[132] An agreement with Lollie was finally struck, by which Sara would stay in the corner of Lily's old room, and Lollie would get 10 percent of the proceeds on sales. As the flags brought £50 each, the deal was profitable for all parties.

When unexpected orders continued to come for Sara, Lollie told Lily that "her girls resented" the sales "very much," a story Lily regarded as fiction. "Her girls have some common sense and ballast in spite of her bad influence."[133] Lily got little willing cooperation from her sister. "If I ask Lolly to bring a piece of linen for me from Cuala that Sara has marked a design on, Lolly mentions at intervals all evening how heavy it made her case and how it made her miss her bus, etc., etc."[134]

Lollie's ways didn't change. Since Rose's death Maria had been the lone servant in Gurteen Dhas. She too was growing old and feeble, so a young girl, Mary Cronin, was brought in to help her out. "Lolly had a maddening way of keeping Mary up in her room for hours on Saturday, looking at her clothes, dusting her books," and otherwise failing to recognize that Mary was there to help Maria, "not attend on Miss Lolly." At Cuala the girls had com-

plained that "one of them is always 'in attendance on Miss Lolly,' "
and so she had "the habit," becoming accustomed to personal service.[135] "In Cuala she really does very little," Lily reported to Ruth,
relying on what the girls and Sara told her, "just potters about, and
always has a girl to wait on her."[136]

Her business practices hadn't changed either. An announcement of a forthcoming Cuala book, *Essays 1931–1936,* by W. B.
Yeats, gave the price as twelve shillings and sixpence. The notice
had to be corrected in ink: *"Note:* Since this announcement was
printed, more Essays have been added and we have had to increase
the price.—E. C. Yeats." The price had been corrected, also in
ink, to "15/-."[137] Lollie was careful to assign responsibility for the
change. She wrote to Philip Sherman, the American collector: "Of
course people will blame me for not printing the right price on the
announcement, but when it was printed we had, we understood,
all the MS. Just lately my brother has added 2 long essays which
delays the book, but makes it a better book, so I cannot complain
—and the way of poets is always a little disconcerting to the poem
publisher."[138]

The pattern never changed for Lily: occasional sales at Cuala,
occasional commissions from people who knew her work, total
proceeds so small as to be negligible. In the spring of 1937, Willie
again tried to help her as he had done two decades earlier, by giving
her a design, by Diana Murphy, of "The Land of Youth." Lily was
skeptical of it but in no position to reject it. "It is queer and
modern, but I am going to do it at once," she told Ruth. Willie
would try to sell it for her, and his arrangement with her guaranteed her no loss. He would pay her £5 for each finished piece she
gave him, and she would refund the sum if the picture was sold.
He planned next to give her a design of "Innisfree,"[139] and paid her
£5 on account when she had finished it, hoping a rich American
would buy it and the others for a higher price.[140] He ended one
letter to her with the words: "I am doing enough for Lolly by
finding her books, etc., to publish. I cannot afford more than
that."[141]

Willie discovered that Lollie was continuing to run up an overdraft at the bank, and that she was dipping without permission
into one of the two accounts at the bank, in violation of an earlier

agreement. A Mr. Scroope of the bank wrote Willie in early December 1937 with the alarming news. WBY responded by guaranteeing that the overdraft would remain fixed until the following 1 April, then asked if the bank would be willing to help him discipline Lollie by prohibiting her from drawing on the second account. "This will make no difference to you," he wrote Scroope, "but will help me very much. I want to get into the heads of the various workers at Cuala that henceforth they can make their business a success without borrowing from anybody." He told him that when he returned to Ireland in April 1938, he would present him with "a scheme for the gradual reduction of the overdraft." [142]

Lollie blamed not herself but Willie for the increase in debt, which had again reached £800, started, she told James Healy, when her brother became ill in 1936 and one of his books was delayed as a result. He had also promised two books for 1937 but had only delivered one. [143] She told an American correspondent that she thought Willie had finally realized the difficulty to her "if books are delayed." She had been put in an impossible position. "One cannot (a *magician* could *not* do it) run Cuala on Prints and Cards alone—and that is practically what *I* had to do this last (1937) year." [144]

So Willie realized some drastic restructuring was needed at the Press, and from 1937 until his death in 1939, he engaged in precise maneuvers to change the system at Cuala so that it would function after he was gone. His health was bad, and he correctly foresaw that he would probably not live much longer. When he hinted to Lollie that some changes would have to be made, she agreed enthusiastically, not realizing that her aims would be incompatible with his. She thought he ought to relinquish his position as editor and give it to someone with whom she could work more amicably. His goal was to reduce her powers and assume more of them himself, passing them on to a successor he would name.

The successor he had in mind was F. R. Higgins, a minor poet, whose *Arable Holdings* had been published by Cuala in 1933. To lay the groundwork for his scheme, he invited Lollie to consult with him about Cuala's future. The first of their meetings took place at WBY's Fitzwilliam Square residence on 28 November 1937, while Higgins was in America. Willie would tell her at the time only

72. William Butler Yeats, about 1937. *Courtesy of Anne B. Yeats.*

that a scheme was in the works but withheld details. He wrote Edith Shackleton Heald about the expected meeting: "Her eyes will be like snails eyes for curiosity but I will tell her nothing until Higgins returns from America." [145]

The meeting of the brother and sister went as one might expect. He asked searching questions about the operation of the Press, which she could not satisfactorily answer, and about the habits of work at the Press, which she defended. She put forward her own scheme for a successful enterprise. "What Cuala needs," she wrote, "is another Director (or Editor if you prefer to use the term) as well as yourself. . . . You want someone who understands the *purely practical side*, the daily working of the place. You say *yourself* that you do not understand the practical side, yet you will not listen to me, and I *do* understand *that side* of Cuala. I don't want to worry you more. *No, I want to take the worry of the thing off your shoulders.*" She ended with a flourish of diplomacy: "Do think over my idea of another Director for Cuala, *to take* the *practical part* off you. You are the *Inspirer*. The whole thing comes from you." [146] The unspoken part of her message, the subtext Willie or anyone else could easily divine, was that Lollie wanted another director who would be favorable to her. [147]

Despite his poor health and the doctor's insistence that he rest, WBY took spirit from the contest with Lollie, whom he called "my excitable sister." "I enjoy the struggle," he told Dorothy Wellesley. "Cuala is the one outpost of chaos left in my life." [148] To Lollie it was her fortress of stability, which she now saw under assault. [149] The contest was an unequal one, for Willie held all the cards.

The effect on Lollie of the uncertainty of affairs was devastating. She wrote on the last day of 1937 to George of a sleepless night in which horrifying visions came to her: "Trains rushed at me belching smoke and sparks. . . . In came a man with a red face—and his long moustache suddenly burst into flame!!" [150]

Having arranged matters temporarily to his own satisfaction, but leaving Lollie dangling like a condemned man on the trapdoor, Willie took off in early January 1938, for the south of France, where the weather was good for his assorted ailments, the "fatal four disorders" (as Ann Saddlemyer has called them) that were to cause his death a year later. He and George found a place at Cap Martin, the Idéal Séjours, "the perfect hotel," he called it, "small, cheap, clean, in the midst of the country." From there he planned further jobs for his sisters, for Lily a Diana Murphy design for *The Happy Townland,* for Lollie an experimental new kind of publication that would prove to be *On the Boiler,* the first in a projected series of miscellaneous prose observations that WBY compared to Ruskin's *Fors Clavigera.* He thought he could "make Cuala prosperous" by publishing one such book "bi-annually," causing his enemies to "hit back" and giving him "the joy of answering them." [151]

Not till Willie returned to Dublin in June 1938 did he fill in the blanks for Lollie. F. R. Higgins would be brought in as a new director, groomed to take WBY's place. Higgins had just returned from America and, Willie said, had an "expert knowledge of printing, etc." Cuala would be turned into a limited company (the same kind of arrangement Lollie had written to John Quinn about years before) with Willie and Higgins as directors. Whether WBY chose Higgins with malice aforethought is hard to know, but he could not have found anyone less temperamentally in tune with Lollie; the two "were so rude to each other that they could not even talk to each other on the phone." [152]

Under the new scheme Cuala would continue to produce its two hand-printed books every year but otherwise would act as publisher only, all printing to be farmed out. The embroidery business would continue as before, with casual work done by Lily and Sara. Lollie would no longer be subject to only her brother's editorial judgment but would have to face a board of directors. [153] Another friend of WBY's, Frank O'Connor, was brought in as adviser to the Press. [154]

At first Lollie didn't realize fully what the changes had wrought on her own position. She wrote cheerfully to James Healy in October, 1938 about the new order.

> At last I have my wish. I wanted badly some such arrangement. It is not perhaps *quite* what I wanted, but I think it will serve, and I will not be in future under such a *strain* as I will share the responsibility [of] Cuala with 3 other Directors, W. B. Yeats, Mrs. W. B. Yeats, F. R. Higgins. The company will not actually be in legal existence till the end of this month, legal formalities etc to be attended to. I *liked* the new auditor, F. R. O'Connor, FSAA, 10 Westmoreland St. [155]

Two weeks later her tune had changed.

> So far things instead of being *better for me are far worse.* I now simply am *advised* to do this and that by Mr. F. R. Higgins and Mrs. W. B. Yeats. W. B. is in London. I *have* to object to some

things and say *what I think*. Really the trouble is that they know nothing at all as yet about the working of a place like Cuala. . . . They appointed a new auditor without consulting me, and so on and so on. I being like W. B. a natural fighter *do* hold my own at the Directors meetings—but I feel ill and exhausted in consequence. *They just want to sweep me aside.* . . . All is so delayed waiting for meetings to make any decisions, printing of new paper also all held up, and the new auditor has done nothing at all. I half wish I had left matters as they stood.[156]

When she discovered that O'Connor was not doing his work in a manner she thought proper, she revised her story to James Healy of how his appointment had come about:

They appointed him Auditor of the new company *at our first meeting*. I felt it was useless to protest. The man was sitting there. I did open my mouth to protest, and Mrs. W. B. put her hand on mine to keep silent. W. B. was of course in an irritable mood —*not at all well*—so she may have felt it best to let things go through, and *I subsided.*[157]

WBY spent two months in London, then returned in the fall of 1938 for his last visit to Dublin. When he and Lily met, both were aware of the effects of their years. As they sat in armchairs facing each other at his home in Fitzwilliam Square, their feet on a stool between them, he indirectly revealed his awareness of his condition, telling her he had written a poem about his wish to be buried in the churchyard at Drumcliff, where his great-grandfather Parson John Yeats had preached a hundred years earlier. He was pleased with the new arrangement at Cuala, "in high spirits," and they "laughed and discussed Lolly, not that she is a laughing matter," Lily told Ruth. Now she would have "less power" and be unable "to act off her own mad hat any more."[158]

Yet, as usual, Willie was not altogether fair to Lollie. Board meetings were generally held once a week, but decisions were not often made, and those discussed in private between Willie and Higgins were not always shared with Lollie.[159] By November she had worked herself "into a frenzy" over the new arrangement. Lily, who wanted peace in the house, tried to work up the courage to ask her not to discuss Cuala until after Christmas but didn't dare. "She comes in," she told Ruth, "and pours out all sorts of nonsense, imaginary wrongs. I can't discuss it with her because one cannot even discuss the weather with her. She will go off the rails if she is not more careful and cooler. The whole truth is that she hates anyone to have any say but herself. It all lies in that nutshell." [160]

When Willie left Dublin in late October for the last time—leaving George to work out details about Cuala with Lollie—Lollie felt totally isolated. With her brother she could at least quarrel. Higgins refused to have anything to do with her. He was probably too busy with other matters to be much bothered by the day-to-day problems at Cuala; but to Lollie, whose own world was the whole world, the apparent snub was greeted with fury. She and Lily both wrote to Willie at Cap Martin in mid-January, 1939. Her letter stands in familiar contrast to Lily's. Lily wrote the kind of cheery, friendly letter she knew her brother would enjoy, mentioning the coming hundredth anniversary of their father's birth on 16 March 1939 and avoiding unpleasant subjects altogether. Lollie, unable to contain her anger and frustration, wrote in a different spirit. Although she knew Willie was seriously ill, she did not ask after his health, confining herself solely to complaints about her treatment by the new Cuala people:

I write this short note to ask you, can you write yourself to F. R. O'Connor—10 Westmoreland St. & F. R. Higgins you have his address. Neither of these gentlemen have kept any one of the promises I myself heard them make to you at the meeting held here in October.

(1) *I have received no Balance Sheet.*

(2) *The Press is idle.* I do not know what the next book is to be?

(3) *I get queries about "On The Boiler"*—and I have no idea how to reply to these letters. I rang up Mr. Higgins on two different days and each time Mr. Gorman said he was not at the Theatre and he had not seen him that day, but he offered to give him a message from me, and he wrote down my message. I saw him in the bus this morning, and he told me he had given my message to Mr. Higgins.

(4) We *have* the blocks for
"Art O'Leary"

but cannot print it as nothing was decided about *paper size, number of copies.*

If I had particulars of "On the Boiler" I *could* get orders.

When she wrote the letter, Willie had only seventy-two hours left to live, yet she ended it with a typical complaint. "I am very worried. Result, I got that violent pain again twice this week."[161] What Willie would have got had he read the letter is not known. One hopes that George kept it from him; its contents might have been enough to carry him off. It was dated 25 January 1939. Willie died on the twenty-eighth. With a single-minded devotion to her own interests, Lollie stayed consistent even in the face of her brother's approaching death.

She remained so even in the face of her own, which took place less than a year later. The weakness in the heart she had first suffered in 1930 after the devastating rejection by the Cork suitor returned in force in 1938, and the unusual stresses placed upon it after she understood WBY's plans for Cuala may have led to its collapse. As early as June 1938, she complained to George Yeats that the bad weather "presses on my heart," and told her she had to "go as slow" as she could.[162] A couple of months later she gave George a vivid description of a heart seizure while she was at a hotel in Kilkeel: "I got that violent pain I sometimes get across my chest —just as I was getting ready for dinner except to throw my dress over my head when it came on. I just sat on my bed and endured it, and got some brandy I had in my case, still it went on just as violent, and the gong rang, and *I couldn't go down.* Suddenly it dimmed away, and I was able to slip on my dress and go down." "I live *really in fear* of it," she told George.[163] After Willie's death she got chest pains on every day when a board meeting was scheduled.

Whether Willie and George intended cruelty to Lollie, the dealings at Cuala could only have added to her anxieties and the physical consequences that flowed from them. The minutes of Cuala after the reorganization trace the development of the rising pressures on her. On 6 October 1938 she had been ordered to close her accounts and have them audited, a slap at her management of finances. On 2 November the directors ordered that a record of all lodgments at the bank be submitted at each meeting, "together with a record of weekly cash transactions," another slap at her cavalier practices. At the second meeting after WBY's death, on 21 March 1939, it was ordered that "no privately printed book orders [were] to be taken except with the approval of the Directors." A month later the directors declared "unsatisfactory" her method of keeping account of the girls' working hours and demanded a "precise record" in the future. When Lollie told them of her correspondence with James A. Healy, they passed a motion "that no Director or official of the Cuala Industries Ltd write on or verbally discuss the financial affairs of the company with any person or firm without the full consent of the Board." [164] As early as 1937 she had objected to the manner in which she was being treated—"I am not a child after all" [165]—yet the treatment continued, and the effect on the overstressed heart can hardly be exaggerated.

Lollie, ever the dreamer, continued to believe she exercised power. She wrote hastily to Healy after being told not to:

> I *really* write this note because I said to you (which is quite true) that I felt we will want more money to carry out the new ideas etc. *Well,* better not mention I said this. I find my co-Directors *rather difficult* so far—and so want to be careful not to "put their backs up." As new brooms they want I think *all* suggestions to come *from themselves,* so I ought not to have said this. I find that after a little time they adopt my suggestion. Just a question of waiting. [166]

George hoped to strengthen the directors by having Jack replace Willie on the board, but he flatly refused. [167] She and F. R. Higgins had to carry on most of the work of Cuala by themselves.

All during 1939, Lollie suffered recurrent heart spasms. In the spring she was forced to give up her painting classes. Her doctor told her she must take it easy, be less bothered by things. Some time later he happened to walk behind her for the length of a street. "She never relaxed a moment," he told Lily. [168] She was put to bed by her doctor and told to stay there. Lily describes what happened: "She had tabloids [*what some call tablets*] to take if the pain began. She ate the whole bottleful except those she lost behind the bed. Then she got it into her head that the tabloid was only chocolate and wrote at 8 a.m. one of her four-page letters to the doctor, enclosing a sample." [169] Lily found the tabloids "a joke, a maddening one." "She never knows how many she has taken." In mid-December Lollie's condition had so deteriorated that the doctor ordered her to betake herself to St. Patrick Duns Hospital. Despite being in pain, she insisted on dressing in her finest clothes, and she strode to the ambulance boldly, head held high. It was the last time the housebound Lily saw her alive.

At the hospital Lollie was "a very difficult patient" and "was so disturbing they thought they would not keep her." Lollie "laid out" the whole staff of the hospital from two in the morning till eight, and was so rude to the doctor that George, embarrassed, wrote him a letter of apology the next morning. "Never did I see a woman in such a temper," said the doctor. He and George spoke severely to her, and after that she quieted down for a while. "As usual," Lily told Ruth, "she has reversed the story and says that it was a good thing she made that row as now she is being properly looked after." [170] Yet she continued to cause trouble. Irritated by the dripping of a tap, [171] she jumped out of bed to tighten it and promptly fell to the floor, and the staff had to be called to get her back to bed. [172] On 16 January 1940 she died, not quite a year after the death of the brother she thought she resembled. [173]

But Lollie was not done. At her funeral in St. Nahi's Church, her coffin rested on a trestle in the middle aisle. One of its legs gave way, and the coffin slanted down at a grotesque angle. Nephew Michael Yeats turned to his sister Anne and said, "Just like Aunt Lollie, troublesome to the end," and she replied, "Aunt Lollie has to have the last word." Lollie went to her final resting place as she would have liked, not only the center of attention but complaining.

Lily was unable to attend her sister's funeral, just as she had been unable to attend the memorial service for Willie the year before in London. Her breathing problems had disabled her almost totally. Yet she could still embroider and write, and she continued to produce pieces to sell and to write weekly letters to her cousin Ruth Lane-Poole. She prepared a memorial pamphlet on Lollie, published by the Cuala Press later that year. Readers not familiar with the lives of the sisters might not notice that virtually the whole account is given over to a history of the Cuala Press rather than to Lollie. Less than a tenth of it mentions her personally, and in that portion the absence of sisterly affection is striking:

The Cuala Press has suffered an immeasurable loss in the death on January 16th, 1940, of its Founder Elizabeth Corbet Yeats. In the Spring of 1903 Elizabeth Corbet Yeats founded the Dun Emer Press. . . .

In spite of wars, depressions, and other adversities, Elizabeth Corbet Yeats's courage and determination kept the Press alive. . . .

About 1906 Elizabeth Corbet Yeats widened the scope of her Press, and began to specialise in hand-coloured prints, Christmas cards, and pamphlets. . . .

The Cuala Press pays tribute to Elizabeth Corbet Yeats for her great achievement and to her loyal helpers Eileen Colum, Esther Ryan, Maire Gill, who have worked with her for thirty years, without whose work the Press could not have succeeded. . . .

When Elizabeth Corbet Yeats started she had no knowledge at all beyond what she learned of the setting up of types in a few lessons at some woman's printing works in London. Of the Press work she knew nothing at all. . . .

Elizabeth Corbet Yeats did many of the designs for her sister's Embroidery and for the Christmas cards and prints, devoting to the development of the Industries all the artistic knowledge and feeling which she showed in her landscape painting and art teaching.[174]

Ruth Lane-Poole caught the lack of warmth at once, and Lily excused it by saying that she had written much more but that George had cut the tribute to save space and that Lily had not had a chance to read the proof. "I had to keep it impersonal," she said; and anyhow "it did what it set out to do, told of her death, the work of the Press, and announced its continuation. That was why it had to be got out at once, to show that the Press was to go on."[175] She told Ruth that in the letters of condolence from Lollie's friends, many noted "how distinguished she looked and how much they admired her, but no one said they loved her."[176] When she responded to a note from Philip Darrell Sherman, an American admirer of Cuala, she was equally reticent about Lollie, saving her favorable comments for George. "The end of the Press would have been very sad to her, and to me. It is living on with Mrs. W. B.

Yeats and others as directors. My sister-in-law is a great woman. . . . Elizabeth had a good life, I think, interesting and active, and she had great health." [177] Lily's real feelings are revealed by what she did not say. When she found the packet of letters from Lollie to her father, she declined to read them, fearing what she might find there. [178]

When Lollie died, the original Cuala Press, the one that grew out of Evelyn Gleeson's Dun Emer, in a sense died with her. With F. R. Higgins's death only a year after Lollie's, George Yeats had to manage Cuala virtually alone until new directors could be brought in. [179] Eileen Colum and others stayed on at the Press, and the operation continued. The business was almost devastated by the Second World War, which broke out four months before Lollie's death. Lily thought George so "full of courage and very active" that she would have succeeded "in normal times." How things might have turned out had Lollie lived she hated to imagine. "George and she never could have worked together," wrote Lily. "Who could work with Lolly? And Lolly could not have run the Press alone. She had no judgment in the choice of books. Willy did all that." [180]

Lily was able to help the Press in a striking way. She remembered that when Dun Emer had started almost four decades earlier, George Bernard Shaw had promised to provide a book someday, correcting the proofs himself "with a view entirely to the look of the page." George asked her to write Shaw and remind him of his pledge. The result was the Cuala publication of his letters to Florence Farr. [181]

William Butler Yeats had been an essential part of the original Cuala, along with Lollie, and with their deaths the most important part of the history of Cuala ended. By then its achievement had been noteworthy. Despite Lollie's inadequacies as a worker and businesswoman, despite the endless struggles to make ends meet, despite everything, she had produced a body of privately printed books that are still regarded as outstanding examples of their kind. [182] They could have been better had she been more devoted to her work and less to her person. Yet few private presses have equalled her balance of beautiful printing and significant literary text. She may not have received during her lifetime the kind of personal adulation she craved; but the continuing admiration for the products of her craft may please her if, as Lily believed, she has found a second existence in another place.[183]

If Lily had hope of immortality through her work, she has been less fortunate than Lollie for reasons already suggested: that embroidery is essentially an anonymous business, its work not being registered or even, in most cases, signed. Yet those who possess her work or have seen examples of it testify to its excellence. Even at the age of seventy-three she could boast of her powers. "It may be vanity," she told Ruth, "but I do not think my skill has left me at all. I find I am as sure as ever, know what I want and rarely take out any work."[184]

Lily was correct in her assessment that except for her physical affliction she was as strong and healthy as any of her long-lived Yeats ancestors. After Lollie's death she was able to take some pleasure out of life despite the continual pain. "The last three and a half years have been a wonder to me," she wrote Ruth on 26 July 1943, "and made me realize what the other part of my life had been." Yet she still felt weak all the time, and at one point she thought her heart might be "feeling the strain" of her breathing. The doctor told her she had nothing to worry about, that "anyone would be glad" to have her heart.[185]

Responsibility for her care was assumed partly by brother Jack but chiefly by George Yeats, WBY's widow. The newly reorganized Cuala gave Lily an allowance of £2.15 "for the good will and all our years of work." That sum added to her other income gave her £300 a year, which allowed for comfortable but not riotous living.[186] The Pollexfen shares held as security for the overdraft proved to be £70 short of what was necessary to clear the Cuala debt, and Lily, who had been left the shares by Lollie, had to sign them over. She also held herself liable for her sister's remaining personal debts, planning to sell Lollie's sketches to meet the obligation. "Her friends would I am sure like to have them in memory of her." None of the friends had ever appeared at Gurteen Dhas, for Lollie's social life was lived outside the home.[187] Ruth was left one of Lollie's paintings, which Jack chose for her. In sending it, Lily repeated her general view of Lollie as an artist. The sketch was "good," she said, but "she never advanced. Her last sketches were no better than her early work, and the last Cuala books no advance on the first. I think she had a curious lack of interest in whatever she did, so busy with herself and merely personal trifles."[188]

George had been careful to make a will years earlier in which Lily and Lollie were specifically excluded as possible guardians for her children, and for a long time, perhaps mostly during the six years when she and everyone else believed Lily was faking her symptoms, thought her "manipulative" and "devious."[189] Yet George found Lily a cheerful patient who made few demands, and shortly after Lollie's death said to her, "Do you know, I am very fond of you?"[190]—a remark that pleased the worried invalid.

Lily reached her seventy-seventh birthday on 25 August 1943, full of spirit. A few days later she suffered a stroke that not only sent her to bed for the rest of her life but also disabled her right hand, "a scurvy trick of fate," she called it,[191] making further embroidering impossible. She was told by the doctors that she would never return even to the unpleasant condition she had learned to endure.[192] She was afraid she would become a burden to those around her. Ruth wrote a revealing letter of sympathy. "You have been no trouble ever to anyone in your life, and it was always a hope that you never would be, and I expect now it distresses you to have so much done for you, but . . . it is done by those who love you, and I am sure you expect the minimum, always thinking of the other person."[193] She lingered more than five years, until the fifth of January (the fatal month for the Yeatses)[194] of 1949, her mind always active, her weekly letters to Ruth, now dictated, continuing to the end.

The long enterprise begun so doubtfully as Dun Emer in 1902 and restarted so hazardously as Cuala in 1908 had survived for more than forty years. The industries managed by Lily and Lollie during the glorious days of the Irish Renaissance constitute a distinctive part of the artistic life of the Dublin world during the most exciting period of Ireland's modern history. That such an achievement should have come from two troubled spinster sisters—one trapped in a life she hated, the other trapped in the life of the first—is not the least of its glories.

Considering her views, it is not surprising that when Lily wrote of her own approaching death, she invariably spoke of once again seeing her father, with whom she wanted to spend eternity. Her mother was not mentioned, nor was Lollie. Lily was vague about the precise topography of Heaven, but she expressed the hope that it would include a section reserved for neurasthenics.[195] Having endured Lollie for so long, Lily was certainly within her rights in wishing that God would place the two of them in different parts of his eternal world.

7

Jack B. Yeats

I am always thinking about Jack. He gives no sign.
You never know how he is. I used to think he was always
happy, and now I don't know what to think.
　　　　　　　　　—John Butler Yeats to Isaac Yeats,
　　　　　　　　　　　　　　　　　　　　3 April 1916

Jack was quite right when he would not stay in the
art schools and become a virtuoso (at the time I did not
think so), and so he is working out his own technique
by painting his convictions. A man learns to write by
having something to say. A man learns painting in the
same way.
　　　　　　　　　—John Butler Yeats to John Quinn,
　　　　　　　　　　　　　　　　　　　14 March 1911

In the early 1950s two American tourists were being shown about
Dublin by an Irish friend. On Grafton Street the friend stopped
to exchange pleasantries with a stooped, slender, elderly man, then
turned to the women to introduce him. "I'd like you to meet Jack
Yeats," he said. "Oh," the first woman responded, "are you related
to the famous poet named Yeats?" The other woman noticed how
Jack Yeats's face stiffened, the muscles in his tight jaw working.
Their guide explained hastily that Mr. Yeats was indeed the brother
of the famous William Butler Yeats but was also himself a distinguished painter. They spoke a few more words and passed on.[1]
　The second woman was a perceptive witness to a display that
must have occurred many times before. Jack Yeats had said nothing
in complaint, his few remarks to the women couched in polite
language. What he thought privately nobody could tell, for he

seldom let people know what he felt. The irony, one of many involving Jack Yeats, is that he was at the time one of Ireland's most distinguished artists, whose paintings commanded high prices and whose fame in the world of art—at least in the Irish and European world—like his brother's in the world of poetry, was considerable. In the decades since his death, the value of his paintings has risen astronomically, and today he is recognized as an important painter of the twentieth century.

Yet in the Yeats family he was always the youngest child, the "kid brother," obscured during most of his life by the dazzling light of his poet brother's reputation. He was accustomed to the treatment accorded him by the American visitor. In late 1937, a little more than a year before WBY's death, another American lady on a visit to Dublin "gushed up" to Jack and said she had longed for years to meet him. Hardened by decades of misidentification, he tried to steer her in the right direction. "It must be my famous brother," he replied. "No," she said. "It is you, and you are just as famous." Jack, unprepared for such a response, managed only a lame reply, "Well, he has kept his hair and I haven't.²

His sister Lily, who had spotted Jack's genius and predicted his future fame when most of the world was unaware of his talents, saw the problem early. Jack was "rather put in the shade by his big brother," she told her cousin Ruth.³ One of his pictures was accepted by the National Gallery in London when he was in his fifties, and Lily thought it a good development. "He wants some success, being rather shadowed by Willy," she wrote Ruth.⁴

Adding to Jack's annoyance was his brother's haughty attitude toward him. Willie was the great poet, the man of international fame, aware of his high position in the literary world. Jack, the brother six years younger, might of course be a good draftsman and possibly a promising artist but was obviously not in the same class as he. Members of the family wrote seldom about the tensions within their group—except of course for Lily's therapeutic complaints to Ruth about Lollie—but the few passages that occur testify to the difficulties between the brothers. John Butler Yeats wrote to Lily in 1909 about a visit her brothers had made to Lady Gregory's estate at Coole. "I would like to know about *Jack and Willie,* though I don't suppose things there will ever alter." Clearly "things" had never been good. "I am perfectly certain Willie is very fond of Jack," the old man continued, "and I suppose Jack has an affection for Willie. Of course Willie irritates Jack as he does many people, whereas Jack never irritates anyone."[5] In his own sharply perceptive way, the father had succinctly described both the relationship and the personalities. Willie, airily confident of his own importance and of his genius and less than appreciative of the talents of others, annoyed people. Jack was universally liked. JBY's apprehensions about their relationship never ended. When Willie visited Jack and his wife in 1915, Papa wrote to Jack: "I would like you and Cottie to tell me about Willie's visit. Did you invite him or did he come of himself? Did you make him happy and were you and Cottie happy?" When he received Jack's report, he was relieved. "I am so glad you and Willie had a good time together. A good time together is the secret of friendship and affection and everything that makes life worth living."[6] Such instances were obviously rare, for the extensive record of the Yeatses' correspondence reveals few examples of the brothers' being in the same place at the same time, and there were few letters between them.[7] Yet Jack, with every right to feel irritated by his brother's cavalier attitude, was unfailingly good-natured, polite, and inoffensive. Hardly a critical word about Willie appears anywhere in Jack's reminiscences. Still, it may not be insignificant that, trivial though the matter may seem, Jack designed bookplates for his two sisters but not for his brother.[8] When in the 1930s he sought a literary agent, he made it clear he would not consider A. P. Watt, who handled his brother's writings. "They are my brother's agents," he explained without further comment, "and I would like a separate agent."[9]

His nephew Michael Yeats, son of the poet, has noted that Jack thought himself as great an artist as his brother was a poet and resented the fact that he commanded much less attention than the world-famous WBY.[10] As late as 1942, when Jack had long since been acknowledged as an original painter, Sir Kenneth Clark refused to separate the two. In a brief critical article on Jack's paintings,[11] he felt it "irresistible" to make a comparison with "the great poet, his brother." WBY had found his best voice, Clark averred, only after a long period of trial and error, "passing through labyrinths of myths and learning." Jack had arrived at the stage "in a leap." His brother began in complexity and ended in simplicity; Jack reversed the process. Clark gratuitously offered his opinion that as a result WBY's work has "a certainty which his brother's painting lacks." Jack was annoyed at the article. "Always a pull-back," he complained to Terence de Vere White;[12] he was not allowed the dignity of independent existence as an artist but had to be judged in comparison to his brother—his apples against Willie's oranges—where no comparison was really valid. "One can see why [Jack] Yeats was not enamoured of Clark's written verdict," White commented dryly.[13] It is no wonder that the "kid brother" felt keenly the irrelevant comparisons; and it is a mark of his inner strength that he made no direct public complaints about the linkage. His feelings were shown without ambiguity in a remark he made a few years later to a critic preparing a catalogue of his works. "I don't want it said about my work that it is pretty good for an Irishman. . . . You hear too often, 'This is a fine work by a man with a wooden leg, or a man with one ear.' " A work should be judged on its merits, he made clear to the critic, "not that this is the work of an Irishman, a national figure, a playwright and the brother of a great poet, but that this is just painting."[14]

Jack could hardly have failed to resent some of the circumstances surrounding the honorary degree awarded him by Trinity in 1946. The citation began with a quotation from Horace, "as painting, so with poetry," and went on: ". . . one house in these last days has given us in a pair of famous brothers a perfect example of either art. . . . To honor the poet we assembled some years ago. He, alas, is no longer with us; but today we confer the same distinction on the painter."[15] Yet when WBY was awarded his degree, Jack was not mentioned.

What Jack might have thought of his brother's appointment to the Senate of the Irish Free State is another of those mysteries his reticence prevents us from unlocking. For of all the Yeatses it was Jack who was the most radically nationalist in politics, supporting the cause of full independence. As early as 1898, when he attended the centenary celebration of the Rising of 1798, he had become a passionate Republican.[16] Willie, who urged others to action but shrank from it himself ("Did that play of mine send out / Certain men the English shot?"), whose connection with the Easter Rising of 1916 was purely verbal and after the event, supported the 1922 Treaty, which was regarded by many Republicans as a betrayal of all that the Rising had fought for, and was appointed to the Senate of the Free State as a reward. Jack, who refused to play an active part in politics, would not have been a candidate for such a post in any event. Yet WBY's appointment must have galled those like him who would not settle for less than complete liberation from the English crown.

Willie had been brought up chiefly by his politically moderate father, who all his life tried unsuccessfully to shape his eldest son to his own purposes. Jack, on the other hand, had spent the formative years of his life in Sligo with his terrifying grandfather William, of whom Lily and all other grandchildren were frightened. Jack was the only one who could speak to him [17] and the only one Grandfather William accepted as a companion. William Pollexfen was a dedicated Unionist who carried a gun at his side—even during church services—against a possible uprising by the Sligo people. He had no sympathy for even the mildest form of Home Rule. Yet Jack, who grew up under his influence, became a radical Republican. The only male of the Yeats family to have been born outside Ireland in two hundred years, [18] he became the most Irish of them all.

As the son of an artist, Jack might have been expected to fall under the influence of his father's theories and methods. Indeed, on several occasions he proclaimed that he became an artist only because his father had been one. Yet the son painted in an entirely different way from his father. Not only were their techniques not the same: JBY painted portraits almost exclusively, his early work in landscape being merely for training; his subjects include almost everyone of importance in the Ireland of his time. [19] The son painted landscapes and dramatic scenes, almost never portraits.

Jack Yeats was the fifth child and third son of JBY and Susan Pollexfen, born at the Fitzroy Road house in Regent's Park, London, on 29 August 1871. There would be another child, Jane Grace, within a year, but she and the second son, Robert Corbet, both died young. The four survivors who grew up as a family were Chesterton's "Willie and Lily and Lollie and Jack." The gap of six

73. Jack Yeats as young child. *Courtesy of Michael B. Yeats.*

years between WBY and Jack was crucial to their relationship. Jack
was always the baby in the family, pampered by the girls, adored
by the grandparents, almost disregarded by the older brother.
When Willie entered his teens Jack was only seven, when he
reached manhood in 1886 Jack was still a boy of sixteen. Though
the difference in age should have meant less and less as the years
went on, still Jack could never escape the feeling that his older

brother regarded him as a person of no particular importance. Indeed, in the writings of William Butler Yeats, including his letters, one is aware of the mother and father and occasionally of Lily, but Jack's existence is hardly noticed.[20] The "things" that would never "alter" were present from the beginning.

For the first eight years of his life Jack grew up with his sisters and brother, first in the Fitzroy Road house in which he was born, then at Edith Villas in the North End, a small and uncomfortable house associated with the death of the youngest Yeats, Jane Grace. During the summers and on some holidays, he joined with them and his mother in visits to his Sligo grandparents while his father either traveled about Ireland to paint portraits or stayed in London to study with other artists.[21] In the summer of 1879 all the children stayed with their parents at Branscombe in Devon, and there Jack showed his talents for art as well as his comic spirit. As already noted, Lily writes in her scrapbook of his painting horses with black paint and of his drawing faces on big stones the sisters were using as dolls. When the sisters bathed the dolls, "off came the faces and Jack put them on again."[22] A short time later, at their new house in Bedford Park, all the children planted flowers in the garden. The others chose single plantings; Jack mixed a variety of seeds together to make "a comic exciting plot."[23]

Shortly after the move to Bedford Park, Jack was sent off to Sligo to live with his grandparents. Save for at least one visit to London (in the summer of 1880, when Willie and Lily stayed in Sligo), he remained there, living under the same roof with his grandparents, for eight years.[24]

So from the age of eight to sixteen Jack lived apart from the rest of his family. The stay was to have vital consequences for him and his relationship with them. By the time he returned to live with them in London, they were all busily employed at studying, writing, or keeping house, and he spent much of his time at art school, so that, as Lily noted later, "we really did not grow up with him."[25] The intimacy that comes from living together under the same roof, shared by Willie and his two sisters, was denied Jack, and the denial erected a kind of wall between him and them.

His long boyhood stay in Sligo was to prove the seminal epoch of his life. There, among the surrounding hills, lakes, and ocean

74. Jack Yeats, about 1880. *Courtesy of Michael B. Yeats.*

inlets, among the streets of Sligo with the bridges across the narrow
Garavogue River, among the shopkeepers and priests and sailors
and Irish peasants, among the stables and the race tracks with
their noble horses, he developed what Marilyn Rose has called his
"memory pools,"[26] rich waters of imagery from which he would
drink for the rest of his life and which constituted almost the sole
subject matter of his paintings and writings. There, as Lily put it,
he "gathered much that has made him."[27]

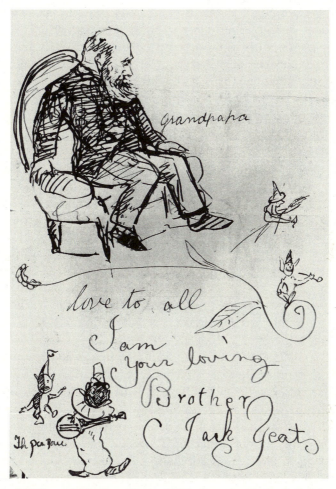

75. William Pollexfen, about 1881. Pen sketch by Jack Yeats, age ten. *Courtesy of Michael B. Yeats.*

He had his grandparents all to himself, for his Pollexfen aunts had all married and left the big house, and of the sons only Uncle George Pollexfen remained. Since George spent most of his time at the company branch office in Ballina, Jack saw little of him and seems not to have been influenced by him at all, in contrast to George's prominent place in the life of William Butler Yeats. In 1886 the Pollexfens left the spacious Merville and took a smaller house, Rathedmond. At both homes Jack was the only Pollexfen descendant in regular residence with his grandparents.

The person with whom he associated most was his grandfather William Pollexfen, he whose temper frightened everyone else in the family. Lily as a girl in Sligo felt terrified in his presence. He was moody and irascible, showing little affection for or interest in his grandchildren. But Jack was a special case. Like his sister Lily, and unlike Willie and Lollie, Jack was one of those people who are instantly likable; perhaps the Yeatsian gene that made his father such a delightful companion had providentially come to him.

People in Sligo remembered years later Jack and his grandfather riding together in a cart, once taking a detour to end up in front of a funeral procession that had blocked their way. He listened at the dining table as his grandfather talked with visiting sea captains of the Sligo Steam Navigation Company (owned by the Pollexfens). The conversation was not, Lily told Joseph Hone, "talk as the Yeatses understood talk" but was rather about "cargoes and ships."[28] He also attended school, to whose demands he paid little attention, sometimes ending up at the foot of his class.[29] Mostly he enjoyed a boyhood of wandering and observing, walking among the quays, meeting sailors from faraway ports, attending the horse races. He told Lily in later life that "when he was a boy he spent hours leaning on the bridge in Sligo spitting into the river, and he wishes he had spent many more hours."[30] And he continued drawing, one of his most fascinating sketches a portrait of his grandfather sitting in an overstuffed chair.[31] The sketch, like others, was included in a letter; all his life he decorated his letters with illustrations, some quite sophisticated.[32] His father, the specialist in the single subject, noted that except for rare instances like the sketch of William Pollexfen, Jack's drawings "were never of one object, one person, or one animal, but of groups engaged in some kind of drama." The tendency toward what Hilary Pyle calls "dramatic groupings," she says, was shown in his early love for dolls, for which he made a house. His interest in the dramatic interplay of people led directly to his later "miniature theater."[33]

Hilary Pyle gives us a vivid picture of the Sligo of Jack's boyhood and of his place in it:

He walked about the country roads, studying the country people, attending fairs, sports, circuses and races. . . . There were weekly markets in Sligo, instituted three centuries before: and four yearly fairs to which Yeats returned for many years afterwards. The race meetings were known as "four pound nineteens," for the prizes not reaching the value of five pounds came under no official rules. Jockeys in brilliant striped costumes lined up on their mounts by the flags and sped off around the poles marking the edges of the strand, at times ending in the sea, if one of the great mists arose. On the shore itself were groups of long low tents, made of bent saplings covered with sacking, where poitín, the twenty-four hour whiskey, was consumed in quantity. Vendors of various kinds travelled the track, with toffee-apples and trinkets; and ballad singers would give their performances, and sell their printed ware.[34]

Not long after his permanent move to London in 1887, Jack returned to Sligo for a vacation, staying with Uncle George at Rosses Point. "It's a jolly place and I get plenty of bathing and that sort of thing." He went to the races on the Strand and wrote Sarah Purser that "after every race the people went to fight," and he drew her a picture of the opposing groups, the winning and losing jockeys surrounded by their followers, squaring off; and he reported going to Lissadell, home of the Gore-Booths, the principal gentry of the neighborhood, for a cricket match.[35] It was standard behavior for Jack: watching people in action, then making sketches of them.

When Jack settled in with his family in London in the autumn of 1887, he was already a practiced artist, and surely few of his craft have had better early preparation for their careers. Out of his long and easy boyhood grew the entire subject matter of his lifetime's work. Almost at once he began drawing menus for local restaurants and submitting drawings to magazines. Through Sarah Purser's good offices, he sent a dozen menus to a friend of Lady Gore's, and Miss Purser bought some cards herself.[36] He was seventeen at the time, but even at that age he showed the persistence of the practiced businessman. He had sent "some hunting sketches" to the *Graphic,* he told Miss Purser, but if they weren't accepted he planned to submit them to the *Pictorial.*[37] His diligence and self-confidence as an artist proud of his wares and eager to be compen-

76. Sarah Purser (1848–1943). Pencil sketch by Josephine Webb. *Courtesy of Society of Friends, Dublin.*

sated for them stood in sharp contrast to his father's aimless drifting as a businessman. In the thirteen months ending December 1890, he earned at least £19.2.8.[38] From then until the end of his life he continued to make money from his art, and he showed from the beginning a sense of economy, a feeling for money, of which his uncertain father was totally innocent. When Frederick Langbridge offered Jack a commission to draw for him, Willie, assuming the role of agent, wrote him: "My brother will draw for you at the rates you name on the understanding that the amount increase if the venture prosper and that the lowest sum paid be 5/-." [39]

It was clear to the others in the household that William Pollexfen's terrifying personality had not rubbed off on Jack. Lollie's diary records Jack's antics, such as his arriving from Sligo with a pocket full of shrimp and his mimicking the actors after a visit to the theatre. Rose Hodgins, the Yeatses' maid, found him delightful; one of the neighbors called him "the Baby," because, she said, "he has such nice sleepy blue eyes." Willie wrote to Katharine Tynan about the humor of his seventeen-year-old brother at dinner: their cousin Geraldine Orr and Jack "kept up a continual joking together," and had "to be kept quiet almost by force." [40] Two small girls staying with the Yeatses at Blenheim Road, Edith Todhunter and Susan Orr (another cousin), wanted to marry Jack when they grew up.

This was the Jack most people saw, the Jack who inspired affection and friendship. But there was another Jack, who existed side by side with the first—the taciturn, private Jack, who never tipped his hand, never revealed what was going on in his mind. This was the Jack who continued to baffle his sisters for the rest of his life. "He is very reticent," Lily told John Quinn, "never talks of himself or his things." [41] "No one seems less mysterious than he does when you see him and talk with him," she told their cousin Ruth, yet one never knew what he was really thinking. [42] One had to consider his actions and make assumptions.

One of the first such actions was his treatment of his mother. Shortly after Jack joined the family at the mean little dwelling in Eardley Crescent, Susan Pollexfen Yeats suffered the first of the strokes that were to bring about her continuing invalidism and end with her death in 1900. She was sent to stay with one of her sisters in Denby and suffered another stroke. Not until the rest of the family had settled in the Blenheim Road house in Bedford Park was she able to be moved, and when she settled there it was to be for the rest of her life. JBY, at the lowest depth of his always low financial resources, could not afford a doctor or nurses. Lily, reflecting on her mother's troubles years later, thought that in a later time her blood pressure could have been treated with medication, but at the time "nothing could be done." Nevertheless, Jack, the youngest in the family, with "his first earnings" hired a specialist to visit his mother.[43] When she died eleven years later, it was he who took charge of the purchase and placement of the plaque to her memory in St. John's Church in Sligo;[44] and for the six months following her death he was unable to work.[45] It is possible to read into his actions a silent rebuke of his hapless father, who stood by and did nothing. They also suggest that Jack, alone in the family, felt a special affection for his mother. Yet he revealed no more of those feelings in words than he did about other personal matters.

Another suggestive event is recorded in her diary by Lollie. Willie and his father had become engaged in a hot dispute over John Ruskin. The father, emotionally overwrought at a stage in his life when everything about him seemed to be crumbling, picked up a framed picture and hit Willie over the head with it, breaking the glass. It was an incident the father later forgot, burying it deep in a subconscious vault he did not wish to see unlocked. Willie remembered it all too well, and his brother and sisters were all aware of what had happened.[46] Shortly afterward the two had another dispute, and Papa challenged his son to a fight. As WBY remembered it, "He squared up to me, and wanted to box, and when I said I could not fight my own father replied, 'I don't see why you should not.' " Jack watched from the sidelines, and after JBY had "fled without speaking," Jack said to Willie, "Mind, not a word till he apologizes."[47] This, from a youth still in his teens, implies little sympathy with a father whom almost everyone regarded as a failure and whom the younger son must have regarded as a failure too. Since Jack played his cards close to the vest, one can never be sure of his inner feelings, but nowhere in his surviving writings is there any word of praise or affection for his father.[48] All his references to him are objective and noncommittal. Even when JBY wrote an approving article on Jack for the *Christian Science Monitor,* the son was not appreciative. Lily told her father she liked the article and that Jack did too, but that Jack had then added: "It is not all true."[49] Being Jack, he gave no further details, but the inference is that the father didn't know the son as well as he thought he did.

Both sons learned from their father's errors the necessity of placing a proper value on their work. Except for private acts of generosity, Jack insisted on payment for everything he did, and the surviving records make clear that he asked good prices and would not compromise. Jack attended an art school in South Kensington, for his father felt a complete education in technique (which he felt he himself had failed to get) was essential to any artist, and later at the Chiswick Art School in Bedford Park and the Westminster School. But, in Hilary Pyle's words, he "had sufficient individuality to avoid the stamp" and never completed a formal course at any of them. He also joined a volunteer military unit, the 20th Middlesex Rifle Volunteer Corps in early 1889, an artists' regiment that gave him an opportunity to draw.[50] JBY admitted in 1908 that Jack had discovered "a style" of his own, "and perhaps he would not have if he had spent more time at art schools."[51] Jack from the beginning drew what he knew, the horses of Sligo, boxers in the ring, sailors on the quays, tradesmen in their shops, people in the streets. He submitted his drawings to magazines and had the satisfaction of seeing them reproduced. In 1892 he accepted a job in Manchester as a poster artist and stayed there till 1894, returning to Bedford Park for holidays whenever he could. It was unsatisfactory work, from which he felt he had learned nothing,[52] but it brought in money, and Jack knew that without the cash which a good sense of money produced, he might wind up like his unsuccessful father.

In 1892 came two important events: the first the deaths of his Pollexfen grandparents; the second his meeting a fellow art student, Mary Cottenham White, nicknamed "Cottie," whom he determined to marry as soon as he could declare himself financially independent. It was to establish his financial credentials that he took the work in Manchester. His two years there testify to his determination and diligence, and to his willingness to make sacrifices to achieve distant ends.

With his marriage to Cottie on 24 August 1894, his direct, daily association with his own family came to an end. By that time he had spent only a small fraction of his life as a member of the immediate Yeats group. After his sixth birthday he spent a total of only about seven years living in the same house with his parents and siblings, and five of these came during the Blenheim Road

77. Jack Yeats, about 1892. *Courtesy of Anne B. Yeats.*

years when all the children spent their days outside the home working: Lily at the Morrises' doing embroidery, Lollie teaching at
schools and private homes, and Willie writing for Irish and American publications and spending much of his time away from home
in pursuit of occult interests. The environment was not of the same
kind as it had been at Branscombe, with its childhood companionship, nor of the same importance.

Cottie told Jack that she was two years older than he, a difference not common in marriages of the time, but one that presented no obstacle to either. They were both artists, and their natures were perfectly compatible with each other's. Their marriage lasted, without known dissension or other difficulty, for almost fifty-three years, until her death in 1947. Not until her final days in the hospital did Jack learn the secret she successfully concealed from him for half a century, that she was not two years older than he but almost five.[53]

Cottie was the beneficiary of a small but more than adequate income from an annuity, out of which she made an allowance to her mother. Perhaps aware of her father-in-law's reputation with money, she had her lawyer draw up papers to remove her mother's portion from her own control. Her income was for life only, the corpus of the trust passing to other hands on her death.[54] It enabled the newlyweds to live without privation while Jack was developing his growing skills as a cartoonist, and Jack never considered it as his own property, diligently working instead to establish his own position and make his own living through his art.

The entry of in-laws into a family is always cause for apprehension. The other members of the Yeats family were never quite sure of their attitude toward Cottie, perhaps because they were unsure of hers toward them. Lily recorded years later that in all the years they had known each other, "We never had as much as a little tiff." The couple "exactly suited each other," she said, and her father always insisted that Cottie was "the perfect wife."[55] JBY called her "exceedingly clever artistically," possessing a talent for which "very few give her credit," but said she was "too timid to claim her rights."[56] She never "bullied" Jack or "anyone else," according to Lily.[57] But the uncertainty was always present. "I hope you liked Jack's wife," wrote JBY to Lady Gregory after the couple had visited Coole. "We liked her better every day. She is genuinely amiable and very intelligent."[58] There is an air of apology in his lines. Did he think Lady Gregory couldn't discover Cottie's qualities without his assistance?

Cottie, unassertive herself, was fiercely protective of her rights to her husband. Whenever the other members of his family tried to interfere, she erected a barricade between them, seemingly afraid "of her rights being infringed."[59] Lily told John Quinn that the members of the family were "on the most friendly terms with her," yet "she is always on the defensive with us, and we only go there when formally asked."[60] There is no record of any member of the family speaking to Jack about Cottie, a liberty he would certainly have met coldly, and no record of either of them ever having been even slightly dissatisfied with the other.

A daughter-in-law or sister-in-law might have had faults annoying to the family, like being overbearing, or being too interested in parties and money and in knowing important people; she might also have been open and free and companionable, as Willie's wife, George, was to prove later. Except for a compulsion to chatter and gossip, Cottie was none of these, but instead a determined wife who wanted only to be with her husband and protect him. She became an enigma to her in-laws, who could find no serious faults in her and yet could not draw her to the bosom of the family. She could on occasion flare up in defense of her husband, though such incidents were apparently rare. Only one suggestive sentence in a letter of Lily's hints at this aspect of her behavior: "I like her all the time," she told Ruth, "and never bear any malice after her attacks." The "attacks" were clearly defensive responses in her husband's interests. "I think she makes Jack happy," Lily continued, "and her house is well run and she gets on with her maids and never nags."[61]

All the members of the family except Lollie, who stayed at home with Mama, attended the wedding at the Emmanuel Church in Gunnersbury. The newlyweds settled in a house called "The Chestnuts," at Eastwort, Chertsey, Surrey, and stayed there until 1898, when they moved to Devon. Jack continued to send his drawings to any magazine that would accept them and also tried his hand at writing. The list of his drawings during this period, given in Hilary Pyle's biography, testifies to his diligence: it covers several pages. Many of the early drawings appeared in obscure publications, but by 1896 he had breached the walls of *Punch,* to which he continued to contribute for decades. His writings too, as listed in Hilary Pyle's index, are so numerous that if he were not today studied primarily as a painter, he would probably be the subject of doctoral dissertations for his writings,[62] which, how-

78. Mary Cottenham White (Mrs. Jack) Yeats ("Cottie"). Pencil by JBY. *Courtesy of Michael B. Yeats.*

ever, never made the impact on the public that his paintings did. Many will share the feeling of Terence de Vere White, who admired Jack as a person and who thought him a great painter: "I must confess an inability to appreciate either his books or his plays."[63]

He also tirelessly promoted his own works, not from flamboy-

79. Jack Yeats rowing a boat, about 1900. *Courtesy of Anne B. Yeats.*

ance or a desire for personal fame, but from a shrewd sense of the realities of life. He did good work, showed it to the world, and urged the world to buy it. Even when he allowed Maurice Bourgeois to reproduce his drawings in a book on Synge, he insisted that they be acknowledged as "reprinted from 'A Broadside,' Cuala Press, Dundrum, Ireland."[64] The man who was so likable and friendly, so comic, was also a sound and uncompromising businessman.

He was also always totally independent. Lady Gregory, who

had already set her sights on Willie Yeats and begun the long process of trying to reshape him to her design, was equally attracted to Jack, whose first exhibition (at the Clifford Gallery in London) she had attended in late 1897. The following year he came to Coole, but he resisted her blandishments, proving as private and unapproachable to her as he did to others who ventured to penetrate from the public man to the private. His father nevertheless thought he saw a change in Jack after the Coole visit. Not only had Lady Gregory given him sixty pounds (presumably for drawings), "but he has ideas, ambitions, hopes, that he never had before." Father admitted that his judgment was inferential. "I have had very little talk with him, but I gather this from his wife as well as himself."[65] At Coole, Jack preferred the company of the younger people, Lady Gregory's son Robert, with whom he fished, and T. Arnold Harvey, later to become Dean of St. Patrick's Cathedral and Bishop of Cashel and Cork. He joined in boat races on the lake, often in a boat in which he and Willie raced against Harvey and Robert Gregory and Robert's cousin.

He also became a good friend of John Masefield. Lily's recollection of Masefield's relationships with the family reveals much about the differences between the two brothers:

> We knew him when first beginning to write. He and Jack were great friends. I think he made himself known to W. B. by just ringing the bell at Woburn Place and asking if he might come in. He admired W. B. greatly and began giving him books. Then he met Jack and transferred his affections to him, took the books he had presented to W. B. from the shelves and gave them to Jack.[66]

In 1898, Jack and Cottie moved to Strete, near Dartmouth, in Devon. They rented a place while a cottage of his own design was being built.[67] He christened it "Snaile's Castle" ("Cashlauna Shelmiddy" in Irish), a small house with a separate studio nearby. Here they stayed until their move to Ireland in 1910. At Snaile's Castle, Jack indulged his talent for miniature theatre, designing and building small stages and puppet characters and giving shows in the neighborhood, among them his own plays.[68] In 1898 he and

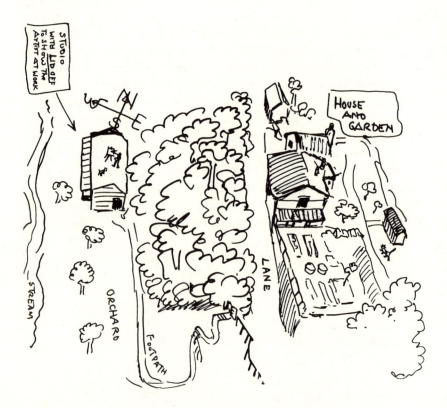

STUDIO WITH LID OFF TO SHOW THE ARTIST AT WORK

HOUSE AND GARDEN

STREAM

ORCHARD

FOOTPATH

LANE

80. Jack Yeats, sketch of house and studio in Strete, Devon. India ink, letter from Jack Yeats to John Quinn, 13 December 1904; collection of New York Public Library. *Courtesy of Anne B. Yeats.*

Cottie paid a visit to Venice and northern Italy, and in 1899 to Paris. Friends came to visit at Strete, among them Masefield and Arnold Harvey, and the members of his own family.

One of Jack's colleagues in art was Pamela Colman ("Pixie") Smith, with whom he collaborated on a single-page publication ("large unfolded sheets," Lollie described them)[69] called *A Broadsheet,* published by Elkin Mathews, the Yeatses' next-door neighbor in Bedford Park. The world at large thought it an equal collabora-

81. Jack Yeats, 1899. Pencil sketch by JBY. *Courtesy of Michael B. Yeats.*

tion. Jack did nothing to dispel the illusion publicly, but he made his feelings clear in a letter to John Quinn in 1902 about the origin of the project.

> Pamela Smith did *not* start the Broad Sheet. I did. In fact I had a weird thing called the Broad Sheet two years ago, just

stencils that I used to print myself. . . . Between you and me
and the wall, as they say, Miss Pamela Smith (though I think a
fine imaginative illustrator with a fine eye for colour, and just
the artist for illuminating verse) is a little bit erratic, and she
being a woman I can't take a very high hand with things, so
there is often a lot of bother about the numbers, and I don't like
being responsible for anything that I have not got absolute control of.[70]

Lily recalls the difficulties with Pixie, a restless, high-strung Jamai-
can, who, though "clever and charming," was also lazy. "When
Jack brought out the Broad Sheet," she wrote, "I used to go to her
studio once a month and colour Jack's picture while she did hers,
only a hundred. Yet she often lay on the sofa and cried because, she
said, I was bullying her and making her work when she did not feel
like work."[71]

Much of Jack's character is revealed in the matter of the *Broadsheet*. He learned not to rely on other people but to work by himself
for himself; he got rid of Pamela Smith without hurting her feelings
and let her retain her pride;[72] and he provided his sister Lily, then
still recovering from her attack of typhoid, with a small income by
hiring her as a colorist. The incident is telling also in what it
suggests of Jack's view of the sexes. His chivalry came straight
out of nineteenth-century notions of the sanctity and inferiority of
womanhood. Working with Pamela Smith had not been easy for
him because he could not deal with her as he would with a man.
When years later he sought an agent to handle some of his manuscripts, he learned that one company suggested to him was ambigu-
ously named. "I did not know that A. M. Heath and Company was
run by a lady," he told a literary adviser unabashedly. "Could you
give me the names of one or two agencies that might be useful to
me and are not run by ladies?"[73]

In 1904, Jack and Cottie made their only visit to America,
encouraged by John Quinn, the financial, artistic, and literary god-
father to the whole family. Jack placed sixty-three pictures on exhibition at Clausen's Gallery at high prices. Of these only twelve
were bought, bringing him a total of $430.[74] The dogmatic Quinn
thought there was something wrong with Jack's habits of work—

82. Jack Yeats, about 1900. *Courtesy of Anne B. Yeats.*

his privacy and his reluctance to accept advice—and tried to reform him but was no more successful than Lady Gregory had been. Jack as always went his own way.[75] The following year he and John Millington Synge took a walking tour through the West of Ireland, where he expanded the "memory pools" of his youth. There is a telling anecdote about their collaboration. Synge suggested that the older of the two be considered the leader of their expedition, know-

83. Catalogue. Jack Yeats, *Sketches of Life in the West of Ireland.*
Exhibition, London, 4 February 1903. *Courtesy of author.*

ing he had been born a few months before Jack. Jack agreed, as the matter was of no importance. Only later did Synge learn that Jack had extracted a higher fee from the *Manchester Guardian* for his drawings than Synge had for his writings.[76]

The *Broadsheet* also provided a precedent for the larger *Broadside* that he produced years later for his sisters at Dun Emer and Cuala.

84. Bookplate for John Quinn by Jack Yeats. *Courtesy of author.*

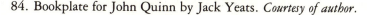

He designed John Quinn's bookplate, the first Dun Emer produced, and he contributed sketches for greeting cards.[77] He donated the use of the sketches but, ever the businessman, kept the originals for sale by himself.[78] It was at the height of his sisters' dispute with Evelyn Gleeson that he hit on the idea of doing the new broadsheet, which he christened *A Broadside,* as a contribution to Lily and Lollie. Altogether, between 1908 and 1915 he produced a total of eighty-four issues, Jack contributing all the drawings for them, 252 in all. He also wrote some of the verses to accompany the drawings, using assumed names.[79]

Yet what Jack contributed was his own work, not money, and he carefully avoided making a financial commitment to the Industries. Perhaps, since everyone in the family knew of Cottie's independent income, it would have been thought indelicate to solicit funds that might come not from their own flesh and blood but from an in-law. In any event, Jack's contribution to Cuala was considerable and brought much-needed income to the sisters, though his out-of-pocket expenses were zero. Later, when it was clear that Lily did not have enough to manage the household at Gurteen Dhas, Jack voluntarily made an allowance of a pound a month.[80] The contribution was small and manageable, but it was given specifically for household expenses, not for Cuala. He saw less of his sisters than even his brother, who confessed that he saw them "only very occasionally."[81] Jack avoided making a long-term commitment that he might not wish to continue. He made clear years later, when people were preparing histories of Dun Emer and Cuala, that "at no time, even during the life of my sister Elizabeth," had he knowledge of "how any wheels turned."[82] When George Yeats asked him to come aboard Cuala in 1939 to fill the directorship left vacant by Willie's death, he declined.[83]

Just before his fortieth birthday Jack announced his desire to leave Devon and live in Ireland. JBY wrote to Lily that he was glad to hear of the development. "It is not good for him to live away from his kind," he commented.[84] And after the move Lily wrote pointedly to John Quinn that Jack and Cottie now "have plenty of friends round them, a pleasant change from the deserts of Devonshire."[85]

The move to Ireland took Jack back to where he belonged. He had thought he wanted the isolation of Devon, but he missed the Irish. Yet in the suburb they chose he saw only a way station to his desired haven. Years earlier he had agreed with John Quinn that England was not the place for him. "I do miss lots of the joy of life . . . from not living in Ireland," he told him. "It's a queer thing to live in an alien country. But I wouldn't give a thrawneen to live in Dublin. I would want to be somewhere in the West and by the sea."[86] Fate would deal him a different hand, though the last card wouldn't fall into place for another seven years, when Dublin at last became their home.

He and Cottie chose "a jolly House" some miles to the south of Dublin, in Greystones, where they settled in the fall of 1910, "such a pleasant happy house, facing the sea with a ploughed field between."[87] It was easy for friends to come from Dublin and for them to take the train north, yet it was just far enough away that they did not see Dubliners regularly, every day. They did not have the opportunity to walk along Grafton Street and meet friends, to attend the Abbey whenever they wanted, to be part of the life of the country's largest city, where almost everybody of importance lived.[88] But Cottie accepted her new country at once. Lollie referred to her as one of "the kind of English people that *take to Ireland* with such gusto that in a short time they will believe *themselves Irish.*"[89]

The period surrounding the move from Devon corresponded with another big change in Jack's artistic life, his move from black-and-white drawings and watercolors to oils, and a more significant move—from realistic depiction to impressionism, a long slow process that was to continue for almost four decades. The art Jack produced at the end of his life is hardly recognizable as the product of the same man who drew broadsides for Cuala, yet the change in both technique and attitude was hardly noticeable from one work to the next. Only a month after the move to Greystones, Jack held a one-man exhibition at Leinster Hall in Dublin, *Pictures of Life in the West of Ireland*. It was his sixteenth exhibition and his ninth in Dublin, but it was the first in which he showed an oil. Lily thought the show a sparkling success: "We are just back from Jack's private view, our faces stiff from smiling at 250 people. . . . The pictures are the best he has ever shown, many of them oil. He paints a fine, vivid, rich style in oil."[90] Quinn was glad to get the news. He had been critical of Jack's sketches and quick to make his displeasure known,[91] so now he was "glad to know" Jack was "going in for oils."[92] The first attempts were in a sense merely the familiar subjects in a new medium, vivid depictions of people, places, and events—evidence that, as Hilary Pyle says, "he tended to regard himself still as a descriptive interpreter, and he did not yet place oil as a medium apart."[93]

To Jack his black-and-white drawings, the newspaper and magazine cartoons, represented only a stage on his journey to the territory of the major artists, the country of oils. When he was ready for great work, he wanted to jettison the earlier baggage. Yet the black-and-white work brought a regular income. In an attempt to

Cashlauna Shelmiddy, Strete, near Dartmouth, South Devon

85. Jack Yeats, cartoon of William Butler Yeats; letter from Jack Yeats to John Quinn, 15 December 1903. *Courtesy of New York Public Library.*

have his cake and eat it too, he continued to send drawings to *Punch* but began using the name "W. Bird." He may have fooled the ordinary reader, but he did not fool Lily Yeats, who recognized his work at once. When she faced Cottie with her discovery in 1913, Cottie "became so red and embarrassed she had to tell." Yet Jack

THE MARCH OF SCIENCE.

86. Jack Yeats, cartoon from *Punch,* 2 November 1910.

himself refused to admit to anyone that he was W. Bird. Two and a half years later, in 1915, she brought Quinn up to date: "Everyone now sees through the W. Bird myth, but I have not heard of him yet as having acknowledged it." [94]

The "W. Bird" cartoons appeared in *Punch* for thirty years, the first in 1910, the last in 1941. In them he drew on his own comic impulses and sense of the ridiculous, recording in black and white

LIFE'S LITTLE ANOMALIES.

How many thousands of pounds have been offered to Carpentier and Dempsey to fight, and now here is a kind old lady giving two boys sixpence each if they'll promise *not* to.

87. Jack Yeats, cartoon from *Punch*, 16 June 1920.

the kind of humor he expressed verbally in society. He had a particularly sharp eye for the absurd. The technique in the last cartoons shows little advance over the first, but Jack was interested not in the artistic possibilities of the cartoon but in making money. He had found a successful formula early, and he stayed with it. His contributions, well over a thousand, brought in a steady income for three decades.

If Jack could be so secretive about a matter as trivial as the identification of his drawings in *Punch*, it is no wonder that he should be so uncommunicative about the more important aspects of his life. Here Lily, who knew both brothers as well as anyone and better than most, saw the wide differences in their personalities: "Willy gives you all that is in his mind, spreads it all out, work, plan, thoughts. Jack keeps all to himself."[95] He left few fingerprints. Alone among the members of his family, he destroyed all

Dashing Native of Bohemian Chelsea. "THERE'S VODKA IN THESE COCKTAILS."
Ordinary Man from somewhere else (a little hard of hearing). "VOLGA? WHY NOT THAMES?"

88. Jack Yeats, cartoon from *Punch,* 19 February 1930.

the personal papers (diaries, letters, manuscripts) that he could lay his hands on, and as a result the curious student is left with less information about him than about anyone else in the family. His nephew Michael Yeats has revealed the extraordinary detail that nobody ever saw Jack read or write, just as no one ever saw him paint (except Cottie when she sat for her portrait). He presented copies of his books to his wife only after they were bound and published.[96] The biographer is forced to engage in that most risky and uncertain business of psychological probing, of attempting to deduce from scanty evidence the nature of a complicated human

"How do I know you're not a parachutist in disguise?"

89. Jack Yeats, cartoon from *Punch*, 20 November 1940.

being, much as a paleontologist reconstructs a mastodon from contemplation of a fossilized piece of shinbone.[97]

So it is not easy to analyze Jack's prolonged illness that lasted from beginning to end for almost two years, from the summer of 1915 to the spring of 1917.[98] When Lily first wrote to Quinn about it, the condition had existed for some time. "He has to rest, and the doctor does not allow him to work more than a couple of hours a day," she told him.[99] The symptoms were the classic ones associated with depression. Lollie noticed that Jack looked "very ill, *very thin, no spirits* at all, and his colour so gray and dark."[100] Lady Gregory told Quinn that Jack was bedridden.[101] He was unable to work, was restless and fatigued. By the spring of 1916 his

90. Jack Yeats with model boat, about 1910. *Courtesy of Anne B. Yeats.*

condition was so poor that he had given up writing to his father, who immediately became apprehensive, sensing at once that the trouble was emotional. "Why do you never write to me?" he asked. "It makes me worry. I think you must be in low spirits, and that you have tumbled into some pits of black melancholy." He insisted —perhaps against his own conviction—that Jack was not a Pollexfen but a Yeats and should therefore be happy.[102] Lady Gregory, Quinn, and his brother and sisters rallied round to help.

The principal obstacle to their enlightenment was Cottie, who proved maddeningly evasive about her husband's condition, refusing to admit that Jack was seriously ill or to insist on the treatment others thought he needed. "Cottie in her letters to me makes such a mystery of it," JBY said of her.[103] Her possessiveness and peculiar personality frustrated them. After a local doctor had ruled out tuberculosis,[104] Willie and the sisters wanted to know what else might be involved. Cottie did nothing. Willie wrote to Jack, asking him to see a specialist, and Quinn cabled Lily, urging medical help. Lily, reluctant to intrude on the protective Cottie, "thought it over" and decided to send the cable and another of Quinn's letters to Cottie. Two weeks passed and still nothing happened.[105]

Quinn and Lily exchanged notes on their feelings about Cottie. "I agree with all you say about Jack," Lily told him. "Cottie's answers to me are just the same as her written answers to you. What is wrong is, I think, she is just limited. I saw her in town and I lunched with her two days ago, and I talked of Jack and a specialist. She did then say what she would not say before, that she would get a specialist *at once* if she thought Jack was not improving." But as Jack had put on weight and seemed better, Cottie made no move.[106] When Lollie wrote, suggesting that Jack consult Dr. Travers-Smith, she had to "beg" Cottie "not to be offended" for her interfering.[107] And Lily wrote Quinn: "When talking to her I always find myself being careful, going back and putting things more carefully as I see her face change and her mind close up." Lily acknowledged that perhaps there was nothing in her behavior directed against the Yeatses personally. "She is just the same with her own people. We think it is English because we can't think of anything else to call it."[108] Quinn had called her "odd," and Lily agreed. She thought children of her own would have strengthened the relationship between Cottie and her in-laws, "mixed us and her."[109] It was some years before the Yeatses dared use the single adjective which they thought explained her shortcomings—spoken only within the family, never committed to print: she was "stupid." It was a key word that unlocked many a door behind which was hidden her otherwise incomprehensible behavior.[110]

By midsummer of 1916 the symptoms had abated. When at last Jack sent a letter to his father that included a sketch, JBY knew the mending had begun; for a long time the few letters he wrote had contained no sketches.[111] But recovery was slow. As late as April 1917, Lily described him as looking "like a man who has been very ill," [112] and Lollie told Elkin Mathews, their former next-door neighbor on Blenheim Road, that Jack was still "far too thin and worn." [113]

The roots of Jack's illness are buried deep. Because it covered the period that included the Easter Rising, there is a generally assumed feeling that political problems must have had something to do with it, though it antedated the Rising by many months. [114] Jack had followed the uncertain fortunes of Ireland's moves toward political independence. The maneuverings of the English and of the Irish Unionists to keep the land in subjection deeply troubled him. [115]

Whether his keen disappointment in the events of the early years of the 1910s was partly responsible for his illness is impossible to know, yet the viewer can sense some of his feeling in his water-color *Bachelor's Walk: In Memory,* painted after the senseless massacre there in 1914. The circumstances surrounding the event illustrated the duplicity of English policy. The Unionists in the North, led by Edward Carson, had illegally imported arms and ammunition at Larne in order to be able to fight a civil war if England should include Ulster in a grant of Home Rule, long promised to the Irish. Though the gunrunning was known to everyone, the English stood by and made no attempt to stop it. Later, when the Irish Republicans tried to smuggle in their own arms at Howth, British forces stopped them; and it was while Irish civilians were taunting British soldiers at Bachelors Walk (only a few yards from O'Connell Bridge) that the soldiers opened fire and killed several people. The barbarity of the massacre and the hypocrisy of it confirmed Jack in feelings he had long held. He had attended meetings of Sinn Fein regularly since coming to Ireland in 1910, and his devotion to the cause of complete independence never wavered, although, like other members of the family, he did not prefer violence as a means of bringing it about.

Lily thought her brother's indisposition was caused merely by his diligence. "He has always worked too hard. That black-and-white work means no break even for a week, and this terrible war like dense fog over all." The kind of work Jack did was not in demand, she complained, so Jack was suffering economically. "No

one wants pictures or any artists' work except for something to put
in 'The Queen's Gift Book' or 'Princess Mary's Scrap Album.' " [116]
Terence White writes of Cottie's speaking "bitterly" of the "public
neglect" of her husband, and he also writes of Jack's generally low
view of man's place in the world, the view that led to his fascination
with and contribution to the literature of the absurd. Marilyn Gaddis Rose and Robin Skelton both point out that the thickest thread
running through Jack's prose works is that of the absurdity of
things as they are, of the apparently meaningless operations of
chance, of the inevitability of final nothingness at the end of life. It
is widely held that the younger Samuel Beckett derived his own
philosophy from Jack. But Beckett was a total absurdist, without
hope of hope. Jack held a low opinion of man in general, but of
man as he was, not as he might be. In his old age he told Terence
de Vere White that "experience of life, if it does not teach you to
believe in God, certainly convinced you of the existence of the
devil." White also repeats the comment of his nurse during his
final illness that he became "increasingly distressed by the wickedness and cruelty of the world and was for ever extolling children
and lamenting their inevitable involvement in the hell their elders
had devised." [117] Man could solve his problems but refused to. [118]
Writing four months after the outbreak of the Second World War,
Jack saw the "muddy clouds on the hilltops and stinking mists in
the valleys of a creaking civilization." [119] Even Lady Gregory, who
admired Jack, saw in his painting "traces of the harsh memories of
famine, of banishment, of some unending war, some latent fierce-
ness in the strong unflattered faces. . . . Traces of the knowledge
of 'the big change' that is coming, that is already begun, of the old
world that is dying without pity, and the young world that is
growing up on its grave." [120] But such a view clashed with the other
world that Jack saw and painted, an equally valid world, of human
activity at its most glorious and varied, of the "living ginger" (one
of his favorite terms) [121] in people in action.

When it was clear that the breakdown had been at least in part
emotional, Lily, like her father, thought she knew the remedy. Jack
must end his isolation, get around more, work less strenuously. "I
think he ought to live where he could see more people and get talk
with men." At Greystones, as at Snaile's Castle, when Jack ended

his daily stint of drawing and painting, he merely took up some other work, pottering about the house. "He wants to play more," Lily insisted; "his present life is too lonely and far off from the world for a man of his kind." What he wanted now, she said, was "idleness,"[122] more variation in his life, less routine, more gadding about, more relaxation. He recovered, slowly, but not until he and Cottie had settled in Dublin had the crisis clearly been passed; from then to the end of his life Jack enjoyed good health.

That move took place in late September 1917, Jack and Cottie taking a house at 61 Marlborough Road in Donnybrook,[123] a suburb of Dublin within walking distance of the center of the city. With the move a new and better life began, though still a simple one. Jack and Cottie never owned a car, and Jack would not allow a telephone in the house until late in his life, when he thought he might need one to call a doctor.[124] It had taken him forty-seven years to arrive at the place where he once thought he would not have given a thrawneen to live, but for the rest of his life he would be part of the excitement of Dublin, one of its most distinguished practicing artists, a popular figure known and liked by everyone of importance in the city.

John Butler Yeats told Cottie that Jack had been "an extraordinary favorite" with the Americans he had met on his visit to New York,[125] and so he proved in Dublin, in contrast to his more crusty brother. Norman Colbeck, an English book collector, has spoken of finding Jack Yeats "open, friendly, delightful." Colbeck on several occasions was in the same room with WBY but never dared introduce himself for fear of being rebuffed, regarding him as "haughty and snobbish."[126] Many others shared his feeling. When Lollie learned that the daughter of one of her American clients was to visit Dublin, she offered to introduce her "to my artist brother and his wife and some other people," but significantly omitted Willie from the list.[127] Lily had to warn Ruth not to ask her to introduce her friends to Willie. He had always been unapproachable, she said, and grew even more so as he aged.[128] Jack was completely approachable. And just as John Masefield had chosen Jack over Willie, so the young Samuel Beckett made the same choice, although he found Cottie and her chatter annoying. He made a point of seeing Jack privately whenever he was in Dublin but avoided WBY because, as his biographer writes, Beckett found him "pompous and posturing, fatuously slobbering over all the whole aspects of Ireland and Irish society." [129]

The testimony to Jack's popularity after he came to Dublin is abundant. He was one of those rare people who is instantly likable. "There are so many people we like because we think well of them," JBY wrote to Lady Gregory. "But from the first moment one likes Jack and we think well of him because we like him, which is the only basis of lasting friendship." [130] His conversation was delightful. "You are not unprepared for anecdote in Dublin," wrote an American admirer, "but the tale-telling of this lean angular figure—whose electric presence is that of a stooped giant—leaves you breathless. There is story upon story—of remembered men and horses of his native Sligo." [131] When he received an honorary degree from Trinity College in 1946, the provost in his public remarks said that Jack "was loved by everyone in Dublin." [132]

His rebirth in the capital city may have provided just the fire he needed after the isolation of Devon and Greystones. "He used to hide himself away and go nowhere, see no one," Lily told John Quinn. After the move to Dublin and the recovery from his emotional problems, he became a changed man. "Now he is everywhere, accepts all invitations and enjoys everything." When his morning stint was finished, he walked into the city and wandered about and saw people. "He is liked by all," Lily told Quinn in 1918, "and looks remarkably well." [133] Lily kept insisting that he "did for himself" by "hard work" but had now learned his lesson, becoming "quite fond of loafing and taking life easy." [134] She tried to impress on Cottie that "Jack must never go back to his old ways" but would have to "play and rest and get more talk." [135] Instead of working every day, now he took one day a week off, "wandering about the quays and off into the country." [136] He always went alone, without Cottie, sometimes going into the country on a bus, "coming back full of honey, like a wise old bee after a day in a sunny garden." [137] Friday was his day off; on other days "he works regular hours as if he worked in an office." [138]

Yet Jack's daily routine had been fixed for some years; in Dublin he merely modified it. In the morning he would retreat to his studio and work for several hours, then assist Cottie about the

91. Jack and Cottie Yeats, about 1920. *Courtesy of Rosemary Hemming.*

house. In the afternoon he walked. If interrupted during the course
of his morning's work, he would stop at once and do no more for
the day, even if the interruption came after only ten minutes of
painting or writing. Cottie learned to avoid him. The two devised
a scheme to keep her away. Jack would wrap a pipe cleaner around
the doorknob so that Cottie would feel its sharp point if she attempted to touch the knob.[139] She entered his studio by invitation

only once. She had teased him that he had never painted her, so one day he beckoned to her and said, "Come in. I will paint you." He painted quickly, almost flinging the paint on the canvas. That was one of the few portraits he painted. Cottie never saw him paint again—and neither did anyone else. His desire for privacy was almost pathological. Yet even his best friends, said Elizabeth Curran Solterer, respected it and knew enough not to push him beyond a certain point. [140]

His niece Anne Yeats describes him: "He always dressed formally in old-fashioned clothes, and when he went out he wore a long black coat with a narrow velvet collar and large pockets. He also wore a brimmed black hat." He was "a tall man, stooped and nearly bald and very thin when I knew him"—Anne was born in 1919—"but with well-kept hands, always very courteous and formal in his manner. He was a well-known figure in Dublin, especially around the Quays, always alone, always watching and sketching. He was once seen at a concert in the front row, drawing the musicians, which annoyed the man who told me the story. 'That Yeats must be tone deaf,' he said—to be drawing and not listening to the musicians, I suppose. He took every Friday off work. His wife went to the cinema and had tea with her friends, while he rambled round the city. He had a characteristic walk. When he was young he adopted, so my father claimed, a gait like a Sligoman or a sailor to remind himself of his Sligo background." [141]

Unlike his brother, Jack was involved in no public projects like the Abbey Theatre and no secret societies like the Golden Dawn. He took no part in the politicking at the Royal Hibernian Academy, to which he had been elected a full member in 1915. He tried to avoid general exhibitions, preferring one-man shows over which he could exercise control. Again unlike Willie, he put himself in a position where it was difficult for him to offend anyone personally. His natural good humor leavened gatherings of which he was a part, but as he kept his remarks impersonal, he was a delightful guest wherever he went. When Ruth Lane-Poole's daughter Charles visited Dublin in the mid-1930s she was fascinated by him, and Lily reported to her mother that Charles's "eyes shone as she listened to his nonsense and funny stories and queer wisdom." [142] Lily wrote of how at another family party "Jack made us all laugh the whole time." "You know how he can just in a few words make things amusing," she wrote Ruth, who had known Jack in her unmarried days.[143] Often he employed pantomime, once "showing us how he had seen a man playing a mechanical piano with feeling and emotion."[144] His books sometimes had the same effect. When Lily's friend Anne Boston ("Phillida") read his *Sligo,* she said the book "made her laugh so much she had to go and read it in her own room for fear she would laugh aloud in the public room."[145]

Yet the private Jack, the one who coexisted harmoniously with the other, had not changed at all. He was still secretive about his painting, letting no one see his work till it was finished to his satisfaction and ready for public inspection, treating his pictures "as if it was counterfeit coin he was making," Lily told Quinn.[146] When one of Jack's pictures was sold in New York, Lily learned of the sale through a note John Sloan, the American painter and friend of Jack's father, added to a Cuala bill. Then she discovered Cottie didn't know about the sale either, and Cottie planned to "have some fun with Jack over it."[147] When Cottie did know how much Jack received for a painting, she was as secretive as he. "He and Cottie are so deep and dark they do not say if he sold one big or small," she told Ruth.[148] When Lily heard that Jack had sold "a big-priced picture," she said she wasn't sure of the price, "and of course he doesn't say."[149] When he was writing *Sailing, Sailing Swiftly* he wouldn't let even Cottie see the proofs but made her wait till the book was published. Lily called him "a dark horse."[150] She could never find out precisely how he stood financially. "Jack is so mysterious you never know. He may be looking about for 6d or he may have a good bank account." Even Cottie didn't know, she told Ruth.[151] When he sold a picture for £250, Cottie learned the price from Constantine Curran's wife, Helen Laird Curran, who had private connections in the art world. When Helen called Lily on May Day in 1941 to tell her Jack had sold between four and five hundred pounds worth of pictures during the preceding few weeks, she added, "Jack I'm sure won't tell you, so I do."[152] He did not look or sound secretive. Lily described a visit from Jack in 1942. "He is well and the best of company with his humour, but nothing of himself he tells. He may have sold a picture for £250 the day before but never mentions that."[153] "Yet he always

92. Helen Laird (Mrs. Constantine) Curran. Pencil sketch by
Josephine Webb. *Courtesy of Society of Friends, Dublin.*

appears to be telling you all the news," she told Ruth. [154]

One of the biggest of Jack's merchandising enterprises was kept
secret from everyone in the family, and even apparently from the
omniscient Helen Curran. In the early 1930s he sent thirty-seven
of his paintings to the Ferargil Galleries in New York City. When
Ferargil proved unsuccessful in selling them they were turned over

to a dealer named Patric Farrell, who made little effort to sell them. Jack managed to retrieve one of the thirty-seven, but Farrell held on to the others, selling none. When Jack inquired about them, Farrell replied with telegrams that said nothing, promising to tell Jack what was going on but never doing so. He ignored Jack's requests for their return. When James A. Healy, the New York stockbroker, began his association with the Yeats family in the late 1930s, Jack sought his advice about recovering the pictures, and through him retained a lawyer in New York to sue for their return. Jack placed a total value of $18,500 on the paintings, so his financial commitment was deep. Yet despite the importance of the matter to him and the frustration of six years, he never said a word about it to anyone in the family.[155]

His anger over Farrell was matched by another conflict, this one with the mighty Macmillan publishing house. It illustrates his remorselessness in pursuing what he regarded as his rights.[156] There were two Macmillans, one in New York, one in London, and though each was an independent company, each had an informal agreement with the other to share publications on the basis of "first refusal." The New York house had published Padraic Colum's *The Big Tree of Bunlahy*, with illustrations by Jack, and Jack had insisted that the use of his drawings, for which he was paid £400, be limited to the New York edition only, securing a letter with that proviso from the editor of children's books. In the spring of 1934 Jack learned that Macmillan of London was advertising copies of the book for sale without having made separate arrangements with him. He immediately wrote to Macmillan of New York to demand a share of the profits from its sale.

The ensuing dispute provides a marvelous example of a Goliath trying to crush an adamant David. New York at first denied knowledge of the special agreement. When faced with the letter to Jack from the children's book editor, it then protested that the agreement had somehow never entered the main files. The London office turned on its transatlantic associate, telling Jack it was sorry that New York "had committed the error" of not informing them of Jack's rights, and mentioning "our unconscious infringement of your rights." The dodging and squirming as each side tried to put the liability on the other, business devices to encourage the complainant to drop his pursuit, only angered Jack the more. New York told him that their Mr. Brett was on his way to London and would "no doubt" get in touch with Jack. When Jack wrote the London Macmillan to ask why Mr. Brett had not communicated with him, London replied that Mr. Brett was on his way back to New York and would "no doubt" write him from there.

Jack's correspondence with Kilham Roberts of the Incorporated Society of Authors, Playwrights, and Composers shows his annoyance at such treatment. He resented the constant shift of focus from one continent to the other. "Writing to both sides of the Atlantic is becoming unpleasant to me," Jack wrote Roberts after three months of fruitless correspondence, and a short time later: "Again you see the matter crosses the Atlantic." He wrote sternly to Macmillan of London, "I am becoming a little impatient at the delay." If they thought Jack could be bulldozed, they were mistaken. "The more they write the more my feeling about them becomes unpleasant," Jack wrote. He hung on like a terrier, refusing to be intimidated, and Macmillan of London finally stopped sale of the book and returned the unsold copies to New York. New York asked Jack what compensation he would settle for, and Jack demanded the same £400 he had received for the American edition.

Mr. Brett, faced with this demand, finally responded, protesting to Jack that because London had sold fewer than a hundred copies and had returned the rest to New York for credit, the expenses had left his company "a very small margin indeed." Would Jack therefore be satisfied with their action in removing the book from the London market? Jack would not. He was angered over the deviousness involved, and as to the profits gained or losses sustained by the two Macmillans because of their failure to recognize his rights, they meant "nothing" to him.

Jack had moved carefully during the negotiations, following Roberts's advice, and when at last he felt that the two companies were determined to persist in what a later generation would call "stonewalling," he placed the matter in the hands of Roberts's Society, to which he paid a fee. The result was a new contract between the London Macmillan and Jack, calling for separate English publication of the book with an advance royalty of £50, a 20 percent royalty on all books sold, bound or unbound, and a guarantee about the book's availability. With a 10 percent fee to the

Society, Jack ended up with £45, which was £45 more than Macmillan had planned to part with at the beginning.

Though the settlement may have been small, Jack persisted until his rights were recognized. But he told nobody in the family or, as far as the record shows, anyone else except Roberts and Healy about his negotiations.

His correspondence with the Society reveals also a business mind interested in all the details of publication. He asked innumerable questions of Roberts. Could he as an artist ask for a royalty as well as a flat payment? If he allowed photographs of his paintings to be reproduced, would he still keep his copyright in them? If he had a photograph made of himself, would he own the copyright in that? He wanted to make sure he got every shilling legally owed him.

Yet in handling specific matters of copyright, he was as always sensitive to the rights and needs of others. When Van Wyck Brooks asked him if he would give permission for the publication of John Butler Yeats's letters, Jack asked Roberts whether he should charge a fee, and if so how much. But he didn't want to hurt Brooks's feelings. "Brooks was I am certain an old and tried friend of my father's and I do not want to do anything in the slightest way unfriendly, ungenerous, or stupid, or retarding to the publication of the letters, and the book may after all just have a small sale among friends—perhaps with difficulty pay for the editing."[157]

Some years later when Joseph Hone, a family friend, edited *J. B. Yeats: Letters to His Son W. B. Yeats,* Jack wanted to know whether he could ask the publisher for an advance payment to himself and his sister Lily and a slice of the royalties as well, on top of what Hone himself was given. But he stressed that Hone was a family friend. When he learned that that could not be done, Hone offered to make the payments himself. Having protected his rights and secured the cash, Jack in his Dr. Jekyll mode turned it over to Lily.[158]

Jack was as careful of his reputation as of his financial position, afraid bad copies of his work would compromise him. No copy could match the original, he thought, and he came to insist that no reproductions of any of his work of any kind be allowed. When the Tate Gallery reproduced his work for a catalogue he wanted to sue, then discovered that galleries or museums automatically acquired the copyright along with the painting. Private collectors ordinarily did not, and Jack thereafter specified in selling his paintings that he retained the copyright.[159]

His privacy, or desire for secrecy, extended in many directions. In the facts and figures he provided for *Who's Who* he would not give the date of his birth,[160] and Lily had to warn Joseph Hone not to give it in the biography of Willie he was preparing.[161] What secret vulnerability his strange behavior implied must be left to the contemplation of divines, yet something may be inferred from one of his remarks about art and literature and the superiority of one to the other:

> Paintings are the most lasting kinds of events—plays and books die out, a picture does not need translation. A creative work happens. It does not need "documentary evidence," dates, photographs of the artist, or what he says about his pictures. It doesn't matter who or what I am. People may think what they will of the pictures.[162]

Lollie described as "odd" another of his peculiarities. "He often will not consent to send pictures," she wrote Professor Alfred De Lurey, a Canadian patron of Cuala. "For example the Belgian Consul here told me that they had tried to get him to send a picture to an Exhibition this year supposed to represent Irish art in Brussels, and that *no one* could induce him to let them have a picture on loan." Lollie could not understand him, calling him "a kind of 'lone bird.' "[163]

When he was looking for a house in Dublin he would tell Lollie nothing except that he was "still negociating." "He and Cottie hate to tell what they are doing," she complained to her father. "I don't know why. They are always like that." Lollie exacerbated matters by interfering. "I have *inundated* him with lists and particulars of *possible houses*," she told Papa. "He is probably mad with me. He and Cottie hate anyone to interfere with them at all."[164] Once, when Jack held a successful exhibition in Birmingham, he told the family nothing about it, not even that it was being held. William Cadbury gave the news of it in casual talk with Lollie.[165] When he was writing books, he told nobody of his plans. "What book has

93. Jack Yeats and William Butler Yeats, in front of Gurteen
Dhas, 1933. *Courtesy of Anne B. Yeats.*

Jack published?" Willie asked Lily when word reached him that
Jack had just produced another volume.[166]

To Lollie, of course, such behavior was maddening. When she
wanted to know how he had done at an exhibition, he would answer
merely, "Good," instead of giving a figure, which Lollie, "full of
curiosity," wanted to know. Despite her persistent questioning,
she could never, according to Lily, "get into his skin." He kept his
humor always. "He never shows irritation, answers all questions
but tells nothing."[167] Jack was also amused at Lily's exasperation
with Lollie at Gurteen Dhas. "I wish he would try it for a week,"
Lily complained to Ruth. "He would find it no laughing matter."[168] He shrewdly kept his distance from their problems. Jack,
usually the life of the party at small gatherings, was sometimes

outmaneuvered by Lollie, who would seize the floor from under him. One Christmas night at Aunt Fanny Gordon's, Jack, "who is so good a talker," and Rupert Gordon, "full of interest and interesting things," were kept silent by Lollie's chatter, "so restless and silly." [169] Cottie and Jack saw in Lollie what everyone else saw. At dinner at Gurteen Dhas on the first Christmas after Lollie's death, Cottie said several times amid the unusual silence, "The house feels so free." [170]

Lily always maintained that Jack never made much money until well past middle age, but there is no question about his business acumen from the beginning. When the Royal Hibernian Academy was destroyed in the Easter Rising of 1916, the insurance company gave him half the value of his lost paintings, and he promptly took steps to get the other half. [171] His father, on the other hand, was surprised to learn that one of his sketches had been lost at a burned-out publishing house, and when the insurance cheque for it came, covering only part of the claimed value, he made no attempt to get more. [172] Jack made use of Lily to try to get Ruth Lane-Poole to persuade the National Gallery of Australia to take one of his oils, Lily making a point of Jack's winning of a silver medal in Paris in 1924 as a selling point. [173]

He preferred one-man shows not only because there only his own pictures were on sale. His insistence on complete independence made him wary of association with others, as he might be considered part of a "group." He advised his young friend Terence de Vere White "to keep out of groups and not to accept positions on committees for good causes," for such groups would only want to use him. "If ever there was an individualist he was one," said White. His principles cost him dearly; White notes that Jack "was left out of at least one exhibition because he insisted that he must be shown alone or not at all." [174] He organized his exhibitions carefully and mailed invitations to prospective customers and to Dublin friends who would talk up his products. He set a price on each of his pictures, prices that his sisters thought "high," and the price was often listed in guineas, not pounds, a device practiced by physicians and other professionals to show that their wares were meant only for those who could afford the best. Often they sold at once, [175] but Jack would not lower his prices if they did not. At the

Engineer's Hall in Dublin in 1925, he sold only one high-priced picture the first day, and a cheaper one at £15.15.[176] Lily's remarks to Ruth on Jack's exhibitions usually included the refrain, "None of his prices are low." Lily admired his persistence. "If Jack can manage to get along he is probably right in his big prices." In 1930, at the Alpine Club Gallery in London, he kept to his principle. "He did not sell many," Lily informed Ruth, "but his pictures are high, so the total may have been fairly good."[177] Lollie made the same observation, wondering whether he would sell anything in his private showing in February 1921. "He had lately put very high prices on his pictures, but he always knows what he is about —or at any rate it is no use discussing prices etc. with him. He goes his own way, and apparently sees his own road clear before him."[178]

Jack's resolute determination to stick to his asking price paid off in a special way in 1930. *The Liffey Swim,* the painting that had won the silver medal in Paris in 1924, was purchased by the National Gallery of Ireland for £250, its first major purchase of one of his works.[179] Thomas Bodkin, Director of the National Library of Ireland, told Lily he watched at auctions for Jack's works and had already "picked up two little ones."[180] More and more, Lily was able to report high prices for sales of Jack's pictures, and more and more sales.

By 1942 he was in such demand that the Currans were afraid he might be running out of pictures to sell, "and his prices were big ones." Lily, a believer in Jack's greatness from the beginning, was glad to get the report. "I am so glad his pictures are selling well now for some time, and that he is recognized as a fine artist in many countries, and that so much fame has come to him in his lifetime." Both her brothers had led long lives in relative impecuniosity, Willie more than Jack, she thought, since Jack had "a good income from very early days by black and white work." "Willy made hardly any money till elderly," she told Ruth, and Jack, who might have made more money by sticking to cartoons and black-and-white sketches, "had his mind made up all the time to be a painter."[181] Late in her life (and Jack's) she exulted, "Isn't it wonderful to think of a Yeats making money?"[182] Jack was not modest, in private at least, about his merit. "I know I am the first living painter in the world," he wrote to Willie in 1925. "And the second is so far away that I am only able to make him out faintly." [183]

Lily never pretended to authority as a critic of either poetry or art and even acknowledged how difficult she found some of Willie's verses. Once Jack turned to oils and moved away from photographic representation, Lily felt equally baffled, yet she never wavered in her conviction that he knew what he was doing and that from the beginning he had the spark of genius in him. She had written sharply to her father as early as 1904 about the misguided attempts of him and Willie and Lady Gregory to tell Jack how he should paint. "He is all right and knows what he is doing," she told Papa. "You say too much. . . . He never drifts. . . . He wants encouragement, and his work is beautiful and his own. When we are all dead and gone great prices will be given for them. I know they will." A decade and a half later, years after her chiding letter to Papa, she told him, "Jack is a big man and his work will live forever." [184] "Jack is really great and will become greater," she told Ruth in 1929. "When we are all dead dealers will wax fat on Jack Yeats." And she quoted Thomas Bodkin: " 'This man has a European mind. Anyone buying his work now is getting something of great value.' " [185] "He is now considered so good he is an investment," Lily wrote Ruth in 1941. Six months before she died, she could write with satisfaction to Ruth, "He is now a famous man." [186]

From Lily's letters to Ruth, one can trace the effect the development in Jack's oils made on ordinary viewers, those who were not specialists in artistic criticism or in theories and movements. She described one of the paintings in the first of Jack's exhibitions in which oils were prominent, the one-man show that opened in Dublin in December 1910: "No. 3, 'An Occupation,' is a beauty, an old circus man going toward a bear in a cage to feed it. He has a bucket and is toiling toward the cage." The painting is a realistic depiction of the event, a work that differed from his earlier watercolors and black-and-whites only in being done in oils, in which, according to Lily, "he paints a fine, rich, vivid style." [187] A decade and a half later she was saying of some of his paintings that they were "very fine, curious many of them." [188] In 1930 she openly expressed bafflement at the oils he showed in a rare exhibition with others at the Royal Hibernian Academy: they had "lovely colour," she said, "but all else a mystery." She deferred to the judgment of AE, who said "they were the only pictures he wanted and he could talk till 4 in the morning about them, while all the rest he could understand by one glance out of the corner of his eye."[189] Two years later she was even more puzzled by an oil called *Tears,* which, again, she called a "mystery." She reported on it to Ruth, quoting Cottie's explanation of it: "it is of people on a verandah listening to a man reading a poem, wine glasses on the table etc., views of cloud-topped hills behind them. It is just a jumble of lovely colour. I made out a wine glass. Still I suppose it all has a meaning and I am not young enough to see it."[190] Jack himself wouldn't tell what his pictures meant, nor talk of his technique, nor hint what prompted him to do a particular painting.[191] Two years later still, Lily was mystified by an oil called *Those Others,* bought by Sarah Purser for £250. It showed a countryside "over which walk a procession of half-seen figures of the lovers of old Irish history, Grania and Dermot, Deirdre, etc. etc. They come majestic, beautiful, as if slowly moving, lovers just leaning toward each other. It is not easy to describe, but it is beautiful to see."[192] Willie responded to Jack's impressionist style—"very strange and beautiful in a wild way," he wrote Lady Gregory in 1929. James Joyce, he told her, said that "he and Jack have the same method" and had bought "two of Jack's pictures of the Liffey."[193] What *Ulysses* was to the world of writing Jack's oils were to the world of art.

John Butler Yeats had always insisted that no matter how impressionist an artist might be, behind everything he painted must be a representation of something; the idea of a factless, featureless painting was beyond his grasp.[194] He had inoculated his sons with the same theory, and John Quinn had to chide Willie for not appreciating JBY's self-portrait because it didn't appear to be an accurate representation:

> The right hand or the left hand has nothing to do with the greatness of the picture. You are still a victim of the notion of representation in art and think of anatomy which has nothing to

do with art. One should never think of the right hand or the left hand in that painting but of the whole painting, the shape of the head and shoulders and the whole poise of the figure and the wonderful richness of color, color that even Renoir never got, for your father's color is cooler than Renoir's. It will grow better as time goes on.[195]

JBY himself disagreed with Quinn. In his letters to Jack he repeatedly emphasized the importance of representation. He expressed his view dogmatically in a letter to Padraic Colum: "There are three things necessary to a work of art—first portraiture, imitation of the concrete fact—and T. S. Eliot &c be damned and all who denounce 'representation.' That is the body, the existence, the specific gravity, and it is identical with the artist's *force.*"[196]

Certainly Jack in all his early and middle works drew sharply defined scenes and portraits. If he indeed continued to accept his father's strictures, then his own later impressionist paintings can be explained, in terms of technique, by a simple development on the basic principle. From the beginning to the end of his impressionist period, Jack's paintings can be seen as following a simple continuum. The viewer sees the early paintings as if through clear air, the next ones through slightly mottled glass. The mottle, mild in the early oils, grows greater with each successive painting until in the last the viewer sees, or thinks he sees, only the mottle and not the thing represented behind it. Yet the thing is always there, even if, as with Lily and her reaction to *Tears,* someone had to explain what it was. The method gave Jack full scope for exercising his talent for shape and color while seeing through half-closed eyes his images of horse and cloud and wave. Lily may not have known what Jack was doing, but she knew it was good. Kenneth Clark thought the continuum ended at last in sheer impressionism: "With the recklessness of advancing years he had a revelation. Why should he be confined to the rules of representational painting? All that mattered was to convey his feelings in their original intensity. And in an amazingly short time he created for himself a new style."[197] *Ulysses* had become *Finnegans Wake.*

•   •   •

Those alive today who remember Jack Yeats bear out the view held by the members of his own family. In a perceptive and sympathetic essay on him by a younger man who came to know him well, Terence de Vere White writes of him with the same affection that exudes from Lily's letters. He was still a youth of college age when he met Jack Yeats.

> I recall the attentiveness of the eye, the total absence of condescension, the grace of manner. In those days people were more inclined to stand upon their advantages in casual contacts; age dominated youth; difference of social position was at once apparent. Yeats was entirely free of every pretension of that character. His presence was ageless and classless, not as if he was unaware of such differences, but as if he was above them. He was the least vulgar of men. I doubt if anyone was ever rude or impertinent to him.

With Terence White he was as protective of his privacy as with the members of his own family:

> He was reticent, not to say secretive about most things. He was a man to whom one hesitated to put any question concerning himself or his work, nor do I recall him ever asking me a personal question, although we spoke intimately, particularly at the time when Mrs. Yeats died. I saw a great deal of him then; but the form his confidence took was to say exactly what he thought about our various acquaintances. He did not talk about himself or expect you to talk about yourself. He was proud. I was told that he disliked any discussion of his painting. This led to not a little insincerity at gatherings in his room. Everyone praised everything equally.

White also discovered a significant difference between the two brothers, noting their uses of and attitudes toward that simple flower, the rose. WBY, he points out, "used it romantically in his lyrical phase, and later linked it to his rambles through occult, eastern and Grecian philosophies and other esoteric playgrounds. For Jack Yeats, if 'a rose is a rose is a rose' was not quite the whole story, his attitude to the flower was less egocentric, his devotion more consistent than his brother's. He was content to look at the rose; to love it for his own sweet sake." One wonders how much of Jack's attachment to the concrete, the immediate, the direct, came from opposition to some of his brother's vaporous yearnings about ancient Irish heroes and heroines, as one wonders how much of his sense of economy sprang from his father's financial imprudence. Can it be that he became the kind of person and artist he was not by a fortuitous concatenation of genes but by a deliberate act of will, quite simply doing the opposite to those things in his father and brother that he most disliked? Again one has to note that Jack seems less like a Yeats than any of the others in his family. If he had not been the son of JBY and the brother of WBY, would the world ever have suspected they were soldiers in the same regiment?

Terence White believes that Jack, despite being present in the late eighties and early nineties at his father's dinner table, "was probably much less influenced by his father than the poet was."

> For one thing he was not with him so much, and there is no evidence of a correspondence such as that which the old Yeats kept up with his sometimes unresponsive elder son. Because W. B. had taken words as his medium of expression the father may have been more concerned to influence his thought. Then it is probable that Jack was not of a didactic turn. He was up and doing rather than talking; he listened, no doubt, but made no attempt to discuss. He had his own ideas about everything; but he did not invite argument, and it was not very easy to argue with him because his ideas were so often whimsical. His nature was more affectionate than W. B.'s and, if entirely self-sufficient, he was not so self-centered. The poet, walking about, or even in company when he wasn't holding forth, would be seen to move his lips in silent recitation; Jack Yeats was ever on the alert; he missed nothing. In a gathering where someone was left out of the conversation if Jack Yeats was present, I can imagine him singling out the neglected person for attention. Not so W. B.[198]

Jack's generosity was of a piece with the rest of his behavior. When Lily incurred heavy expenses at the Roseneath Nursing Home, he stood aside and let Willie bear most of the expenses. Since Willie had just come into his Nobel Prize money, he was at that moment in a better position than Jack anyhow, and the fact would not have been lost on Jack. His own preference was for the unexpected gift when it was most needed. In 1921, Lily came down with a bad case of boils, one of the many afflictions from which she suffered before her major attack in 1923. Jack visited her, found her with a high fever, and promptly booked her for a week at the Grand Hotel in Malahide, "a luxury, not a necessity," Lily told her father, "—and all a bit of goodness of Jack's." [199] When Lollie died, Jack paid for her tombstone and the inscription, [200] as he had paid for his mother's plaque years before. Terence White tells of Jack's contributing to an old woman who had "fallen on hard times," and to an artist who was ill. Jack sent White £50 toward a fund for the woman and gave him £25 to buy the artist's pictures but pretend they were for White himself, not Jack, who "never wanted to see them." [201] When Joseph Hone paid £25 for the use of John Butler Yeats's letters, Jack, as already noted, gave his share to Lily. [202] When a church—to which Jack did not belong—needed renovation, Jack "arranged all the colouring for the decoration" and pleased the other painters and decorators so much that they included his name in a book acknowledging his contribution. Lily learned of his act by accident; Jack told no one about it. [203]

Yet he always kept the two sides of his life separate, the personal and the business. He seldom gave away the fruits of his labors. Even Cottie owned only two of Jack's paintings, one the oil of herself. [204] Terence White tells an illuminating story. White visited Jack after Cottie's death and saw on the wall a picture he liked. "We talked and then Yeats went out of the room and came back and said, without any show of emotion: 'Cottie never made a will, but I know what she wanted me to do, and she would have liked you to have that as a little remembrance.' He handed me a cheque for £100." That was the kindly, generous Jack Yeats, wanting to show his affection for the much younger man whose friendship he valued. White then, "on an impulse," asked if he might spend the money on purchasing the picture on the wall. Instantly the circumstances altered, although there was no change in Yeats's expression. He took back the hundred pounds and gave White the picture, [205] a business transaction of the most conventional kind. Another man might have thrown in the painting with the gift of money, but there were three men involved in this transaction, White one of them, the two Jacks the others—the friend and the businessman.

Samuel Beckett ran up against Jack the businessman in the same way, with a similar result. At one of his intimate talks with Jack at Fitzwilliam Square, Beckett fell in love with a new painting by Jack called *Morning*. It carried a price tag of £30, which Beckett didn't have. He let Jack know how much he liked the picture and how much he wanted to have it. Jack said nothing, made no move. A week later they met by chance at the National Library, and Beckett mentioned the picture again, "but still Yeats said nothing." The price was £30, and, until the money was produced, the picture would not be given up. Finally Beckett brought two friends with him to Fitzwilliam Square, asked if he could have the picture and pay for it in installments. Jack instantly yielded, and Beckett borrowed the money from his friends, preferring to owe them rather than Jack.[206] Beckett got the picture he wanted, but there was no uncertainty about the deal being strictly one of business.

Elizabeth Curran Solterer has told of another instance in which Jack the private man gave way to Jack the businessman. He possessed "an enormous he-man's chest," which he never opened in anyone else's presence until 1945, when Miss Curran, managing his 50th Anniversary Retrospective, needed to check the ownership of some of his works. Jack opened the chest for her. In it, neatly arranged, were records, organized by year, of everything he ever sold, with title, sale, buyer (if known), and price realized. Jack was extremely businesslike throughout. He would not have opened the trunk except that Miss Curran needed the information for an important professional purpose, and so he was willing to share it.[207]

Jack not only provided the week in Malahide for Lily when she fell ill, he also provided his subsidy of a pound a month to her and came forward at other times when help was needed. In 1946 their cousin Ruth in Australia, knowing only of Lily's invalidism and impecuniosity, charged that Jack was selfish, and Lily was aroused to a spirited defense. "Till three years ago he never made a good income, and the shows with frames etc. must have been a loss. Now of course he is doing very well, but he must put by for a time when perhaps he won't be able to paint at all. Since March last year he sent me two cheques amounting to £190, and also for years he has sent me a bottle of brandy a month, and I have been able to pay the rent, taxes, the electric light, telephone, grocer, chemist." [208]

Always at Jack's side was Cottie, a source of discomfort to her in-laws but of strength to him. They knew where they stood with each other, and few marriages have lasted as long and been as successful as theirs. William Butler Yeats's checkered and, at times, sensational love life was not paralleled by his brother's. Terence White has remarked that, if he "were called upon to testify," the evidence he was aware of "would be that there had been one woman and only one in his long life." [209] Lady Gregory, who disliked women generally, had paid little attention to Cottie when Jack first visited Coole with her, and Jack quietly showed his displeasure by not accepting her next imperious invitation. John Butler Yeats told Lily years later that Jack may have been responding subtly to her "too obvious dislike—at least *repulse*—of Cottie." Jack, he said, "ought to be much attached" to Lady Gregory "for all her goodness, but he can't forget that she snubbed Cottie." [210]

The two were not only inseparable but, if only two people can be so, clannish. She resented what she saw as a failure by the Establishment (that is, the English art world) to recognize her husband's genius, not realizing that to the English anything Irish was automatically regarded as inferior. In any event, as Terence White notes, it was only during the Second World War, when Jack was in his seventies, that fame and fortune came to him, so it is no wonder that Cottie, enduring the years of neglect, was embittered for her husband's sake and protected and defended him with spirit. Lily thought Cottie herself was "clever" as an artist, [211] yet she subordinated her own career completely to his, never trying to make a name for herself. Lily's letters to Ruth, over a period of almost four decades, are peppered with the phrase "Jack and Cottie." They lived together, stayed together, went places together. Only when Cottie visited her mother in London from time to time, and when Jack took his solitary Friday walks, were they apart. It was her protectiveness and sense of ownership of her husband that had so troubled Jack's family at the time of his breakdown. Yet if they were disturbed by her behavior, he wasn't. Nowhere in the family correspondence or the recollections of those who knew them is there the slightest indication that they were ever less than totally devoted to each other. She even preferred not having domestic help intrude on their lives. When they received notice to leave their first Dublin flat, Cottie was glad because she could get rid of Maggie, the maid, by claiming the new quarters were too small.[212] In 1929 they moved into a small flat on Fitzwilliam Square, "just three rooms, bathroom and kitchenette with stove," though "Jack's room is big and he can show his pictures well there."[213] The kitchen was tiny, and henceforth Cottie had to prepare meals there,[214] but neither she nor Jack complained.[215]

She wrote good letters when she wrote them, which was seldom.[216] The sisters found it not always safe to talk to her, for she might repeat confidences. "I like Cottie greatly," Lily told Ruth, "and she is reliable and kind and the best of wives, but I don't tell her anything I don't want repeated." In this way she was quite different from the more freewheeling George Yeats, who never violated a confidence.[217] So the peculiar relationship persisted, everyone in the family admiring and liking Cottie, but all wary of her and never sure of her affection for them. She was a sturdy prop for her husband, but at the same time a wall separating him from his brother and sisters.

Cottie's health had always been good, save for one bout of pneumonia in the early twenties.[218] So it came as a shock to everyone when she entered the Portobello Nursing Home in March 1947, after having experienced a chill.[219] A week later someone reported to Lily that she was "resting well,"[220] but in fact she was dying. When Jack visited Lily, she saw how "lonely" he was, his "perfect wife" away from him "for the first time."[221] She had apparently "been going downhill" for two years,[222] and once in Portobello she declined fast, falling asleep even when Jack was visiting her.[223] On 28 April 1947 she died, rather suddenly, before Jack could be summoned.[224]

"It will be dreadful for Jack," Lily told Ruth, "53 years of their marriage, which was perfectly happy. They exactly suited each other. She was, as Papa said, the perfect wife." Despite his long struggle as an artist, there were compensations. "She saw Jack become famous and receive honours, so I suppose we cannot expect much more." Lily took refuge in her one firm belief. "We have

94. Jack Yeats in studio, 1950. *Courtesy of Anne B. Yeats.*

faith that there is another and better life after this one."[225]

Cottie was given an impressive funeral, the president sending his aide-de-camp, and the prime minister his representative. The Abbey Theatre company was present, Lord and Lady Moyne, the Gogartys and Currans, and "crowds of others." Jack walked between his sister-in-law George Yeats and his nephew Michael, and at one point it looked as if he would break down, "but he just turned his back for a moment and recovered."[226]

Thereafter Jack slowly declined until his death on 28 March 1957. He continued to paint and to exhibit, but at a slower rate. More honors were bestowed on him as his art came to be more widely appreciated.[227] Thomas MacGreevy, later to become director of the National Gallery, became his faithful overseer. In late 1947,

Jack joined the University Club, and Lily was happy to report that he was its "pride."[228] After Lily's death in the first days of 1949, he felt alone and almost bereft, the last survivor of a remarkable generation of Yeatses. His affection for his niece Anne remained strong; he felt that her talent as an artist was a reflection of his own, and, when he died on 28 March 1957, he left most of his unsold paintings to her. It is pleasing to note that during his final days at the Portobello Nursing Home, his grandniece Caítríona, a young girl of six—later to become a distinguished harpist—brought him a spray of flowers picked from her own garden. It was an appropriate linking of the generations. Jack and Cottie had never had children, although they and everyone else in the family had always hoped for them.[229] Willie's children, and then Michael's, had served as substitutes.

The contrast between the two brothers may have been marked. Jack was laconic, Willie open and voluble; Jack could keep a secret, Willie couldn't. But perhaps Jack's refusal to open himself to others may have proved a blessing for him, for when he did reveal his mind he displayed a landscape of misanthropy, a battlefield on which the few and powerful wicked preyed on the many and powerless good. Although he favored goodness and wanted it to prevail, he believed it would not.

The one person who saw this other side of Jack and who could compare him fairly with his older brother was the perceptive father of both, John Butler Yeats. JBY wrote letters to all his children, but fewer to Jack than to the others; he wrote a dozen letters to Willie for every one to Jack. With Willie he was open and uninhibited, with Jack cautious and tentative, not quite sure how his words would be received. So it is illuminating to read the comments he made to Rosa Butt, the only correspondent to whom he wrote in absolute frankness, comments he believed would never be read by later generations: "It is curious, but I find Willie with all his faults more lovable than Jack. The latter was too long in Sligo and so full of ill will towards all his fellow creatures, and suspicion and contempt." Willie, on the other hand, he continued, "thinks well of his fellow creatures except when he is fighting them, at any rate has a high opinion of human nature and believes it has a noble destiny." His younger brother's response to the world was perhaps a defensive disguise. "Jack of course sticks manfully to duty, which makes him an admirable fellow citizen, but then it makes him a little cold and a little self-complacent."[230]

He remained the same elusive Jack Yeats to the end. Lily Yeats saved everything connected with her family—every letter, every newspaper clipping, every scrap of any interest, including Jack's boyhood diary and some of his early letters. He destroyed everything of his, except his paintings, that he could lay his hands on. The few surviving letters of his are found in libraries around the world only because he had no control over them. He told his niece Anne that he wished to be remembered and understood by his paintings, though he never provided his admirers with the key for cracking the code concealed in them. The letters of the other members of his family are often personal, even intimate, and through them we are able to understand much of their inner lives. The surviving letters of Jack's are mostly impersonal. He has compelled us to do his bidding. Like Christopher Wren, he has said essentially to the students of his life, "If you would seek my monument, look about you." He carried with him to the grave the secret of his double personality, the lighter man of social attractiveness and humour and gaiety, the darker one of pessimism and misanthropy. He remains the most mysterious member of his remarkable family.

8

John Butler Yeats and Rosa Butt

"I am always wanting a woman to whom I can talk
freely and have never found her. It was impossible with
my poor wife."
                                        —John Butler Yeats to Rosa Butt

One of the best-kept secrets in the Yeats family was the lengthy
but platonic love affair between John Butler Yeats and Rosa
Butt, daughter of Isaac Butt, founder of the political movement for
Home Rule for Ireland. Tantalizing phrases in two letters suggest
that Lily may have been made privy to the relationship,[1] but nowhere in the voluminous family correspondence is there any evidence that anyone else in the family knew what was going on
between them. Only the survival of his letters to her confirms
existence of the affair. In the late 1920s rumors spread in Dublin
that the two had planned to marry, but apparently little of the
gossip surfaced until after Jack's death in 1957.

   None of the story would have been revealed if Rosa Butt, a lady
of stern Victorian morality, had not broken a solemn promise made
to her ardent suitor. For more than twenty years they wrote letters
to each other regularly. They had come to an agreement that they
would write with absolute frankness, as if indeed they were husband
and wife sharing the most intimate secrets, and each agreed to burn
the other's letters as soon as read. John Butler Yeats kept his
promise; Rosa Butt did not. No letters of hers to him survive;
almost all of his to her do. A few she apparently destroyed, perhaps
because she thought them shocking, perhaps damaging to people
who might be hurt by their revelations. Yet even the letters she
saved, a little more than two hundred,[2] are certainly by the stan-

328

dards of the times unusually intimate and gossipy, and some are downright steamy, more than enough to bring a blush to maidenly cheeks of a properly brought-up lady of the nineteenth century.

After Rosa's death in 1926, the letters passed into the hands of her cousin Mary Swanzy, the painter, who refused to let anyone read them, replying to requests, "Some things ought to remain private, don't you think?"[3] Yet she allowed their existence to be known and even gave some people in Dublin a cryptic description of their contents; and she denied them the ultimate privacy of destruction by depositing them in the Bodleian Library at Oxford, with a stern prohibition that nobody could look at them until 1979.[4]

The story the letters tell is a fascinating one, not only of the two lovers but of Susan Pollexfen Yeats, of Willie and Lily and Lollie and Jack, of Dun Emer and Cuala, of the Abbey Theatre, of life in New York City in the early decades of the twentieth century, of John Quinn and John Sloan and dozens of others. Of the letters of John Butler Yeats, who was regarded as one of the most engaging correspondents of his time, these are certainly among the best. Despite whatever Rabelaisian quivers they may have induced in the lady who received them, most readers today would find them inoffensively mild even while recognizing the author's intention to shock. Why Rosa Butt did not destroy them, and why Mary Swanzy preserved them, make interesting questions for psychologists, but perhaps a longing for immortality played its part. Without the letters Rosa Butt would be forgotten. Even with them it is hard to capture with accuracy what her remarkable qualities must have been, and it is cause for regret that JBY didn't break his promise too. The course of their affair must be found in his letters only, but they are enough to keep alive the memory of Rosa Butt, who never wrote a novel or composed a sonata or met a payroll—whose only distinction was to be loved by John Butler Yeats.

•   •   •

John Butler Yeats and Rosa Butt were of almost the same age. Born on 16 March 1839, he was younger than she by only three months.[5] When she died in 1926, she had outlived him by a little more than four years.

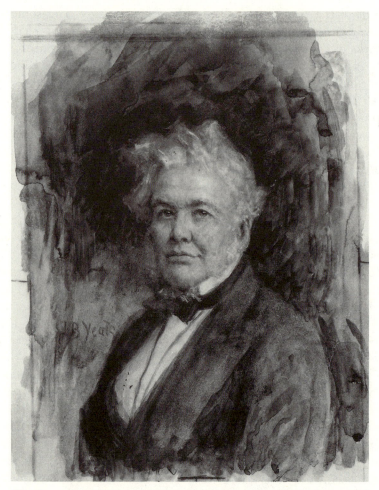

95. Isaac Butt (1813–1879). Chalk sketch by JBY. *Courtesy of J. Robert Maguire.*

Each came from an eminent Anglo-Irish family. JBY was the son and grandson of Church of Ireland clergymen, landlord of Butler properties in County Kildare. Rosa Butt was the daughter of one of the most talented barristers of the time, Isaac Butt (1813–1879). Butt, a close friend and schoolmate of Yeats's father, the Reverend William Butler Yeats, had been born a firm believer in the superiority of English culture and in the justice of England's claims to sovereignty over Ireland, but at the same time he was a defender of the rights of the Irish people to have a voice in their own government. His sympathies for the plight of Ireland grew, and at the height of his career as a member of the British Parliament, he founded what came to be known as the Home Rule movement. Displaced by Charles Stewart Parnell, he died at the age of sixty-six a few years after his fall from influence. The members of his family, including his daughter Rosa, never forgave Parnell for his usurpation of what they regarded as Isaac's personal property, and their bitterness toward him is reflected in their correspondence.[6] Isaac Butt left behind a number of tracts whose titles suggest his interests: *Land Tenure in Ireland: A Plea for the Celtic Race* (1866); *The Irish People and the Irish Land* (1867); *A Practical Treatise on the New Law of Compensation to Tenants in Ireland* (1870); and, perhaps most important, *Home Government for Ireland: Irish Federalism! Its Meaning, Its Objects, and Its Hopes* (1874).

Like Parnell, whose fall from political power was owing to an extramarital association, Butt was a man of many interests, a principal one of which was women. His reputation as a philanderer was widespread, so much so that his exploits made the single and quite understandable indiscretion of Parnell seem mild, as indeed it was and would have been so regarded anywhere except in Joyce's "priest-ridden" Ireland. Butt, for example, had been caught by his wife *in flagrante delicto* with Miss Jane Francesca Elgee,[7] later to become wife of Sir William Wilde and mother of Oscar. Mary Swanzy told Olive Purser that Butt "had two establishments," and that "you had to be careful when he approached which one he was with."[8] His reputation may have had much to do with the circumspect behavior of his daughter Rosa toward the insistent John Butler Yeats.

Despite his flouting of the conventions, the structure of Butt's family life fell into familiar British patterns. He married Elizabeth Swanzy, of an Ulster family. One of his sons became a lieutenant in the British army and later a barrister. Another became a member of the Bengal Civil Service. One of his grandsons became a lieutenant in the Indian Medical Service, and a granddaughter married a man who won the Medal of the Order of the British Empire and became

King's Remembrancer and Master of the Supreme Court. Of the three daughters who survived to adulthood, the only one who married, Elizabeth, chose a Scotsman, Thomas Colquhoun. No matter what Butt's own views might have been, the members of his family were saturated with notions of English and Anglo-Irish superiority, and Rosa was not exempted from the delusion.

So it was not surprising that the Yeats and Butt families should know each other. One genealogist has observed that almost every Anglo-Irish family is related to every other. There were few families to feed the gene pool, and intermarriage within a small group was inevitable.[9] The Butts often visited JBY's uncle Robert Corbet at Sandymount Castle, and when JBY became a barrister he "deviled" for (that is, served as junior counsel to) Butt.

Nevertheless, there is no evidence that John Butler Yeats met Rosa Butt until he was about twenty years old. Proper Anglo-Irish boys were sent away to school, so JBY spent his boyhood and youth in schools at Liverpool and on the Isle of Man. He did not appear on the Dublin scene until he was ready to enter Trinity College. His recollections of their first encounter suggest that it may have taken place about 1861 or 1862, certainly before his marriage to Susan Pollexfen. "When I first saw you," he wrote to her years later, "you were a woman grown (as well as growing) and I a hobbledehoy." He thought her at the time "the most beautiful woman" he had ever seen.[10] Nothing came of the meeting.

The impressions of her gained from their first meeting never left him; they might have been "often forgotten and out of sight" but were "yet *still there*."[11] She developed an affection for him only later, but she came "early" into his "amorous thoughts," he told her in later years.[12] Even in the early 1880s, when he visited Rosa's parents regularly, "I used to listen to every word that concerned you," he told her.[13] We know that he saw her in 1887, when he showed her a sketch he had made of himself. She had told him she thought he looked too old, and that as they were contemporaries she did not like to see him "made too old."[14] We know too that he saw her in 1889, for Lollie's diary records a visit he made "to the Butts in Oakley Street" on 3 February of that year. When he began to see her regularly years later, the old fires were rekindled; from then until the day of his death Rosa Butt remained the sole object of his amorous affection.

His marriage to Susan Pollexfen was so unsatisfying that during its early years he strayed into an illicit affair with another woman, unmarried at the time, "that one transitory passion," he called it, a *"source of misery"* to him.[15] "We parted on principle," he wrote of it to Rosa in 1910. "It all took place nearly forty years ago," and after they parted he did not speak "as many as twenty words" to her, but as he was able to describe her as "a grandmother,"[16] it is clear that she came from his own society and that he knew the details of her later life. She had not been merely a slip that passed in the night.

The unhappy marriage of JBY and Susan Pollexfen was rendered more so by the stroke she suffered in 1887 and her growing invalidism in the coming decade. Never an amiable companion, she became more and more withdrawn during the 1890s until, in the last few years of her life, she was living virtually in a world of her own.[17] So it is not surprising that when Rosa Butt entered JBY's life again in the late 1890s she should inflame the old desires. The circumstances of their renewed meeting are unclear, but we know that in 1897 he and York Powell were together with her at a railway station in London, apparently escorting her to a train to take her back to the city after a visit to Bedford Park. When the train departed, York Powell said to JBY, "What a beautiful face," and JBY deliberately repeated the compliment to Rosa, hoping she would realize that he regarded Powell's opinion as an echo of his own.[18]

Letters, tentative ones, began to pass between them. In late December 1899, only two weeks before Susan's death, he belatedly wrote Rosa to thank her for a letter, but his principal message was to tell her that he had heard from his cousin Ellie Yeats that Rosa had expressed her disappointment in not hearing from him.[19]

Then Susan Pollexfen Yeats died, on 3 January 1900, and everything changed utterly. By the middle of the year he and Rosa were corresponding with increasing frequency. When a letter for him arrived at Jack's place in Devon in July 1900 as he, Lily, Cottie, Ruth Pollexfen, and Jack were leaving the house for a stroll, he let the others walk on while he "fell behind" to read her letter. He was "very much disposed to read between the lines and find all sorts of pleasant meanings."[20] His wording was suggestive, the putting of a toe in the water—hesitant, yet fervent and invita-

96. Rosa Butt (1838–1926). *Courtesy of Michael B. Yeats.*

tional. As if to dismiss the importance of their age, he ended the main body of the letter: "So now, old friend, who to me are not old, farewell." Then, in a postscript, he threw out another baited hook: "I did not say I liked writing letters but that I liked writing to you."[21]

By November he was writing her that an amateur fortune-teller had warned him that he was "very fond of some person" who did not care about him. He wondered who it was, but the seer was unable even to say whether it was man or woman. "I made no remark," he wrote Rosa, "but had I done so would have said affection is its own reward. I am content to be the person charmed."

But he wouldn't let the letter end without a strong hint of his intentions. "Besides, a man cannot be deprived of his hopes."[22]

He found her next letter "the best" he had ever got, making him feel "buoyant" and "*exalted.*" He was so dazzled by it that as he thought of what he would write in reply, he would "in thoughts" begin his letter "My *dearest* Rosa." At this, he told her, "I would stop aghast, and then would ensue such labyrinthine musings."[23] Shortly afterward he wrote what was to become a recurring theme in his letters, that he wished she had been able to say "*all you felt.*" Her letters were like her father's, he said, with the "same vital quality, each sentence like a spark struck from an anvil." As for himself, he wrote to her, "You must not think I write to anyone as I write to you or *ever have done so.*"[24] By the end of the year, he was painting her portrait,[25] finding greater pleasure than usual in the endless revisions that are the hallmark of his work.

The correspondence between them makes clear that most of their meetings were in the presence of others. Rosa was living in Battersea with her two sisters: Amy, unmarried, and Lizzie, the widow of Thomas Colquhoun. Amy liked John Butler Yeats and enjoyed his visits, but Lizzie was a stern and unflagging chaperone who viewed JBY's presence with distaste. She apparently enjoyed widowhood more than marriage, and she clearly did not want her sister to get caught up in the kind of activity she herself had so loathed in her days with the unfortunate Mr. Colquhoun. She constantly reminded Rosa of her age, hinting strongly that physical pleasures were now beyond her. On one occasion when JBY visited their home in Battersea, Lizzie sent JBY into her room to wash rather than Rosa's room, where he would much have preferred to be.[26] She disapproved of their corresponding. "What will Lizzy say?" he asked Rosa as letters flowed between them. "She will feel she has new grounds to be really indignant. At our age we ought to know better, she will say."[27] He charged that Lizzie would have stopped their correspondence "if she could."[28] Once, when he asked Lizzie to give Rosa his "love," he noticed the "indignant silence" that fell upon her.[29] She disliked not only his courtship of Rosa but the views he held: "I fancy she would be hostile to me and my ideas," he told Rosa.[30] He preferred to see Rosa in London rather than Dublin except that "Lizzie is a difficulty."[31] He spoke of her "presence" and "tyranny,"[32] and regretted that Rosa could not get clear of her and lead her own life. To him she was "a nuisance every way,"[33] a "hysterical, unreasonable" woman.[34] When Lizzie went off on a vacation, Rosa's letters increased, both in number and fervor. "I impute the improvement in your spirits to the absence of Lizzie," he told her. "She is an incubus."[35] So he preferred going into the city with Rosa to seeing her at her home. They often visited art galleries, and he later recalled one of their days in the National Gallery, where their favorite picture was of "three lovely goddesses" and "the handsome Pan." She was angry that the goddesses were nude but Pan was not.[36]

His behavior toward her in those early days suggests the infatuation of the teenage schoolboy. In London one day, they had to separate when he, "as a matter of stern duty," had to attend a talk to which she had not been invited. Years later he recalled the occasion: "I remember so well that day I went to the lecture and at the door of the Lecture Hall looked back at you as you went away, and felt so full of affection for you and of my pleasure in your company that I as near as possible renounced the lecture and returned to you."[37]

Yet nothing was more effective at keeping the lovers from each other than their own timidity. Before he left London for Dublin in early 1902, they had gone further than Rosa would have dared admit. When he asked her to come to Dublin to visit because he needed someone to talk to, he spoke to her in terms suggesting what had already happened and would probably be repeated. "Had I anyone to talk to, I should recover my courage and get to work. I should pass my hand over your shoulder and bosom and then be at peace."[38] She wrote to him of her "strong nature" and of her "vision of a storm," and the words, at first baffling to him, encouraged him when he came to realize what they meant.[39] His passion mounted. He called her visits to him "a fearful joy" that made him "feel like a raging tiger." "I want to devour you," he insisted. Yet at the time, he said, she would hardly allow him to kiss her, so his other fleshly invasions must have been made surreptitiously, he looking the other way and she pretending not to notice.[40]

Time passed. Their letters became more and more intimate. At

97. Rosa Butt, about 1904. Pencil sketch by JBY. *Courtesy of Michael B. Yeats.*

length, in the spring of 1906, Rosa was able to schedule a visit to Ireland, ostensibly to see friends but in fact to be able to be alone with JBY in his studio. JBY was in a state of high excitement awaiting her arrival. "You must come early," he wrote her. "Then I am sure to be alone, or if there is a model it is easy to send her away." He tried to prepare her for his expectations. "You must not *torture* me by treating me as if we were not something more, something much closer, than lovers. In your letters you now treat me as I treat you, that is, as if there is between us an absolute intimacy. And you must do this when we meet. . . . I feel myself to be yours *body and soul.*"[41]

The big moment came. At last they were alone in his studio on Stephens Green. Things happened, the recollection of which sustained John Butler Yeats during the starved years that lay ahead. Two influences kept matters from getting completely out of hand: he was too cautious and considerate of her reputation, waiting for a specific invitation before proceeding; she was imprisoned in the cell of her upbringing. "I once had a chance with you and my courage failed," he said years later, remembering his lost opportunity.[42] She eagerly accepted his embraces only to a certain point and no further. Rosa's lifetime of immersion in a sea of Victorian prudery, coupled perhaps with JBY's fears of Lizzie's frowns, preserved her virtue. The flesh was willing, but the spirit was weak.

Enough had happened to encourage him to pursue matters further, though after that day the pursuit was by correspondence. The morning after the incident in the studio, she had to leave Dublin, fearful that if she lingered, tongues would begin wagging. He urged her to pay another visit to his studio before going back to Battersea, and in view of what had happened, he thought they should declare themselves "an engaged couple." In that case, he told her, *"people would help us to meet."* She insisted she must return directly to London. He was afraid she was merely showing her timidity, that "this hurry to London is mere panic." He had a simple solution, that she should tell the facts to the people with whom she was staying. "Take some of them, *even one of them,* into your confidence, and I will come down, and we shall see each other for some hours. *The bond between us is a sacred one."* Openness would help their cause. "Tell them all about it, how it has gone on for years, and that we write constantly and see each other hardly ever. If they are human they will do something to help you and bring us together." He concluded his argument with a revealing sentence. "In fact, a confidence of this sort might help us to get married."[43]

The wording suggests that she had agreed, in a moment of intimacy in the studio, that they might indeed someday become

98. John Butler Yeats in studio, 7 Stephen's Green, Dublin, about 1906. *Courtesy of author.*

husband and wife, though his own circumstances—his lack of money and of the means to make it—and hers—her own advanced age and her obligation to her sisters—made realization of the dream difficult. Yet no matter what indiscreet promises she may have made to him in the studio, she now refused to remain in Dublin but went straight to London. He wrote that he was "bitterly disappointed." "I believe on my soul that it is only your own faintheart-edness. It is perfect nonsense to say you can't stay another four and twenty hours." If she would allow him, he would even write to Lizzie and tell her everything.[44] Instead, she fled to Battersea, and that marked the end of the physical part of their romance.

In her John Butler Yeats found two Rosa Butts, the "real" one and the "artificial" one.[45] The first was the passionate, affectionate Rosa who delighted in the physical manifestations of love, the other the repressed Victorian, the outer shell that contained the smoldering spirit within. The "real" Rosa liked his frank letters, the "false" one pretended to be shocked by them. Between the two was a wall he could never quite breach.

Lizzie and other obstacles kept them separated after the delicious days of 1906, and there is no evidence that the marvels were repeated before JBY left Dublin for the six-week visit to New York that turned into a permanent stay. He never saw Rosa again, but that only intensified the ardor of his letters, which continued until his death.

There is no doubt about what happened during their Dublin meetings. When in later times he recollected the days in the studio, he was quite specific about details: "You are bright-eyed and alert, muscled and deliciously plump," he wrote her in 1912. "You are so comely and so inviting, and so pleasant and plump in the places where you ought to be plump." He continued: "By this time you know I am not a saint, and is not that the reason that I love you and that you love me? For *I know* you are not a saint, though you try to think you are."[46] He fantasized to her: "If I was with you and we were alone I would coax you into good spirits. I would place my hand round your waist—one hand—and the other hand would distractedly find its way, however forbidden, into your bosom. And fighting with me would put you into good spirits and me into bad spirits."[47] At another time he wrote, "If you and I were together and by ourselves I would give you such a loving embrace that all youth would start up in your veins. Ah, I won't say what thoughts are now in my head, *and in my veins.*"[48] He liked what happened when she yielded but not what didn't happen when she resisted. "I am instinctively constant and think *only* of you, cruel though you have always been."[49]

His letters from New York constituted a kind of verbal foreplay to a seduction that was never consummated, though he hoped someday it would be. They constituted also an attempt at educating a woman who, in his view, had allowed her natural instincts to be crushed under the heavy hand of a faulty upbringing. For while she had partly accepted his advances and made clear that she was by no means displeased with them, and had accepted his importunate letters and responded to them, she had always withheld an ultimate enthusiasm. At the studio she had played the old game of what used to be called, in the days before the sexual revolution, "Now you see it, now you don't," and, in replying to his letters, she either hinted that his remarks were too broad or pretended that he had never written them.[50]

One of the reasons he was attracted to Rosa was that he found in her a potential conversationalist (even though she often disappointed him when the subject grew improper). "I am always wanting a woman to whom I can talk freely," he told her, "and have never found her. It was impossible with my poor wife."[51] With Susan he could only bring up matters that were "quite trivial." "If I showed her my real thoughts she became quite silent and silent for days, though inwardly furious." Unfortunately, he told Rosa, he found some of the same faults in her. "My real thoughts you dislike. They offend you."[52] Even with her the harsh censor of propriety acted as a deterrent on his speech. "I have not a woman friend in the world, and in fact have never had one, to whom I could tell everything in free hearted intimacy. I loved my wife but told her nothing."[53]

In early 1906, JBY had given a talk in Dublin at an exhibition of the paintings of George Watts and had shocked his conventional audience by discussing the virtues of "temptation." Beatrice Elvery, a young artist who knew JBY well and heard his talk, recalled with excitement how the old man had openly discussed matters "unusual for the time," speaking of "love, desire, women, and sex."[54] The substance can be summarized by a few of his sentences:

> The moralist says: I teach morality, without which society would not hold together. The trader says: I teach trade, without which there would be no wealth. . . . The religious teacher: I

teach religion, without which people would forget that there was another world or a judgment to come. And the scientist says: I teach truth, which is the basis of everything.

What can the artist say? . . . He works only to please himself, and regards it as the most egregious folly—indeed, a kind of wickedness—to try and please anybody else; he admires wrong as often as right; . . . he inculcates no lessons, and preaches no dogma. . . . Art seems to say, with all its strength and with all its voices: "Seek temptation; run to meet it; we are here to be tempted." Art does not say—"Be happy, or be miserable, or be wise, or be prudent"; but it says—"Live, have it out with fortune, don't spare yourself, be no laggard or coward, have no fear."[55]

His letters to Rosa from New York are filled with commentary and footnotes to the talk on Watts. He resolutely stuck to his determination to educate her away from her restricted views on morality. When she protested the frankness of one of his letters, he replied: "Fancy Rosa denying Venus!—Oh you humbug. You are full of Venus. Old age has not tamed you, and were I with you I would make you acknowledge it. Without Venus life would be a poor thing."[56] He would not let her avoid the physical realities of love, which he thought proper and enjoyable and she enjoyable and improper. He stuck to his dramatic assumption that they were an old married couple and in one letter restated his position:

One of the charms of marriage is that two people can talk to each other of things that the woman would not talk of to other women or the man to other men, and that is why I insisted on our letters being burnt, so that you and I could write to each other as if in married frankness: and I do write to you as if you were my real wife and one flesh with me (which also you are not in reality). You on your side are a little too maidenly and proper. Not for worlds would you write these words: "bottom" or "thigh," nor would you allude to your breasts. How I would like to make a portrait of them with the little pink nipples![57]

He compared her to the one person whose behavior embarrassed the Butt daughters. "Your father was untameable because he had so much human nature. To meet him was to recognize your own self, only on a far larger scale. You are like your father, and in my letters I am always trying to break the shell of timidity and get into it as one opens a door to blow up the furnace. Alas! that we did not marry. You would have made a man of me, and I would have made you the woman you are and that you do not know you are."[58] He defended Butt and explained his behavior. "Christ we learn was tempted in all things. Your father was tempted in all things but, not being divine, could not escape the consequences. Have you ever realized that the majority of men keep straight precisely because they are not tempted?" He thought Butt's reputation had not been damaged as much as people thought. "I can remember that Parnell rose in men's estimate and *especially in women's* when it was known that he had his weakness for another man's wife." Her father's only enemies, he maintained, were "the people endowed with all the *mean* virtues."[59]

She pretended he never wrote such letters, and he objected to the blandness of her replies: "You are early Victorian with a vengeance, that is to say, you think the correct thing for a woman, when she writes a letter, is to say nothing and to do it over a long letter."[60] In the very next letter, he apologized for having written so crossly, then persisted in his criticism: "I know no more about you than I did years ago. You give me *no* confidences, and when I give you my confidences, judging by your letters, you don't seem a bit interested. And on one occasion you were quite angry that I gave you my confidence, and in fact let me know that you wished me to keep to ordinary and everyday things in our correspondence. The greatest pleasure in life for a man like me is friendship and intimacy with a charming woman, and you won't have it so."[61]

When he wrote her with approval about unmarried lovers he knew in New York, she avoided replying. "You see I have not the slightest objection to lovers being happy in their own way and would help them all I could, because I don't hate human nature," he told her. "Probably these 'lax' views will disgust you. At any rate you would die sooner than write to me about them. There are so many things forbid in your conscience that I don't know what to write about. Ah me!"[62] He wrote of one manifestation of the sexual revolution in America: "Everyone in America talks quite frankly about the prevention of births in married life, at table, anywhere. Men and women are quite frank about it, and so are many of the magazines. In every shop syringes are sold to be used by ladies, great piles of them."[63] She refused to acknowledge that she would read such things. "What are you thinking of?" he demanded to know. "Every letter I write I tell you things and say things for the very purpose that you in your reply would say *something about them* —and you never say anything, unless indeed I happen to say I have a toothache or a head ache or am in bad spirits."[64] He charged that she thought some of his frank letters were "inspired by a desire to vex" her,[65] but he reminded her of their joint promise. "When I asked you to agree that letters on both sides should be burned at once I thought this would make us both write freely and that we would be both of us like married people without secrets with each other. And I have destroyed all your letters. There is not one in existence."[66] Yet she kept all his, even those in which he revealed the shape, firmness, and color of parts of her anatomy. He would not let up on his insistence that love could not be merely spiritual, that she and he had bodies that must partake of it too. When he saw a cartoon of a demasculinized Cupid, he took advantage of it to drive the point home:

> Yesterday I saw a paper with a little boy in it, a sort of Cupid. I thought of sending it to you. Other people put on the male a fig leaf. Here they do better. They remove the offending thing and so a fig leaf is unnecessary. Tell me what you think about it. Are you in your feelings inclined to think that Americans are right in *censoring the &ccc?* Arrows shot by a Cupid so mistreated would be without any effect, I think, just as men so treated would have no sweethearts and not want to have any, whatever they may say. The soul depends on the body.[67]

All this was heady stuff for poor Rosa, locked in the arid flat with her sisters. "I sometimes wonder how much of my letters you impart to Amy," he wrote. "There is a good deal I know you don't impart, yet some you might tell her. Lizzy no! she is too hard and censorious."[68] He told Rosa he often dreamed that he was "young and naked and unashamed," together with her "in love and intimacy," that he thought of drawing them so, and that they might then look at the drawings and "kiss each other just as if we were young and in a way that would shock Lizzie." He thought Lizzie's education had been ruined despite her experience. "She thinks she knows everything and she knows nothing, even though she was married." [69] He believed her sister's malign influence was inhibiting Rosa's letters, and he became annoyed at writing frankly to her only to have her not respond in kind: "I want you to answer this letter by return of Post and tell me if you have destroyed all my letters. I liked the idea of writing to you as frankly as if we were old married people, but you never took to it, as was perhaps natural." [70] She disregarded his request and brought forth an uncharacteristically intemperate outburst:

> You are too provoking. In my last letter I asked two things that you would answer by return of post, and that you would tell me whether you have destroyed all my letters, and you have neither answered by return nor told me whether or not you destroyed all my letters.
>
> It spoils my pleasure in writing to you that you never answer any of my questions or make any reference to what I say in my letters. It is not nice or sympathetic to treat me in such a way. I have really tried all along to make my letters amusing to you, but I will try no longer. I give it up. You don't encourage me enough.
>
> It seems to me that your practice is to read my letter and toss it away, and then after some weeks when you have completely forgotten all I have written to set about answering it.
>
> As soon as you have told me that you have destroyed all my letters, I will write again—and *not till then*. So there. [71]

She responded with a "lovely letter," but JBY neglected to let posterity know how she replied about her promise to destroy his letters. Whatever she may have said, she continued to hold on to them, [72] and he continued to write boldly. "I love you with my soul and with my body, and I love your body," he told her almost ten years after the ecstasy of the studio. "I like to kiss you and to touch your hands, and to think about it. Don't worry about stupid vulgar people. You always think too much about them. They frighten you.

I despise them. I could not get along with them so comfortably as I do, if *I did not despise them.*"[73] When she sent him a letter that could have been interpreted as he wished it to be, he seized the opportunity to reply. "In today's letter there was just *one* sentence which pleased me. You said you would like to sit beside a fire, your feet on the fender, and a friend, platonic or *otherwise,* beside you. You know I am not satisfied to be platonic, and that the attempt to keep me platonic makes me mad, notwithstanding our years. In the real sense we are both as young as ever."[74] He threatened to send her some lines of Walt Whitman, who had "honest courage about love and the facts of life." But he warned her not to show them to Lizzie. "She has sold herself to the devil, in spite of her better nature, just like those people I abhor."[75]

He maintained that he wrote two letters to every one of hers and sometimes even more,[76] and despite an occasional letter from her that pleased him, she continued to decline commenting on the racier parts of his. He described at some length the scandalous personal life of President Woodrow Wilson (as that life was told to him by Wilson's detractors at Princeton), but she not only failed to respond to his comments on it but even delayed writing at all for a longer period than usual.[77] He refused to let up on his education of her. "I always feel sorry for women who have not husbands, or lovers," he wrote her in 1916. "Over here a woman always manages to have at any rate a lover, and whether the relations are innocent no one knows, and that is because no one cares. In this matter of the sexes a silent revolution has been going on for a long time, and no one can stop it, no more than King Canute could stop the tide."[78] He pursued the subject in his next letter, telling of a married couple, "young, well-educated, and well-born." In conversation with a friend the husband said, "casually," "I and Lilly lived together for a year before we were married," and another guest in his boarding house, "a Harvard man very polished and ceremonious," remarked "in the best Harvard way" that "he and his wife lived together some time before they were married."[79] "Quite 'nice' young girls will go from one lover to another, living with each of them, and *not lose the respect of her friends.*" He assumed that there was a certain "moderation" in these affairs, "though it would be impossible to say what is and what is not moderation." He himself

99. John Butler Yeats dining at Petitpas, about 1914. *Courtesy of author.*

approved what he saw. "It is like my opinions on drink. I would lynch a drunkard, but so would I a teetotaller. And they like a moderate lover as I do a moderate drinker."[80] Hearing no response to these titillations, he wrote in exasperation, "I can't write more, for I don't know what to write about, although had I your sympathy I could write of many things."[81]

She had been quite different when they were together, and he dreamed of what it would be like when they were reunited. "I am always in vision seeing you and me sitting together under a shading tree on a bench in your park while I tell you some of what I hear in America, and I hear your mocking and humorous laugh."[82]

That laugh was what was missing in her letters. He confided in her that the weakness of his character was "vanity," and that when he achieved something he wanted her approval. Yet she always withheld it. "You never praise me," he complained. "Years ago I wrote a very appreciative article on your father, . . . and I sent it to you and thought to myself, 'How Rosa will like this and how she will reward me with praise and compliments.' But no, not a word from Rosa. 'Well,' I said to myself, 'no matter, virtue is its own reward.' " Then he arranged for Lollie to send her a copy of the selection from his letters made by Ezra Pound, a book that had received glowing reviews from all the best people, including the rising young T. S. Eliot.[83] He recounted what happened.

> You get my book, and you are good enough to tell me that you had received it, and you said it was sent by Lolly, and you quite ignored the fact that it was sent because Lolly knew I would wish you to get it and also that I had paid for it. And in that book are several paragraphs all written in sympathy and admiration for your magnanimous and noble-hearted father. But you did not give a word of praise. All you said was to object to the word 'damn' in the first sentence.
>
> Yet if I happen to say anything you disliked, as when I ventured to say a good word for Parnell, I would get a reply by *return of post* and a scolding that left no mistake as to your feelings. If you want to keep me you must praise. Constantly I have taken a bit of trouble to make a letter interesting to you and then said to myself, "Rosa will reward me with her praise and affection." But you never do, and you never did. All was silence— blank silence.[84]

A short time later he modified his stance, perhaps feeling he had been too extreme in his vanity. "Of course I don't want you to praise me. I don't care for praise. I get plenty of it. It rolls like water off a duck's back. But when I write so much about your father, I should have liked to hear what you thought, at any rate that you liked or disliked, and that I think is not being very unreasonable."[85] Yet she grew more reticent with the years, and his disappointment continued.

* * *

One of the virtues of JBY's letters to Rosa is that, because of their frankness, he reveals more in them than he does elsewhere. In them, for example, we get his comparison between Willie and Jack and his preference for the former.[86] In them too we find the clearest and most complete picture—as drawn by him—of his unhappy marriage to Susan Pollexfen Yeats, unsatisfying in equal measure to both. Susan, as a Pollexfen, did not write. She has left no letters, diaries, or essays to explain her position, and so her husband was left an open field for criticisms of her.

Like most of the Pollexfens, he told Rosa, Susan was completely "self-centered." She "did not notice any person outside the few people she liked," and they, he added, *"were very few."* She was critical of people regardless of their class, never seeing a difference "between a lord and a labourer that was not to the advantage of the labourer." She generally held a poor opinion of everybody, in this regard being "most undeviating and impartially unfair." These qualities he admired, as he hated all signs of class distinction himself, but there was one deficiency that kept her from becoming "something very remarkable": she had no "intellect."[87] "I used to enjoy hearing my poor wife talk of other people. She was always wrong, but her mistakes were more interesting than other people's right judgment."[88]

From her general distrust of mankind came a practice she shared with her daughter Lollie: "I remember that my wife never failed to tell you bad news. If there was good news it did not seem to her worth talking about. It was only when things were going wrong that she spoke."[89] "I used to 'put off' opening a letter of Susan's, and I do the same with Lollie's letters, and in both cases their peculiarity has its source in the same fine quality, a determination in their own lives to continually face the disagreeable and turn away from the agreeable." "At the same time," he added, "it is as well there are not too many of these people."[90] But where Lollie insisted on talking all the time and annoying people with her insecurities, Susan Pollexfen retreated into silence "and so was not so hard to live with," as Lollie was. For a long time JBY could not understand his wife's strange behavior. "I used to wonder what was the matter with her, and why she hated so many people and said such vitriolic things. It is only since I have seen and observed Lollie that I have known why she was so strange and difficult, and ready to hate every one."[91]

Despite the casual remark that he had loved Susan,—"I loved

my wife but told her nothing,"[92] repeated as a matter of form
whenever the occasion demanded—in one indiscreet moment he
told a different story: "I became engaged on two or three days
acquaintance, and it was not first love or love at all (this really *entre
nous*—I have never confessed it to anyone) but just destiny."[93]

He often spoke of the Pollexfens' stern sense of duty, yet John
Butler Yeats showed as much as they. Having married Susan Pollexfen, he accepted the permanence of his obligation. "I have always
been chaste," he assured Rosa. "I was faithful to my dear wife,
except for that one transitory passion which was to me a *source of
misery* at the time, and I have always been faithful to you."[94] For
Susan he felt a "conjugal affection," even learning not to mind
"when Susan insulted me and my friends."[95] He had expressed the
idea more fully in a letter to Willie in 1916:

> People seem to me to have quite forgotten *what a wife is*. A
> man may admire one woman and be in love with another, and all
> sorts of wanton fancies in his restless heart may play continually
> about a third. There is one woman whom *he accepts* and she is his
> wife—all her limitations, her want of intellect, even her want of
> heart. All her infirmities and all her waywardness he accepts and
> would not have them altered. If there be such a woman she is his
> wife. The feeling grows slowly. It is not affection as it is not
> passion. It is just *husband's feeling,* and she has doubtless a corres-
> ponding *wife's feeling.*[96]

• • •

The letters are filled too with marvelous commentary about
America, which to him was a Utopia. At a time when many Americans were fleeing their country because they found it too repressive,
too conservative, he had fled English and Anglo-Irish civilization
because he found in them what American dissidents saw in their
own country. In America, he said, "The skies are nearly always
blue and the sun nearly always shining. The women have no affecta-
tion and can talk seriously, and the men have no pretension, and
people meet together to talk." He found to his delight that "old
men are popular here, in the streets and everywhere, a breezy sort
of popularity, as if they thought it was jolly to be old and to have
so long survived pneumonia and cancer and consumption and

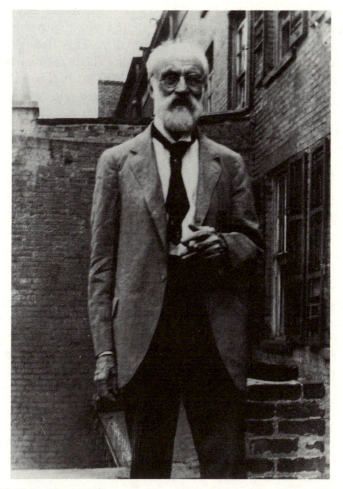

100. John Butler Yeats on roof of Petitpas Boarding House, 317
West 29th Street, New York City, about 1917. *Courtesy of author.*

drink, and all the evils flesh is heir to."[97] After seven years among
its inhabitants, he wrote enthusiastically that "the American de-
mocracy is *extraordinarily* intelligent, and America is far and away
the most intelligent country in the world."[98] He spent almost all
of his fourteen American years in New York and absorbed its prejudices about other places, notably Boston. "They [Bostonians] are

always careful of their dollars," he wrote. "The richer they are the worse they are. And then they are so pleased with themselves. They don't know that in my eyes they are dirt. They hate England intensely. That is the only interesting thing about them. I am told by everyone that it is terrible to live in Boston, it is so infernally dull. I suppose they have a good side but I have not as yet discovered it." [99]

He found America to be a giant fair. "I reach out towards America as it were hands of longing. Till I came here I never realized the meaning of the words 'human destiny.' " [100] Yet as time went on he began to find warts on the face of his adopted country. He scorned Woodrow Wilson for his cowardice in refusing to enter the war early, [101] and he disliked the coming of Prohibition. "How the devil are you to make friends among new acquaintances? All strangers are hostile till you drink with them." [102] Toward the end he had developed the disillusionment of the ordinary American with his country. "I hate the crude in women and artists and children and in painting and literature. I am highly civilized, and America is not enough civilized for my taste." [103] When a vast explosion took the lives of thirty-seven women in a downtown New York factory, he charged that such incidents were "mere bagatelles, mere nothings, parts of the daily life, a little amusement provided for U.S.A." John Quinn's office was close to the explosion, and Quinn, who saw the smoke, "was delighted to tell about it." JBY was depressed by what he saw as indifference. "The slaughter of 37 innocent chicks, and pretty stenographer girls hurrying along full of talk and laughter and with eager anticipation of the good daily lunch all suddenly caught up and hurled into cold graves—what about it? Among a nation of a hundred millions, by this they are all forgotten, except here and there where the heart of a mother or father is still bleeding. Their sweethearts have by this time got someone else. That is life in the U.S.A., where nothing is taken very seriously." [104]

He also reveals to Rosa those qualities of mind and thought that brought him ostracism in fashionable Dublin society. He thought English civilization "a nightmare," [105] a view not likely to find favor among the settled and prosperous Anglo-Irish class of which he was supposed to be a member. He couldn't understand why rich people were admired by others, even the stingy ones like his distant cousin Vyvyan Stewart, while a poor man was not, even the generous ones like his Uncle Matthew. "That is why I am a radical," he said, "and say the whole world must be turned upside down before it will be a fit place to live in." [106] He made some remarkable pronouncements, one in particular that can be excused on the grounds that it was delivered two years before the November "revolution" that transferred power from one set of despots to another. "The civilization of the future will come from Russia. They are the real enemies of Germany. England is only another Prussia, and they can't endure each other, because they are both of them thieves. In both the people are selfish and self-centered, and utterly indifferent to the feelings of anyone other than themselves, though the Germans are infinitely more wicked." [107]

He liked to call himself a "socialist," but there is little evidence that he knew what the term meant, nor did he ever specify exactly how his ideal world would have been organized. He knew only that unworthy men were rewarded while the just and gifted were not; as he was one of the unrewarded, he was dissatisfied with the existing system. In Dublin he had made himself unpopular with the powers at Trinity College by openly expressing his opinions about what he thought its mediocrity. In his letters to Rosa, he gives us a sample of the kind of utterance that irritated the powerful of Dublin: "University education is nearly always bad education. TCD is chiefly occupied in making mediocre men still more mediocre, whereas it very successfully strangles any original talent that has the bad luck to enter its gates." [108] He believed his country's association with England had corrupted the Anglo-Irish. "I have always said that I am for Home Rule in order to rescue Irish Protestants from greed and vulgarity. . . . I think Irish Protestants are the meanest people on Earth, and have always thought so." [109] In a society where the lines between classes were clearly marked, and where he himself could have occupied the space above the top line, he chose to attack the divisions. "I hate *class feeling* and have always done my best not to allow myself to be influenced by it. I have chosen my friends without thinking of class considerations. One reason why I get irritated with Merrion Square is that it is full of class feeling. In my young days a man said he was a gentleman because his father had been a gentleman. This of course was folly, but at any rate it was antique, besides which it meant that a man, being a gentleman, need not make any further push to be something else."[110] He thought Rosa's own political persona had been determined by her surroundings. "A person living in Merrion Square will be as others there. In those magnificent abodes I am as a tainted person—a radical and a Home Ruler and Pro Boer."[111] He returned to the subject whenever Rosa aroused him to it. "You may have said it with innocent intentions, but I don't like being accused of a taste for fashionable society, and it is a sort of passion with you. I detest all the qualities that are *class,* the self-complacency and vulgar self-assertion of the middle class, the insolence of the upper, and the sullen selfishness of the lower class. What I like is the intellect playing *disinterestedly* all round life and thought. That fascinates me, even if it be as the candle does the moth."[112]

He approved of women's suffrage at a time when the campaign for it was anathema to all right-thinking citizens; yet he managed to insert a few needles under Rosa's skin while defending it. "I am glad you are in favor of women getting votes. It is the first bit of common sense on politics that I have ever heard you utter. Of course the women should have votes. The churches are entirely in their hands. This business of running everything has made the woman much less attractive to the male. . . . Women having *direct power* into their hands don't trouble about exercising the old arts of indirect power, and the result is to me most curious. . . . Goethe said the last thing man would civilize is woman. Well, here [in America] she is, frankly, a tiger, out in the open. In Europe she keeps back in covert, in ambush ready to spring, or, if she appears in the open she hides her savage nature under a sleek skin and movements of her body full of grace and deception."[113] Yet Rosa herself, with her unfortunate background and upbringing, might not be able to exercise her franchise intelligently. "When I say you are not literary, . . . I only mean that I wish you took some interest in ideas, the idea of progress for instance. Ireland is progressing, beginning to take an interest in intellectual things, in poetry and art, but all this is to you nothing. You are about as interested in ideas as if you were a nun, or a priest, or a Swanzy. That's why you are so often in low spirits."[114] It certainly did not occur to him that his definition of "progress" as a general increase of interest in ideas was hardly one that would have been accepted by the movers and shakers. In his world all that mattered were art and intelligence. In his strange prophecy about Russia, he apparently thought that when the czar's empire collapsed it would be succeeded by a brave new world run by the Dostoievskis and Tolstoys; the very idea of a Lenin would have been so repugnant to him that he would not have accepted its possibility. When the event happened, he expressed his displeasure, calling "Bolshevism" a system that "likes nothing better than to shoot down clergymen and professors and artists and poets."[115]

Another reason for the world to be grateful for JBY's letters to Rosa is that in them he strikes off the occasional sparkling remark or the unexpected anecdote that tells us things we have long wanted to know. Students of the Abbey have often wondered why Annie Horniman aroused such antagonism among the Irish beyond the fact of her mean behavior to them. JBY put the matter in a simple phrase. She is "a woman of the best principles and actions, nothing to object to except herself."[116] In another letter he managed to give the back of his hand to the unpopular German wife of the great Celtic scholar Douglas Hyde by comparing her to a Mrs. Merrington, another woman he disliked. "She is a great friend of Mrs. Douglas Hyde, because they have a subject in common—abuse of the Irish people."[117] Of Mrs. Merrington he wrote: "She acts on one's nerves like the scraping of pots."[118] He sculpts George Moore in a few phrases: "He is the most old maidish and pernickety man you ever met. It is almost impossible to please him with anything or anybody. . . . He never says on any subject what he does not think."[119]

He occasionally repeats gossip about scandalous subjects of interest to followers of Irish history. Maud Gonne had sought a separation from her husband, Major John MacBride, and wanted custody of their son Séan. She had earlier borne Lucien Millevoye's illegitimate child, Iseult, of whom the court had no official cognizance. "The major has taken care to let some things be known over here," JBY told Rosa. "For instance at one of the enquiries he was asked had he not been offered a chance of seeing his child. He answered, 'Yes, but at the house where she keeps her other child,' " thereby letting the cat out of the bag.[120]

●　　●　　●

At length the years took their toll on both lovers, the one who burned the cool letters and the one who kept the burning ones. By May 1918 he acknowledged that age was catching up with them. "You have given up writing and abandoned me for good and all. I know what is the matter. We have the same complaint. It is our last birthday and thinking about the next one." He had been ill, had indeed almost died of influenza, and recovery was slow. "All the latter part of last winter I felt bad. I walked slowly and was glad to lean on my stick. I struggled against it and would strengthen myself and walk briskly. I said to myself, 'This is nerves, it is hysteria.' All the same I could not shake off my depression, and there were other symptoms, too horrible to think about." Yet he summoned up his old optimism. "And now I am all right and am firmly convinced that old age is a delusion. If I was near enough to you, I would call for you every morning and take you for a walk and then in the afternoon take you for another walk and should tell you merry stories about the people of New York, and you would be young again."[121]

But the tide could not be turned back. Amy, Rosa's friendly sister, suffered a stroke in 1919 and lost control of her speech. "You are now all alone," JBY wrote Rosa, and your *evenings will be alone.* Often writing to you I said to myself, 'This will perhaps interest Amy,' and so I would write thinking of her as well as you, but never of Lizzie."[122] Rosa's letters decreased in number even more, and Amy's death in 1920[123] was a kind of writing on the wall. "You have long ceased writing to me," he complained a month before Amy died. "And getting no letters from you I have followed your example, for I have begun to think that my letters are only a bore. I write illegibly, and you don't care about America, and I have only America to write about. I suppose it pleases Lizzie to see that our correspondence has ceased."[124] Yet all things are relative. The letter in which these words appear was almost eight

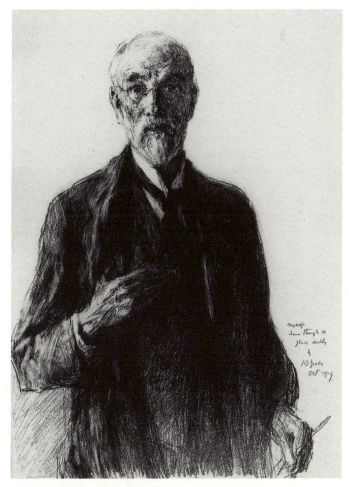

101. John Butler Yeats, 1919. Pencil sketch by JBY. *Courtesy of author.*

hundred words long, and in the year and a half between it and his last letter, he managed to fire off another dozen totaling almost ten thousand words. He tried to stave off the inevitable by putting on a brave front. "The old are expected to be cheerful," he told Rosa. "I think the reason we are sometimes cheerful is that in order to keep ourselves alive we have to be cheerful. The young can afford to be dismal and play that kind of trick with themselves. *We can't.*"[125]

He hoped she would imitate him in writing about herself and telling him interesting things that had happened.

> I like greatly getting letters from you, and like you I am old. I am much happier than you are, because I am here by myself with no one to torment or distress me, only my work to do. I constantly think about you and would write constantly, only it stops me and discourages me that you do not write, because I can't help thinking that my letters are only a bore, and that you prefer being left to yourself and to your own sadness. I think you would be more at peace if you told me things. You are too reticent. You never tell me anything, never confide in me. Shakespeare says that sorrow if it is not communicated whispers the o'erfraught heart and bids it break. And besides, since you let me know nothing about yourself, the effect is that when I sit down to write to you I am all at sea and do not know what to say to you. That is why I don't write. Of all the people I write to, you are the one I know least about, and *yet you are the one I am most curious about.* Whenever in the old days we were together *I was always trying to find out* what you felt and what you thought, but you always kept away from me, telling me nothing. I could never induce you to trust me. I sometimes thought that though you persuaded yourself you liked me you really distrusted me. I suppose it is the Ulster blood and the Swanzy influence.
>
> Had we married I would have had a great struggle with you and never rested till I had won your confidence. I really am profoundly affectionate or would have been so, certainly with you, had we lived together like married folk who do not separate night or day.[126]

His dreams and illusions were fixed at the year when he last saw her. "You are lonely and sad and I suppose old. I wish I was near you. We should see each other every day. When we found ourselves alone we should exchange kisses, and defy all scandal. What things I would tell you about the USA and people here, and how you would laugh, notwithstanding your age and your primness. I don't believe you are old and prim as if I were with you you would be as young as ever, and you would think me young. I remember perfectly what it tastes to kiss you." [127] She responded with a letter beginning "My dear old lover," delighting him. He agreed. "And we are lovers. And if we meet and when we meet, we shall kiss and be young in that kiss, our bodies and souls not." [128]

These words were written by a frail old man with not many months to live, who was expected by family and friends to return to Dublin to die in dignity near his children. Yet nothing stopped the active mind from living its own life on its own terms. "You don't know how much affection I have for you. It has been growing all these years, notwithstanding the wide Atlantic. If I get to London I will come to you." [129]

Of course, he never got to London, or to Dublin either. He resisted every effort by his family and by a thoroughly irritated John Quinn (who had spent most of his adult life watching over the feckless painter and wanted to be rid of his burden) to leave New York, and had finally put his foot down so thoroughly on the idea of returning that they gave up the attempt. He died on 3 February 1922 in his little bedroom in the Petitpas lodging house on West 29th Street. For the last three months of his life he had written Rosa nothing.

•   •   •

What is to be made of this remarkable, almost totally epistolary yet passionate affair? Professing undying fealty to Rosa, John Butler Yeats nevertheless moved three thousand miles away from her and never seriously tried to return. He talked marriage but never attempted it. He was beyond doubt a sincere lover, for he became troubled when he did not hear from Rosa, and there is no reason to question the anguish and longing for her so clearly reflected in the letters. Yet one can hardly place this charming couple in the company of Abelard and Héloise, Romeo and Juliet, Lancelot and Guinevere, or Tristan and Iseult. There were no obstacles of religion, social standing, or inconvenient spouses blocking their way. Money was a deterrent, but other great passions have triumphed over poverty. It is true that Rosa resided with the two sisters—one as daunting as the Berlin wall—but when have sisters stood in the way of great passions? Some of the most moving poetry in the

English language has been written about the enforced renunciation of lovers (including his own son's "When you are old and gray"), yet his separation from Rosa was not enforced at all. Perhaps his affair with her can be considered as merely another of John Butler Yeats's unfinished projects, the last in a long line beginning with his fragmentary novels of the 1870s, his many tentative oil portraits, his uncompleted autobiography. Like them, it has the virtue of being utterly fascinating and, like the works of art, we are the richer for having it even while wondering how it came about or why it developed as it did.

Why Rosa kept his letters despite her solemn promise may be a mystery to be unraveled only by students of psychology who specialize in the female mind. Whatever her reasons, the world is grateful to her for having provided an outlet for the confidences of John Butler Yeats, who, for all his boasting about freedom, was remarkably loath to discuss intimate matters either in his other letters or in his memoirs. He may not have said all he wanted to say to Rosa, but he has said enough to make the world grateful to her for her violation of a sacred trust.

Epilogue

Many families are notable for their production of financiers, politicians, or athletes: the Rothschilds and Harrimans, the Churchills and Kennedys, the Shulas and Ripkens. Not many produce writers or artists. The Huxleys and Arnolds, Macaulay and the Trevelyans come to mind and, of course, in the United States, the Jameses: Henry, William, and Alice. To this last group can be added the Yeatses, who may in sheer numbers—and diversity—have surpassed the rest. Not many families can boast of a father who was both a noted portraitist, conversationalist, and letter writer, one son considered by many to be the greatest poet of his age, another regarded with growing appreciation as one of the finest painters of his time, and two daughters of unusual talents in embroidery and printing.

The five were part of the Dublin artistic, literary, and intellectual establishment for decades and left an indelible mark on its cultural life. William Butler Yeats won fame not only in his own country but in the entire English-speaking world and was honored for his achievements with the Nobel Prize in Literature. Jack Yeats's fame as a painter is as marked in England as it is in Ireland (though it has not yet penetrated the United States). The products of Dun Emer and Cuala are still sought by collectors. "We are quite a remarkable family," Lily boasted to her cousin Ruth Pollexfen, accurately if immodestly.[1]

How did such an improbable development come about? Probably there is no answer that will satisfy everyone. Was it nature or nurture or, more likely, a combination of both, and in what proportions? Yet there can be little doubt that the overpowering personality of John Butler Yeats and his insistence on a particular kind of life for his children had more to do with their choice of careers than any other single force. Without his overwhelming presence and influence they would certainly have developed otherwise. Good Anglo-Irish families of their time—like the Butts, for example—produced lawyers and physicians, members of the British civil service, military officers. Sarah Purser complained to John Butler Yeats that he could have turned his elder son into a doctor at small expense. He replied by showing her a copy of a poem Willie had written, as if to unmask her own pretensions as idiosyncratic.[2] When Willie declined to accept a salaried nine-to-five job that York Powell could have secured for him, his father breathed a sigh of relief. For Willie, and for all his children, JBY desired a life of freedom, of residence in an intellectual and artistic universe. He himself knew that if he had remained with the law, he would have advanced to the bench, as many of his King's Inns classmates had. But then, he reflected triumphantly, his sons would probably have grown up to be commonplace money-grubbing citizens too.[3]

So nurture had much to do with his children's fate. Yet the father was fortunate in the material he had to work with—precious ore waiting to be refined. Nature too had made its contribution, though its precise components are hard to enumerate and define. John Butler Yeats felt that a happy combination of genes had met and united in his children, and that he himself had been but one small element in its shaping—and not necessarily the most important one, merely a link in a long chain that would carry the medallion of greatness in the form of his children.[4]

JBY put his views simply, reducing the complementary parts of his children's nature to the two names "Yeats" and "Pollexfen," the one humane, generous, open, inspired; the other somber, absorbed, profound, forbidding, yet full of a suppressed poetry and vibrant with life. He referred to them as "those two kinds of civilization, each with its own values."[5] His own family he knew well. The Yeatses, he told his son the poet, were "The Good People."[6] Of his uncles Thomas and John he wrote to his daughter Lily: "You would be proud to have their blood. They were so clever and so innocent. I never knew and never will know any people so attractive."[7] That family, with its Taylor, Armstrong, Corbet, and Butler lines, was composed of Castle officials, clergymen, high military officers, stockbrokers, all in the Anglo-Irish tradition, unsullied by diversions into poetry or art. Its members were generous, sentimental, sympathetic. JBY's grandfather, Parson John Yeats of St. Columba's Church in Drumcliff, made it a practice to cough loudly before entering a room where he knew two of his servants might be engaged in unseemly behavior, and at his death he left an unpaid bill of £400 for liquor.[8] The parson's son William Butler Yeats, also a clergyman, "sat down by the road and cried, grown man though he was," when he saw the favorite horse of his youth reduced years later to hauling carts of turf.[9] JBY's uncle Matthew defended tenants from the indignities their landlords tried to inflict on them.[10] The Yeatses were genteel, civilized, and kind.

Yet their very humanity worked against them in one way. Although they were loved, JBY told Willie, they were not feared, and so passed "making no mark."[11] They lacked toughness and were too amiable to have left an impression on the world.

That weakness, according to JBY, was more than compensated for by the Pollexfens. Brooding, morose, sternly moral, puritanical, interested in "getting on," they were nevertheless full of what John Butler Yeats called "magnetism," of suppressed poetry, which he believed they transmitted to his children. It says much for their power over John Butler Yeats that when Edward Dowden praised his son's early poetry, JBY should have attributed the gift to his wife's family rather than his own.[12]

Lily thought the credit belonged largely to her father. "When I look back at Papa's life I marvel at his gay courage, talking literature and art and life, and no income, an invalid wife, four children growing up without education or prospects. If we had not that spark, or whatever it is that we have, we would have gone down out of our class. Anyway, he lived to see Willie famous, Jack a fine painter whose work will live, and Lollie and I are not nonentities."[13]

While Susan Pollexfen Yeats may have contributed little to the character of her children and almost nothing to their intellectual development, yet the family heritage she bequeathed them exercised perhaps a more profound influence on them than that of their father. JBY, seeing in them the marks of his wife's family, continually reminded them not only of its virtues but of its short-comings. Possessing his own articulateness and, at times, his bubbling enthusiasm, all his children—with the possible exception of the cheerful Lily—showed the intensity, the solemnity, the tendency to melancholia of the Pollexfens, which stuck to them like burrs.

We do not know much about the workings of genes and chromosomes. Every living person is a bewildering combination of his ancestors, the immediate remembered and the past unknown. Against the claims of individuality, we have all seen at times how a child, like Shakespeare's fox, no matter how tame, how "cherish'd and lock'd up, will have a wild trick of his ancestors." JBY attributed the ebullience in his children to their Yeats heritage but found the source of his older son's crustiness and his younger daughter's psychopathy in the imperfect protoplasm of his wife's family, even as he found their poetry there.

John Butler Yeats may have been too modest about his own contribution to the talents and achievements of his children, for it was he who insisted on the life of conversation and intellect, who argued for the supremacy of art over the mundane, who almost willfully regarded money as an enemy to art and did his best to rid himself of it. It was his talk that became her education, Lily has written, the environment in his household that provided a college course for Susan Mitchell and Ruth Pollexfen. In New York City, John Butler Yeats made such a name as an inspiration to writers and artists that sixty-nine years after his death the mayor of the city proclaimed a day in his honor, and a plaque was installed on a building there in which he had once lived.[14] All who knew him, even those exasperated by his peccadilloes, found him a stimulating presence.

He was closer to his environment than we, and perhaps we should consider, even if with some skepticism, his own judgment about his junction with his wife's family. The Yeatses may have been "The Good People," but, he wrote his brother Isaac, they "are doomed to be like water spilled on the ground."[15] It was the other family that was possessed of "brooding imagination," of a "native, an indestructible and wholly unconscious spontaneity."[16]

"I have hoped," he told Isaac, "that by some good chance one of [the Yeatses] might marry and meet thereby with the right kind of mate, so that the Yeats essence or elixir shall be saved and not spilled on the ground." And he added, with a quiet satisfaction that the world has endorsed: "I think I myself mated well when I married with the Pollexfens. You yourself can see that in my daughters and sons." [17]

Appendix
Notes
Bibliography
Index

Appendix
The Yeatses and the Occult

My father's unbelief had set me thinking about the evidence of religion, and I weighed the matter perpetually with great anxiety, for I did not think I could live without religion.

— William Butler Yeats, *Autobiographies*

The mystical life is the centre of all that I do and all that I think and all that I write.

— William Butler Yeats to John O'Leary

I am sorry you are returning to mysticism. Mysticism means a relaxed intellect.

— John Butler Yeats to William Butler Yeats

Yeats will be quite sensible till some question of ghosts or occultism comes up, and then he is subject to a curious excitement, twists everything to his theory, usually quality of mind goes.

— Ezra Pound to John Quinn

The hummingbird in migration is guided by an instinct which in my mind is exactly like the *psychic* power by which some people, Lily for one, foresee what is going to happen—a power we all possess in some degree more or less.

— John Butler Yeats to Isaac Butt Yeats

Lily is too intelligent and too well taught to believe in the supernatural, so her words are, "It is something the Marconis of the future will make use of."

— John Butler Yeats to Frank Yeats

369

In some circles William Butler Yeats is as well known for his interest in the spirit world as for his poetry. His works are studied by occult societies, and his activities with organizations like the Order of the Golden Dawn are the subject of an extensive literature.[1] His prose work, *A Vision,* is based on "automatic writing" passing from a higher spirit through the pen of his wife, George, and from it come many of what he called "metaphors for poetry."[2] If he had not become a famous poet, he would still be remembered today, though perhaps only in an occasional footnote, for his association with spiritual studies.

In his own family his activities drew a double response. His sister Lily, who possessed strange powers of her own, shared his belief in the working of outside invisible powers on men's lives. His rationalist father, on the other hand, was appalled at what he regarded as his son's bizarre conduct, regarding it as evidence of a mind in trouble, perhaps a symptom of part of his Pollexfen heritage. The subject constitutes a thread running through the family correspondence and provides its own narrative attraction. It was a drama of unresolved conflicts, for at the end of their lives, none of the Yeatses had changed the mind of any of the others, though JBY modified his own views mildly.

Jack and Lollie usually stood on the sidelines while the game was being played. If Jack thought anything about the subject, he said nothing, characteristically keeping his ideas to himself. Lollie on one or two occasions shared her sister's experience of seeing a seabird in her room at the time of a relative's death, but she was too absorbed with her earthly problems to worry about messages from beyond. Papa and Lily and Willie were all inclined to think there was something more to the universe than the accidental colliding of electrons. Like most Irish of their day (not to say most people anywhere), they shared some common folk superstitions not related to broader occult beliefs. For instance, the Yeats sisters would never begin a book on a Friday. The one time they varied from the practice, under pressure, in the publication of J. M. Synge's *Poems and Translations* (1909), WBY noted that, "Do what they could, it would not come right."[3] Synge died while the book was being set in type.

WBY's occult studies have been thoroughly investigated and need no repeating here. Less well-known are the conflicts between his father and himself on the subject, and the opinions of even his most sympathetic friends on the unusual passion of his pursuit of what he himself acknowledged as, after his poetry, the main interest of his life.

John Butler Yeats was the archetype of the rational-superstitious man. As he was a disciple of Darwin and Huxley, his mind told him that all was material, that everything could be explained by natural laws. As a human being he saw strange coincidences hard to explain, and like all people he was laced with the genes of superstition. When JBY was in New York City, he regularly visited fortune-tellers and cheerfully paid their fees from his scanty resources. His correspondence is full of accounts of such visits and payments. He went out of his way to consult Mrs. Charles Johnston, Madame Blavatsky's niece, who had a reputation as a seer, and, whenever he found a new expert, he hurried to spend his money for a reading.[4] Like many thoroughgoing rationalists, John Butler Yeats was every twelfth inch a spiritualist. Yet he continued to live his life as if the predictions of astrologers never existed, and he resolutely objected to his son's more serious dabblings.[5]

Lily, while charitably accepting her father's amusing accounts of his adventures with readers of palms and tea leaves, was at her mordant best when commenting on fortune-tellers, particularly those claiming to hear voices from the spirit world. She wrote her father about a visit from a friend of hers whose prognostications came from what she thought a deranged mind.

> She has been quite mad for a while and away from home, but is said to be quite sane again. That spiritualism of hers is most dangerous for her, I think, and fearful nonsense in any case. She and her friends call up Parnell and Gladstone. . . . She looked at me one day and said, "You will marry a man with kind eyes and a taste for agriculture." "Must be Horace Plunkett," I said, "I'll start in pursuit tomorrow." But she would not even smile.[6]

Papa and Lily wrote to each other about their dreams. When he dreamed of fish, he thought money was about to come his way.[7]

Lily had dreams or visions too, though of a somewhat different kind, believing them, with good reason, to be predictive and therefore indicative of a world more than merely material, and her father found them persuasive too. In his father, therefore, Willie did not face a mere materialist scornful of a son's peculiar obsession but rather a paternal caretaker concerned for a son's sanity.

JBY's aversion to his son's dabblings with the occult began early and never ended. He boasted to his brother Isaac in 1918 that he had helped Willie grow. "I abolished religion and insincerity," he declared.[8] Yet, as he knew only too well, he had merely abolished Christianity—his son calling himself "a churchless mystic"[9] —and other conventional forms of religion from which vast numbers of people take comfort in the face of the insoluble mysteries of human existence. He had not abolished William Butler Yeats's hunger for religion, which the son sought to feed through magic and mysticism. His later association with the Order of the Golden Dawn was an inevitable consequence of his earlier interest, and one not easily accepted by his father.

In his Sligo boyhood in Merville, Willie had seen through an open window his first "fay," or fairy, "moving down a moonbeam toward him,"[10] and no assertions of his father's could convince him that such beings did not exist. In the mid-1880s, Willie read A. P. Sinnett's *Esoteric Buddhism,* and in 1885, influenced by its contents, founded the Hermetic Society in Dublin with a friend named Charles Johnston.[11] It was not "theosophical" in the sense applied to their organization by H. S. Olcott and Mme. Helena Blavatsky,[12] but it was replete with incantations, with the absorbing of "the Odic Force," and with other mystical trappings, including the inevitable philosopher from the Mysterious East in the person of a Persian professor at Trinity College, Dublin.[13] Willie had found a religion that was to give him infinite satisfaction until the end of his days and occupy him almost as much as, if not more than, his poetry. When his father disapproved of what he heard about his son's doings, the son retreated into silence.

As early as 1892 the evidence of his father's dislike of Willie's practices is clear. John O'Leary had apparently suggested—in a letter to WBY now lost—that his protégé sprinkle cold water upon the heat and flame of his occultism. Yeats's reply to O'Leary, one of the most frequently quoted of his passages, is worth quoting again:

> Now as to Magic. It is surely absurd to hold me "weak" or otherwise because I chose to persist in a study which I decided deliberately four or five years ago to make, next to my poetry, the most important pursuit of my life. Whether it be, or be not, bad for my health can only be decided by one who knows what magic is and not at all by any amateur. The probable explanation however of your somewhat testy postcard is that you were out at Bedford Park and heard my father discoursing about my magical pursuits out of the immense depths of his ignorance as to everything that I am doing and thinking.

He admitted there were ambiguities in the words he used that might explain aversions to his pursuits.

> The mystical life is the centre of all that I do and all that I think and all that I write. It holds to my work the same relation that the philosophy of Godwin held to the work of Shelley and I have always considered myself a voice of what I believe to be a greater renaissance—the revolt of the soul against the intellect—now beginning in the world. By all this I have however probably called down upon myself another reproving postcard which shall be like to the other in all things. It is my own fault I dare say for I sometimes forget that the word "magic" which sounds so familiar to my ears has a very outlandish sound to others.[14]

Father described his son's attitude toward the occult as "hot and credulous."[15] His opinion of Willie and the equally mystical George Russell is hinted at indirectly in his letter to Sarah Purser of 7 July 1897: "I don't know where Willie is or what he is doing. The last I heard was that he and Russell had gone west (Sligo or thereabouts) to find a new God."[16] When he learned that Willie was writing a novel about his occult adventures (*The Speckled Bird*), he wrote to Lady Gregory: "I am full of curiosity as to his novel—I may say *anxiety*. Mysticism may become a rank vegetation destroying the vital principle. A novel with elaborate notes and a commentary would be a portentous kind of art." He hastened to add: "And besides, I am no enemy to mysticism."[17] If his son was a mystic and his father disapproved of what he was doing yet approved of mysticism, then clearly the word "mysticism" needed definition. It was not the search JBY objected to but the method used for it.

A quarter century later his attitude had not changed. When Lady Gregory sent him newspaper clippings about WBY's book *Per Amica Silentia Lunae,* he wrote his son sadly:

> I am sorry you are returning to mysticism. Mysticism means a relaxed intellect. It [is] of course very different from the sentimentalism of the affections and the senses which is the common sort, but it is sentimentalism all the same, a sentimentalism of the intellect. *"I will make the unknown known, for I will present it under such symmetrical forms that everyone will be convinced—and what is more important I shall convince myself."* So speaks the mystic, according to my idea. AE is a man of genius marred by mysticism, at least forced down into a lower grade. I must respect my poet, I must feel to my core that he has a vigorous character and an intellect clear as crystal. Otherwise I soon tire of his melodious verses.[18]

Since father and son seldom discussed details of their disagreement, it is not easy to know precisely what studies troubled the older man. WBY made clear to John O'Leary that he didn't believe in mesmerism, for example: "You need not be afraid of my going in for mesmerism. It interests me but slightly. No fear of Madame Blavatsky drawing me into such matters—she is very much against them and hates spiritualism vehemently—says mediumship and insanity are the same thing."[19] And he could write with telling humor about the oddities of other people's beliefs: "A sad accident happened at Madame Blavatsky's lately, I hear. A big materialist sat on the astral double of a poor young Indian. It was sitting on the sofa and he was too material to be able to see it. Certainly a sad accident!"[20]

He was attracted to Madame Blavatsky's Theosophical Society but critical of it. When he wrote an article for *Lucifer,* the Society's journal, he was asked to promise never to criticize the Society again. He declined and gave up his membership instead. "I refused," he told O'Leary, "because I looked upon request as undue claim to control right of individual to think as best pleased him." He told his former colleagues "they were turning a good philosophy into a bad religion," a remark that had "not been well taken by some of the fiercer sort."[21]

Shortly before writing O'Leary, Willie had shaved off his beard at the urging of Katharine Tynan and others. Madame Blavatsky told him the loss of the beard would bring him "disaster in matter of health through loss of 'magnetism' or for some other eccentric reason of the same kind." So, he told Miss Tynan, she could "see now what you and my other friends have got upon your souls."[22] Despite his joshing, he was apparently regarded by others as one who sought theological answers outside the accepted institutions and so inspired respect and fear. Edwin Ellis's wife grew "white with terror" at the sight of him, suffering from "a curious delusion," as WBY called it, "that I had some mesmeric power over her that made her ill." He tried avoiding her company. "She is so horribly hysterical and has had her head turned by a too constant and wholly unthinking sense of the unseen universe and of its unknown powers."[23]

But all humor vanished when he spoke of his own activities: "My own occult art," he wrote John O'Leary, "(though I cannot expect you to accept the evidences) has again and again for a longish time now been telling me of many curious coming events and as some have come true (all that have had time) I rather expect the others to follow suit."[24]

Those words were written just before the violent paragraph about JBY's meddling in his studies. By then WBY was already deep in his involvement with the Order of the Golden Dawn as a member of its Isis-Urania Temple, an air of the ludicrous emanating from its very title. Its rituals were secret, and in any event Willie would not have discussed them with his father, but some notion of what went on there can be gathered from WBY's letters to other members. To one of these, W. T. Horton, he gave a partial explanation of its position. "Our order is not, as you seem to think, 'spiritist' in any sense but wholly opposed to spiritism. . . . Nor is our Order anti-Christian. That very pentagram which I suggested your using is itself, as you would presently have learned, a symbol of Christ. I am convinced however that for you progress lies not in dependence upon a Christ outside yourself but upon the Christ in your own breast, in the power of your own divine will and divine imagination, and not in some external will or imagination however divine." He included a significant sentence that constitutes a paradox of his own assertions and actions: "The uttermost danger lies for you in emotional religion, which will sap your will and wreck your self-control." [25] Such religion was that to be found in the conventional church, of any denomination, barred to him forever by his father's teachings. "My father's unbelief had set me thinking about the evidences of religion, and I weighed the matter perpetually with great anxiety, for I did not think I could live without religion." [26]

When he wrote about what he was actually practicing, the language became bizarre. He held a meeting in London in his rooms at Woburn Buildings on 3 January 1898, at which Sarojini Chattopâdyây would be present, and invited Mrs. Dorothy Hunter and her husband to come along. He told Mrs. Hunter what was in the works: "I want to talk to you and your husband about a certain part of our Celtic project in which you can be of great help. I am following out a plan laid down long ago, and after consultation with our chiefs. It is going to be a great movement in the end." Then he branched into another matter in language that would have curled his father's beard:

> I have had a number of visions on the way home, greatly extending the symbolism we got tonight. The souls of ordinary people remain after death in the waters and these waters become an organized world if you gather up the flames that come from the waters of the well when the berries fall upon it, and make them into a flaming heart, and explore the waters with this as a lamp. They are the waters of emotion and passion, in which all but purified souls are entangled, and have the same relation to our plane of fixed material form as the Divine World of fluid fire has to the heroic world of fixed intellectual form. [27]

A few weeks later he wrote to George Russell (AE) that he was "deep in 'Celtic Mysticism,' " and was on his way to Ireland with

Maud Gonne "to get as you do the forms of gods and spirits and to get sacred earth for our invocation."[28] If his father got only a whiff of these goings-on, his concern would be understandable. Willie tried to keep as much of it from him as possible. He did, however, tell him of his curing Uncle George Pollexfen of an illness suffered from an impure smallpox vaccine, as his father relates: "Willie cast symbols and invoked 'divine names connected with the Kabalistic system with the moon.' George attributed the cure to his nephew's magic, and the event cemented their friendship."[29]

WBY's experiences in the Order of the Golden Dawn having been fully explored elsewhere, it is sufficient to say here that its mumbo jumbo, its secrecy, its vague language, its evocation of the spirits of the universe, were qualities appealing to him but appalling to his father. The estrangement between them over this single issue of occultism was never resolved, though WBY took heart from a possible visit to him by his father's ghost in 1924. Willie attended a séance at the home of a friend:

> Somebody came claiming to be my mother and spoke apparently of Lolly. I asked if she meant "Polly," and she said "Oh no no no," and then I was told my father would materialize. In a moment a hand came, quite distinct against some vague luminous object. It was like my father's hand but seemed smaller than life size. It touched me and was there for some time—very exciting and strange, the sudden appearance of a solid hand out of nothing. It touched my hand on the side opposite to the medium, who remained perfectly motionless. I had hoped for a message for Lily.[30]

Of another such experience he wrote, "I was at a séance and various spirits came, one claiming to be our mother, and another our Sligo grandmother, who spoke of Spot the dog, and also of a black cat when I was fourteen."[31] Five years after George Pollexfen's death, he heard from George's ghost. "It insisted that it would appear to me when alone and insisted that I would be able to see. I have seen nothing yet."[32]

He neglected no aspect of "Magic." When a trio of medicos in London marveled at Lily's mysterious illness without finding its cause, Willie cast her horoscope for a revelation from the stars. The answer it gave him was no worse than theirs, but the method of diagnosis would have disconcerted his father. When Cuala made its temporary move to his home on Merrion Square, he tried to forecast its fate astrologically.[33] His father's attitude, he said, had driven him "from speculation to the direct experience of the mystics"[34] and hence caused him to extract communication from unwilling, not to say nonexistent, spirits.

John Butler Yeats recognized and acknowledged the importance to a poet of an imagined world out of which he could generate the surface substance of his poetry. His apprehension at his son's occultism arose from a quite different source—from a fear that it might mean a disorder of the poet's intellect or personality, even a manifestation of the mental instability of the Pollexfens. For Willie was not able, despite his protestations, to keep his activities within the bounds of stability. Even in his most mature years, he displayed superemotional behavior in his search for metaphysical truths. One person who observed his antics closely was Ezra Pound, who served as his secretary and confidant for a number of years. Willie was working out his theories on lunar phases to explain human characteristics—work that would later reach publication as *A Vision*— and Pound was present at the creation. Pound, not recognized as a model of psychic stability, made an interesting observation about WBY in a letter to John Quinn, the hardheaded New York lawyer who befriended and partly subsidized the Yeats family. "Bit queer in the head about 'moon,' " he wrote, "whole new metaphysics about 'moon,' very very very bughouse."[35] Pound noted how WBY's attitude would change when a nonsecular subject arose: "Yeats will be quite sensible till some question of ghosts or occultism comes up," he wrote to Quinn, "and then he is subject to a curious excitement, twists everything to his theory, usually quality of mind goes."[36] Katharine Tynan writes of an occasion when Mrs. George Sigerson told WBY that she saw in a crystal ball golden bars and jewels "of the most glorious color." WBY's excitement was "prodigious" until Dr. Sigerson remarked "in his cool dry voice" that what shone in the crystal ball was a reflection from the building across the street.[37]

The subject of the occult would of course be a touchy one

between father and son. It was seldom alluded to in correspondence, though the shards of evidence over a period of thirty-five years suggest a clear pattern.[38] Whenever JBY suspected his son's dabbling in mysticism was getting out-of-hand, he fired darts at it, seldom doing damage. Willie was determined to keep his father in the dark.

It is tempting to believe that JBY's objections to WBY's mysticism arose naturally out of his own deconversion from Christianity, which he regarded as "myth and Fable." He had adopted the methods of Mill, Comte, and Darwin long before it had become fashionable to do so among the intellectual community, accepted their conclusions, and stuck with them in great measure throughout his life. It would be easy to accept the proposition that his distaste for his son's metaphysical extravagances was a simple outgrowth of his own agnosticism, a mere disagreement with a prejudice that didn't coincide with his own.

Such a conclusion collapses when one considers JBY's attitude toward the parasensory experiences of Lily, his favorite child and Willie's favorite sister. Because of what happened to her, John Butler Yeats in the last few decades of his life listened with respect to those who asserted ties with another world or another dimension, though never deserting his disbelief in the metaphysical and insisting that all such ties be subject to rational investigation.

Lily Yeats was a forthright, observant lady of unusual common sense, straightforward in nature, but gifted with a nice sense of irony. Utterly without pretension as intellectual, writer, or metaphysician, she took life as it came and exhibited remarkable courage and forbearance in circumstances that might have shattered others. When a person of her humor and rationalism had "visions" that proved either accurate replays of past events of which she had no knowledge or remarkable predictions of future ones, yet made no special claims about them or her own powers, those about her would naturally pay attention, as her father did. He found an interesting parallel between her gift and the migration of the hummingbird, which was "guided by an instinct which in my mind is exactly like the *psychic* power by which some people, Lily for one, foresee what is going to happen—a power we all possess in some degree more or less. It is common among peasants."[39]

Lily Yeats left behind no detailed body of written description of her experiences, though she and her father alluded to them often. Nevertheless, we have several letters and notes that shed light on their nature, and for a couple at least we have corroborative evidence of their retrospective or predictive accuracy.

Lily's experiences can be divided into three broad categories. The first can be subdivided into two groups: the simple dream fantasy, the kind of thing common to us all—a jumble of irrational and sometimes frightening events, often rising to the intensity of nightmare; and the type of vision that is a visual sensation of something not objectively present, the sensation occurring either in a waking state or in the state of half-waking just before sleep in which the experiences are not easily referable to external people or events. Since there is no way to analyze such visions rationally, the category can be disregarded as inconsequential.[40]

The second category is that of the vision in which an object seems to be a significant symbol of an external, observable event. Lily had a "sort of dream" just before the death of her mother, Susan Pollexfen Yeats, in 1900, in which a white seabird was "flapping its wings" in her face. A few weeks later the bird appeared again, and a day or so later her uncle John Pollexfen died in Liverpool. In 1910 she dreamed again of the strange bird, and Uncle George Pollexfen kept the association consistent by conveniently dying.[41]

Then, in February 1913, Lollie, who seldom received messages from beyond, was visited by the bird, which she had never seen before. She "woke with a scream and said there was a great wingless bird in her room, a penguin, she thought." The following night Lily woke up "feeling sure there was a sea-swallow on the table by my bed." Because of her three previous experiences, she confidently waited to hear of the death of another Pollexfen. More than four months passed and she had almost forgotten the vision when she got word from the family lawyers that Uncle William Middleton Pollexfen, incurably mad for almost forty years in a hospital in Northampton, had died in February. When Lollie lay dying in a Dublin hospital, she told her doctor "that a duck was in the room all day." Lily didn't tell the doctor about the family's experiences with seabirds but confided to her cousin Ruth Lane-Poole that she herself had been "sure in the night I had a dead wild duck in my arms."[42]

The third class of vision, and by far the most interesting, is that in which events and people fairly easy to identify—or to find parallels for—are seen clearly by Lily in either vision or dream. This class can be subdivided into three groups: the first the vision or dream of events in the distant past; the second of events in the near future; the third of events in the distant future.

Lily described one of the first kind to Oliver Elton in 1916. The vision itself had come to her two years earlier.

One Sunday in July 1914 Lolly and I got into an outside car and drove to Glencullen to see the Joseph Campbells, who had not long [since] moved into the house there. It was a most beautiful hot calm day. We went about four miles up into the hills and found the house, very lonely and buried away, a big old house with a view of the Sugarloaf mountains. It was partly furnished by the Campbells and partly by furniture belonging to the land-lord. We only looked into the house, and then went into the garden, where we stayed for our whole visit. . . .

The moment I got there I felt in touch with some other world—a most pleasant feeling, almost an exalted feeling; but I could get no quiet, and so saw nothing. This feeling remained with me all the time, and almost all the time of the drive home, and till I went to bed.

The moment I was in darkness, I saw I was back again at the house. The house was closed, but (I thought) furnished—only closed up for a time. Then round the side of the house came a lady, a tall woman in the dress of (I judged) the forties or early fifties. She was not handsome, not a girl; elegant, full of charm, and, I thought, something of a personage. With her was a man younger than she.—Then I seemed to get out of my own mind and into hers. I saw with her mind and felt with it. She was very unhappy, and full of thoughts of an old love-story of her youth, and at the same time trying to talk cleverly to the man—I think he was more or less a stranger—all the time her mind full of sorrow. France and Ireland were woven in and out of each other, one moment France then Glencullen. I saw her lover—young man, thick set, very sallow, fine head, rather big; I thought he was a Pole or a Frenchman, and a musician or artist, and I felt she knew George Sand. I saw him ill on a sofa—a lingering illness, slow consumption perhaps. I knew they had lived together, and knew no one knew. Then I saw his funeral. It seemed to leave the steps of the Glencullen house, and yet it was France —a very country place, but I thought not far from Paris. I saw the coffin and on it a tossed laurel wreath tied with a tricolour. A priest and two acolytes in red followed, that was all. The priest and the boys looked rough peasants, as if they had come from working on the land, freckled and sunburnt, not very well washed. There it ended.

Next day Lily went to work to learn what she could about Glencullen and its history. Without letting the Campbells know the contents of her dream—merely telling them she had had one —she asked them whether the house had had connections with France in the forties or fifties. They knew nothing but referred her question to the owner, Mr. O'Connell FitzSimon. "He said his grandmother had lived there and was a daughter of Dan O'Connell and had been in France in her youth, been very happy there and knew many literary people."

Lily thereupon described her vision to the Campbells. They searched through the books in the house and found a volume of poems by Mrs. FitzSimon. One poem was "addressed to a friend who had died alone in France." A neighbor in Dundrum provided Lily with further information about O'Connell's family. His daughter Ellen, he reported, married Christopher FitzSimon of Glencullen; she died on 27 June 1883. William Butler Yeats helped to confirm some of the details of the vision:

> I have been looking into a life of O'Connell. A daughter of his "a few" years after his wife's death (1835) became melancholy because of some "sin." There are two very moving letters by O'Connell to her urging her to submit to the directions of her confessor, and speaking of salvation and repentance. She was married and had a child or children.

The coincidences are startling. Some people Lily spoke to about her dream ascribed it to indigestion or fright, but she disagreed. "I can't explain it," she told Elton. "Lobster suppers and rats—both fail. What has the sceptic left? He better believe. It is the easiest."[43]

Under questioning by Elton, Lily expanded on the dream and her discoveries after it:

> No. I had no knowledge of the history of the house. I did not even know the [word omitted] of the house. I knew of the O'Connell FitzSimons, and knew Mr. FitzSimon but did not know their relationship to the great Dan. I never even saw Dr. FitzSimon till the rebellion [of 1916] . . . He has the same nose that the lady of my vision had, but he is short and she was tall. . . . Her nose had a rather unexpected sort of sharp end, which her grandson has.
>
> No, I thought she had not seen the funeral. That seemed to be my own bit of vision, but of that I can't be sure. . . .
>
> Sorrow and regret and misery of mind were what I felt the vision lady had in acute form, and also the feeling that it was her great secret known to no one. This feeling was very strong. The whole story was her sad secret I think.
>
> She wore a gray dress, loose straightjacket, and a bonnet rather of the wide poke shape. She was graceful. Elegant is, I am sure, the word of her day with the meaning of her day that would describe her best.[44]

Equally startling was a vision of 1906 that was followed within a fortnight by a chillingly suggestive set of events. While Lollie was visiting in New York in the fall of that year, Lily wrote her of a vision—not a dream—in which she had seen "a funeral come out of the Dun Emer gate," with a "light-coloured coffin" in evidence. About a week after Lily's vision, Miss Gleeson learned that her only brother had been taken ill. The next day he died suddenly. Lily was "relieved," she told Lollie, as "now my vision is out." It was easier to absorb the death of someone she didn't know well than of one of the people at Dun Emer whom she saw every day. But it developed that the vision was not "out." Less than a week after Mr. Gleeson's death, a seventeen-year-old nephew of Miss Gleeson's arrived at Dun Emer to be taken care of. He had been sent down from Clongowes School with a letter from the doctor there containing "an alarming account of his health." The boy was large and slow and had been behaving strangely. Miss Gleeson promptly took him into Dublin, where three physicians examined him. All pronounced him healthy, telling Miss Gleeson he was merely "hysterical."

The next morning at Dun Emer, the boy died, the victim of a brain tumor. When Lily reached Dun Emer that morning, she knew immediately what had happened, for she saw three doctors standing together at the Dun Emer gate. At the time she had the vision, she was hardly aware of the nephew's existence and did not know he was ill.[45]

Another experience, reported at second hand and not mentioned in the family records, was Lily's apparent vision of a ghost while visiting Anne Boston's home at St. Wyburn. "She asked Anne who the elderly man was with the clipped moustache whom she had seen about the house and going up and down the stairs. She had described Anne's father, whom she had never seen in her life and who had been dead for some years."[46]

Two other visions, for which we have specific records, are equally interesting, perhaps more so, as they involve predictions of the future, one of a quite distant future. Both Lily and her father had for years been desolate at the possibility that the Yeats family line, at least the branch descended from him, would die out. Willie shared the family concern and suffered in addition a twinge of guilt. The first poem in *Responsibilities,* "Pardon, old fathers," was his cry of remorse for having failed to produce descendants to carry on the family name. It ended with a passage alluding to his unsuccessful pursuit of Maud Gonne:

> Pardon that for a barren passion's sake,
> Although I have come close on forty-nine,
> I have no child, I have nothing but a book,
> Nothing but that to prove your blood and mine.

At forty-nine he was still unmarried, as were Lily and Lollie. Jack and Cottie had been married for two decades but were childless. Prospects for a line descending from John Butler Yeats were, in those days, poor.

Then, in the fall of 1917, William Butler Yeats married Bertha Georgie Hyde-Lees, twenty-seven years his junior. A few months later Lily had a dream in which she saw "a high stone tower, on the top of it a Herald blowing a trumpet. Out of the trumpet came not notes but the words, 'The Yeatses are not dead.' " She sent the account to her father. "Wasn't that good?" she asked.[47] Not long afterward Mrs. William Butler Yeats announced to those in the family that there was to be a child born to her and the poet. The following February, Anne Butler Yeats was born. Lily thought the dream must have foretold her birth.

But of course anyone can dream of a newly married couple having a child. It was the long paragraph that followed that is by far the most impressive of Lily's visions, one that came to her in 1911, when Willie was forty-six years old and viewed by family and friends as a perpetual bachelor. Here are her words, written to her father on 22 September 1918:

> Then I'll tell you another story that will please you. Seven years ago next month, I was in London at an exhibition of women's work. I lodged near Victoria and used to walk up every day into Bond St. One morning I was going up to Hyde Park Corner when I thought it was a sad pity you had no grandchildren, when in a flash I saw a grandson of yours. He was like Willy, only taller, bigger features and more colour, blue eyes. I thought he was a brilliant man, perhaps a statesman, and that he was in and out of the Embassies that are all about Hyde Park there. He was almost forty in my glimpse, a man of great vitality. In another flash I saw he had my portrait on his wall, a dark wall, panelled I think, and thought a great deal of it.[48]

Students of the Yeats family may well be astonished by this vision. Almost exactly ten years after Lily experienced it, and three years after she recorded it, Michael Butler Yeats, the poet's first (and only) son and second child, was born.[49] Lily died in January 1949, when her nephew was twenty-eight. Her letters, kept neatly in manila envelopes, remained in the home of Mrs. William Butler Yeats until her death in August 1968. In the interval nobody consulted them. There is no question about the authenticity of Lily's letters or the unplanned nature of the parallels to what appears in them.

The facts are that Michael Yeats was (and still is) tall and dark, strongly resembling his father. During a long life in public service, he was a member of the Senate of the Republic of Ireland, its president for many years, the Irish representative to the European Parliament and a vice-president of that body—in other words, a "statesman." In the music room of Senator Yeats's home in Dalkey, County Dublin, on a paneled wall, hangs John Butler Yeats's oil portrait of Lily. Lily's vision has proved eerily accurate.[50]

•   •   •

John Butler Yeats was impressed by his daughter's gift. He wrote to his cousin Frank Yeats in 1920: "My daughter Lily is psychic, extraordinarily psychic and can foresee the future of which I could give you many instances. But she is too intelligent and too well taught to believe in the supernatural. Her words are, 'It is something which the Marconis of the future will make use of.' "[51] The emanations she received, like radio waves, were physical phenomena, he believed, and Lily never accepted them as anything else. Indeed, she shared her father's feelings about people who thought they had contact with the spirit world, like the woman who "called up" Parnell and Gladstone. Van Wyck Brooks, the American literary historian and critic who knew John Butler Yeats intimately during his last years, observed that despite his involvement with palm readers and fortune-tellers, he never fell over the cliff. He had a combination of interests, Brooks wrote, "that made for an infinite, if a somewhat bewildering wit—a wit, however, that, where spirits were concerned, drew the line just the other side of the banshee."[52]

JBY thought the gift of "second sight" lay quite within the range of man's material powers. If he lacked it himself, he could not disregard it in Lily, and he thought the Pollexfens possessed it beyond the ordinary. In his unpublished memoirs he recounts a dream his wife had one night when Jack, then a schoolboy, was traveling from London to Liverpool to spend a night with the John Pollexfens. "My wife remained restlessly awake till long past midnight, being convinced that he had lost himself. Afterward we found it was true and that when he found his aunt's house it was precisely at the time when she consented to fall asleep." He continued:

I think perhaps that we have at birth the gift of second sight, but that we become immersed in the multitudinous details of everyday life and so neglect it—but that my wife's family being not much interested in these distractions retain and exercise the gift. Yet this doesn't fully explain it, for my daughters have the liveliest sense of everything that passes and yet have the gift—of which I could give you many instances from my daughter Lily's experiences. I am certain that we all have this gift but that we are carefully taught to abandon it and forget it.[53]

Lily herself had one vivid dream about a woman committing suicide, the tragedy being confirmed in all details by a newspaper account a few days later.[54] Yet in his early years of marriage to Susan Pollexfen, JBY had pooh-poohed those who thought dreams and visions had meaning. His early recognition of the Pollexfen tendency to place faith in them, and his own skepticism about their powers, is revealed in a letter he wrote his wife in 1873, in reply to one of hers that has disappeared:

You must not dream dreams, although, whether from your mother or from some old fashioned aunt or from some servant like Nellie, you have all learned to have a kind of half belief in dreams and so worry yourself and others with narratives of your dreams. You are all great dreamers, and yet they have never helped any of you to divine correctly anything.[55]

It is unfortunate that we do not know the content of Susan Pollexfen's dream, for just sixteen days later, on 3 March, Robert Corbet Yeats, their second son, died suddenly of croup at the age of three.

Whatever his earlier feelings, John Butler Yeats's opinions had been modified by Lily's experiences.[56] The question that arises is why he showed such sympathy for hers and so little for his son's. If there was such a thing as otherworldly "truth" that could be apprehended by those with special gifts, why shouldn't Willie's activities be granted equal approval?

Clearly, in JBY's mind there was a sharp distinction between the two. He did not object to "psychics," only to "mystics." A "psychic" was one who, like Lily, received visions effortlessly, one to whom things happened unsought and unforced. A "mystic," on the other hand, was one who, like Willie, deliberately looked for

signs from the other world, stared into crystal balls (as he did for
years with his uncle George Pollexfen), consulted astrological
charts, waved "magic" wands about, joined eccentric societies like
the Order of the Golden Dawn, and regarded with awe and rever-
ence Indian swamis who brought in their train the wisdom of the
Mysterious East. The first was a normal person who simply recorded
what happened; the second was one to whom little happened but
who went "bughouse" trying to induce supernatural experiences.
Like an earlier Celtic poet who took his claim to magical powers
with equal seriousness, W. B. Yeats thought he could "call spirits
from the vasty deep." In the family drama John Butler Yeats was
confined to playing the role of Hotspur, with about as much success
as his Shakespearean counterpart.

Readers of *The Speckled Bird,* that intense, astonishingly personal, autobiographical novel,[57] will understand and appreciate the
depth, earnestness, and sincerity of the poet's attempt to establish
a link with the powers of a world on a different plane. But they
will understand also the fears of his father, who after 1890 was
virtually cut off from intimate knowledge of his son's mystical
pursuits. Yet it was not only his father—and Ezra Pound—who
saw WBY as he never saw himself. Father would have been vexed,
if also partly amused, by Joseph Holloway's account in his diary of
remarks made by George Russell at a gathering at Con Curran's
house in January 1918. Russell, according to Holloway, "told
many strange and droll incidents of Yeats's adventures in search of
'spookish' experiences. . . . AE has the saving grace of humour to
keep him sane and cool on such subjects. He thinks that they
[i.e., mystics] must be very ill-informed if they can't give a clearer
message from the unknown than those."[58]

John Butler Yeats, the perpetual artist, feared that his son's
mysticism might weaken his poetry by making it "vague" and
"insincere." In a long letter to WBY critical of the Syrian painter
and poet Kahlil Gibran, he spoke indirectly to his son:

Vagueness is always insincerity, and of it are two kinds. When a
man does not take the trouble to think or to know precisely, he
is vague—and if this come from human weakness or laziness or
because it is so soothing in itself to a disturbed mind, then it is

so human as to be likeable or even lovable, and great poets have shown themselves not averse—only with this condition, that as honest men they must not pretend that it is a conviction, or, as some of your second-class mystics, that it is a religion. There is another kind of vagueness which no poet or artist should touch with his delicate and sensitive fingers: that is where there is calculation that vagueness may be of popular advantage to the writer. . . . Cleverness itself is an insincerity (it was the bane of Edwin Ellis) since its aim is not the essential truth but success. Of course the Poet rules over a wide Kingdom and may at will and according to his artistic judgment practice all the insincerities; only he must never be their dupe.[59]

Happily, Willie's father was spared most of the details of what went on behind the mystical curtains. He was unaware, for instance, that when Willie married George Yeats, the two engaged in "automatic handwriting." Padraic Colum saw the emotional hunger behind the experiment: "W. B. had to create for himself an imaginative belief that included, not only his own version of God, Freedom, and Immortality, but esoteric doctrines and magical practices." Whether Willie was the dupe of mysticism or not must be left to the judgment of the dispassionate student. All that can fairly be said is that John Butler Yeats was lucky to have died before parts of the automatic writing found their way into print as *A Vision*. Of that book, with its earnest analyses of the phases of the moon and their effect on historical figures, filled with the lingo of medieval astrology—a book that is almost unreadable and would be of no interest to the world if it were not the work of a great writer who mined it for "metaphors" to be used in his poetry—Colum declared that "nothing could be further from J. B.'s serene and uncritical rationalism" than it.[60] If JBY had lived to see it published, the shock would surely have killed him.

Notes

Designations for Depositories

ABY	Collection of Anne Butler Yeats
Brown	Brown University Library
Delaware	University of Delaware
	Hugh M. Morris Library
MBY	Collection of Michael Butler Yeats
NLI	National Library of Ireland
NYPL	New York Public Library
Princeton	Princeton University Library
Reading	University of Reading
	Elkin Mathews Collection
Stanford	Stanford University
	James A. Healy Collection of Irish Literature
TCD	Library of Trinity College, Dublin
Texas	University of Texas Libraries
	Humanities Research Center
Toronto	University of Toronto
	Thomas Fisher Rare Book Library
	De Lurey Collection
Yale	Yale University
	Beinecke Library
Victoria	University of Victoria, British Columbia
	McPherson Library

1. The Yeatses, the Pollexfens, and Sligo

Sources for this chapter include the letters of the Yeats family, Lily Yeats's scrapbooks and other memorabilia, John Butler Yeats's unpublished memoirs, the records of the King's Inns in Dublin, and the people and publications listed below. Three of my publications, out-of-print or hard to obtain, contain some of

391

the material in this essay: *The Yeats Family and the Pollexfens of Sligo* (Dublin: Dolmen, 1971); "The Ancestry of William Butler Yeats," in *Yeats and the 1890s,* ed. Robert O'Driscoll and Lorna Reynolds (Shannon: Irish University Press, 1971), 1–19; and " 'In Memory of Alfred Pollexfen': W. B. Yeats and the Theme of Family," *Irish University Review,* 1, no. 1 (Autumn, 1970): 30–47. Lily's letters to Joseph Hone (Texas) repeat much of the information found in her scrapbooks; I cite the Hone letters only when they contain information not found elsewhere in Lily's writings.

1. G. K. Chesterton, *Autobiography* (New York: Sheed and Ward, 1936), 140.
2. JBY to Lily, 15 Sept. 1916, MBY. Part of the letter appears in J. M. Hone, ed., *J. B. Yeats: Letters to His Son W. B. Yeats and Others* (New York: Dutton, 1946), 229, where the punch line is omitted.
3. Lily remarks almost offhandedly in her "Scrapbook" (MBY), "I think it was from the Corbets the artistic interest came." For Lily's three casual notebooks, see chap. 2, n. 11.
4. Two reviews of William M. Murphy, *The Yeats Family and the Pollexfens of Sligo* (Dublin: Dolmen, 1971), make note of the simple division. Donald Torchiana expresses his dissent from the view that the family can be thus simply explained (*Newsletter of the American Committee of Irish Studies,* 3, Feb. 1973: 3), and Richard Ellmann (*Notes and Queries,* May 1975: 226) calls the view "biological cocksureness," but each seems to believe that it was one conceived by the author rather than by the Yeatses.
5. JBY to WBY, 24 Mar. 1909, MBY.
6. JBY to Lily, 15 Sept. 1916, MBY. Quoted in Hone, *JBY: Letters.* "They were like wild snow drops,—*capricious* and *gentle* and *pure.* Merely to be with them was to me a happiness" (JBY to Lily, 10 Oct. 1917, MBY); "They all of them in every fibre of their being were 'the Good people' " (JBY to WBY, 24 Mar. 1909, MBY; Hone, *JBY: Letters,* 117).
7. JBY to Isaac Yeats, 28 Apr. 1911, ABY. See also his letter to Lollie two weeks earlier (14 Apr., MBY): "In you are two races, the Yeats and the Pollexfen. The first always makes the best of things, and the second makes the worst of things. The first would impel you to like your fellow creatures and live in gay harmony with them. The other impels you to dislike them and get into discomfortable relations with them."
8. Two other children did not survive childhood, Robert Corbet Yeats (1870–1873) and Jane Grace Yeats (1875–1876). Because JBY and Jack bore the same name and were both artists, they are repeatedly confused. In the catalogues of art galleries and auction houses, Jack's paintings are often listed as by "J. B. Yeats," a mistake. The father was called or called himself "J. B. Yeats" or "John Butler Yeats" and (except on only one occasion, paradoxically by an act for their convenience by his own daughters) never "John B. Yeats." He was familiarly known about Dublin as "JBY," "JB," or "Old JB."
Jack was never (except when required on legal documents) called "John Butler Yeats," or "John" in any combination, and never "JBY" or "JB." He was

called or called himself "Jack B. Yeats" (his own preference), or "Jack Yeats," or, less frequently, "Jack Butler Yeats."

John Butler Yeats spent the last fourteen years of his life as a sage in a New York lodging house. Jack visited New York briefly a few years before his father's arrival there. Yet an article by Lucius Beebe in *American Heritage* (August 1965), contains the following paragraph: "Downtown in the Village there was an almost infinite variety of home-style French restaurants where liquor was available, such as that of Mlle. Petitpas, who ran a boarding house upstairs and set a creditable bourgeois French table that achieved celebrity because for a number of years the king of the premises was a swaggering Bohemian wit, Jack Yeats, younger brother of the Irish poet" (65). The Petitpas boarding house was not "downtown in the Village" but on West 29th Street; there were three Mesdemoiselles Petitpas, not one; and few who knew JBY or Jack would describe either as a "swaggering" wit. Jack never set foot in the Petitpas establishment. Lucius Beebe was more noted for evocation of atmosphere than for slavish adherence to fact.

9. Frances-Jane French, the genealogist, has found references to Yeatses in Dublin (under the spellings "Yeats," "Yeates," and "Yeatts") as early as 1671. She believes Jervis's ancestors, but not Jervis, came to Ireland from Yorkshire. Conversation with author, 1968.

10. The family tradition may possibly have reflected the facts, but no direct line has ever been traced, the records being murky or incomplete. WBY spent much energy trying to find a connection with the Ormonde Butlers, and Lily helped him, but he finally abandoned the search. He wrote her (9 Mar. 1928, MBY): "George [Mrs. William Butler Yeats] thinks you should not put the Duke of Ormonde story in the family book . . . as we have no real evidence." Four years earlier (10 June 1924, MBY) he had optimistically assured her: "There should be no difficulty in tracing the Butlers back." See Lord Dunboyne, *Butler Family History* (Kilkenny, 1966), 16–17, where the poet is said to be descended from James Butler (d. 1338), first earl of Ormonde, through his eldest (though technically illegitimate) son Edmund. The evidence presented is unconvincing; it is possible Lord Dunboyne was as eager to connect the poet to his family as the poet was to be connected.

Mary Butler Yeats came into the Kildare properties through the will of John Humphrey [*sic*] of Dublin, dated 14 May 1775, registered at the Registry of Deeds on 27 September 1775. The will mentions a nephew, the Rev. Richard Humphreys [*sic*], and two other Humphreyses, and names "My kinsman John Butler, my Godson Henry Butler, third son of said John Butler." He leaves certain property to "Mary, eldest daughter of the said John Butler and wife of Benjamin Yeates [*sic*] of Dublin." Among the executors is "*Cousin:* John Butler of Dublin."

Lily Yeats gives these details in her Scrapbook but neglects to say whether there were other bequests in the will, the original of which I have not seen. Nor does she say whether Humphreys's property was part of the ancient Ormonde Butler holdings, or how it might have passed to him rather than a Butler.

In a letter to Lily (20 May 1909, MBY), JBY writes: "My greatgrandmother

Mary Butler, married to Benjamin Yeats, and *last of the Ormonde Butlers* [italics mine], is named in the Peerage." JBY in typical fashion provides no details. The letter is quoted in Lily Yeats's Scrapbook.

11. See the fuller account in William M. Murphy, "The Ancestry of William Butler Yeats," in *Yeats and the 1890s,* ed. Robert O'Driscoll and Lorna Reynolds (Shannon: Irish University Press, 1971) and *Prodigal Father: The Life of John Butler Yeats* (Ithaca and London: Cornell Univ. Press, 1978), passim. The Thomastown lands in Kildare consisted of 346 acres, 2 roods and 25 perches Irish measure (about 560 acres English or American measure), producing an income of about £470 a year. The house in Dorset Street brought in £30; JBY sold it, after having thoroughly mortgaged it, in 1877. The Thomastown lands were sold to their tenants under the Ashbourne Act, the final payment made in 1907, nine months before JBY left Ireland for America.

12. Lily Yeats, Draft Scrapbook, "Grandmother Yeats" (MBY). See also Lily Yeats, "Scrapbook," 'Grandmother Yeats' (MBY). Despite her account of the visit to Grandmother Yeats, who died in 1876, Lily wrote to John Quinn (9 Feb. 1915, NYPL): "Our Yeats grandparents we never knew. Papa's father died before Papa's marriage and his mother not long after." See also n. 17 below.

13. Lily remembers Lollie throwing a stool out the nursery window and recalls Jack "sleeping by Mama in her bed, he rolled in a pale blue shawl" (Scrapbook, 'Where We Lived'.) Willie remembers looking out a window of the Fitzroy Road home (*Autobiographies* [London: Macmillan, 1966], 5). Lily also told Oliver Edwards of remembering Edwin Ellis with books and candle. (Oliver Edwards, "A Few Chapters from 'Yeats: His Life and Poetry,' " unpublished typescript, p. 20). I am grateful to the late Dr. Edwards for his kindness in letting me read and quote from his typescript.

14. Lily to Ruth, 23 June 1936, MBY.

15. Lily Yeats, Draft Scrapbook, "Mary (Aunt Mickey) Yeats."

16. Lily Yeats, Draft Scrapbook, "At Matthew Yeats's." Apparently Matthew's children had some "bitter feud" with the Wynnes. JBY's children had no feeling one way or the other but joined in the fray anyhow. See Murphy, "The Ancestry of William Butler Yeats," *Yeats and the 1890s,* ed. O'Driscoll and Reynolds, 1–19. Matt's children were about the same age as JBY's, though a generation separated them. "He married late," Lollie explained to Prof. Alfred De Lurey (29 Dec. 1932; Toronto), "so his children and we four are not very different in age." Two of Matt's sons emigrated to Canada, one (Dr. Frank Yeats) becoming mayor of Dunham, P.Q.

17. JBY to Jack, 17 Oct. 1917, ABY. In their adult years the Yeatses saw much of their father's sisters Fanny Gordon and Grace Jane and Jane Grace Yeats, and of his brother Isaac Butt Yeats. They were all fervent Unionists, conservative and conventional. Relationships with them were always pleasant, but there is no evidence that they exercised influence of any kind on the Yeats children.

18. JBY to Edward Dowden, 3 Jan. and 7 Jan. 1884, Dowden Correspondence, TCD.

19. Lily describes Merville in a letter to Joseph Hone (19 May 1939, Texas): "In our day it was a solid house, big rooms, about 14 bedrooms, stone kitchen and offices, and a glorious laundry smelling of soap, full of white steam, a clean coke fire with rows of irons heating at it, our grandmother's store room like a village shop, a place with windows and fireplace, shelves and drawers and a delicious smell of coffee. The house was of blue-gray limestone—the local stone —60 acres of land round it, a very fine view of Ben Bulben from the front of the house." I cite Lily's letters to Hone only when they contain information not found elsewhere in Lily's writings.

20. See George Mills Harper's admirable monograph, *"Go Back to Where You Belong": Yeats's Return from Exile"* (Dublin: Dolmen, 1973). I have discussed the Pollexfens at length in *Yeats Family and the Pollexfens*, and *Prodigal Father*.

21. WBY, *Autobiographies*, 7–8; and Lily Yeats, "Scrapbook," 'Grandmama Pollexfen's Brothers and Sister.'

22. WBY, *Autobiographies*, 17.

23. JBY to Lily, 11 Sept. 1920, MBY.

24. JBY to WBY, 10 Feb. 1918, MBY.

25. Lily Yeats, "Scrapbook," 'Grandmother Yeats.'

26. JBY to Lily, 30 Oct. 1912, MBY. He repeats Ellen's remark in many other places.

27. JBY, "Memoirs," unpublished.

28. JBY to Lily, 25 Nov. 1919, MBY.

29. WBY, *Autobiographies*, 9.

30. Lily Yeats, "Scrapbook," 'Grandfather William Pollexfen.'

31. See chap. 7 below.

32. Lily Yeats, "Scrapbook," 'Grandfather William Pollexfen.'

33. Lily Yeats, "Scrapbook," 'Grandfather William Pollexfen.'

34. Lily Yeats, "Scrapbook," 'Our Grandmother Elizabeth Pollexfen—born Middleton.'

35. JBY to WBY, 13 June 1914, MBY.

36. JBY to WBY, 30 July 1915, 5 Mar. 1909, MBY.

37. JBY to Lily, 25 June 1910, MBY.

38. JBY to Isaac Yeats, 3 Apr. 1916, ABY.

39. JBY, "Memoirs," unpublished, MBY.

40. JBY to WBY, 3 Aug. 1906, MBY.

41. JBY to WBY, 6 Sept. 1916, MBY.

42. WBY, *Autobiographies*, 10.

43. Alan Roberts and W. S. Ferguson, " 'Mr Alfred': A Poetic Connection," *Foyle and Londonderry College Former Pupils Association Magazine*, Feb. 1991: 20–22. I thank Dr. Robert C. Montgomery for calling this article to my attention and providing me with a copy.

44. JBY to WBY, 20 Apr. 1916, MBY.

45. JBY wrote in his "Memoirs" [unpublished]: "My son inherited this ear for rhyme."

46. JBY to WBY (n.d., "This is why I said . . ."), MBY.

47. Lily to JBY, 19 Sept. 1916, MBY.
48. JBY to WBY, 12 Feb. 1919, MBY.
49. JBY to WBY (n.d., "This is why I said . . .", MBY).
50. JBY to Lily, 30 Aug. 1916, MBY.
51. Lily to JBY, 13 July 1916, MBY.
52. JBY to WBY, 25 Apr. 1915, MBY.
53. JBY to WBY, 11 Aug. 1908, MBY. The passage is quoted in Joseph
Hone, *W. B. Yeats, 1865–1939* (London: Macmillan, 1965), 16. For a fuller
discussion of Alfred, see William M. Murphy, " 'In Memory of Alfred Pollexfen': W. B. Yeats and the Theme of Family," *Irish University Review*, 1, no. 1
(1970): 30–47.
54. JBY to WBY, 18 Sept. 1916 (second letter of this date, beginning
"Why am I writing . . ."), MBY.
55. JBY to WBY, 6 Sept. 1915 (first letter of this date, beginning "I am
writing . . ."), MBY.
56. Hone, *JBY: Letters*, 48–49.
57. JBY to WBY, 21 Sept. 1916, MBY.
58. See, for example, JBY to Isaac Yeats, 10 July 1912, ABY: "Lily never
speaks of it to anyone, and to me always speaks of it as nerves, as I to her—but
it is depressive mania, and it affected more or less most of the Pollexfens. Three
of them were in Asylums." Even George spent time in a hospital because of
depression.
59. WBY, *Autobiographies*, 10.
60. Lily Yeats, "Scrapbook," 'Our Grandmother Elizabeth Pollexfen—born
Middleton.'
61. For details about the date and place of William Middleton Pollexfen's
death, I am indebted to the late Oliver Edwards.
62. A copy of William Pollexfen's will is in the possession of Michael Butler
Yeats.
63. Lily Yeats, "Scrapbook," 'Our Grandmother Elizabeth Pollexfen'.
64. Lily to JBY, 9 July 1913, MBY.
65. Could the errant gene have come from William Pollexfen? See JBY to
Isaac Yeats, 30 June 1911, ABY: "A great doctor here . . . says mind and
digestion are closely connected. He has cured several cases of insanity of *long
standing*, simply by attending to their digestion. . . . It was by treating his
digestion that old Wm. Pollexfen was cured." Also JBY to Isaac Yeats, 12 Dec.
[1911], ABY: "Lollie is an abiding anxiety. Long ago I several times was most
anxious about her—she is so constantly unhappy, too like 'Grandpapa.' " See
chap. 4, below.
66. JBY to Isaac Yeats, 5 Aug. 1911, ABY.
67. JBY to WBY, 20 Sept. 1916 and 11 Aug. 1908, MBY.
68. JBY to Lily, 25 June 1910, MBY.
69. Lily writes to Ruth, 7 Feb. 1938 (letter no. 1 of this date), MBY, that
her daughter Charles Lane-Poole was "amused at Uncle Arthur's way of speaking
of Willy as 'poor Willy Yeats.' To him Willy was of no account." On Jackson's
"manner," see Lily to Ruth, 5 Aug. 1935.

70. Lily to Ruth, 13 Aug. 1929 and 27 Oct. 1928, MBY. Lily was unduly harsh in her judgment of Jackson. As an employee of the Belfast firm of Richardson Sons and Owden, he was sent to Sligo as their representative. When the Pollexfen firms floundered in the late eighties and early nineties, he was brought in to rescue them, and did so with remarkable success. He was highly regarded by those who knew him well and dealt with him. He became a Harbour Commissioner for Sligo and served as Chairman of the Commission for fourteen consecutive years. In addition to running the Pollexfen and Sligo Steam Navigation companies, he was also a director of the Midland Great Western Railway, the Sligo Gas Company, and the London and Lancashire Insurance Company. He served as High Sheriff for Sligo in 1899 and was also Deputy Lieutenant for the county. When the Irish Free State was established, he was named one of its original senators and served for six years.

It is reported that Jackson introduced half-day closings at the Sligo companies, a rarity in those days. On the day of his daughter's wedding, he gave each of his 131 employees a day's holiday and a gift of a half sovereign to celebrate the occasion. He appears less limited than Lily describes him.

I thank Mr. Gerald Bryan, Jackson's grandson, for providing me with a copy of an unpublished typescript, "The Jackson Family," and also for the photographs of Arthur and Alice Pollexfen Jackson.

71. JBY to Lily, 6 Nov. 1910, MBY. A later letter to her elaborated: "Fred would have been a good man if his parents had taken a little interest in him, but there was no one to advise him except his brother Charles, and Charles was never a good influence at any time. I once told George that I thought Charles had been Fred's ruin, and it annoyed George very much *because he knew it was true.* Charles was the bad influence in the family. I saw that from the first" (1 Feb. 1922, MBY).

72. Alan Roberts and W. S. Ferguson, " 'Mr. Alfred': A Poetic Connection," *Foyle and Londonderry Former Pupils* Association *Magazine, Feb. 1991,* 20—22.

73. Mrs. Ida Varley Dewar-Durie (daughter of Isabella Pollexfen), conversation with author; Lyme Station, Scotland, 1968.

74. Mr. Edward Fawcett Brown (of Sligo, son-in-law of Agnes Pollexfen Gorman), conversation with author, 1968.

75. JBY to WBY, 20 Sept. 1916, MBY.

76. JBY, "Memoirs."

77. John Butler Yeats, *Early Memories* (Dublin: Cuala, 1923), 12, 13.

78. JBY, "Memoirs." This is a characteristic embellished misquotation of Wordsworth's *Excursion,* I, 80.

79. JBY, *Early Memories,* 13, 16, 17, 18.

80. JBY to Isaac Yeats, 25 Dec. 1917, ABY. "This I know is Willie's opinion and it certainly is mine. We Yeatses have the *idealistic* imagination. The Pollexfen mind is *realistic.*" To Lady Gregory he wrote (22 Aug. 1907, NYPL), "George Pollexfen is a man of genius though he does not know it."

81. JBY, "Memoirs." In a letter to Edward Dowden (8 Jan. 1884, Dowden Correspondence, TCD), he had written that the Pollexfens were as solid and powerful as the sea-cliffs; "but hitherto they are altogether dumb. To give them

a voice is like giving a voice to the sea-cliffs, when what wild babblings must break forth." This is apparently the earliest use of the metaphor.

82. WBY to Lady Gregory [29 Sept. 1910] (Allan Wade, ed., *The Letters of W. B. Yeats*, [London: Rupert Hart-Davis, 1954], 553).

83. JBY to Lily, 1 Feb. 1922, MBY; WBY to Lady Gregory [28 Sept. 1910] (Wade, *Letters of WBY*, 552).

84. JBY, *Early Memories*, 96. George Moore alludes to George Pollexfen as "a celebrated occultist whose predictions were always fulfilled" (*Ave* [New York: Boni and Liveright, 1923], 24).

85. WBY to Lily [20 Jan. 1895] (Wade, *Letters of WBY*, 245).

86. JBY to WBY, 29 Apr. 1921, MBY.

87. George Pollexfen had been close to Lucy Middleton, who herself had visions or previsions that WBY called "verifiable," and she and Willie often spoke of visions and magic. See *William Butler Yeats, Memoirs*, transcribed and edited by Denis Donoghue (New York: Macmillan, 1972), 76. See also the appendix below.

88. Donoghue, *WBY: Memoirs*, 79.

89. WBY to Katharine Tynan [after 6 Sept. 1888] (Wade, *Letters of WBY*, 87).

90. Edward Fawcett Brown, conversation with author, 1968.

91. JBY, *Early Memories*, 93.

92. JBY to Jack, 31 May 1916, ABY.

93. JBY to Lily, 13 July 1917, MBY.

94. George left Fred's share in trust, with the bulk going to his children. Fred protested, and Arthur Jackson, the executor, brought a suit in Chancery to have the terms of the will accepted, Jack allowing himself to stand as defendant (since the Yeats sons were granted only half as much as their sisters and hence had standing).

John W. Purser (*The Literary Works of Jack Yeats*, [Gerrards Cross England,: Colin Smythe, 1991], pp. 10, 141) thinks Jack was more sympathetic to Fred than has hitherto been thought, both because of Jack's role as defendant and because Jack makes use in his novel *The Amaranthers* of a situation like Fred's. Undoubtedly Jack would have been attracted to the wild career of Fred and had some sympathy for him, as Purser says (p. 141), but on the issue of the hearing in the Court of Chancery the evidence is unmistakable, not only Lily's own account of it but the record of the hearing itself (High Court of Justice in Ireland, Chancery Division, 1910, No. 1005: Notice of Judgement December 7, 1910: Estate of George Thomas Pollexfen, between Arthur Jackson, plaintiff, and John Butler Yeats Jr., defendant). At the hearing Fred's lawyer, a Mr. Matheson, suggested that his client be made a defendant also, but Jack's lawyer objected, a certain sign that in the matter of George's will, Jack was not sympathetic to Fred. The judge accepted the will, Fred being allowed merely "to attend inquiry at his own expense." Lily adds a note to her record of the hearing: "Friendly action taken to put the snuffer on Fredrick Pollexfen."

Purser's excellent study appeared after this essay was prepared for publication. Unhappily, I have been able to make only limited use of it.

95. On George Pollexfen's death and his will, see the notes in Lily Yeats's "Scrapbook;" JBY to WBY, 6 Sept. 1916, 20 Sept. 1912, MBY; and JBY's memoirs.

96. JBY to Lily, 15 Sept. 1916, MBY. Hone's *JBY: Letters* contains part of the letter but not the quoted passage. See also JBY to Oliver Elton, 9 Apr. 1911, collection of Leonard Elton: The Pollexfens "hated, positively hated" Willie.

97. Lily Yeats, "Scrapbook," 'Our Grandmother Elizabeth Pollexfen—born Middleton.'

98. Lollie to Paul Lemperley, 8 Jan. 1913, Stanford.

99. Lily to Ruth, 23 June 1926, MBY.

100. Lily to Ruth, 4 Feb. 1939, MBY. A *rath* is a pre-historic earth fort or mound, supposed by Irish peasants to be inhabited by fairies.

101. WBY, *Autobiographies*, 22.

102. Lily to James A. Healy, 5 Apr. 1938, Stanford.

103. Lily Yeats, "Scrapbook," 'Our Grandmother Elizabeth Pollexfen—born Middleton.'

104. Jack to James A. Healy, 18 June 1940, Stanford.

105. WBY, *Autobiographies*, 52. For a fuller treatment of Yeats's feelings about Sligo, see Harper, *"Go Back to Where You Belong."*

2. Home Life among the Yeatses

1. Lily to Joseph Hone, 26 Feb. 1942, Texas. She told Hone that WBY was also "very hopeful," though "not quite to the extent Papa was" (19 May; 1942; Texas).

2. Lily Yeats, Scrapbook, "Mama's Health and Other Things." For treatment of the subject generally, see also James Lovic Allen, "All In The Family: Artistic Interaction Between W. B. Yeats and His Siblings," *Yeats Eliot Review* 5, no. 1 (1978): 32–43; and Murphy, *Prodigal Father*, passim.

3. C. P. Curran, conversation with author, Dublin, 1966. Curran was a Dubliner married to Helen Laird, a friend of Lily and Lollie. He was close to James Joyce.

4. Ida Dewar-Durie, daughter of Isabella Pollexfen Varley, has remarked that Susan was quiet, gentle, and sweet—milder than the other daughters in the family and never able to stand up for herself (conversation with author, Lyme Station, Scotland, 1968.).

5. John Todhunter to Edward Dowden, 14 Jan. 1870 (Dowden Correspondence, no. 60, TCD).

6. JBY to Rosa Butt, 20 Oct., no. 110, 17 Nov. 1910, no. 112; 29 Nov. 1915, no. 161 Bodleian. See chap. 8.

7. John Todhunter to Edward Dowden, 27 Sept. 1869 (Dowden Correspondence, no. 55, TCD).

8. For the birth and death records and their significance (and for many other acts of kindness and generosity), I am indebted to the late Dr. Oliver Edwards.

9. Lily to Joseph Hone, 21 Feb. 1942, Texas. She describes in that letter the ride of Uncle Fred Pollexfen on a galloping horse to fetch aid for baby Robert, in such a hurry he didn't wait to saddle the horse. She wrote Hone a short time later (26 Feb.) of how, years afterward, she saw a performance of WBY's *Purgatory* at the Abbey. "You will remember there is the sound at the beginning and again at the end of a galloping horse. When that came, all round me melted away and I felt myself back nearly seventy years in my cot on that March morning hearing the galloping of the horse going too late for the doctor for my baby brother. It shows what deep impressions children get while seeming to see or feel nothing."

10. They made their own mark on Sligo while they were still young. One newcomer, reluctant to go to church in the rain, was admonished, "Don't be lazy. The Yeats children are worth getting wet to see" (Lily Yeats, Scrapbook entry).

11. Lily's final version, handwritten and placed in a scrapbook, is called here her "Scrapbook." Earlier versions of some of the entries appear in what I have called the "Draft Scrapbook." Another manuscript, entitled by her "Odds and Ends," also contains her memories. Sometimes there are different versions of the same general entries in the three manuscripts (all three MBY). I make use of those that seem most appropriate.

12. Lily Yeats, "Odds and Ends": 'The tenth bridesmaid.'

13. Lily Yeats, "Odds and Ends": 'By Sea to Sligo.'

14. Lily Yeats, Draft Scrapbook, "The Frost on Lough Gill."

15. Lily Yeats, Draft Scrapbook, "Walks with Papa."

16. In his *Autobiographies* WBY calls 14 Edith Villas "the first house we lived in," forgetting Fitzroy Road. Edith Villas is a block-long street in what used to be called North End and is now West Kensington. The street, a short distance from the Kensington Underground Station, still stands, but No. 14 was destroyed by German bombing during the Second World War.

17. Lily Yeats, "Odds and Ends": 'The National Gallery.'

18. Lily Yeats, "Odds and Ends": 'The Moonbeam.'

19. Lily Yeats, "Scrapbook," 'Our Education.'

20. Murphy, *Prodigal Father*, 110, 112.

21. Lily Yeats, "Odds and Ends": 'Miss Jowitt.'

22. Lily Yeats, "Odds and Ends": 'The wry mouth family.'

23. Lily Yeats, "Scrapbook," 'Mama's Health.'

24. Lily Yeats, "Scrapbook," 'Mama's Health and Other Things.'

25. JBY to Lily, 19 Dec. 1913, MBY. See Murphy, *Prodigal Father*, 113, 115.

26. See Murphy, *Prodigal Father*, 105–9.

27. Lily Yeats, "Odds and Ends": "Miss Jowitt." They always remembered Miss Jowitt, and she them, keeping in touch by card and letter. Forty years later she visited them in Dublin to discuss old times (JBY to Jack, 2 May 1921, ABY).

28. Lily Yeats, "Odds and Ends": 'Miss Jowitt.'

29. Lily Yeats, "Odds and Ends": 'Miss Jowitt.'

30. Draft scrapbook, "Odds and Ends," and Lily to JBY, 26 May 1917, MBY.

31. Lily Yeats, Draft Scrapbook, "In the summer of 1879."

32. Lily Yeats, Draft Scrapbook, "In the summer of 1879"; "Odds and Ends": 'Branscombe, Devon.'

33. Lily Yeats, Draft Scrapbook, "In the summer of 1879"; "Odds and Ends": 'Branscombe, Devon.'

34. Lily Yeats to JBY, 26 May 1917, MBY.

35. These drawings are reproduced in Murphy, *Prodigal Father*, 119.

36. Lily Yeats, "Odds and Ends": 'Branscombe, Devon.'

37. Lily Yeats, Draft Scrapbook, "In the summer of 1979"; "Odds and Ends": 'Branscombe, Devon.'

38. Lily Yeats, "Scrapbook," 'Our Education.'

39. Lily Yeats, "Odds and Ends": 'The York Street Studio.'

40. Lollie Yeats, Diary, 24 Oct. and 6 Dec. 1888, MBY.

41. Lily Yeats, Scrapbook, "Where We Lived." The address in Terenure was 10 Ashfield Terrace (now 418 Harold's Cross Road).

42. JBY, "Memoirs." See Murphy, *Prodigal Father*, 137.

43. JBY to Isaac Yeats, 1 July 1915, no. 2 of this date ("When I write to you . . ."), ABY.

44. The matter of Susan Pollexfen has been covered in Murphy, *Prodigal Father*, but not convincingly enough for all readers. See Helen Vendler, "J. B. Y.," *New Yorker*, 8 Jan. 1979, 66–77, and my reply, "Home Life Among the Yeatses," in *Yeats, Sligo and Ireland*, ed. A. Norman Jeffares (Gerrards Cross, England: Colin Smythe, 1980), 170–88.

45. WBY, *Autobiographies*, 167.

46. Susan Pollexfen Yeats to Matthew Yeats, 21 Aug. 1880, MBY.

47. JBY to Isaac Yeats, 29 Dec. 1915, ABY; Murphy, *Prodigal Father*, 56.

48. WBY, *Autobiographies*, 61.

49. See Murphy, *Prodigal Father*, 60–71, for an account of the unpleasant relationship between Susan Pollexfen Yeats and Edwin Ellis. See also WBY, *Autobiographies*, 58: "I was asked to write an essay on 'Men may rise on stepping-stones of their dead selves to higher things.' My father read the subject to my mother, who had no interest in such matters." Writing to Rosa Butt with unusual candor, JBY said, "Had my poor wife a little more intellect she would have been something very remarkable" (ca. 1903, date unclear, letter beginning "More letters . . .," no 18, Bodleian).

50. John Todhunter to Edward Dowden, 14 Jan. 1870, Dowden Correspondence, TDC; see Murphy, *Prodigal Father*, 71.

51. Oliver Elton, preface to Hone, *JBY: Letters*, 5.

52. JBY to WBY, 25 Apr. 1915, MBY; quoted in Murphy, *Yeats Family and the Pollexfens*, 87.

53. WBY, *Autobiographies*, 61.

54. Metropolitan School of Art, Index Register, session 1882–1883, nos. 2996–2997.

55. JBY to Matthew Yeats, 3 Oct. 1883, MBY.

402   Notes to Pages 53–57

56. Isabella may have gained her own interest from her husband's father, also named John Varley and also a painter. Earlier he had similarly influenced Sir Richard Burton, the explorer and linguist. See Edward Rice, *Captain Sir Richard Francis Burton* (New York: Scribner, 1990), 22.

57. See Murphy, *Prodigal Father,* 137ff., and passim; Murphy, "Psychic Daughter, Mystic Son, Sceptic Father," in *Yeats and the Occult,* ed. George Mills Harper (Toronto: Macmillan of Canada, 1975); and the appendix.

58. See Metropolitan School of Art, Index Register, May 1884-Apr. 1886.

59. Murphy, *Prodigal Father,* 132–33, 568–69; Wade calls Laura "a distant cousin" (*Letters of WBY,* 117 n). See also JBY to John Quinn, 3 Dec. 1917, NYPL; WBY to Katharine Tynan, 21 Mar. 1889 (Wade, *Letters of WBY,* 117; John Kelly, *The Collected Letters of W. B. Yeats* (Oxford: Clarendon Press, 1986), 1:155). Laura's letter to WBY is dated 10 Aug. 1884 (Wade, *Letters of WBY,* 117 n; Kelly, 1, 155). Under her inspiration he wrote "Time and the Witch Vivien" and "The Island of Statues." Her full name was Edith Laura Armstrong; her first husband was named Byrne. See Murphy, "William Butler Yeats's *John Sherman:* An Irish Poet's Declaration of Independence," *Irish University Review* 9, no. 1 (Spring 1979): 92–111; reprinted in *Image and Illusion: A Festschrift for Roger McHugh* (Dublin: Wolfhound Press, 1979), 92–111.

60. The terms are JBY's (JBY to John Quinn, 3 Dec. 1917, NYPL).

61. Quoted by Pamela Hinkson, "The Friendship of Yeats and Katharine Tynan, I: Early Days of the Irish Literary Revival," *Fortnightly Review,* Oct. 1953, 253.

62. The most prominent of the illustrated works was the *Romances and Narratives of Daniel Defoe,* sixteen volumes, edited by George A. Aitken, with illustrations by J. B. Yeats (London: J. M. Dent and Co., 1895).

63. WBY to Katharine Tynan [after 6 Sept. 1888] (Wade, *Letters of WBY,* 85; Kelly, 1: 95).

64. Lily to Joseph Hone, 7 Nov. 1941, Texas.

65. WBY to Katharine Tynan, 21 Apr. 1889 (Wade. *Letters of WBY,* 34; Kelly, 1: 111).

66. See chaps. 4 and 5, on Cuala, below.

67. JBY to John O'Leary, 20 Mar. 1888, NLIr.

68. Lily Yeats, Draft Scrapbook, "In 1887 . . ."; also in Lily Yeats, "Scrapbook," 'Return to London, 1887.'

69. WBY to Katharine Tynan, 8 May 1887 (Wade, *Letters of WBY,* 35; Kelly, 1: 13).

70. WBY to Katharine Tynan, 18 May 1887 (Wade, *Letters of WBY,* 36; Kelly, 1: 15).

71. WBY to Katharine Tynan, 18 May 1887 (Wade, *Letters of WBY,* 36; Kelly, 1: 16).

72. WBY to Katharine Tynan, 20 Apr. 1888 (Wade, *Letters of WBY,* 68; Kelly, 1: 62).

73. WBY to Ellen O'Leary, 1 May 1888 (Wade, *Letters of WBY,* 70; Kelly, 1: 64).

74. WBY to Katharine Tynan, 19 May 1888, and [June] 1888 (Wade, *Letters of WBY*, 73, 75; Kelly, 1: 70, 71).
75. Lily Yeats, Draft Scrapbook, "Lady Wilde's Saturday Afternoon."
76. WBY to Katharine Tynan, 12 Feb. 1888 (Wade, *Letters of WBY*, 60; Kelly, 1: 50).
77. Donoghue, *WBY: Memoirs*, 31.
78. See Murphy, *Prodigal Father*, 154ff.
79. JBY to Isaac Yeats, 25 Dec. 1917, ABY. Also, Susan Mitchell, "John Butler Yeats," unpublished talk: one version in Sligo County Museum, the other, virtually identical, in MBY. Both are holographs.
80. For details of *Dhoya* and the writing and publication of *John Sherman*, I am indebted to Richard Finneran's edition, *William Butler Yeats: John Sherman and Dhoya* (Detroit: Wayne State Univ. Press, 1969). I make use also of my own essay on the longer novel, "William Butler Yeats's *John Sherman*."
81. Allan Wade, *A Bibliography of the Writings of W. B. Yeats* (London: Rupert Hart-Davis, 1968), 22.
82. WBY to Katharine Tynan, 12 Feb. 1888 (Wade, *Letters of WBY*, 60; Kelly, 1: 50).
83. WBY to Katharine Tynan [?Feb. 1888] (Wade, *Letters of WBY*, 61; Kelly, 1: 52, where it is dated "[?20 Feb. 1888]").
84. WBY to Father Matthew Russell, 6 Mar. [1888] (Wade, *Letters of WBY*, 62; Kelly, 1: 53). See also WBY to John O'Leary [19] November [1888] (Wade, Letters of WBY, 94–95; Kelly, 1: 110): "my hatred of London." After he had spent fifteen years in London, WBY apparently relented, for in declaring that the novel had been written when he was "very young and knew no better," he seems to be saying that London is not so bad after all. It is noteworthy that from the time he returned to London in 1887 until he bought his castle in Ireland to be "among my people" a period of thirty years elapsed, during most of which he lived in London. The greatest Irish poet of his time spent the three decades of his life after reaching manhood outside the country he wrote about. See Richard Finneran's illuminating discussion of the novel in his edition, 21–32.
85. WBY to Katharine Tynan, 25 Aug. [1888] (Wade, *Letters of WBY*, 81–82; Kelly, 1: 92, notes it is enclosed in the letter of 30 Aug. 1888).
86. One of the most perceptive critics of Yeats's prose, James Olney, has noted Yeats's underappreciated sense of humor, finding it of paramount importance in those passages of the *Autobiographies* in which he responds to George Moore's malicious attacks on him ("The Uses of Comedy and Irony in *Autobiographies and Autobiography*," in *Yeats: An Annual of Critical and Textual Studies*, ed. Richard J. Finneran, vol. 2, 1984, [Ithaca, N.Y.: Cornell Univ. Press, 1984], 195–208.) Olney notes that Hazard Adams, "almost alone among Yeats commentators," has also recognized his use of comedy in "Some Yeatsian versions of Comedy," in *In Excited Reverie*, ed. A. Norman Jeffares and K. G. W. Cross (London: Macmillan; New York; St. Martin, 1965), pp. 152–70.
87. There are many identifiable parallels in the novel: the Imperial Hotel of

the book is the Imperial Hotel of Sligo (Finneran. p. 43); the firm of Sherman and Saunders, ship-brokers, is a combination of W. and G. T. Pollexfen and Co. and the Sligo Steam Navigation Company (p. 60); St. Peter's Church in London is the name of the church in Dublin where Laura Armstrong was married (p. 66); the church members who turned against their rector (p. 86) correspond to the Calry Parish churchgoers in Sligo who hated John Dowden for views they thought too High Church. When WBY described the harmonium and the "twenty children . . . singing in shrill voices" (p. 53), he was describing his own brief experience in "singing school," later remembered in "Sailing to Byzantium." His description of Mary Carton as of "a type that in country towns does not get married at all," "its beauty too lacking in pink and white" fitted Katharine Tynan in its essentials. Sherman's voyage to Liverpool among squealing pigs (p. 58) is paralleled in the family's real experiences on the family steamers. When the old woman on the ship asks John Sherman why he is leaving Ballah ("Why are ye goin' among them savages in London, Misther John? Why don't ye stay among your own people—for what have we in this life but a mouthful of air?") (p. 59), Willie is remembering a Pollexfen aunt's remark to him when the family moved to London in 1874: "You are going to London. Here you are somebody. There you will be nobody at all." WBY doesn't name the aunt, who is almost certainly Agnes. See WBY, *Autobiographies,* 27.

88. The first full critical edition of *The Speckled Bird* was not published until 1976 (ed. William H. O'Donnell, *The Speckled Bird, by William Butler Yeats,* Canada: McClelland and Stewart, 1976). In the same year appeared O'Donnell's *Literatim Transcription of the Manuscripts of William Butler Yeats's The Speckled Bird* (Delmar, New York: Scholars Facsimiles and Reprints, 1976); his limited edition of the novel, without critical apparatus, was published by the Cuala Press in 1974. I am grateful to Dr. O'Donnell for having let me consult his complete transcript of all versions of *The Speckled Bird* and for sharing his findings with me. WBY began writing some time before 7 July 1898 (JBY to Lady Gregory, 7 July 1898, NYPL.

From both books the biographer can learn much. An astute scholar of the subject, James Olney, has pointed out that autobiographies are notoriously untrustworthy, as the writer unavoidably tries to paint a picture of himself as he would like to be seen, a temptation to which WBY was not immune. The novelist makes use of a hundred little falsehoods to arrive at a greater truth, the autobiographer of a hundred little truths to arrive at a greater falsehood.

89. WBY did, however, recount the story in a radio broadcast.

90. Miss Acostos's words are approximate. See Lily to Ruth, 17 June 1930, MBY. The first version of the poem was completed shortly before 21 Dec. 1888; neither it nor the incident of the reading is mentioned in Lollie's diary. WBY sent a full copy of this early version to Katharine Tynan in his letter to her of 21 Dec. 1888 (Wade, *Letters of WBY,* 100; Kelly, 1: 121). If that is the poem he read to the ladies, it is not surprising that they should be unimpressed, for it is awkward and unmusical, with uncertain metrical properties. Wade notes that the final version, not printed till 13 December 1890 (Wade mistakenly gives the

date as 12 Sept. 1891), "shows Yeats's skill in revision at its best" (*Letters of WBY*, 100 n).

91. The original of the diary is in the possession of Michael Butler Yeats. I refer in the text to the dates of her entries.

92. On Jack at Bedford Park see chap. 7, below.

93. Jack mentions having to go "off to school" in a letter to Sarah Purser, 7 June 1889, Victoria.

94. WBY to Katharine Tynan, 25 July [1888] (Wade, *Letters of WBY*, 80; Kelly, 1: 88).

95. WBY to Katharine Tynan, 9 May [1889] (Wade, *Letters of WBY*, 126; Kelly, 1: 166, and note, where Kelly cites Miss Tynan's piece in *The Sketch*, 29 Nov. 1893). Jack's diary entry for 26 May 1889 is said to show his sketch of the ceiling, but I have not seen it.

96. WBY to Katharine Tynan, 31 Jan. 1889 (Wade, *Letters of WBY*, 107; Kelly, 1: 136).

97. WBY to John O'Leary [after 26 Jan. 1888] (Wade, *Letters of WBY*, 56; Kelly 1: 45). WBY to Katharine Tynan, 25 June 1887 (Wade, *Letters of WBY*, 41; Kelly, 1: 22).

98. WBY, *Autobiographies*, 141. For an excellent summary of the relationship, see William Dumbleton, "William Morris and the Yeatses," an unpublished paper read at Albany Institute of History and Art, 16 Apr. 1987. Although WBY admired Morris, their political ideas were quite at variance; see Peter Faulkner, *William Morris and W. B. Yeats* (Dublin: Dolmen, 1962).

99. WBY to John Quinn, 30 Sept. 1921, quoted from B. L. Reid, *The Man from New York* (New York: Oxford Univ. Press, 1968), 493–94. Yeats saw Henley at Henley's house in Chiswick, a place he did not enjoy as much as Kelmscott. See WBY to Katharine Tynan [after 6 Sept. 1888 (Wade, *Letters of WBY*, 89; Kelly, 1: 99, where it is dated "[?22–28 Sept. 1888]").

100. Lily Yeats, "Scrapbook," 'My Six Years I Spent with May Morris.'

101. WBY to Katharine Tynan, 25 June 1887, postscript 1 July (Wade, *Letters of WBY*, 42; Kelly, 1: 23).

102. Lily Yeats, "Scrapbook," 'My Six Years I Spent with May Morris.'

103. Lily to JBY, 9 Oct. 1910, MBY.

104. Lily Yeats, "Scrapbook," 'My Six Years I Spent with May Morris.'

105. WBY to Katharine Tynan, 11 Apr. 1888 (Wade, *Letters of WBY*, 66; Kelly, 1: 59).

106. WBY to Katharine Tynan, 13 Jan. 1889 (Wade, *Letters of WBY*, 101; Kelly, 1: 123).

107. "She is to be a kind of assistant of hers," WBY wrote Katharine Tynan on 13 Jan. 1889 (Wade, *Letters of WBY*, 101; Kelly, 1: 123). Other girls worked for May too; Lily Mason was already there when Lily arrived but did not stay for long. Florence Farr (Mrs. Edward Emery), sister-in-law of H. M. Paget, was one of those who worked with May. Miss Mason's mother arranged for her daughter to leave, feeling the job made her unable to "attend to her social duties," or, as Lily put it, "meaning she would never get a husband sitting on a chair doing

embroidery" (Lily Yeats, "Scrapbook," 'My Six Years I Spent with May Morris'). The mother was right. Miss Mason married, Lily did not. Lily was the only assistant who stayed for a long period (see Murphy, *Prodigal Father,* 160, 164–66, 180–82).

108. Lily Yeats, "My Six Years I Spent with May Morris." For an account of May from a different point of view, see Linda Parry, *William Morris Textiles* (London: Weidenfeld and Nicolson, 1983), 30–35. Miss Parry did not know of Lily's experiences with May. I thank Dr. Nicola Gordon Bowe for calling this article to my attention and providing me with a copy.

109. WBY to Katharine Tynan, 13 Jan. [1889] (Wade, *Letters of WBY,* 101; Kelly, 1: 123).

110. Lily Yeats, "Scrapbook," 'My Six Years I Spent with May Morris.'

111. Lily Yeats, "Scrapbook," 'My Six Years I Spent with May Morris.'

112. Lily Yeats, "Scrapbook," 'My Six Years I Spent with May Morris.'

113. Lily Yeats, Draft Scrapbook, "Lily and May Morris."

114. Lily to Ruth, 8 Mar. 1932, MBY.

115. Lily Yeats, "Scrapbook," 'My Six Years I Spent with May Morris.'

116. WBY to Katharine Tynan, 4 Dec. [1888] (Wade, *Letters of WBY,* 95; Kelly 1: 111).

117. Lily Yeats, "Scrapbook," 'My Six Years I Spent with May Morris.'

118. Lily Yeats, "Scrapbook," 'My Six Years I Spent with May Morris.' "I used to call her 'The Gorgon,' " Lily wrote James A. Healy (4 Dec. 1938, Stanford). The dating of Lily's week-long stay is precise: "Lilly is staying for a week at the Morris's" [*sic*], WBY wrote Katharine Tynan on Thursday, 27 Feb. 1890 (Wade, *Letters of WBY,* 149; Kelly, 1: 210). She returned to Blenheim Road on 3 March, a Monday. Her stay as chaperone probably lasted from Friday, 21 Feb. (or Saturday, 22 Feb.) through the weekend ending 2 Mar. As Monday was a workday, Lily would have put in her regular hours before returning home.

119. Lily Yeats, "Scrapbook," 'My Six Years I Spent with May Morris.' Lily preferred Kelmscott to Hammersmith. "I lunched . . . with [the Morrises] and so met many interesting people. Bernard Shaw was one, then very hard up and doing musical criticism for a paper. . . . [He] came in like a refreshing breeze, with his brains and wit and easy Irish manners. The house was delightful. In the room I worked in were three fine Rossetti pictures" (Lily to James A. Healy, 4 Dec. 1938, Stanford).

120. Lily Yeats, Draft Scrapbook, "Lily and May Morris."

121. Lily Yeats, "Scrapbook," 'My Six Years I Spent with May Morris.'

122. JBY to WBY, 2 Sept. 1892 (William M. Murphy, ed., *Letters from Bedford Park* [Dublin: Cuala, 1973], 7).

123. See Murphy, *Prodigal Father,* 157, 574.

124. I have corrected the spelling and added punctuation where necessary. Lollie spells Maud's last name as "Goonne," implying an imperfect personal knowledge of her while her parenthetical remark shows knowledge of her reputation. She also shows the spellings "immence," "handsome" (for "hansom"), and "complection."

125. "I hate to be smiled on, a sort of royal smile," was Lily's comment on Maud Gonne (Lily to JBY, 14 Nov. 1910, MBY). Miss Gonne's name seldom appears in the correspondence between the members of the family. In the more than two million words of family correspondence (not including WBY's writings) there cannot be more than half a dozen or so references to her. In one, from JBY to Lady Gregory, 2 August 1898 (Murphy, *Letters from Bedford Park*, 43, 75n), he says of her, comparing her to another woman: "I know other ladies, one especially, of unsurpassed brilliancy, who seems to have come straight from Purgatorial fires. But then Purgatory is the way to Heaven." There was an unspoken accusation of blame against her for having swayed the affections of Willie; yet it was he who pursued her in the hopeless affair, for she never showed the slightest emotional interest in him. The family did not approve of her love of violence as a political weapon nor of her plans for Irish independence. (In fact, an impartial observer might note that Maud's political position and her activities were indeed extreme and irrational and might wonder whether, if she had been as homely as, for example, a Katharine Tynan or a Sarah Purser, she would have had any influence at all. She was a kind of political Marilyn Monroe who, not content to be a mere beauty to be stared at, used her staggering appearance and vocal talents to entice men into supporting her causes).

126. Lily Yeats, "Scrapbook," 'Our Education.' Lily writes fifty years after the event, "Lollie went as student mistress [i.e., student teacher] to the High School in Bedford Park and also to the Froebel College." Which came first is not clear. On 21 Mar. 1889, WBY wrote Katharine Tynan, "Lolly is teaching at Kindergarten School in Bedford Park" (Wade, *Letters of WBY*, 118; Kelly, 1: 155). Lollie's diary entries suggest limited time at school: "In from school 12.30" (21 May 1889); "At school till 1.30. Went to Grammar class" (22 May). In her vita Lollie lists teaching at the "Chiswick High School, Bedford Park," and this is perhaps the high school Lily had in mind. The only certificates Lollie mentions holding are the "Elementary and Higher" from the Froebel Society (listed in a document, "Vita Brevis," in Lollie's own hand, in the Evelyn Gleeson Papers [collection of Dr. Patrick Kelly]); she claims no diploma from the high school.)

127. WBY to Katharine Tynan, 21 Mar. 1889 (Wade, *Letters of WBY*, 118; Kelly, 1: 155–56).

128. Lollie Yeats, "Vita Brevis," Gleeson Papers.

129. Lollie to George (Mrs. William Butler) Yeats, n.d. [ca. 1938.] (Cuala Press Archives 1902–1986, Press A Cuala Arch, Box 8, TCD).

130. WBY to Katharine Tynan, 10 Apr. [1889] (Wade, *Letters of WBY*, 120; Kelly, 1: 158).

131. The method was simple but apparently novel at the time. The student would draw directly with the brush, not being allowed to make a preliminary sketch on the paper. Lollie's first private student was Mariella ("Cuckoo") Powell, daughter of York Powell (diary, 11 Sept. 1890).

132. The accounts of Lollie's income and expenses, and those of Willie and Jack, not always easy to date precisely, are given in Lollie's hand on the pages of her diary after the daily entries end.

133. JBY to WBY, 24 June 1921, MBY.

134. JBY to Isaac Yeats, 1 Aug. 1921, ABY.

135. Hilary Pyle, *Jack B. Yeats* (London: Routledge and Kegan Paul: 1970), 37.

136. JBY to Lily, 1 Aug. 1894 (Murphy, *Letters from Bedford Park,* 12).

137. See chap. 7, below.

138. I thank Dr. Maureen O'Rourke Murphy for providing me with this information.

139. Lily Yeats, diary, 6 Dec. 1895.

140. Lily Yeats, "Scrapbook," 'My Six Years I Spent with May Morris.' See Murphy, *Prodigal Father,* 180, 182. May had a brief affair with John Quinn, who dropped her (see Reid, *The Man from New York,* New York: Oxford Univ. Press, 1968, 76n, 80–84), then moved in different circles. Forty years later Lily gave Ruth Pollexfen Lane-Poole her opinion of May's tastes and standards: "May always had some inferior as a confidant in my day, a woman hairdresser who used to bring her vulgar gossip and tittle tattle about the Burne-Joneses, and all the people May disliked and was jealous of, which was all she knew." When Lily wrote the letter, May was "living with Lollo, known as 'Daughter of the Plough,' wears knickers all the time, is quite uneducated and is very rough" (Lily to Ruth, 4 Nov. 1935, MBY).

141. Lily's diary has regular entries—some long, some short—almost daily from 1 Aug. 1895 until 27 Jan. 1896. The next entry is dated five months later, 22 May 1896, and consists of two lines; the next, a long passage, is 11 July 1896, two months later. After that the entries become fairly detailed once again but separated by weeks rather than days. These entries continue until 10 December 1896. The next and penultimate entry is for 15 April 1897. The gaps were brought about by her illness in France and her later relapse in Bedford Park. The pages after the 15 Apr. 1897 entry are filled with notes about the Ormonde, Yeats, and Pollexfen families; these are followed by one final diary entry of 26 June 1897. The last pages of the notebook contain three fortunes "told by W. B.," dated 18 Sept., 23 Aug., and 23 Aug. (the date is repeated), in that order. In the text I cite the date of each entry quoted.

142. Lily to JBY, 30 Oct. 1910, MBY. See chap. 2, n.62, above.

143. JBY described his problems to John Quinn in an undated letter written about April 1919, beginning "All thro' the worst part of my illness. . . ." See Murphy, *Prodigal Father,* 494.

144. T. W. Rolleston to Elkin Mathews, 6 July 1894 (Reading, Elkin Mathews Collection.)

145. Robert Louis Stevenson to W. B. Yeats, 14 Apr. 1894. Typescript copy in Elkin Mathews Collection, Reading f. 676.

146. See Murphy, *Prodigal Father,* 183ff. and passim.

147. WBY to John O'Leary, 5 [Jan.] 1894 (Wade, *Letters of WBY,* 229); Kelly (1: 229) gives the date as "February".

148. Another four lines in the entry were scratched out so vigorously that they challenge decipherment.

149. Lily Yeats, end of Diary, after entry for 26 June 1897.

150. See Murphy, *Prodigal Father,* 185–86.

151. I thank Dr. John Kelly for calling this passage to my attention, along with the observation about WBY's part in Lady Gregory's use of the word "dangerous."

152. Jack to Lily, 24 Mar. 1900, MBY.

153. T. R. Ablett, "Introduction," *Brushwork* (1896), by E. C. Yeats. See next note.

154. All three were published by George Philip and Son, London.

155. JBY to Lady Gregory, 16 June 1899, NYPL; (Murphy, *Letters from Bedford Park,* 50–51).

156. JBY to Lady Gregory, 29 July 1898, NYPL; Murphy, (*Letters from Bedford Park,* 41).

157. WBY to John Quinn, 30 Sept. 1921 (from Reid, *Man from New York,* 493–94).

158. Leonard Elton, conversation with author, London, 1968.

159. Susan Mitchell, "John Butler Yeats" (1919), unpublished talk (Sligo County Museum; MBY).

160. Chesterton, *Autobiography,* 139–41.

161. Lily Yeats, "Scrapbook," 'Mama's Health.'

162. JBY to WBY, 2 Feb. 1921, MBY.

163. WBY, *Autobiographies,* 31.

164. WBY to Mabel Dickinson, 11 May 1908, Bancroft Library, University of California at Berkeley. I thank Professor Phillip L. Marcus for calling this passage to my attention. See Murphy, *Prodigal Father,* 215–17.

165. JBY to Clare Marsh, 26 July 1900 and an undated letter [July 1900], ("Can you forgive me . . ."), TCD.

166. JBY to WBY, 19 July 1907, MBY.

167. JBY to Isaac Yeats, 25 Dec. 1917, ABY. "She now says, 'I have only one home, and Lily I regard as my mother.' "

168. See the chaps. 3, 4, 5, and 6, below.

169. On the back of a watercolor sketch of Jack and Lily in 1900 sitting by a fireplace at Fuge Farm is a note by Lily: "Papa, Ruth Pollexfen then a little girl, and I went to Devon for a holiday and took rooms in Fuge Farm near Jack's house." Lily gave the picture to Willie on his birthday in 1935.

3. Dun Emer, 1902–1906

AH: Augustine Henry.

EG: Evelyn Gleeson.

Pim: Sheila Pim, *The Wood and the Trees: A Biography of Augustine Henry* (Kilkenny, Ireland: Boethius Press), 2nd edition, 1984.

Miller: Liam Miller, *The Dun Emer, Later the Cuala Press* (Dublin: Dolmen, 1973).

Sources for this chapter include the letters of Augustine Henry to Evelyn Gleeson: National Library of Ireland, NLI MS 13,698 (the Henry papers); further letters AH to EG: Dr. Patrick H. Kelly (private collection) (the Gleeson papers); Yeats family correspondence); other material as specified below.

"Dun Emer" is pronounced to rhyme with "soon dreamer," "Cuala" to rhyme with "Moo'-uh-luh," the last two vowels like the schwa (inverted "e").

1. Confusion about the two Industries, and the part of the two sisters in them, is common. *The Reader's Catalogue* of Cahill and Co., Christmas 1990, contains the sentence: "The Cuala . . . was founded in 1903 by Susan and Elizabeth Yeats." Cuala was not founded until 1908. Dun Emer (which the writer evidently had in mind) was founded not in 1903 but 1902. In her *Lady Gregory: A Literary Portrait,* 2d ed. (London: Secker and Warburg, 1966), p. 197, Elizabeth Coxhead writes that Lady Gregory's memoirs were brought out by "Miss Yeats," and identifies her in the index as "Lily," when Lollie is the one meant.

2. The sisters thought Evelyn Gleeson was much older, Lollie writing in 1938 that she was "about 60" when they began their association with her (Lollie to James A. Healy, 3 Dec. 1938, Stanford). She was in fact only 47.

3. Sheila Pim has mined this material for her definitive study, *The Wood and the Trees: A Biography of Augustine Henry* (Kilkenny, Ireland: Boethius Press, 2nd edition, 1984). Appendix 1 of that edition, "The Dun Emer Settlement" (205–16), is the most authoritative account of the founding of Dun Emer and its subsequent history. I am grateful to Miss Pim for her kindness in leading me to the Henry letters in the National Library of Ireland (MS 13,698) and giving me the benefit of her extensive knowledge of the subject. I thank Dr. Barbara Phillips of Bath, Dr. Henry's greatniece, for permission to quote from his letters. Dr. Patrick H. Kelly generously gave me access to his collection, an absolutely essential supplement to the Henry Papers. In these notes I refer to the NLI material as the "Henry Papers," and to Dr. Kelly's as the "Gleeson Papers." Until the appearance of Miss Pim's book, Liam Miller's monograph, *The Dun Emer Press, Later the Cuala Press* (Dublin: Cuala, 1973), was the principal source of our knowledge of the enterprise. His work was limited by its focus on the Press and by the fact that he was unaware of the Henry and Gleeson Papers, and of Lily Yeats's letters to Ruth Pollexfen Lane-Poole, the second principal source of our knowledge. All students of the subject are deeply indebted to the late Mr. Miller for his pioneer research on Dun Emer and Cuala.

4. Pim, *The Wood and the Trees,* 99, 106. Evelyn Gleeson underwent two operations, in 1900 and 1901, the nature unspecified, though Miss Pim calls them "major." Miss Gleeson had respiratory problems and some difficulties with a congenitally weak foot.

5. "The London air was killing me," she wrote two decades later (EG to Mr. Gwynn, 16 July 1924, Gleeson Papers).

6. Pim, *The Wood and the Trees,* 206.

7. AH to EG, 21 Jan. (postmark) 1902, Gleeson Papers; quoted by Pim,

The Wood and the Trees, 206. Henry's letter was in fact addressed to only one of the Yeats sisters. As Lily had given up her work with May Morris five years earlier, I suspect the letter was written to Lollie, who was active as a teacher of painting.

8. See Murphy, *Prodigal Father,* 231–37.

9. JBY to Lollie, 7 Jan. 1902, MBY. See also Murphy, *Prodigal Father,* 237.

10. JBY to Rosa Butt, n.d., ca. late Jan. 1902 ("After Monday . . ."), no. 9, Bodleian.

11. EG to Mr. Gwynn, 16 July 1924, Gleeson Papers.

12. WBY to Lady Gregory, 8 Feb. 1904; Wade, *Letters of WBY,* 431; see Murphy, *Prodigal Father,* 240–41.

13. AH to EG, 7 Nov. 1902, Henry Papers, NLI.

14. AH to EG, 20 Mar. 1902, Henry Papers, NLI.

15. Lily Yeats, *Elizabeth Corbet Yeats* (Dublin: Cuala, 1 Feb. 1940), quoted in Miller, *Dun Emer Press,* 95. See also Lollie to "Dear Sir" [? Holbrook Jackson], 11 Nov. 1903 (Lockwood Memorial Library, State University of New York at Buffalo): "I had never even seen a Press worked until we had nearly finished 'In the Seven Woods.' " See Murphy, *Prodigal Father,* 240.

16. In all the correspondence that passed between the sisters on the one hand and Henry and Miss Gleeson on the other, apparently only one letter was written by Lily (Lily to EG, 22 Mar. 1903 [date taken from stamp on receipt], Gleeson Papers).

17. AH to EG, 9 Apr. and 3 Nov. 1902, Henry Papers, NLI.

18. Lily to EG, 22 Mar. (date taken from stamp on receipt), Gleeson Papers.

19. AH to EG, 6 Apr. 1902, Henry Papers, NLI.

20. "Articles of the Society," draft in ink with occasional interlineations in pencil, Gleeson Papers. It is not in the hand of either Lily or Lollie. It is undated, but Miss Pim gives it a date between 19 and 26 Apr. (*The Wood and the Trees,* 215). As Lollie's letter dated "Easter Monday" mentions the order for embroidery that Lily had received from an American woman, and as Miss Gleeson had sent money to Lily to purchase materials for it by 22 Mar., the preliminary meeting to discuss the partnership must precede that date. I quote passages without correction of grammar or spelling. All the Irish of that period, including Miss Gleeson and Dr. Henry—and the English too—seem to have been baffled by the spelling of plurals and possessives of names ending in "s." What should have been "Yeatses" is written as "Yeats" or "Yeats' " but never "Yeatses." So we have "the Yeats," "the Yeats'," and "the Yeats's." For "Miss Yeats's book" or "the Yeatses' book" we have a variety of creative spellings, none correct. Dr. Henry and Miss Gleeson might be forgiven for failing to master the intricacies of a name so unlike their own, but none of the Yeatses ever mastered them either. They all spell as if they had been educated in American schools. The part of the document about the loan to the Yeats sisters is quoted in Pim, p. 207.

21. Lollie to EG, Easter Monday 1902, Gleeson Papers.

22. AH to EG, 20 July 1902, Henry Papers, NLI. The source of Henry's bounty is hard to explain unless he came into possession of the estate of his first wife, Caroline Orridge. They were married in June 1891; she died in May 1894 (Pim, *The Wood and the Trees,* 43, 51, 53). But Sheila Pim declares the evidence suggests that Caroline left no money.

23. Alexander Millar to EG, 29 Apr. 1902, Gleeson Papers. Pim quotes extensively from Millar's letter and discusses it (*The Wood and the Trees,* 207–208).

24. AH to EG, 6 Apr. 1902, Henry Papers. Partly quoted by Pim, *The Wood and the Trees,* 208.

25. Henry acknowledged Yeats's talents, but it is interesting to observe that his opinions of him as a person match those of other critics. "You amuse me about W. B.," he wrote Miss Gleeson. "He is a genius, and his ways in society are to be excused *completely*—and you must not blame him. He is probably in the clouds. Of course he is much spoiled by admiration of women" (7 Nov. 1902, Henry Papers). His remarks about Yeats's notion of artistic drama are curiously like some of Joseph Holloway's (see Murphy, *Prodigal Father,* 211, and Robert Hogan and Michael J. O'Neill, eds., *Joseph Holloway's Abbey Theatre: A Selection from His Unpublished Journal,* [Carbondale: Southern Illinois Univ. Press, 1967]): "I have a complaint [about the Irish National Theatre Society]," he wrote Miss Gleeson. "They preach about art for art's sake, which is rubbish. The theatre is meant to amuse or to instruct. I wish there was some one with the dramatic gift, who would put on the boards a series of plays representing Ireland as it is—the poor house as it works so stupidly, the Shoneens, the things in general that want mending" (AH to EG, 22 Oct. 1902, Henry Papers, NLI).

26. EG to AH, 15 Nov. 1903, Henry Papers, NLI.

27. Pim, *The Wood and the Trees,* 207. As late as 1939, Lollie hadn't learned Miss Gleeson's age, calling her "about 90 now" (Lollie to James A. Healy, 19 Jan. 1939, Stanford). She was in fact 84.

28. JBY to Lily, 25 June 1910 (postmarked June 24), MBY. In this long letter JBY gives a remarkable dissection of those whose lives are ruined by notions of class.

29. AH to EG, 31 July 1902 (date in alien hand; postmark Aug. 2), Henry Papers, NLI.

30. AH to EG, 1 and 22 Aug. 1902, Henry Papers, NLI.

31. AH to EG, 5 June and 26 July 1902, Henry Papers, NLI.

32. JBY to WBY, ca. 15 Aug. 1902 ("I send you . . ."), MBY; see also Murphy, *Prodigal Father,* 241.

33. AH to EG, 29 Jan. 1903, Henry Papers, NLI.

34. Pim, *The Wood and the Trees,* 133–34.

35. By December 1903 thirteen girls were listed in a Christmas annual produced by Lollie (TCD: Press A Cuala Arch, box 1a). Listed as weavers were Margery Gallagher, Rosie Gallagher, Katie Dempsey, Alice Redmond, Frances Cassidy, Christina Byrne, Mary Keane; as "Embroideresses": Margaret McCabe, Ellen McCabe, Mary Little; Printers: Esther Ryan, Beatrice Cassidy. A year later

there were only six weavers, but Lily had added two embroideresses, Eileen Colum and Annie Ryan. Esther ("Essie") Ryan had joined the staff as part of Lollie's press crew in early January of 1903 as a fourteen-year-old. She worked on the first book printed in 1903, *In The Seven Woods,* and on the last (of the original series), Elizabeth Rivers's *Stranger in Aran,* in 1946. When the Press suspended publication in that year, Essie worked at colored prints until her death in 1961. Hers was the longest service, but many other young girls devoted a large part of their lives to either Dun Emer or the later Cuala, so that the goals of Henry and Miss Gleeson were to a great extent realized. In Lollie Yeats's 1905 Book of Dun Emer, ten weavers are listed in addition to Miss Gleeson, six embroideresses with Lily, the same two helpers at the Press with Lollie. The material on Essie Ryan comes from Miller, *Dun Emer Press,* 24.

36. JBY to WBY, ca. 6 or 13 Aug. 1906 ("Many thanks for your letters . . ."), MBY. "It was at the commencement of the work at Dun Emer, and Miss Gleeson was obviously drinking, and we thought that to this was due many things, her queerness over money and business, and her explosions of violent temper." Hone prints most of the letter in *JBY: Letters* (p. 97) but omits this passage and the entire paragraph in which it appears.

37. Lily to Ruth, 18 Jan. 1933, MBY: "We only found out about Mrs. McCormack's drinking habits a few days before we left London for here. If we had known earlier I don't suppose we would have started on the venture at all."

38. Murphy, *Prodigal Father,* 241–42.

39. AH to EG, 3 and 14 Nov. 1902, Henry Papers, NLI. In the second of these letters, Henry writes: "we agree pretty well about her [i.e., Lollie's] character. Caroline was as *definite."*

40. WBY to Lady Gregory, 4 Dec. 1902 (Wade, *Letters of WBY,* 387); see also Murphy, *Prodigal Father,* 242.

41. WBY to Lady Gregory, 3 and 6 Jan. 1903 (Wade, *Letters of WBY,* 391–95; see Miller, *Dun Emer Press,* 25–26).

42. Lily to JBY, 27 July 1904, MBY. Partly quoted in Murphy, *Prodigal Father,* 267.

43. Miller, *Dun Emer Press,* 14–15. George Russell, one of WBY's early partners in occult studies, wrote and painted under the pseudonym AE.

44. Lollie to John Quinn, 26 May 1903, NYPL, where the number "ten" is specifically mentioned. Pim gives twenty-four as the number of banners (*The Wood and the Trees,* 209). In a letter to Ruth, 25 Aug. 1925 (MBY), Lily asks: "Do you remember the 20 or more banners I did 20 years ago for Loughrea?," confusing the issue further.

45. Lily to James A. Healy, 4 Dec. 1938, Stanford. When the banners were returned to Cuala thirty years later for repair, Lily was pleased to see "they looked very well and had worn well." Lily also told of a priest at Loughrea who may have been the same one who had the design changed. "They were ordered by the then Priest Father O'Donovan. He not long after left the church entirely and went to live in London. So—oh no—he is never mentioned. He was a clever cultivated man."

46. Pim, *The Wood and the Trees*, 209. The banners, designed by Jack Yeats and his wife Cottie, are a splendid example of the high quality of Dun Emer's work. They can be seen still in an outbuilding at the cathedral.

47. AH to EG, 18 Dec. 1902, Henry Papers, NLI.

48. AH to EG, 26 Nov. 1902, Henry Papers, NLI. Miss Gleeson had introduced Henry to Gill, who had used his influence to get Henry appointed to the Forestry School in Nancy, France. When Henry wanted to justify his help to Miss Gleeson (which he would have given anyhow), he told her it was his way of repaying the favor she had done him (Pim, *The Wood and the Trees*, 206.)

49. AH to EG, 28 Dec. 1902, Henry Papers, NLI.

50. AH to EG, 29 Jan. 1903, Henry Papers, NLI.

51. AH to EG, 14 Feb. 1903, Henry Papers, NLI.

52. Draft copy of questionnaire, ca. mid-1903, Gleeson Papers.

53. AH to EG, 18 Mar. 1903, Henry Papers, NLI.

54. JBY to Lady Gregory, 3 Jan. 1903 [misdated "1902"], NYPL.

55. Lollie Yeats, ed., "The Second Number of the Book of Dun Emer," Dec. 1904 (single copy only), Cuala Archive TCD.

56. WBY to Sydney Cockerell (Wade, *Letters of WBY*, 397–98; Miller, *Dun Emer Press*, 26). Lollie had finished a "pile of printing" in mid-May when "some stupid person" put a weight on it "and spoilt the whole of ten days work" (Lollie to John Quinn, 26 May 1903, NYPL). It was precisely the kind of blunder Alexander Millar knew would be committed and had warned about.

57. EG to AH, 24 May 1903, quoted by Pim (*The Wood and the Trees*, 210). The disputed device was never used by the Press.

58. AH to EG, 8 Aug. 1903, Henry Papers, NLI.

59. AH to EG, 13 Aug. 1903, Henry Papers, NLI.

60. Inscription by WBY in presentation copy to John Quinn of *In the Seven Woods* (from Allan Wade, *A Bibliography of the Writings of W. B. Yeats*, [London: Rupert Hart-Davis, 1968], 67); Miller, *Dun Emer Press*, 33.

61. Special books, like *A Lament for Art O'Leary* and *On the Boiler*, and the single sheet *Broadsides* were printed in their own format. See Miller, *Dun Emer Press*, 23, 114, 115, 116, 120, 122.

62. AH to EG, 30 Nov. 1903, Henry Papers, NLI. The colophon, which inspired Joyce's first reference to the sisters in *Ulysses*, ended with the words: "Finished the sixteenth day of July, in the year of the big wind, 1903."

63. Yeats had made an exclusive arrangement with A. P. Watt, concluded by late December of 1901, to serve as agent for his works. See WBY to Lady Gregory, 21 May [date from postmark] 1901 (Wade, *Letters of WBY*, 351). Watt, not Yeats, would have been the one to assess the royalty.

64. WBY to Stephen Gwynn, 13 June 1906 (Wade, *Letters of WBY*, 473).

65. Gleeson Papers. An earlier accounting among the Cuala Press papers, in Lollie's hand, is almost the same, except that under "Money Received" Lollie shows £28.8.5 instead of £33.8.5, for a total of £178.0.5 instead of £184.0.5; and in the right hand column she shows for "Authors Royalties" £34.2.6 and her own pay as £125, for a total spent of £232.12.3 (Miller, *Dun Emer Press*, 23–24.

66. AH to EG, 21 Sept. 1903, Henry Papers, NLI. From the Henry and
Gleeson Papers it is clear that virtually everybody who was anybody in Dublin
knew about Dun Emer and followed it with interest. Some of the names that
turn up in the correspondence are Frank Fay, Susan Mitchell, Roger Casement,
Sarah Purser, Padraic Colum, and Alice Stopford Green.

67. AH to EG, 2 Oct. 1903, Henry Papers, NLI.
68. EG to AH, 15 Nov. 1903, Henry Papers, NLI.
69. AH to EG, 15 Nov. 1903, Henry Papers, NLI.
70. AH to EG, 24 Nov. 1903, Henry Papers, NLI. The punctuation in
this passage is typical of Henry's throughout. He admitted many times that he
was not a literary artist. Like others similarly deprived, he tried to spice up his
writing by bizarre decoration, like college freshmen who submit badly written
papers in green ink. Henry's prose is in need of a colonic irrigation.

71. George Russell to John Quinn, 17 May 1903 (Alan Denson, ed., *Letters
from AE* [London: Abelard-Schuman], 48). See also Murphy, *Prodigal Father,*
260.

72. Pim, *The Wood and the Trees,* 210, where she lists AH to EG, 7 Mar.
1904 as reference.

73. JBY to Rosa Butt, n.d., ca. 1904 ("Are you unwell . . ."), no. 28,
Bodleian.

74. JBY to John Quinn, 30 Aug. 1906, Foster-Murphy Collection, NYPL.
See Murphy, *Prodigal Father,* 266. JBY, watching all from the living room
of Gurteen Dhas, commented to Rosa Butt (n.d., ca. Mar. 1904, "Your last
letter . . . ," no. 17, Bodleian): "Lilly and Lollie have their minds much exercised on the question whether or not Dun Emer should accept a grant from the
Agricultural Board. I fancy it would mean a certain loss of freedom. This is
serious, or would be so if Miss Gleeson was any good."

75. AH to EG, 26 Jan. 1904, Gleeson Papers.
76. T. W. Rolleston to "Miss Yeats" (pencil copy sent in letter of about 4
Mar. 1904 from AH to EG), Gleeson Papers. The money was supposed to have
been funneled to the sisters through a private fund administered by the Arts and
Crafts Society under Sir Horace Plunkett but was thought to have come from
some unnamed American benefactor (AH to EG, 7 Mar. 1904, second letter of
this date).

77. Pim, *The Wood and the Trees,* 210–11; AH to EG, 7 Mar. 1904.
78. AH to EG, 7 Mar. 1904, Gleeson Papers.
79. AH to EG, 7 Mar. 1904 (second letter of this date), Gleeson Papers.
80. Lollie to EG, n.d., ca. Mar. 1904, Gleeson Papers. As Lollie was not
the kind to apologize voluntarily or even to know she ought to apologize, I
suspect that Lily or her father persuaded her to write this letter, here quoted in
full.

81. WBY to Lady Gregory, 8 Feb. 1904 (Wade, *Letters of WBY,* 430).
Quoted in Miller, *Dun Emer Press,* 37–38.

82. WBY to Elkin Mathews, 19 July 1904, Reading, Elkin Mathews Collection. WBY wrote that he was "merely" literary adviser, but the admission
was private. The sisters complained that he thought he was running the show.

83. WBY to Lady Gregory, 8 Feb. 1904; passage not quoted by Miller. See Murphy, *Prodigal Father,* 263–67.
84. JBY to WBY, 1 June 1904 MBY; see Murphy, *Prodigal Father,* 264–65.
85. Lily to John Quinn, 4 Jan. 1909, NYPL.
86. AH to EG, 21 Feb. 1904, Gleeson Papers.
87. AH to EG, 9 Feb. 1904, Gleeson Papers.
88. AH to EG, 17 Feb. 1904, Gleeson Papers.
89. AH to EG, 26 Feb. 1904 (date from postmark), Gleeson Papers.
90. AH to EG, 27 Feb. 1904, Gleeson Papers.
91. Flier, MBY.
92. "Stock taken over from Miss Gleeson at formation of Dun Emer Industries," sheet of paper among Gleeson Papers. A sheet of scrap paper, also among the papers, gives a less complete accounting that shows £940.10.2.
93. AH to EG, 27 Sept. 1904, Gleeson Papers. Pim, *The Wood and the Trees,* 211, quotes from this letter.
94. "Account Sheet August 1902 till 17 Sept 1904," Gleeson Papers.
95. AH to EG, 15 and 28 Aug. 1904, Gleeson Papers.
96. In this letter (27 Feb. 1904) Henry had specifically mentioned lending £120 to the sisters in the new enterprise and giving them £80 as a gift. Perhaps the £200 loan is this sum, Miss Gleeson having the caution, born of experience, to treat the £80 portion of it as a loan until the time came, if it ever came, to announce it as a gift.
97. The official division was not signed till 2 Dec. 1904. It is a legal Memo of Agreement (stamped 2 Jan. 1904 by an official who forgot to move the year on his stamp to 1905). It is signed by Evelyn Gleeson, E. C. Yeats, Lily Yeats, Essie Ryan, and Maire Walker, and at the bottom is signed again by Miss Gleeson and Lollie. The schedule of debts which the sisters agree to assume for business connected with embroidery and the Press includes Miller and Sons for £2.0.7, Galway and Co. for £7.2.10, Pearsall for £1.13.4, Dr. Duglas [*sic*] [Hyde] for £23.12.6, Eason and Sons £12.3.11, H. W. Caston & Co. 10s.7d., and W. Yeates [*sic*] £60 (for Royalties). Miss Gleeson's solicitor, Daniel S. Doyle, drew up the document. Gleeson Papers.
98. Lollie to John Quinn, 17 Aug. 1906, NYPL.
99. Miller, *Dun Emer Press,* 40–41. Miller (pp. 39–40) gives the complete minutes of the 29 Sept. 1904 meeting of the "Provisional Meeting."
100. Draft of letter, EG to "Sir," Ref. No. 28142/04, Gleeson Papers. Miss Gleeson enclosed a copy of Lollie Yeats's "Vita Brevis," written by Lollie. In it, after listing every client and every school where she taught, Lollie adds grandly, "and other colleges too numerous to mention."
101. Sheet attached to grant application. The girls in weaving were Frances Cassidy, Kate Dempsey, Rose Gallagher, and Bridget MacLoughlin; in printing Beatrice Cassidy and Esther Ryan; in embroidery Eileen Colum, Jane [*sic*: for "Molly"?] Gill, Mary Little, Margaret MacCabe, and Maire Walker. The last of these was the Abbey Theatre actress Maire nic Shiubhlaigh; Eileen Colum was

the sister of Padraic. Beatrice Cassidy and Esther Ryan stayed with the printing department for decades.

102. AH to EG, 19 Dec. 1904; Henry Papers, NLI.

103. Pim, *The Wood and the Trees,* 211.

104. AH to EG, 3 Nov. and 20 Oct. 1904, 26 Mar. 1905, Gleeson Papers.

105. AH to EG, 20 Oct. 1904, Henry Papers.

106. AH to EG, 26 Mar. 1905, Gleeson Papers.

107. Miller, *Dun Emer Press,* 43.

108. 25 Mar. [1905], in Evelyn Gleeson's scrapbook, Gleeson Papers.

109. The review, from about May 1905, appears in an unidentified English newspaper. It is pasted in Miss Gleeson's scrapbook.

110. Pim, *The Wood and the Trees,* 211.

111. Lily to John Quinn, 11 Oct. 1904, 11 Jan. 1906, and 31 Jan. 1905, NYPL.

112. Lily to John Quinn, 13 Aug. 1905, NYPL.

113. Lollie to John Quinn, 14 Aug. 1905, NYPL. Quinn had told the sisters that a friend of his, a Mr. Robertson, would visit them in Ireland and that he had money to spend. Yet Robertson talked JBY into doing two pencil sketches for which he paid nothing, and bought only 30/- at the Industries. "I hope you don't think we look at people from a commercial point of view only," Lily wrote Quinn (11 Jan. 1906, NYPL), "but you told us the Robertsons were reputed to have money and that we were to get them to spend some with us if possible."

114. AH to EG, 12 Feb. [from postmark] 1906, Gleeson Papers.

115. AH to EG, 22 June 1906, Gleeson Papers.

116. JBY to WBY, 2 July 1906 (from Hone, JBY; *Letters,* 75); as quoted in Miller, *Dun Emer Press,* 45.

117. JBY to Oliver Elton 28 June 1906, collection of Leonard Elton. See Murphy, *Prodigal Father,* 303.

118. JBY to WBY, n.d., ca. 2 Aug. 1906 ("My letter written . . . ."), MBY. See Murphy, *Prodigal Father,* 304. Miller quotes from an undated letter (Hone, *JBY: Letters,* 97): "Lolly has courage, and courage to the bystander, indifferent or not, always seems indiscretion." He quotes also from a letter of 6 Aug. JBY to WBY: ". . . peace must be patched up between you and Lolly. I think also you should treat Russell and Magee with great respect. After all a writer knows his own work and he should be anxiously consulted. . . . You must keep strictly to advising, otherwise you wreck everything" (*Dun Emer Press,* 46, 57).

119. JBY to WBY, 3 Aug. 1906, MBY. See Murphy, *Prodigal Father,* 304–306. Annie Horniman had found a kind of "Nietzscheanism" in WBY after his visit with John Quinn in New York. Quinn had recommended Nietzsche's works to WBY and obviously sympathized with them. If there were indeed Supermen, then clearly he and WBY were members of the clan. One of the ironies of WBY's meddling with Dun Emer was that, no matter how superior his literary judgments might be to his sister's, he himself has been the subject of

negative criticism for what some regard as his bizarre selections for *The Oxford Book of Modern Verse*.

120. JBY to WBY, 8 Aug. 1906, MBY. See Murphy, *Prodigal Father*, 306. Hone reprints the letter, badly edited, as no. 51 in *JBY: Letters*, 97–98, where he dates it 6 Aug.

121. WBY to Katharine Tynan, 24 Aug. 1906 (Miller, *Dun Emer Press*, 46–47). The original of the letter is in the Delyte W. Morris Library at Southern Illinois University (Irish Literary Renaissance Collection, 55/9/6). There is also a draft copy, written from Coole, a fragment of two pages with corrections in WBY's hand, in the collection of MBY (quoted in Murphy, *Prodigal Father*, 306; part also quoted in Miller, 46–47).

.   122. WBY to Katharine Tynan [Hinkson], 28 Aug. 1906 (from a draft copy, written from Coole, a fragment of two pages with corrections in WBY's hand, MBY). See Murphy, *Prodigal Father*, 306; also quoted in Miller, *Dun Emer Press*, 46–47.

123. JBY to WBY, 8 Aug. 1906; see Hone, *JBY: Letters*, 97–98, and n. 120 above. Lollie included Lily in the complaint, but Lily told her cousin Ruth years later (18 Apr. 1943) that she had made no such objection to Willie's easy life; Lollie had invented Lily's disapproval for her own purposes. See chap. 4, n. 142, below; also Murphy, *Prodigal Father*, 306.

124. The informal accounting of *In the Seven Woods* (ca. Aug. 1903, Gleeson Papers) shows a royalty to WBY of £31.10 (Miller, *Dun Emer Press*, 24, using another accounting from the Cuala records, shows £34.2.6). A rough accounting for *The Nuts of Knowledge* (ca. 1 Dec. 1903, Gleeson Papers) lists Russell's royalty as £13.15.3. The Memo of Agreement of 2 Dec. 1904 lists royalties owed to Douglas Hyde of £23.12.6 (Gleeson Papers).

125. Lollie to John Quinn, 29 Oct. 1906, NYPL.

126. WBY to Katharine Tynan, 24 Aug. 1906 (Miller, *Dun Emer Press*, 46–47).

127. Lollie to John Quinn, 25 Nov. 1906, NYPL.

128. Lily to John Quinn, 1 Jan. 1907, NYPL.

129. For accounts of John Quinn, see Reid's biography, *The Man from New York*, and Murphy, *Prodigal Father*.

130. Lollie to JBY, 19 Mar. 1921, MBY. See Murphy, *Prodigal Father*, 307.

131. Newspaper cutting, undated, Gleeson Papers.

132. AH to EG, 14 June 1907, Henry Papers, NLI; and AH to EG, 23 June 1907, Henry Papers, NLI.

133. Lollie to John Quinn, 25 Nov. 1906, NYPL. See Murphy, *Prodigal Father*, 308. See also the appendix below.

134. JBY to Rosa Butt, n.d. [1907] ("That young man . . ."), Bodleian.

135. 13 July 1907, cutting from unidentified newspaper, scrapbook, Gleeson Papers.

136. *British Warehouseman,* Export Number, 1907 (no month or day), scrapbook, Gleeson Papers.

137. Lily to John Quinn, 13 Sept. 1907, NYPL.

138. JBY to Rosa Butt, 13 Sept. 1907, no. 43, Bodleian.

139. JBY to Rosa Butt, 15 Dec. 1907, no. 52, Bodleian.

140. JBY to Rosa Butt, ca. 20 Sept. 1907 ("I know your talents . . .") no. 46, Bodleian.

141. JBY to Rosa Butt, 18 Sept. 1907, no. 45, Bodleian.

142. JBY to Rosa Butt, 3 Dec. 1907, no. 51, Bodleian.

143. JBY to Rosa Butt, 15 Dec. 1907 (from postmark), no. 52, Bodleian.

144. JBY to Rosa Butt, 15 Dec. 1907, no. 52, Bodleian.

145. Lily to Lollie, 4 Jan. 1908, MBY.

146. An account of Mark Twain's visit, "while reporters stood round us," appears in Lily's letter to James A. Healy, 4 Dec. 1938, Stanford. "He asked me to a 'musical riot' at his house, but I could not get away. In no time the evening papers came out with his portrait and mine and what we had said—quite a long story."

147. JBY to Rosa Butt, 9 Jan. 1908, no. 55, Bodleian. JBY and Lily often visited Julia (Mrs. Simeon) Ford, with whom Lollie had stayed on her visit to New York. JBY's comment: "Lilly and I both like Mrs. Ford and their house very much and don't find Mrs. Ford to be a bore at all. In fact we like her too much. Yet to Lollie she was obviously a terrible trial."

148. Lily to Lollie, 28 Jan. 1908, MBY. Lily wrote after the exhibition was over that she knew "nothing of the Gleeson lot," but gave an almost final report of her own success. "We came out as we expected at invoiced price and may be well satisfied, I think, don't you? We have got rid of a lot of things we would have had on our hands for ages and might never have sold, and they must make something out of us. So I will send you over £100 on Tuesday, and J. Q. still owes me almost £11, which I will send on. You have to just make up the fair divisions to the different parts of the Industry from the invoice. I will send you a list of some expenses I had with the stall, and the money orders cost a lot, a £1 on what I have already sent. Then I owe the fund almost £5. They tell me I did almost the best of all. I certainly made some money for them. Counting the vestment I got in over £200. . . . I have sent you, not counting J.Q.'s first fan, £98.15 and will now send £107 odd and John Quinn's £11 as soon as I get it which will bring the total to about £218. Then I owe the Industry something and had some expenses, which makes it right" Lily to Lollie, 6 Feb. 1908, MBY.

149. *Boston Herald,* 3 Feb. 1908, scrapbook, Gleeson Papers.

150. *Pilot,* 15 Feb. 1908, scrapbook, Gleeson Papers.

151. JBY to Rosa Butt, 18 Feb. 1908, no. 57, Bodleian.

152. Lily to John Quinn, 13 May 1908, NYPL.

153. For an account of JBY's life in New York, see Murphy, *Prodigal Father,* and Reid, *Man from New York.*

154. JBY to Rosa Butt, 18 Feb. 1908, no. 57, Bodleian. Pim, *The Wood*

and the Trees, 214, says Miss Gleeson was back at Dun Emer "by the beginning of April."

155. Rough sheet with accounts of "Weaving Industry." N.d. [after 31 Mar. 1908 and before 30 June 1908], Gleeson Papers. The 1908 accounting is for three months only.

156. Lollie Yeats, Letter to Editor, about Spring 1908, *Freeman's Journal,* Gleeson Papers. Her letter is mentioned but not quoted by Pim, *The Wood and the Trees,* 213.

157. Pim, *The Wood and the Trees,* 214.

158. JBY to Rosa Butt, 25 May 1908, no. 62, Bodleian. "At last Lollie has left Dun Emer, or does so in a few days when she will be at Lackeen Cottage which is close to us." I thank Dr. Maureen Murphy for the information about the cottage that became Cuala.

159. For the details of the breakup and settlement, see AH to EG, 8, 25, 28 May; 1, 2 June 1908, Henry Papers, NLI. A copy of a letter of Henry's to Lollie is included in the 2 June letter to Miss Gleeson. In it he writes: "In your letter you say that Miss Gleeson threatens to sue for £185 of my money, which your society still owes. This is an erroneous statement, as the sum is due to Miss Gleeson. In my opinion you should settle amicably with her."

160. Sheet of notepaper, date uncertain, Gleeson Papers.

161. AH to EG, 2 June 1908 (see n. 159 above).

162. "Memo of Agreement," Hamilton and Craig, Solicitors, 6 July 1908, "Between 1st part Evelyn Gleeson, 2nd Constance MacCormack, 3rd Dun Emer Industries Ltd.; 4th Dun Emer Guild Ltd.; 5th Lily Yeats and Elizabeth C. Yeats," Gleeson Papers.

Miller's account of the split omits the details: "By 1908 the difficulties in the Dun Emer Industries generally, and the difficulties in the Press in particular, had grown to such an extent that it was no longer practical to continue all the work at the home of Miss Gleeson. The division eventually [*sic*] proposed by J. B. Yeats early in 1904 was put into effect and the Yeats sisters separated their parts of the venture from the Dun Emer Industries and established the Cuala Industries at Churchtown near Dundrum in County Dublin. The change of name was necessary because Miss Gleeson had made the name 'Dun Emer' her own, and, as noted above, had altered the name of her house to 'Dun Emer' " (*Dun Emer Press,* 49–50.)

163. Scrap of paper, n.d. [ca. July 1908], Gleeson Papers.

164. Lollie to Paul Lemperly, 7 Jan. 1909; to John Shelley, 22 Aug. 1912, Stanford.

165. Lily to John Quinn, 5 July 1908, NYPL.

166. Lollie to James A. Healy, 2 Dec. 1938, Stanford. The account is a good example of JBY's analysis of the Pollexfen trait as he saw it in his wife and Lollie: "the most truthful people I ever met, but . . . I wouldn't believe a word they said" (JBY to Rosa Butt, n.d., ca. 1904 ["Are you unwell . . ."], no. 28, Bodleian.

167. Sheila Pim observes that Miss Gleeson's nieces "were extremely reti-

cent" in writing of the quarrels, but that "Lolly protested too much, as if the matter was on her conscience." ("Dun Emer—the Origins," *Irish Arts Review* 2, no. 2 [Summer 1985]: 22). In a letter to the author (7 Oct. 1980), Miss Pim summarizes things as evenhandedly as possible: "Henry once or twice reproaches her [Miss Gleeson] for being too 'sensitive,' in other words touchy. The Yeatses *were* apt to be high-handed, but maybe Miss Gleeson was also apt to take offense. I don't think she was a good businesswoman. The Yeatses felt they could run the centre better. But if they thought her grasping she thought them spongers. They didn't lose financially. And in the long run I don't think Cuala got on any better than Dun Emer."

168. Lily to John Quinn, 4 Jan. 1909, NYPL.

4. William Butler Yeats and "The Weird Sisters."

1. G. K. Chesterton, *Autobiography,* 140. Chesterton also tells us that he "knew and admired those sisters of the poet who maintained in the Cuala industry a school of decoration and drapery not unworthy of the great lines about the heavens' embroidered cloths." He says nothing of the Cuala Press, Lollie's enterprise.

2. I use the spellings JBY chose during his later years in his letters to his daughters, consistent with the spellings in Murphy, *Prodigal Father.*

3. James Joyce, *Ulysses* (New York: Modern Library, 1940), 14, 417. The second passage reads: "To be printed and bound at the Druiddrum press by two designing females. Calf covers of pissedon green. Last word in art shades, most beautiful book come out of Ireland at any time." One wonders whether Joyce was aware of the sly paradox of his double-entendre: the woman who did the designing was not the "designing" woman, and the one who didn't do the designing was.

4. JBY to Susan Pollexfen Yeats, n.d., from 23 Fitzroy Road, Regent's Park, "Yesterday I wrote. . . ," MBY.

5. WBY to Dorothy Wellesley, 17 Dec. 1937, private collection. I thank Dr. John Kelly for providing me with a copy of this revealing letter. Willie made a similar, briefer remark to Lily (Lily to Ruth, 14 Dec. 1937, MBY).

6. Lily to Ruth, 18 Oct. 1938, MBY.

7. Lily to Ruth, 14 Sept. 1936, MBY.

8. Lily to Ruth, 27 Apr. 1936, MBY.

9. Lily to Ruth, 26 Nov. 1925, MBY.

10. JBY to Isaac Yeats, 2 July 1908, ABY.

11. JBY to Lily and Lollie, 6 July 1908, MBY.

12. Lily to Ruth, 7 Feb. 1928, MBY.

13. Lollie to JBY, 19 Mar. 1921, MBY. See also chap. 3, above, and chap. 3, n. 130.

14. Lily to Ruth, 1 Jan. 1929; 16 Oct. 1937, MBY. An actress, Mary Merrill, visiting Lily a year and a half before her death, told her she "was

beautiful and always had been, which," Lily added, "was a great surprise to me to hear" (Lily to Ruth, 13 Apr. 1947, MBY).

15. Lily to Ruth, 30 Mar. 1936, MBY.
16. JBY to Lily, Lollie, and Ruth Pollexfen, 13 July 1908, MBY.
17. Lily to Ruth, 24 Oct. (P.S. of 25 Oct.) 1937, MBY.
18. Leonard Elton, conversation with author, London, 1968.
19. Nancy Morgan to Ruth Pollexfen Lane-Poole, 6 Jan. 1949, MBY.
20. Lily to Ruth, 14 Feb. 1945, MBY.
21. Lily to James A. Healy, 4 Dec. 1938, Stanford.
22. Jack to James A. Healy, 21 May 1949, Stanford.
23. JBY to Rosa Butt, 13 Apr. 1910, no. 100; Bodleian. When Lollie was deep in the neurosis that forced her to leave Cuala and travel abroad, JBY told Rosa Butt, at whose London home Lollie was visiting, what he thought Lollie should do: "I think that she ought after a bit to 'move on' to someone else. She is enterprising and practical, and if she moved on she might manage to do sketches that would sell. Lilly is a peaceable person, soothing to other people, and only asks to keep quiet and enjoy her friends and her surroundings" (JBY to Rosa Butt, 27 Jan. 1911, no. 117, Bodleian).
24. JBY to Rosa Butt, 9 Jan. 1908, no. 55, Bodleian.
25. JBY to Isaac Yeats, 29 Dec. 1915, 15 July 1919, ABY.
26. Lily to Ruth, 23 June 1936, MBY.
27. Lollie Yeats, Diary, 3 Feb. 1889.
28. Lily to Ruth, 26 Sept. 1923, MBY.
29. WBY to Lily [29 Dec. 1914, 11 Nov. 1914?], MBY. Dates on original letters in hand of Allan Wade.
30. See Murphy, " 'In Memory of Alfred Pollexfen,' " 30–47. The closeness of Lily's relationship to WBY finds expression in a letter to Ruth (10 Apr. 1939) after his death, which "has taken all the salt out of things and increased my loneliness." Willie's widow, George, could not prove an adequate substitute, for "we did not grow up together on the same floor."
31. Lily to Ruth, 23 July 1938, MBY.
32. JBY to Isaac Yeats, 18 May 1910, 11 July 1912, ABY.
33. Donoghue, *WBY: Memoirs,* 20.
34. JBY to Isaac Yeats, 12 Aug. 1915, ABY.
35. Lily to Ruth, 8 Oct. 1927, 15 May 1928, MBY.
36. Lily to JBY, 30 Jan. 1917, MBY.
37. Lily to JBY, 3 Jan. 1917, MBY.
38. Lily to Lollie, 24 Feb. 1908, MBY.
39. JBY to Isaac Yeats, 11 Dec. 1909, ABY.
40. Lily to JBY, 15 Aug. 1913, MBY.
41. JBY to Lily, 2 Dec. 1913, MBY.
42. Lollie to Frederick A. King, 3 July 1917, Stanford.
43. JBY to Isaac Yeats, 5 Dec. 1917, ABY.
44. Lily to John Quinn, 28 Aug. 1914, NYPL.
45. Lily to Ruth, 9 July 1929, MBY

46. Lily to Ruth, 20 Sept. 1929, MBY.
47. Lily to Ruth, 22 July 1929, MBY.
48. Lily to Joseph Hone, 9 May 1939, Texas.
49. Lily to Ruth, 30 Apr. 1929, MBY.
50. Lily to Ruth, 20 May 1930, MBY.
51. Lily to Ruth, 17 Apr. 1934, MBY.
52. Lily to JBY, 12 May 1917, Princeton. Also in Lily to Ruth, same date, MBY.
53. Lily to Ruth, 29 July 1917, MBY.
54. Lollie attended St. Nahi's, Lily the Taney Parish church.
55. JBY to Isaac Yeats, 28 Feb. 1916, ABY.
56. JBY to Lady Gregory, 20 Oct. 1917, NYPL.
57. While Lily believed in immortality and reincarnation, JBY wasn't sure what he believed. He retained his skepticism to the end. In complaining that he had never had his fling he came as close as he ever would to expressing a hope for an afterlife: "It is not one man *in a thousand who gets his fling*—and it is because none of us gets his fling that I have a hope that there may be a hereafter—a very faint hope" (JBY to John Sloan, 14 Aug. 1917, Princeton). He once wrote a friend: "There are things for which I would thank God if I knew where to find him" (JBY to Martha Fletcher Bellinger, 26 Aug. 1916, Princeton). As he entered "on the last stretch before that harbour which sooner or later will receive us all" (JBY to Isaac Yeats, 29 July 1921, ABY) he became somewhat less pessimistic, but there is no doubt about his basic feeling. "I have never thought about my soul," he wrote eight months before his death. "I am neither an early Christian nor a modern. I am as little interested in my soul as if I were a vegetable—just to live and go on clinging to my environment is all I want" (JBY to Martha Fletcher Bellinger, 10 June 1921, Princeton).
58. See the appendix below.
59. Lily to Ruth, 23 May 1933, MBY.
60. Lily to JBY, 6 Apr. 1919, Princeton.
61. Lily to WBY, 23 Feb. 1922, MBY.
62. Lily to Ruth, 15 Feb. 1937, 26 June 1941, MBY.
63. Lily to Joseph Hone, 30 May 1939, Texas.
64. Lily to Ruth, 13 Oct. 1938, MBY.
65. Lily to Ruth, 2 Apr. 1935, MBY.
66. Lily to Ruth, 10 Mar. 1936, MBY.
67. Lily to Ruth, 27 Feb. 1939, MBY.
68. Lily to Ruth, 7 Apr. 1938, MBY.
69. Lily to Ruth, 27 Aug. 1929, MBY.
70. Lily to Ruth, 16 May 1942, MBY.
71. Lily to Ruth, 25 Dec. 1934, MBY.
72. See Lily to Ruth, 27 Oct. 1931, MBY: "TCD is one-third R.C. students now. George [Mrs. William Butler Yeats] was speaking of this difficulty only this week. . . . Of course there are many very delightful Catholics, but still———."

73. JBY to Lily, 25 June 1910, MBY.
74. JBY to Isaac Yeats, 8 Feb. 1920, ABY.
75. Lily to Ruth, 1 Mar. 1939, MBY.
76. Lily to Ruth, 7 Apr. 1938, MBY.
77. Lily to Ruth, 7 May 1938, MBY.
78. WBY to Dorothy Wellesley, 21 Dec. [1937], private collection. I thank Dr. John Kelly for providing me with a copy of this letter.
79. Lollie to James A. Healy, 25 Jan. 1939, Stanford.
80. JBY to Lady Gregory, 29 Sept. 1919, NYPL.
81. According to Lily, Lollie "never even wore a shabby thing" (to Ruth, 23 Nov. 1946, MBY).
82. Mrs. Ruth Jameson quotes JBY as saying to her: "Lollie is very good as a housekeeper but for nothing else" (conversation with author, Dun Laoghaire, 1966).
83. Chesterton, *Autobiography*, 150ff; Lily to Ruth, 24 Nov. 1936, MBY. Chesterton describes the club as a debating society where he himself "first tried my crude ideas with even cruder rhetoric." It is not surprising that Lollie would be denied membership in a club where the floor was open to anyone. The name had no significance (though theosophists could think of it as "India's Divine Karma" and Socialists as "Individualists deserve kicking"); members were supposed to reply "I don't know" when asked what the letters meant.
84. Lily to Ruth, 4 Aug. 1936, MBY. Lollie went to the party dressed as "Ireland," but as she carried a harp lent her by the daughter of the Lord Mayor of London she was thought to be St. Cecilia, the patron saint of music (Lily to Ruth, 12 Oct. 1936, MBY).
85. JBY to Rosa Butt, 27 Jan. 1911, no. 117, Bodleian.
86. Lily to Ruth, 28 Oct. 1938, MBY.
87. Lily to Louis Purser, 22 Mar. 1910 (in possession of the late Olive Purser, Louis's niece). Miss Purser kindly provided me with a copy of this letter. For a fuller discussion of the affair, see Murphy, *Prodigal Father*, 242, 373–74.
88. Lily to JBY, 27 July 1904; JBY to WBY, n.d. [ca. 30 Oct. 1904] ("I should be very much. . . ."). See Murphy, *Prodigal Father*, 267.
89. JBY to WBY, about 6 or 13 Aug. 1906, "Many thanks for your letters . . ."; see Murphy, *Prodigal Father*, 307. JBY is quoting Miss Mitchell.
90. JBY to Isaac Yeats, 11 July 1911, 29 Dec. 1915, 18 May 1911, ABY.
91. JBY to Rosa Butt, 27 Jan. 1911, no. 117, Bodleian.
92. Lily to Ruth, 17 Sept. 1940, MBY.
93. Hannah Cadbury Taylor to the author, conversation, Birmingham, England, 1985.
94. Lily to Ruth, 17 Sept. 1940, MBY.
95. Anne Yeats, Gráinne Yeats, and Hannah Cadbury Taylor have all expressed such feelings to the author. Mrs. Taylor recalls a time in the late 1920s or early 1930s when Lollie poured out her griefs to her mother, Emmeline Cadbury, telling her of her hopes, her loves, her disappointments. Mrs. Cadbury, realizing the depths of her unhappiness and fearing she might suffer a total

breakdown, supported Lollie financially and emotionally for many years thereafter (conversation with author, 1985; see n. 93).

96. JBY to Isaac Yeats, 10 July 1911, ABY.

97. Lily to Ruth, 4 Mar. 1925, MBY.

98. Lily to Ruth, 15 Feb. 1930, MBY. Lollie liked only happy plays. She often went with Lily to the Abbey, complaining beforehand that she might not want to attend because she might be disappointed. "Any play that is not as simple and pretty as Cinderella is spoken of by Lolly as 'sordid,' and in the end of course she comes and takes half the pleasure out of the evening." (Lily to Ruth, 3 July 1938, MBY).

99. JBY to Isaac Yeats, 11 Dec. 1909, ABY.

100. JBY to Isaac Yeats, 12 Dec. [1911], ABY.

101. JBY to Isaac Yeats, 18 Jan. 1911 [for "1912"?], ABY.

102. JBY to Isaac Yeats, 10 July 1912, undated fragment, "Had I liked. . . . ," ABY.

103. Lily to Ruth, 14 Sept. 1936. See also Lily to Joseph Hone, 28 Feb. 1942, Texas: "Lolly was highly explosive, Grandfather Pollexfen over again, only cleverer. He was kept in check by a wholesome fear of the wrath of God. She had no such fear."

104. JBY to Isaac Yeats, 10 July 1912, ABY.

105. JBY to Isaac Yeats, 11 July 1912, ABY.

106. Thomas MacGreevy, conversation with the author, Dublin, 1966. Anne Yeats and Gráinne Yeats confirm MacGreevy's adjective. MacGreevy, friend of Jack Yeats, was Director of the National Gallery of Ireland.

107. Lily reports on her sister's effect on a family pet. "Kate (the cat) used to strike the floor with her hind legs when irritated by Lolly, who would tease her. I never heard of a cat doing such a thing before. It was like a rabbit's warning knock" (Lily to Ruth, 14 Feb. 1945, MBY).

108. See, e.g., Lily to Ruth, 6 Feb. 1934, MBY. WBY, in a letter to Edith Shackleton Heald (28 Nov. [1932], private collection), compares her eyes to "snails." I thank Dr. John Kelly for calling this letter to my attention and providing me with a copy. Uses of the term "her mouth no bigger than her eye," occur in Lily to Ruth, 5 Mar. and 13 Mar. 1934.

109. Lily to Ruth, 5 Mar. 1934, MBY.

110. Anne Yeats to author, conversation, Schenectady, N.Y., 1987.

111. Lily to Ruth, 23 Sept. 1925, MBY.

112. Lily to Ruth, 9 Aug. 1923, MBY.

113. Lily to Ruth, 2 Sept. 1946, MBY.

114. Lily to Ruth, 9 Aug. 1923: "Her hatred of Phillida [Lily's nickname for Miss Boston] is as intense as hers of you when you are here. . . ." Lollie even hoped Miss Boston would "fail in her moderatorship" at TCD.

115. Lily to Ruth, 19 Jan. 1927, MBY.

116. Lily to Ruth, 6 Mar. 1927, MBY.

117. Lily to Ruth, 15 Jan. 1930, MBY.

118. See chap. 6, below.

119. See, e.g., Lily to Ruth, 25 Aug. 1931, MBY.
120. Lily to Ruth, 12 Aug. 1935, MBY.
121. Lily to Ruth, 21 July 1936, MBY.
122. Lollie to James A. Healy, 19 Jan. 1939, Stanford.
123. Lollie to Frederick A. King, 3 July 1917, Stanford. Lily does not mention the compliment in any of her letters to her father or to Ruth Pollexfen Lane-Poole or, as far as I know, anywhere else. Lollie may very well not have passed it on.
124. Lily to Ruth, 28 July 1928, MBY.
125. Lily to Ruth, 9 Jan. 1929, MBY.
126. Lily to Ruth, 21 July 1931, MBY.
127. Lily to Ruth, 6 July 1936, MBY
128. Lily to Ruth, 17 Jan. 1937, MBY.
129. Lily to Ruth, 6 Mar. 1936, MBY.
130. Lily to Ruth, 26 Aug. 1926, MBY. Characteristically, Lollie not only gave her opinion but George Yeats's as well, which she misrepresented. "She says it is very dull there and she doesn't like it much, and that George didn't like it. George told me yesterday that she liked it greatly and thinks the house beautiful and full of peace. She said Lolly was obviously bored and wanted to be at something all the time."
131. Lily to Ruth, 25 Feb. 1930, MBY.
132. Lily to Ruth, 9 June 1931, MBY.
133. Lily to Ruth, 18 Sept. 1929, MBY. "I expect Lolly had to play second fiddle and got no innings."
134. Lily to Ruth, 25 Jan. 1927, MBY.
135. Lily to Ruth, 28 June 1933, MBY.
136. Kathleen Franks, conversation with the author, Dublin, 23 Sept. 1988.
137. Lily to Ruth, 26 Oct. 1932, MBY.
138. Lily to Ruth, 14 Nov. 1933, MBY. The letter ends with the familiar words, *"Burn this."* She wrote Ruth on 15 October 1934 about the swain's returning to Gurteen Dhas after an evening at the Abbey: "And after all what is a kiss these days? As he didn't come again or write and pretended his visit had been the usual formal friendly affair, she ought to have accepted it and kept her head and remembered her age and not been such a complete idiot."
139. Lily to Ruth, 29 Aug. 1933, MBY.
140. Lily to Ruth, 7 Aug. 1934, MBY.
141. Lily to Ruth, 20 June 1933, MBY.
142. JBY to WBY 8 Aug. 1906, MBY (badly edited in Hone, *JBY: Letters,* 97–98, where it is dated 6 Aug.). Lollie had written her father that she and Lily resented WBY's freedom and public acceptance, but she was not justified in including Lily in her complaint. It was another example of Lollie's tendency to stretch the truth. Joseph Hone had sent the proofs of his book, *J. B. Yeats: Letters to His Son W. B. Yeats and Others* to Lily, who wrote to Ruth: "I saw some of the proofs of Papa's letters, and after thinking it over for some time I got one

letter taken out. It was to W. B. asking him to make his peace with his sisters, as they thought he was having a good time while they worked hard for very little. Well, one of the sisters never made any such complaint, as she hated such petty jealousies, and the other had a way of bolstering up her jealousies and complaints by bracketing the sister's name with hers. Also, W. B. was also working very hard for very little and had all the troubles over the theatre, such bitter disappointments, and the infernal Maud through it all. I was just in time to get it left out." (18 Apr. 1943, MBY). See chap. 3, above, 129, and chap. 3, n. 123.

143. "William Butler Yeats," in *Scattering Branches,*ed. Stephen L. Gwynn (New York: Macmillan, 1940; reprint 1981), 221. See Murphy, *ProdigalFather,* 264.

144. Lily to Ruth, 3 Apr. 1934, MBY.

145. The kindly Constantine Curran suggested to the author that "perhaps Willie's nearsightedness made him seem more calculating than he was," but not many of Willie's enemies would be as generous (conversation with author, Dublin, 1966).

146. Yeats made an enemy of Duncan S. MacColl, even though he was brother-in-law of Oliver Elton, one of JBY's oldest friends. After Hugh Lane's death on the *Lusitania,* Lady Gregory and Yeats sought out MacColl to do a biography or memoir of Lane. MacColl agreed but then took an active part in the controversy over whether Lane's collection of paintings should go to Ireland or England, his witnessed will having named England, his later but unnotarized codicil naming Ireland. MacColl addressed the controversy in literary journals, and Yeats responded with his customary lack of diplomacy. MacColl, protesting he had been defamed, announced he would not proceed with the biography unless Yeats publicly apologized. Yeats not only refused but wrote a rather cavalier letter to MacColl, suggesting that MacColl ought to apologize to him. The upshot was that MacColl withdrew from the Lane project and Lady Gregory ended up writing Lane's biography herself.

The dignity of Lady Gregory's letters to MacColl stands in strong contrast to those of Yeats, but she ultimately—as she always did—stood with Yeats.

The dispute casts light on the controversy over Lane's pictures. The English had them on loan, and although no one disputed the authenticity of Lane's codicil, the lack of a notarization gave legal grounds for the English to keep them. MacColl's argument, worked out tortuously, was that Lane, had he lived and had more time to think maturely about his decision, would surely have chosen the superior English over the uncultivated Irish and that it was therefore quite proper that the pictures remain in London. The Irish were no more to be trusted with the paintings than the Greeks with their Elgin Marbles. MacColl was Scottish before he was British, but British before he was Irish. The dispute is recorded in the Duncan MacColl letters in the Library of the University of Glasgow, to whose kindness I am indebted for providing me with copies of them; and I am indebted too to Avis Berman for having called the collection to my attention.

147. Nora Connolly O'Brien's father James, wounded in the Easter Rising, was executed by firing squad while strapped to a chair in the jail courtyard. She told the author how shocked and offended she was by WBY's comments on Constance Gore-Booth, whose failure to be executed with the others for her part in the Rising, he told her, "ruined the symmetry of the rebels' deaths," and so made her "not a fit subject for a poem." She remembered his remarks with bitterness a half century later (conversation with author, Dublin, 1968).

WBY did not confine his dislikes to private conversation. There is a revealing letter about WBY's effect on others from Alfred Perceval Graves to Mrs. John Todhunter, 31 July 1922: "I cannot tell you how annoyed I have been at Yeats' attacks on his old friends in the London *Mercury*, J. F. Taylor and your husband, and his vulgar if true revelations of Lionel Johnston's goings-on. I wonder Squire printed them: it is a record of self-glorification as regards the Irish Literary Society, for which Willie Rolleston and I worked hardest—tho' no doubt he did a good deal, though I should imagine very injudiciously, for the National Literary Society of Dublin" (Elkin Mathews Papers, MS 202/1/1, ff. 788–790, Reading).

148. JBY to Lily, 23 Oct. 1908, MBY. George Russell, in a letter to Quinn (4 June 1909, NYPL) writes that he and WBY "had drifted apart," and adds: "None of my friends, George Moore, John Eglinton, Colum, O'Sullivan, Stephens, are on what could be called friendly terms with WBY." I thank Harry Diakoff for providing me with a copy of this letter before his gift of it to NYPL.

149. Murphy, *Prodigal Father*, 277–78; Hogan and O'Neill, *Joseph Holloway's Abbey Theatre*, journal entry for 31 Oct. 1904, p. 45; see also entry for 15 Apr. 1904, p. 39. The company was not at the time called the Abbey but the Irish National Theatre Society. For simplicity, I make use of the better known name.

150. Lily to Ruth, 31 July 1934, MBY. Elizabeth Curran Solterer recalled (to the author, telephone, 1987) that George Yeats had also told this story to her mother. On another occasion George delayed a visit to Ballylee in order to be present at a meeting between WBY and Lollie and her auditor: "The help is partly to take the form of drawing off Lolly that I may be alone with the auditor" (WBY to Lady Gregory, 26 June [1923], private collection); I thank Dr. John Kelly for having provided me with a copy of this letter.

151. Lily to Ruth, 3 Sept. 1934, MBY.

152. Lily to Ruth, 18 Aug. 1929, MBY.

153. JBY to Isaac Yeats, 29 Dec. 1915, ABY.

154. JBY to Lily, ca. Apr. 1896, "Willie has been staying . . ." (Murphy, *Letters from Bedford Park*, 29).

155. JBY to Rosa, n.d., ca. fall 1907, "Miss Merrington's friend . . ." In a letter to Isaac (1 Dec. 1910, ABY) JBY alludes darkly to his son's Pollexfen heritage: "Willie also likes fighting. He does not get it from me." JBY's observation confirms what the student of WBY's life also sees, that Willie was at his most vigorous, and perhaps happiest, when he had a clearly identifiable enemy. One can make a partial roll call of the names: Edward Dowden, John F. Taylor, MacGregor Mathers, James Cousins, the Fays, Annie Horniman. See WBY to

Stephen Gwynn, 13 June 1906 (quoted in Joan Coldwell, " 'The Art of Happy Desire': Yeats and the Little Magazine," in *The World of W. B. Yeats,* ed. Robin Skelton and Ann Saddlemyer. [Seattle: Univ. of Washington Press, 1965], 37): "What Dublin wants is some man who knows his own mind and has an intolerable tongue and a delight in enemies." See Murphy, *Prodigal Father,* p. 37.

156. Lily to Ruth, 12 Dec. 1932, MBY.

157. Lily to Ruth, 29 Oct 1944, MBY.

158. Kathleen Franks, conversation with author, Dublin, 1988.

159. *Daily Telegraph,* 27 Oct. 1967, MBY.

160. Donoghue, *WBY: Memoirs,* 157.

161. JBY to Rosa Butt, [week of 21 July] 1917, no. 182, Bodleian.

162. WBY's "A Journal 1908–1914," Item 44, 1909 [undated, between 31 Jan. and 3 Feb.], in Donoghue, *WBY: Memoirs,* 156–57. Other passages from his journal that should be read in the light of Lollie's problems are the following:

"I have had a curious breakdown of some sort. I had been working hard, and suddenly I found I could not use my mind on any serious subject" (140).

"I must stop writing and lie down, or go out and walk. I have the old stopping of my faculties when I ask for serious thought. I have a slight headache also, and palpitations" (160).

"Headache again, brought on by very slight amount of work. I begin to think that the worry of years, trying to do too many different things, has upset my nervous system. For years now I have had the most intense desire for a life of routine in which it would be possible to live undisturbed the life of imagination. For years I have had for long periods a kind of fright, a sense of spiritual loss" (171).

"Made another attempt to work at play and failed. I think it may be partly health, as I have that slight headache I used to have at the time of my breakdown. The mood of creation is very fragile" (191).

"Last night, walking home late, I felt as I passed the canal bridge a desire to throw a ring which I value more than anything I possess, because of her that gave it, into the canal. It passed off in a moment or two, but it was also as strong as the desire I felt when at San Marino to throw myself from the cliff. Once when I was walking in a wood with a dear friend, holding an axe in my hand, the impulse had for a moment a homicidal form, which passed off the moment I held the axe by the head instead of the handle. My father says that when he is on the top of an omnibus and another passes he wants to jump from one to the other. Is there violent madness at the root of every mind, waiting for some breaking of the leash?" (235–36).

163. Donoghue, *WBY: Memoirs,* 33.

164. JBY to Rosa Butt, ca. Feb. 1906, "Are you unwell . . . ," no. 29, Bodleian.

165. See the letter to WBY, 2 Nov. 1933, MBY, in which the writer exhibits several different handwritings in a long rambling letter.

166. Lily to Ruth, 17 Sept. 1940, MBY.

5. Cuala: The Partnership, 1908–1923

1. Sources for this chapter are the letters to and from members of the Yeats family, Liam Miller's *The Dun Emer Press, Later the Cuala Press* (Dublin: Cuala, 1973); Vincent Kinane, "Some Aspects of the Cuala Press," *The Private Library* (Quarterly Journal of the Private Libraries Association, London), 4th ser., vol. 2, no. 3 (Autumn 1989): 119–29; and others as listed in the notes below. Discussions of the artistic work of Cuala (and Dun Emer) can be found in W. G. Blaikie Murdoch, "The Cuala Press," *Bookman's Journal and Print Collector* 6, no. 10 (July 1922): 107–11; Aileen M. Goodwin, "The Cuala Press in Ireland: A Woman's Contribution to Fine Printing," *Birmingham Post* [1915]; and in several articles by Nicola Gordon Bowe: "The Irish Arts and Crafts Movement (1886–1925)," *Irish Arts Review Yearbook,* 1990–1991, 172–84; "Two Early Twentieth Century Irish Arts and Crafts Workshops in Context: An Tur Gloine and the Dun Emer Guild and Industries," *Journal of Design History* 2: nos. 2 and 3 (1989): 193–206. For other early articles on both Dun Emer and Cuala, see K. G. W. Cross and R. T. Dunlop, *A Bibliography of Yeats Criticism 1887–1965* (London: Macmillan, 1971).

2. Lily to Frederick A. King, 28 May 1910, Stanford. The new cottage was "only four miles out of the city."

3. In this chapter, as in chap. 3, I correct remarks I made in *Prodigal Father,* this the one on p. 534 that in the separation "Miss Gleeson seems to have emerged with the better part of the bargain."

4. Miss Gleeson directed Dun Emer till her death in May 1944; her niece Katharine MacCormack kept it in operation for more than a decade longer. (See the letter from Katharine MacCormack to the Editor, *Irish Times,* 16 Sept. 1953; quoted in Miller, *Dun Emer Press,* 54).

5. WBY also thought of himself as a "political nationalist" but was never part of the group that planned the Rising or ran the Free State and the Republic. His appointment to the Senate was an honor given him for his distinction, not his views. See Adrian Frazier, "The Ascendancy Poetry of W.B. Yeats," *Sewanee Review* 88, no. 1 (Jan.-Mar. 1980): 67–85, an enhanced version of his "Irish Poetry After Yeats," *Literary Review* 2, no. 2 (Winter 1979): 133–44. Yeats's purely "political" activities were confined to and determined by his association with Maud Gonne, whose favor he courted. Once, when she wanted him to remain with her in Ulster for a political rally, he returned to Dublin instead to look into a problem with the Abbey Theatre, which he thought more important

than haranguing peasants from the stump (Elizabeth Curran Solterer to author, telephone, 1987).

6. Lily to JBY, 18 Jan. 1910, MBY. The "good hater" phrase is from JBY to Lily, 26 Jan. 1910, MBY. In the spring of 1911, Lily attended a meeting of the Arts and Crafts Society in the Shelbourne Hotel. "I put on my very best, thinking that old devil Evelyn Gleeson would be there and hoping she would think we were coining money, but she never came" (Lily to JBY, 8 Mar. 1911, MBY).

7. JBY to Lily, 10 June 1908, and JBY to Lily and Lollie, 18 July 1908 (both MBY) are the earliest occurrences of these epithets for Evelyn Gleeson, but they continued for years. He predicted that Miss Gleeson would "sink in an ocean of general contempt, firing broadsides of lies as she goes down." He thought her support would be limited. "She is not a good Catholic—too lazy— so the Priests won't trouble about her." He cautioned his daughters to say little about her. "If anyone became her champion it would be because you were against her" (JBY to Lily and Lollie, 24 July 1908, MBY). When Lily reported to her father that Miss Gleeson was ill with neuralgia, she mischievously added that the affliction "came out of the same bottle as Mr. Lane-Poole's sciatica," another allusion to her bibulousness. Even Quinn called her the "Mother Abbess" when commenting on the split (John Quinn to Lily, 20 Dec. 1908, MBY).

8. JBY to Lily, 20 Aug. 1914, MBY.

9. Lily recognized the fact clearly. In 1935 (19 Aug., MBY) she wrote to Ruth about one of her embroideries: "I think my name ought to be on the bedspread. Perhaps you could sometime manage to put it on. It will add to the value and interest in the future. My name is famous. I am not, but the name is and will be so for ages." Some measure of the difficulty is suggested by Lily's attempt to inform James A. Healy about the location of her work: "Mr. Gogarty's Hotel at Renvyle, Co. Galway, has several things of mine, needle pictures, a St. Francis of Assisi, St. Columcille, The Madonna and some landscapes, a Garden, a Meadow, and an Orchard. The National Museum in Dublin has a St. Columcille of mine designed by Jack. . . . Then we did a great many Masonic banners and Boys Brigade flags. . . . Also Glasgow Museum has a little picture of mine called 'The Sea Chanty.' These are all I can think of. Of course many things are scattered about in private houses, where I don't know. I have no photographs of my things in Canberra or Loughrea—I never had the money to get them done."

10. Lily to John Quinn, 5 July 1908, NYPL.

11. Lily thought the Irish government "very pious" and hence inclined to favor Dun Emer (Lily to Ruth, 21 Oct. 1930, MBY).

12. Lollie to John Quinn, 28 Jan. 1918, NYPL.

13. Lily to Ruth, 2 Apr. 1928, MBY.

14. John Quinn to Lily, 23 June 1909, MBY. The nature of Quinn's private propagandizing for Cuala is suggested by his treatment of its edition of Synge's poems. Of the fifteen copies he bought, "I sent one to James Huneker, who wrote a good article on Synge in the Sunday Sun; one to Gregg, who

reviewed the book; one to Paul Elmer More of the Evening Post; and one to Francis Hackett, the Editor of the Literary Supplement of the Chicago Evening Post. . . . At my request Gregg mentioned your press by name so that the advertising you get out of it won't go amiss. If More reviews the book, I will send you copies of his article also" (John Quinn to Lily, 23 June 1909, MBY).

15. Lily to John Quinn, 12 Feb., 28 Mar., 8 May, 23 Aug., 28 Sept. 1916; 27 Mar., 17 Apr. 1917, NYPL. In the last of these, Lily writes: "I feel it is very unfair to let you pay me for a screen that has been sent to the bottom by our common enemy the German, or else stolen." When the replacement screen arrived, Lily wrote: "I don't feel it is at all right or fair for you to pay the whole cost of the lost screen. Not only do you do this, but you pay me extra for this one, which is very generous of you. I hope you like the screen. I think it one of Morris's best embroidery designs. The colouring is my own" (11 Mar. 1918, NYPL). She did not offer to return the payment and made no further comment about it. The screen is now in the possession of Thomas Conroy, Quinn's great-nephew.

16. John Quinn to Lily, 20 Dec. 1908, MBY.

17. Lily to John Quinn, 12 Mar. 1909, NYPL. The lettering for the poems she mentioned to Quinn was done by a Mr. Braithwaite of Belfast. Jack Yeats came to be the principal contributing artist for the cards.

18. Lollie to James A. Healy, 18 May 1938, Stanford. Lollie admitted that the books were the most valuable part of Cuala, but when WBY criticized the cards in his last fight with Lollie, she pointed out that the "despised" cards had brought in £400 in 1938 (Lollie to James A. Healy, 3 Dec. 1938, Stanford). See also Lollie to Paul Lemperly, 15 June 1917, Stanford, in which she lists fourteen prints, some plain, some colored.

19. Miller, *Dun Emer Press*, 64, 66.

20. Lollie to James A. Healy, 3 May 1938, Stanford.

21. Lollie to Frederick A. King, 17 Jan. 1928, Stanford.

22. Lollie to James A. Healy, enclosure in letter of 18 May 1938, Stanford.

23. Lollie to James A. Healy [after 15 July, before 12 Aug.] 1938, Stanford.

24. Lollie to JBY, 23 Apr. 1920, MBY.

25. Lollie to James A. Healy [after 15 July, before 12 Aug.] 1938, Stanford.

26. For instance, in the spring of 1909, Cuala held a sale in Inverness that did "fairly well" and in June rented a stall at the Oxford Arts and Crafts (Lily to John Quinn, 6 May 1909, NYPL). Before the June event a private sale was held at the home of the Chestertons, "just a few people but they sold £10 worth of small things, better than we expected" (Lily to JBY, 26 May 1909, MBY). In August, Lollie represented Cuala at a sale of goods at the Exhibition of Women's Work at the Olympia in London (Lily to JBY, 26 Aug. 1909, MBY). Later in the year Lily took charge at a sale in Edinburgh in the flat of a Mr. Paterson, a friend of WBY's and Synge's (Lily to JBY, 29 Nov. 1909). It was a success,

bringing in over £46. "The Patersons took a great deal of trouble and had a crowd of the well-to-do who treated the work with great respect. I never had a sale where things were less upset. Generally people tumble everything about, but here they looked and did not touch" (Lily to JBY, 2 Dec. 1909, MBY). JBY was apprehensive about the sale, for he thought Lily not as good a salesman as Lollie: "When customers come she holds them with her glittering eye like the Ancient Mariner" (JBY to Lily, 7 Dec. 1909). The effort was exhausting. "Sales are always fatiguing, packing and unpacking the work and then standing all day showing it" (Lollie to JBY, 26 June 1910, MBY).

27. Lollie to Paul Lemperly, 21 Aug. 1911, Stanford. See Liam Miller's account of this work *Dun Emer Press*, 58–62.

28. Miller, *Dun Emer Press*, 56.

29. Miller, *Dun Emer Press*, 57.

30. Miller, *Dun Emer Press*, 58–59.

31. Lily to John Quinn, 6 May 1909, 10 June 1910, NYPL.

32. Lily to JBY, 18 Jan. 1910, MBY.

33. Miller, *Dun Emer Press*, 63. The new press was in operation by March 1910. Because of the interest in Synge, who had died in the spring of 1909, it produced his *Deirdre of the Sorrows* and a print of Synge made by Emery Walker in photogravure after a sketch by John Butler Yeats (see illustration 58). Miller notes that these and other productions were offered at a sale in Leinster Hall in March 1910. The new press cost £15, according to Lily. "We got it yesterday, such panting and blowing and bumping that went on, three men. We had to move the old press into the kitchen and put the new one in its place" (Lily to JBY, 18 Jan. 1910, MBY).

34. Lily to Ruth, 18 Mar. 1941, MBY.

35. Lollie to JBY, 20 June 1917, MBY.

36. Lily to JBY, 26 Aug. 1909, MBY.

37. Lily to Louis Purser, 22 Mar. 1910, collection of Olive Purser. See the chapter within, "William Butler Yeats and 'The Weird Sisters.'" See also Murphy, *Prodigal Father*, 373–74. I am grateful to the late Miss Purser for having provided me with a copy of this most important letter.

38. Lily to JBY, 10 Jan. 1910, MBY. JBY gave Lily most of the credit for the union. "I congratulate *you*. I think everyone will do so. You are a good matchmaking Mama. Or rather, for the match was of no one's making, you know how to bring up a girl so that she may make a good sort to marry" (JBY to Lily, 23 Jan. 1910, MBY).

39. Lily to Ruth, 17 Nov. 1916, MBY. "I can never talk of those six years with her. Could you?" If Lily's numbers are right, Ruth's departure in 1911 would fix the onset of Lollie's troubles at 1905, three years before the final break with Miss Gleeson.

40. The account of George's last days and subsequent events is vividly told by Lily in her letters to her father, 20, 22, 30 Aug.; 5, 12, 20, 22, 26, 29, and 9 Oct. 1910, MBY.

41. Lily to JBY, 9 Oct. 1910, MBY. See chap. 7, below.

42. WBY to Lily, n.d. [ca. Oct. 1910] ("I think George . . ."), MBY.
43. Lily to JBY, 9 Oct. 1910, MBY.
44. Lily to JBY, 5 Dec. 1910, MBY.
45. JBY to Lollie, 10 Dec. 1910, MBY.
46. JBY to WBY, 13 Dec. 1910, MBY.
47. JBY to Julia (Mrs. Simeon) Ford, 17 Jan. 1911, Stanford.
48. Lily to JBY, 3 Jan. 1911, MBY.
49. Lily, who was not supposed to be in charge of the Press's books, had to write Quinn in early 1911 to explain what had happened to one account. She blamed the trouble on "the girls in charge," who "had not remembered your cheque for £4 sent June 15th 1909" (11 Jan. 1911, NYPL). That of course was a year and a half earlier, and in all that time nobody had caught the error. In response Quinn noted that Cuala was cheating itself of £2.11.3. He admitted that his own method of paying—waiting till the bills piled up and sending a check for what he thought was the balance—may have been partly the cause of the discrepancies and suggested that henceforth he pay immediately on receipt of each item. Yet it was not Quinn's business, but Cuala's, to see that proper payments were made.

Two and a half years later the system had not been corrected. Lollie wrote Quinn in one of her breathless sentences: "I think you have really sent us a little too much money as we gave you a small discount as you get so many books and the books would be to you 6/9 instead of 7/6 a copy, and they are supposed to be port free" (25 Aug. 1913, NYPL). And later still, in August 1914, she had to apologize again for sending an incorrect bill; he had not returned the bill with his remittance and Lollie had neglected to keep a copy (17 Aug. 1914, NYPL). She protested too much about the error: "You may think from this confusion over your account that we often make mistakes, but it is not so—not by any means. It is ages and ages since we have had a mistake of this kind. If you had returned the account with the cheque we would have known exactly what it was you were paying for" (7 Oct. 1914, NYPL).

As late as 1928 one of her customers, Mrs. Julia Ford, complained of a mistake in the billing. "It is Miss Ryan's fault," Lollie responded. "She does the accounts and she forgot to mark 'Paid' in the book" (28 Jan. 1928, Yale). But Essie Ryan was a footsoldier in the ranks; Lollie was the general.

50. JBY to Isaac Yeats, 28 Apr. 1911, ABY.
51. Lily to JBY, 22 Jan. 1911, MBY.
52. Lily to JBY, 29 Mar. 1911 (from Kildevin, Westmeath), MBY.
53. JBY to Isaac Yeats, 28 Apr., 18 May 1911, ABY.
54. Lily to JBY, 23 July 1911, MBY.
55. Lollie to John Quinn, 29 July 1911, NYPL.
56. Lollie to John Quinn, 21 Aug. 1911, NYPL.
57. Lollie to John Quinn, 28 Nov. 1911, NYPL. "I didn't agree to Mr. Kennerley's offer. It would be only selling the book at a loss. He owes us £55.1.2. I wish he would pay before Xmas. It would help our Balance Sheet to have a more respectable appearance."

58. Lily to John Quinn, 22 Nov. 1911, NYPL. Earlier she had reported Lollie's enforced vacation without comment: "Lolly is home again and quite well after her three months trip" (Lily to John Quinn, 19 Apr. 1911, NYPL).

59. Lily to John Quinn, 22 Nov. 1911, NYPL.

60. Lily to John Quinn, 4 Jan. 1913, NYPL.

61. At the height of his career, Dowden had put his name forward for a Chair at Oxford, unaware that the committee sought a proper Englishman for the post. (See Dowden Correspondence, TCD.)

62. WBY to Lollie, 25 Oct. 1913, MBY. I have discussed the event at length in *Prodigal Father*, 407–409. To assuage WBY's feelings Lollie included in the next Cuala catalogue the sentence: "This book is not a part of the Cuala series arranged by W. B. Yeats." When WBY inscribed James A. Healy's copy, he wrote: "Had nothing to do with this book, a temporary rebellion on the part of my sisters" (*W. B. Yeats and the Irish Renaissance*, ed. Michael Stanford [Stanford University Library, 1990], 12). He may have meant "sister's," for the rebellion was Lollie's, not Lily's. See also the following note.

63. Lollie made only a perfunctory effort to follow her brother's instructions, for copies were sold without the disclaiming circular. When, with Lollie's assistance, William Maxwell published his list of Cuala books in 1932, his note on *A Woman's Reliquary* makes no mention of the dispute or the disclaimer (*A Complete List of the Books, Pamphlets, Leaflets, & Broadsides printed by Miss Yeats, with Some Notes by the Compiler,* privately printed, 1932). The colophon reads: "Privately Printed in Edinburgh for Presentation Only." I thank George Mills Harper for allowing me to consult his copy of this rare book. A Cuala Press flyer dated Spring 1914 (Stanford) lists Dowden's book as available and adds: "This book is not part of the Cuala Series arranged by W. B. Yeats." Although the book disappears from most lists during the twenties, when Lollie wrote James A. Healy in 1939 (n.d., with the incorrect salutation "Dear Mr. Higgins"), she noted that she still had "a few copies left," as also of *Certain Noble Plays of Japan* and *The Kiltartan Poetry Book.*

64. WBY to Lily, 1 Dec. 1913, MBY. For a fuller discussion see Murphy, *Prodigal Father*, 409. WBY helped Cuala in a special way. When he struck a deal with Macmillan for the publication of his works, he included a provision allowing him to publish any of his writings with Cuala first (WBY to James S. Starkey [Seamus O'Sullivan], 20 Feb. [postmark 1932]; Wade, 792).

65. Lollie to Mr. John J. Gallagher, 28 Jan. 1938, Stanford. Wade, *Bibliography*, 114, gives the number of copies as fifty.

66. Lollie to Paul Lemperly, 19 Jan. 1922, Stanford.

67. Listed in Maxwell's *Complete List* (1932), 33–41, and in Miller, *Dun Emer Press*, 122–24. From 1902 to 1932 there were nine publications "privately printed for their authors" (Maxwell, *Complete List,* 39), and twenty "Booklets and Pamphlets Privately Printed." Among the twenty-nine were Susan Mitchell's *Frankincense and Myrrh* (1912); WBY's *Poems Written in Discouragement* (1913); WBY's *Hour-Glass* (1914), Katharine Tynan's *Flower of Youth* (1916); "Aftermath of Easter Week," published for the benefit of the Irish Volunteers Dependents

Fund (1917); "Requiescat" (1921) for Michael O'Callaghan (1879–1921), first Republican Mayor of Limerick, printed for his widow, and a collection for Mrs. Emmeline Cadbury, *A Message for Everyday* (1923). I thank Mrs. Hannah Cadbury Taylor for showing me a copy of her mother's Cuala book. See also Lollie to James A. Healy, 14 Sept. 1939, Stanford.

68. See Murphy, *Prodigal Father*, 422, 625; and Wade, *Bibliography*, no. 110, p. 116.

69. JBY to Lollie, 4 May 1914, MBY.

70. Lily to John Quinn, 26 May 1914, NYPL.

71. Lily to John Quinn, 28 Aug. 1914, NYPL.

72. Lollie to John Quinn, 13 Nov. 1914, NYPL.

73. Lily to JBY, 1 Nov. 1915, MBY.

74. Lily to John Quinn, 5 Apr. 1915, NYPL.

75. Lollie to John Quinn, 7 Oct. 1914, NYPL; Lily to John Quinn, 8 Nov. 1914, NYPL.

76. Lollie to John Quinn, 13 Nov. 1914, NYPL.

77. Lily to JBY, 23 Aug. 1915, MBY.

78. Lily to John Quinn, 13 Jan. 1915, NYPL. In the fall of 1915, the sisters fell ill simultaneously, Lollie with sciatica, Lily with a recurrence of boils; Cuala had to operate without them.

79. George Moore, *Vale* (New York: Boni and Liveright, 1923), 135–46 and passim. See Murphy, *Prodigal Father*, 418ff.

80. WBY to Lily, 28 July [1914: year from postmark], MBY.

81. Lily to Ruth, 26 Sept. 1923, MBY. "George said Willy said it was a shame the way he picked my brains for his book 'Reveries.' Most of the early part is my memory, not his, and I am very glad to have helped, and don't tell."

82. Lily to JBY, 2 Aug. 1914, MBY. Her description of it to John Quinn (30 July 1914, NYPL) was more detailed: "It was the Rosses Point as Jack saw it when a child, the sun shining, the thatch like gold, a ship coming to anchor, the pilot boat going out, the sea captain in his shore going clothes off to town on a car, the Islands, the lighthouse, everything visible and everything happening at the same time and all at its best. The Rosses Point to us as children was paradise, and I think to us all when we look back is as Jack painted it."

83. WBY to Lollie, 27 Oct. 1914, MBY. Filson Young had written a book called *Memory Harbour.*

84. WBY to Lollie, n.d., ca. 1913, from Stone Cottage, Coleman's Hatch, Surrey, ("It is not 100 copies . . ."), MBY.

85. WBY to Lily, 29 Dec. [1914] (Wade's dating of year), MBY.

86. WBY to Lily [?11 Nov. 1914] (Wade's dating), MBY.

87. WBY to JBY, 18 Jan. 1915 [date taken from alien hand above salutation], MBY. The letter, from Stone Cottage, Coleman's Hatch, was typed by Ezra Pound. See Lily to John Quinn, 19 Feb. 1915, NYPL: "Willy read me about half of his book of memories about a month ago. It is very good, I think, very interesting, of lasting interest. It ends with our grandparents (Pollexfens) death. They died within six weeks of each other in 1891, and with them went

Sligo for us and all its charm and beauty, and our childhood seemed pushed back into space."

88. WBY to Lily, 28 July [postmarked 1914], MBY. He used similar excuses often. "As I have sealed up my letter to Lolly, she will not mind if I add something which is more especially her business," he wrote Lily on 1 Dec. 1913 (MBY). In another letter to Lily about Rabindranath Tagore's Cuala book (10 Aug. 1914, MBY), he opened with the words: "I write to you as I conclude Lolly is still away." When he and his wife, George, were contemplating a move from Oxford to Dublin, he wrote Lily to ask her to look into prices for hiring furniture, even though Lollie was in better health and might have been able to give more energy to the job (WBY to Lily, 4 Feb. 1918, MBY). When he wanted to borrow a copy of one of his own books, he preferred to ask Lily for her copy rather than Lollie (WBY to Lily, 4 Mar. [postmarked 1923], MBY).

89. Lily to WBY, 12 Jan. 1915, MBY. Lily's claim was not entirely accurate. Mary Yeats, a younger sister of JBY's, had married Robert Blakely Wise, a wastrel. Their daughter Edith, who married Meredith Johnston, spent the last years of her life under care for an emotional disturbance (Lily to Ruth, 12 Feb. 1929, MBY). And Lily includes Lollie among the sane.

90. Lollie to John Quinn, 3 Aug. 1915, NYPL. WBY admitted his part in the delays of production of the books. After acknowledging that "a hand press prints very slowly," he continued, "I revise in proof a great deal" (WBY to Ernest Boyd, 26 Sept. [1915]; Wade, 601).

Reveries Over Childhood and Youth was the first publication since Synge's *Deirdre* to include additional nonliterary material. In a separate portfolio were three prints, and a note by WBY. The prints included a portrait of John Butler Yeats from a watercolor self-portrait, a pencil sketch of Susan Pollexfen Yeats, and a reduced reproduction in color of Jack's *Memory Harbour* mounted on heavy black paper. The note by WBY explained Jack's painting. The volume became the first in the series of books that make up WBY's *Autobiographies*.

91. Lollie to John Quinn, 19 Oct. 1915, NYPL.

92. Lollie to John Quinn, 3 Aug. 1915, NYPL. The debt had been reduced to £350 at the outbreak of the war, but in 1916 Lollie had to put up further security for a £500 overdraft. The interest on the sum was a constant drain. Lollie floated the idea of a limited company before Paul Lemperly (8 Jan. 1917, Stanford): "Our dream is some time somehow to be able to raise £1,000 perhaps by forming a small private company." She thought if "25 friends" would invest £25 in one-pound shares, the debt could be wiped out and the investors paid a "small dividend." Lemperly didn't bite. Lollie was never able to persuade investors that Cuala was a worthy risk. She approached Quinn again on the subject (16 Jan. 1923, NYPL) but again met with no enthusiasm.

Altogether, 1915 was a bad year for Cuala. Sales at exhibitions were down, and the Press put out no new cards at Christmas because Lily thought people wouldn't send them "this terrible year." Beatrice Cassidy, Lollie's "head girl," who had been with the Press from the beginning and had set the type, died suddenly in the fall of 1915, shortly after she had married Padraic Colum's brother (Lily to John Quinn, 29 Nov., 13 Dec. 1915; Lollie to John Quinn, 13 Jan. 1915, NYPL).

93. Beatrice Lady Glenavy, conversation with author, Dalkey, 1966.

94. Leonard Elton, conversation with author, London, 1968.

95. WBY to Lily, 25 Dec. [1915], from "Stone Cottage, Coleman's Hatch, Surrey", ("I had hoped . . ."), MBY. See Wade, *Letters of WBY,* 603–604.

96. WBY to Lily, 25 Dec. [1915], MBY. One of the offshoots of Willie's idea was the displaying of Lily's embroidery in shop windows. She reported in some surprise to Ruth in early 1917 that Violet Crichton Jameson had bought one of her ten-pound screens ("The Wood") after seeing it in Freke's window, and that the display (in connection with a promotion of the Irish language) "got lots of attention." She also continued to ship embroidered goods to customers in England (Lily to Ruth, 18 Mar. 1917, MBY).

97. JBY to Isaac Yeats, 27 Mar. 1916, ABY. See also JBY to Rosa Butt, no. 117, 27 Jan. 1911, Bodleian: "She cannot live without movement and excitement and visible success."

98. Roy Foster, *Modern Ireland 1600–1972* (London: Allen Lane: Penguin, 1988), 3.

99. George W. Russell ("AE") to Thomas Bodkin, 6 Aug. 1930; Thomas Bodkin and others to George Russell, [after 6 Aug.] 1930 (Denson, *Letters from AE,* 187–88). Russell had sent invitations to Bodkin and other Irish Roman Catholics to join an organization "For the Realization of Peace and Brotherhood through Understanding and Neighbourliness—between people of *ALL* Nationalities, Races, Cultures, Classes, Conditions and Creeds." In London, Russell told Bodkin, 1,200 people had attended a meeting for "World Unity," with representatives "of Eight Religions and Seven Countries."

It was a simple do-good organization of which the world has had, and has, many, and the naïve AE supposed that any person of ordinary goodwill would be happy to join in so inoffensive a cause. The reply of Bodkin and his friends must have curled his whiskers:

> You show a sad misunderstanding of the Catholic position. As Catholics we are as anxious as you are to promote "the realisation of peace and brotherhood throughout the world." But we do not, for an instant, admit that such a consummation can be brought about by "a fellowship of faiths." We believe in one true church, out of which . . . there is no hope for humanity. We regard our faith as the only God-appointed way to real peace, here or hereafter. Our efforts toward peace can only be made under the guidance, and by the authority of the Catholic Church, universal and apostolic.
>
> Membership of your association would, therefore, mean for us an admission that mankind's highest aspirations can be realised outside the Church.
>
> So, while recognising the good motives which, no doubt, prompted your invitation, we must decline it, as we have no pretensions to "the appreciation of other faiths."

AE apologized for his effrontery.

On 26 May 1924, WBY had told Olivia Shakespear (Wade, *Letters of WBY,* 705) that he and Russell had been accused "of being in a conspiracy to destroy the Catholic faith through free education." At least he was "told" of the charge, for, he said, "I never see the popular Catholic press." In 1936 a similar accusation was leveled against him indirectly: in a letter to Dorothy Wellesley on 9 Dec. [1936] (Wade, *Letters of WBY,* 871), he describes the behavior of a movement in Ireland called the "Christian Front," which had been quite properly exercised over atrocities committed during the Spanish Civil War but one of whose publications had then asserted: "Those responsible for the outraging of nuns in Spain are all the intellectuals since the Renaissance who have opposed the supernatural." Yeats continued his summary of their remarks: ". . . and then came sentences which are supposed to refer to the Irish Academy of Letters and to myself. We were told we were watched, and that the Catholics of Ireland would not be always patient." Yeats of course approved of the supernatural but not in a way acceptable to the Christian Front. That organization might be described as an extreme right-wing branch of Catholicism if it were not that the reaction of Bodkin and his friends to Russell's invitation raises questions about the location of the center.

An instructive sidelight on the division, a subject seldom discussed in Irish studies, emanates from an article by Kevin Costelloe (as published in the *Gazette,* Schenectady, N.Y., 21 July 1990) about Jews in Dublin:

> Ronit Lentin, an Israeli married to an Irish Jew who is a television producer, says she feels an "undercurrent of anti-semitism."
>
> "My husband can still be told by people, 'But you're not really Irish,' " she said. 'Now, how Irish is Irish? He was born in Ireland and his father was born in Ireland. When do you become Irish? When you become Catholic, this is the answer.' "

Lily Yeats made an interesting observation to Ruth (21 May 1929, MBY) on Lennox Robinson's play, *The Big House:* "I think Lennox wants to show how we Protestants are as Irish as the Catholics and as much of the country and as full of love for it." She did not explain why such a demonstration should be necessary, or who needed to be persuaded.

100. James Joyce, *A Portrait of the Artist as a Young Man* (New York: Modern Library, 1928), 219–21. "The language in which we are speaking is his before it is mine. . . . His language, so familiar and so foreign, will always be for me an acquired speech. I have not made or accepted its words. My voice holds them at bay. My soul frets in the shadow of his language."

101. Lily to Ruth, 16 May 1916, MBY: "We [the English and Irish] can never understand each other. I felt that when I was a girl and an Englishman wanted me to have him. I felt we could never understand each other. He would have thought he understood me the whole time, which would have been maddening."

102. Lily to John Quinn, 1 June 1917, NYPL.

103. JBY to Lady Gregory, 14 Aug. 1920, NYPL.

104. *Sinn Fein,* 20 June 1917. See Murphy, *Prodigal Father,* 346–48. The words were part of a devastating attack on WBY. Lily Yeats was furious at Susan Mitchell, her closest friend, and blamed the article on the influence of George Russell. He, however, insisted he had had nothing to do with the attack on Yeats, which Miss Mitchell, a first-class satirist, was quite capable of on her own. In a long and somewhat angry letter to Quinn (4 June 1909, NYPL), Russell vehemently denied the charge. (I thank Harry Diakoff for providing me with a copy of this letter, given by Quinn to Jeanne Robert Foster, by her to Diakoff, and by him to NYPL).

Miss Mitchell's relationship with Russell is usually discreetly avoided by Irish biographers, but there was no question that the two were close. The Yeatses were never in doubt about it. "I suppose Susan was the woman he wanted," Lily wrote Ruth (16 July 1935, MBY) in reporting that Russell was dying, but knowing Miss Mitchell's independence added: "I don't think she would ever have married him or any man." When JBY sailed for Liverpool on his way to America, Miss Mitchell and Russell came to see him off. His comments to Rosa Butt are suggestive: "I am sure they are a great happiness to each other. I think everyone is glad that it is so." Russell's wife was apparently in the dark. She "never knows anything about anybody and finds her children and life generally a bore." JBY asked Rosa to keep his remarks in "her faithful bosom." "You must not betray them" (20 Dec. 1907, no. 53, Bodleian). When Miss Mitchell lay dying in a nursing home in Dublin, Russell was the only member outside her family allowed to visit her (Lollie to Julia Ford, 23 Feb. 1926, Yale).

In his letter to Quinn Russell provides positive evidence, long missing but widely suspected, that it was his influence that caused the Irish National Theatre Society to elect WBY its president, despite Yeats's unpopularity with its members.

105. Lily to JBY, 26 Apr. 1916, MBY.

106. Lily Yeats, "Scrapbook," 'The Rebellion of 1916.' See also Lily to Ruth, undated fragment, ca. Apr. 1916 (". . . this whole work here . . ."), MBY. Lily also describes the aftermath of the Rising vividly in letters to her father of 1 and 29 May 1916 (Princeton).

107. Lily to John Quinn, 8 May 1916, NYPL.

108. Jack, though opposed to bloodshed on general principles, was the most radical politically of the Yeatses and the most favorable to complete independence. See chap. 7, below.

109. Lily Yeats, "Scrapbook," 'The Rebellion of 1916.' See also Murphy, *Prodigal Father,* 448–54, for a discussion of the reactions of members of the Yeats family to the Rising.

110. Lily to Oliver Elton, 26 May 1916, collection of Leonard Elton.

111. Lollie to JBY, 4 May 1916, MBY.

112. Lily wrote her father (8 Oct. 1916, MBY) about the effect of English policy on the Irish. "One of my girls has just come back from her holidays in Co. Kildare. She says that last night a lot of soldiers marched from the Curragh

to Dublin and passed through the Village she was in. There were so many of them they were two hours going through the Village. For those two hours not one single person opened their doors or even looked out. Every door was closed, not a sound. And yet England goes on being as stupid as ever she was, still thinking we can be taken in by sentiment and won by violence—described as 'firmness and kindness.' "

The knee-jerk reaction of the official, public Anglo-Irish was to condemn the Rising, and the Irish Guild of the Protestant Church did just that. Two years later, when conditions in Ireland had changed, the Guild changed its position too. Not everyone went along. The Rt. Rev. Dr. Sterling Berry, Protestant Bishop of Killaloe, resigned from the Guild as a result of the rescission. As he had been chairing the meeting, a crisis developed when he stepped down; Susan Mitchell replaced him and conducted the rest of the meeting (Lily to John Quinn, 15 May 1918, with cutting from the *Telegraph,* dated only "Wednesday," with an account of the meeting, NYPL).

113. WBY's *Cathleen ni Houlihan* (1902) was an unabashedly patriotic and somewhat incendiary Irish play that probably inspired many Irish youths to a devotion to the cause of Irish freedom. But Yeats may have been attributing too much influence to it when he wrote years later:

> Did that play of mine send out
> Certain men the English shot?
> ("The Man and the Echo,"
> *Collected Poems of W. B. Yeats*
> [London: Macmillan, 1965], 393).

The imagined connection, if it existed, was surely a distant one. There is no evidence that the fathers of the Rising paid the slightest attention to WBY's views or opinions when they planned it, and there is little reason to believe the Rising would not have taken place had Yeats not written his play.

114. Lily never changed her opinion of the Rising and its aftermath as a piece of folly on both sides. Two years later, in telling her father of Maud Gonne's search for a house in Dublin, she told him Maud "was rearing" up her son Séan "for martyrdom." She hoped Maud's plans wouldn't work. "May he disappoint her and give himself body and soul to the growing of tulips or anything of that kind. We have 99 martyrs in this country for one tulip grower. I wish it were the other way." She thought the new status of John MacBride, Séan's father, a joke, "now elevated to a martyr of the first water. Before the bullet he was a villain of the darkest dye" (Lily to JBY, 7 Feb. 1918, MBY).

115. Lily to JBY, 13 July 1916, MBY. "Coal is £2 a ton. Ponder that. And turf 1/2 a sod. It is a very cold evening and I have just set fire to 1ᵈ worth of turf."

116. Lollie to John Quinn, 18 Sept. 1916, NYPL. Cuala could no longer post on its own account but had to go through an accredited bookstore, Hodges and Figgis.

117. Lily to John Quinn, 28 Sept. 1916, NYPL.

118. Lily to JBY, 23 Jan. 1917, MBY. The legacy took four years to distribute. The original estimate for each portion was £60, "but Fredrick jumped into things since and much has vanished by law."

119. Lily to Ruth, 18 Sept. 1916, MBY. "I now have an order from an agent in Australia," Lily wrote Quinn (17 Apr. 1917, NYPL). The agent was Ruth, but Lily made it sound as if an independent entrepreneur had been retained.

120. Lily to JBY, 23 May 1918, MBY.

121. Lollie to Paul Lemperly, 8 Jan. 1917, Stanford.

122. Lollie to John Quinn, 3 Aug. 1915, NYPL. A wall was knocked out downstairs to make the living room measure 28 by 17 feet, large enough to accommodate the guests at their occasional parties.

123. Lily to JBY, 20 Feb., 7 Apr. 1917, MBY. Lily sent Anne Boston a copy of Susan Mitchell's *The Living Chalice* (1913) inscribed " 'Philadelphia' with love from Lily Yeats March 1917. Dundrum, Dublin." The page also contains a poem written and autographed by Susan Mitchell. I am indebted to Rosemary Hemming for providing me with a copy of this page and for giving me extensive information about Anne Boston, her great-aunt. The significance of the nickname, given to her before she met Lily, is unknown; it was later shortened to "Phillida" and always appears so in the letters.

124. WBY to Lollie, n.d. ("My only free evening . . ."), MBY.

125. Lollie to JBY, 26 May 1917, MBY.

126. Lollie to JBY, 3 May 1917, MBY.

127. Lily to John Quinn, 7 May 1917, NYPL.

128. Lollie to JBY, 26 June 1917, MBY. See Murphy, *Prodigal Father,* 461–66. On p. 635 there I have supplied names for the disguising initials.

129. The word was "self-deserting." Louis Purser had questioned the word as it appeared, "self-deserving," but Pound grandly swept his pen through the correction (Lollie to JBY, 20 June 1917, MBY).

130. Lollie to JBY, 20 June 1917, MBY.

131. Ezra Pound to Lollie, 21 June 1917, MBY.

132. WBY to Lily, 4 Oct. [1917], MBY. The book that wasn't selling was Pound's first Cuala publication, *Certain Noble Plays of Japan* (1916). The JBY book sold well. Pound's *Plays* and Dowden's *Reliquary* were still advertised as available in 1918.

133. Lily to John Quinn, 1 June 1917, NYPL.

134. JBY to Lady Gregory, 11 June 1917, NYPL.

135. Lily to John Quinn, 9 July 1917, NYPL. The following day she added: "I am very pleased you like my father's book and that you think Ezra Pound was the right man to edit it. Everyone else seems to object to him. I had letters from all sorts of people saying things like 'in spite of Ezra Pound the book is delightful.' *One after another people wrote like this.* The few exceptions were our Uncle Isaac Yeats who said he had done the selecting very well, and Louis Purser (who liked the Japanese plays). Ezra Pound was a most trying and cheeky proof

corrector, and quite the worst proof corrector I ever came across, and was rather rude into the bargain. But all ended well, and I got quite to like him towards the end. I only know him through his letters" (Lily to John Quinn, 10 July 1917, NYPL).

When Quinn sent her a copy of Pound's *Lustra,* she responded: "He is certainly himself whatever he writes, and I think and hope the hectic eye and blazing brain with which he sees women is quite his own. If he sees truly we are just dangerous animals. As his view it is interesting and amusing, and I shall read it with pleasure. I like the dedication. In it he is again himself" (Lily to John Quinn, 27 Nov. 1917, NYPL).

136. Lollie to Elkin Mathews, 26 Mar. 1917, Elkin Mathews Collection, Reading.

137. Lily to Quinn , 1 Aug., 20 Sept. 1917, NYPL.

138. WBY to JBY, n.d., [probably either 8 or 15 Oct. 1917], Foster-Murphy Collection, NYPL. JBY didn't receive it till after the wedding.

139. JBY to WBY, 15 Nov. 1917, MBY.

140. Lily to JBY, 28 Sept. 1918, MBY. The next night there was a dinner at the Arts Club in Chesterton's honor, at which both he and WBY spoke. "He is nowhere as a speaker compared to Willy," Lily told her father.

141. Lollie to JBY, 29 Dec. 1918, MBY.

142. For a full account of JBY's illness, see Murphy, *Prodigal Father,* 487–90.

143. Miller, *Dun Emer Press,* 110.

144. Lily to John Quinn, 16 Oct. 1919, NYPL.

145. Lily to John Quinn, 30 Dec. 1918, NYPL.

146. Lily to JBY, 7 June 1920, MBY.

147. Lollie to John Quinn, 15 Apr. 1919, NYPL.

148. Lollie to JBY, 10 January 1919, MBY.

149. Lily to Ruth, 17 Oct. 1928, MBY.

150. Lily to JBY, 13 Sept. 1920, MBY.

151. Lollie to JBY, 15 June 1921, MBY.

152. Lollie to JBY, 28 Oct. 1920, MBY. See Murphy, *Prodigal Father,* 511–12.

153. Lily to JBY, 23 Nov. 1920, MBY.

154. Lily to JBY, 17 Oct. 1920, MBY. "Dr. Gogarty was so careful he was in six times the first day, and he had a special nurse for day and night." The operation took place on 13 Oct. (Lily to John Quinn, 14 Oct. 1920, NYPL).

155. Lily to JBY, 13 Feb., 8 Mar. 1921, MBY. In June 1921 there were thirty-five at another Gurteen Dhas party (Lily to JBY, 8 June 1921, MBY).

156. Lily to JBY, 20 Oct. 1920, MBY. Though Lily and Miss Boston were fast friends, the incidental advantage to her living at Gurteen Dhas as a paying guest was considerable. When she returned to England after a term at Trinity, Lily wrote her father: "We miss her very much. When she is here, as well as her companionship I can pay *every* bill on Saturdays and put away the rent under lock and key. So you see I have two very good reasons for missing her" (Lily to JBY,

30 May 1921, MBY). In the fall of 1921, Phillida became ill and was ordered away by her doctor. "So she telegraphed to her married sister in Staffordshire and went off yesterday morning. And I was saving up so delightfully for the rent out of her money. So go the little plans of poor weak man" (Lily to JBY, 8 Nov. 1921). In Lily to JBY, 30 Aug. and 13 Sept. 1920 (MBY) she writes more about Phillida.

157. Lily to JBY, 20 Oct. 1920, MBY.

158. Lily to JBY, 23 Nov. 1920, MBY.

159. Lily to JBY, 9 December 1920, MBY. "I saw in Clare Street [in Dublin] a motor lorry of Black and Tans, all with revolvers in their hands, not in their pockets or belts but in their hands, going as if driven by a man in a frenzy and written on its side in white chalk letters of almost two feet high, 'Reprisals galore.' I saw two other such lorries minus the charming motto, otherwise the same. I was only in town for an hour and only in a small area." She closed: "Some day I suppose we will be free again in this country and able to go about our own country as we wish without being fired at or insulted."

160. Lily to JBY, 1 Mar. 1921, MBY.

161. Lily to JBY, 23 Aug. 1921, MBY.

162. WBY to Lily, 25 Jan. 1912 [date from postmark; WBY incorrectly dates the letter "Feb. 25" even though he refers to "the third week in February" as in the future], MBY.

163. WBY to Lollie, 23 Dec. 1921 (after the month and day is written in Wade's hand: "[22 *(sic)* Dec 1921]"), MBY. For a fuller discussion of the whole matter of Lollie's editing, see Murphy, *Prodigal Father*, 524, 528–30.

164. WBY to Lollie, 10 June [1921] (year in Wade's hand on original letter), MBY. Willie added: "(I would, of course, always sign for the Cadburys if they like)."

165. WBY to Lollie, 8 July [1921] (year in Wade's hand on original letter), MBY.

166. Lily to JBY, 4 Sept. 1921, MBY.

167. Lily to JBY, 4 Sept. 1921, MBY.

168. Lily to JBY, 21 Dec. 1921, MBY.

169. Lily to JBY, 10 Jan. 1922, MBY.

170. Lily to Ruth, 4 Mar. 1925, MBY.

171. Lily to JBY, 18 Jan. 1922, MBY.

172. Lily to JBY, 16 Oct. 1921, MBY.

173. Lily to John Quinn, 13 Aug. 1922, NYPL.

174. Lily to John Quinn, 13 Aug. 1922, NYPL.

175. Lollie to John Quinn, 15 Feb. 1922, NYPL.

176. Lily to JBY, 10 Jan. 1922, MBY.

177. Lollie to Philip D. Sherman 7 July 1922, 24 Aug. 1922, 30 Mar. 1932, Brown. After De Valera won an election in 1937, Lily wrote Ruth (6 July, MYB): "It is curious how he holds the illiterate. He is a dull speaker, and his own family must hate the sight of him. His wife or family never go anywhere with him, never see him off, even when he goes on long travels."

178. Lollie to John Quinn, 18 July, 4 Aug. 1922, NYPL.
179. WBY to Olivia Shakespear, 17 Feb. [1922]; Wade, *Letters of WBY,*
678: "I shall arrange his autobiographical chapters for Cuala."
180. John Quinn to WBY, 19 Nov. 1923, MBY.
181. Lily to John Quinn, 13 Aug. 1922, NYPL.
182. Lily to John Quinn, 13 Aug. 1922, NYPL.
183. Lollie to John Quinn, 16 Jan. 1923, NYPL. The marriage, on 10 Jan.
1923, took place at Taney Church, Dundrum, Lily's church. (Lollie attended St.
Nahi's Church). The reception was supposed to have been held at WBY's house,
82 Merrion Square, but had to be shifted to Gurteen Dhas because of Anne's
illness with scarlet fever.
184. Lily Yeats, "Scrapbook," 'The Raid on Cuala.'
185. Lily Yeats, "The Raid on Cuala."
186. Lily Yeats, "The Raid on Cuala."
187. Lollie to John Quinn, 31 July 1923, NYPL.

6. Cuala: The Separation, 1924–1940

Sources for this section are the same as for the preceding one, with the
addition of the Cuala Archive at the Library of Trinity College Dublin.

1. Lollie to John Quinn, 16 Jan. 1923, NYPL.
2. WBY to Lady Gregory, 17 July [1923], private collection. For this letter
and those following to Lady Gregory, to and from Dr. Robert Simpson, and to
E. D. Waggett, I am indebted to Dr. John Kelly, who generously called them
to my attention and provided copies.
3. WBY to Lady Gregory, 19 July [1923], private collection.
4. WBY to Edmund Gosse, 23 Nov. [1923]; Wade, *Letters of WBY,* 701.
5. WBY to Lady Gregory, 17 July [1923], private collection.
6. *Irish Literary Portraits,* ed. W. R. Rodgers (New York: Taplinger, 1972),
10. Deirdre Bair, in her biography of Samuel Beckett, repeats what she calls "an
apocryphal story popular in the pubs of Dublin." "According to legend, the lord
mayor of Dublin was the first person to receive the news, telephoned from
Stockholm. He dressed in his ceremonial robes and carried the badges of his
office through the streets in a horse-drawn carriage to Yeats's house. When he
arrived, he stood on the steps and in ringing tones proclaimed Yeats to the
curious crowd that had followed his carriage. Beckett's version of the story had
Yeats hopping anxiously from one foot to the other, until, unable to contain
himself any longer, he interrupted the long and boring speech to demand, 'Yes,
yes, just tell me what it's worth! How much will I get?' (*Samuel Beckett* [New
York: Summit, 1990], 610).
7. Lily to Oliver Elton, 22 Dec. 1923, collection of Leonard Elton.
8. John Quinn to WBY, 19 Nov. 1923, MBY. The letter is full of Quinn's
bluff, heavy-handed humor as well as of unsolicited medical advice about Lily's

condition. "Anatole France kept his money though he was a Socialist and to have a capital of $40,000 was quite contrary to Socialist principles. But you are not a Socialist and you are not as old as Anatole France is and you are not a wealthy old codger with a priceless collection of art and bronzes and marbles as Anatole France is and you have a wife, a legitimate honest to God wife, and two legitimate children, and France has no children that he acknowledges and a wife who doesn't need anything from him." He insisted several times, with heavy capitalizations and underlinings (some in his own hand to supplement the typewriter's) that Lily be sent away from London at once.

9. WBY wrote Lady Gregory on 13 Jan. [1924] (Wade, *Letters of WBY,* 701) that he had invested £6,000 of the prize money "and kept £500 to pay off the debt on this house [52 Merrion Square] or pay Lily's expenses, as the case may be." He and George had spent £400 on the trip to Sweden and on furnishings for the Merrion Square house, and for the purchase of something he had always wanted, a "sufficient reference library."

10. Lily, "My wishes," MBY. Lily told Joseph Hone (16 May 1942, Texas) that after she returned home from Roseneath she discovered that Maria had stolen many things from the house. "We ought to have sent her flying twenty years ago —but as we could not give her a character [i.e., a character reference] kept her."

11. Lily Yeats, "My wishes," unpublished, MBY.

12. Lollie to John Quinn, 31 July 1923, NYPL. In another letter to Quinn (24 Mar. 1924, NYPL), she calls Lily's illness "a *nerve malady.*"

13. WBY to Lady Gregory, 9 Feb. 1924, MBY.

14. Dr. Robert Simpson to WBY, 20 Mar. 1924, private collection.

15. Dr. Robert Simpson to WBY, 20 Mar. 1924, private collection.

16. E. D. Waggett to WBY, 26 Mar. 1924, private collection.

17. Lily to Ruth, 30 Apr. 1929, MBY.

18. WBY to E. D. Waggett, 3 Apr. 1924, private collection.

19. WBY to Dr. Robert Simpson, 3 Apr. 1924, private collection.

20. Lollie's account of her visit to London appears in a letter to John Quinn (24 Mar. 1924, NYPL). "W.B. has been most generous and paid these two doctors and also gave me a cheque to go to London on. But he never speaks to me of Lily. Neither does George. They *seem* vexed I interfered, but I *had to.*" Years later, in reporting Waggett's death to Ruth, he having learned by then "what a fool he had been," Lily wrote, "If Lolly had not interfered I would have been saved much mental suffering" (18 July 1942, MBY).

21. WBY to George (Mrs. W. B.) Yeats, 27 July [1923], MBY.

22. WBY to Lily, 15 June 1924, MBY.

23. WBY to Sturge Moore, 18 Aug. 1923, Texas. I thank Dr. John Kelly for calling this letter to my attention and providing a copy. WBY's financial problems at this time, despite the Nobel Prize money, are suggested in his letter to John Quinn (3 Nov. 1923, NYPL): "Neither George nor I has forgotten that we owe you much money (paid out by you for my father) but we must ask you to leave it for a little till this illness of my sister has been paid for. Cuala, which

was nearly killed by war and civil war, has begun to do well and to pay its debts, and we shall pay ours."

24. Lily to John Quinn, 14 June 1924, NYPL.

25. Lollie to John Quinn, 24 Mar. 1924, NYPL.

26. Lollie to James A. Healy, 12 May 1938, Stanford. Quinn's last letter to WBY was dated 23 Nov. 1923 (postscript to 19 Nov.), NYPL. For a full account of Quinn, see Murphy, *Prodigal Father,* and Reid, *Man from New York.*

27. George (Mrs. W.B.) Yeats to WBY, 21 Aug. 1924, MBY, where she quotes Lily's letter. I thank Ann Saddlemyer for providing me with a copy of this letter.

28. Lily to Ruth, 4 Mar. 1925, MBY.

29. WBY to Lily, 26 Mar. [1925], MBY.

30. Lily to Ruth, 4 Mar., 23 June 1925, MBY.

31. Lily to Ruth, 2 Apr. 1925, MBY.

32. Lily to Ruth, 16, 21, 28 May 1925, MBY. For example, Cuala had to pay a fee for the use of the Irish Trade Mark, and bureaucratic demands made record keeping tiresome.

33. Lily to Ruth, 29 Nov. 1925, 4 Feb. 1926, MBY.

34. Lily to Ruth, 7 Apr. 1925, MBY.

35. Lily to Ruth, 7 Apr. 1925, MBY.

36. Lily to Ruth, 29 July 1925, MBY.

37. Lily to Ruth, 19 Aug. 1926, MBY.

38. Lily to Ruth, 28 Oct. 1926, MBY.

39. Lily to Ruth, 26 Sept. 1923 (postscript of 27 Sept.), MBY.

40. The details are spelled out in an Indenture, dated 13 Oct. 1925, between Susan Mary Yeats and Elizabeth Corbet Yeats, "Mortgagors," and W. B. Yeats, "Mortgagee." Their debt to the bank is given as £1,976. He paid the debt but insisted on the security of the Pollexfen and Steamer shares. He guaranteed their overdraft at the bank but not for more than £200 at a time. (TCD: Cuala Press Archive 1902–1986: Press A Cuala Arch, box no. 8).

41. Lily to Ruth, 17 Dec. 1925, MBY.

42. Lily to Ruth, 26 Nov., 5 Dec. 1925; 28 June 1926, MBY.

43. Lily to Ruth, 21 Nov. 1927, 5 Dec. 1926, MBY.

44. Michael B. Yeats, preface to Miller, *Dun Emer Press,* 8.

45. Lily to Ruth, 13 July 1926, MBY. A Mrs. Ball visited Dublin in July and stopped in at Cuala every morning to chat with Lily, and ordered "rest gowns" for her friends that were like the one Lily had already made for her.

46. Lily to Ruth, 17 Apr. 1928, MBY. Chesterton himself also purchased, probably on another visit, "a Sacred Heart designed by Jack, which Gilbert gave to some church in England."

47. Lily to Ruth, 30 June 1925, MBY.

48. Lily to Ruth, 30 June 1925, MBY.

49. Lily to Ruth, 23 Sept. 1925, MBY.

50. WBY to "My dear Sisters," 29 Oct. [1925], MBY. The sum spent on

Lily's care (£245) would be roughly the equivalent of $10,000 (U.S.) in 1990 values.

51. WBY to "My dear Sisters," 29 Oct. 1925, MBY.

52. Lollie to Philip D. Sherman, 7 Jan. 1924, Brown; Lollie to Kate Buss, 2 July 1935, Stanford.

53. Lollie to Van Wyck Brooks, 30 Apr. 1924, estate of Van Wyck Brooks. She told Gogarty also (Lollie to O. St. J. Gogarty, 30 July 1924, private collection). I thank Dr. John Kelly for calling the Gogarty letter to my attention and providing a copy.

54. Lollie to James A. Healy, 2 Dec. 1938, Stanford. Gibbon's book, *The Masterpiece and the Man: Yeats As I Knew Him* (London: Rupert Hart-Davis, 1959), is an unfriendly account of his dealings with WBY, showing resentment at Yeats's dismissal of him as a poet. Gibbon naturally had a high opinion of his own work and did not relish what he saw as WBY's rejection of it. What he did not know was that WBY thought well of Gibbon's verse and told Lily so (Lily to Ruth, 4 Mar. 1925, MBY), though he apparently never told Gibbon. Whether Gibbon's portrait would have shown a kinder, gentler Yeats if Cuala had been allowed to publish his book is a matter for the psychologist to decide. WBY's target may have been Lollie rather than Gibbon. Whatever the reasons, WBY's admiration did not extend to the ultimate blessing of inclusion in the Cuala series.

Whatever WBY told Lily about his opinion of Gibbon's verse, he succeeded in offending him in an unusual way. Gibbon had given him an inscribed copy of a book of his poems. Some months later Gibbon visited at Merrion Square, saw the gift book on a shelf, took it down, and discovered the pages were uncut. He was furious. George told her daughter Anne that it "served him right, as he had no business taking down the book" (ABY, to author).

55. George Yeats to Ezra Pound, 19 Aug. 1928, private collection. I thank Dr. Ann Saddlemyer for calling this letter to my attention and providing me with a copy.

56. Lily to Ruth, 5 July 1927, MBY.

57. Lily to Ruth, 29 Nov. 1925, MBY.

58. Lily to Ruth, 13 Mar. 1928, MBY.

59. Lily to Ruth, 4 Feb. 1926, MBY.

60. Lily to Ruth, 29 Jan. 1927, MBY.

61. Lily to Ruth, 13 July 1926, MBY.

62. Lily to Ruth, 5 July 1927, MBY.

63. Lily to Ruth, 3 Dec. 1928, enclosure of catalogue of Cuala sale at Keswick, 10–15 Sept. 1928, MBY. To James A. Healy she wrote (4 Dec. 1938, Stanford): "I did the quite beautiful bedspreads. On each had to go the Royal crown. I was sent from Buckingham Palace a coloured sketch of the correct form and colour." She also provided firescreens for the new capital building in Canberra in the early 1930s.

64. Enclosure in Lily to Ruth, 28 Oct. 1926, MBY.

65. Lily to Ruth, 5 July 1927, MBY.

66. Lily to James A. Healy, 17 Jan. 1939, Stanford.

67. Lily to Ruth, 19 July 1927, MBY.

68. Michael B. Yeats, preface to Miller, *Dun Emer Press, 7.*

69. Vincent Kinane, "Some Aspects of the Cuala Press," *The Private Library,* 4th series, 2:3 (Autumn 1989), 121.

70. Lollie Yeats to Philip D. Sherman, 7 July 1922, Brown.

71. Lollie to Prof. Alfred De Lurey, 29 Dec. 1932, Toronto.

72. Michael B. Yeats, in Miller, *Dun Emer Press, 7–8.*

73. Lily to Ruth, 24 Oct. 1927, MBY.

74. Lily to Ruth, 2 Jan. 1928, MBY.

75. Lily to Ruth, 12 Dec. 1927, MBY.

76. Lily to Ruth, 30 Sept. (postscript Monday [3 Oct.]) 1938, MBY. See also chap. 4, above.

77. Lily to Ruth, 27 Jan. 1929, MBY.

78. Lily to Ruth, 27 Jan. 1929, MBY.

79. Lily to Ruth, 10 May 1929, MBY.

80. Lily to Ruth, 27 Jan. 1929, MBY.

81. Lily to Ruth, 21 Feb. 1929, MBY.

82. Lily to Ruth, 25 June 1929, MBY, and in many other letters. See, e.g., 19 Aug. 1935, MBY: "I do think my work is original and good, and I never let the standard drop, did I?—in the face of all the difficulties, wars, strikes, and no capital, and finally no trade because of tariffs and depressions."

83. Lily to Ruth, 1 Dec. 1930, MBY.

84. Lily to Ruth, 15 Dec. 1930, MBY.

85. Lily to Ruth, 28 Apr. 193[1], MBY.

86. Lily to Ruth, 12 May 1931, MBY.

87. Lily to Ruth, 12 May, 9 June 1931, MBY.

88. Lily to Ruth, 27 Jan. 1931, MBY.

89. Lily to Ruth, 15 Sept. 1931, MBY. Among the odd jobs were napkins for Emmeline Cadbury, a wedding gift for her daughter Hannah ("Joy") Cadbury, who married Christopher Taylor. Mrs. Taylor has been most generous in sharing information about her family's role in Cuala.

90. Lily to Ruth, 4 Sept. 1931, MBY.

91. Lily to Ruth, 27 Sept. 1931, MBY.

92. Lily to Ruth, 20 Oct. 1931, MBY.

93. Lily to Ruth, 17 Nov. 1931, MBY.

94. George Yeats to WBY, 4 Jan. 1932, MBY. I thank Dr. Ann Saddlemyer for bringing this letter to my attention and providing me with a copy. It is important in showing as it does that George, not WBY, was the one who worked out the details.

95. Lollie to James A. Healy, 2 and 3 Dec. 1938, Stanford.

96. Lollie to James A. Healy, 3 Dec. 1938, Stanford.

97. Lily to Ruth, 29 Nov. 1925, MBY.

98. Lily to Ruth, 27 Sept. 1931, MBY.

99. Lily to Ruth, 27 Sept. 1931, MBY.

100. Lily to Ruth, 4 Jan. 1932, MBY. The Customs House and Abbey pictures were drawn for Lily by Dorothy Blackman.

101. Lily to Ruth, 8 Mar. 1932, MBY.

102. Lily to Ruth, 15 Dec. 1931, MBY.

103. Lily to James A. Healy, 4 Dec. 1938, Stanford.

104. WBY to Lily, 6 Jan. [1932] (year provided on original letter in hand of Allan Wade), from Coole, MBY.

105. Lily to Ruth, 4 Jan. 1932, MBY.

106. Lily to Ruth, 4 Jan. 1932, MBY.

107. Lily to Ruth, 18 Jan. 1932, MBY.

108. Lily to Ruth, 18 Jan. 1932, MBY.

109. The "rich American" was Mrs. Nicholas Brady. The Stations were placed in a memorial chapel in Wernersville, Pennsylvania (Lily to James A. Healy, 17 Oct. 1938, Stanford).

110. Lily to Ruth, 29 June 1932, MBY.

111. Lily to Ruth, 5 July 1932, MBY.

112. Lily to Ruth, 5 July 1932, MBY.

113. Lily to Ruth, 19 Sept. 1933, MBY. Rossi's book proved hard to sell. In 1938, Lollie still had 82 copies on hand out of 300 (Lollie to James A. Healy, 31 Mar. 1938, on flier enclosed with letter, Stanford). Liam Miller notes that in 1946 the book was still in print, the price reduced from 10s. 6d. to 5s. 6d. (Miller, *Dun Emer Press,* 113). The 1938 list of unsold books included, in addition to Rossi's, Higgins's *Arable Holdings* (1933), 36 copies; WBY's *Stories of Michael Robartes and His Friends* (1931), 67 copies; WBY's *King of the Great Clock Tower* (1934), 24 copies; and *Passages from the Letters of AE to W. B. Yeats* (1936), 25 copies. Three other titles were unadvertised, as only "a few copies" were available: Dowden's *Woman's Reliquary,* Pound's *Certain Noble Plays of Japan,* and Lady Gregory's *Kiltartan Tales* (Lollie to James A. Healy, n.d., [1939], Stanford).

114. Lily to Ruth, 21 Dec. 1933, MBY.

115. Lily to Ruth, 1 Oct. 1935, MBY.

116. Lily to Ruth, 3 Sept. 1934, MBY.

117. Lily to Ruth, 3 Sept. 1934, MBY.

118. Miller, *Dun Emer Press,* 114–15.

119. Lily to Ruth, 3 Sept. 1934, MBY.

120. Lily to Ruth, 1 May 1934, MBY.

121. Lily to Ruth, 1 May 1934, MBY.

122. Lily to Ruth, 3 Apr. 1934, MBY. WBY thought Lollie "not at all safe over the money side," yet she would never ask for advice, and "only the very brave can offer it." Donaghy's bill was still unpaid after WBY's death, but the new directors went after him for payment even though he had no funds.

123. Lily to Ruth, 25 Sept. 1934, MBY.

124. Lily to Ruth, 27 Nov. 1934, MBY.

125. Lily to Ruth, undated fragment, probably late 1934 (". . . and she said that she thinks. . . ."), MBY. Lollie persuaded the Franks family that Lily's

behavior was the cause of Maureen's unhappiness, and they accepted her version, even though Lily and Maureen saw little of each other. Lily noticed that the Frankses grew increasingly cold to her and assumed correctly that Lollie was the cause. See chap. 4, above.

126. Lily to Ruth, 31 July 1934, MBY. See chap. 4, above.
127. Lily to Ruth, 25 Feb. 1935, MBY.
128. Lily to Ruth, 15 Jan. 1935, MBY.
129. Lily to Ruth, 7 May 1935, MBY.
130. Lily to Ruth, 17 June 1935, MBY.
131. Lily to Ruth, 5 Aug. 1935, MBY.
132. Lily to Ruth, 1 Oct. 1935, MBY.
133. Lily to Ruth, 29 June 1936, MBY.
134. Lily to Ruth, 1 Mar. 1936, no. 2 of two letters of this date, MBY.
135. Lily to Ruth, 4 Oct. 1937, MBY.
136. Lily to Ruth, 31 Jan. 1938, MBY.
137. Announcement of Cuala Press, undated, enclosed with letter, Lollie to Philip D. Sherman, 21 June 1937, Brown.
138. Lollie to Philip D. Sherman, 21 June 1937, Brown.
139. Lily to Ruth, 30 Aug. 1937, MBY. In March, WBY wrote from the Idéal Séjour of Diane Murphy's design for "The Happy Townland." He paid Lily £5.5 for the embroidering of it (WBY to Lily, 3 Mar. 1938, MBY): "Some rich American may buy the lot." Another letter (WBY to Lily, 23 July [1938], MBY) gives further information about "Innisfree" and also "The Post Office" and "The Abbey Theatre." "I do not mind if they do not sell."
140. WBY to Lily, 3 Mar. [1938], MBY.
141. WBY to Lily, 20 Aug. [1937], MBY.
142. WBY to Mr. Scroope, 2 Jan. 1938 (draft copy of a letter, unsigned), MBY.
143. Lollie to James A. Healy, 21 Oct. 1937, Stanford.
144. Lollie to John J. Gallagher, 10 Jan. 1938, Stanford.
145. WBY to Edith Shackleton Heald, 28 Nov. [1937], Houghton Library, Harvard University; partly in Wade, *Letters of WBY,* 900–901, but not this passage. I thank Dr. John Kelly for providing me with a typescript of this letter. Frederick Robert Higgins, born in 1897, died in 1941, only a year after Lollie.
146. Lollie to WBY, 30 Nov. 1937, MBY.
147. Lollie told Lily she had been "most dove-like" at their meeting, and "Willy inflated with vanity" (Lily to Ruth, 4 Dec. 1937, MBY).
148. WBY to Dorothy Wellesley, 21 Dec. [1937], private collection. I thank Dr. John Kelly for calling this letter to my attention and providing me with a copy.
149. While negotiations were proceeding, one of WBY's admirers was seeking to help the Cuala Press. James A. Healy, a New York stockbroker devoted to his Irish-born parents, had long thought highly of W. B. Yeats and had begun collecting books and manuscripts associated with him. When he

heard of Cuala's difficulties, he began corresponding independently with Lollie, offering to attempt to raise money to erase the overdraft. One suggestion was that each of a number of Americans contribute $50 to the Press and in return be given copies of all Cuala publications (Lollie to James A. Healy, 18 May 1938, Stanford). Lollie countered by suggesting that they be allowed to purchase at cost copies of everything produced by the Press. Healy, with some of the others who had banded together earlier to help WBY by helping him financially, formed the Cuala Associates "to foster a broader appreciation of Cuala's achievement in America" (typescript of first draft of article on Cuala, Stanford). Nothing significant came of either scheme, largely because of WBY's death in January 1939 and Lollie's a year later.

The earlier committee, "The Testimonial Committee for William Butler Yeats," consisting of some fifty Americans of Irish ancestry, was organized in 1937 under the chairmanship of the novelist James T. Farrell "to enable the poet to continue his productive activities without economic worries" (*New York Sun,* 4 Jan. 1939).

150. Lollie to George Yeats, 31 Dec. 1937, from Vincent Kinane, "Some Aspects of the Cuala Press," *The Private Library* (Quarterly Journal of the Private Libraries Association, London), 4th ser., vol. 2, no. 3 (Autumn 1989): 124.

151. WBY to Dorothy Wellesley, 11 Nov. 1937; Wade, *Letters of WBY,* 900. He apparently thought the "bi-annual" book would make up the £150 a year the Press would need (WBY to Ethel Mannin, 17 Dec. [1937]; Wade, *Letters of WBY,* 903). *On The Boiler* was published but not printed by Cuala (WBY to Lily, 3 Mar. 1938, MBY) and provided ammunition for his detractors without his having the opportunity to find "joy in answering them," for it was issued after his death.

In commenting on the book, Conor Cruise O'Brien, in a well-known essay, "Passion and Cunning," implies without openly saying so that Yeats was a fascist. The essay first appeared in 1965 in *In Excited Reverie,* ed. A. N. Jeffares and K. G. W. Cross (see Conor Cruise O'Brien's *Passion and Cunning: Essays on Nationalism, Terrorism and Revolution,* [New York: Simon and Schuster, 1988]). His accusation led to an avalanche of replies, rebuttals, and counterrebuttals. Yeats probably spoke merely from an Irish, anti-English point of view, but his remarks were at best injudicious.

152. Lily to Ruth, 3 July 1938, MBY. Lollie proposed another scheme to her brother—that Cuala become a commercial printer. She said Monk Gibbon might be a willing investor. (Lollie to WBY, 9 May 1938; from Kinane, "Some Aspects of the Cuala Press," 124). Nothing more is heard of the plan.

153. Lily to Ruth, 3 July 1938, MBY.

154. Lollie to WBY, 25 Jan. 1939, MBY.

155. Lollie to James A. Healy, 19 Oct. 1938, Stanford.

156. Lollie to James A. Healy, 4 Nov. 1938, Stanford.

157. Lollie to James A. Healy, 19 Jan. 1939, Stanford.

158. Lily to Ruth, 21 Sept. 1938. The ever generous Emmeline Cadbury sent £100 to the newly organized company, half to buy shares for Lollie, the

other half for shares "for the girls who have worked so faithfully under you in the Printing Room" (Emmeline Cadbury to Lollie Yeats, 16 Nov. 1938; TCD: Cuala Collection: Press A Cuala Arch, box 2). Cecil Harmsworth lent £150, to which the directors assigned an interest rate of 5 percent (note by Lollie in Press A Cuala Arch, box 2), and Anne Boston made a loan also (meeting of 10 Mar. 1939).

159. Records of Cuala Meetings, 1938–39 (TCD: Cuala Archive).

160. Lily to Ruth, 12 Nov. 1938, MBY.

161. Lollie to WBY, 25 Jan. 1939, MBY.

162. Lollie to George Yeats, 10 June 1938 (TCD: Press A Cuala Arch, box 2).

163. Lollie to George Yeats, undated, ca. Aug. 1938 (TCD: Press A Cuala Arch, box 2).

164. All these letters and documents are from the Trinity College Dublin Cuala Collection (Press A Cuala Arch, box 2).

165. Lollie to George Yeats, 31 Dec. 1937 (TCD: Press A Cuala Arch, box 2).

166. Lollie to James A. Healy, 5 Apr. 1939, Stanford.

167. Lollie to James A. Healy, 5 Apr. 1939, Stanford.

168. Lily to Ruth, 1 July 1943, MBY.

169. Lily to Ruth, 17, 22 Nov. 1939, MBY.

170. Lily to Ruth, 28 Dec. 1939, MBY.

171. Lily to Ruth, 6 Jan. 1940, no. 1, ("Lollie is doing well. . . ."), MBY.

172. Lily to Ruth, 6 Jan. 1940, MBY, both letters of this date.

173. Lily to Ruth, 15 Jan. 1940; and postscript to the letter of 17 Jan., MBY.

174. Lily Yeats, *Elizabeth Corbet Yeats* (printed brochure, 4pp.), Cuala Press, 1939.

175. Lily to Ruth, 10 June 1940, MBY.

176. Lily to Ruth, 23 Nov. 1946, MBY.

177. Lily to Philip D. Sherman, 13 Mar. 1940, Brown.

178. Lily to Joseph Hone, 8 Apr. 1942, Texas. "They may be full of skeletons."

179. Miller, *Dun Emer Press,* 97.

180. Lily to Ruth, 13 Sept. 1940, MBY.

181. Lily to Ruth, 13 Sept. 1940, MBY. The book was *Florence Farr, Bernard Shaw, and W. B. Yeats,* letters edited by Clifford Bax, which appeared in November 1941 (Miller, *Dun Emer Press,* 117). Shaw also sent a gift to the Press of £300 through Lily (F. R. O'Connor to Cuala Directors, 13 Feb. 1940, and notation thereon, TCD: Press A Cuala Arch, box 2).

182. From *Reader's Catalogue for Christmas,* Cahill and Company, 1990, 51: "The distinguished and witty American critic Hugh Kenner recently shocked and delighted an audience of the Grolier Club, serious book collectors all, by asserting that the most beautiful printing in modern times is being accomplished

by a small Dublin firm called the Cuala Press." The copywriter for the advertisement should have either continued with Kenner's prose or stopped completely, for he goes on to write: "The Cuala (pronounced Coo-uh-la) Press was founded in 1903 by Susan and Elizabeth Yeats." The copywriter thus achieves three errors in a single sentence. Cuala was founded not in 1903 but 1908; Dun Emer (which the writer obviously had in mind) was founded not in 1903 but 1902; and Elizabeth Yeats, not Lily, was the founder of the Press. The pronunciation, however, is correct, so he bats .250. (Hugh Kenner is not a witty American but a witty Canadian). The mistake about the founding of Dun Emer may have come from Lily's tribute to Lollie, where the date is also given as 1903. The first book was published in 1903, but the Press was founded in 1902.

183. George Yeats carried on the work of the Press until her death in August 1968 and produced work of perhaps higher quality than Lollie because she brooked no carelessness in typesetting or inking of the kind Lollie had fallen into. When the lease on the Baggot Street building expired, she moved the business to her home at 46 Palmerston Road, Dublin, on 1 Jan. 1942. The Cuala series of books was suspended in 1945 (with the publication of Elizabeth Rivers's *Stranger in Aran),* but the hand-colored prints and greeting cards continued to be sold. After George's death her children, Anne and Michael, resumed the publication of books. In 1989 they closed down the business permanently, leaving the press itself and a collection of documents relating to the business to the library of Trinity College, Dublin.

184. Lily to Ruth, 11 Aug. 1939, MBY.

185. Lily to Ruth, 26 July 1944, MBY.

186. Lily to Ruth, 11 Feb. 1940, MBY.

187. Lily to Ruth, 22 Apr. 1940, MBY. An undated clipping about the presentation of Lollie's books to the Margaret Cunningham Library at Trinity Hall speaks of "the friendship of Elizabeth Yeats and Margaret Cunningham"; yet Miss Cunningham's name seldom appears in the family correspondence (e.g. Lily to Ruth, 2 Oct. 1934). Lollie's will specified that her books were to constitute the "Elizabeth Yeats Library." Although the will was dated 25 Mar. 1937 (before the final unpleasant years) and names Lily, Jack, Michael, and Anne, Willie is cut out completely.

188. Lily to Ruth, 17 Sept. 1940 (fragment), MBY.

189. MBY, to author, Dalkey, 1970.

190. Lily to Ruth, 19 Feb. 1940, MBY.

191. Lily to Ruth, 25 Sept. 1944, MBY.

192. Lily to Ruth, 3 May 1944, MBY. She wrote to Charles Lane-Poole (15 July 1947, MBY) on her illness: "You wonder how I can stand it. I often wonder myself. The many years standing Lolly broke me in."

193. Ruth to Lily, 21 Feb. 1944, MBY.

194. Lily died on 5 January. Susan Pollexfen Yeats, Willie, Lily, and Lollie all died in January. JBY overshot into February by three days.

195. Lily to Ruth, 18 Nov. 1930, MBY: "I hope in the next world I will be left with those of calm nerves and not egotists. I have had enough. I hope to

be surrounded by calm, comfortable angels, and no fuss. Lolly probably hopes for a circus, organs, barrels, merry-go-rounds, not literally so, but racket round her and she in the middle on a pivot." See also 14 June 1932, MBY: "I do hope in the next life I will be among people with easy nerves and tempers and I no longer ill. What a joyful time we will have."

7. Jack B. Yeats

Sources for this chapter include my own *The Yeats Family and the Pollexfens of Sligo* (1971) and *Prodigal Father* (1978), the family correspondence, and specific works mentioned below. John W. Purser's *The Literary Works of Jack B. Yeats* (Gerrards Cross: Colin Smythe, 1991), appeared too late for me to be able to make substantial use of it, but I have incorporated parts of it herein. Anne Yeats provided me with a typescript of her essay, "My Uncle Jack: Some Reminiscences." Terence de Vere White's "The Personality of Jack B. Yeats" (*Jack B. Yeats: A Centenary Gathering,* Dublin: Dolmen, 1971, pp. 22–50) is a most valuable short study of Jack Yeats on which I have relied heavily. Hilary Pyle's indispensable *Jack B. Yeats: A Biography* (London: Routledge and Kegan Paul, 1970) is the principal authority for facts and figures unless otherwise noted.

1. Eloise Bender, conversation with author, 1966.
2. Lily to Ruth, 28 Nov. 1937, MBY.
3. Lily to Ruth, 17 Mar. 1925, MBY.
4. Lily to Ruth, 17 Mar. 1925, MBY.
5. JBY to Lily, 25 Aug. 1909, MBY.
6. JBY to Jack, 16 June, 22 July 1915, ABY.
7. Ann Saddlemyer notes that Jack and Cottie "kept on friendly if somewhat distant family terms" with his brother. Once when a political issue was brewing, George Yeats wrote her husband: "Jack and Cottie are keeping themselves to themselves at the moment" (Ann Saddlemyer, in *Omnium Gatherum: Essays for Richard Ellmann,* ed. Susan Dick et al., [Gerrard's Cross, England: Colin Smythe, 1989]). I thank Dr. Saddlemyer for letting me see a typescript copy of her essay.
8. Jack to James A. Healy, 21 Feb. 1940, Stanford. He drew Lily's bookplate while she was still a girl (Lily to James A. Healy, 5 Apr. 1938, Stanford). When Willie wanted a bookplate—the one he admitted looked like a "life-belt" —it was Sturge Moore to whom he turned for the design (WBY to Lily, 18 Feb. [1915: year on original letter in hand of Allan Wade], MBY).
9. Jack to Kilham Roberts, 8 June 1934, Delaware.
10. Michael B. Yeats, talk at American Conference on Irish Studies (ACIS), Fort Lauderdale, Fla., 31 Jan. 1990.
11. Kenneth Clark, "Jack Yeats," *Horizon* 5, no. 25 (Jan. 1942): 40–42.
12. Terence de Vere White, "The Personality of Jack B. Yeats," in Roger McHugh, ed., *Jack B. Yeats: A Centenary Gathering* (Dublin: Dolmen, 1971), 38.

13. White, "The Personality of Jack B. Yeats," 38.

14. J. S. P., "Jack Yeats," in *Jack B. Yeats: A First Retrospective American Exhibition 1951–1952,* Institute of Contemporary Art, Boston, and National Academy, New York, 27 May to 21 June 1952 (Stanford).

15. Transcript from Lily Yeats's Scrapbook.

16. Pyle, *Jack B. Yeats,* 54. Pyle comments: "Home Rule would never be enough for him."

17. Joseph Hone, notes on talks with Lily Yeats, Texas.

18. Lily to JBY, 28 Sept. 1918, MBY.

19. The only two important subjects to escape JBY's pencil or brush were James Joyce and Maud Gonne, the first because the opportunity was lacking, the second because he had no desire to paint her. A sketch of a woman, full-length in a long dress, in the National Gallery of Ireland is said to be of Maud Gonne, but there is no external evidence of its identity and I find myself unable to agree with the ascription. In any event, the face in the drawing is quite small and the "portrait" portion quite insignificant. John Butler Yeats did not like Maud Gonne.

20. The numerous references to Jack in WBY's letters (47 in Wade) are to his drawings or are casual notices. Almost none suggest that the two saw much of each other.

21. See Murphy, *Prodigal Father,* passim. I have made use of my earlier book in recounting the details of Jack's life and will refer to it when appropriate. Otherwise, unless specifically noted differently, factual information for this chapter, such as dates of Jack's exhibitions, accounts of his travels and changes of residence, I take from Hilary Pyle's fine study, *Jack B. Yeats: A Biography* (London: Routledge and Kegan Paul, 1970).

22. Lily to JBY, 26 May 1917, MBY. See chap. 2, above.

23. Lily Yeats, "Odds and Ends": "Miss Jowitt."

24. Murphy, *Prodigal Father,* 120, 566.

25. Lily to Ruth, 23 Sept. 1925, MBY.

26. Marilyn Gaddis Rose, *Jack B. Yeats: Painter and Poet* (Berne: Herbert Lange; Frankfurt am Main: Peter Lang, 1972).

27. Lily to J. M. Hone, 21 Feb. 1942, Texas. Cp. "[John Butler Yeats], The Education of Jack B. Yeats," *Christian Science Monitor,* 20 Nov. 1920 (the article is unsigned). Jack, his father said, had been born "to observe and paint," and Sligo provided all he needed, "the dramatic skies, all cloud and storm and sunshine and all the life of that little town and its people, with so many 'characters,' and humourists half tragic, half comic."

28. J. M. Hone, Notes on talks with Lily Yeats, Texas. See also Lily Yeats, scrapbook, draft scrapbook, and "Odds and Ends."

29. JBY to Isaac Yeats, 25 Dec. 1917, ABY.

30. Lily to John Quinn, 15 May 1918, NYPL. Jack remembered the advantages of the bridge and continued counseling people to imitate him. "Once when I went down to Devon to stay," Lily wrote Ruth (13 Mar. 1934, MBY) "Jack the first morning said to me to go down to the Valley and lean on the bridge and spit into the river for an hour and a half, it would do me lots of good."

31. Jack to Lily, undated letter, about 1881. See illustration 75.

32. The illustrations in his father's letters are far more unfinished, done quickly and haphazardly. Jack's were elaborate, often colored. See, for example, those to John Quinn in the Foster-Murphy Collection in the New York Public Library.

33. Pyle, *Jack B. Yeats,* 13 (from which the passage from JBY is quoted).

34. Pyle, *Jack B. Yeats,* 15.

35. Jack to Sarah Purser, 9 Sept. 1888, Victoria.

36. Jack to Sarah Purser, 24 Dec. 1888, Victoria. She had sent him a cheque for "doyleys" earlier (Jack to Sarah Purser, 25 Oct. 1888, Victoria), and he had sent menus to her for her inspection (9 Sept. 1888, Victoria).

37. Jack to Sarah Purser, 17 Sept. 1888, Victoria.

38. From Lollie Yeats's diary. See Murphy, *Prodigal Father,* 164, 576. Though her listing of Jack's income is sporadic and hence probably incomplete, she records twenty-three separate payments.

39. WBY to Frederick Langbridge, 12 Oct. [1893] (Kelly, 1: 365–366).

40. WBY to Katharine Tynan [ca. 15] June [1888] (Kelly, 1: 72; Wade, *Letters of WBY,* 75).

41. Lily to John Quinn, 5 Apr. 1915, NYPL.

42. Lily to Ruth, 1 Oct. 1942, MBY.

43. Lily to Ruth, 15 Oct. 1934, MBY.

44. Jack to Lily, 16 Apr. 1900, MBY. Jack waited till his father was in Paris to write to her about the plaque. Cf. Murphy, *Prodigal Father,* 216, 587.

45. Pyle, *Jack B. Yeats,* 58.

46. WBY attributed their dispute to a difference between generations. "In old days at Bedford Park he once broke a picture glass with the back of my head, and another night, as Jack will tell you, wanted to fight me because of the quite legitimate difference between the ideas of his generation and mine. The cause of the dispute was entirely abstract and impersonal" (WBY to Lollie, 13 July [1921: year in Wade's hand on original letter.], MBY).

47. Murphy, *Prodigal Father,* 161. The events are described in WBY's *Autobiographies,* 111–95; JBY to John Quinn, ca. Apr. 1919 ("All thro' the worst part of my illness . . ."), NYPL; Lollie Yeats, Diary, 8 and 18 Sept. 1888; WBY to Lollie, 13 July 1921, MBY; and WBY, *Memoirs,* 19.

48. When Joseph Hone was preparing an edition of JBY's letters and was having trouble finding someone to write an introductory essay, Lily suggested he ask Jack (Lily to Joseph Hone, 11 Mar. 1942, Texas). As nothing further appears in the record, I suspect that Hone asked Jack in person and that Jack declined.

49. Lily to JBY, 6 Jan. 1921, MBY.

50. WBY to Katharine Tynan, 21 Apr. [1889] (Kelly, 1: 62, and note; Wade, *Letters of WBY,* 124). Jack's enlistment in an English regiment suggests that his nationalist feelings had not yet developed.

51. JBY to Cottie Yeats, 24 Nov. 1908, ABY.

52. Pyle, *Jack B. Yeats,* 37. See chap. 2, above.

53. Lily to Ruth, 8 Apr. 1947, MBY. The estimates of her seniority over Jack vary. Lily gave four years, Anne Yeats eight (conversation with author,

Dalkey, 1976). The marriage certificate lists his age as "22 years," hers as "about 25 years" (information for which I am indebted to the late Oliver Edwards).

54. JBY to Lily, 1 Aug. 1894 (Murphy, *Letters from Bedford Park,* p. 12).

55. Lily to Ruth, 8 Apr. 1947, MBY. She had made a similar remark thirty years earlier: "We have never had anything approaching a tiff with her."

56. JBY to Oliver Elton, 23 Sept. 1910, collection of Leonard Elton.

57. Lily to John Quinn, 28 [29?] Mar. 1916, NYPL.

58. JBY to Lady Gregory, 19 May 1899, NYPL. Also in Murphy, *Letters from Bedford Park,* 47.

59. Lily to John Quinn, 28 [29?] Mar. 1916, NYPL.

60. Lily to John Quinn, 16 Mar. 1916, NYPL.

61. Lily to Ruth, 7 Apr. 1925, MBY.

62. Marilyn Gaddis Rose has in fact written a most perceptive essay on Jack Yeats as a writer ("Mixed Metaphors; Jack B. Yeats's Writings," in McHugh, *Jack B. Yeats: A Centenary Gathering,* 92–106), in which she suggests that, although Jack does not succeed in blending his materials successfully in his writings as he does in his paintings, he was a precursor of the literature of "the Absurd," a man much ahead of his time. She notes that late in life he tried to downplay his own confidence in his writings: "I wish they'd forget this stuff. . . . They should remember me as a painter" (105). Nevertheless, Jack devoted so much of his time to writing and was so persistent in publishing what he wrote that one may be justified in seeing in these remarks a melancholy recognition that the world had not accepted him as a writer.

Another fine critical study of Jack's writings is John W. Purser, *The Literary Works of Jack B. Yeats.*

63. White, "The Personality of Jack B. Yeats," 45. Jack's letters in the University of Delaware Library reveal that none of his novels was a success. He had difficulty finding publishers, and his books were remaindered soon after they were written, to his great disappointment. Perhaps if they had succeeded he would not have insisted that he wanted to be remembered only as a painter.

64. Jack to M. Bourgeois (after 2 May), 1913, Stanford.

65. JBY to Lady Gregory, 27 May 1899, NYPL (Murphy, *Letters from Bedford Park,* 48). JBY liked to dabble in fortune-telling and other popular methods for not arriving at the truth. This time he made use of physical appearance. "Jack having this very short upper lip is not quick at *explaining* himself."

66. Lily to Ruth, 7 Feb. 1928, MBY.

67. Lollie to John Shell[e]y, 27 Feb. 1905, Stanford.

68. See Robin Skelton, ed., *The Collected Plays of Jack B. Yeats* (London: Secker and Warburg, 1971), 2–4.

69. Lollie to Mr. [.G. S.] Tomkinson, 25 Mar. 1926, University of Kansas.

70. Jack to John Quinn, 15 Dec. 1902, Foster-Murphy Collection, NYPL.

71. Lily to Ruth, 15 Nov. 1937 (postscript of 16 Nov.), MBY.

72. Pamela Smith soon set up shop in London at 3 Park Mansions Arcade, Knightsbridge, "for the sale of Hand-Coloured Prints and other Engravings, Drawings, and Pictures, Books, &c . . . Orders taken . . . for Christmas and

Invitation Cards, Menus, Ball Programs, Book Labels, and every kind of Decorative Printing and Hand-Colouring. Sign Boards Painted, and the Decoration of Rooms, and Illustration of Books undertaken" (Flier, Reading). Elkin Mathews Collection.

73. Jack to Kilham Roberts, 30 May 1934, Delaware.

74. See Pyle, *Jack B. Yeats*, 83–86, and *The Man from New York*, 21.

75. See Murphy, *Prodigal Father*, 267; and Lily to JBY, 27 July 1904, MBY.

76. Pyle, *Jack B. Yeats*, p. 87.

77. Lollie to Paul Lemperly 15 June 1917 (Stanford). He also designed bookplates for Lily and for Lennox Robinson, (Miller, *Dun Emer* 125; Jack to James A. Healy, 21 February 1940, Stanford). In a perceptive paper, "The Art of Resistance: Jack Yeats, W. B. Yeats and the Cuala Press Broadsides," Elizabeth Bergmann Loizeaux calls attention to Jack's sketches to accompany cards bearing his brother's poetry. WBY's lines were often sentimental, Jack's drawings hard-headed and unsparing (see *Yeats: An Annual of Critical and Textural Studies*, ed. Richard Finneran [Ann Arbor: Univ. of Michigan Press, 12, forthcoming]).

78. Advertising sheet enclosed in Lollie to Paul Lemperly 15 June 1917, Stanford.

79. Miller, *Dun Emer Press*, 120. Contributors to the *Broadsides* were not paid. (Norman Colbeck to author, Vancouver, 1980). See also Lollie to Paul Lemperly, 7 Jan. 1909, and to John Shelley, 22 Aug. 1912, Stanford.

80. Lily to John Quinn, 5 Apr. 1915, NYPL. There may have been a hiatus in his monthly donation. In a letter to Ruth on 19 Nov. 1935 (MBY), Lily mentions all her sources of income but says nothing of a monthly donation from Jack. Yet in 1946 letters to Ruth (MBY) she again mentions taking an allowance from Jack (3 Mar.) and speaks of many unexpected gifts she has received from him (23 Aug.).

81. WBY to JBY, 5 Mar. 1912, MBY.

82. Jack to James A. Healy, 11 Nov. 1948, Stanford.

83. Lollie to James A. Healy, 16 Mar. 1939, Stanford. Lollie gave the reasons for wanting him, the very reasons that persuaded Jack to decline. "He is a very calm and collected person and so will act as a deterrent on F. R. Higgins, who has a queer temper, and he could (if he accepts) attend meetings regularly. He, Mrs. WBY and myself could do most of the business. . . . My brother Jack is very sane on such matters, and *nothing* can put him out of temper, a very useful quality to have as a Director." She got the bad news soon afterward: "Jack B. Yeats will not alas! consent to be our 4th Director" (Lollie to James A. Healy, 5 Apr. 1939, Stanford).

84. JBY to Lily, 10 Apr. 1910, MBY.

85. Lily to John Quinn, 6 Dec. 1911, NYPL.

86. Jack to John Quinn, 7 Sept. 1906, Delaware.

87. Lily to Frederick A. King, 3 Jan. 1910, Stanford.

88. Lollie to John Quinn, 28 Nov. 1911, NYPL.

89. Lollie to JBY, 25 Aug. 1917, MBY.

90. Lily to John Quinn, 7 Dec. 1910, NYPL.
91. See, for example, John Quinn to Lily, 23 Apr. 1909, MBY: "As a rule I like Jack's drawings tremendously, but this one I don't like at all. The younger of the two tinkers looks like an idiot, has the wild, vacant stare and open mouth of an idiot. It seemed to me very bad. The other tinker is good. If that drawing is published with Synge's book it will hurt the book itself and you will find the hostile reviewers referring to the drawing and the idiot boy depicted in it as typical of the poems."
92. John Quinn to Lily, 5 Feb. 1911, MBY.
93. Pyle, *Jack B. Yeats,* 105.
94. Lily to John Quinn, 5 Apr. 1915, 10 Dec. 1917, NYPL. Jack's cartoon, "Willy lecturing on Speaking to the Psaltery in the Wild and Wooly West" in his letter to John Quinn of 15 Dec. 1903, NYPL (see illus. 85) is a splendid unpublished example of his wicked eye.
95. Lily to John Quinn, 5 Apr. 1915, NYPL.
96. MBY, talk, ACIS, Fort Lauderdale, Fla., 31 Jan. 1990.
97. Psychoanalytic probing is a dangerous business, more likely to lead to autobiography than to revelation. It is an enterprise from which Marxists, Freudians, Deconstructionists, New Historicists, and assorted other "-ists" and "-ians" do not shrink, but one which the person of ordinary common sense approaches with caution. The reconstructionist's pride in his work is almost always greater than the reliability of his conclusions.
98. Hilary Pyle writes briefly of Jack's illness:

> Besides the emotional strain overwork caused Yeats's illness in 1916. He had been putting out the monthly *Broadsides* for years, gathering material and colouring his illustrations singlehanded. He had been painting a good deal in oil and his work received no more attention than it had done when he started out as a watercolourist.
>
> On 18 August Lily Yeats wrote to Thomas Bodkin to tell him that Jack was recovering and that she would bring him to Greystones to introduce him to her brother and to show him Jack's pictures (119–20).

My own account of it in *Prodigal Father* is equally brief and unsatisfactory (455). Robin Skelton is even briefer: "In 1910 he moved from Devon to Dublin, where in 1916 he fell seriously ill. After his recovery he did little work for five years" (4).

John W. Purser gives a measured and sensible account of the illness:

> It has been assumed that the Easter 1916 Rising was the cause of a nervous collapse in Jack Yeats. Yeats was indeed ill at the time, but too much has been read into it and it is important to correct this impression. In fact his illness had started as early as November 1915 and in June 1916 he wrote . . . that he was "much better and getting better all the time now." . . . There is nothing to indicate that the Rising caused his illness when the evidence of his correspondence is

that he was ill before it and getting better after it. JBY and others have assumed that he was depressed . . . If it was depression, one could speculate reasonably on other grounds. For instance, at about this time any prospect of Cottie becoming pregnant would be near its end. Loneliness could have been a cause; and we know that he felt isolated in Greystones. Also the 1914–18 War depressed sales of paintings and may have left Yeats more dependent on Cottie's personal income. At the age of forty-four Yeats might have suffered a "mid-life crisis." Or he might simply have been the victim of a durable virus (*The Literary Works of Jack B. Yeats*, 3–4, 9).

99. Lily to John Quinn, 29 Nov. 1915, NYPL.
100. Lollie to John Quinn, 21 Jan. 1916, NYPL.
101. As reported to Lily by Lady Gregory, 28 Mar. Lily to John Quinn, 28 Mar. 1916, NYPL.
102. JBY to Jack, 1 Mar. 1916, ABY.
103. JBY to Lily, 2 May 1916, MBY.
104. Lily to John Quinn, 17 Jan. 1916, NYPL; Lollie to John Quinn, 21 Jan. 1916, NYPL.
105. Lily to John Quinn, 17 Jan., 3 Feb. 1916, NYPL.
106. Lily to John Quinn, 16 Mar. 1916, NYPL.
107. Lollie to John Quinn, 21 Jan. 1916, NYPL.
108. Lily to John Quinn, 28 [29?] Mar. 1916, NYPL.
109. Lily to John Quinn, 16 Mar. 1916, NYPL.
110. Michael B. Yeats, talk, ACIS, Fort Lauderdale, Fla., 31 Jan. 1990.
111. JBY to Jack, 18 July 1916, ABY. Also JBY to Lady Gregory, 20 Oct. 1917, NYPL: [After receiving a letter from Jack with a sketch]: "His letters used to be full of sketches. His wife *can* write most amusing letters—but latterly her letters were void of any interest, which I interpreted to mean that Jack was not himself."
112. Lily to John Quinn, 17 Apr. 1917, NYPL.
113. Lollie to Elkin Mathews, 26 Mar. 1917, Reading, Elkin Mathews Collection.
114. For instance, in the *Times Literary Supplement,* 19 Apr. 1991, p. 18, Timothy Hyman writes: ". . . after a mid-life breakdown (coinciding with the Easter Rising). . . ."
115. Jack disliked the politicians connected, as he saw it, with those who favored England, consciously or unconsciously. During his last years at Portobello House, the *Irish Times* published a series of "profiles" of Irish political leaders. One was of William Cosgrave, of whose views Jack disapproved. When his nephew Michael visited him, Jack asked, "Did you see the piece on Cosgrave?", then added bitterly, "Next thing you know they'll be doing one on Sadleir and Keogh" (MBY, to author, conversation, Pompano Beach, Fla. 1990). The latter two were Irishmen of the nineteenth century widely regarded by Irish nationalists as "traitors" to their country.
116. Lily to John Quinn, 29 Nov. 1915, NYPL.

117. White, "The Personality of Jack B. Yeats," 43.

118. See Bair, *Samuel Beckett,* 121–22: "It had often been noted among Irish writers and critics how strong the strain of metaphysical irony is in Jack B. Yeats, predating Beckett by some twenty-odd years. Yeats's humor, tinged with irony and enigma, and the ability of his characters to persevere with pragmatic optimism in the face of often grim distresses have been suggested as possible precursors of Beckett's postwar fiction. What these writers and critics fail to consider, however, is the strong strain of moral affirmation that runs through Yeats's writing and is its strongest characteristic. The popularity of Yeats's writing in Dublin was significantly hindered by his constant head-on confrontation with the ugly side of life as his readers preferred to see the portrayal of sickness, suffering and despair for what it meant to him—the necessary foil for affirmations of life's goodness. Beckett was aware of the blackness in Yeats's writing, but he realized what it was and what purpose it served, and when he wrote about Yeats, he praised him."

119. Jack to James A. Healy, 1 Jan. 1940, Stanford. Cp. Lily to Joseph Hone, 28 Apr. 1942, Texas: "Jack says that if he said what he feels about the war in the language he thinks of it in no one would speak to him again."

120. Typed page, Lennox Robinson Papers, folder 26, Delaware.

121. Hilary Pyle quotes Jack's letter to John Quinn of 7 Sept. 1906, NYPL: "I believe that all fine pictures, and fine literature too, to be fine must have some of the living ginger of Life in them." Almost a half century later, in writing to Van Wyck Brooks to thank him for Brooks's *John Sloan: A Painter's Life,* he made use of the same term: "Your book is the best biography I have read of any painter. All you show of the give and take 'gentle words' which seemed to always be so necessary to the living ginger of the relationship of my father and Sloan, rings well and strongly" (30 Mar. 1955, estate of Van Wyck Brooks).

122. Lily to John Quinn, 17 Jan. 1916, NYPL.

123. Lily to John Quinn, 20 Sept. 1917, NYPL: "Jack has taken a house in Dublin, 61 Marlborough Road, Donnybrook. They move there next week." On 25 October she told Quinn they had moved in.

124. About the telephone Anne Yeats comments: "In fact when he did feel ill one night he insisted on waiting until eight in the morning before ringing the doctor so as not to inconvenience the poor man!" ("My Uncle Jack: Some Reminiscences," typescript).

125. JBY to Cottie Yeats, 24 Nov. 1908, ABY.

126. Norman Colbeck, conversation with author, Vancouver, 30 Sept. 1980. Mr. Colbeck was the Curator of the Colbeck Collection at the University of British Columbia in Vancouver, which includes extensive holdings in Anglo-Irish Literature, among them Dun Emer and Cuala publications.

127. Lollie Yeats to Philip Darrell Sherman, 13 July 1938, Brown.

128. Lily to Ruth, 1 Oct. 1925, MBY. "He was never very approachable, now he is very unapproachable. He has to rest in the afternoon and must protect himself from callers. He could get no peace."

129. Bair, *Samuel Beckett,* p. 121. She adds: "Beckett actually met W. B. Yeats only once, during a brief encounter in Killiney, where he was disgusted

with the way W. B. Yeats simpered over his wife and made an inordinate fuss with his children." She gives as source Beckett's letter to H. O. White, 15 Apr. 1947, TCD.

130. JBY to Lady Gregory, 16 June 1899, NYPL. (Murphy, *Letters from Bedford Park*, 50–51). "Everyone likes him," Lily told Quinn (14 Feb. 1918, NYPL). To Ruth she wrote, "People love Jack" (23 July 1928, MBY), and "Jack never did a mean thing in his life, has no enemies." (5 Aug. 1946, MBY).

131. J. S. P., "Jack Yeats," in *First Retrospective.*

132. Lily to Ruth, 5 Aug. 1946, MBY.

133. Lily to John Quinn, 14 Feb. 1918, NYPL.

134. Lily to John Quinn, 15 May 1918, NYPL.

135. Lily to John Quinn, 16 Mar. 1916, NYPL.

136. Lily to Ruth, 27 Apr. 1937, MBY.

137. Lily to WBY, 27 Dec. 1938, MBY. Lily thought Jack's nephew Michael resembled him in his silences, his solitary trips, his imperturbability. Other references to the resemblance appear in Lily to Ruth: 10 Aug. 1936, 27 Apr. 1937, 16 Jan. 1938, 23 July 1938, 27 Mar. 1942, and 14 Apr. 1942, MBY.

138. Lily to Ruth, 14 Dec. 1946, MBY.

139. Anne Yeats, conversation with author, Dalkey, 1975.

140. Elizabeth Curran Solterer, conversation with author, 1987.

141. Anne Yeats, "My Uncle Jack: Some Reminiscences."

142. Lily to Ruth, 25 Dec. 1934, MBY.

143. Lily to Ruth, 15 Mar. 1935, MBY.

144. Lily to Ruth, 27 Dec. 1937, MBY.

145. Lily to Ruth, 1 July 1930, MBY.

146. Lily to John Quinn, 5 Apr. 1915, NYPL.

147. Lily to JBY, 14 June 1921, MBY.

148. Lily to Ruth, 20 Mar. 1928, MBY.

149. Lily to Ruth, 29 July 1925, MBY. The picture was "The Pilot Boat," showing "the boat at Rosses Point going out at dawn."

150. Lily to Ruth, 14 Feb. 1933, MBY.

151. Lily to Ruth, 14 Sept. 1936, MBY.

152. Lily to Ruth, 28 Dec. 1939, 6 May 1941, MBY. "Helen Curran generally tells me," she told Ruth (11 Jan. 1942, MBY).

153. Lily to Ruth, 11 Jan. 1942, MBY.

154. Lily to Ruth, 28 May 1941, MBY.

155. The story of the New York pictures is revealed in Jack's letters to James A. Healy and to the lawyer John Caldwell Myers; 8 June 1938 (two letters: 16 Aug. 1938 and 10 July 1939, Stanford). The exhibition and sale of Jack's thirty-seven paintings was held at the Ferargil Galleries, 63 East 57th Street, New York, from 29 Feb. to 14 Mar. 1932. I take the spelling from a contemporary handbill giving the titles of the paintings (collection of author). Hilary Pyle gives "Ferragail" as the spelling and Jack in his correspondence "Faragil."

156. The details of the dispute are found in the collection of Jack's letters

in the University of Delaware Library. Most are to Kilham Robarts, secretary of the Incorporated Society of Authors, Playwrights, and Composers; some to and from George Brett and both the English and American branches as corporations.

157. Jack to Kilham Roberts, 21 May 1941, Delaware.

158. The matter of Jack's royalties from Hone is also dealt with in the letters at the University of Delaware. I thank L. Rebecca Johnson for her kindness in providing me with copies and Elizabeth Bergmann Loizeaux for calling them to my attention.

159. Michael B. Yeats, talk, ACIS, Fort Lauderdale, Fla., 31 Jan. 1990.

160. Lily to Ruth, 26 Oct. 1936, MBY.

161. Lily to Joseph M. Hone, 19 May 1937, Texas.

162. J. S. P., "Jack Yeats," in *First Retrospective.*

163. Lollie to Prof. Alfred De Lurey, 20 Nov. 1930, Toronto.

164. Lollie to JBY, 25 August 1917, MBY.

165. Lollie to JBY, 2 Sept. 1917, MBY. "I tell people too much and Jack too little." She and WBY were alike in more ways than one. "Willie tells *almost all* his own affairs, but generally with great apparent secrecy, and then one finds he has told ever so many people the same thing 'as a secret.' " Lily, the best letter writer of all, did not escape Lollie's scalpel. "Lily makes a witty story of it all, which is so unlike the real truth that no one can accuse her of telling anything at all."

166. WBY to Lily, 1 Jan. [1916], MBY.

167. Lily to Ruth, 5 May 1937, MBY.

168. Lily to Ruth, 10 Mar. 1936, MBY.

169. Lily to Ruth, 1 Jan. 1939, MBY.

170. Lily to Ruth, 31 Dec. 1940, MBY.

171. Lily to John Quinn, 16 Feb. 1917, NYPL.

172. Jack lost four paintings (Lily to Lollie, 9 May; Lily to JBY, 12 May 1916, MBY). JBY's sketch showed Horace Plunkett, Edward Martyn, and WBY together. It was in the offices of Maunsel and Company on Middle Abbey Street (Murphy, *Prodigal Father,* 453, 632).

173. Lily to Ruth, 17 Feb. 1925, MBY.

174. White, "The Personality of Jack B. Yeats," 40.

175. Lollie to JBY, 31 Mar 1918, MBY. In the exhibition of spring 1918, he sold pictures to Mr. William Cadbury, the Lord Chancellor, Oliver St. John Gogarty, and a rich American living in Bray.

176. Lily to Ruth, 15 Oct. 1925, MBY.

177. Lily to Ruth, 19 Feb. 1929, 7 Oct. 1929, 22 July 1930, MBY.

178. Lollie to JBY, 16 Feb. 1921, MBY.

179. Lily to Ruth, 15 Dec. 1930, MBY. Lily had earlier noted to Ruth (7 Oct. 1929): "Dublin has no good picture of his."

180. Lily to Ruth, 15 Dec. 1930, MBY.

181. Lily to Ruth, 1 Oct. 1942, MBY.

182. Lily to Ruth, 2 Nov. 1946, MBY.

183. Jack to WBY, 31 Oct. 1925 (from Pyle, *Jack B. Yeats,* 124).

184. Lily to JBY, 27 July 1904, 30 Aug. 1920, MBY.

185. Lily to Ruth, 7 Oct. 1929, MBY.

186. Lily to Ruth, 6 May 1941, 28 June 1948, MBY.

187. Lily to Ruth, 7 Dec. 1910, MBY. The show is described as a "private view." Since Commissioner William A. Bailey, a Dubliner, and Lollie are both named as being present and as the letter is written from Dublin it is clear that the exhibition was held in Dublin, too. In Hilary Pyle's list of Jack's exhibitions, none is listed for December 1910. She gives the London showing of 12 Oct.–20 Nov. 1910 (209) and the New York and London shows (undated) of 1910, followed by the Belfast Exhibition of 1911. The Royal Hibernian Academy Exhibition of 1911 is listed also (210), but this does not appear to be a private show of Jack's.

188. Lily to Ruth, 15 Oct. 1925, MBY.

189. Lily to Ruth, 8 Apr. 1930, MBY. This exhibition of Jack's paintings also does not appear in Hilary Pyle's list.

190. Lily to Ruth, 30 Mar. 1932, MBY.

191. Elizabeth Curran Solterer, conversation with author, 1987.

192. Lily to Ruth, 15 Oct. 1934, MBY.

193. WBY to Lady Gregory, 19 May [postmarked "1929"] (Wade, *Letters of WBY,* 764).

194. Copying geometrical forms, even if representational, were also not acceptable under JBY's formula. In late 1921 he wrote "an article against Cubists, the whole crowd" (JBY to Jack, 2 May 1921, ABY).

195. John Quinn to WBY, 19 Nov. 1923, postscript of 23 Nov. (Alan Himber, ed., *The Letters of John Quinn to William Butler Yeats,* [Ann Arbor: UMI Research Press, 1983], 292).

196. JBY to Padraic Colum, 12 Aug. 1921, NYPL. The two other necessaries he insists upon are "creation . . . the spirit issuing from the heavy mould of the portraiture," and "the mind, the point of view, of the artist himself."

197. Kenneth Clark, "Jack Yeats," 40.

198. White, "The Personality of Jack B. Yeats," 22–50. I have perforce quoted but little from this essay, but it is required reading for anyone who wishes to know Jack Yeats. Hilary Pyle, who never knew Jack Yeats, has given us in her biography a complete account of Jack Yeats's life and of his art; it too is required reading. What she says about Jack and what I (who also did not know Jack Yeats) have said about him here confirm the late Terence White's splendid essay, which I think comes closer to capturing the spirit of his personality than any other work written by one who knew him.

199. Lily to JBY, 30 May 1921, MBY.

200. Lily to Ruth, 22 Jan., 12 Mar., 31 Mar. 1941, MBY.

201. White, "The Personality of Jack B. Yeats," 34.

202. Lily to Ruth, 27 Mar. 1942, MBY.

203. Lily to Ruth, 1 Oct. 1942, MBY.

204. Elizabeth Curran Solterer, conversation with author, 1987.

205. White, "The Personality of Jack B. Yeats," 48–49.

206. Bair, *Samuel Beckett,* 201–202.

207. Elizabeth Solterer, conversation with author, 1987.

208. Lily to Ruth, 5 Aug. 1946, MBY.
209. White, "The Personality of Jack B. Yeats," 43.
210. JBY to Lily, 22 Nov. 1917 (quoted in Murphy, *Prodigal Father,* 585).
211. Lily to Ruth, 7 Apr. 1925, MBY. She echoed the words her father had written years earlier to Oliver Elton (23 Sept. 1910, collection of Leonard Elton): "She is full of good qualities and exceedingly clever artistically, and very few give her credit for it, and she is too timid to claim her rights."
212. Lily to Ruth, 23 Apr. 1929, MBY.
213. Lily to Ruth, 17 Dec. 1929, MBY.
214. Lily to Ruth, 27 Jan. 1932, MBY.
215. See Lily to Ruth, 12 Mar. 1947; MBY: "Cottie ought to have a good maid. Jack, as you know, is the nicest person in the world and never grumbles. Where they are now it is impossible to have anyone living in the house."
216. Lollie to John Quinn, 5 July 1916, NYPL. Lily to Ruth, 19 Mar. 1934, MBY: "I am glad Cottie wrote to you, an honour as she is very bad at letter-writing, but quite good when she does do it."
217. Lily to Ruth, 12 Oct. 1936, MBY. George Yeats was in fact so different from her sister-in-law, gregarious and outgoing, that they never disagreed, each keeping to her own world yet comfortable with the other. Lollie thought Cottie might resent George and noted how when they first met on 10 Mar. 1918 she thought Cottie "self-conscious," "nervous and fussed up." But "George was so nice Cottie [was] soon quite at ease, and not afraid the new sister-in-law would try to supplant her with all of us" (Lollie to JBY, 13 Mar. 1918, MBY).
218. Lily to JBY, 14 June 1921, MBY.
219. Lily to Ruth, 12 Mar. 1947, MBY.
220. Lily to Ruth, 20 Mar. 1947, MBY.
221. Lily to Ruth, 12 Mar. 1947, MBY.
222. Lily to Ruth, 8 Apr. 1947, MBY.
223. Lily to Ruth, 17 Apr. 1947, MBY.
224. Lily to Ruth, 29 Apr. 1947, MBY.
225. Lily to Ruth, 8 Apr. 1947, MBY.
226. Lily to Ruth, 3 May 1947, MBY.
227. Among other honors was the Retrospective Exhibition of 1951–1952 in Boston and New York. Among lenders of pictures to it were the Aberdeen Art Gallery, the Capuchin Annual Office, Dublin Municipal Gallery of Modern Art and National Gallery of Ireland, the Phillips Collection, Washington, the Tel Aviv Museum, and the Toledo Museum of Art; and, of private owners: Lady Christabel Aberconway, Lady Cusack Smyth, Bryan Guinness (Lord Moyne), Z. Lewinter-Frankl (of Belfast), William McQuilty, Esq., Richard McGonigal, Marchioness of Normanby (London); Mrs. A. V. Ryan, Mrs. Mabel Spiro, Mr. and Mrs. Martin Lederman, Mr. and Mrs. F. L. Vickerman, Victor Waddington, Burgess Meredith, and Anita Loos. Jack himself lent eleven (Stanford).
228. Lily to Ruth, 19 Dec. 1947, MBY.
229. Lily to John Quinn, 16 Mar. 1916, NYPL.

230. JBY to Rosa Butt, 4 Dec. 1907 [date from postmark], letter no. 51, Bodleian. I cannot resist the temptation to close this essay with the fine and compassionate words with which John W. Purser closes his book:

> Yeats has also seemed to me a good companion over these years, but a tricky one; and the subtlety and complexity of his imagery frequently leave one having to be content with the sensation of little waves washing the sand away from under one's bare feet. It is a pleasurable sensation: and it is also nice to feel assured that the sad day, when all that is worth knowing about Jack Yeats is known, will never arrive. His was a fascinating and teasing mind which started up many hares; but he was a gentle man and would sooner have raised his hat to them as they disappeared over his horizon, than track them down: and though I have merely stood in the next field watching them race by, I hope I have started a few myself that will survive to enjoy their own freedom (197).

8. John Butler Yeats and Rosa Butt

References to JBY's letters to Rosa Butt are to the collection in the Bodleian Library, Oxford, where they are catalogued as MS Eng. Lett: e.87: [1883] 1897–1903; e.88: 1905–1907; c.194: 1908–1912; c.195: 1913–1921.

Unless noted otherwise, information about the Butt family is from Terence de Vere White, *The Road of Excess* (Dublin: Browne and Nolan, [1945]), appendix, 381. Isaac Butt (1813–1879), married Elizabeth Swanzy (died 1897, aged 89).

Children:

1. Robert Berkeley Butt, Lieut., R.A., afterwards Barrister-at-Law, born 9 Nov. 1837, died unmarried 27 May 1896.
2. Henry Butt, born 14 Apr. 1840, died young.
3. George Butt, born 8 Oct. 1842; died 26 Jan. 1879; married, 21 Sept. 1875, Annie Frances, daughter of Robert Ball.
   i. George Berkeley Butt, Lieut. Indian Medical Service, born 3 July 1878; died 28 Aug. 1902.
   ii. Kathleen Mary Butt, married, 9 Oct. 1903, her first cousin William Valentine Ball, O.B.E., King's Remembrancer and Master of the Supreme Court, son of Robert Ball the astronomer.
4. Berkeley Isaac Butt, 1847–1861.
5. Rosa Butt, died 1926, aged 88 [born Dec. 1838 (from JBY to Rosa Butt, 14 June 1900), died May 1926 (from Lily Yeats to Jeanne Robert Foster, 17 May 1926, (Foster-Murphy Collection, NYPL].
6. Elizabeth Butt, married Thomas Colquhoun, Solicitor; died 1925.
7. Amie [*sic*] Butt, died 1920.
8. Mary Butt, died 1864.

1. The evidence is inconclusive. In JBY to Rosa, [17 Sept. 1907 (date in alien hand?), no. 44], he writes: "Lily knows you know." Earlier he had written her: "When I told Lilly about Amy, she said she would give me her blessing" (JBY to Rosa, n.d. ["There is no fear. . . ."], no. 24). The ambiguity of the pronouns makes interpretation difficult. A broad reading of the two passages might suggest that JBY had confided to Lily about his love for Rosa, that Lily had assured him Rosa's sister Amy would view his suit favorably, and that JBY had told Rosa of Lily's knowledge and that Lily knew he had told her. Since the passages could just as well refer to another subject altogether, it is unwise to make pronouncements. Aside from these two passages, there is nothing in the whole mountain of Yeats documents to suggest that anyone in the family knew of the affair.

2. The letters end with no. 213, but some fragments have survived that add to the total.

3. Mary Swanzy, conversation with author, London, 1968. In a footnote to *Prodigal Father* (1978), I wrote: "A rumor circulated in Dublin for years that the widowed JBY proposed marriage to Rosa Butt and was rejected. On the face of it there is nothing unreasonable or unlikely about the story, but no evidence of it has surfaced. JBY's letters to Miss Butt are in the Bodleian Library at Oxford under lock and key till 1979. In them perhaps may lie the truth about the rumor" (588n). I have Terence de Vere White to thank for having told me of the rumor and given me Miss Swanzy's name, and I thank Michael Yeats for giving me access to the letters on their liberation in 1979. I thank also Cornelia Stark, Keeper of Western Manuscripts at the Bodleian, for her help in arranging for the reproduction of the letters. Dr. John Kelly of St. John's College, Oxford, and Professor Phillip L. Marcus of Cornell University also used their good offices in helping me to track down the letters.

4. R. W. Hunt, Keeper of Western MSS, to author, 5 May 1966.

5. See, e.g., JBY to Rosa, 16 Aug. 1917, no. 184.

6. See, e.g., JBY to Rosa, 9 Jan. 1915, no. 149, and 16 Aug. 1917, no. 185, JBY.

7. JBY to WBY, 30 May 1921 (*JBY: Letters*, 277–78, where Hone has hopelessly garbled the transcription). The passage in the original reads: "When she was Miss Elgee, Mrs. Butt found her with her husband when the circumstances were not doubtful, and told my mother about it," MBY. See also Murphy, *Prodigal Father*, 31, 551.

8. Olive Purser, conversation with author, Hotel Ivanhoe, Dublin, 1966.

9. John Butler Yeats was related to the Reverend William Gibbon, pastor of Taney's Church in Dundrum, which Lily attended. Stopford Brooke, the Anglo-Saxon scholar, was another distant relative, and the Corbets and Armstrongs threw out tentacles to many other ascendancy families. Isaac Butt's son George was married to Annie Ball, daughter of Robert Ball the astronomer, whose sister was the first wife of JBY's old friend John Todhunter, and George's daughter Kathleen married her cousin William Ball, another son of Robert's. The relationships resembled a spider's web, and a Dublin Anglo-Irishman touching one strand of it caused the others to vibrate.

10. JBY to Rosa, Dec. 1900, ("Yesterday I was . . .") no. 6. Some years later JBY, in a rare burst of confidence, told Edwin Ellis that he had fallen in love with a young woman in a "blameless," "delightful," and "beautiful" affair, and its unrequited ending affected him for long afterward (Edwin Ellis to JBY, 16 Feb. 1870, MBY). Tempting though it is to identify the young lady as Rosa Butt, the evidence of his later letters to her makes clear that she was not the one. See also Murphy, *Prodigal Father*, 552, where I have noted that one of JBY's short pieces of fiction, "John Whiteside," appears to be a disguised account of the affair. JBY had also experienced "puppy love" for a cousin when he was thirteen (JBY to WBY, 12 Mar. 1918, MBY).

11. JBY to Rosa, Dec. 1900 ("Yesterday I was . . ."), no. 6.
12. JBY to Rosa, 14 Oct. 1912, no. 120.
13. JBY to Rosa, 20 Oct. 1913, no. 131.
14. JBY to Rosa, 18 Mar. 1921, no. 211.
15. JBY to Rosa, 29 Nov. 1915, no. 155.
16. JBY to Rosa, 17 Nov. 1910, no. 112. He had impulsively mentioned the affair to Rosa in a letter of 20 Oct. 1910 (no. 110): "There was another woman *but of her you must never ask me.* It was over many years ago and happened when I was very young." He refused to elaborate: "It would be dishonourable and treacherous in me to tell you more, and it would be just as bad for you to ask me" (17 Nov. 1910). (See also letters, week of 17 July 1917, no. 182; 20 Oct. 1910, no. 110; 17 Nov. 1910, no. 112).
17. For an account of Susan Pollexfen Yeats, full except for what appears here, see Murphy, *Yeats Family and the Pollexfens* and *Prodigal Father,* and the earlier chapters herein.
18. JBY to Rosa, 29 July 1897, no. 1.
19. JBY to Rosa, 20 Dec. 1899, no. 2.
20. JBY to Rosa, 11 July 1900, no. 4.
21. JBY to Rosa, 11 July 1900, no. 4.
22. JBY to Rosa, Nov. [1900] ("Many thanks for . . ."), no. 5.
23. JBY to Rosa, Dec. 1900 ("Yesterday I was . . ."), no. 6.
24. JBY to Rosa, 1 Dec. 1900, no. 6.
25. JBY to Sarah Purser, 24 Dec. 1900, MBY.
26. JBY to Rosa, 7 Nov. 1909, no. 93.
27. JBY to Rosa, n.d. ("More letters . . ."), no. 18.
28. JBY to Rosa, 13 Apr. 1910, no. 100.
29. JBY to Rosa, n.d. ("No commissions . . ."), no. 11.
30. JBY to Rosa, [11 Aug. 1903], no. 19.
31. JBY to Rosa, n.d. (beginning of letter illegible), no. 25.
32. JBY to Rosa, 15 Oct. 1917, no. 185.
33. JBY to Rosa, 15 Oct. 1917, no. 185.
34. JBY to Rosa, 13 Nov. 1917, no. 186.
35. JBY to Rosa, n.d. ("At last a letter . . ."), no. 191.
36. JBY to Rosa, 8 May 1914, no. 138.
37. JBY to Rosa, 24 July 1918, no. 190.

38. JBY to Rosa, [11 May 1902], no. 15.
39. JBY to Rosa, n.d. ("Your last letter . . ."), no. 17.
40. JBY to Rosa, n.d. ("I know your talents . . ."), no. 45.
41. JBY to Rosa, n.d. [probably between Jan. and Mar. 1906], no. 57.
42. JBY to Rosa, 12 Mar. 1910, no. 99.
43. JBY to Rosa, n.d. [probably between Jan. and Mar. 1906] ("I am bitterly disappointed . . ."), no. 57.
44. JBY to Rosa, n.d. [probably between Jan. and Mar. 1906] ("I am bitterly disappointed . . ."), no. 57.
45. The division of people into "real" and "artificial" personalities was one JBY was fond of; he spoke of the "real" Edward Dowden and the "false" one, of the "real" and "unreal" George Russell. George Moore, the Irish novelist, was one of the few people who was integrated, always himself.
46. JBY to Rosa, 27 May 1912, no. 105.
47. JBY to Rosa, 26 Aug. 1910, no. 109.
48. JBY to Rosa, 16 Oct. 1912, no. 121.
49. JBY to Rosa, 16 Oct. 1912, no. 122.
50. JBY to Rosa, 17 Oct. 1914, no. 143.
51. JBY to Rosa, 20 Oct. 1910, no. 110.
52. JBY to Rosa, 10 June 1914, no. 140.
53. JBY to Rosa, 20 May 1915, no. 155.
54. Beatrice Lady Glenavy (née Elvery), conversation with author, Dublin, 1966. For a fuller account of the talk, see Murphy, *Prodigal Father*, 295, 601.
55. John Butler Yeats, "Watts and the Method of Art," *Essays Irish and American* (Dublin: Talbot; London: T. Fisher Unwin, 1918), 79–86.
56. JBY to Rosa, 21 Nov. 1913, no. 133.
57. JBY to Rosa, 26 Jan. 1914, no. 134.
58. JBY to Rosa, 21 Feb. 1914, no. 135.
59. JBY to Rosa, 21 Feb. 1914, no. 135.
60. JBY to Rosa, 17 Oct. 1914, no. 143.
61. JBY to Rosa, 17 Oct. 1914, no. 143.
62. JBY to Rosa, 19 Oct. 1914, no. 144.
63. JBY to Rosa, 20 Apr. 1915, no. 154.
64. JBY to Rosa, 20 May 1915, no. 155.
65. JBY to Rosa, 20 May 1915, no. 155.
66. JBY to Rosa, 11 Nov. 1914, no. 146.
67. JBY to Rosa, 22 Dec. 1914, no. 148.
68. JBY to Rosa, 13 Jan. 1913, no. 127.
69. JBY to Rosa, 9 Jan. 1915, no. 149.
70. JBY to Rosa, 26 Jan. 1915, no. 150.
71. JBY to Rosa, 18 Feb. 1915, no. 151.
72. JBY to Rosa, 23 Mar. 1915, no. 153.
73. JBY to Rosa, 29 Nov. 1915, no. 161.
74. JBY to Rosa, 26 Aug. 1910, no. 109.
75. JBY to Rosa, 29 Nov. 1915, no. 161.

76. JBY to Rosa, 1 Aug. 1917, no. 183; and 30 Dec. 1916, no. 175.

77. JBY to Rosa, 3 May 1916, no. 169.

78. JBY to Rosa, 1 Feb. 1916, no. 166.

79. JBY to Rosa, 16 Feb. 1916, no. 167.

80. JBY to Rosa, 5 Jan. 1918, no. 187.

81. JBY to Rosa, 3 May 1916, no. 169.

82. JBY to Rosa, 17 Feb. 1917, no. 178.

83. T. S. Eliot, "The Letters of J. B. Yeats," *Egoist,* June 1917, 89–90. See Murphy, *Prodigal Father,* 462–63, 634.

84. JBY to Rosa, 16 Aug. 1917, no. 184.

85. JBY to Rosa, 15 Oct. 1917, no. 185.

86. See chap. 7, above.

87. JBY to Rosa, n.d. [ca. 1903] ("More letters . . ."), no. 18.

88. JBY to Rosa, 3 Oct. 1918, no. 192.

89. JBY to Rosa, 23 Nov. 1908, no. 75.

90. JBY to Rosa, 13 Apr. 1910, no. 100.

91. JBY to Rosa, week of 21 July 1917, no. 182.

92. JBY to Rosa, 20 May 1915, no. 155.

93. JBY to Rosa, 3 Oct. 1918, no. 192.

94. JBY to Rosa, 29 Nov. 1915, no. 161.

95. JBY to Rosa, week of 21 July 1917, no. 182.

96. JBY to WBY, 15 Jan. 1916, MBY. See Murphy, *Prodigal Father,* 216, and 586 n. 100, where part of his letter to Lady Gregory, 30 Sept. 1919 is quoted: "The man and the woman become bound by the interchange of gifts—like great chiefs—the man's strength for the woman's subtlety, his slowness quickened by her rapidity, his longing helped by her fancy that seems to possess what he desires. He is self-centered, she is sympathetic. And so it goes on, each keeping the other alive. *Love . . . is really the highest form of companionship.*"

97. JBY to Rosa, 19 Feb. 1908, no. 58.

98. JBY to Rosa, 22 Dec. 1914, no. 148.

99. JBY to Rosa, 25 May 1908, no. 62.

100. JBY to Rosa, 1 Feb. 1910, no. 97.

101. JBY to Rosa, 11 Apr. 1917, no. 180. "We are at last in the war, and I find that the President's admirers who loved him because 'he kept us out of the war' are now enthusiastic for him because he has brought us into the war. Two years ago I said and so did many of us that he was drifting straight for war. One always drifts —drifting. He drifted into war with Mexico and then drifted out of it. It is his special hobby. He has a genius for it."

102. JBY to Rosa, 11 Apr. 1917, no. 180.

103. JBY to Rosa, 3 July 1919, no. 197.

104. JBY to Rosa, 4 Oct. 1920, no. 205.

105. JBY to Rosa, n.d. ("Your last letter . . ."), no. 17.

106. JBY to Rosa, [6 Mar. 1906, from postmark; arrived in London 7 Mar.], no. 29.

107. JBY to Rosa, 30 Dec. 1915, no. 164.

108. JBY to Rosa, 27 Aug. 1907, no. 39.
109. JBY to Rosa, 11 Jan. 1916, no. 165.
110. JBY to Rosa, 11 July 1908, no. 64.
111. JBY to Rosa, Sunday [27 Apr. 1902, postmarked 7 AM Apr. 28 (Monday)], no. 13
112. JBY to Rosa, 17 July 1908, no. 65.
113. JBY to Rosa, 17 July 1908, no. 65.
114. JBY to Rosa, 13 Jan. 1913, no. 126.
115. JBY to Rosa, 3 July 1919, no. 197.
116. JBY to Rosa, 18 Sept. 1907, no. 45.
117. JBY to Rosa, n.d. [ca. fall 1907] ("I know your talents . . ."), no. 46.
118. JBY to Rosa, n.d., postmarked Oct 25 (?) [1907] ("Your letter today . . ."), no. 48.
119. JBY to Rosa, n.d. ("I thought perhaps . . ."), no. 13.
120. JBY to Rosa, 20 May 1905, no. 26. Maud had replied in court, "I told you before I married about that child." JBY informed Rosa, that some people in Dublin knew ("very unfortunately," in his view) that "she used to live with Millevoye, the Socialist Deputy."
121. JBY to Rosa, 19 May 1918, no. 189.
122. JBY to Rosa, 9 Mar. 1919, no. 195.
123. JBY to Rosa, 16 July 1920, no. 202.
124. JBY to Rosa, 23 June 1920, no. 201.
125. JBY to Rosa, 20 Dec. 1919, no. 199.
126. JBY to Rosa, 23 June 1920, no. 201.
127. JBY to Rosa, 2 Nov. 1920, no. 206.
128. JBY to Rosa, n.d. ("I like your letter . . ."), no. 208.
129. JBY to Rosa, 10 Jan. 1921, no. 209.

Epilogue

1. Lily to Ruth, 11 Oct. 1938, MBX.
2. JBY, "Memoirs." Hone (*W. B. Yeats: 1865–1939*, 41) mentions the incident without identifying Miss Purser.
3. JBY to Isaac Yeats, 15 July 1919 (quoted as epigraph to chap. 2), ABY.
4. JBY to Lady Gregory, 20 Oct. 1917, NYPL.
5. JBY to Jack, 12 July 1981, ABY.
6. JBY to WBY, 24 Mar. 1909, MBY.
7. JBY to Lily, 15 Sept. 1916, MBY.
8. Lily Yeats, "Scrapbook," 'Grandfather Yeats.'
9. Lily Yeats, "Odds and Ends," 'Death of Grandfather Yeats.'
10. JBY, "Memoirs."
11. JBY to WBY, 24 Mar. 1909, MBY.
12. JBY to Edward Dowden, 8 Jan. 1884, MBY.

13. Lily to Ruth, 15 April 1935, MBY.

14. April 23, 1991 was proclaimed "John Butler Yeats Day" in the City of New York by Mayor David Dinkins, and in Manhattan by Borough President Ruth Messinger. A special program honoring JBY was held at the Harvard Club, across the street from a building where JBY had lived and where the bronze plaque is affixed.

15. JBY to Isaac Yeats, 4 May 1920 ("Willie dined her last night . . ."), ABY.

16. JBY to WBY, 18 Sept. 1916, MBY.

17. JBY to Isaac Yeats, 4 May 1920 ("Willie dined her last night . . ."), ABY.

Appendix: The Yeatses and the Occult

Much of the material in this essay has already been published in George Mills Harper, ed., *Yeats and the Occult* (Toronto: Macmillan of Canada, 1975), in the chapter "Psychic Daughter, Mystic Son, Sceptic Father," 11–26. The present chapter supplements and expands on what is written there.

1. See George Mills Harper, *Yeats's Golden Dawn* (London: Macmillan, 1974), and *W. B. Yeats and W. T. Horton: The Record of a Friendship* (London: Macmillan, 1980); and George Mills Harper, ed., *Yeats's 'Vision' Papers,* 3 vols., (London: Macmillan; Iowa City: Univ. of Iowa Press, 1992).

2. See Helen Vendler, *Yeats's "Vision" and the Later Plays* (Cambridge, Mass.: Harvard Univ. Press, 1963); and George Mills Harper, *The Making of Yeats's "A Vision": A Study of the Automatic Script,* 2 vols. (Carbondale and Edwardsville: Southern Illinois Univ. Press, 1987); and George Mills Harper, ed., *A Critical Edition of Yeats's "A Vision" (1925)* (London: Macmillan, 1978).

3. Miller, *Dun Emer Press,* 62.

4. There is nothing unusual about the phenomenon. Buildings—even in sophisticated New York City, regarded as the capital of materialism—routinely neglect to contain a thirteenth floor (either choosing the number 12-A or going directly to 14), and almost every newspaper in America, run by skeptical publishers, carries a daily column of astrological forecasts, knowing its circulation will fall sharply if the column is dropped.

5. Jeanne Robert Foster, a devout occultist herself, spent much time with JBY in New York in the decade before his death. She regretted that he did not take the subject seriously: "JBY, at Petitpas, 'read hands,' palmistry, and was quite skillful and listened to fortune tellers. I remember his giving me a quick palmistry reading. Yet he could not look at the authentic occult." (JRF, letter to Richard Londraville, 5 Feb. 1968). I thank Dr. Londraville for showing me this letter.

6. Lily to JBY, 14 Nov. 1910, MBY.

7. See, e.g., JBY to Lily, 20 May 1910, MBY.

8. JBY to Isaac Yeats, 28 Jan. 1918, ABY.

9. WBY to Katharine Tynan [July 1891] (Wade, *Letters of WBY,* 173); in Kelly, 1: 255, it is dated "early July 1891".

10. The late Professor Joseph Doty to author (conversation, 1966), reporting on a talk given by WBY at Oxford when Doty was a Rhodes Scholar there. See Murphy, *Prodigal Father,* 561–62.

11. Ernest Boyd, *Ireland's Literary Renaissance* (New York: Knopf, 1922), 213–14. See Murphy, *Prodigal Father,* 137, 139.

12. WBY to Ernest Boyd, Feb. 1915 (Wade, *Letters of WBY,* 592).

13. WBY, *Autobiographies,* 90, 91–92.

14. WBY to John O'Leary, week of 23 July 1892 (Wade, *Letters of WBY,* 210–11; Kelly, 1: 303).

15. JBY to Lily, 1 Aug. 1894 (Murphy, *Letters from Bedford Park,* 12). Jeanne Robert Foster, on reading the letters of JBY to his son almost fifty years after his death, found her impression reinforced of the father's antagonism to his son's pursuits: "In these volumes of letters I am reading, he continually tries to drag Willie away from an interest in and study of occultism and he records that Willie continually 'refused to be dragged' " (JRF, letter to Richard Londraville, 13 Jan. 1968. I thank Dr. Londraville for letting me see this letter).

16. JBY to Sarah Purser, 7 July 1897 (Murphy, *Letters from Bedford Park,* 12).

17. JBY to Lady Gregory, 9 Jan. 1899, NYPL (Murphy, *Letters from Bedford Park,* 45).

18. JBY to WBY, 27 Apr. 1918, MBY.

19. WBY to John O'Leary, 7 May [1889] (Wade, *Letters of WBY,* 125; Kelly, 1: 164).

20. WBY to Katharine Tynan, 12 Feb. [1888] (Wade, *Letters of WBY,* 59; Kelly, 1: 49).

21. WBY to John O'Leary, [ca. 8] Nov. [1890] (Wade, *Letters of WBY,* 160; Kelly, 1: 234).

22. WBY to Katharine Tynan, 4 Dec. 1890 (Wade, *Letters of WBY,* 162; Kelly, 1: 238).

23. WBY to Katharine Tynan, 5 Mar. [1891] (Wade, *Letters of WBY,* 164–65; Kelly, 1: 244).

24. WBY to John O'Leary, [week ending 23 July 1892] (Wade, *Letters of WBY,* 209; Kelly, 1: 303).

25. WBY to W. T. Horton, [*undated*] (Wade, *Letters of WBY,* 263. See Harper, *W. B. Yeats and W. T. Horton,* 8 and passim).

26. WBY, *Autobiographies,* 24, 25–26.

27. WBY to Dorothy Hunter, 1 Jan. 1898 (Wade, *Letters of WBY,* 293–94. See Murphy, *Prodigal Father,* 201, 203).

28. WBY to George Russell, 22 Jan. 1898 (Wade, *Letters of WBY,* 295).

29. JBY, *Early Memories,* 97.

30. WBY to George Hyde-Lees (Mrs. W. B.) Yeats, 28 Aug. 1924, MBY. I thank Dr. John Kelly for providing me with a copy of this letter.

31. WBY to Lily, 16 Feb. [1923?], MBY. "Spot" appears in a photograph with Willie and Fred Pollexfen, reproduced in Murphy, *Prodigal Father*, 82.

32. WBY to Lily, 21 Aug. [1915], MBY. See also Murphy, *Prodigal Father*, 437.

33. A copy of the chart is on file at the Library of the State University of New York at Stony Brook, W. B. Yeats MC 294, sub-group 1, series 3, subseries 4, no. 1102040. I thank Peggy McMullen, Cataloguer of the Collection, for calling this chart to my attention and providing me with a copy. The time of Cuala's move, given in WBY's hand, was "August 23, 1923, 11.5. D.M.T."

34. W. B. Yeats, *A Vision* (New York: Macmillan, 1938), 12; Murphy, *Prodigal Father*, 640.

35. Ezra Pound to John Quinn, 13 Dec. 1919; (from Reid, *Man from New York*, 389). Reid also quotes George Russell on WBY: "His mind is subtle but never very clear in its thought" (George Russell to John Quinn, 10 July 1919), 386–87.

36. Ezra Pound to John Quinn, 15 Nov. 1915 (from Reid, *Man from New York*, 352).

37. Quoted in Kelly, 1: 263n.

38. See, for instance, JBY to WBY, 6 Sept. 1915 (second letter of this date, beginning, "I hope I am not . . . "), MBY: "A mystic is a man who believes what he likes to believe and makes a system of it and plumes himself on doing so."

39. JBY to Isaac Yeats, 26 Sept. 1916, ABY.

40. Lily has left a long account of two "visions" involving "The Red Rose" and "The White Rose." Since these seem to be related to nothing external, I omit discussing them here. It should be noted that WBY told Lily that the plots of *Cathleen ni Houlihan* and *The Cap and Bells* came from dreams (Lily to Joseph Hone, 10 July 1939, Texas).

41. See Murphy, " 'In Memory of Alfred Pollexfen.' " The last lines of Yeats's ode are:

> At all these death-beds women heard
> A visionary white sea-bird
> Lamenting that a man should die;
> And with that cry I have raised my cry.

George Pollexfen died 26 Sept. 1910. Lily also thought she heard the banshee wail a day earlier.

Omens of their relatives' deaths seem to have been programmed into the Pollexfens. On the night that Susan Pollexfen Yeats died in London, her sister Elizabeth Orr said she heard the banshee outside her window.

42. Lily to Ruth, 11 Feb. 1940, MBY.

43. Lily to Oliver Elton, 28 Aug. 1916, collection of Leonard Elton. With this letter is also "Account of a Vision Seen by Me, Lily Yeats, in July 1914," dated at Dundrum, 28 Aug. 1916. I have referred here to a copy of her account

typed by Oliver Elton, 29 Aug. 1916. The reference to WBY's undated letter to Lily and to the letter of G. E. Hamilton to Lily, 22 Oct. 1915, are taken from the same copy. I thank Mr. Leonard Elton for providing me with a copy of it.

44. Lily to Oliver Elton, 30 Aug. 1916, collection of Leonard Elton. As a postscript she wrote: "Show my vision to anyone interested, of course."

45. Lollie to John Quinn, 25 Nov. 1906, NYPL. She repeats the account in a letter to Julia (Mrs. Simeon) Ford, 1907, n.d. ("We got in . . .), Yale.

46. I thank Rosemary Hemming, a great-niece of Anne Boston, for this account (letter to author, 27 June 1990). Lily had another such experience at the Grand Union Hotel in New York in late 1907: "I saw a ghost the first night I slept in the hotel, a man who had hung himself in the open doorway between my room and the bathroom. I asked Mr. Ford if anybody had hung themselves in that room. He said many people came to the city, spent all their money in other hotels and then came and committed suicide in his" (Lily to Joseph Hone, 23 May 1942, Texas).

47. Lily to JBY, 22 Sept. 1918, MBY.

48. Lily to JBY, 22 Sept. 1918, MBY.

49. After Michael's birth (on 22 Aug. 1921) Lily wrote Willie promptly about her vision. He replied that he thought "the boy's horoscope . . . quite compatible with a diplomatic career" (WBY to Lily, 1 Sept. [1921], MBY).

50. For those interested in combinations, permutations, and probabilities, a further note might be added here. In July of 1969, at my summer home in Nova Scotia, I was deciphering the letter cited above and dictating its contents into a recording machine. In the middle of the transcription, just after Lily's account of the dream and before that of the vision, the tape ended, and I decided it was as good a time as any to walk to the foot of the long lane and pick up the day's mail. In it was a letter from Michael Yeats. Immediately after reading it I returned to the transcription and came upon the account of the vision of the "statesman." I offer this footnote without commentary to occultists and mathematicians who might find food for thought in it.

51. JBY to Frank Yeats, 8 Sept. 1910, collection of Harry Yeats. In an interview with Marguerite Wilkinson, JBY is cited as saying that Willie spoke Lily's words, obviously a misprint or a misunderstanding of what JBY told her (Marguerite Wilkinson, "A Talk with John Butler Yeats," *The Touchstone* [Oct. 1919]: 10–17).

52. Van Wyck Brooks, "A Reviewer's Notebook," *The Freeman,* 1 Mar. 1922, 599.

53. JBY, Memoirs.

54. Lily to JBY, 23 Mar., 19 Apr. 1910, MBY.

55. JBY to Susan Pollexfen Yeats, 15 Feb. 1873, MBY.

56. For interesting parallels to Lily's experiences, see J. W. Dunne, *An Experiment with Time* (London: Macmillan, 1936).

57. I am indebted to Professor William H. O'Donnell for sharing with me his findings on Yeats's novel, which he transcribed and edited for publication by the Cuala Press in 1974; it was later published as part of the Yeats Studies Series by McClelland Stewart, Canada, in 1976.

58. *Joseph Holloway's Abbey Theatre: A Selection from His Unpublished Journal,* ed. Robert Hogan and Michael J. O'Neill (Carbondale: Southern Illinois Univ. Press), 202.

59. JBY to WBY, 12 Feb. 1919, MBY.

60. Padraic Colum, "John Butler Yeats," *Atlantic Monthly,* no. 172 (July 1943), 82.

Bibliography

S ources for this volume are chiefly the unpublished letters, documents, and other material of the members of the Yeats family, particularly two large sets of letters hitherto unstudied, the Rosa Butt and Ruth Pollexfen Lane-Poole collections. These and other similar material are listed below.

A bibliography of W. B. Yeats's works fills a good-sized volume, and no attempt is made here to list it. The published works noted below are those of which I have made particular use. Other works, referred to once or twice, are described in the appropriate footnote.

Some of the material in the book has appeared in other publications of my own, listed below. I have made use of these as I would of any secondary sources.

Manuscripts

Jack Yeats. Letters to John Quinn. New York Public Library.
Jack Yeats. Letters to Kilham Roberts. University of Delaware Library.
Jack Yeats. Letters. University of Victoria Library.
John Butler Yeats. Letters to William Butler Yeats, Lily Yeats, Lollie Yeats, Susan Pollexfen Yeats, and others. Collection of Michael Butler Yeats.
John Butler Yeats. Letters to Jack Yeats and Isaac Butt Yeats. Collection of Anne Butler Yeats.
John Butler Yeats. Unpublished memoirs and unfinished stories. Collection of Michael Butler Yeats.
John Butler Yeats. Letters to Rosa Butt. Bodleian Library, Oxford.
John Butler Yeats. Letters to John Quinn and others. New York Public Library and Princeton University Library.
Lily Yeats. Letters to Ruth Pollexfen Lane-Poole. Collection of Michael Butler Yeats.

479

Lily Yeats. Letters to her father and others; her three notebooks: "Scrapbook," the Draft Scrapbook, and "Odds and Ends"; and her Diary. Collection of Michael Butler Yeats.
Lily Yeats. Letters to John Quinn. New York Public Library.
Lily Yeats. Letters to James A. Healy. Stanford University Library.
Lily Yeats. Letters to Joseph Hone. University of Texas Library.
Lollie Yeats. Letters to members of the family and her diary. Collection of Michael Butler Yeats.
Lollie Yeats. Letters to John Quinn. New York Public Library.
Lollie Yeats. Letters to James A Healy and others. Stanford University Library.
William Butler Yeats. Unpublished letters. Collection of Michael Butler Yeats and others in various collections.
Letters and other material involving the Yeatses in the National Library of Ireland, the New York Public Library, and the following university libraries: Brown; California at Berkeley; Delaware; Glasgow; Harvard; Kansas; State University of New York at Buffalo and at Stony Brook; Princeton; Reading; Southern Illinois; Stanford; Texas; Trinity College, Dublin; Victoria, British Columbia; Yale.
Letters, photographs, and other material involving Evelyn Gleeson and the Dun Emer Industries in the collection of Dr. Patrick H. Kelly of Trinity College, Dublin.
Letters and other material involving the Dun Emer Industries, chiefly the letters of Augustine Henry, in the National Library of Ireland.

Books and Articles

Bair, Deirdre. *Samuel Beckett*. New York: Summit, 1990.
Chesterton, Gilbert Keith. *Autobiography*. New York: Sheed and Ward, 1936.
Denson, Alan, ed. *Letters from AE*. London: Abelard-Schuman, 1961.
Donoghue, Denis, ed. *William Butler Yeats, Memoirs*. New York: Macmillan, 1972.
Finneran, Richard, ed. *William Butler Yeats: John Sherman and Dhoya*. Detroit: Wayne State Univ. Press, 1969.
Gwynn, Stephen, ed. *Scattering Branches*. New York: Macmillan, 1940.
Harper, George Mills, ed. *A Critical Edition of Yeats's "A Vision" (1925)*. London: Macmillan, 1978.
————, *The Making of Yeats's "A Vision": A Study of the Automatic Script*. 2 vols. Carbondale and Edwardsville: Southern Illinois Univ. Press, 1987.

————, *W. B. Yeats and W. T. Horton: The Record of a Friendship*. London: Macmillan, 1980.

————, ed. *Yeats and the Occult*. Toronto: Macmillan of Canada, 1975.

————, *Yeats's Golden Dawn*. London: Macmillan, 1974.

————, ed. *Yeats's "Vision" Papers*. 3 vols. London: Macmillan; Iowa City: Univ. of Iowa Press, 1992.

Himber, Alan, ed. *The Letters of John Quinn to William Butler Yeats*. Ann Arbor: UMI Research Press, 1983.

Hogan, Robert, and Michael J. O'Neill, eds. *Joseph Holloway's Abbey Theatre: A Selection from His Unpublished Journal*. Carbondale: Southern Illinois Univ. Press; London and Amsterdam: Feiffer and Simons, 1967.

Hone, Joseph. *J. B. Yeats: Letters to His Son W. B. Yeats and Others*. New York: Dutton, 1946.

Hone, Joseph, *W. B. Yeats 1865–1939*. London: Macmillan, 1965.

Kelly, John. *The Collected Letters of W. B. Yeats*. Vol. 1, 1865–1895. Oxford: Clarendon Press, 1986.

McHugh, Roger, ed. *Jack B. Yeats. A Centenary Gathering*. Dublin: Dolmen, 1971.

Miller, Liam. *The Dun Emer, Later the Cuala Press*. Dublin: Dolmen, 1973.

Murphy, William M. "The Ancestry of William Butler Yeats." In *Yeats and the 1890s*, edited by Robert O'Driscoll and Lorna Reynolds, 1–19. Shannon: Irish University Press, 1971.

————. "Home Life Among the Yeatses." In *Yeats, Sligo, and Ireland*, ed. A. Norman Jeffares, 170–88. Gerrards Cross: Colin Smythe, 1980.

————. " 'In Memory of Alfred Pollexfen': W.B. Yeats and the Theme of Family." *Irish University Review* 1, no. 1 (Autumn 1970): 30–47.

————, ed., *Letters from Bedford Park*. Dublin: Cuala, 1973.

————, *Prodigal Father: The Life of John Butler Yeats*. Ithaca and London: Cornell Univ. Press, 1978.

————. "Psychic Daughter, Mystic Son, Sceptic Father." In *Yeats and the Occult*, edited by George Mills Harper, 11–26. Toronto: Macmillan of Canada, 1975.

————. "William Butler Yeats's *John Sherman*: An Irish Poet's Declaration of Independence." *Irish University Review*, 9, no. 1 (Spring 1979): 92–111. Also published in *Image and Illusion: A Festschrift for Roger McHugh*, 92–111. Dublin: Wolfhound Press, 1979.

————. *The Yeats Family and the Pollexfens of Sligo*. Dublin: Dolmen, 1971.

O'Donnell, William H., ed. *The Speckled Bird, by William Butler Yeats.* 2 vols. Dublin: Cuala, 1974. Toronto: McClelland Stewart, 1976.

Pim, Sheila. *The Wood and the Trees: A Biography of Augustine Henry.* 2d ed. Kilkenny, Ireland: Boethius Press, 1984.

Purser, John W. *The Literary Works of Jack Yeats.* Gerrards Cross: Colin Smythe, 1991.

Pyle, Hilary. *Jack B. Yeats: A Biography.* London: Routledge and Kegan Paul, 1970.

Reid, B. L. *The Man from New York.* New York: Oxford Univ. Press, 1968.

Rodgers, W. R., ed. *Irish Literary Portraits.* New York: Taplinger, 1972.

Rose, Marilyn Gaddis. *Jack B. Yeats: Painter and Poet.* Berne: Herbert Lange; Frankfurt am Main: Peter Lang, 1972.

Skelton, Robin. *The Collected Plays of Jack B. Yeats.* London: Secker and Warburg, 1971.

Skelton, Robin, and Ann Saddlemyer, eds. *The World of W. B. Yeats.* Seattle: Univ. of Washington Press, 1965.

Wade, Allan. *A Bibliography of the Writings of W. B. Yeats.* London: Rupert Hart-Davis, 1968.

————, ed. *The Letters of W. B. Yeats.* London: Rupert Hart-Davis. 1954.

White, Terence de Vere. *The Road of Excess.* Dublin: Browne and Nolan, [1945].

Yeats, John Butler. *Early Memories.* Dublin: Cuala, 1923.

Yeats, W. B. *A Vision.* New York: Macmillan, 1938.

Index

A number in *boldface italics* indicates a page on which an illustration appears. The number may refer to the subject of the illustration or the artist responsible for it.

Gleeson, Evelyn (*continued*)
89; and loan to Lily and
Lollie, 123, 131, 140; and
Lucania, 133, 135; and
Constance MacCormack, 81,
95; and Katharine
MacCormack, 430; and
Milan, 125; and Alexander
Millar, 88, 94, 96–98; and
William Morris, 88; as
"Mother Abbess," 126, 131,
142, 180; and her name
("Miss Gleeson"), 99; and
New York City, 133, 135,
137, 138; and newspaper
battle with Lily and Lollie,
131, 137, 138; and Barry
O'Brien, 91, 98, 98–99; and
occult, 383–84; and *The
Pilot,* 137; and P. T. Power,
132–33; and purpose of Dun
Emer, 89, 125; and Press at
Dun Emer, 105, 181; and
John Quinn, 117, 123, 125,
126, 183, 431; and
"Runnymede," 99, *99;* and
"St. Patrick," 104; and 1904
separation from Yeats sisters,
122; and 1908 separation
from Yeats sisters, 420; and
"The Settlement," 89, 100;
as the "Spider," 126, 131,
180; and tapestry, 87–88,
180; and Technical
Department, 117; and trust
fund, 87, 91, 115, 131; and
weaving, 87, 88; and
workers at Dun Emer, 99,
124, 134–35; and Jack
Yeats, 84–85, 91; and John
Butler Yeats, 99, 101, 117,

131, 133, 134–35, 138,
180, 431; and Lily Yeats,
85, 86, 92, 94, 95, 96, 98,
99, 101, 104, 108, 115,
117, 119, 124, 126, 127,
131, 131–33, 135, 137,
138, 140, 141, 141–42,
142–43, 144, 180, 181,
291, 383–84, 431; and
Lollie Yeats, 62, 84–85, 86,
92–93, 94, 95, 98, 99, 100,
101, 105, 108, 109, 111–
12, 113, 114–15, 115, 117,
118, 119, 123–24, 124,
126, 127, 131, 133, 137,
138, 138–39, 140, 141,
142, 143, 144, 164, 167,
185; and William Butler
Yeats, 86, 89, 91, 101, 120
Gleeson, James ("Jim"), 87
Gleeson, Monsignor (of Buffalo),
137
Glenavy, Beatrice Lady, 197,
341
Glenbeigh, 124
Glencullen, 381–82
Glendower, Owen, 388
Godolphin School, 45, 47
Godwin, William, 373
Goff, Dr. Arthur, 214–15, 243
Gogarty, Oliver St. John, 211,
234, 235
Golden Dawn. *See* Order of the
Golden Dawn
Gonne, Iseult, xxiii, xxvi, 355–
56, 472
Gonne, Maud, xxiii, xxiv, xxvi,
30, 60, 61, 73, *74,* 355–56,
377, 407, 427, 430, 441,
472
Gordon, Fanny Yeats, 314, 394

512   *Index*

White, Mary Cottenham
  ("Cottie"). *See* Yeats, Cottie
White, Terence de Vere, 268,
  283, 302, 314, 319–20,
  321–22, 323, 465
"Whiteside, John." *See* "John
  Whiteside"
Whitman, Walt, 346
Who's Who, 312
Wilde, Lady Francesca (Mrs.
  William), 57. *See also* Elgee,
  Jane Francesca
Wilde, Oscar, 57, 331
Wilde, Sir William, 331
"William Howard" (character in
  John Sherman), 60
Wilson, Woodrow, 346, 352
Wise, Edith, 437
Wise, Mary (sister of JBY), 437
Wise, Robert Blakely, 437
Woburn Buildings (London),
  285, 376
Woburn Place. *See* Woburn
  Buildings
Woman's Reliquary, A (Dowden),
  191–92, 195, 435
Women's Health Committee
  (Dundrum), 194
Women's Printing Society
  (London), 102
"Wood, The" (embroidery),
  184
Woodstock Road (Bedford Park),
  46–47, 58
World War I, 194, 205–6, 208
World War II, 261, 323
Wren, Christopher, 327
Wright, Ellen, 76
Wuthering Heights (E. Brontë),
  154
Wynne family (Sligo), 9, 394

Yeats (name and reputation),
  136–37, 172, 181–82, 246
Yeats ancestry, 5–6, 393
Yeats, Anne Butler (1919–),
  xxvi, 167, 209, 233, 235,
  259, 306, 326, 327, 385,
  424, 445
Yeats, Benjamin (son of
  Benjamin), 6, 393
Yeats, Benjamin (son of Jervis),
  6
Yeats, Bertha Georgie Hyde-Lees
  (1892–1968) (Mrs. William
  Butler). *See* Yeats, George
Yeats, Caitríona Dill, 326
Yeats, Cottie (1867?–1947)
  (Mrs. Jack Yeats), *305, 383;*
  her age, 281, 457, 458; as
  artist, 136, 236, 323; and
  Australia, 236; and Samuel
  Beckett, 303; character,
  personality, 281–82, 323,
  466; and childlessness, 300,
  326, 384; and
  confidentiality, 324; and
  Coole, 281; her death, 281,
  324, 324–25; and Dublin,
  303, 324; and English, 323;
  and Fitzwilliam Square, 324;
  her funeral, 325; and Lady
  Augusta Gregory, 281, 323;
  and Gurteen Dhas, 314; and
  Ireland, 293; and Ruth Lane-
  Poole, 333; her legacy, 76,
  281; as letter-writer, 324;
  and Loughrea Cathedral,
  414; and Maggie the maid,
  324; and *Manchester
  Guardian,* 236; and
  Marlborough Street, 303; her
  marriage, 76, 279, 281,

confusion of name with father, 392–93; his conversation, 304, 306–7, 313; and Coole, 256, 285; and William Cosgrave, 461; and Cuala (*see* Jack Yeats *under all* Cuala *entries*); his death, 325; and Devon, 76, 83, 282, 292, 304; and Diary (Lollie Yeats), 61, 62, 75, 277; drawings, 48, 75, 183; and Dublin, 292, 303, 304, 306, 312, 324; and Dun Emer (*see under* Dun Emer: Jack Yeats); and Eardley Crescent, 277; and Earl's Court, 56–57; and Easter Rising, 314; and Eastwort, 282; and Edith Villas, 271; and education, 62, 265, 274, 279; and Engineers Hall (Dublin), 314; and the English, 301, 323; and exhibitions, 285, 288, *290,* 293–94, 312, 314, 316; and Patric Farrell, 309; and Ferargil Galleries, 308; and finances, 72, 75, 279, 293–94, 307, 309, 315, 316; and Fitzwilliam Square, 322, 324; his generosity, 194, 288, 291–92, 320–21, 321, 321–22, 322–23; and Evelyn Gleeson (*see under* Gleeson, Evelyn: Jack Yeats); and Aunt Fanny Yeats Gordon, 314; and Rupert Gordon, 314; and Grafton Street (Dublin), 265; and Lady Augusta Gregory, 285, 298, 299, 302, 316,

323; and Robert Gregory, 285; and Greystones, 292, 302–3, 304; and Gurteen Dhas, 182, 194, 292, 313, 314; and T. Arnold Harvey, 285, 286; his health, 298–303, 323, 325, 460–61; and A. M. Heath, 288; and Joseph Hone, 274, 312, 321; his humor, 277, 306–7; and income, 275–77; his independence, 285, 312, 314, 319; and Ireland, 292; and Irish Free State, 268; and *Irish Independent,* 125; and Italy, 286; and Arthur Jackson, 398; and "John Sherman," 60; and James Joyce, 317; and Kensington, 62; and William Keogh, M. P., 461; and Ruth Lane-Poole, 262, 314, 316, 322; and Frederick Langbridge, 276–77; and Leinster Hall (Dublin), 293–94; his letters, 327, 457, 461; his lifestyle, 303, 304, 304–5; and Liffey River, 317; and *The Liffey Swim,* 315; and Lissadell, 275; and Liverpool, 386; and Lollie's Diary (*see above* Diary); and London, 62, 269, 271, 275; and Loughrea, 104, 414; his love life, 323; and Macmillan Publ. Co., 309–10; and Maggie the maid, 324; and Malahide, 321–22; and Manchester, 76, 279; and *Manchester Guardian,* 290; and Marlborough Street

271; and *British Warehouseman,* 131; and *Broadsides* (1908–15), 141, 197, 291; and Buckingham Palace, 448; and Rosa Butt, 328, 329, 468; and Cadbury family, 212; and Cambridge-Oxford boat race, 71; and S.S. *Campania,* 133; and Campbells, 381–82; and Catholic (*see below* Roman Catholic); character, personality, 68–69, 148–60, 165, 217, 422, 433; and G. K. and Mrs. Chesterton, 81; and Christianity, 158; and Churchtown, 101, 140; and Mrs. Crichton, 171; and May Courtney, 243–44, 248; and Cuala (*see* Lily Yeats *under all* Cuala *entries*); death, 325; and *Deirdre* (Synge), 186; and Denby, 57; and Eamon De Valera, 216, 444; and Devon, 83, 292; diary, 61, 77–78, 408; and Lollie's diary, 61, 62; Draft Scrapbook, 400; and drinking, 101, 413; and John Doran, 50; and Dublin, 176, 209, 263; and *Dubliners* (Joyce), 199–200; and Dundrum, 194; and Dun Emer (*see under* Dun Emer: Lily Yeats); and Easter Rising, 200–202; and Mrs. Eaton, 171; and Edith Villas, 44–45; and education, 47, 49, 407; and Una Ellis-Fermor, 150–51; and embroidery, 67–71, 76–77,

94, 95, 103, 104, 108, 149, 181, 187, 197, 222, 236, 241, 243–44, 245, 246, 253, 262, 438, 448, 449; and FitzSimon family, 282–83; and Fitzwilliam Square, 255; and Julia Ford, 419; and Franks family, 171, 450–51; and Maureen Franks, 248; and Freke, 236, 438; and Gamble family, 62; and "Garden" (embroidery), 241; and Germany, 189; and T. P. Gill, 117; and Gleeson, Evelyn (*see under* Gleeson, Evelyn: Lily Yeats); and Beatrice Lady Glenavy, 197; and Glencullen, 281–82; and Dr. Arthur Goff, 214–15, 243; and Maud Gonne, 73, 427, 441; and Grand Union Hotel (New York), 476; and Frederick Gregg, 153; and Lady Augusta Gregory, 80, 103, 221, 316; and Gurteen Dhas, 167, 169, 173, 182, 210, 218, 229, 230, 245; and Hammersmith (London), 61, 71; and *Happy Townland* (embroidery), 253; health, 42, 49–50, 80, 145, 151, 160, 168–69, 171, 176, 195, 214–15, 221–27, 228, 240–43, 259, 262, 263, 321, 378–79; and Augustine Henry (*see under* Henry, Augustine: Lily Yeats); and Adolf Hitler, 159; and Joseph Hone, 312, 321; and A. E. F.

Yeats, Lollie (*continued*)
254, 255, 256; and *The
Hour-Glass* (WBY), 195; and
Sara Hyland, 243, 247, 249;
and I. D. K. Club, 161; and
In the Seven Woods, 103;
insecurity, 165; irrationality,
130–31; isolation, 42, 160,
176, 256, 262; and Italy,
189, 191; jealousy, 83, 167,
203, 211, 218, 418; and
James Joyce, 146, 177, 414,
421; and Kelmscott House
(London), 66–67; and
Mitchell Kennerley, 191,
434; and Kilkeel, 257; and
Frederick A. King, 170,
426; and "Lake Isle of
Innisfree" (WBY), 60; and
Charles Lane-Poole (daughter
of Ruth Lane-Poole), 150;
and Mary Lane-Poole, 150;
and Ruth Pollexfen Lane-
Poole, 83, 150, 159, 167,
182, 203, 211, 218, 223–
24, 260, 262; laziness, 234;
and Paul Lemperly, 437;
letters, 86, 130, 138–39,
160, 189; and "Lollipop,"
148; and London, 40, 126,
224, 226; and Lord Mayor of
Dublin, 248; and Constance
MacCormack, 95, 101, 413;
and Thomas MacDonagh,
202; and Annie McElheron,
167–68; maliciousness, 169,
170, 224–27; as manager,
187, 194, 195, 196–97,
213, 214, 229, 250;
mannerisms, 42, 166–67,
177–78, 189, 214, 247; and

Margaret Cunningham
Library, 454; and Elkin
Matthews, 301; meanness,
169–70, 245;
meddlesomeness, 209–10;
and "Memoirs" (JBY), 176–
77; mendacity, 170–71,
215, 230, 426, 426–27,
450–51; and Merrion
Square, 229–30; and
Metropolitan School of Art,
54; and Alexander Millar,
97; as "Miss Lolly," 187,
248, 249–50; and Susan
Mitchell, 150, 163, 203; and
William Morris, 67; name,
146, 187; and New York
City, 129, 130; and Notting
Hill, 75; and occult, 370,
380; and Frank O'Connor,
254, 255; and *Offering of
Swans* (Gogarty), 234; and *On
the Boiler* (WBY), 253, 256;
and Sir Lambert Ormesby,
170; and Caroline (Mrs.
Augustine Henry) Orridge,
413; as seen by others, 80,
80–81, 86, 124, 130, 137,
145–46, 148, 160–61, 163,
166, 171–72, 233–34, 260;
and overdrafts, 247, 250–51;
and *Packet for Ezra Pound*
(WBY), 235; painting, 93–
94, 177, 262; and Padraic
Pearse, 202; personality, 80–
81, 86, 161–67; philosophy,
80, 189–90; and *The Pilot,*
137; and *Pleiades,* 71; and
Poems (Synge), 185; and
Alfred Pollexfen, 202; and
George Pollexfen, 188; and